The Politics of United States Foreign Policy

Seventh Edition

This one is for Elizabeth.
—J.M.S.

Sara Miller McCune founded SAGE Publishing in 1965 to support the dissemination of usable knowledge and educate a global community. SAGE publishes more than 1000 journals and over 600 new books each year, spanning a wide range of subject areas. Our growing selection of library products includes archives, data, case studies and video. SAGE remains majority owned by our founder and after her lifetime will become owned by a charitable trust that secures the company's continued independence.

Los Angeles | London | New Delhi | Singapore | Washington DC | Melbourne

The Politics of United States Foreign Policy

Seventh Edition

James M. Scott
Texas Christian University

Jerel A. Rosati
University of South Carolina

FOR INFORMATION:

CQ Press
An imprint of SAGE Publications, Inc.
2455 Teller Road
Thousand Oaks, California 91320
E-mail: order@sagepub.com

SAGE Publications Ltd.
1 Oliver's Yard
55 City Road
London EC1Y 1SP
United Kingdom

SAGE Publications India Pvt. Ltd.
B 1/I 1 Mohan Cooperative Industrial Area
Mathura Road, New Delhi 110 044
India

SAGE Publications Asia-Pacific Pte. Ltd.
18 Cross Street #10-10/11/12
China Square Central
Singapore 048423

Printed in Canada

ISBN: 9781544374550

LCCN: 2019037307

Acquisitions Editor: Anna Villarruel
Content Development Editor: Alissa Nance
Editorial Assistant: Lauren Younker
Production Editor: Bennie Clark Allen
Copy Editor: Amy Marks
Typesetter: C&M Digitals (P) Ltd.
Proofreader: Sue Schon
Indexer: Jean Casalegno
Cover Designer: Candice Harman
Marketing Manager: Jennifer Jones

20 21 22 23 24 10 9 8 7 6 5 4 3 2 1

Brief Contents

Detailed Contents

Preface to the Seventh Edition

Welcome to the seventh edition of *The Politics of United States Foreign Policy!*

The Politics of United States Foreign Policy engages students of American foreign policy to consider the players, processes, and politics that drive US decisions and involvement in the global political system. This emphasis on the politics and processes of US foreign policy brings a distinct focus to this text. In this endeavor, we emphasize that a variety of actors play a role, and that the struggle over competing values, purposes, meanings, and interests is never far from the surface of foreign policy. Indeed, politics, and the processes that follow, are even more important than ever in today's world, and they shape US foreign policy choices and behavior in profound ways.

APPROACH

While our approach includes rich discussion of the policies and problems the United States has addressed in its foreign policy over time and in the contemporary context, we approach these aspects through our focus on policymaking and the political process through which they occur. Accordingly, we organize our text around efforts to

- Provide substantive description of problems, policies, and patterns and their explanations in the foreign policymaking process

- Address the global context, government, and society as key levels of analysis, focusing on how they interact and impact the real world of politics and the policymaking process

- Emphasize the political process and the prospects for and challenges to presidential management in the face of the engagement and influence of other institutions; actors; and forces in the government, domestic society, and world— with special attention to how these actors and forces operate, interact, conflict, win, compromise, and lose, and how the competing and complementary beliefs, personalities, and preferences of these actors within and outside government shape foreign policy decisions

- Integrate theory and practice throughout so as to encourage students to think analytically and theoretically to make sense of the foreign policy choices of the United States over time and in different contexts, and to think about and formulate answers to the questions of "how?" and "why?"

How does one study and understand the complex politics of US foreign policy? Three different approaches to the study of US foreign policy have predominated over the years: the policy approach, the historical approach, and the social science approach.

- The *policy approach* predominates among practitioners and those involved in politics and the policy world. Policy analysts tend to concern themselves primarily with contemporary affairs; emphasize the present and the near future; make policy recommendations; and write for policymakers and a broad, general audience.

- The *historical approach* to US foreign policy comes out of the scholarly tradition of diplomatic history and the humanities within academia. It tends to emphasize a historical understanding of US foreign policy, attempts to recapture the specifics of the times, recognizes a wealth of factors influencing foreign policy, relies heavily on primary source documentation (such as government documents and private papers), and results often in well-written narratives for a scholarly and more general audience.

- Finally, the *social science approach* to US foreign policy tends to be focused on identifying and explaining basic patterns in foreign policy and policymaking.

Each approach or orientation has something important to contribute, and synthesizing the three approaches so that they complement each other is key to acquiring breadth and depth of knowledge and understanding. Our orientation to the study of foreign policy is that of a social scientist sensitive to the importance of history and practice, so our text is sensitive to broad patterns and specific information about the politics of US foreign policy, contemporary and past politics, a theoretical and historical understanding, and competing policy views and recommendations.

Overall, while we weave together substantive, historical, and theoretical knowledge to maximize understanding and critical thinking, we approach foreign policy from a policy-making perspective. In essence, a single overarching question informs and leads us: *What are the factors that shape and determine the foreign policy choices of the United States?* We thus stress analytical and theoretical thinking about cause-and-effect in policymaking, integrating factors from the international and domestic contexts with institutional, organizational, and individual dynamics and characteristics.

The Politics of United States Foreign Policy fosters and supports the groundwork to describe what the United States has done, does, or might do, and to evaluate the merits of one policy over another, but we privilege the examination and explanation of *how* and *why* those choices are made at any given time. Underlying this is our fundamental philosophy, organized around student engagement and active learning, and efforts to facilitate subject mastery and the development of critical/analytical thinking generated when students ask "why?" questions and formulate answers. Our text therefore enables a rich array of opportunities for student thinking; active classroom activities such as case-based analysis, simulations, and other approaches; and writing assignments.

NEW TO THIS EDITION

This text (now in its seventh edition) has long received a very warm reception from students, instructors, and practitioners, holding a place among the most successful textbooks on US foreign policy since its inception. In the new edition, we maintain our overall approach and general outline, while making key changes to strengthen and improve the text and thus ensure its continued relevance and success. The revisions we made include the following:

- *Chapter reorganization* to improve the thematic coherence of the text.

- *A new analytical/conceptual framework* to examine and understand the complex and shifting politics of US foreign policymaking.

- *Streamlining and focusing the text for readability*, resulting in a leaner, more accessible book that is more tightly presented even as it maintains breadth and depth of coverage.

- *Timely updates to cover developments since the end of the Obama administration and the first three years of the Trump administration and the unique politics, personnel, and processes it has involved*, woven into every chapter, making the revised version as up-to-date as possible.

- *New and expanded attention to the challenges of changing international and domestic contexts* and their impact on the foreign policy agenda, foreign policy orientations, executive branch structures, legislative-executive interactions, societal concerns and engagement, and the increasingly partisan and polarized political environment in which US foreign policy is made.

- *New and updated figures, tables, maps, and other supporting material throughout.*

- *New and updated boxed features throughout*, with each box ending with critical thinking questions to spur analysis and discussion. **A Closer Look** boxes (all new or newly revised) consider significant issues or developments in more detail. **A Different Perspective** boxes (all new or newly revised) explore competing or alternative viewpoints. **Think About This** chapter-ending boxes (wholly new to this edition) prompt reflection and engagement and facilitate critical thinking.

All told, this major revision not only brings the text up to date, but it also delivers a more readable, better focused, and pedagogically helpful book. It draws on our many years of collective experience in the classroom and the success we have enjoyed working together with our students to examine the nature and consequences of the US foreign policymaking process. We hope that you find it helpful in your classes and that it contributes to your efforts to engage your students on this subject as well.

FEATURES AND PEDAGOGY

This book continues to rely on a variety of pedagogical features:

- *Examples and historical context* aid students in understanding the nature of the institutions involved, the dynamics of the process, and the larger themes addressed.

- *Overviews and summaries* are provided in the introduction and concluding section of each chapter.

- *Theory and practice are integrated and discussed* throughout the book.

- *Key terms* have been streamlined and *boldfaced* in the text, and they are listed at the end of each chapter.

- *Boxed features offer opportunities for critical thinking and writing exercises in and out of class.*

- *End-of-chapter puzzles offer opportunities for reflection and application.*

DIGITAL RESOURCES

A password-protected resource site available at **https://edge.sagepub.com/scottrosati7e** provides high-quality content for instructors. This book includes the following instructor resources:

- **Test banks** provide a diverse range of pre-written options as well as the opportunity to edit any question and/or insert your own personalized questions to effectively assess students' progress and understanding

- **Instructor's manual** provides lecture notes outlining key concepts and includes engaging discussion questions and class activities

- Editable, chapter-specific **PowerPoint® slides** offer complete flexibility for creating a multimedia presentation for the course

- **Tables and figures** from the book are available for download

Acknowledgments

We are indebted to a large number of people who inspired us, from whom we have learned, and who took the time and effort to directly assist and support us in the writing of this book.

We also very much appreciate the following reviewers:

Stewart Dippel, University of the Ozarks

Adrien M. Ratsimbaharison, Benedict College

Michael J. Struett, North Carolina State University

Luca Zini, Florida International University

Reviewers of previous editions include:

Andrew Bennett

Douglas Borer

Philip Brenner

Dan Caldwell

Steve Chan

Renato Corbetta

John Creed

Larry Elowitz

John Gilbert

J. Joseph Hewitt

Samuel B. Hoff

David Houghton

Christopher M. Jones

George Kieh

Martin Kyre

J. Patrice McSherry

Dean Minix

B. David Myers

Andrew L. Oros

Martin Sampson

David Skidmore

Donald Sylvan

Larry Taulbee

David W. Thornton

Steve Twing

Lane Van Tassell

Walter F. Weiker

Matthew C. Zierler

Finally, crucial psychological support has been essential and provided by our families and our friends. Altogether, it has been an incredibly satisfying and taxing experience involving the help of many people to produce a book on the politics of US foreign policy for which we alone take complete responsibility.

About the Authors

James M. Scott is the Herman Brown Chair and Professor of Political Science at Texas Christian University. His primary research and teaching interests are in international relations and foreign policy analysis, and he has special interests in US foreign policymaking, the role of Congress, and US democracy promotion. He has authored/coauthored seven books and more than 150 journal articles, book chapters, other nonrefereed publications, review essays, and conference papers. During his career, Dr. Scott has earned more than two dozen awards from students, faculty, administration, and professional associations including, most recently, the 2019 Textbook Excellence Award from the Textbook and Academic Authors Association (for *IR: International, Economic, and Human Security in a Changing World*, 3rd edition, coauthored with Ralph G. Carter and A. Cooper Drury); the 2018–2019 Distinguished Faculty Lecture Award (AddRan College of Liberal Arts, Texas Christian University); the 2018 Excellence in Teaching and Mentoring Award (International Studies Association–Midwest); the 2018 and 2019 AddRan College of Liberal Arts Division of Social Sciences Award for Distinguished Achievement as a Creative Teacher and Scholar (Texas Christian University); and the 2012 Quincy Wright Distinguished Scholar Award (International Studies Association–Midwest). Dr. Scott has been active in professional associations, serving on the governing boards, as conference program chair, and as president of both the International Studies Association–Midwest (2000) and the Foreign Policy Analysis Section (2001) of the International Studies Association, and as a councillor for the Council on Undergraduate Research (2017–2019). He served as associate editor of *Foreign Policy Analysis* (2009–2015), coeditor of *Political Research Quarterly* (2015–2018), and lead editor of *International Studies Perspectives* (2020–present). From 2004 to 2013, he was the director of the annual National Science Foundation–funded Democracy and World Politics Summer Research Experience for Undergraduates Program.

Jerel A. Rosati is Professor Emeritus of International Studies and Political Science at the University of South Carolina. His area of specialization is the theory and practice of foreign policy, focusing on the US policymaking process. He has been a Fulbright Senior Specialist in Argentina and Colombia, and a Visiting Scholar in Argentina, Armenia, China, and Somalia (in 1984). He also has been a research associate in the Foreign Affairs and National Defense Division (FAND) of the Library of Congress's Congressional Research Service (CRS) in Washington, DC; president of the International Studies Association's (ISA) Foreign Policy Analysis Section; and president of the Southern region of ISA. He was the principal investigator, program director, and academic director of a six-week US Department of State Fulbright American Studies Institute on US Foreign Policy for six years for 108 scholar-practitioners from more than sixty countries. He is the author of more than seventy articles and chapters, as well as five books. The recipient of numerous outstanding teaching awards, Dr. Rosati has been the director and reader of more than fifty PhD dissertations and more than fifty master's theses, and has mentored many more individuals in their academic and professional careers within the United States and throughout the world.

PART I

Introduction

THE CONTEXT OF US FOREIGN POLICYMAKING

Chapter 1 introduces US foreign policymaking and the underlying analytical framework used to understand the complex politics through which it is shaped. Chapter 2 discusses the international context, considering the historical and global-power contexts and major patterns in the US foreign policy response to them.

Understanding the Politics of US Foreign Policy

PHOTO 1.1 **How does the United States decide what to do in foreign policy?**

Illbusca/DigitalVision Vectors/Getty Images

LEARNING OBJECTIVES

1. Know the meaning and significance of foreign policy.

2. Understand the foundations of the politics of foreign policymaking.

3. Identify a framework for understanding the politics of foreign policy.

INTRODUCTION: THE IMPORTANCE OF FOREIGN POLICY

What is foreign policy, and why should people care about it and the politics that shape it?

Very simply, **foreign policy**, or foreign relations, refers to the scope of involvement abroad and the collection of goals, strategies, and instruments that are selected by governmental policymakers (see Rosenau 1976). To understand the foreign policy of a country, one needs to recognize who decides and acts. To say "the United States intervened" is part of our everyday language. But what do people mean when they use this phrase? In reality, countries do not act; people act. What the phrase usually means is that certain governmental officials, representing the state—that is, the United States—acted. A state is a legal concept that refers to the governmental institutions through which policymakers act in the name of the people of a given territory. The **foreign policy process**, or the politics of foreign policy, therefore, refers to how governmental decisions and policies get on the agenda, are formulated, and are implemented—which is the focus of this book. Nevertheless, while we stress process and politics, the substance of policy is woven throughout.

Although it may not seem so to either Americans or people from other countries, US foreign policy engagement in the world profoundly affects their lives in many ways. Thus, studying how and why the United States chooses to do what it does in foreign policy—the politics of US foreign policy—is important for both Americans and the world.

For example, in 2018, the United States spent about $700 billion on defense (not counting military-related expenditures in departments other than the Department of Defense), close to 40 percent of the world's total military expenditures. About 200,000 American troops (roughly one sixth of the US armed forces) are stationed worldwide in around 800 US military bases, big and small. Since the 1930s, the US has been engaged in numerous conflicts, including five major wars, which required millions of personnel to serve in the military and potentially place their lives at risk. World War II resulted in more than 400,000 US battle deaths, and the United States has sustained more than 400,000 military casualties since then. More than 35,000 Americans died during the Korean War, more than 58,000 died during the Vietnam War, and about 7,000 Americans have died in the Afghan and Iraqi wars as of 2019. In addition to those who died, many suffered physical and psychological injuries in each of these major wars as well.

The American standard of living is also heavily affected by the world economy, which is affected by US foreign economic policies involving trade in goods and services, investment in companies and capital, monetary policies and currency fluctuations, and access to raw materials and energy. In fact, as the global economy has expanded, the American economy has become increasingly more dependent on foreign markets and investment. Today, about one third of the US gross domestic product (GDP) comes from the import and export of goods and services. Although the United States now imports about a third of its oil, much of it from the Middle East, that figure was as high as 60 percent as recently as 2006.

Other important areas of foreign policy impact Americans beyond security and war or economics. Some areas that come to mind are immigration and population dynamics, the drug trade, the spread of AIDS, travel and tourism, and transnational issues such as global climate change. Additionally, times of war and national emergency are also times of greater presidential power and political tension at home when the demands of democracy often conflict with the demands of national security. This affects individual freedom, liberties, and civil rights guaranteed in the US Constitution.

Not only does US foreign policy have significance for Americans, but it also impacts the lives of people throughout the world. Because the United States is much more powerful and wealthy than most other societies and peoples, Americans must understand that US foreign policy can affect societies and lives all around the world—sometimes for the better, sometimes for the worse. In fact, the impact can be quite profound on the lives as well as the "perceptions and attitudes" of others, including Americans. Certainly the September 11 terrorist attacks, the subsequent war on terrorism, the wars in Afghanistan and Iraq, and the economic crisis of 2008–2010 clearly highlight the importance of America's connection to and policies toward the world. In sum, US foreign policy involves many activities and issues throughout the world that have implications—sometimes more immediate and direct, sometimes more indirect and underlying—for the everyday lives and futures of Americans.

Finally, our focus on the politics and processes of US foreign policy is motivated by several other foundational insights. Clearly, "what" the United States chooses to do in its foreign policy is quite consequential. But, policy—choices about the scope of involvement abroad and the collection of goals, strategies, and instruments to pursue it—is conditioned by "how," the process by which those choices are made. And the process is, in turn, conditioned by who is deciding—the characteristics of the individuals, agencies, and institutions that interact to make foreign policy choices. Since those individuals, agencies, and institutions have different preferences and perspectives, their interactions in the process are highly political; policy, therefore, is ultimately politics.

UNDERSTANDING US FOREIGN POLICY

How should we try to understand the politics of US foreign policy? Let us begin with two simple, but very important, points about the nature of the US foreign policy process:

- It is a very complex process.
- It is a very political process.

First, the US foreign policy process is complex and extremely messy. Many Americans initially tend to hold a very simple view of the foreign policy process: that US foreign policy is made and defined at the top of the political hierarchy, especially by the president. According to Roger Hilsman (1964:5), former assistant secretary of state for Far Eastern affairs in the John Kennedy administration, "As Americans, we think it only reasonable that the procedures for making national decisions should be orderly, with clear lines of responsibility and authority." We expect decisions to be made by "the proper, official, and authorized persons, and to know that the really big decisions will be made at the top . . . with each of the participants having roles and powers so well and precisely defined that they can be held accountable for their actions by their superiors and eventually by the electorate."

Clearly, the president is important, and presidential leadership is central to the politics of US foreign policy. The individual characteristics and beliefs of the individual elected to hold the office of the presidency play a crucial role in the making of US foreign policy. However, the president does not make US foreign policy alone, and presidential leadership in foreign policy is more a variable than a constant. President Lyndon Johnson colorfully put it this way:

Before you get to be president you think you can do anything. You think you're the most powerful leader since God. But when you get in that tall chair, as you're gonna find out, Mr. President, you can't count on people. You'll find your hands tied and people cussin' you. The office is kinda like the little country boy found the hoochie-koochie show at the carnival, once he'd paid his dime and got inside the tent: "It ain't exactly as it was advertised." (quoted in Cronin [1979], 381)

As President Johnson's description suggests, the reality is that many other individuals and institutions within the government and throughout society are involved in the foreign policy process. In the United States, these include presidential advisers, employees in the White House, the foreign policy bureaucracies, and other bureaucratic agencies in the executive branch; members of Congress and their staffs in the House of Representatives and the Senate; the courts; the public, political parties, and interest groups; the media; and even state and local governments at times. From outside the US, international actors such as foreign leaders, allies, and international organizations can also play a role. It is in this sense that the making of US foreign policy is a complex process. It is also a messy process, for the variety of individuals and institutions that affect US foreign policy do not stand still but constantly interact with and have an impact on one another. In other words, the policymaking process is not static but, as the word *process* implies, is dynamic.

Second, the foreign policy process in the United States is a very political process. What is politics? One common definition of **politics** is "who gets what, when, and how" (Lasswell 1938). This definition emphasizes that politics is, as Hedrick Smith (1988:xvi) says in *The Power Game*, a "serious game with high stakes, one in which the winners and losers affect many lives—yours, mine, those of the people down the street, and of people all over the world." Politics might also be defined as *the competition for power and shared meaning*. This simple but meaningful definition emphasizes the importance that ideas and symbolism play in the policy process. A final definition might describe politics as *competition between different individuals and groups for support of the public and influence throughout society in order to control the government and policymaking process for certain ends*. This is the broadest of the three definitions, emphasizing the role of different goal-oriented individuals and groups and the various arenas in which the political process takes place.

The three definitions are complementary and contribute to an understanding of what politics is all about. Together they illustrate that the politics of US foreign policy involves competition among differently motivated individuals and groups, that politics involves the flow of power and symbolism throughout government and society, and that it involves winners and losers. Such politics defines the **national interest**—a concept that is supposed to represent what is best for the country. However, policymakers will often invoke the idea of "the" national interest to justify and gain support for their particular preference from other policymakers or society. Different people, groups, and institutions have competing conceptions of what is best for the country, and it is through politics that such competing interests are "resolved" into policy choices. Ultimately, US foreign policy (and the so-called national interest) tends to reflect the goals and priorities of those individuals and groups who are the most successful in influencing the political process within government and throughout society.

The Changing Politics of US Foreign Policy

Clearly, the making of US foreign policy is a complex process inseparable from politics. This has been a dominant theme that most of the early theorists—including Gabriel Almond (1960); Richard Snyder (1958); Charles Lindblom (1959); Richard Neustadt (1960); Warner Schilling, Paul Hammond, and Glenn Snyder (1962); Roger Hilsman (1964); and Stanley Hoffmann (1968)—emphasized throughout their work on the US foreign policymaking process during the "high Cold War" period of the 1950s and 1960s, when the world seemed simpler, a time when presidential power and the Cold War consensus were at their apex.

Since the Vietnam War, the policy process has become increasingly complex, political, and visible. One consequence is that it has become very difficult for a president to govern successfully and lead the country in foreign policy. In the words of I. M. Destler, Leslie H. Gelb, and Anthony Lake (1984:20), "The making of American foreign policy [has] entered a new and far more ideological and political phase." Or as Hedrick Smith (1988:xvi) likewise observed, "Presidents now have much greater difficulty marshalling governing coalitions" for "it is a much looser power game now, more wide open, harder to manage and manipulate than it was a quarter of a century ago when I came to town."

The complex politics of US foreign policy, if anything, has been heightened with the collapse of the Cold War, the war on terrorism, the challenges of globalization, and the rising **political polarization** with which Presidents George W. Bush, Barack Obama, and Donald Trump have had to contend. Indeed, with its roots in the domestic reaction to the Vietnam War, polarization in foreign policymaking has increased steadily. With the end of the Cold War, the glue of anticommunism largely disappeared and polarization in foreign policymaking increased further, while ideological and partisan differences amplified the complexity and consequences of foreign policy politics.

A Framework for Understanding US Foreign Policymaking

How will we make sense of the complex politics of US foreign policy? We use a general **analytical framework** that provides the basic structure or frame of reference for organizing and thinking about (i.e., analyzing, conceptualizing, and synthesizing) the information and knowledge available in order to understand the politics of US foreign policy. As we noted, it is common practice to refer to the preeminence of presidents over American foreign policy. In fact, a common framework of US foreign policymaking is the **Presidential Preeminence** framework, illustrated on the left side of Figure 1.1. This framework is depicted as a series of concentric circles beginning with the president and expanding outward to include advisers, bureaucracies, Congress, and the public. According to this framework, the influence and relevance of actors decreases with the distance from the center of the circles, suggesting that the president dominates policymaking. Because we understand that presidential leadership is more a variable than a constant in the politics of US foreign policy, we adopt the analytical framework shown on the right side of Figure 1.1, which we call **Shifting Leadership and Politics**.

Unlike the Presidential Preeminence framework, the Shifting Leadership and Politics framework recognizes the complex and messy politics of the US foreign policy process and the varying roles and leadership of the president, presidential advisers, the agencies of the foreign policy bureaucracy, Congress and its members, societal forces and actors such as public opinion, interest groups and the media, and international factors as well. Our framework indicates that the White House *may* dominate, but it does not necessarily *always* dominate. Thus, while presidential leadership is a key aspect of US foreign policymaking, our analytical framework encourages consideration of the conditions under which it is more or less likely, as well as the roles and resources of other players in the foreign policy

FIGURE 1.1

Two Frameworks for Understanding US Foreign Policymaking: Presidential Preeminence (left) and Shifting Leadership and Politics (right)

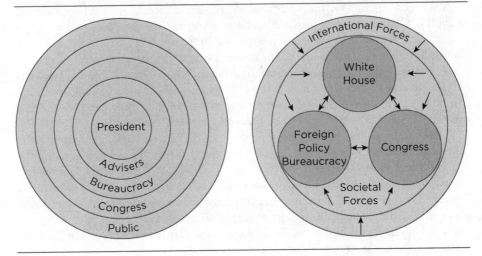

process, including the foreign policy bureaucracy and Congress, and the roles and resources they bring to the process as well.

Organized by this analytical framework, our examination of the players and process of US foreign policy addresses two central and overarching themes: (1) the patterns and changes in the politics of US foreign policy, and (2) the conditions for and challenges to presidential leadership of foreign policy. We begin our examination of the politics and processes of US foreign policy with the international and historical contexts, which set the stage and provide the foundation for understanding the politics of US foreign policy. Chapter 2 briefly provides the global and historical context, focusing on an overview of international settings, US orientations to roles in the world, and the major historical patterns of US foreign policy since the founding of the country. Our discussion in Chapter 2 thus incorporates factors and forces from the international and societal circles of our analytical framework.

In Part II of our text, we turn to the inner core of our analytical framework, focusing on the three circles at the center of the policymaking process: the major governmental institutions and players from the White House, the foreign policy bureaucracy, and Congress.

The White House. The role of the president and top aides and advisers stems from the president's position as the chief executive. The person of the president and his or her individual characteristics and the nature of the presidency and its institutional characteristics are important aspects that affect the politics and processes of US foreign policy and the opportunities for presidential leadership.

The Foreign Policy Bureaucracy. This circle consists of the State Department, the Defense Department, the Central Intelligence Agency, as well as economic agencies created to provide advice and implement policy decisions. The bureaucracy's expertise and control of information place it in a position to shape the formulation of policy by performing much of the generation and consideration of policy alternatives. Moreover, the various agencies of the foreign policy bureaucracy shape policy with their primary role in its day-to-day implementation. In both of these roles, the role and influence of the officials and agencies of the foreign policy bureaucracy are affected by the nature and organizational characteristics of bureaucracy.

Congress. This circle includes the leadership, committees, individual members, and staff of both houses of Congress. While Congress and its members are affected by many structural characteristics and electoral constraints, including its size, decentralized nature, limited access to information, and procedures, the institution and its individual members have access to potentially potent avenues of influence. These include tools such as the ability to pass laws; the constitutional and statutory authority to hold oversight hearings, require reports, and request individual briefings; the advise-and-consent authority over treaties and appointments; and the "power of the purse."

Our framework invites consideration of the opportunities and challenges of presidential—or White House (i.e., the president and top staff/advisers)—leadership, and we devote considerable attention to the conditions under which White House leadership is enhanced but also constrained. However, our framework also directs consideration to foreign policy leadership by the foreign policy bureaucracy and by Congress, as well as competition among some or all of the three governmental circles over foreign policy influence. Thus, our framework highlights the importance of presidential leadership and management, but it accounts for shifting patterns of leadership and influence among the governmental actors. In effect, we treat presidential leadership as a variable, not a given.

We examine the players and institutions at the center of the foreign policy process in the eight chapters that make up Part II of our text. Chapter 3 examines presidential power and the president's ability to direct US foreign policy. This sets the stage for examination of the major institutions of the foreign policy bureaucracy and their input in the policy process: the State Department in Chapter 4, the military establishment in Chapter 5, and the intelligence community in Chapter 6. Chapter 7 discusses how the president attempts to manage foreign policy and makes use of the National Security Council within the executive branch. Chapter 8 focuses on the players, institutions, and processes of foreign economic policymaking. Chapter 9 examines the role of Congress in foreign policy and the nature of interbranch politics. Part II concludes with Chapter 10, which offers a summary overview and theoretical synthesis of presidential, bureaucratic, and congressional policymaking power and employs different policymaking models to discuss the interaction of these actors and the opportunities for leadership to explain the dynamics of the policymaking process.

Part III turns to the examination of how the larger society and domestic politics affect the government and the foreign policymaking process. We begin in Chapter 11 with the significant and often underestimated role of the public and its beliefs—public opinion, political ideology, and American national style—in the making of US foreign policy. Then we examine the role and influence of interest groups and group politics in Chapter 12. Chapter 13 addresses the nature and effects of the media and the role of communications in the politics of US foreign policy.

The book concludes in Part IV with Chapter 14, which provides a summary of all that we have covered. In the concluding chapter, we synthesize our discussions of the global, governmental, and societal factors; we explore key patterns of influence and the shifting leadership that our analytical framework leads us to, returning to the two central themes of our text; and we also offer final insights on the politics of US foreign policy for the future.

POLITICS AND UNCERTAINTY IN THE TWENTY-FIRST CENTURY

Our text is organized by our Shifting Leadership and Politics framework and the two themes we build around throughout its pages. The analytical framework thus provides a meaningful way to make sense of the complexity and politics of US foreign policy. We hope the net result will be your acquisition of better insights into and understanding of how and why the United States engages in foreign policy as it does.

This is a particularly interesting time to examine the complex politics of US foreign policy because the Cold War has come to an end, the United States has entered the twenty-first century, and the nation has experienced the September 11 terrorist attacks and the Great Recession. Significant changes in global politics and power have ensued, and disagreement and uncertainty about the role of the US and its engagement in the world have heightened throughout the presidencies of George W. Bush, Barack Obama, and Donald Trump. How has the global context shaped the patterns and politics of US foreign policy? How will the interaction of global context, government, and society shape the future patterns of the politics of US foreign policy and presidential leadership? We take up these questions throughout this book.

THINK ABOUT THIS

Hubert Humphrey, who served in the US Senate from 1949 to 1964 and from 1971 to 1978, and as vice president from 1965 to 1969, once said, "Foreign policy is really domestic policy with its hat on." Think about the nature of the foreign policy process as we have initially presented it in this chapter.

What makes the politics of US foreign policy complex and messy?

KEY TERMS

analytical framework 7

foreign policy 3

foreign policy process 3

national interest 6

political polarization 7

politics 6

Visit **edge.sagepub.com/scottrosati7e** to help you accomplish your coursework goals in an easy-to-use learning environment.

The Global and Historical Context

POWER, ROLE, AND POLITICS ON THE WORLD STAGE

US Navy photo by Mass Communication Specialist Seaman Zachary A. Anderson/Released/Flickr

PHOTO 2.1 The USS *Abraham Lincoln*, F/A 18 Hornets, and MH-60S helicopters project US global power.

LEARNING OBJECTIVES

1. Know the meaning and significance of the global context as a factor in US foreign policy.

2. Understand the meaning and limits of the isolationism-internationalism debate.

3. Identify the nature and characteristics of the Continental, Regional, and Global eras of US foreign policy.

4. Assess the relationship between the global context and the historical patterns of US foreign policy.

INTRODUCTION: THE GLOBAL AND HISTORICAL CONTEXT OF THE CONTEMPORARY CHALLENGE

Since his surprise election victory in 2016, President Donald Trump has pursued a broad, often controversial agenda to reverse the course of current policies in many arenas. In foreign policy, the Trump administration retreated from decades of bipartisan commitment to free trade, the North Atlantic Treaty Organization, and support for the European Union, to name a few examples. The administration's inconsistent approaches to Russia, China, and other important states have generated uncertainty at home and abroad. According to some observers, President Trump's pursuit of a muscular nationalism "seems determined to challenge the policies and practices that have cemented America's vast power and influence in the 20th and 21st centuries" (Sestanovich 2017). President Trump did little to allay such fears when he asserted that the post–World War II international order, which all presidents since Harry Truman have been committed to building and sustaining, is "not working at all" (Landler 2017).

As at numerous points in history, US policymakers now grapple with questions about the nature of world politics and United States's role in the world. After seventy years of relative consensus over US global leadership and engagement, significant debates over the nature and purpose of US involvement in world affairs and the United States's relationship to the rest of the world raise questions about almost all aspects of US foreign policy. Some observers point to potentially far-reaching shifts in global power and to problems and potentially major changes in the United States's relationships with its allies and friends, competitors, and adversaries that impact US security, freedom, and prosperity as well as the United States's roles and policies in the international arena.

Contemporary American foreign policymakers have strategic choices to make about US foreign policy engagement and policy in this current time of transition and change. Understanding the politics and processes of US foreign policy choices in this critical time begins with understanding the broad global context—the outer circle of our analytical framework introduced in Chapter 1 (see Figure 1.1). The present and future of US foreign policy is shaped in part by this context and by the past decisions and actions of US policy-makers in response to it. In this chapter, we consider how and why US foreign policy—in national security and economics—evolved after independence as the United States became a global power in the twentieth century, and how the global environment has affected American policy and power from the Cold War into the twenty-first century.

THE GLOBAL CONTEXT: PATTERNS AND DEBATES IN US FOREIGN POLICY

The **global context**—or setting, environment, or milieu—refers to phenomena external to the institutions, beliefs, and processes of human interaction in government and society. This context refers to such elements as the country's power (military and economic), resources, and level of technology, and to the larger global arena of which the United States is a part, all of which influence the complex politics of US foreign policy in the past, present, and future.

The global environment plays a significant role in the politics of US foreign policy in two principal ways. First, global structures and patterns set the underlying conditions or parameters of likely US foreign policy. For example, the general patterns that prevail throughout the globe affect American power and the United States's international role, thus setting the stage on which the politics of US foreign policy operates in society and government. Second, particular world events and relationships often have an immediate impact on domestic politics and the US policymaking process. For example, **international crises** (commonly defined in terms of surprise, a threat to values, and little time to respond) are events that catapult an issue onto the political agenda and often play an influential role in the politics of US foreign policy. Similarly, **international conflict** and war present problems and challenges to which the United States might respond and shape the politics and processes of those responses. Therefore, both general patterns and immediate events in America's global context affect one another and are often mutually reinforcing (see Gilpin 1981; Hermann 1969; Lebow 1981; Morse 1973; Waltz 1959). Set in this global context, the foreign policy of the United States has a long and rich history since American independence, and understanding the connections between the international system and US foreign policy through the rise of American power is important to understanding where we are today.

A Different Perspective

COMPETING GLOBAL THEORIES

In the aftermath of World War II, the study of international relations became a serious discipline, especially within the United States and academia. Since the 1970s, **three different global theoretical approaches (or perspectives or paradigms)** have dominated: (1) classical realism, (2) liberal idealism (or internationalism), and (3) social globalism (see Knutsen 1997).

Classical realism tends to see the world as relatively anarchical and conflictual. In this view, the primary actors are (sovereign and independent) states, the most important issues revolve around national security and the use of force, and the principal motivation is the promotion of national power and wealth and prestige. So-called realists focus on the tremendously uneven distribution of power among states, on great power conflicts (and alliances and empires), the rise and decline of power, the maintenance of stability and order, and the utility of force as a means to settle disputes and international conflict. Conservative realists tend to be more pessimistic about the future possibilities of a world of greater peace, prosperity, and human development. According to Michael Doyle (1997:18) in *Ways of War and Peace*, to realists it is "the nature of humanity, or the character of states, or the structure of international order (or all three together) that allows

wars to occur. This possibility of war requires that states follow 'realpolitik': be self-interested, prepare for war, and calculate relative balances of power."

Liberal idealism (or internationalism) tends to see a world of more cooperation and complex interdependence. Although they see states as important actors, liberal idealists contend that the dominance of states has diminished with the advent of other influential actors, such as international organizations (governmental actors like the United Nations or the International Monetary Fund, and nongovernmental ones like private voluntary organizations), multinational corporations, and ethnic groups. Such complexity allows for a much more interdependent (capitalist) international political economy, in which a variety of issues may be significant, including not just national security but political, economic, social, and cultural issues as well. This suggests that despite a world of considerable conflict, there is also much cooperation and order that regularly does and can occur—hence, the importance of such forces as international law; international norms and rules; international networks; international markets, finance, and commerce; and democratic institutions. Liberal idealists tend to be much more optimistic about the potential

(Continued)

(Continued)

for greater cooperation and peace, prosperity, and human development throughout the world. In their view, the state is not a hypothetical single, rational, national actor in a state of war (as it is in the classical realist view) but, instead, is a coalition or conglomerate of coalitions and interests, representing individuals and groups and transnational actors.

Social globalism tends to see the existence of a global system, but one in which power and wealth is incredibly unevenly distributed throughout the world. The world is often divided into different classes: a small, wealthy class of powerful or "core" states (and actors—basically the "developed countries" or "First World"); a predominantly poor class of weak or "peripheral" states (and actors—the "developing countries" or "Third World"); and a small group of industrializing or "semiperiphery" states (and actors—such as India and Brazil). These political and especially economic distinctions between different classes of people also seem to exist within different countries and societies. The emphasis is on the international political economy, the dominance of the capitalist system, and the inherent inequalities and dependencies that result for the poor relative to the wealthy that are difficult to change. Social globalists are extremely pessimistic about the future, given the global system of inequality and injustice; at the same time, they remain optimistic or hopeful that major or radical changes can occur to dramatically increase peace, prosperity, and human development for all.

What are the implications of these three competing perspectives for American power and US foreign policy?

From Isolationism to Internationalism?

The original thirteen colonies—established as a result of European (especially English and French) colonial expansion—rebelled against England in the American Revolution. The issues that over time incited the American revolutionaries, formerly loyal British subjects, involved the nature of the imperial relationship with the "mother" country. From the perspective of the British crown, the thirteen colonies were an integral part of the British colonial and mercantile empire that increasingly spanned the globe. Therefore, the colonists rightfully were subjects of British imperial rule. From the perspective of the colonists, who increasingly saw themselves as possessing the rights of Englishmen, the British increasingly were abusing their power as they denied representation, taxed the colonies, and controlled trade with the rest of the world.

Eventually the political and economic conflicts escalated to the point of a formal Declaration of Independence in 1776. With significant French assistance, the ensuing five-year "war of independence" resulted in American independence and official recognition with the signing of the Treaty of Paris of 1783 (by England, France, Spain, and the United States). The treaty gave the United States territory from the upper Great Lakes almost to the Gulf of Mexico (Spain held Florida and the Gulf Coast) and reaching westward to the Mississippi. European expansion and power politics were heavily involved in the creation of the United States and would continue to play an important role in US foreign policy after independence.

In his 1796 farewell address, America's first president, George Washington, offered the following advice: "The great rule of conduct for us in regard to foreign nations is in extending our commercial relations, to have with them as little political connection as possible .... It is our true policy to steer clear of permanent alliances with any portion of the foreign world." In 1801, President Thomas Jefferson used his inaugural address to call for "peace, commerce, and honest friendship with all nations—entangling alliances with none." Two decades later, then–Secretary of State John Quincy Adams emphasized similar limits on US involvement in world affairs, declaring, "Wherever the standard of freedom and independence has been or shall be unfurled, there will her heart, her benedictions and her prayers be. But she goes not abroad in search of monsters to destroy. She is the well-wisher to the freedom and independence of all. She is the champion and vindicator only of her own." Taken together, comments such as these, and some of the ensuing features of US foreign policy in the nineteenth and early twentieth centuries, have led some observers to characterize the US approach to the world as a contest between isolationism and internationalism. In this perspective, isolationism dominated until World War II, with a brief period of engagement around the end of World War I, and internationalism has dominated since then.

However, as most US diplomatic historians argue, this simple breakdown of US foreign policy over time distorts much more than it enlightens. If one defines **isolationism** to mean noninvolvement abroad, the United States has never truly been isolationist during its history. Even if one defines isolationism more narrowly to mean *no* involvement in European political affairs, it would still be stretching reality to conclude that US foreign policy was isolationist. In fact, the United States was never uninvolved with Europe, whether in North America or across the Atlantic. As historian A. J. Bacevich (1994:75) stated,

> Only by the loosest conceivable definition of the term, however, could "isolation" be said to represent the reality of United States policy during the first century-and-a-half of American independence. A nation that by 1900 had quadrupled its land mass at the expense of other claimants, engaged in multiple wars of conquest, vigorously pursued access to markets in every quarter of the globe, and acquired by force an overseas empire could hardly be said to have been "isolated" in any meaningful sense.

For example, consider the regular use of US armed forces outside the country between 1798 and World War II (see Table 2.1). Before World War II, US armed forces were used abroad 163 times. Before the Spanish-American War of 1898, there were 98 uses of US armed forces abroad. Overall, the frequency of US armed intervention has remained pretty much the same over time—an average of about one "armed intervention" per year for more than 140 years. Although many of the cases might be considered "minor" incidents, especially from a twenty-first-century perspective, they all involved the "official" use of US armed forces in conflicts with other states while pursuing American interests. Moreover, this list does not include the use of US armed forces against Native American people as the United States expanded westward during the nineteenth century.

TABLE 2.1

US Military Interventions Before World War II

1798–1801—Undeclared naval war with France	1843—China
	1843—Africa
1801–1805—Tripoli	1844—Mexico
1806—Mexico	1846–1848—Mexico
1806–1810—Gulf of Mexico	1849—Smyrna
1810—West Florida (Spanish Territory)	1851—Turkey
1812—East Florida (Spanish Territory)	1851—Johanna Island
1812–1815—Great Britain	1852–1853—Argentina
1813—West Florida (Spain)	1853—Nicaragua
1813–1815—Marquesas Islands	1853–1854—Japan
1815—Tripoli	1853–1854—Ryukyu and Bonin Islands
1816—Spanish Florida	1854—China
1816–1818—Spanish Florida (First Seminole War)	1854—Nicaragua
	1855—China
1817—Amelia Island (Spanish Territory)	1855—Fiji Islands
1818—Oregon	1855—Uruguay
1820–1823—Africa	1856—Panama
1822—Cuba	1856—China
1823—Cuba	1857—Nicaragua
1824—Cuba	1858—Uruguay
1824—Puerto Rico	1858—Fiji Islands
1825—Cuba	1858–1859—Turkey
1827—Greece	1859—Paraguay
1831–1832—Falkland Islands	1859—Mexico
1832—Sumatra	1859—China
1833—Argentina	1860—Angola, Portuguese West Africa
1835–1836—Peru	1860—Colombia
1836—Mexico	1863—Japan
1838–1839—Sumatra	1864—Japan
1840—Fiji Islands	1865—Panama
1841—Drummond Islands	1866—Mexico
1841—Samoa	1866—China
1842—Mexico	

1867—Nicaragua	1901-1902—Colombia
1868—Japan	1903—Honduras
1868—Uruguay	1903—Dominican Republic
1868—Colombia	1903—Syria
1870—Mexico	1903-1904—Abyssinia
1870—Hawaiian Islands	1903-1914— Panama
1871—Korea	1904—Dominican Republic
1873—Colombia	1904—Tangier, Morocco
1873—Mexico	1904—Panama
1874—Hawaiian Islands	1904-1905—Korea
1876—Mexico	1906-1909—Cuba
1882—Egypt	1907—Honduras
1885—Panama	1910—Nicaragua
1888—Korea	1911—Honduras
1888—Haiti	1911—China
1888-1889—Samoa	1912—Honduras
1889—Hawaiian Islands	1912—Panama
1890—Argentina	1912—Cuba
1891—Haiti	1912—China
1891—Bering Sea	1912—Turkey
1891—Chile	1912-1941—China
1893—Hawaii	1913—Mexico
1894—Brazil	1914—Haiti
1894—Nicaragua	1914—Dominican Republic
1894-1895—China	1914-1917— Mexico
1894-1896—Korea	1915-1934—Haiti
1895—Colombia	1916—China
1896—Nicaragua	1916-1924—Dominican Republic
1898—Spain	1917—China
1898-1899—China	1917-1918—World War I
1899—Nicaragua	1917-1922—Cuba
1899—Samoa	1918-1919—Mexico
1899-1901—Philippines	1918-1920—Panama
1900—China	1918-1920—Soviet Russia

(Continued)

TABLE 2.1

(Continued)

1919—Dalmatia	1926—China
1919—Turkey	1926-1933—Nicaragua
1919—Honduras	1927—China
1920—China	1932—China
1920—Guatemala	1933—Cuba
1920-1922—Russia	1934—China
1921—Panama, Costa Rica	1940—Newfoundland, Bermuda, St. Lucia, Bahamas, Jamaica, Antigua, Trinidad, and British Guiana
1922—Turkey	
1922-1923—China	1941—Greenland
1924—Honduras	1941—Dutch Guiana
1924—China	1941—Iceland
1925—Honduras	1941—Germany
1925—Panama	1941-1945—World War II

Source: US Congress, House, Committee on Foreign Relations, *Background Information on the Use of U.S. Armed Forces in Foreign Countries*, 1975 Revision, Committee Print (94th Cong., 1st Sess., 1975).

The extent of the US government's use of military force throughout the world since independence may come as a surprise to many Americans. Although the scope of armed intervention tended to be concentrated in the Western Hemisphere and Asia, Table 2.1 shows that the United States intervened in other parts of the world as well. Such interventionist behavior indicates that the US was quite active internationally (see Braumoeller 2010).

Instead of the simple—and misleading—distinction between isolationism and internationalism, another way to think about the development and trajectory of US foreign policy after independence is to divide it into **three major eras since independence**: (1) the Continental Era, 1776–1865; (2) the Regional Era, 1865–1940; and (3) the Global Era, 1941–present.

The Continental Era, 1776–1865

From its earliest days as an independent state, the United States had an active foreign policy. Indeed, the noted addresses by George Washington and Thomas Jefferson might be better interpreted as arguments for "nonalignment"—whereby the US should avoid permanent alliances and entanglements—rather than for isolationism. During this period, most US actions focused on the surrounding North American continent until the latter half of the nineteenth century. During this time, American leaders tended to focus on two general goals: nation-building and continental expansion.

Nation-building was critical since the United States was a new and relatively weak (emerging) country at the turn of the nineteenth century. It had won its national independence from the global superpower of its time, England, but it faced many of the problems that any new country with a colonial history faces upon gaining independence. Although far from Europe, the former thirteen colonies were surrounded by territories that England, France, Spain, and Russia coveted and fought over. As Walter LaFeber (1994:11) has stated, "From the beginning of their history, Americans lived not in any splendid isolation, far from the turmoil and corruption of Europe many had hoped to escape. They instead had to live in settlements that were surrounded by great and ambitious European powers."

The economy of the North American colonies also was dependent on the English economy. In addition, the new country was attempting to implement the first democratic experiment in the modern world. Given this environment, a priority for most Americans was nation-building: to build an independent country safe from its neighbors, construct a strong national economy, and establish a stable democratic polity. Therefore, much of the focus was on strengthening the internal situation in the United States.

The second goal, **continental expansion**, was closely linked to nation-building. What better way to protect the nation from potentially hostile neighbors than to expand its territory and push the British, French, Spanish, and Russians (as well as the Mexicans and Native Americans) farther and farther away from the eastern seaboard, preferably off the North American continent and out of the Western Hemisphere? What better way to build a strong economy than through the acquisition of more land that could be put to work? Strengthening national security and the national economy also contributed to political stability. But this meant that "Americans—whether they liked it or not—were part of European power politics even as they moved into the forests and fertile lands beyond the Appalachian Mountains. They could not separate their destiny from the destiny of those they had left behind in Europe" (LaFeber 1994:12; see also Weeks 1996).

Up to and including the purchase of Alaska from Russia in 1867, US foreign policy aimed at acquiring and/or annexing increasing amounts of territory throughout the North American continent. Although such territory was inhabited predominantly by Native Americans, the United States acquired it from European states: from England in the North and Northwest, such as northern Maine and the Oregon territories; from France in the Louisiana Territory to the west; from Spain in the Florida territories to the south; from Mexico in the Southwest, such as Texas and the southwestern territories (including California); and from Russia in the farthest reaches of the Northwest (Alaska) (see Figure 2.1). Native American peoples suffered the most from this expansion. According to Walter LaFeber (1994:10), "A central theme of American diplomatic history must be the clash between the European settlers and the Native Americans"—a population estimated to be between 8 million and 10 million inhabitants throughout North America by the time Christopher Columbus first arrived. Clashes were constant with Native Americans—misnamed "Indians"—as Americans expanded westward. As Thomas Jefferson put it to James Madison in 1801:

However our present interests may restrain us within our limits, it is impossible not to look forward to distant times, when our rapid multiplication will expand it beyond those limits, and cover the whole northern if not the southern continent, with people speaking the same language, governed in similar forms, and by similar laws. (quoted in Van Alstyne 1974:87)

The agents of US continental expansion were not only the government, especially the army, but also thousands of private and entrepreneurial Americans spilling westward in search of land, gold, profit, and freedom. The net result was that by the 1860s the United States had grown from thirteen colonies on the eastern seaboard to a country that spanned the continent. In the words of diplomatic historian Thomas Bailey (1961:3), "The point is often missed that during the nineteenth century the United States practiced internal colonialism and imperialism on a continental scale."

During the Continental Era, the United States was active outside North America as well, but this activity was more sporadic in nature. American commerce and merchants were active in all areas of the globe, especially Europe, the West Indies (i.e., the Caribbean), the Orient (i.e., Asia), and the slave trade of Africa. "During the eighteenth and nineteenth centuries," according to Alfred Eckes (1995:1), "the founders of U.S. foreign policy pressed

FIGURE 2.1

US Territorial and Continental Expansion by the Mid-Nineteenth Century

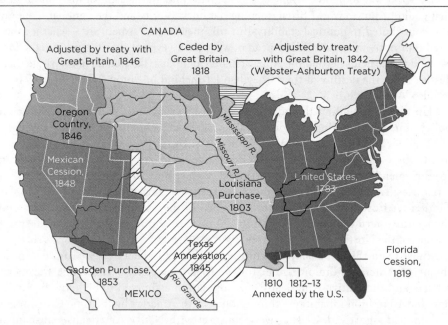

Source: Walter LaFeber, *The American Age: United States Foreign Policy at Home and Abroad,* 2nd ed. (New York: W.W. Norton, 1994), p. 132.

to open markets and attacked mercantilistic barriers abroad in order to bolster the domestic economy and secure independence." Interruption of American commerce by the British during the Napoleonic War, for example, was a major cause of the War of 1812 between the United States and England.

Despite the "spirit of commerce" since colonial times, American merchants were unable to open up the mercantilist control of trade by the European powers and increasingly adopted a policy of **economic nationalism**, including the use of tariffs to encourage (and protect) the growth of domestic manufactures. Increasingly, tariff policy became trade policy in the nineteenth century (e.g., Eckes 1995; Kindleberger 1977).

The US government was also politically and militarily active beyond the continent, especially through the Navy. The first diplomatic consulate established overseas by the new government was in Canton, China, in 1789. As early as 1821, "the navy began operating a squadron off the west coast of South America; and by 1835 intercourse with China and the East Indies reached the point where it justified the establishment of a separate East India squadron" (Van Alstyne 1974:126).

Regarding Latin America, the **Monroe Doctrine** (declared in 1823) insisted on an end to European interference and colonization in the Western Hemisphere, for which the United States promised noninterference in European affairs. As early as 1850, the US negotiated the Clayton-Bulwer Treaty for rights to build an interoceanic canal. And attempts also were made to annex Cuba and Santo Domingo (now known as the Dominican Republic) to the US republic. In Asia, the United States, led by Daniel Webster, negotiated the 1844 Treaty of Wanghia, giving Americans "most favored nation" status (like other European countries) in trade and extraterritorial rights with China. Americans, led by Commodore Matthew C. Perry, forced Japan to open its ports to foreigners and commerce in 1854; and the Hawaiian and Midway Islands were occupied as transit points for American commerce with Asia.

The Regional Era, 1865–1940

By the latter half of the nineteenth century, the United States had been quite successful in building an independent and transcontinental country that was growing more powerful. By the end of the Civil War, the United States no longer faced any immediate threats from its neighbors in the hemisphere. The Civil War also settled the divisions between the North and the South, allowing political stability at the national level. The national economy was vibrant and growing, and the transcontinental railroad was completed in 1869. According to Van Alstyne (1960:10), as the US "entered its period of consolidation and centralization, it began developing its internal economy intensively, and abroad it soon joined in the international scramble for material wealth and power," best exemplified by the Spanish-American War of 1898 in which Cuba and the Philippines became US colonies.

As the United States reached the limits of continental expansion, more and more Americans during the latter half of the nineteenth century were beginning to speak of the future of the United States in terms of a **manifest destiny**. According to William Weeks (1996:61), "Manifest Destiny was founded on the a priori conviction of the uniqueness of the American nation and the necessity of an American empire." Such an orientation reflected three key themes (see also Stephanson 1995):

> The special virtues of the American people and their institutions; their mission to redeem and remake the world in the image of America; and the American destiny under God to accomplish this sublime task. Under the aegis of virtue, mission, and destiny evolved a powerful nationalist mythology that was virtually impossible to oppose. (Weeks 1996:61)

In fact, the foundation for ideas of US **exceptionalism**, mission, and destiny had existed from the time of the Puritan settlements in New England. They were popularized by John Winthrop's sermon in 1631 that the Puritan colony in Massachusetts Bay represented a "city upon a hill" from which the regeneration of the world might proceed. Many Americans came to characterize the United States as a special place where human society might begin anew, uncorrupted by Old World institutions and ideas, giving it a special mission and role in the world.

Following the Civil War, US foreign policy actively promoted political stability and economic expansion abroad, especially in Latin America and Asia. US foreign policy increasingly became a presence on the global stage. The US government and American business dramatically increased their presence in Latin America throughout Central America and the Caribbean. The US government promoted friendly political regimes in the region that would be unresponsive to European involvement, open to American trade and investment, and stable enough to pay back their American bank loans. In turn, American business intensified with the rapid expansion of American trade, loans, and investment in the region.

Increased US involvement in Latin America—a region that was experiencing decolonization, nation-building by independent states, and considerable political instability—resulted in frequent American military intervention and occupation, especially after the turn of the century. As Secretary of State Richard Olney proclaimed in 1895, "The United States is practically sovereign on this continent, and its fiat is law upon the subjects to which it confines its interposition." The Olney Proclamation reinforced the original purpose of the Monroe Doctrine, that the United States had the right, and now the power, to intervene in and dominate its "own backyard"—foreshadowing what was to come with the Spanish-American War and after.

From President Theodore Roosevelt's "Big Stick" policies to William Howard Taft's "Dollar Diplomacy" and Woodrow Wilson's "New Freedom," through the Warren Harding, Calvin Coolidge, and Herbert Hoover administrations, the United States regularly sent the Marines to crush local rebellions, prop up old or new regimes, and restore political stability in virtually every major state in Central America and the Caribbean, often only to return again and again. Military intervention usually meant that the local "customs houses" were subsequently run by US government (usually Treasury Department) officials to guarantee that revenues from tariffs and duties were collected to repay American loans. Financial supervision, for example, lasted thirteen years in Nicaragua (1911–1924), twenty-five years in Haiti (1916–1941), thirty-six years in the Dominican Republic (1905–1941), and sixty years in America's colony of Cuba (1898–1958). American leaders so badly wanted a canal to connect the Atlantic and Pacific oceans that in 1903 President Roosevelt actively instigated and supported Panamanian secession from Colombia. He then immediately recognized the new country and signed a treaty giving Panama $10 million, plus $250,000 a year for rights "in perpetuity" for a ten-mile-wide strip—which became the Panama Canal Zone—that cut the new country literally in half.

Thus, American involvement and power had carved out a regional **sphere of influence**. This was the period during which the United States acquired its earliest colonial possessions (and "protectorates") in the area, including Cuba, Puerto Rico, and the Virgin Islands. Not until the 1920s and 1930s, under Herbert Hoover and then Franklin Roosevelt's "Good Neighbor" policy, was direct intervention of American troops into the domestic affairs of US neighbors temporarily abandoned.

American foreign policy was in search of political stability and US economic expansion in Asia as well, with China being the major prize. "Merchants, missionaries, adventurers, sea captains, naval officers, and consular officers crowded into the Pacific during the nineteenth century and spun a web whose strands extended to every part of the ocean" (Van Alstyne 1974:125). Unlike Latin America, which was Christianized by the Spanish, there was a large American missionary presence in Asia, particularly in Japan and in China (over 3,000 by 1905). And during the crisis with Spain over Cuba, the US Navy, just before the Spanish-American War began, attacked the remnants of the Spanish empire in Asia, producing American Samoa, Guam, Wake Island, and, most important, the Philippines as colonies of the United States (see also Rosenberg 1982).

However, American involvement in Asia and the Pacific resulted in more limited uses of force because of the region's distance from American shores and the strong military presence of England, France, Russia, and Japan. US foreign policy in China, for example, emphasized an **Open Door** approach in order to maximize American involvement and trade (Williams 1988). Therefore, America's military and commercial involvement resulted in fewer costs as well as fewer gains. The United States, nevertheless, sent more than 120,000 American troops from 1899 to 1902 to fight its first noncontinental counterinsurgency war, eventually defeating a national independence movement in the Philippines to preserve its new colonial control.

Even though US foreign policy was oriented toward the regions to its immediate south and distant west, the final two decades of the Regional Era saw increasing engagement in European and world affairs as well. Entering the twentieth century, France and especially Great Britain were the two global powers that dominated the global status quo. At the same time, Japan and Germany rapidly grew in power and challenged Great Britain, France, and the status quo. Ironically, the resulting two world wars contributed to the shift from Europe as the center of world politics to the rise of American power and the international leadership of the United States.

While officially neutral during the early part of World War I, the United States eventually became a major participant in bringing about the war's outcome. Woodrow Wilson was, in fact, highly instrumental in influencing the Treaty of Versailles, which officially ended the war and attempted to create a new liberal world order through the League of Nations. During 1918–1919, the United States even sent 14,000 troops—along with the British, Canadians, French, Czechs, and Japanese—to occupy part of the newly declared Soviet Union in an effort to aid the anti-Bolsheviks and reestablish a Russian front against Germany.

After World War I, the 1920s and 1930s are popularly thought of as a return to isolationism. The US rejection of American participation in the League of Nations, the rise of isolationist sentiment among the American public and a strong peace movement, and American reluctance to become actively involved in European conflicts (especially during the Great Depression and the early years of World War II) provide good evidence of the more isolationist orientation during the interwar period. However, as diplomatic historian William Cohen (1987:xii) has argued, "rejection of the Treaty of Versailles and lack of membership in the League had little impact . . . on American involvement in world affairs in the decade that followed. In the 1920s the United States was more profoundly engaged in international matters than in any peacetime era in its history."

In addition to the active regional foreign policy engagement already discussed, the United States undertook a number of important global diplomatic initiatives. From November 1921 to February 1922, the US hosted and actively promoted a major naval disarmament conference in Washington, DC, that resulted in the first major arms control treaty in modern times, along with the Four Power Treaty and the Nine Power Treaty involving Pacific island possessions and the rivalry in China). In 1928, the United States and France jointly sponsored the Kellogg-Briand Pact in an effort to outlaw war. The US also began to play a more active, though unofficial, role in League of Nation activities.

Just as important, the United States became increasingly important to the international political economy following World War I, which was still dominated by the Europeans. As a result of the debts and damage incurred by the war, European economies became increasingly dependent on the US government and on American business as a source of trade and finance. According to Cohen (1987:41), "Clearly, the impact of American trade, investments, and tourism on the world economy in the 1920s was enormous. No other nation even approximated the United States in economic importance." Nevertheless, as the British role declined, the United States also continued its embrace of **protectionism** in trade—especially in the 1930s—and refrained from taking a strong political leadership role in the international economy, which contributed to the world falling into a great depression (Kindleberger 1977).

The Global Era, 1941–present

World War II ended the Regional Era of US foreign policy, and its consequences for European power and the global system contributed to the rise of American leadership and engagement in world politics. With the decline of Europe following World War II, the Soviet Union and the United States filled the political vacuum in world affairs. The ascendance of the Soviet Union and the United States in the wake of the European collapse resulted in a global context of bipolarity in which American assertiveness in world politics and an American-Soviet conflict of some type were almost inevitable.

World War II lifted the American economy out of the Great Depression of the 1930s and catapulted it into unprecedented prosperity. American economic production was the key to Allied success in the war and was responsible for producing almost half the value of the world's goods and services following the conflict. As Godfrey Hodgson (1976:19) observed:

> In 1945, the United States was bulging with an abundance of every resource that held the key to power in the modern world: with land, food, raw materials, industrial plant, monetary reserves, scientific talent, and trained manpower. It was in the war years that the United States shot ahead of all its rivals economically. In four years, national income, national wealth, and industrial production all doubled or more than doubled. In the same period, . . . every other industrial nation came out of the war poorer and weaker than when it went in.

American multinational corporations and financial investment, which had been expanding since the turn of the century, came to dominate the postwar international marketplace. The United States emerged from World War II not only as a superpower but as the **hegemonic power** of its time (Ikenberry 1989).

After the US entered World War II, the Soviet Union and the United States were cautious partners who found themselves in an alliance of convenience during the war. The United States set its sights not only on defeating Germany and Japan but also on establishing a postwar order that would promote stability and security. Under President Franklin Roosevelt, the US took an active leadership role in planning for a global order that learned the lessons of the interwar period and their consequences for the Great Depression and World War II. Thus, the Roosevelt administration sought to establish structures and practices that would better ensure economic stability and prosperity and promote peace and multilateral cooperation.

In the world economy, the American strategy, arrived at in Bretton Woods, New Hampshire, in 1944, was to promote multilateral efforts with American allies to restore and manage an increasingly liberal, global market economy, based on a new system of fixed exchange rates and open, free trade. What came to be called the **Bretton Woods system** would provide necessary assistance and rules for economic transactions principally through the creation of three multilateral international organizations: the International Bank for Reconstruction and Development (IBRD, known as the World Bank) to make loans for economic recovery and development, the International Monetary Fund (IMF) to support the stability of national currencies based on gold, and the General Agreement on Tariffs and Trade (GATT) to promote and govern open trade (originally the ITO, International Trade Organization, was to be created but was opposed by the US Senate). Success on the economic front in promoting a liberal capitalist world order was thought to be crucial for ensuring peace and minimizing threats to international stability, as had occurred when the Great Depression led to the rise of Adolf Hitler (Gardner 1980; Ikenberry 1992).

The United States also sought to construct a new international political order that would promote cooperation and prevent the outbreak of further wars. Under Roosevelt, the US initially emphasized a strategy of multilateral cooperation based on a sphere-of-influence approach and the creation of a new international organization to replace the League of Nations—the United Nations. Roosevelt's strategy depended on global cooperation among members of the "Grand Alliance" during the war: the United States, the Soviet Union, Great Britain, France, and China. The instrument for maintaining cooperation among the "big five" and preventing a challenge to the status quo, which could lead to the outbreak of a new war, was the high-level diplomacy and creation of the United Nations, and especially the operation of the United Nations Security Council (a body in which each of the big five held veto power). Roosevelt also assumed that each of the five so-called great powers would exercise power over its regional sphere of influence: the United States in Latin America, the Soviet Union in Eastern Europe, Great Britain and France in Europe and their colonial possessions, and China in East Asia.

Before his death in April 1945, Roosevelt laid the foundation for the post–World War II US foreign policy and international leadership. However, Roosevelt's death left the White House to Harry Truman, who was unfamiliar with Roosevelt's postwar plans and lacked Roosevelt's considerable experience. Moreover, as war ended, it was soon clear that the European economies were in much worse shape than most people had thought and were in need of assistance beyond that which the Bretton Woods–devised multilateral international organizations were capable of providing.

Finally, hope for lasting cooperation among members of the Grand Alliance to achieve national security eroded quickly as distrust, fear, and conflict between the United States and the Soviet Union escalated. Roosevelt's grand strategy gave way to the realities of the postwar context. Specific international events and crises reflecting these World War II and postwar developments influenced domestic politics and the government policymaking process in such a way that they spurred the onset of the Cold War. Within the United States, for example, disputes over postwar European economic reconstruction; the fate of Germany; the rise of communism in Eastern Europe; the Soviet-American conflict over Iran, Greece, and Turkey; the fall of Chiang Kai-shek and the Nationalist government in China; the North Korean attack on South Korea; and the Soviet explosion of an atomic bomb all contributed to the growing Cold War environment both abroad and at home.

American foreign policy was soon dominated by a view of the Soviet Union as no longer an ally but an evil enemy attempting to achieve world empire. Americans in both government and society saw a "free world" led by the United States pitted against a "totalitarian world" led by the Soviet Union in a global Cold War throughout the 1950s and early 1960s. Thus, soon after World War II, the Global Era of US foreign policy emphasized American **internationalism** in the form of engagement and leadership or hegemony. Since the early postwar years, the US approach to the world has passed through four phases: (1) the Cold War Consensus, 1947–1968; (2) the Cold War Dissensus, 1969–1989; (3) the post–Cold War years, 1990–2001; and (4) the post-9/11 years, 2002–present.

The Cold War Consensus, 1947–1968. For roughly twenty years, through the administrations of President Truman and President Lyndon Johnson, US foreign policy experienced considerable continuity based on the twin goals of national security and economic prosperity. The twin goals were based on the quest for global security and stability from a perception of the rising "threat" of Soviet communist expansionism and the promotion of a liberal international market economy based on the principles of free, open trade and fixed exchange rates. The Cold War era also represented the height of the president's power to lead the country in foreign policy, as we discuss further in subsequent chapters.

Following the war, for the first time since independence and the Continental Era, Americans began to perceive an external threat to their national security: the advance of Soviet communism. In the postwar international context—a **bipolar world** with two "superpowers"—US engagement became more important. Because the new fear of Soviet communism became the key problem for most Americans, national security concerns drove US foreign policy and was defined in terms of global security and stability. In the bipolar world, the threat was perceived to be global and American leaders believed that, with the collapse of the British and French empires, only the United States had the power to respond. Although the United States and the Soviet Union never engaged in a "hot war" (i.e., a direct military clash), the United States prepared for a direct military confrontation with the Soviet Union and engaged in a global **Cold War**.

The US foreign policy strategy during this phase rested on a broad policy consensus that had four central pillars. First, US policymakers broadly shared a commitment to American engagement and leadership in world affairs. Although elements of both the left and the right in American politics dissented, a substantial bipartisan consensus supported internationalism and active American leadership, and the importance of American power to the security and stability of the international order.

Second, under American leadership, a **containment strategy** was developed that aimed to deter, by the threat of coercion, the spread of Soviet communism, first in Europe, then in Asia with the Korean War, and eventually throughout the world. The containment strategy was initially embodied in the Truman Doctrine, announced in 1947 and directed at containing Soviet expansion in the eastern Mediterranean countries of Greece and Turkey. In the words of one analyst, its future implications for US foreign policy were to be global and quite profound:

> The Truman Doctrine contained the seeds of American aid, economic or military, to more than one hundred countries; of mutual defense treaties with more than forty of them; of the great regional pacts, alliances, and unilateral commitments: to NATO, to the Middle East, to the Western Hemisphere, and to Southeast Asia. It justified fleets of carriers patrolling the Mediterranean and the South China Sea, nuclear submarines under the polar icecap, air bases in the Thai jungle, and police advisers in Uruguay and Bolivia. In support of it, an average of a million soldiers were deployed for twenty-five years in some four thousand bases in thirty countries. It contained the seeds of a habit of intervention: clandestine in Iran, Guatemala, Cuba, the Philippines, Chile, and the CIA alone knows where else; overt in Korea, Lebanon, the Dominican Republic, Laos, Cambodia and Vietnam. (Hodgson 1976:32)

Resting in part on the foundation of **anti-communism**, the focus of the first strand was to surround the Soviet Union and its allies in Eastern Europe and mainland Asia with American allies, alliances, and military (conventional and nuclear) forces in order to deter the Soviet Union from initiating a military strike and possibly triggering World War III—which came to be known as "deterrence theory." In the Third World, where the US-Soviet confrontation tended to be fought more indirectly over the "hearts and minds" of local elites and peoples, the United States relied on foreign assistance, counterinsurgency, and the use of covert paramilitary operations to promote friendly regimes. The United States also pursued containment of the Soviet Union and its allies (such as in Eastern Europe and Cuba) through the use of broad economic sanctions (i.e., boycotts). Diplomacy and other less coercive instruments of policy were put aside by the United States in East-West relations and superseded by the threat and use of coercion to deter and contain what American leaders saw as major challenges to American national security commitments and national interests (see George and Smoke 1974; Jentleson 1987; Mastanduno 1985).

Third, the bipartisan US global strategy involved a commitment to a **liberal international economic order (LIEO)**. As Western European economies struggled to recover from the Great Depression and the war, the United States took the lead in unilaterally sustaining and expanding Roosevelt's Bretton Woods system to promote a stable and prosperous international market economy built around economic openness and multilateral management. The original Bretton Woods system was to be based on a multilateral effort by the Europeans and Americans, but the war-torn European economies were in need of recovery, and the Soviet bloc remained outside the system, which prevented the Bretton Woods system from operating as originally agreed. Instead, the US shifted to **Bretton Woods II**, in which the strength of the American economy allowed the United States to unilaterally support the Bretton Woods system and focus on European economic recovery.

The Bretton Woods II liberal international economic order was to be accomplished by providing massive capital outlays (of dollars) in the form of American assistance (such as the Marshall Plan for aid to Europe), private investment and loans by US multinational corporations, and trade based on opening the US domestic market to foreign imports. Therefore, the Bretton Woods international economic system based on free trade and fixed exchange rates became dependent on the United States acting as the world's banker. Although primarily European oriented, and later also Japanese oriented, US foreign economic policy was also active in promoting a market system in the Third World through its support of private investment and development abroad (see Kuttner 1991; Spero and Hart 2009).

Fourth, the Cold War Consensus also included a commitment to liberal norms and values. This pillar included broad agreement on the importance of **multilateralism** through cooperative international institutions, and a rules-based international order, as well as commitment to the importance of democracy and human rights. Unfortunately, while the first strand was actively embraced, the second was often relegated to the back seat as the United States pursued its anti-communist/anti-Soviet containment strategy in the political and economic world. To be sure, rhetorical support for freedom, democracy, and human rights was central to American policies. In practice, however, that support was often compromised by more strategic concerns for power and prosperity in the Cold War calculations of the period.

A Closer Look

WAR, PEACE, AND THE PENDULUM EFFECT

As a country founded on the principles of liberty and limited government, the United States has grappled regularly with the tension between the requirements of those principles and the demands of national security in an anarchic and dangerous world. One way to understand the consequences of the tension and trade-offs between democracy and national security is to examine the patterns in terms of a pendulum effect. During times of war and danger when perceptions, real and imagined, of threat and fear of enemies increase, US leaders have tended to embrace policies to curtail the civil rights and liberties of Americans, sometimes dramatically, in the name of national security. As the periods of national emergency and danger pass, and perceptions of threat decline, leaders have generally taken steps to restore and protect liberties and roll back the security measures that were adopted. Thus, the pendulum swings between these two competing objectives, as it has done throughout US history (see Farber 2008; Stone 2007).

We could trace this pattern back to the earliest days of the United States (e.g., the passage of the Alien and Sedition Acts in 1798; measures such as the suspension of the writ of habeas corpus and the imposition of martial law during, and after, the American Civil War), but let's consider examples of this pendulum effect from the last 100 years or so. These examples illustrate the actions and reactions that form the pattern and make for a good discussion of the dilemmas between liberty and security over the course of American history.

- During World War I, the US government imposed a broad array of restrictions on socialist, anarchist, and other groups, including German Americans, in the name of security. This included the Espionage Act of 1917 and the Sedition Act of 1918 (regulating antigovernment speech and opinion) and continued with the anti-Bolshevik and anti-socialist Palmer Raids in 1919–1920 led by J. Edgar Hoover and the early FBI. In the years following World War I, almost all of these restrictions were rolled back by the Supreme Court and Congress.

- World War II led to the infamous presidential decision in Executive Order 9066 to relocate and intern more than 100,000 Japanese Americans in a series of "War Relocation Camps," actions later rescinded in 1945, and the Smith (or Alien Registration) Act of 1940, which required non-US citizens to register with the government and established criminal penalties for advocating—or belonging to a group advocating—the overthrow of the US government.

- During the early Cold War, the threat and fear of communism led to numerous congressional investigations (such as by the House Committee on Un-American Activities); loyalty oaths; official lists of supposed subversive organizations; informal "blacklists"; and domestic surveillance, investigations, and infiltration of thousands of individuals and groups by the government and local leaders (such as *Operation Cointelpro* under J. Edgar Hoover and the FBI). This came to be known as McCarthyism and produced a powerful backlash with the rise of the civil rights and anti–Vietnam War movements.

- After 9/11, the Bush administration quickly submitted an antiterrorism bill known as the **USA Patriot Act** (which stands for United and Strengthening America by Providing Appropriate Tools Required to Intercept and Obstruct Terrorism), which became

(Continued)

law in October 2001. The USA Patriot Act increased penalties for acts of terrorism and for harboring or financing terrorists or terrorist organizations. It expanded the government's ability to conduct electronic surveillance; get subpoenas for e-mail, Internet, and telephone communications; acquire nationwide search warrants; detain immigrants without charges; and penetrate (and sanction) money-laundering banks. It also permitted government officials to share grand jury information to thwart terrorism and relax the conditions under which judges may authorize intelligence wiretaps. Beginning in 2005, when the Iraq War went badly, the act became increasingly controversial and was later challenged and modified (but not outright eliminated).

According to Geoffrey Stone (2007), it is almost as if the United States has two constitutions: one for war and one for peace. Or as Richard Hofstadter (1965) has found, times of fear and perceived threats to national security are often accompanied by what he has called "the paranoid style in American politics." This typically occurs because most segments of society tend to rally behind the president and the government in order to fight the enemy abroad (and at home). War and national emergencies, in particular, tend to be times when fear increases and little tolerance exists for individuals and groups that publicly criticize or challenge the government's foreign policy or the status quo within society. Clearly, leaders and citizens of the United States continue to struggle with the dilemmas of liberty and security.

Is the United States currently in a time of war, a time of peace, or "war in a time of peace"? What should be the appropriate balance between the demands of liberty and security for conducting a war on terrorism?

For twenty years, American leaders from both political parties broadly embraced this strategy of "**liberal hegemony**" (Posen 2018). As Ikenberry (2017) summarized, American power and leadership was directed to a "liberal international order" organized around economic openness, multilateral institutions, security cooperation, democratic solidarity, and internationalist ideals. Global containment and deterrence were at the core of US national security policies as American policymakers emphasized trying to prevent the Soviet Union from expanding its communist empire. American policymakers believed that protecting other countries from the Soviet threat indirectly protected the United States and enhanced its national security. Hence, the United States drew lines, labeled countries as friend or foe, and made national commitments to and alliances with friendly regimes. And when foreign threats were perceived, the United States responded. Moreover, the broad bipartisan policy consensus also led to a procedural consensus in which presidential leadership—even preeminence—in the politics and processes of US foreign policymaking flourished (e.g., Melanson 2015).

This policy and procedural consensus centered on US leadership, global containment, and the liberal international economic order inevitably led to American interventionism abroad and the tragic involvement of the United States in the Vietnam War. Over four different presidential administrations from the late 1940s to the mid-1960s, the steady and increasing American commitment to South Vietnam was never seriously challenged within the executive branch or by members of Congress. American policymakers were operating within the Cold War Consensus in which South Vietnam was seen as an independent state threatened by the expansionist designs of a communist monolith (North Vietnam, China, and the Soviet Union). Therefore, the United States could not afford to appease the so-called expansion anywhere in the world for fear that this would feed the appetite of the aggressor and allow other countries to fall (like dominoes) to communism.

The Cold War Dissensus, 1969–1989. Changes in the global context and the effects of international events had significant consequences for US foreign policy and its politics. The most important changes in the global context included perceived parity between the United States and the Soviet Union; the economic recovery and rising power of Europe and Japan; growing economic influence from the newly industrializing countries of the developing world and the Organization of Petroleum Exporting Countries (OPEC); and the growth of Third World nationalism and independence. Between the 1960s and the 1980s, the relative decline of American power and a more pluralistic and interdependent world made it increasingly difficult for the United States to pursue its Cold War policies abroad.

As the world became noticeably more pluralistic and interdependent from the 1960s through the 1980s, the United States's economic and military ability to influence the world declined relative to its post–World War II apex. The US decline was not in "absolute" or real terms but was "relative" to changes occurring in the global environment. In some respects, the decline of American power was inevitable. The immensity of American power in the late 1940s and early 1950s was clearly extraordinary—and temporary—given the devastation wrought by the war throughout most of the world. As Europe, Japan, and the Soviet Union recovered from the war, American power could only decline in comparison. The United States continued to be the most powerful country in the world but no longer was as able to exercise the kind of economic, political, and military influence that it enjoyed at its height during the late 1940s and 1950s.

In many ways, the Cuban Missile Crisis (with its crystal ball–like revelations about the potential consequences of unrestrained US-Soviet confrontation) and the growth in Soviet military power contributed to perceived parity between the United States and the Soviet Union. Economically, although the United States remained the preeminent power, its economic influence nonetheless declined quite dramatically during the 1960s and 1970s from its post–World War II peak. Between 1950 and 1976, for example, America's economic role in the world declined in the following ways:

- The percentage of total world economic production produced within the United States declined from almost 50 percent to 24 percent.

- The American share of world crude steel production fell from 45 percent to 17 percent.

- American iron ore production shrank from 42 percent to 10 percent of the world total.

- Crude petroleum production declined from 53 percent to 14 percent.

- The percentage of international financial reserves decreased from 49 percent to 7 percent.

- American exports fell from 18 percent to 11 percent of world trade.

- Even American wheat production as a percentage of global production declined from 17 percent to 14 percent. (Krasner 1982:38).

- Very simply, economic production had increased more rapidly in Europe and Japan and throughout the world than in the United States.

The American failure in the Vietnam War (with its harsh exposure of the costs of the logic of global containment) and the rising nationalism and independence of the Third World highlighted the limits to the ability of the United States to achieve its goals and control outcomes in the developing world. The Vietnam War was the first time in its history that the United States lost a war. Simply put, after investing as much as $30 billion a year and more than 500,000 troops during the height of American involvement in a war that lasted at least fifteen years, the United States's containment strategy was unsuccessful in keeping South Vietnam an independent, noncommunist country. As a result of America's failure in Vietnam, the policy of global containment of Soviet communism, which had prevailed since World War II, was challenged by competing foreign policy perspectives.

At the time, this challenge was probably best represented by J. William Fulbright, chairman of the Senate Foreign Relations Committee and the first prominent critic to receive popular attention. In *The Arrogance of Power* in 1966, Fulbright argued that there were two Americas: one, generous, humane, and judicious; the other, narrowly egotistical and self-righteous. For Fulbright (1966:3), Cold War policies and US interventionism abroad indicated that an aggressive and self-righteous America was prevailing in US foreign policy. This perspective fueled dissensus over the ends and means of US foreign policy.

Economically, the **relative decline** of the United States and the rise of new forces in the developing world and the international economy led to major changes to US foreign economic policy. In 1971, President Richard Nixon responded to increasing international pressure on the US economy by discarding the convertibility of the US dollar to gold and placing a 10 percent surcharge on Japanese imports. In doing so, he violated the principles of fixed exchange rates and free trade, contributing to a situation in which the Bretton Woods system could no longer be sustained. This reflected a "relative" decline in the US economy, the economic recovery of Europe and Japan, and the rise of OPEC. Currencies would now float: The German Deutschmark, the British pound, the French franc, and the Japanese yen increased in value relative to the dominance of the US dollar (the euro did not exist until 1999). The price of oil would rise periodically. International trade and investment grew tremendously between the increasingly developed countries, while developing countries increased their foreign debt. In summary, the international economic system became increasingly market oriented, complex, and open to periods of rapid growth and prosperity at the same time that economic instability, recessions, and the periodic collapse of different economies occurred throughout the world. The United States and a recovered Europe (the Group of 7 or G-7) found it increasingly difficult to manage these changes—a trend that has intensified to the present day.

A similar pattern occurred with respect to ability of the United States to threaten and use force successfully abroad after the Vietnam War. The US government found it increasingly difficult to promote political stability and to exercise overt and covert military force. In Iran, for example, the United States was able to covertly overthrow the Iranian government with relative ease, restoring the shah to power in 1953. Twenty-five years later, however, the United States could not stop the Iranian revolution and the rise of the Ayatollah Khomeini, triggering the Iran hostage crisis in American politics. Even in Central America, the traditional region of American hegemony, the United States faced new obstacles to the exercise of foreign policy influence. Small military or covert US operations had determined the fate of Central American countries throughout most of the twentieth century; by the 1980s, however, the Ronald Reagan administration's covert war in Nicaragua involving more than 10,000 Contras was unable to defeat militarily the Sandinistas. Clearly, quick, and easy military victories, such as in Grenada and Panama, were still possible, but they were becoming more costly politically and, with the rise of global complexity, they were becoming the exception to the rule.

These changes in the global context, and the US foreign policy response to them, resulted in major challenges to the policy and policymaking procedures of the Cold War Consensus. First, with each new administration, there was a modification in the direction of US national security policy. Although a policy of containment continued to have its share of advocates, other policy orientations gained legitimacy and influenced the policymaking process (e.g., Melanson 2015). Second, with the growth of economic problems at home and abroad, foreign economic policy grew in importance to the foreign policy agenda. Although most American leaders continued to see the need for a stable and liberal international market economy, they were often unsure over the particular strategy and means to promote economic stability. Third, in contrast to the Cold War years, after the Vietnam War it became very difficult for any president or administration to dominate foreign policymaking, devise a foreign policy that responded successfully to changes in the global environment, and obtain substantial domestic support over time. Indeed, concerns over the excesses of US foreign policy during the Cold War Consensus—including the United States's reliance on the use of force and interventionism and the growth of what many viewed as excessive presidential power and influence over policy—led to both substantive and policy debates and challenges as well as efforts to challenge and limit the dominance of an "**imperial presidency**" (e.g., Schlesinger 1989). These things forced every president to change or modify US foreign policy during his term, usually toward the political center, and increased the inconsistency and incoherence of US foreign policy since Vietnam.

Although US foreign economic policy became more important in the Cold War Dissensus phase, it tended to lack coherence in an increasingly globalized economy despite the simple rhetoric of "free markets." This is because of the growing difficulty that governments have addressing complex and intractable economic issues—such as inflation, unemployment, energy needs, deficits, currency fluctuations, "bull" and "bear" markets, environmental concerns, and the like—in both the domestic and international arenas. This meant that US foreign economic policy has tended to be reactive to domestic and international economic problems as they have arisen.

In the national security area, incoherence and inconsistency in US foreign policy also has been visible. The Nixon and Ford administrations represented the first real change from the Cold War emphasis on containment of Soviet communism to ensure global security to a "realpolitik" orientation and a policy of **détente** focused on counterbalancing the Soviet Union as a traditional great power in order to promote global stability and order. Although there was much disagreement during the early 1980s as to the nature of the Carter administration's foreign policy, a broad consensus has recently emerged that the administration entered office with a relatively optimistic vision of global change and a liberal internationalist orientation. In 1981, US foreign policy under the Reagan administration fully returned to an emphasis on global containment of Soviet communism through the threat and use of force reminiscent of the Cold War era of the 1950s and 1960s, while retreating from multilateralism as well, until the latter years when greater cooperation with the Soviet Union emerged with the rise of Mikhail Gorbachev.

Thus, the Global Era in US foreign policy that began with American involvement in World War II resulted in two globally oriented foreign policy periods separated by the Vietnam War. From World War II until Vietnam, American national security policy was devoted to containing the threat of Soviet communism throughout the globe and was supported by a foreign economic policy based on American leadership of the international political economy. Changes in the global context and events like the Vietnam War and the breakdown of the Bretton Woods system challenged the United States's ability to promote a global containment policy and to maintain economic prosperity at home. After Vietnam, successive administrations embraced different foreign policy initiatives to address the new context, and foreign economic policy was restored to a significant place on the foreign policy agenda.

The Post–Cold War Years, 1990–2001. With the collapse of communism in Eastern Europe and the collapse of the Soviet Union, the United States entered a new phase of its Global Era in foreign policy. The end of the Cold War in 1989 and 1990 made the world an even more complex place, with contradictory implications for American power and US foreign policy. Two key features of the post–Cold War global context have been most important for the politics of US foreign policy: (1) the collapse of communism and the Soviet Union, and (2) the rise of globalization.

The most significant long-term development in the global environment has been the collapse of communism and the Soviet Union. After Mikhail Gorbachev came to power as the leader of the Soviet Union in 1985, he embarked on a course of domestic and foreign policy reforms to improve Soviet political and economic structures, policies, and performance and the Soviet Union's relations with the United States and Europe. Gorbachev led efforts to decentralize economic policymaking and open greater political participation, freedom of speech, and freedom of the press at home. He also sought to reduce Cold War tensions and improve cooperation with the United States and Western Europe, while rejecting the so-called Brezhnev Doctrine, which asserted the Soviet Union's right to intervene militarily in other communist countries (e.g., in Eastern Europe, Afghanistan, and elsewhere) if their Marxist-Leninist governments were under threat.

In 1989, the Soviet-aligned governments of Central and Eastern Europe fell peacefully to popular movements seeking to replace them, although the revolution to remove the Ceausescu regime in Romania turned violent. The Soviet Union did not interfere, even as

East Germany and West Germany began the process of reunification while remaining in the NATO alliance. However, as the movements for independence spread to the republics of the Soviet Union, Gorbachev resisted, facing opposition from hard-line military and Communist Party leaders. In August 1991, the hard-liners attempted a coup against Gorbachev, which failed largely due to the resistance of Boris Yeltsin, the elected president of the Soviet Republic of Russia. Yeltsin pushed hard with other republic leaders for the dissolution of the Soviet Union and, in December 1991, Gorbachev resigned as president of the Soviet Union, which was dissolved in favor of a loose federation of its former republics, now independent, in the Commonwealth of Independent States.

This dramatic change removed the central challenger to American power and influence in world politics and led to dramatic changes in the global context. Widely regarded as an American and Western victory in the Cold War, the collapse of communism and the Soviet Union led to what columnist Charles Krauthammer (1990) called a "**unipolar moment**": "The true geopolitical structure of the post–Cold War world . . . [is] a single pole of world power that consists of the United States at the apex of the industrial West. Perhaps it is more accurate to say the United States and behind it the West." Others went even further and hailed this change in the global context as "the end of mankind's ideological evolution and the universalization of Western liberal democracy as the final form of government" (Fukuyama 1989:3).

The end of the Cold War also expanded and accelerated **globalization** (Keohane and Nye 2011), which had been under way for decades. The collapse of the Soviet Union and the ensuing changes resulted in a single, integrated international political economy of growing interdependence and complexity. For at least forty years after World War II, the Soviet Union attempted to withdraw and minimize its interaction with the larger, capitalist global economy dominated by the West and the United States—creating its own separate political economy made up of communist and socialist states. The collapse of communism in the Soviet Union and Eastern Europe, along with the economic transition within China since the death of Mao Zedong, reintegrated these areas of the world within the larger international political economy, and accelerated the integration of other areas of the world deprived of an alternative to the US-led liberal international economic order. This change was reinforced further by the tremendous rise of international economic transactions and trade with countries such as China as well as the development of the North American Free Trade Agreement (NAFTA) and the creation of the World Trade Organization (WTO). This means that all states and parts of the world, including the United States, were increasingly interdependent economically as the world has become a single global economy.

In this context, the end of the Cold War provided the United States with new opportunities and constraints in the conduct of foreign policy. Certainly, the central axis of US foreign policy after World War II was removed, opening opportunities for US leadership and greater cooperation in the rules-based liberal international order. However, the end of the Cold War also removed the central strategic focus of post–World War II US foreign policy—the containment of the Soviet Union—leading to uncertainty over the direction of policy. In fact, the Cold War's end led to a world of greater complexity, where global issues proliferated and power became more diffused. One key area of greater concern soon emerged—transnational terrorism. In addition, other types of problems become more salient, including the following:

- Disputes arising from traditional rivalries and state boundaries such as in the Middle East and between India and Pakistan

- Changes in the power and influence of state actors, such as in China, Russia, and the European Union

- Nuclear proliferation, such as in Iraq, Iran, and North Korea

- Ethnic groups and loyalties, over and within state boundaries

- Movements and migrations of peoples, demographic changes, and the growth of refugee populations

- Demands and needs for scarce resources such as water

- Economic competition and growing inequality between rich and poor, around the globe and within regions and states

- International economic instability and limits to growth, not just for poorer countries but also for developing and developed countries, especially the core economies of the United States and the European Union

- Profound technological developments occurring with greater speed and uncertainty, especially in information and communications technology

- Environment and pollution problems including deforestation and global warming and more

Clearly, the end of the Cold War created increasing global complexity and the rise of globalization, but it also resulted in the proliferation of global conflicts, crises, wars, and lots of future uncertainty. As James Woolsey, director of the Central Intelligence Agency from 1993 to 1995 noted, "We have slain a large dragon, but we live now in a jungle filled with a bewildering variety of poisonous snakes. And in many ways, the dragon was easier to keep track of" (Jehl 1993). These new challenges posed new issues for the exercise of American power and leadership.

President George H. W. Bush directed his administration's attention to managing the disruptions generated by the collapse of the Soviet Union; ensuring peaceful transitions in Europe, including the reunification of Germany; and taking steps toward greater cooperation in what he called a "**new world order**." The Bush administration was driven by a pragmatic approach committed to managing the effects of the dramatic changes in the Soviet Union and elsewhere (Beschloss and Talbott 1994). Not surprisingly, as David Halberstam (2001:59) described in *War in a Time of Peace,*

> The top civilians in the Bush administration were cautious in general, befitting men who had grown up and come to power during a prolonged period of relentless Cold War tensions, tensions made ever more dangerous by the mutual

availability of nuclear weapons. . . . The principal military men were cautious, too, but in a different way, befitting men who had experienced the full bitterness of the Vietnam War.

Beyond that, confronting and reversing Iraq's invasion of Kuwait in 1991 was seen not only as an important step to resist international aggression but also as "a big idea; a new world order . . . [with] new ways of working with other nations . . . peaceful settlement of disputes, solidarity against aggression, reduced and controlled arsenals and just treatment of all peoples" (President Bush, quoted in Nye, 1992).

The Bill Clinton administration sought to direct American attention to liberal internationalist goals in the post–Cold War global context. However, as its predecessor found, the Clinton administration faced an increasingly complex international and domestic environment in which the days of the Cold War's grand design gave way to a more pragmatic time of muddling through (Danner 1997; Layne 1997; Rosati 1997; J. Scott 1998). President Clinton aimed US foreign policy at preserving and extending American leadership and engagement in world affairs, expanding free trade and the cooperative structures and institutions of the global economy, empowering multilateral cooperation and problem-solving, and the support for and promotion of democratic governance. The president highlighted the dilemma in a 1993 interview, commenting on the implications of the loss of the anti-Soviet foreign policy framework that dominated the preceding forty years: "Gosh, I miss the Cold War. Finding a workable framework for this new era and sorting out America's role could take years" (Devroy and Smith 1993).

President Clinton did manage to initiate several significant foreign policy actions in Haiti, Mexico, Bosnia, and the Middle East. Also, the administration had great difficulty in responding to the continuing Yugoslavian crisis, and in getting its NATO allies to work together multilaterally, until war resulted in Kosovo through a massive bombing campaign. For the most part, major national security failures were avoided while the administration highlighted domestic policy and international economics. Most prominent in this regard were passage of NAFTA and the Uruguay Round of GATT, which produced the WTO. However, the Clinton administration was accused of considerable vacillation and hesitancy in the conduct of US foreign policy and often tended to be reactive rather than proactive abroad.

In the post–Cold War context, both President Bush and President Clinton faced another set of challenges as well, this time centered on the politics of US foreign policy and the prospects and challenges for presidential leadership. In this global context, consensus over the proper role, important interests, and necessary actions of the United States in the world was noticeably lacking. As noted by Holsti and Rosenau (1984) and Holsti (1994), policymakers and the public are increasingly divided—and increasingly along partisan lines—on the basic issue of the United States's appropriate role in the world and on what constitutes acceptable foreign policy goals, actions, and instruments. Hence, great debate over foreign policy has ensued and presidents have faced growing challenges to their leadership of foreign policymaking.

The Post-9/11 Years, 2002–Present. For US foreign policy, the September 11, 2001, terrorist attacks on New York City and Washington, DC, mark another significant shift in the global context. For the administrations of George W. Bush and Barack Obama, three central features of this context were most salient. First, ten years after the end of the Cold War, American power remained dominant in world politics. Indeed, the historian Paul Kennedy, who once wrote of the imperial overstretch and decline of US power (Kennedy 1987), characterized it this way: "Nothing has ever existed like this disparity of power; nothing" (Kennedy 2002). As Brooks and Wohlforth (2002) put it, "If today's American primacy does not constitute unipolarity, then nothing ever will." Second, the post-9/11 global context was characterized by the continued broadening and deepening of globalization. Finally, the global context after 9/11 highlighted the growing challenges of **transnational terrorism** and **nuclear proliferation**. Together, these features of the global context created a complex array of challenging dynamics for US foreign policy.

During George W. Bush's 2000 election campaign, much emphasis was on the need to lessen commitments, emphasize vital national interests, and exercise greater humility abroad in response to what was commonly described as a more benign and favorable international environment (see Rice 2000). However, in reaction to the September 11 attacks, the administration openly embraced a more aggressive foreign policy, revolving around a global war on terrorism, preemption, and the pursuit of international primacy and unilateralism. In the words of National Security Adviser Condoleezza Rice: "I really think that this period is analogous to 1945 to 1947 in that the events so clearly demonstrated that there is a big global threat, and that it's a big global threat to a lot of countries that you would not have normally thought of as being in the coalition. That has started shifting the tectonic plates in international politics" (quoted in Lemann 2002:44). Numerous members of the administration tended to view power, especially military power, as the essential ingredient for American security, while also rejecting traditional emphases on deterrence, containment, multilateralism, and international rules and agreements. It was, in short, a view fundamentally committed to maintaining a unipolar world and acting unilaterally (see Daalder and Lindsay 2003; Ikenberry 2011).

New enemies—Osama bin Laden and al-Qaeda, Saddam Hussein and Iraq, and terrorism—replaced the old enemy of communism. The new foreign policy orientation was based on deterrence, containment, and preemptive strikes on terrorism and alleged terrorist threats throughout the world. After 9/11, in the minds of members of the Bush administration, "the United States was [now] faced with an irreconcilable enemy; the sort of black-and-white challenge that had supposedly been transcended in the post–Cold War period, when the great clash of ideologies [had] ended, [and] had now reappeared with shocking suddenness" (Hirsh 2002:18). Bush's global war on terrorism resulted in a major defense buildup, an emphasis on "homeland security," an effort to distinguish between friends and foes, and a heavy reliance on the use of force abroad, especially in Afghanistan and Iraq. The administration's strategy became much more unilateral in orientation, saw little relevance of international organizations like the United Nations, and officially emphasized the threat and use of preemptive (or preventive) strikes.

This policy orientation became known as the **Bush Doctrine**, reflected in Bush's 2002 foreign policy address at West Point. The war on terrorism became the core and the mantra of the Bush administration's foreign policy, to the neglect of numerous other foreign policy issues and approaches, including the international political economy. In the words of one critic, "The Bush Doctrine has been used to justify a new assertiveness abroad unprecedented since the early days of the Cold War—amounting nearly to the declaration of American hegemony—and it has redefined US relationships around the world" (Hirsh 2002:19).

At first, the public and Congress rallied around this action. However, with the initial military campaign over, the more difficult task of rebuilding the Iraqi government and nation-building ensued. Moreover, Bush's rejection of the international community left the United States isolated and widely distrusted overseas. For example, by late 2006, citizens in thirty-three of thirty-five countries surveyed believed that the war in Iraq had increased the likelihood of terrorist attacks around the world (Program on International Policy Attitudes 2006). Ninety-eight percent of European Commission members and 68 percent of members in the European Parliament disapproved of Bush's foreign policies (Center for the Study of Political Change 2006). At home, a July 2008 survey found "improving America's standing in the world" to be the general public's top US foreign policy priority (Chicago Council on Global Affairs 2008).

With the costs of the war spiraling upward, Bush began to face increased unrest and challenges, and his public approval began to decline steadily. Distance from the 9/11 attacks, coupled with increasing costs in Iraq, persistent questions about the success of his global war on terrorism, and the decline of American prestige and reputation around the world (along with domestic economic problems and other challenges) eroded Bush's support. It exacerbated his lame-duck status to the point that his presidency was effectively crippled in November 2006, when the Democrats seized control of both houses of Congress in a stunning political backlash against Bush.

Riding public discontent with the Bush administration, Obama emerged as the victor in the 2008 presidential elections and promised to restore American prestige and reputation and reengage with the world so as to repair relations with friends and allies and assert American power and influence in a softer and more conciliatory fashion. While contending with the so-called Great Recession of 2008–2010, Obama effectively sought "indispensability" instead of primacy or dominance. Although the problems Obama faced as he began his efforts were not so dramatic as those of the economic depression and global war of the 1930s and 1940s, few presidents since World War II have faced such a daunting array of challenges.

The administration's first priority was to prevent the economic situation from deteriorating further and potentially collapsing into a great depression reminiscent of the 1930s. The Obama administration emphasized the need for Keynesian governmental spending and involvement as the primary source for calming the markets, restoring confidence, and increasing the likelihood of an economic recovery—in a pragmatic and experimental way. The administration also highlighted the need for a multilateral response (through the Group of 20 [G-20] countries and international financial institutions) since the economic collapse was global in its scope and the United States could not address the problem unilaterally, given the spread of globalization.

In addition to urgently needed attention to foreign economic policy, the Obama administration also had to deal with a variety of national security issues inherited from previous administrations. These included contending with the legacy of the Iraq invasion; challenges stemming from the deteriorating situation in Afghanistan and Pakistan (where the Taliban and al-Qaeda had reemerged as viable opponents); and regional security and nonproliferation challenges in North Korea, Iran, and changes in the Arab world with the onset of the Arab Spring in 2011. In addition, other issues needed to be addressed, including the Arab-Israeli conflict, the future of Russia, oil dependency, immigration, and urgent environmental issues such as global warming. Furthermore, substantive debates and divisions deepened on questions about the proper nature, uses, and balance of foreign instruments, including diplomacy, force, aid, and others. Obama also confronted a political environment in Washington, DC, more divided along partisan lines than ever before in recent memory.

The Obama administration actively tried to restore confidence in US leadership and renegotiate the liberal international order to reestablish US leadership and promote multilateral responses to address such global problems (Ikenberry 2011). In contrast to Bush, Obama argued that American power was applied most effectively in the velvet glove of cooperation, relying more on **soft power** based on persuasion and ideational appeal, and with greater concern for global problems than American dominance (Walt 2005). He thus aggressively pursued diplomatic engagement and multilateral cooperation. The new administration stressed a conception of American national interest that incorporated transnational concerns, a conception of power that included soft as well as hard forms of power, an emphasis on diplomacy and economic statecraft to a greater degree relative to military power, and greater involvement in multilateral institutions and support for international law (Hook and Scott 2012; Ikenberry 2011).

As President Obama (2009) articulated early on:

> The United States remains the most powerful, wealthiest nation on Earth, but we're only one nation, and . . . the problems that we confront, whether it's drug cartels, climate change, terrorism, you name it, can't be solved just by one country. And I think if you start with that approach, then you are inclined to listen and not just talk. . . . Countries are going to have interests, and changes in foreign policy approaches by my administration aren't suddenly going to make all those interests that may diverge from ours disappear. What it does mean, though, is, at the margins, they are more likely to want to cooperate than not cooperate.

It is unclear how much the Obama administration was driven by an idealistic worldview or by pragmatic efforts to react to the plateful of national security and economic issues it faced. For example, in an August 12, 2010, memorandum written by Obama for his staff in response to the reform movements known as the Arab Spring, the goals of democracy and reform were couched in the language of US interests rather than in the sharp moral language that presidents often use in public:

> Increased repression could threaten the political and economic stability of some of our allies, leave us with fewer capable, credible partners who can support our regional priorities, and further alienate citizens in the region. . . . Moreover, our regional and international credibility will be undermined if we are seen or perceived to be backing repressive regimes and ignoring the rights and aspirations of citizens. (Lizza, 2011)

Indeed, President Obama appeared to seek a delicate balance: to talk like an idealist while often acting like a realist. During the 2012 election campaign, President Obama blended these elements of idealism and pragmatism as he defended his foreign policy record against his rival, former Massachusetts governor Mitt Romney. While the 2012 election focused on economic issues, President Obama stressed his administration's practical approach to trade, his aggressive efforts in the war on terrorism—including the successful raid that killed Osama bin Laden in Pakistan—and his commitments to a strong defense. At the same time, he also stressed his successful engagement and multilateral cooperation with allies, friends, and others to address complicated problems.

The Trump Response to the Post-9/11 Global Context

After Donald Trump's unexpected victory in the 2016 presidential election, the global context facing his administration was dominated by questions of American power and the nature and consequences of globalization and transnational issues, especially terrorism. Surely, the United States remains the most powerful single actor on the global stage. It is the only complete superpower, and its military and economic might are still formidable. However, US power and leadership have faced growing challenges, as other states have taken increasingly assertive stances in world politics.

Understanding these challenges involves important factors related to the nature of the global context. As Richard Betts (2002:33) wrote early in the post-9/11 years, "Not all the world sees U.S. primacy as benign." Three reactions are often generated in response to hegemonic power, in this case, the United States, especially in the post–Cold War and post-9/11 years. First, the predominance of American strength might prompt other powers to accommodate and cooperate with the United States, "bandwagoning" (joining in), "bonding" (build close ties and hope to influence US decision-making as a trusted ally), or attempting to "penetrate" American politics (taking advantage of the open society and multiple access points to American officials in the executive branch and Congress to persuade decision makers to adopt favorable policies). Second, US hegemony might trigger efforts by other states to rein in American power and resist American domination. These efforts might take the form of "binding"—attempting to use norms and institutions such as the United Nations and others to constrain American freedom of action. They could also resort to "blackmail," which involves threatening to take action that Washington opposes unless the United States offers compensation. They might also prompt efforts at "balancing" American power, "balking" (ignoring US requests), or "foot-dragging" in response to American requests to hinder American efforts. Third, to encourage and spread resistance to American leadership, others might attempt "delegitimization," portraying the United States as irresponsible, arrogant, and selfish (see Walt 2005).

By 2016, over two-and-a-half decades of the "unipolar moment" contributed to significant increases in the second and third types of reactions to hegemony. Continuing trends from the end of the Cold War Consensus years, friends and allies in Europe and Asia took more independent roles on a variety of issues. China's rapid growth in economic and political power led it to challenge US leadership on a variety of matters, while other regional powers such as Brazil, India, and Iran pursued more assertive policies as well.

Vladimir Putin's Russia engaged in increasingly aggressive challenges to the liberal international order and US leadership and policy, including its sophisticated campaign of cyber-attacks on the 2016 US presidential elections and its aggression against its neighbors in Georgia, Ukraine, the Baltic states, and others. The expansion of these types of reactions to hegemony fueled concerns that the global environment was undergoing a significant power transition, which would have major consequences for the international order and for the patterns of cooperation, competition, and conflict in it (e.g., Allison 2017; Ikenberry 2011; Tammen et al., 2000).

The second key feature of the global context involved the accelerating effects and consequences of globalization and transnational issues. The forces of globalization have unleashed a more complex and uncontrollable world of interdependence; technological change; uneven development; identity and culture clashes; and transnational issues and forces, including transnational terrorism, global environmental problems, and challenges generated by the movement of people across borders. Economically, for the United States, economic competition from increasingly wealthy states, the consequences of trade competition for American jobs and workers, and growing inequality between the wealthiest Americans and the rest of society spurred significant public disillusionment with the liberal international economic order. Issues of sustainability, security, stability, and culture generated by the transnational problems fostered by globalization further fueled societal tension, fear, and conflict and amplified the disagreements and lack of consensus among US policymakers over goals and policy responses.

Trump seized on these matters during the 2016 presidential election campaign, adopting a more populist, nativist, and unilateralist approach. In office, the Trump administration's foreign policy response suffered from significant incoherence, as the president and contending factions of advisers struggled to formulate policy without well-structured policymaking processes. Nevertheless, the administration's overall approach reflected a two-pronged response to the challenges of the global context.

First, the Trump administration largely rejected the post–World War II American commitment to a liberal international order. Convinced that the US commitment to this order long resulted in America "losing" to others, the Trump administration's embrace of an "**America First**" strategy largely repudiated the foundations of American foreign policy on which most preceding administrations had built. In their place, the Trump administration fully embraced unilateralism and abandoned support for the institutions and cooperative practices of post–World War II multilateralism (e.g., Ikenberry 2017). In addition, the Trump administration pursued a blend of primacy and neoisolationism disconnected from the liberal norms of support for democracy, human rights, or international institutions; long-standing American alliance commitments to NATO, Japan, and South Korea; and the US commitment to global problem-solving—all in pursuit of "**illiberal hegemony**" and an "independent America" (e.g., Bremmer, 2016; Posen 2018). Finally, the Trump administration adopted an amoral transactionalism, implementing an improvisational foreign policy framework that stressed discrete wins rather than coherent strategy; treated foreign relations bilaterally and without distinction between democracy and autocracy, allies or nonallies; and resisted the alignment of means and ends (Zenko and Lissner 2017).

Second, the Trump administration pursued foreign policies aimed at economic nationalism, extreme homeland security, and a muscular but constrained American military. The Trump administration abandoned the long post–World War II commitment to a global free trade regime, which it viewed as a threat to US economic success, instead withdrawing from trade deals and negotiations and implementing tariffs and other pressure on trade partners. Motivated by a focus on the dangers of radical Islamic terrorism and immigration, the administration advocated for and enacted harsh border security policies including a ban on refugees and immigrants from (mostly) Muslim countries and the construction of a wall along the US-Mexico border. The administration also sought the expansion of US military power and increased defense spending, while seeking to withdraw American military commitments and deployments around the world (e.g., Kahl and Brands 2017; Lissner and Rapp-Hooper 2018; Posen 2018; Zenko and Lissner 2017).

The Trump response to the post-9/11 global context generated controversy and conflict at home and abroad. In one key consequence related to the global context and questions of American power, leadership, and influence, by 2019 the administration's foreign policy course had substantially eroded American support and prestige around the world. According to the Pew Research Center, for example, confidence in US leadership from key American allies plummeted from levels achieved during the Obama administration, reaching lows at or below those during George W. Bush's presidency (see Figure 2.2). Perhaps even more troubling, Pew Research Center polling indicates major shifts in how a

FIGURE 2.2

Confidence in Trump Remains Low in Key European Union Countries

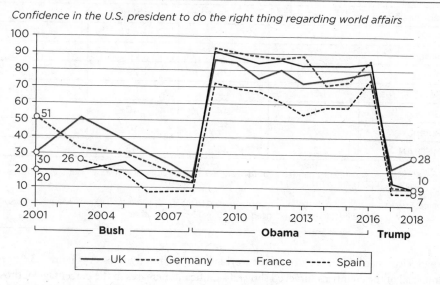

Source: Spring 2018 Global Attitudes Survey. Q35a. https://www.pewglobal.org/2018/10/01/trumps-international-ratings-remain-low-especially-among-key-allies/pg_2018-10-1_u-s-image_0-5/.

FIGURE 2.3

US Power and Influence as a Major Threat to Our Country

People see U.S. power and influence as a greater threat In the Trump era

	2013 %	2017 %	2018 %	'13–'18 Change
Germany	19	35	49	+*30*
France	20	36	49	+*29*
Mexico	38	61	64	+*26*
Brazil	27	47	53	+*26*
Tunisia	36	50	61	+*25*
Spain	17	59	42	+*25*
Canada	23	38	46	+*23*
Nigeria	17	38	39	+*22*
South Africa	24	35	42	+*18*
Japan	49	62	66	+*17*
Australia	19	35	36	+*17*
Argentina	41	49	57	+*16*
UK	22	35	37	+*15*
Italy	10	20	22	+*12*
Kenya	31	45	41	+*10*
Indonesia	44	55	52	+8
Russia	37	37	43	+6
Israel	9	17	15	+6
Philippines	25	25	29	+4
South Korea	66	70	67	+1
Greece	49	44	48	+1
Poland	23	15	18	−5
MEDIAN	**25**	**38**	**45**	

Note: Statistically significant changes in **bold**. Hungary, Netherlands, and Sweden not included due to lack of trend data from 2013.

Source: Pew Research Center, https://www.pewglobal.org/2019/02/10/climate-change-still-seen-as-the-top-global-threat-but-cyberattacks-a-rising-concern/pg_2019-02-10_global-threats-2018_0-04/.

broad selection of countries around the world view the United States. As Figure 2.3 shows, almost all of the countries surveyed showed significant increases in the percentage of those seeing US power and influence as a threat. Indeed, under Trump, America was viewed as a threat by 49 percent or more of respondents in countries as diverse as Germany, France, Mexico, Brazil, Tunisia, Japan, Argentina, Indonesia, and South Korea.

SUMMARY: THE GLOBAL CONTEXT AND THE CHALLENGE FOR US FOREIGN POLICY

As we have seen, the global environment plays a significant role in the policies and politics of US foreign policy. US foreign policy responds to the nature of the global context, and the dynamics, threats, and problems of the global context affect foreign policymaking. The long and rich history of US foreign policy has played out against the backdrop of the international system, which has contributed to the patterns and developments we have discussed in this chapter. Although the future of the United States is both promising and full of challenges, the patterns that have unfolded over time, especially in the Global Era of the post–World War II years, signal an uncertain future.

However, several things seem relatively clear. We may have entered a time of world history when the future of the United States will probably be unlike that experienced by any other previous great power. Throughout history, great powers in decline have traditionally faced a great power war that accelerated their fall—a most unlikely future scenario for the United States given key aspects of the global context, including the deterrent effect of nuclear weapons and the increasing interdependence of the world. At the same time, as the United States seeks to apply its power and influence in the global arena, the old levers of power and influence are harder to identify and still harder to apply, and reliable foreign policy instruments such as military force face new constraints at home and abroad in their application.

Finally, the differing approaches of recent administrations to the post–Cold War and post-9/11 environments highlight the centrality of the politics and processes of US foreign policymaking. Our analytical framework places the players of the governmental institutions at the center, and their nature, characteristics, occupants, and actions are at the heart of understanding US foreign policy. In Part II, we turn to major governmental institutions and players from the White House, the foreign policy bureaucracy, and Congress to examine their characteristics, roles, and interactions in the complex and messy politics of US foreign policy.

THINK ABOUT THIS

In 1993, President Bill Clinton said, "Gosh I miss the Cold War!" Think about the nature of world politics, the role of the United States in the world, and US foreign policy discussed in this chapter.

What might explain President Clinton's nostalgia for the Cold War?

KEY TERMS

America First   42

anti-communism   27

bipolar world   27

Bretton Woods II   28

Bretton Woods system   25

Bush Doctrine   38

classical realism   13

Cold War   27

containment strategy   27

continental expansion   19

détente   34

economic nationalism   21

exceptionalism   22

global context   12

globalization   35

hegemonic power   25

illiberal hegemony   42

imperial presidency   33

international conflict   12

international crises   12

internationalism   26

isolationism   15

liberal hegemony   30

liberal idealism   13

Visit **edge.sagepub.com/scottrosati7e** to help you accomplish your coursework goals in an easy-to-use learning environment.

Government and the Policymaking Process

Part II examines the core of the policymaking process, beginning with the White House and moving to the foreign policy bureaucracy and then to Congress. Chapter 3 discusses the president and White House leadership, highlighting the paradox of presidential power. The next three chapters focus on the core agencies of the foreign policy bureaucracy: the State Department (Chapter 4), the military establishment (Chapter 5), and the intelligence community (Chapter 6). Chapter 7 discusses the National Security Council system and process, focusing on the significance and challenges of White House leadership and management. Chapter 8 focuses on the growing role of the foreign economic bureaucracy and the development of the National Economic Council. Chapter 9 discusses the role of Congress and the nature of legislative-executive relations. Part II concludes with Chapter 10, which provides a synthesis of the patterns of policymaking, discussing important theoretical elements and policymaking models for better understanding and explaining the politics of US foreign policy.

The President and White House Leadership

PHOTO 3.1 President Donald Trump listens during a White House meeting.

Zach Gibson/Bloomberg/Getty Images

LEARNING OBJECTIVES

1. Know the meaning and significance of the paradox of presidential power.

2. Understand the nature of the president's individual characteristics and style and the office of the presidency and their importance to US foreign policymaking.

3. Identify the elements of presidential and White House leadership.

4. Assess and explain key patterns of White House leadership in US foreign policy.

INTRODUCTION: THE PRESIDENT AND THE POLITICS OF US FOREIGN POLICY

Most Americans believe that the president is the most powerful political figure in the United States. In fact, many of us acquire an image of an almost omnipotent president. As Stanley Hoffmann (1968:289) observed more than fifty years ago, "The American system of government seems unable to prevent a kind of hand-wringing, starry-eyed, and slightly embarrassing deification of the man in the White House, a doleful celebration of his solitude and his burdens." Naturally, Hoffmann added parenthetically, "when things go badly, there is, of course, a tendency to besmirch the fallen idol." As we suggested in Chapter 1, many Americans have a simple view of the foreign policy process—that US foreign policy is made by the president—and scholars commonly refer to the preeminence of presidents over American foreign policy (review Figure 1.1).

We know that the president and the White House are central to the politics and processes of US foreign policy, but we also know that presidential leadership is a variable rather than a constant. In this chapter, we examine the president and White House leadership. We discuss the paradox of presidential power, the role of presidential personality and the president's circle of staff and top advisers, and how these affect foreign policymaking and White House leadership.

THE PARADOX OF PRESIDENTIAL POWER

In his last year as president, Harry Truman briefly commented on what Dwight Eisenhower—the front-runner in the 1952 campaign—would experience were he to win the election:

> He'll sit here and he'll say, "Do this! Do that!" And nothing will happen. Poor Ike—it won't be a bit like the Army. . . . I sit here all day trying to persuade people to do the things they ought to have the sense to do without my persuading them. That's all the powers of the President amount to. (quoted in Neustadt 1991:10)

President Truman's warning nicely captures the tension between the powers and constraints that make up the paradox of presidential power.

When it comes to US foreign policy, the starting point for understanding why presidential power and White House leadership is a variable and not a constant is the **paradox of presidential power**. The president is the most powerful political actor in the United States with many constitutional roles and capabilities. However, presidents also face many constraints that limit their power. Moreover, the successful exercise of presidential power and White House leadership becomes even more problematic when one considers uncertain elements that sometimes strengthen the president's hand and at other times weaken it. At times the White House is able to successfully influence—even dominate—the policy process, but at other times the president may have little impact on that process (e.g., Cronin and Genovese 2009; Neustadt 1991; Pious 1979). President John Kennedy understood that the president has "extraordinary powers. Yet it is also true that [the president] must wield those powers under extraordinary limitations" (quoted in Sorensen 1963:xii). To better understand this paradox, and its implications for White House leadership over foreign policy, let's consider the elements of presidential power, important limits and constraints on it, and uncertain factors that complicate the president's ability to lead.

Formal Roles and Powers

Presidents wear many different hats that enable them to exercise considerable power. The most important roles include head of state, chief diplomat, commander in chief, chief executive, and chief legislator. These roles have their origins in Article II of the US Constitution and have evolved throughout US history through constitutional amendments, legislation, judicial rulings, and changes in custom (see Rossiter 1960).

Head of State. The president is the "head of state" and represents the United States of America. Although this role is primarily symbolic, symbolism should not be downplayed because the outcomes of politics are heavily a function of its successful use. To compare Great Britain and the United States, for example, when a foreign head of government arrives in Great Britain, the first official visit, according to the diplomatic protocols of international behavior, is with the queen, for she represents the state. In contrast, the same foreign leader coming to the United States will pay official respects first to the president. Similarly, the president or the president's designee represents the United States in many ceremonial functions, both at home and abroad, including such things as state funerals.

Chief Diplomat. The president also is often referred to as the chief diplomat, or chief negotiator representing the United States. This role originates with the president's constitutional duty to nominate the secretary of state and ambassadors to countries abroad and to receive foreign ambassadors. The president also has the right to offer, or withdraw, official US diplomatic relations with foreign governments. Finally, the president can enter into executive agreements with foreign governments and, with the advice and consent of the Senate, can negotiate treaties that are binding on the United States and have the force of law (more on this in Chapter 9 on Congress).

The president has personally headed American diplomatic delegations and negotiated with foreign leaders, something that has increased in frequency over the past four decades with the rise of "summitry." For example, in 1972 President Richard Nixon led the American delegation to Moscow to complete the first Strategic Arms Limitation Talks (SALT) with the Soviet Union. President Jimmy Carter spent thirteen days negotiating with President Anwar Sadat of Egypt and Prime Minister Menachem Begin of Israel in 1978 to produce the Camp David Accords. President Reagan had four major summits with Soviet leader Mikhail Gorbachev between 1985 and 1989 (more than any previous president since Franklin Roosevelt). President Clinton led the American delegation that attempted to bring a settlement to the Israeli-Palestinian conflict. President Obama traveled extensively throughout the world, meeting with foreign leaders concerning a variety of national security and economic issues. Most recently, President Trump has engaged in high-level meetings with American allies in Europe and Asia, the leaders of countries in the Middle East, and others such as North Korean dictator Kim Jong Un and Russian president Vladimir Putin. Finally, US presidents participate every year with leaders from the world's top industrial economies (G-7/G-8) and its most important economies (G-20) in summits to discuss cooperative measures to contribute to the stability and growth of the global economy.

Commander in Chief. According to the Constitution, the president is the commander in chief of the US military with significant authority over the use of American armed forces. Although Congress also has constitutional powers over war and the military, this important power establishes civilian commands of US armed forces and means that, when the president gives an order, members of the military and the Department of Defense must comply. Since World War II, the president has exercised the powers as commander in chief very broadly.

For example, President Truman decided to send American troops to Korea in 1950, whereas American escalation and the use of armed force in Vietnam throughout the 1950s, 1960s, and 1970s was a result of decisions made by Presidents Eisenhower, Kennedy, Johnson, and Nixon. The decision to send US forces to Lebanon (1982) and the Persian Gulf (1987), to invade Grenada (1983) and bomb Libya (1986), and to secretly support the Contras in their effort to overthrow the Sandinistas in Nicaragua were all made by President Reagan. President George H. W. Bush invaded Panama in 1989 and Iraq in the Persian Gulf War of 1991, the latter with congressional authorization. President Clinton led a major NATO bombing campaign in the war in Kosovo in 1999. President George W. Bush led a global war on terrorism punctuated by two major military operations in Afghanistan and Iraq. President Obama escalated American military involvement in Afghanistan and Pakistan and committed US forces to military action in support of Libyan rebels seeking to overthrow Moammar Ghaddafi in 2011. President Trump ordered air strikes against Syria in 2017. Although the Constitution provides Congress the powers to declare wars, raise and support armies, and make rules for their activities, all these examples represent presidential decisions with limited involvement by the US Congress, which authorized the use of force in only a few of these instances and has formally declared war in none since World War II.

Chief Executive. The president is also the chief executive, or head of government, which means the president has authority over the executive branch. So, in theory, all the governmental agencies within the executive branch, all the cabinet secretaries, and all the bureaucrats take their direction from the president. One of the major ways the president exercises this administrative power is through appointments. The president selects personal staff, nominates cabinet secretaries, and appoints most of the high-level officials in each of the departments and agencies that make up the executive branch. The president also establishes the structure and process by which policy is formulated and implemented, which reinforces the roles of commander in chief and chief diplomat.

Chief Legislator. Although not a member of Congress, the president occupies the role of de facto "chief legislator" because of the ability to both initiate and veto legislation. In the modern relationship between the legislative and executive branches, much of the legislation before Congress originates in the executive branch and is submitted by the president—such as the budget of the US government, as well as programs for defense spending and foreign assistance. Therefore, Congress often responds to the president's agenda, which provides some political advantage in gaining congressional acceptance and support. The president also has the constitutional right to "veto" legislation. Congress may override a presidential veto with a two-thirds affirmative vote for the legislation in the House of Representatives and in the Senate, but this happens infrequently. For this reason, the president has great power to stop undesired legislation or persuade members of Congress to modify legislation, an important exercise of presidential power in the legislative area.

Informal Sources of Leadership

The White House also provides the president with a cluster of informal powers that provide leadership opportunities. Let's think about five somewhat interrelated powers:

- **Singularity:** The president is the only government official elected nationally and, as president, is the only individual occupying the position.

- **"Bully pulpit":** The president has an unrivaled ability to speak and gain attention when doing so.

- Initiative: The president can take or order action—commanding staff, advisers, and bureaucratic agencies to do things, forcing others to react.

- Speed and information: As Alexander Hamilton put it in *Federalist* No. 70, the president has the advantages of "decision, activity, secrecy, and dispatch," with more readily available, often classified, information and the ability to issue orders.

- Persuasion: The president can rely on reputation and the trappings of the office to convene meetings with almost anyone and can rely on both formal and informal powers to bargain and persuade, including using campaign promises and threats to win support from others.

The combination of these formal and informal sources of power is potent. Take a moment and consider how they might be employed, alone or together, in White House leadership over US foreign policy.

Limits and Constraints

Clearly, the president has formal and informal roles and authority that enable considerable power and leadership in US foreign policymaking. However, as the paradox of presidential power suggests, presidents face a number of limits and constraints that make it difficult to get their way. These limits and constraints on presidential power tend to be strongest when it comes to domestic policy, but they are significant for foreign policy as well. We'll consider several important limits and constraints in the sections that follow.

Time. The president's first major problem is insufficient time to complete all the tasks necessary to govern successfully. The president has one of the most demanding jobs imaginable: governing a complex society of more than 300 million people and representing the United States throughout the globe. However, like any human being, the president has only so much time to devote to the hundreds of issues and individuals in need of attention. Beyond eating and sleeping and attending to other personal needs, the president has a complicated, full-time occupation seven days a week, usually starting early in the morning and lasting late into the night.

For example, President Obama generally awoke early for exercise and breakfast, arrived at the Oval Office to begin the day's formal schedule about 8:30 a.m., received a daily intelligence briefing around 10:00 a.m., and then proceeded through a busy schedule of phone calls and meetings with staff, advisers, and members Congress. President Obama also typically met with people and/or groups for greetings and photos at various times throughout the day, occasionally giving talks. Some days signing legislation, giving a public speech, and meeting with a world leader were also on the schedule, as were short trips away from Washington, DC. Generally, President Obama ended his work day around 6:00 p.m., heading to the White House residence for dinner and time with his family. After that, the president typically engaged in additional work—reading, completing paperwork, or writing—until 11:30 p.m., often finishing his day with some leisurely reading before retiring to bed around midnight (Szoldra, 2015). For a more detailed example of the rigors of a president's day, see "A Different Perspective: Time Constraints and the President's Daily Schedule."

A Different Perspective

TIME CONSTRAINTS AND THE PRESIDENT'S DAILY SCHEDULE

The presidency may be the most demanding job in the world. The following schedule records the daily activity of President George H. W. Bush on Tuesday, January 8, 1991, just prior to the beginning of the Persian Gulf War:

Time	Activity
7:04 a.m.	The president went to the south grounds of the White House.
7:07	The president went to the Oval Office.
7:12	The president telephoned Senator Malcolm Wallop, Senator John Chafee, and Rep. Mel Levine.
7:21–7:31	The president talked with Senator Wallop.
7:31–7:32	The president talked with Mrs. Virginia Chafee.
7:33–7:56	The president met with John B. Adler.
7:57–8:06	The president talked with Rep. Levine.
8:05–8:24	The president met for an intelligence briefing with William Webster, Director, CIA; [name deleted], briefer, CIA; Brent Scowcroft, Assistant for National Security Affairs; Robert M. Gates, Deputy Assistant for National Security Affairs; John Sununu, Chief of Staff.
8:24–9:10	The president met for a national security briefing with Mr. Scowcroft; Mr. Gates; Mr. Sununu.
9:10–9:48	The president met with Mr. Sununu; David F. Demarest, Assistant for Communications.

Time	Activity
9:52–10:10	The president went to Room 450 in the Old Executive Office Building to participate in a message taping session for the community of nations united against Iraqi aggression. The message will be broadcast over the US Information Agency WORLDNET satellite network.
10:14	The president returned to the Oval Office.
10:16–11:09	The president participated in a meeting to discuss the proposed National Energy Strategy with the Economic Policy Council in the Cabinet Room.
11:09–11:17	The president met with Richard B. Cheney, Secretary of Defense; Mr. Sununu in the Oval Office.
11:17–12:04	The president met to discuss congressional strategy on the Persian Gulf with administration officials in the Cabinet Room.
12:04–12:10	The president met with Secretary Cheney; Lawrence Eagleburger, Deputy Secretary of State; Mr. Scowcroft; Mr. Gates; Mr. Sununu, in the Oval Office.
12:10	The president telephoned Rep. Thomas Foley and Rep. Robert Michel.
12:10–12:19	The president talked with Senator Robert Dole.
12:14–12:37	The president met with Mr. Scowcroft.
12:17–12:29	The president met with Mr. Sununu.
12:24–12:26	The president met with Marlin Fitzwater, Assistant and Press Secretary.
12:19–12:21	The president talked with Senator George Mitchell.
12:22–12:26	The president talked with Rep. Foley.
12:30–12:33	The president talked with Rep. Michel.
12:37–12:39	The president met with [names deleted].
12:39–1:26	The presidential party went to the White House Mess for lunch.
1:27–1:33	The president returned to the Oval Office to meet with Mr. Webster; General Colin Powell, Chairman Joint Chiefs of Staff.
1:33–2:35	The president participated in a meeting with administration officials and Mideast experts.
2:35–2:43	The president met with Secretary Cheney; Mr. Eagleburger.
2:35–2:46	The president met with Mr. Sununu.
2:35–2:54	The president met with Mr. Scowcroft.
2:35–2:49	The president met with Mr. Gates and Richard Haass.
2:54–2:57	The president met with Andrew Card, Asst. and Deputy Chief of Staff
3:00–3:06	The president talked with Charles Black, Jr., Acting Chairman of the RNC.
3:28–3:33	The president met with Robert B. "Bobby" Holt, Chairman of the Republican Eagles.

(Continued)

(Continued)

Time	Activity
3:33–3:55	The president and the First Lady met with the leadership of the RNC Eagles in the Roosevelt Room.
3:50–3:55	The president returned to the Oval Office to participate in a photo opportunity with the Republican Eagles.
4:15–4:23	The president met with Mr. Sununu; Edward Derwinski, Secretary of Veterans Affairs.
4:52–5:02	The president met with Mr. Sununu.
5:02–5:43	The president went to the barber shop for a haircut.
5:11–5:16	The president talked with Secretary of State James Baker in Geneva, Switzerland.
5:43–5:50	The president returned to the Oval Office and met with Mr. Scowcroft.
5:50–5:55	The president went to Mr. Fitzwater's office.
5:55	The president returned to the second floor Residence.
6:45–6:47	The president talked with his physician, Dr. Burton J. Lee III.
10:10	The president retired.
10:27–10:29	The president talked with his brother, William H. T. "Bucky" Bush.

Think about the president's perspective on this schedule and ask yourself: How do you think the need to attend to so many different issues in such a crowded schedule affects a president's leadership and decision making?

Source: US White House, George H. W. Bush, *The President's Schedule* (George H. Bush Presidential Library, Texas A&M).

Although each president has a personal style, the job demands a great deal of time and energy, especially if the president wants to govern successfully. These time demands and their importance for (and constraints on) presidential leadership help to explain the controversy surrounding President Trump's typical schedule, which presents a stark contrast with the examples of Barack Obama and George H. W. Bush we have just considered. In fact, no president in modern times has been less engaged in the tasks of the working presidency, as indicated by the public leak of about three months of Trump's daily schedules from 2018 to 2019 (McCammond & Swan 2019). According to these schedules, about 60 percent of President Trump's day is devoted to unstructured "executive time"—mostly in the White House residence—during which he watches television, reads the papers, and responds to what he sees and reads by engaging on Twitter and talking on the phone to aides and advisers, members of Congress, and friends (see Figure 3.1). President Trump also spent significant and regular time away from the White House at his Mar-a-Lago estate in Florida or one his many golf clubs.

FIGURE 3.1

Donald Trump's Schedule

President Trump's 8am–5pm schedule since the midterm election

■ Executive time　　□ Meetings, events, travel, etc.　　□ No data

Source: "Scoop Insider leaks Trump's `Executive time'-filled private schedules." Alexi McCammond, Jonathan Swan, Axios, https://www.axios.com/donald-trump-private-schedules-leak-executive-time-34e67fbb-3af6-48df-aefb-52e02c334255.html.

The president's time is limited not only from a daily perspective but also in terms of time in office. Presidents have just a term or two (plus a maximum of two years of their predecessor's term, according to the Twenty-Second Amendment to the Constitution) to accomplish all they want. Moreover, as we discuss later, presidents tend to have more opportunity early in their terms. Therefore, presidents are forced to be selective as to how they will occupy their time. They may exercise considerable power over issues to which they are extremely attentive. However, for the remaining issues (those for which they lack interest or time), the president may feel president in name only.

Information. Another limitation on presidential power involves information. Despite having relevant experience such as being a governor, a member of Congress, or a vice president, much of the president's knowledge is acquired through "on-the-job training" because, unfortunately, there is no existing occupation that can adequately prepare one for becoming president of the United States. This means that presidents must use valuable time and require much staff support to obtain information and advice.

The president faces three problems in terms of information: scarcity, overabundance, and understanding. At times, a president may lack adequate information for decisions. This is quite common, especially in the area of foreign policy. Presidents often have great difficulty getting sufficient information about international events, particularly during crises, when time becomes even more limited and important. Yet a president may have no choice but to make decisions. Presidents may also get too much information and lack the time or ability to weigh and digest it. Finally, because presidents have varying backgrounds and experience, they may struggle to understand the meaning of or connections between information, which forces them to rely on others. All these issues make it that much more difficult for the president to exercise power and leadership successfully.

The Bureaucracy. A third major constraint is the bureaucracy. As chief executive and administrator, the president has great capacity to initiate action. However, the bureaucracy has also become so large and entrenched that it is often unresponsive to presidents and their personal staffs and policy advisers, with contradictory consequences for presidential power. The bureaucracy can be of great value to the president as commander in chief, chief diplomat, chief administrator, or chief legislator, yet it can also be extremely unresponsive to presidential requests or commands. Hence, all presidents must grapple with the problem of creating a structure and process to manage and control the far-flung administrative agencies as much as possible (see Chapters 7 and 8).

Such efforts are never completely successful, however, because bureaucratic organizations have a number of advantages that allow them to remain relatively autonomous and free of presidential control (see Chapters 4–6 and 10). First, a new president enters office with a set of policies and programs administered by the bureaucracy already in place under previous presidents. Second, each bureaucratic organization tends to have its own goals, subculture, and tasks over time that may be at odds with the policies preferred by the current president. Third, the president is heavily dependent on the bureaucracy for information. The bureaucracy determines not only the quantity of information available to the president but also its quality and the range of viable options for presidential consideration (often protecting and reflecting the agency's position). Fourth, members of the bureaucracy have the advantage of time. Presidents and their personal staffs are there for only four, perhaps eight, years, but bureaucrats are career employees who may occupy their positions for ten, twenty, or thirty years (and as members of the civil service they have tenure or other rights that make it very difficult for presidents to fire them—even for incompetence). A fifth advantage is that bureaucrats often have close relationships with members of Congress, who ultimately must approve the programs and funding for the executive branch bureaucracy. Therefore, it is not unusual for networks to develop between executive branch employees and members of Congress (and interest groups) around various issues, each dependent on the others. The final advantage is that some bureaucratic organizations enjoy official independence (at least in daily operations) from presidential authority, such as the powerful Federal Reserve Board. These officially autonomous organizations not only can resist the president's exercise of power but also may have the legal right to ignore presidential requests.

Congress. Simply put, the president and Congress share power. In fact, there is no constitutional power provided to the president that the Congress does not share in some way. Therefore, Congress is often a major constraint on the exercise of presidential power. When entering office, the president usually enjoys a brief honeymoon period (see our discussion of this concept later in the chapter) with Congress, during which members from both parties are more likely to be responsive to presidential requests. However, the honeymoon rarely lasts more than a few months, if that long, and then it is back to business as usual in which the president finds that Congress is often unresponsive and, at times, quite obstructionist. In addition, Congress became much more independent and assertive in foreign policy following the Vietnam War and Watergate. Furthermore, since the Vietnam War, the US government has usually been divided (with a Republican president and a Democrat-run Congress, or vice versa), making it that much more difficult for the president to be effective. In sum, the fact that the legislature is an independent branch with independent power means that Congress and the president will be involved in a constant power struggle (as we discuss in greater depth in Chapter 9).

Other Factors. A number of other factors also constrain White House leadership. First, because the framers of the Constitution created a federal system of government in which two sets of governments, each with its own sovereignty and authority, were established, the president has little legal authority over *state and local governments*, which can play a particularly important role in economics and other issue areas. Second, although presidents are nominally the head of their political party, American *political parties*, whether Democratic or Republican, are decentralized and weak, which means that presidents cannot force members of their own party to support them in Congress or elsewhere. Third, the United States has thousands of *interest groups* and *social movements* that promote their own interests and seek to influence state and local governments, Congress, the executive branch, the media, and the American public, defending existing policy or advocating for change (see Chapter 12).

Uncertain Elements

In addition to these limits and constraints, a number of elements that presidents cannot control affect their ability to govern. Sometimes these uncertain elements may work to enhance the president's power; other times they work against the president, acting as another constraint on presidential power. These uncertain elements in the makeup of presidential power include the global and historical context, the courts, public opinion, and the media.

Global and Historical Context. As we discussed in Chapter 2, the global and historical context plays a role in the politics and processes of US foreign policy. Related to that, it also affects White House leadership, sometimes enhancing and other times constraining it. First, American power and its role in the world, along with the nature of global threats and opportunities, may impact presidential leadership. For example, Truman, Eisenhower, Kennedy, and Johnson each had the good fortune to be president during a period of US global leadership in which a broad Cold War Consensus and common enemy united American allies as well as US policymakers, enhancing presidential leadership. The global context after Vietnam presented an increasingly complex and globalized world that fostered disagreement rather than consensus and detracted from White House leadership. In addition, presidents often must react to events and developments as they occur abroad. Sometimes international events strengthen the president's exercise of power, as in crises, and other times they create problems. Finally, all presidents have to contend with the legacy of past policies and problems, which may or may not constrain their leadership.

The Courts. Although the president nominates all federal judges and the Senate tends to approve the nominations, with an occasional controversial exception, this does not guarantee that judges' rulings will support presidential policies (see Chapter 9 for more on that). The classic example of an appointment run amok, at least from the president's perspective, was President Eisenhower's appointment of Earl Warren as chief justice of the Supreme Court. Eisenhower thought he was appointing a political moderate, but Earl Warren led the Supreme Court in a liberal direction over the course of the next two decades. The uncertainty of predicting the future legal decisions of judicial appointees is reinforced by the fact that most judicial rulings are made by federal judges who were appointed by previous presidents. Thus, the impact of judicial rulings on presidential power varies.

Public Opinion. The public is a potentially important source of presidential power. The public elects presidents, and public support can empower them. Yet public opinion can also turn against a sitting president, as Johnson, Nixon, Ford, Carter, George H. W. Bush, Clinton, George W. Bush, Obama, and Trump all discovered. Public opinion tends to be most supportive of the president right after successful elections and during crises, but it tends to decline over time. Partisan opposition, policy failures, scandals, and other events can also hurt public support, while policy success and other factors can improve it. Popular presidents and policies gather supporters; increasingly unpopular presidents and unpopular policies invite opposition, as well as defection by otherwise supportive individuals and groups.

The Media. The media represent another source of uncertainty in the exercise of White House leadership. Remember that different individuals and groups within government and throughout society try to influence the media and the communications process to gain control of the government and influence domestic politics. Presidents, in particular, are heavily dependent on the media to help them promote a positive image—while campaigning and while governing—if they want to win and exercise power. However, while the media can be a crucial source of presidential power, their attention can also be critical and negative, making them a source of much difficulty as well.

THE PRESIDENCY: THE PERSON AND THE OFFICE

As we suggested in the introduction to this chapter, White House leadership in foreign policy depends not only on the president's formal and informal sources of power but also on factors related to the person of the president and the office of the presidency.

The Person: Individual Characteristics

Of course, presidents matter in US foreign policy. But *who* is president matters as well. Individual presidents bring to office particular combinations of background experience, personality, and style that affect both how they do the job and how successfully they manage and lead the politics and processes of foreign policy. As Greenstein (1992:124) put it: "Political institutions and processes operate through human agency. It would be remarkable if they were *not* influenced by the properties that distinguish one individual from another." According to Margaret Hermann (1986), understanding leadership demands knowing about the leader's personality and background. Individual factors such as the leader's personal qualities and characteristics contribute to varying **presidential styles**, which have important consequences for the politics of US foreign policy (Preston 2017).

Take a moment and think about the kinds of individual characteristics that might affect how a president approaches his or her role, and what kinds and outcomes of leadership might ensue. Without doubt, such things as family background, education, professional and personal experiences, personality traits (of a wide variety), cognitive approaches, and others probably come to mind. Indeed, psychobiographies and analyses of many kinds explore such factors as they relate to presidents.

Because we are interested in understanding and explaining the patterns of US foreign policymaking, we are especially interested in how these individual characteristics relate to various types of leadership styles, which we can use to consider and compare different presidents. As Alexander George (1980b) and Richard T. Johnson (1974) argued, President Franklin Roosevelt's experiences and personality led him to rely on a competitive model pitting advisers against each other to gain the president's ear and support. Similarly, President Truman adopted a formal model with each agency head responsible for a particular jurisdiction, advising the president through formal channels so that he could synthesize and decide. Presidents Eisenhower and Nixon embraced similar formal models but with the addition of a "chief of staff" responsible for managing, coordinating, and synthesizing agency heads so that the president could focus on the decision, not the formulation of options or implementation. President Kennedy's personality and approach led him to employ a collegial model emphasizing teamwork and shared responsibility rather than formal chains of command, with the president at the center of a circle of advisers who considered information and policy options together.

One early effort to assess these individual characteristics and construct a typology of leadership styles connected to them came from the work of James David Barber (1972), whose categorization of "**presidential character**" was based on two dimensions: (1) the energy and effort the president puts into the job (active or passive) and (2) the personal satisfaction the president derives from presidential duties (positive or negative). These two dimensions combine to create four types of presidential character:

- *Active-positives* (high energy and high satisfaction from the role), who exhibit optimism and readiness to act.

- *Passive-positives* (low energy and high satisfaction from the role), who exhibit optimism, agreeability, and cooperation.

- *Active-negatives* (high energy and low satisfaction), who tend to be rigid and exhibit aggressive, power-seeking behavior.

- *Passive-negatives* (low energy and low satisfaction), who tend to display low self-esteem, a strong sense of duty and service, and an aversion to the job.

Which presidents would you place in each category?

Another influential approach is that of Margaret Hermann and Thomas Preston (1994) and Preston (1997). These authors weigh involvement in the policymaking process, willingness to tolerate conflict, motivation for leading, strategies for managing information, and strategies for resolving conflict to differentiate four leadership styles based on how presidents prefer to coordinate policy (formal versus informal) and the focus of policy coordination (political process versus substance of problem/decision) (see Table 3.1).

- **Chief executive officers** prefer formal authority patterns (hierarchy) and a focus on the process. Examples include Truman and Nixon.

TABLE 3.1

Hermann and Preston's Classification of Presidential Styles

	Authority Pattern/Hierarchy	
	Formal	Informal
Focus on Political Process	The Chief Executive Officer (Truman and Nixon)	The Team-Builder and Player (Johnson, Ford, and Carter)
Focus on Substance of Problem	The Director/Ideologue (Reagan and Wilson)	The Analyst/Innovator (Franklin Roosevelt and Clinton)

Source: Preston, T. (1997) "Following the Leader": The Impact of U.S. Presidential Style Upon Advisory Group Dynamics, Structure, and Decision. In P. 't Hart, E. Stern, and B. Sundelius (eds.) *Beyond Groupthink: Political Group Dynamics and Foreign Policymaking.* Ann Arbor: University of Michigan Press, pp. 191–248. Hermann, M.G., and Preston, T. (1994) Presidents, Advisers, and Foreign Policy: The Effect of Leadership Style on Executive Arrangements. *Political Psychology* 15 (1), 75–96.

- **Director/ideologues** prefer formal authority patterns (hierarchy) and a focus on the substance of the problem/decision. Examples include Reagan and Wilson.

- **Team-builder/players** prefer informal authority patterns (collegial) and a focus on the process. Examples include Johnson, Ford, and Carter.

- **Analyst/innovators** prefer informal authority patterns (collegial) and a focus on the substance of the problem/decision. Examples include Franklin Roosevelt and Clinton.

Where would you place other presidents from the post–World War II period? George W. Bush? Barack Obama? Donald Trump? More generally, how might these individual styles affect foreign policymaking and presidential leadership?

The Office: Presidential Staff and Advisers

Surely the nature of the person who occupies the office of the presidency is important. However, the job of president depends on more than just one person. As our analytical framework indicates, both the person of the president and the presidential staff and advisers who work most closely with that person are central to the role of the White House in US foreign policy. White House leadership involves both, because the president (as an individual) operates within the institution or office of the presidency, which includes the president and other individuals and organizations working for the president. Therefore, presidential choices about who to appoint as staff and advisers are quite critical.

In deciding who will serve in the administration, a president must make three general sets of presidential appointments:

- Personal presidential staff

- Major policy advisers

- High–level officials responsible for other cabinet departments and executive agencies

These individuals affect the president's ability to manage the bureaucracy and exercise presidential leadership and power. Consequently, with each new president there is turnover in presidential staff and top-level personnel, so presidents can surround themselves with aides and advisers of their own choosing. Even leaving aside mid- and lower-level appointees (we will consider them in subsequent chapters), consider, for example, that although the United States has had ten presidents since John Kennedy's assassination, they have appointed seventeen secretaries of state, nineteen secretaries of defense, twenty-two directors of the Central Intelligence Agency (and five directors of national intelligence), and twenty-one national security advisers (President Reagan alone appointed six in his eight years, and President Trump had four in his first three years).

Building on the recommendations of the 1936 Brownlow Commission, Franklin Roosevelt was the first modern president to expand his personal staff by creating the **Executive Office of the Presidency (EOP)** to cope with a rapidly growing bureaucracy. Today, the EOP contains the people and organizations that a president tends to rely on most in managing the bureaucracy and governing, including the White House Office, National Security Council (NSC), National Economic Council (NEC), Office of the Director of National Intelligence (ODNI), Office of Management and Budget (OMB), and US Trade Representative (USTR) (see Figure 3.2). All told, about 2,000 people work in the EOP, and its budget has grown from about $12 million in 1962 to more than $3.5 billion today.

The president relies most directly on personal staff, who occupy positions in the **White House Office** and therefore play a unique role within the EOP. These are the people who act as the president's eyes and ears and who are preoccupied with protecting and promoting the president's professional reputation, public prestige, and presidential choices. They are responsible for the president's daily activities and help the president prepare for public appearances. Given their proximity and importance to the president, they have also become significantly more involved in the making of US foreign policy (e.g., Cohen, Dolan, and Rosati 2002; Walcott, Warshaw, and Wayne 2001).

The **chief of staff** is the most significant of the president's personal staff and interacts with the president more frequently than anyone else. The chief of staff is responsible for the president's daily schedule and oversees the rest of the White House staff. This is an influential position because the chief of staff usually acts as the intermediary between the president and all staff and advisers who interact with the president. Since the 1970s, the chief of staff has frequently played a more important role in foreign policy as well, often using the **gatekeeping** role to great advantage.

FIGURE 3.2

The Executive Branch

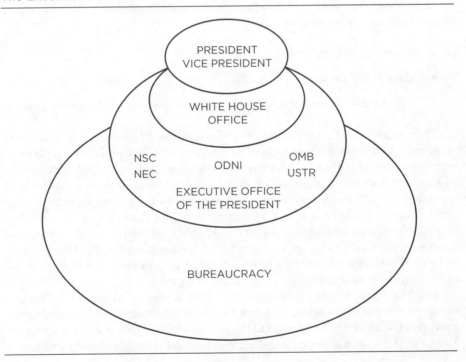

For example, Leon Panetta, President Clinton's second chief of staff, and each of his successors were made formal members of the NSC Principals Committee (see our discussion in Chapter 7). Panetta also instituted a structure that required all paperwork to route through his office (including foreign policy paperwork), and he carefully controlled access to the president. Similarly, George W. Bush's first chief of staff—Andrew Card—was a formal member of the NSC and a valued informal adviser, and his successor, Joshua Bolten, played a comparable role. In the Obama administration, the White House staff was heavily involved in foreign policy discussions and President Obama had four chiefs of staff—Rahm Emanuel, William Daley, Jacob Lew, and Denis McDonough—each of whom was similarly engaged. President Trump had three chiefs of staff in his first three years: Reince Priebus, John Kelly, and Mike Mulvaney (acting). Finally, another position that has become increasingly central to foreign policy for the most recent presidents (with both positive and negative consequences) is that of the **office of the vice president** (see "A Closer Look: Transforming the Vice Presidency, from Gore to Cheney to Biden to Pence").

A Closer Look

TRANSFORMING THE VICE PRESIDENCY, FROM GORE TO CHENEY TO BIDEN TO PENCE

Throughout much of American history, the vice president has been a relatively insignificant player in the policymaking process, usually chosen to "balance" the ticket for the presidential election and relegated to symbolic and unimportant activities (such as to preside over the Senate as stipulated in the Constitution). Thomas Marshall, vice president under Woodrow Wilson, described the job by saying, "The only business of the vice president is to ring the White House bell every morning and ask what is the state of health of the president." This began to change with Presidents Jimmy Carter and Ronald Reagan, who turned increasingly to their vice presidents—Walter Mondale and George H. W. Bush, respectively—for counsel and political support. However, under the past four presidents, the office of the vice president has become a much enhanced position of power and respect.

Albert Gore Jr. was selected as Bill Clinton's running mate in 1992 and became an active participant and trusted adviser in the Clinton White House. Perhaps Gore's most defining issue was his commitment to the environment and to "reinvent government" by lessening red tape and making governmental bodies more efficient. However, Gore was also an active participant in most foreign policy debates. Gore was one of the first vice presidents to effectively promote high-profile national issues.

Under President George W. Bush, Dick Cheney became the most powerful vice president ever, especially in foreign policy. Cheney entered office with broad experience and moved aggressively to strengthen his role in the formal policy process as well. He expanded the office of the vice president, hiring a dozen staff members to create what some consider a mini National Security Council staff of his own. He then ensured that he and his staff had representation in the NSC committees and even lobbied (unsuccessfully) to be the chair of the NSC Principals Committee, which would have put the national security adviser under his direction. An assertive adviser—described by one observer to Bob

(Continued)

Woodward as "the most important, the Cadillac" of the participants in foreign policymaking—he used his staff to work outside the official interagency process to gain even more influence.

With a long record of public service and experience on foreign policy issues in the Senate, Joe Biden played an important role in the Obama administration. As vice president, Biden was "'a total utility player,' as Mrs. Clinton described Mr. Biden, or 'the guy who does a bunch of things that don't show up on the stat sheet,' as Mr. Obama once put it" (Leibovich 2012). Among other things, these roles included designated contrarian in policy discussions, including the Afghanistan War, and advice on dealing with Congress.

In the Trump administration, Mike Pence continued the more active role of his predecessors. Pence carefully fit himself to President Trump's volatile style but played a significant and growing role in foreign policy. A participant in the NSC system and its committees, Pence was regularly present during meetings and conversations with foreign leaders and received the daily intelligence briefing. He also followed his immediate predecessors and established his own national security adviser and a team of advisers. Mostly detailed from other parts of the foreign policy bureaucracy, his "mini-NSC" staff managed issue areas delineated by region or function, similar to the NSC staff itself.

What are the main consequences of this changing vice presidential role for presidential power and management of the foreign policy process?

Source: Daalder and Lindsay (2003), Light (1984), Rogin (2017), and Woodward (2004).

The president must also decide who will occupy major policy positions in the US government and act as top policy advisers. Of the many appointments a president makes, six key foreign policy appointments stand out:

1. National security adviser (sometimes called the NSC adviser)

2. Secretary of state

3. Secretary of defense

4. Director of central intelligence and, since 2005, the director of national intelligence

5. Special assistant to the president for economic affairs (called the national economic adviser or NEC adviser)

6. Secretary of the treasury

These officials are the central players in the president's foreign policy team and are responsible for the most important foreign policy organizations within the executive branch. They are the people with whom the president interacts most on a daily basis in making foreign policy, with the national economic adviser and the secretary of the treasury most instrumental for foreign economic policy and the other officials more consequential in the national security area.

The president also appoints hundreds of other high-level officials to fill positions throughout the executive branch. For most agencies, the president appoints the head or director and the positions at the next three or four hierarchical levels within the agency, usually collaborating with agency heads to select nominees. We consider these appointees in the subsequent chapters of Part II. These appointments do not guarantee presidential control, as we will see in greater depth in the next few chapters, because the bureaucracy has a life of its own and often "captures" appointees to reflect bureaucratic interests. Yet these appointments are one of the key means available for a president to manage the bureaucracy (Patterson and Pfiffner 2001).

Certain selection criteria tend to influence presidential appointments. Presidents generally try to appoint people who are knowledgeable and who share their ideological outlook and worldview. They also usually select people with whom they are comfortable and whom they believe to be loyal, a characteristic particularly important to the current president, Donald Trump. Most members of the White House staff, for example, usually consist of people with whom the president has grown familiar and comfortable, often recruited from the president's campaign team. Quite commonly the chief of staff, and maybe one or two others on the White House staff, are the president's close personal friends and, consequently, may also act as trusted policy advisers. The people who during the campaign acted as advisers (for both domestic and foreign policy), wrote foreign policy speeches and provided briefs, and represented the candidate are appointed to key positions and become major policy advisers. For other high-level officials, the president must rely on personal staff for information and recommendations, and most come from the following professions: law, business, politics and government, and academia and research institutes (see Table 3.2 for President Trump's major staff and foreign policy advisers during his first term).

Time also affects these decisions and presidential management, for many of these decisions are made by the president-elect during the brief transition period. And there is no guarantee that people will accept when asked—President Clinton repeatedly struggled to find a director of central intelligence, for example, and President George W. Bush did not secure his first choice for the new director of national intelligence position either, settling on John Negroponte only after others had declined. For Trump, his controversial style and policy views alienated a major portion of experienced conservative national security and foreign policy experts, many of whom took very public positions opposing him during the 2016 campaign. As a consequence, many of them refused to join the administration or were passed over by the administration because of their public opposition. Such developments affect the success of presidents in moving forward on their agendas.

Another important issue is Senate approval. Appointments to staff agencies within the EOP, such as the White House Office and the NSC, do not require Senate approval. From a constitutional perspective, these personnel and agencies are considered the president's personal staff. Most other high-level appointments in the executive branch require the **advice and consent** of the Senate. Presidents try to nominate people who will gain Senate approval as soon as possible, thereby getting their people in position to help them manage the bureaucracy. As we discuss in Chapter 9, approval is the norm, but most presidents have experienced difficulty with a few appointments.

TABLE 3.2

President Trump's Major Staff and Foreign Policy Advisers, 2017–2019

Position	Name	Background
Vice President	Mike Pence	Law, politics, government, media
Chief of Staff	Reince Priebus	Law, politics
	John Kelly	Military
	Mick Mulvaney (acting)	Politics, government
Senior Advisers and Counselors	Steve Bannon	Media, campaign team
	Stephen Miller	Politics, campaign team
	Jared Kushner	Family member
	Ivanka Trump	Family member
	Kellyanne Conway	Pollster, political consultant, campaign team
	Johnny DeStefano	Politics
White House Counselor	Don McGahn	Law, politics, government
	Emmet Flood	Law, politics, government
	Pat Cipollone	Law, government
Communications Director	Sean Spicer	Politics
	Mike Dubke	Political consultant
	Anthony Scaramucci	Business, political consultant, campaign team
	Hope Hicks	Public relations, campaign team
	Bill Shine	Media
	Stephanie Grisham	Public relations, politics
Press Secretary	Sean Spicer	Politics
	Sarah Huckabee Sanders	Political consultant, campaign team
	Stephanie Grisham	Public relations, politics
National Security Adviser	Michael Flynn	Military, political consultant, campaign team
	H. R. McMaster	Military
	John Bolton	Politics, government
	Robert O'Brien	Law, government
National Economic Adviser	Gary Cohn	Business
	Larry Kudlow	Business, media
Secretary of State	Rex Tillerson	Oil industry
	Mike Pompeo	Business, politics, government
Secretary of Defense	James Mattis	Military
	Patrick Shanahan (acting)	Defense industry
	Mark Esper	Military, politics, defense industry
Chairman of the Joint Chiefs of Staff	Joseph Dunford	Military
	Mark Milley	Military
CIA Director	Mike Pompeo	Politics, government
	Gina Haspel	Intelligence (CIA)
Director of National Intelligence	Dan Coats	Politics, government
	Joseph Maguire (acting)	Military
Secretary of the Treasury	Steven Mnuchin	Business

FIGURE 3.3

White House Staff and Offices in the West Wing

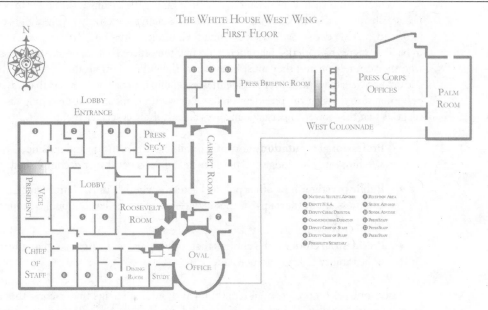

Source: US National Park Service. https://commons.wikimedia.org/wiki/File:NPS_white-house-west-wing-map.gif.

The major staff and advisers to the president who work in the White House tend to get, and often fight for, the largest, nicest, most prominent, and closest offices to the president (usually an indication of prestige and power). Figure 3.3 shows a general floor plan of White House staff and offices in the **West Wing**. Notice the location of the offices of the most prominent personal staff and foreign policy advisers. Naturally, cabinet secretaries and the chair of the Joint Chiefs of Staff have the most prominent offices within their main departmental buildings separate from the White House. For the office locations of presidential staff and advisers early in the Trump administration, see Zeleny (2017).

LEADERSHIP FROM THE WHITE HOUSE

Given the paradox of presidential power, presidential personality, and staff/advisers, how do presidents maximize their strengths and capabilities, minimize the constraints they face, and force the uncertain elements to work in their favor so that they can exercise leadership. Remember the quote from Truman about presidential power early in this chapter? Truman's insight from his experience in the White House is embodied in Richard Neustadt's (1960, 1991) classic statement on presidential leadership. Neustadt's basic argument is that the key to presidential power is the **power to persuade**. Presidents who enter office and expect to "command" are quickly disappointed and frustrated. In fact, as Neustadt points out, efforts at exerting presidential power through command may be an indication of presidential weakness, since presidents should rely on their legal and formal authority only as a last resort.

According to Neustadt, understanding White House leadership as the power to persuade necessarily means that effective presidents must be "active"—actively involved in becoming informed, making decisions, and supervising their implementation. "Passive" presidents tend to be little more than "clerks" who merely occupy the office. To lead, presidents must know who they can rely on and they must be aware of the political implications of what they say and do. For Neustadt, the key for presidential leadership is to persuade others that it is in their best interest to do what the president prefers. Neustadt's work and our preceding discussion suggests that this power to persuade involves at least three crucial elements:

- **Professional reputation:** how other political actors inside and outside Washington, DC, judge the president's ability to get things accomplished

- **Public prestige:** how other political actors—whether in the bureaucracy, Congress, interest groups, or the media—perceive the level of public support for the president

- **Presidential choices:** the choices that only a president can make that affect his or her ability to lead and persuade

The emphasis on professional reputation and public prestige underscores the importance of presidential style, and perceptions and images that have always been important in politics, but with the rise of the electronic media, the importance of symbolism and "symbolic politics" has grown. Leadership involves the ability to create the illusion of being powerful. Presidents' professional reputation and public prestige are largely a function of their personalities and particular styles of operating and presenting themselves. The effect of presidents' personal characteristics on their leadership style can contribute to or hinder their professional reputation and public prestige. Presidents with a reputation for being skillful in exercising power and for having to be reckoned with when opposed are most persuasive. Presidents with a positive public image are more powerful because high credibility and popular support throughout the country enable them to use professional reputation and public prestige to persuade (see Greenstein 2009; Skowronek 2011). The choices presidents make also affect their professional reputations and public prestige. Ultimately, this requires that presidents and their staffs skillfully manage the executive branch and the decision-making process; build coalitions and interact productively with other players in and out of Washington, DC; and effectively communicate priorities and preferences to other policymakers, the American society, and the world.

Richard Pious (1979) extends these insights and argues that the paradox of presidential power has become so constraining that presidents must exercise prerogative government if they want to govern and lead the country (see also Edwards 2009; Fisher 2007). By **prerogative government**, Pious means that presidents must be very active and arrive at decisions that push the Constitution—which is an ambiguous document—to its limits in exercising presidential power. Presidents are more likely to exercise presidential power and prerogative government during times of crisis and war. Many of the most successful and highly rated presidents held a more expansive view of presidential power. However, part of exercising presidential choice involves the careful balancing between activism and going too far. Those who fail to find that balance run the political risk of abusing their power, which can damage or destroy them.

Abusing prerogative power can lead to what Pious (1979) called "frontlash," backlash, or overshoot and collapse. Frontlash can occur if presidents push prerogative government too far during national emergencies such as war. While the urgency of the situation may allow presidents to exercise extraordinary powers, they can expect Congress and domestic politics to reassert themselves during times of normalcy, constraining presidential power. This is what happened under Presidents Abraham Lincoln, Franklin Roosevelt, and George W. Bush, and what may well befall President Trump with his efforts to treat border security and immigration as a national emergency. Presidents may also experience political backlash if they exercise prerogative government, especially over domestic policy. Presidents with an expansive view of the Constitution during domestic emergencies will eventually be perceived as abusing power and may expect to suffer severe political setbacks. Finally, presidents run the risk of overshoot and collapse when exercising prerogative government, resulting in a president's fall from power. This risk is most likely to occur when there is no perception of emergency in society. Presidents who exercise prerogative government under these conditions will be widely perceived as abusing their power and oath of office, and political resistance is likely to be so severe that those who do so may have to fight for their political lives.

In the post–Vietnam War era, for example, President Nixon suffered from overshoot and collapse as a result of Watergate, and President Reagan faced this possibility with the Iran-Contra affair and survived. Similarly, President Clinton was faced with—and also was able to survive—the Monica Lewinsky affair. President George W. Bush's troubles peaked in his second term after Democrats gained control of both chambers of Congress in the November 2006 election and originated, at least in part, in the controversies over the extensive prerogative power sought in the global war on terrorism and aggressive administration actions in making and defending the case for the invasion of Iraq. Donald Trump's controversial policies, aggressive use of presidential power, and suspect activities resulted in a sweeping victory for Democrats in the 2018 elections for the House of Representatives (Republicans held the Senate). This led to a series of investigations of corruption, conflicts of interests, connections to Russian interference in the 2016 elections, and efforts to enlist Ukrainian interference in the 2020 election, eventually culminating in the initiation of the impeachment process in the House in Fall 2019.

THE PARADOX IN PRACTICE: PATTERNS AND PERFORMANCE

The president may be able to exercise White House leadership. But such leadership varies far more greatly than is suggested by the simple conventional wisdom we introduced at the beginning of this chapter suggests. What patterns and dynamics characterize the variations in practice?

Power, Issue Area, and White House Leadership

The notion of paradox provides us with a general understanding of the nature of presidential power and White House leadership, but when and where is the president most able, and least able, to exercise power? The answer to this question turns in part on understanding the nature of power. **Power**, very simply, is the ability to influence the surrounding environment in ways one prefers. The exercise of power can be accomplished in one of two ways: positive power and negative power. The "positive" exercise of power is the ability to initiate, implement, and make something happen. Another way to exercise power may be called "negative" power, which is the ability to block others from doing something against one's wishes.

The White House has substantial opportunities for both kinds of power, but it has a distinct advantage in negative power. In the American political system, initiating and implementing policy requires the support of others—a tall order that runs the president head on into the constraints and uncertainties of the paradox presidential power. The exercise of negative power, by contrast, is less demanding. Presidents do not need to build or maintain extensive political coalitions to block something. Preventing an initiative from surfacing on the political agenda or stopping it after it has surfaced is a much simpler task. The president, for example, has the unique ability to block virtually any piece of legislation through the use of the veto, which is rarely overridden. The chief executive, chief diplomat, and commander-in-chief roles of the president make it hard for others to initiate policy without presidential action.

The answer to the question of when and where presidents are most and least able to exercise power also turns in part on the domain, or **issue area**, at hand. For some issues, presidents are likely to be powerful political figures; on other issues, they may lack much power (Evangelista 1989; Ripley and Lindsay 1993; Manning 1977; Ripley and Franklin 1990). There are a number of different ways to categorize issues, but one relatively simple approach distinguishes among three issue areas: domestic issues, foreign policy issues, and intermestic issues.

As many observers and analysts have concluded, the president tends to have greater strengths and fewer weaknesses in the exercise of power in foreign policy in general and national security policy in particular. Three of the constitutional roles contributing to presidential power really involve only foreign affairs: commander in chief, chief diplomat, and chief of state. Although two of these areas are shared with Congress, these roles typically allow the president to exercise more power, both positive and negative, in the foreign policy area, especially during crises. Furthermore, other players, especially Congress, the courts, state and local governments, the public, political parties, the media, and interest groups, all play independent roles in the making of US foreign policy, but they tend to be more active and influential concerning domestic policies.

With globalization and the major technological revolutions of the late twentieth century in information, communication, and transportation, an increasing array of issues straddles this traditional foreign and domestic policy divide. Issues involving economics, trade, immigration, the environment, and others are both international and domestic in orientation and are often referred to as **intermestic issues** (Manning 1977). When it comes to formulating policies to cope with such issues, everyone gets into the act and attempts to influence the outcomes. On such issues, presidents must increasingly grapple with interest groups (especially corporate, financial, and labor), members of Congress, public opinion, and more within the United States, not to mention foreign governments, multinational corporations, international nongovernmental organizations, and international financial institutions.

We can synthesize these two insights into a simple, yet valuable, three-by-two classification scheme for making better sense of the paradox of presidential power (see Figure 3.4). The president is most powerful in areas of foreign and national security policy, most constrained in the domestic policy arena, and somewhere in between for intermestic issues. Moreover, the president is most successful in exercising power opposing the initiatives of others, and requires more help, skill, and even luck to initiate and sustain policies.

The Presidential Life Cycle and White House Leadership

Another important pattern in the paradox of presidential power involves time. Most presidents find that their ability to exercise power tends to go through a cyclical process over the course of their term of office. In this **presidential life cycle**, a president enters office with all constitutional roles fully available, constraints at their weakest, and most of the uncertain elements working favorably. Newly elected presidents usually proclaim an **electoral mandate** for themselves and enjoy a so-called **honeymoon period**, not only with Congress but with the media and the public as well. People tend to be hopeful, and the president enters a relatively hospitable political environment with considerable leeway to initiate new policies. Within a short period of time—and one that seems to have grown shorter in more recent decades with greater partisanship—the honeymoon is over. Congress begins to challenge the president, especially if the majority party is different from the president's party. Members of the media soon spend more time addressing the issues and critically analyzing presidential policies. Interest groups and social movements descend on the policymaking process. As the political environment becomes more critical and uncontrollable, presidents find that their public approval ratings also tend to decline.

Lyndon Johnson, a former majority leader in the US Senate and a shrewd observer of American politics, once gave the following portrayal of the presidential life cycle after his 1964 landslide victory:

> When you win big you can have anything you want for a time. You come home with that big landslide and there isn't a one of them [in Congress] who'll stand in your way. No, they'll be glad to be aboard and to have their photograph taken

FIGURE 3.4

Categorizing Presidential Power

Issue Area		The Exercise of Power	
		Positive	**Negative**
	Foreign Policy	Moderate	High
	Intermestic Policy	Moderate	Moderate
	Domestic Policy	Low	Moderate

with you and be part of all that victory. They'll come along and they'll give you almost everything you want for a while and then they'll turn on you. They always do. They'll lay in waiting, waiting for you to make a slip and you will. They'll give you almost everything and then they'll make you pay for it. They'll get tired of all those columnists writing how smart you are and how weak they are and then the pendulum will swing back. (quoted in Halberstam 1969:424)

As this honeymoon period fades, the president's strengths diminish, constraints intensify, and the uncertain elements tend to work more unfavorably. The decline of public support is a bumpy process, with peaks and valleys. The major exception to this pattern occurs during times of national emergency and crisis, when the constraints on presidential power are temporarily reduced as the public rallies behind the president for leadership and crisis resolution. These spurts of public approval during crises tend to be reinforced by congressional deference to the president, especially in foreign policy. However, once the crisis subsides, normal politics usually resurface and the downward pattern tends to continue. By the end of their terms, presidents may be so weak that they are reduced to **lame-duck** status.

Figure 3.5 demonstrates the overall decline in public approval that every contemporary president has faced through this life cycle. With the exception of President Clinton, the trajectory has been downward for every president (obviously, the downward trend has been stronger for some presidents than others). For example, even with the tremendous political impact of the September 11, 2001, terrorist attacks, President George W. Bush was not able to escape the presidential life cycle. Bush's approval skyrocketed to more than 90 percent after the attacks, as the country and Congress rallied around the president and the global war on terror, but then public approval declined steadily, dropping below 50 percent in early 2005 and down to the mid-30s by the summer of 2006 until the end of his term of office. Trump, by comparison, assumed office with the lowest approval rating of any president in the figure and still saw his approval drop from there.

This cyclical pattern is largely a function of presidential promises and expectations—in the minds of political leaders, the politically involved and active, and especially members of the general public (Brody 1991). During the presidential nomination and general election campaigns, all candidates promise the American people that, if elected, they will improve the quality of voters' lives. They may promise to restore or maintain economic prosperity, clean up the environment, improve the quality of education, prevent American men and women from dying abroad, build a wall, or "make America great again." These promises create expectations among the public that presidents find very difficult, if not impossible, to fulfill.

Why? Because presidents are neither powerful enough nor in office long enough. The process of promoting expectations that are likely to remain unfulfilled reinforces the vicious life cycle of presidential power. The inability to fulfill the optimism and high expectations created early on means that much of the American public eventually will grow disenchanted with the incumbent president and impatient to see a new individual as president, often from the other party. This sets the stage for a repeat performance of the presidential life cycle for the new president—early optimism eventually replaced by

FIGURE 3.5

Public Approval of Presidential Performance

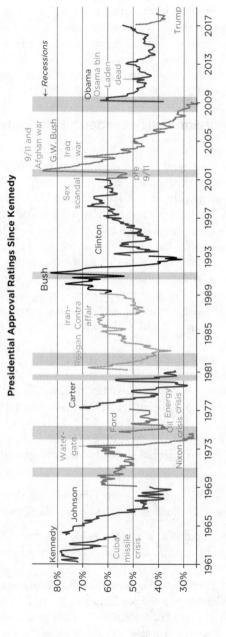

Presidential Approval Ratings Since Kennedy

Source: Gregor Aisch, Datawrapper, https://www.datawrapper.de/_/Wa2Ci/.

pessimism and frustration. The consequence? Again, Lyndon Johnson had an instinctive feel for this pattern:

> "You've got to give it all you can, that first year," Johnson told Harry McPherson, a top aide. "Doesn't matter what kind of majority you come in with. You've got just one year when they treat you right and before they start worrying about themselves. The third year, you lose votes. . . . The fourth's all politics. You can't put anything through when half the Congress is thinking how to beat you." (quoted in Smith 1988:333)

White House Foreign Policy Leadership in Context

What are the implications for presidential power in foreign policy? Historically, it is important to understand that the president has not consistently dominated the foreign policy process throughout American history, especially before World War II. As we discuss in greater depth in Chapter 9, the US Constitution produced a central government with "separate institutions sharing powers," resulting in an "invitation to struggle" between the executive and legislative branches. In fact, executive-legislative relations in foreign policy have been characterized by a kind of "pendulum or cyclical effect" (Schlesinger 1989). In times of national emergency, particularly war, power tends to flow toward the president and the executive branch. During times of peace, when conflict has subsided, power tends to flow back to Congress. Yet while Congress tends to reassert its constitutional authority and power following war, increases in presidential power during periods of conflict tend to be so extensive that it seldom returns to prewar levels.

The cyclical ebb and flow in executive relations in foreign policy has enabled presidents to steadily accumulate greater power over time, especially on issues of foreign policy and national security affairs. Since the global Great Depression and World War II, presidential power in foreign policy has gone through three general stages:

1. During World War II (1939–1946) and the Cold War Consensus years (1947–1968), presidential power and leadership in the making of foreign policy flourished.

2. In the Cold War Dissensus years (1969–1989), White House leadership over foreign policy declined and become much more complex.

3. In the post–Cold War years (1990–2001) and post–9/11 (2002–present) the challenges of the paradox of presidential power have further intensified.

The concepts of presidential style, professional reputation, public prestige, and choices are helpful for understanding the president's ability to lead and govern in general and in foreign affairs in particular. These elements of presidential leadership help to explain why Franklin Roosevelt was the most successful president in modern times; why Presidents Truman, Eisenhower, and Kennedy were able to dominate foreign policy during the Cold

War; why the situation began to change under President Johnson; and why it has been so difficult for presidents to lead in foreign policy since the Vietnam War.

World War II and the Cold War Consensus

As a result of World War II and the rise of the Cold War, the president became dominant in the making of foreign policy. According to Aaron Wildavsky (1966) and his **two presidencies thesis**, this led to a powerful presidency in foreign policy and a weak presidency in domestic policy. Examining the legislative-executive relationship during the 1950s and 1960s, Wildavsky found that presidents were much more successful in influencing foreign policy legislation than domestic legislation. According to the two presidencies thesis, the paradox and life cycle of presidential power were operative predominantly in the realm of domestic policy, but the president was able to exercise leadership when it came to foreign policy (see also Shull 1991).

Before World War II, few governmental institutions were oriented toward foreign affairs and national security—the policymaking elite was extremely small and centered in the State Department. World War II changed this dramatically. Overnight, the US government was redirected to devote itself to fighting a global war: The military expanded enormously, and civilian agencies were established to assist the president in fighting the war. The governmental war effort, in turn, put the economy and society on a war footing to provide the personnel, equipment, and services necessary to achieve US victory.

In this context, Franklin Roosevelt enjoyed a strong professional reputation and high public prestige, and he operated during times of domestic and international emergency allowing him to exercise prerogative government (see Burns 1989; Leuchtenburg 2009; Pious 2002). An activist president, Roosevelt was an effective politician and he capitalized on the crises of the Great Depression and World War II to exercise leadership and initiative.

After World War II, mutual suspicion and fear between the United States and the Soviet Union escalated, leading the expansion of efforts to fight a global Cold War—another time of national emergency in the minds of most Americans—and a substantial policy consensus over doing so. This consensus and sense of national emergency gave presidents during the 1950s and 1960s extraordinary powers of leadership in national security and foreign policy, accounting for the popularity of the two presidencies thesis. During this time the president exerted considerable powers as commander in chief, head of state, chief diplomat, and chief executive. The foreign policy bureaucracy expanded and became an important tool for implementing the Cold War containment policies. Congress developed a bipartisan consensus largely supportive of most presidential initiatives in foreign policy. Constraints were relatively weak, and the uncertain elements tended to be supportive of presidential efforts to contain the threat of communism. A strong anti-communist consensus also developed among the mass and elite publics, resulting in strong public, media, and interest group support of a policy of containment and presidential actions abroad (while state and local governments and the courts were relatively inactive in foreign policy).

Presidential leadership flourished in the Cold War Consensus years. It is not that Truman, Eisenhower, and Kennedy had uniformly great leadership skills stemming from professional reputation and public prestige—the personal situation varied from president to president. Indeed, Truman, for example, had quite low public approval ratings for much of his presidency. A key factor was the public perception that the Cold War represented a contest that the United States and the free world could not afford to lose. It was fought through the strategy of containment, which emphasized the threat and use of force. These Cold War beliefs and policies required a strong president who was able to combat the enemy quickly and secretly with public support and little opposition; therefore, the demands of national security took precedence.

The Cold War Consensus years of American globalism were thus a time of extraordinary presidential power in foreign affairs—certainly not the norm in the history of US foreign policy. This is not to say that the president faced no opposition or that he controlled all foreign policy issues. Nonetheless, the president was clearly the dominant political figure and exercised a disproportionate amount of influence over US foreign policy. With some exceptions, presidents had the ability to formulate and implement policies in accordance with their Cold War beliefs (see Hodgson 1976; Piper 1994).

Ironically, the Vietnam War represented not only the height of presidential power but also the beginning of the end of the extraordinary exercise of prerogative power in foreign affairs. Because of the Vietnam War, presidents were challenged about their conduct in foreign policy for the first time in more than twenty years. Once the bipartisan, Cold War consensus shattered, what had been accepted as a legitimate exercise of presidential power in the political climate of the Cold War years increasingly became considered presidential abuse of power in the political climate of the post–Vietnam War years. The uncertainties and constraints on presidential power, either silent or supportive of the president during the Cold War, resurfaced.

At the end of the Cold War Consensus years, President Lyndon Johnson was in office for both the height and decline of what became referred to as the **imperial presidency** (Schlesinger 1989, 2005). He was the first victim of the changed political environment facing the president. Known from his days as Senate majority leader for his ability to wheel and deal in Washington's corridors of power, his professional reputation was a result of his overall aggressiveness and strong style of personal interaction. However, his public prestige was low. He lacked charisma and was unable to display a sense of confidence in public appearances and, as his administration's handling of the Vietnam War was increasingly challenged, his popularity and ability to lead declined severely (e.g., Kearns 1976, updated in 1991). Johnson was so deeply affected by his loss of support that, rather than fight the political changes that were taking place around him, he declined to seek the Democratic presidential nomination for the 1968 election and withdrew from public life.

The Cold War Dissensus and the Struggle for White House Leadership

The collapse of the anti-communist consensus produced a reassertive Congress, new and varied interest groups and social movements, a more critical media, and a cynical public. In the past, given the strength of anti-communism and the national security state, the president could lead the country, but only in the direction of fervent anti-communism, containment, and interventionism. After Vietnam, every president tried but failed to generate a new consensus or sustained support for foreign policies. As Destler, Gelb, and Lake (1984:50) argued, "The making of American foreign policy [grew] far more political—or more precisely, far more partisan and ideological." Hence, according to Alexander George (1980b:236), "The necessity for ad hoc day-to-day building of consensus under these circumstances makes it virtually impossible for the President to conduct long-range foreign policy in a coherent, effective manner."

The Cold War Dissensus years mark the rise of divided government and partisanship, which created persistent challenges for White House leadership. After the Vietnam War and Watergate, **divided government**, in which the president and the majority in at least one house of Congress are from opposing political parties, became the norm. Partisanship escalated in just about every way imaginable: among party leaders, in congressional voting behavior, and throughout the political arena (see Table 3.3).

Thus, the era of two presidencies and extraordinary White House leadership in foreign policy ended and the high levels of positive and negative power in foreign affairs enjoyed by presidents during the Cold War Consensus diminished after Vietnam. In fact, studies examining the two presidencies thesis after the Vietnam War tended to restrict—or even reject—the argument (Fleisher, Bond, Krutz, and Hanna 2000; Shull 1991). Even the original author of the idea has acknowledged its limits, concluding that "foreign policy has become much more like domestic policy—a realm marked by serious partisan divisions in which the president cannot count on a free ride" (Oldfield and Wildavsky 1991:188).

Without the policy consensus and sense of permanent emergency, the context, presidential skills, reputation, public prestige, and choices became much more important. Presidents Nixon, Ford, and Carter had poor skills, reputation, and prestige and struggled to exercise leadership. Nixon was known for his ruthless exercise of power within Washington, but his professional reputation was poor, and his public prestige declined over the time of his presidency. As his predecessors during the Cold War Consensus had, Nixon tried to govern foreign policy with a free hand, while more and more Americans doubted the validity of communism as the major threat to the United States and questioned the basis of twenty years of containment policies and of presidential prerogative government in foreign affairs. The antiwar movement reached its height, calling for the immediate withdrawal of all US forces from Indochina and challenging American interventionism abroad. Nixon, a scrappy fighter from his earliest political days, believed the traditional authority of presidential power in national security affairs was being challenged and he responded by attacking the domestic opposition as if it were the enemy. This led to a number of illegal and unconstitutional activities by the Nixon White House and came to be known as **Watergate**. Revelations about Nixon's abuse of presidential power led to his downfall and the diminution of presidential power (see "A Closer Look: The Watergate Crisis"). He resigned in 1974, fearing a near-certain House of Representatives vote in favor of impeachment followed by conviction in the Senate.

Neither President Ford nor President Carter fared much better in terms of presidential leadership. Gerald Ford was a likable but passive president with low levels of professional reputation and public prestige. Catapulted into the presidency by Nixon's resignation—which came after Ford replaced Vice President Spiro Agnew, who resigned

TABLE 3.3

Party Control of the Presidency and Congress in the Twentieth Century

Congress	Years	President	Party	Senate			House		
				D	R	Other	D	R	Other
59th	1905–1907	T. Roosevelt	R	32	58	—	136	250	—
60th	1907–1909	T. Roosevelt	R	31	61	—	164	222	—
61st	1909–1911	Taft	R	32	60	—	172	219	—
62d	1911–1913	Taft	R	44	52	—	228‡	162	1
63d	1913–1915	Wilson	D	51	44	1	290	127	18
64th	1915–1917	Wilson	D	56	40		231	193	8
65th	1917–1919	Wilson	D	54	42		210	216	9
66th	1919–1921	Wilson	D	47	49‡		191	237‡	7
67th	1921–1923	Harding	R	37	59	—	132	300	1
68th	1923–1925	Coolidge	R	42	53	1	207	225	3
69th	1925–1927	Coolidge	R	41	54	1	183	247	5
70th	1927–1929	Coolidge	R	46	48	1	195	237	3
71st	1929–1931	Hoover	R	39	56	1	163	267	1
72d	1931–1933	Hoover	R	47	48	1	216‡	218	1
73d	1933–1935	F. Roosevelt	D	59	36	1	313	117	5
74th	1935–1937	F. Roosevelt	D	69	25	2	322	103	10
75th	1937–1939	F. Roosevelt	D	76	16	4	333	89	13
76th	1939–1941	F. Roosevelt	D	69	23	4	262	169	4
77th	1941–1943	F. Roosevelt	D	66	28	2	267	162	6
78th	1943–1945	F. Roosevelt	D	57	38	1	222	209	4
79th	1945–1947	Truman	D	57	38	1	243	190	2
80th	1947–1949	Truman	D	45	51‡	—	188	246‡	1
81st	1949–1951	Truman	D	54	42	—	263	171	1
82d	1951–1953	Truman	D	49	47		234	199	2
83d	1953–1955	Eisenhower	R	47	48	1	213	221	1
84th	1955–1957	Eisenhower	R	48‡	47	1	232‡	203	—
85th	1957–1959	Eisenhower	R	49‡	47	—	234‡	201	—
86th	1959–1961	Eisenhower	R	65‡	35	—	283‡	153	—
87th	1961–1963	Kennedy	D	64	36	—	262	175	—
88th	1963–1965	Kennedy	D	66	34	—	258	176	—

Congress	Years	President	Party	Senate D	Senate R	Senate Other	House D	House R	House Other
		Johnson	D						
89th	1965–1967	Johnson	D	68	32	—	295	140	—
90th	1967–1969	Johnson	D	64	36	—	248	187	—
91st	1969–1971	Nixon	R	57‡	43	—	243‡	192	—
92d	1971–1973	Nixon	R	54‡	44	2	255‡	180	—
93d	1973–1975	Nixon	R	56‡	42	2	242‡	192	1
		Ford	R						
94th	1975–1977	Ford	R	60‡	38	2	291‡	144	—
95th	1977–1979	Carter	D	61	38	1	292	143	—
96th	1979–1981	Carter	D	58	41	1	277	158	—
97th	1981–1983	Reagan	R	46	53	1	243‡	192	—
98th	1983–1985	Reagan	R	46	54	—	268‡	167	—
99th	1985–1987	Reagan	R	47	53	—	253‡	182	—
100th	1987–1989	Reagan	R	55‡	45	—	258‡	177	—
101st	1989–1991	George Bush	R	55‡	45	—	260‡	175	—
102d	1991–1993	George Bush	R	56‡	44	—	267‡	167	1
103d	1993–1995	Clinton	D	57	43	—	258	176	1
104th	1995–1997	Clinton	D	48	52‡	—	204	230‡	1
105th	1997–1999	Clinton	D	45	55‡	—	206	228‡	1
106th	1999–2001	Clinton	D	45	55‡	—	211	222‡	2
107th	2001–2003	George W. Bush	R	50‡	49	1	212	221	2
108th	2003–2005	George W. Bush	R	48	51	1	204	229	1
109th	2005–2007	George W. Bush	R	44	55	1	202	231	1
110th	2007–2009	George W. Bush	R	49‡	49	2	233‡	202	—
111th	2009–2011	Obama	D	58	40	2	256	178	—
112th	2011–2013	Obama	D	51	47	2	198	241‡	2
113th	2013–2015	Obama	D	53	47	2	201	234‡	
114th	2015–2017	Obama	D	44	54‡	2	188	247‡	
115th	2017–2019	Trump	R	48	52		194	241	
116th	2019–2020	Trump	R	45	53	2	235‡	198	

D = Democrat, R = Republican

‡Chamber controlled by party other than that of the president.

* Represents a two-year period, since Congress officially convenes in January.

Source: US House of Representatives; US Senate.

even before Nixon in a scandal of his own in 1973—President Ford was unable to overcome the stigma of Watergate and his pardon of President Nixon. In fact, Ford barely survived a challenge by Ronald Reagan for the Republican presidential nomination and was voted out of office in 1976.

A Closer Look

THE WATERGATE CRISIS

As opposition to his Vietnamization policy grew, especially with military escalation, President Nixon responded by turning to members of his White House staff to conduct a series of illegal and unconstitutional activities. First, Nixon ordered wiretaps of members of the National Security Council staff and a number of journalists in an effort to determine who was leaking information to the media (about the secret US bombing of Cambodia)—hence, referred to as the "plumbers." Second, these efforts soon grew into broader attempts to discredit, disrupt, and derail the antiwar movement and critics of the Nixon administration.

Eventually, given the growing antiwar opposition throughout the country, President Nixon's reelection fears resulted in White House involvement in a number of dirty tricks and illegal activities designed to ensure the president's reelection in 1972. Taking no chances, the Nixon White House attempted to sabotage the campaigns of the political opposition, including Edward Kennedy and Edmund Muskie. This strategy led to the 1972 burglary of the Democratic Party headquarters in the Watergate Hotel in Washington, DC, which gave the ensuing scandal its name and publicly exposed the wide-ranging illegalities and subsequent cover-up by President Nixon. From wiretapping, to an "enemies project," to efforts to ensure the reelection of the president, and finally to the cover-up and obstruction of justice, the legacy of these illegal and unconstitutional activities was a destroyed president.

What does the Watergate episode suggest about the paradox of presidential power and the exercise of prerogative powers?

Source: Emery (1994) and Woodward and Bernstein (1974).

Jimmy Carter attempted to put Vietnam and Watergate behind the country by instilling in the office a new spirit of honesty and idealism, represented by his commitment to human rights and peace. A true "outsider" to national politics, his political experience had been as governor of Georgia. He entered office resistant to the politics of Washington, with few political friends but a public presence that initially instilled hope and high public expectations. President Carter entered office as an activist president with relatively high public prestige and very low professional reputation. Early on, he antagonized members of Congress and the bureaucracy, and he was unable to build consensus around human rights and a more accommodating approach to the Cold War competition with the Soviet Union. Despite the initial popularity of his human rights campaign and foreign policy successes such as the Camp David accords establishing peace between Egypt and Israel, by the end of his administration the US economy went into a tailspin with double-digit inflation and unemployment. The public's perception of his mishandling of US foreign policy abroad also haunted him, especially the Iran hostage crisis and the Soviet Union's invasion of Afghanistan in 1979. President Carter never recovered politically and lost the 1980 election to Ronald Reagan (see Glad 1980; Jordan 1982; Rosati 1987).

During the Cold War Dissensus years, only President Reagan was able to overcome the paradox and life cycle of presidential power. But even Reagan experienced a major crisis of governance during his administration—the Iran-Contra affair—where at the height of the crisis in 1987 it was unclear whether he would survive politically (Cannon 1991; Wills 1988). Reagan's relatively high levels of professional reputation and public prestige—despite concerns over his attentiveness and engagement—are part of the reason he was able to overcome the constraints and uncertainties of his term of office. Although he did not immerse himself in the issues and was relatively uninvolved in the daily operations of presidential governance, he recruited a strong presidential staff and capitalized on his public popularity and ability to communicate.

President Reagan assumed office prepared to initiate a new conservative Cold War agenda: to build foreign policy consensus around strengthening American defense forces, renewing America's efforts to combat communism, while restoring economic prosperity at home. Congressional resistance—especially from Democrats—led to administration efforts to exercise prerogative government and limit or circumvent congressional influence. This set the stage for the **Iran-Contra affair**, in which the administration covertly organized and supported the rebel Contras in an effort to overthrow the leftist Sandinista government in Nicaragua (these operations are discussed in greater depth in Chapter 6, on the intelligence community). In addition, to get around a congressional ban on aid to the Contras, the administration concocted a plan to sell arms to Iran to free some American hostages held in Lebanon and to divert the proceeds of the arms sales to support the Contras. After news of these actions became public, President Reagan and his administration were badly shaken and on the defensive about Iran-Contra for almost a year, facing investigations and congressional hearings. Ultimately, Reagan was able to survive the crisis and complete his term, though he was considerably diminished in power and public prestige and ended his time in office less popular than earlier in his term.

The Post–Cold War and Post-9/11 Years

The end of the Cold War created new opportunities for US foreign policy, but it also exacerbated the difficulties for White House leadership. As we discussed in Chapter 2, lack of consensus on foreign policy, more diffuse international security risks, and an interdependent world economy combined to increase the constraints and challenges facing presidents, while the sense of permanent crisis disappeared with the collapse of the Soviet Union and the Cold War. Of course, crises still occur and allow presidents to be extremely powerful, but this tends to be only temporary and for limited foreign-policy scope.

Freed from the burdens of the Cold War, the past five presidents have had more flexibility to pursue a wider range of foreign policy options abroad. At the same time, the lack of consensus and an increasingly polarized and partisan environment have resulted in great disagreement and significant challenges over the means and ends of US foreign policy (e.g., Scott 1998; Skowronek 2011). The new challenges of the international context, reinforced by the complexity of the domestic environment, reduced the space for White House leadership and presidential success. This has been reinforced by the complex and multifaceted nature of contemporary foreign policy as the differences between foreign and domestic policy are less clear and the issue agenda is less obviously dominated by security concerns. The net result of this crisis of leadership has been that with each new administration, as well as over the course of the same administration, US foreign policy has tended to become increasingly reactive—as opposed to proactive.

George H. W. Bush was skilled and experienced in the realm of foreign policy, but after his victorious 1988 campaign for the presidency, he was ultimately unable to take advantage of the favorable post–Cold War environment and a successful war in the Persian Gulf and lost his bid for reelection in 1992. Bush's leadership style was active and hands-on, informal and open to discussion and deliberation, and less ideological than his predecessor. Often criticized for his pragmatism and lack of broad foreign policy vision, President Bush approached the momentous changes of the end of the Cold War with caution and political sensitivity. Early on, his leadership style paid off with high levels of public and governmental support. His public approval ratings approached 90 percent in his third year, then an all-time high for post–World War II presidents, driven in large part by the success of the American-led war to reverse Saddam Hussein's invasion of Kuwait in the Persian Gulf. However, he was not a particularly good public speaker and, moreover, did not develop an active domestic agenda and faced an economic recession. His pragmatic, realpolitik approach to foreign policy, while successful, did not inspire confidence or passion and often appeared reactive to events and initiatives taken by others. Thus, despite his effective management of the changes generated by the end of the Cold War, the victory in the Persian Gulf War, and public approval ratings approaching 90 percent, Bush was voted out of office after just one term, largely due to perceptions that he did little to address the nation's domestic ills.

President Bill Clinton entered office in 1993 with far less experience in international affairs than his predecessor. Although he had a strong interest in and concern for both policy and politics, he was much more comfortable with domestic policy than foreign policy. In the words of Jack Watson (1993:431), a former White House chief of staff, Clinton was "exuberant, informal, interactive, nonhierarchical, and indefatigable." A self-described "policy wonk," he relished discussion and deliberation and spent significant time considering options to respond to problems. He was also politically pragmatic and emphasized the "doable" in his policy preferences. At the same time, Clinton was undisciplined and often unfocused and was criticized for vacillation and hesitancy in the conduct of US foreign policy, especially in his first term (Greenstein 1994). Highly publicized failures in Somalia and what appeared to be a two-year equivocation on the crisis in the former Yugoslavia were among the early setbacks stemming in part from efforts to promote a more multilateral foreign policy.

Throughout his two terms as president, Clinton faced significant congressional opposition, especially after the 1994 midterm elections in which the Republican Party gained control of both the Senate and the House of Representatives for the first time since 1954, producing divided government once again. President Clinton was forced to tack carefully in the challenging political environment, even facing two government shutdowns when congressional Republicans pushed their own policy solutions. With public attention fixed on the US economy and other domestic issues, the Clinton administration avoided major foreign policy failures—especially after the Somalia episode in 1993—and emphasized domestic policy and international economics. In foreign policy, the administration sought to strengthen multilateralism and American engagement in democracy promotion and human rights; expand the NATO alliance to bring in former Soviet allies in Eastern and Central Europe; and expand international trade through NAFTA, the Uruguay round of GATT, which produced the World Trade Organization, and normalized trade relations with China, among others.

The Monica Lewinsky affair—involving the president's sexual relations with a White House intern—could have destroyed the Clinton presidency but, despite investigations and impeachment proceedings, Clinton managed to escape the scandal and the presidential life cycle. The beneficiary of a relatively placid international environment and an expanding US economy with a first-in-decades budget surplus (see Harris 2005; Renshon 2000), Clinton was the first Democratic president to be reelected since FDR, more than fifty years earlier—and the only president since World War II to leave office with higher public approval than when he entered.

George W. Bush defeated sitting Vice President Al Gore in the highly controversial 2000 election despite winning a smaller share of the popular vote than Gore. His Electoral College victory, which ultimately required a contentious 5–4 Supreme Court decision before it was official, resulted in his presidency beginning with a rather low sense of national legitimacy. Although Bush was previously governor of Texas and ran for president as a "compassionate conservative," he was not widely respected or admired for his political focus, background, or knowledge—especially in the area of foreign policy. As president, Bush embraced a formal, structured style in which he preferred to play a CEO-type role—depending on his advisers for analysis and options—and focus on making decisions. His "I am the decider" approach emphasized loyalty, approval, and support, while his inexperience and formal style emphasized the role of his advisers in policy formulation. The conventional wisdom was that he picked a seasoned foreign policy team that would make up for what he lacked in knowledge about US foreign policy and world politics, and his focus seemed to be on domestic politics—in particular, successfully passing a large tax cut.

The terrorist strikes on the United States on September 11, 2001, transformed the Bush presidency. Quickly reacting to the disaster and ensuing crisis, George W. Bush became the "war president" focused on the global war on terrorism (see Conley 2004; Renshon 2004). The Bush administration framed the new context as a new Cold War–like era of national emergency and crisis. As one reporter noted, "On a wide variety of fronts, the administration ... moved to seize power that it has shared with other branches of government" (Milbank 2001:A1; see also Daalder and Lindsay 2003; Fisher 2007; Goldsmith 2007; Yoo 1996, 2005). Administration officials, including the president, embraced a new vision of a **"unitary executive theory"** in which the president had virtually unlimited ability to exercise prerogative government and could ignore or override laws of Congress that interfere with his duties as commander in chief.

Bush immediately set about refocusing his administration to engage in a global war on terrorism, beginning with Afghanistan to overthrow the Taliban in 2001 before turning to

Iraq to depose Saddam Hussein in 2003 (e.g., Woodward 2004). The public and Congress initially rallied around the military action. Although the initial military campaign succeeded quickly, the more difficult task of rebuilding the Iraqi government and nation-building proved much more difficult. Resistance to the American occupation soon grew, and violence seemed to increase daily. Moreover, the weapons of mass destruction (WMDs) that Iraq was alleged to possess were never found, and the American-led search units soon officially concluded that the WMDs had never been there. Nor were any ties to al-Qaeda discovered, although al-Qaeda soon became active in the insurgency against the US forces and the Iraqi regime that the United States sought to empower. Indeed, far from justifying the president's decision, postwar events cast doubt on the administration's prewar claims and justifications (e.g., Powers 2003).

With the costs of the war thus spiraling upward, Bush began to face increased unrest and challenges, and his public approval began to decline steadily. Although he was able to secure a victory in the bitterly contested 2004 presidential election over Democratic nominee John Kerry, Bush's popularity continued to decline soon after. Distance from the 9/11 attacks, coupled with increasing costs in Iraq, persistent questions about the success of his global war on terrorism, and lingering concerns about the administration's use (or misuse) of intelligence (and other national security powers) combined with natural disasters such as Hurricane Katrina and a collapsing economy to erode Bush's support and exacerbate his lame-duck status to the point that he was essentially ineffective by the end of his term in office. In fact, his presidency was effectively crippled in November 2006, when the Democrats seized control of both houses of Congress in a stunning political backlash against Bush. Hence, while the initial years of the post-9/11 period appeared to be a time of crisis and national emergency ripe for White House leadership, the changing sense of threat, coupled with declining policy success, led to increased criticism even within the Republican-led Congress. Bush's inability to prevail on a variety of policy initiatives in his second term, the increasing opposition to his signature policies on the global war on terror, and concerns over his relative neglect of other domestic and foreign policy issues—especially the economic crisis that began in 2008—provide ample evidence of the challenging environment for presidential leadership.

President Barack Obama entered office in 2009 determined to break with the policies of his predecessor and chart a new course. In a flurry of activity, the Obama administration attempted to take advantage of the honeymoon period to advance an ambitious agenda somewhat reminiscent of the FDR administration and its "first 100 days." Although the problems Obama faced as he began his efforts were not as dramatic as those of the economic depression and global war of the 1930s and 1940s, few presidents since World War II have faced such a daunting array of challenges. In addition to contending with the legacy of the Iraq invasion, Obama faced challenges stemming from the deteriorating situation in Afghanistan and Pakistan (where the Taliban and al-Qaeda had reemerged as viable opponents), a severe global economic crisis, urgent environmental and energy policy issues, continuing global terrorism problems, and regional security and nonproliferation challenges in North Korea and Iran, among other problems. Obama also faced a political environment in Washington, DC, more polarized and divided along partisan lines than ever before in recent memory.

Throughout his two terms, Barack Obama led an activist presidency and administration. His hands-on approach put his White House at the hub of information gathering and deliberation, and his deliberative approach valued the expertise of advisers and consideration of multiple perspectives throughout the policy formulation and decision process. President Obama's leadership style initially seemed to resonate with much of the American people (and much of the world). From the start, he was an effective communicator who appeared active, calm, patient, and thoughtful. In response to the challenging problems his administration faced, he pursued an expansive presidential agenda.

However, while Obama tried to take advantage of his initial honeymoon period, positive professional reputation, and high levels of public approval at the outset of his presidency, the realities of the bitter partisan political environment and the presidential life cycle soon took their toll. He took initial efforts to prevent further economic collapse and stimulate economic recovery and, while they led to the stabilization and then growth of the American economy, they also triggered intense opposition from conservatives and the Republican Party. In national security affairs, the Obama administration took efforts to improve the "soft power" of the United States in the world, emphasizing leadership, engagement, and multilateralism, while implementing plans to withdraw American troops from Iraq by 2010. At the same time, Obama also made early decisions to intensify the American "footprint" in Afghanistan and Pakistan, dispatching an additional 21,000 troops in early 2009 and a subsequent surge of 40,000 troops in the fall of the same year in an effort to prevent further destabilization. In his second term, Obama undertook efforts to address global climate change, resulting in the 2015 Paris Accord, and to complete a multilateral agreement preventing Iran from acquiring nuclear weapons. However, the Obama administration also faced new challenges on terrorism with the rise of the Islamic State and its growing strength and violence in Iraq and Syria, which the administration was less successful in addressing.

At home, Obama's public prestige and professional reputation suffered from Republican opposition in Congress, and intense public disapproval from the most conservative elements of society. The Republican Party consistently fought the initiatives and legislation of the Democrats and Obama. Republicans gained control of the House of Representatives in the 2010 election and won the majority in the Senate in the 2014 midterms. Partisanship worsened, and presidential-legislative relations were marked by endless political battles and stalemates. For example, partisanship was extremely evident when every Republican in the House and all but three in the Senate voted against Obama's stimulus package at the very beginning of his presidency, despite the crisis in the US economy. Even his successful conclusion of a "New START" treaty with Russia to dramatically reduce nuclear arsenals on both sides—a goal that every president since Richard Nixon had sought—faced a fierce partisan debate before it was ratified by the US Senate, and then only after the addition of amendments to placate some Republicans, and only by a 71–26 vote, barely clearing the 67-vote threshold needed for treaty ratification. No Democrats voted against the treaty.

As a consequence, the president turned to the exercise of prerogative power across many fronts, including immigration, climate change, nuclear proliferation in Iran, and relations with Cuba. Although this approach yielded results, it also heightened Republican hostility and opposition. President Obama won a second term in 2012—marking the third straight two-term presidency, something that had not occurred since the early nineteenth century—but he and his administration fell prey to the paradox of presidential power and the presidential life cycle.

The Trump Challenge

Donald Trump narrowly defeated Hillary Clinton, while losing the popular vote by more than 2 percent (about 3 million votes), to become the forty-fifth president of the United States. The least experienced person to ever win the presidency (in terms of public service), Trump was especially inexperienced in foreign affairs. A polarizing candidate and president in an increasingly polarized political context, President Trump embraced a confrontational style of leadership. Inattentive to policy detail and the policymaking process, Trump nevertheless embraced a formal approach that emphasized his preferences and his role as the decision maker. With little willingness to tolerate conflict or dissent, Trump prized personal loyalty among his advisers. He also showed himself to be intensely political, concerned about approval and support and his own power and status. At the same time, he consistently demonstrated his resistance to experts, to information and facts, or to persuasion. Despite his embrace of formal hierarchy and his own power and authority, Trump also established an unstructured, shambolic process with a high rate of personnel turnover, even among his top advisers (see Table 3.2), and leaned heavily on loyal and close personal advisers, including his own children.

Controversial and mercurial, President Trump began his administration with low levels of professional reputation and public prestige. Although he had the strong support and approval of a committed wing of the Republican Party, Trump's public approval ratings in his first two years were the lowest of modern presidents, never exceeding 50 percent, even in his so-called honeymoon period, and mostly ranging from 35 to 44 percent. Although Republicans controlled the White House and both chambers of Congress during Trump's first two years in office, his controversial approach, low professional reputation, and unpopularity—combined with concerns about the nature of his victorious campaign, corruption in his administration, and multiple investigations into misconduct (including those led by the Southern District of New York, the Federal Bureau of Investigation, the Department of Justice, and a special counsel's office)—led to challenges to his leadership culminating in the start of impeachment proceedings by the House of Representatives in Fall 2019.

As we discussed in Chapter 2, President Trump sought dramatic changes to US foreign policy, abandoning core commitments to American engagement and leadership that his predecessors from both parties had embraced. His own inexperience and style, the truncated presidential life cycle he faced, and the nature of the paradox of presidential power that worked against him complicated his ability to exercise effective White House leadership. He increasingly embraced the prerogative power of the presidency, seeking to take advantage of presidential authority, the opportunities of presidential initiative, and aggressive executive orders to accomplish what he could not persuade the rest of the government to support. Ironically, President Obama's resort to these prerogative powers to achieve progress in areas such as climate change and nuclear proliferation meant that President Trump was able to use those same powers to reverse the Obama-era policies by executive fiat.

However, in the 2018 midterm elections, Democrats swept into the majority in the House of Representatives, gaining a net of forty seats to reestablish divided government and open new challenges to White House leadership. Early in 2019, the new majority in the House began a broad series of hearings and investigations designed to challenge the administration, many of which had foreign policy connections and implications. Stymied in domestic policy, Trump turned to the exercise of prerogative powers and the relatively greater freedom of international affairs to seek opportunities for leadership, declaring a national emergency on border security and immigration, and attempting to engage in high-level diplomacy with North Korean dictator Kim Jong Un, among other assertive actions. However, his efforts to escape his unpopularity and evade limits on presidential power and leadership led him to turn to a series of controversial actions that resulted in the start of impeachment hearings in the House of Representatives in Fall 2019.

SUMMARY: THE CHALLENGES OF PRESIDENTIAL LEADERSHIP

The paradox of presidential power, factors related to presidential style and leadership approaches and patterns, and the changing political context mean that the president and the White House are central to the politics and processes of US foreign policy, but White House leadership is a variable rather than a constant. Our examination of the presidency suggests that the changing political and foreign policy context establishes another paradox. As our discussion has indicated, especially since Vietnam, presidents have increasingly turned to prerogative powers to escape or overcome the limits that lack of consensus and the more complicated political environment have created. At the same time, it also appears increasingly difficult for presidents to exercise power and prerogative government in the name of national security or crises/emergencies without risking considerable political backlash.

There is no sign that the fragmented, polarized, and pluralist political environment that has prevailed since the Vietnam War will soon change. Foreign policy opportunities come packaged with political challenges and risks for presidents and American leadership abroad. Much will depend on the nature of threat in the world; a president's policies, leadership style, and skills; and domestic political matters like party control of the branches of government. "Who" is president matters greatly, and "who" holds other positions in the US government is also increasingly important. Even within the executive branch, this is the case, and one area that is of particular importance for foreign policymaking and White House leadership is the foreign policy bureaucracy and its management. We turn to those matters in the next five chapters.

THINK ABOUT THIS

The forty-first president of the United States—George H. W. Bush—once said, "It is my duty as President to conduct the foreign policy of the United States as I see fit." In light of this chapter's material, think about this statement.

What factors shape and condition the role and leadership of the president in foreign policy?

KEY TERMS

advice and consent   67

analyst/innovators   63

bully pulpit   53

chief executive officers   62

chief of staff   64

director/ideologues   63

divided government   79

electoral mandate   73

Executive Office of the
   Presidency (EOP)   63

gatekeeping   64

honeymoon period   73

imperial presidency   78

intermestic issues   72

Iran-Contra affair   83

issue area   72

lame-duck   74

office of the vice president   65

paradox of presidential
   power   50

power   72

power to persuade   69

prerogative government   70

presidential character   62

presidential choices   70

presidential life cycle   73

presidential styles   61

professional reputation   70

public prestige   70

singularity   53

team-builder/players   63

two presidencies thesis   77

unitary executive theory   85

Watergate   79

West Wing   69

White House Office   64

Visit **edge.sagepub.com/scottrosati7e** to help you accomplish your coursework goals in an easy-to-use learning environment.

Understanding the Foreign Policy Bureaucracy

THE DEPARTMENT OF STATE

PHOTO 4.1 Secretary of State Mike Pompeo at his swearing-in ceremony.

US Department of State

LEARNING OBJECTIVES

1. Know the nature, purpose, and main characteristics of bureaucracy.

2. Understand the functions, structures, and processes of the US Department of State.

3. Identify the foreign service subculture and its consequences.

4. Assess and explain key patterns in the role and influence of the Department of State in US foreign policymaking.

5. Describe the role of the secretary of state.

INTRODUCTION: THE FOREIGN POLICY BUREAUCRACY AND THE DEPARTMENT OF STATE

Understanding the foreign policy bureaucracy is essential for comprehending the foreign policymaking process. The foreign policy bureaucracy is large and complex and poses many management challenges for the country's elected leaders, especially the president. After all, it is the bureaucracy that is responsible for most governmental behavior, and it is central to both the formulation and implementation of governmental policies. Over the next five chapters, we examine the key players in the foreign policy bureaucracy, as well as the central institutions and processes for the management and coordination of these agencies. This chapter begins with a general overview of the key features of bureaucracy that make its management so important—and so challenging—and then we focus on the US Department of State to consider its organization and operation, and its role and influence in US foreign policymaking.

UNDERSTANDING BUREAUCRACY

To begin, let's consider why bureaucracy exists. A **bureaucracy** is an administrative organization responsible for carrying out the day-to-day business of government. Often referred to as the "fourth branch," it is, in effect, the eyes, ears, hands, and feet of the government. The current US bureaucracy consists of fifteen cabinet departments and many other independent executive and regulatory agencies, commissions, and government corporations employing almost 3 million nonmilitary individuals, and another 2 million or so active and reserve military personnel. Bureaucratic agencies collect information, conduct analysis and reporting, provide advice, and carry out policy decisions and actions. Bureaucrats, who are career employees, bring expertise to their jobs (or develop it on the job), and they serve policymakers regardless of their political party affiliation. Modern government relies on bureaucracy because of the complexity of the problems and policies it faces.

Three characteristics form the foundation of bureaucratic structure and processes (e.g., Halperin 1974; Heclo 1977; Wilson 1989):

- **Hierarchy:** Bureaucratic organizations usually are hierarchically structured with formal chains of command and divisions of authority and labor specified throughout. Hierarchy involves a top-down division of authority in which every official occupies a particular role and answers to a superior. People in positions near the top of the organization not only enjoy more authority, but they also require more general knowledge and skills since they deal with large questions and the "bigger picture."

- **Specialization:** Bureaucracies themselves are established to focus on particular problems. Between bureaucratic agencies, specialization means that their roles, tasks, and perspectives are differentiated, and each agency emphasizes its own responsibilities. Within an agency, the structure of a bureaucratic organization generally reflects formal divisions, each of which is assigned a particular part of the agency's responsibility. As one moves down the bureaucratic hierarchy, positions become increasingly specialized.

- **Routinization:** Bureaucracies tend to develop repertoires, or standard processes for engaging in their duties. These routines regularize the way that individuals and offices address recurring issues and problems. Moving down the hierarchy, individuals and offices not only have more and more specific tasks and focus, but they have less and less authority to act independently of superiors and are increasingly likely to repeatedly perform the same tasks to address the slice of policy for which they have responsibility.

Together, the features and foundations of bureaucracy are intended to improve efficiency, accountability, competence, consistency, and fairness. However, while these complex organizations are central to governance, the combination of the three key characteristics creates challenges—"pathologies" that tend to manifest themselves in their operations and that create problems for their management. For example, there are **coordination issues** that arise from the jurisdictions and assignments of the agencies, each of which is independent of the others and targets particular problems or parts of problems. Such "turf" matters can create divisions, competition, and conflict among different agencies. Agencies also tend to develop often-competing senses of **mission** and subcultures, both between bureaucratic organizations and within specialized parts of a particular one. This can result in parochialism and friction among agencies and offices. The hierarchy and routines on which agencies rely to promote accountability and efficiency can result in bureaucratic "red tape," the reliance on **standard operating procedures,** and bureaucratic "buck-passing" that makes it hard for agencies to be efficient or to be responsive or innovative. Finally, the career nature of bureaucratic employment can create tension and conflict between the career bureaucrats and the elected and appointed officials of a particular administration (e.g., Allison 1971; Allison and Zelikow 1999; Halperin 1974).

Bureaucratic Size

The president is the chief administrator of this sprawling bureaucracy, much of which is beyond direct presidential control. The president presides over 5 million personnel, located in fifteen major departments and hundreds of other organizations and agencies, who now spend close to $5 trillion a year on thousands of programs and policies throughout the United States and the world. The executive branch is so large that the president cannot manage it alone. Within this sprawling array of organizations, the **foreign policy bureaucracy** is made up of those agencies that have foreign policy roles. The main elements of the foreign policy bureaucracy include the Department of Defense (DOD), which is the largest of all executive branch organizations. It employs more than three million civilian and military personnel (including reserves) throughout the world and now spends over $700 billion a year. Along with the DOD, the foreign policy bureaucracy includes the Department of State, with its professional diplomatic corps, and the Central Intelligence Agency (CIA) and other specialized parts of the intelligence community, which engage in intelligence gathering and analysis devoted to foreign affairs. Other agencies have important foreign policy roles as well, including the Department of the Treasury and the Department of Homeland Security, created in 2002. These are just the most obvious agencies: Virtually every department and agency in the executive branch contains an international component.

As Table 4.1 reveals, many agencies are involved in foreign policy. For example, the Department of Transportation is responsible for the government's policy on international aviation and maritime issues through the Office of the Assistant Secretary for Aviation and International Affairs, the Federal Aviation Administration, and the Maritime Administration. The Department of Justice contains the Federal Bureau of Investigation (FBI), which plays an important role in counterterrorism and counterintelligence, and the Drug Enforcement Administration, the lead agency in fighting the drug war. As noted in Table 4.1, a number of independent agencies and governmental corporations have a role in global affairs, including the Environmental Protection Agency, the Federal Maritime Commission (which regulates waterborne domestic and foreign commerce), and the National Endowment for Democracy (a quasi-governmental foundation that distributes democracy assistance grants). We're talking about a huge foreign policy bureaucracy.

TABLE 4.1

The Foreign Policy Bureaucracy

	Internationally Oriented Agencies	Domestically Oriented Agencies
Executive Office of the President	National Security Council National Economic Council White House Office of Global Communications Office of the Director of National Intelligence Office of the US Trade Representative	White House Office Office of Management and Budget Office of Science and Technology Policy Office of National Drug Control Policy Office of National AIDS Policy
Presidential Departments and Agencies	Department of State Department of Defense Department of the Treasury Department of Energy Department of Homeland Security Central Intelligence Agency US Agency for International Development Peace Corps	Department of Agriculture Department of Commerce Department of Labor Department of Justice Department of Veterans Affairs Department of Transportation Department of Health and Human Services
Independent Agencies	International Trade Commission Export-Import Bank Overseas Protection Investment Corporation Trade and Development Agency International Broadcasting Bureau National Endowment for Democracy African Development Foundation Inter-American Foundation Panama Canal Commission US Institute for Peace	Federal Reserve Board National Aeronautics and Space Administration Environmental Protection Agency Federal Maritime Commission

Source: United States Government Manual.

Bureaucratic Complexity

The bureaucracy is also incredibly complex. Whatever their specific size, each agency and department has its subculture, and sometimes more than one, as well as its own set of goals and missions. Although specialization means agencies have particular roles and assignments, many times the tasks of different organizations overlap, and agencies often compete with each other and sometimes have problems coordinating their activities. For instance, the intelligence community, discussed in Chapter 6, is made up of many executive branch organizations that contribute information and analyses to high-level policymakers. This problem also occurs within an agency, as different bureaus and offices can have overlapping responsibilities as well. These various organizations also have different levels of autonomy from presidential authority. The president has legal authority within the executive branch over those organizations located in the Executive Office of the President, classified as cabinet departments, or presidential agencies. However, most of the organizations classified as independent agencies in Table 4.1 are independent of presidential authority.

The forces of globalization and interdependence have added to the complexity of the foreign policy bureaucracy over the past several decades by fostering the fading distinction between foreign and domestic policy bureaucracies. Once, traditional national security bureaucracies were easy to identify, such as the State Department, the military, and, after World War II, the intelligence community. However, with the growth of interdependence and the boundary-reducing forces of globalization, these distinctions have lost much of their meaning. US foreign policy now involves intermestic policies in such areas as economics, immigration, the environment, transportation and communications, technology, and narcotics, and a host of bureaucratic agencies that have responsibilities in these areas. Now, in part because of the **internationalization of domestic bureaucracies** and the development of global networks of bureaucratic (personnel) interaction, especially in the "principal areas of food, energy, finance, communication, environment, economic growth, and the spread of technology" (Hopkins 1978:31), most of the departments and ministries of modern governments associated with predominantly domestic areas have some kind of international bureau. In fact, the rise in the importance of the foreign economic bureaucracy, which we discuss in Chapter 7, is one of the main consequences of this shift.

Historical Development of the Bureaucracy

Two hundred years ago the US government was tiny compared to what it is today. It was composed of the president, the vice president, a small personal staff, and four small departments: State, Treasury, War, and Justice. Prior to World War II, foreign policy was conducted by

> the president and secretary of state; a handful of administration appointees in the Department of State and major embassies; the senior diplomats of a tiny but adequate Foreign Service; a few military and naval officers serving in important commands or as attaches; and a constellation of influential lawyers and bankers, involved in the Council on Foreign Relations and largely residing on the East Coast. (Maechling 1976:6)

Since the nineteenth century, most bureaucratic growth has taken place in four successive waves:

1. In domestic and economic agencies as a result of the New Deal legislation of the 1930s under President Roosevelt

2. In national security and foreign affairs during World War II and the Cold War under Presidents Roosevelt, Truman, and Eisenhower (Zegart 1999)

3. As a consequence of President Johnson's Great Society programs of the 1960s

4. In the post-9/11 context with President George W. Bush's global war on terrorism and President Obama's response to the global economic recession

In each of these waves, the expansion of the bureaucracy came from the government's responses to the urgency of events and the times. New bureaucratic agencies with new organizational goals and missions were created to respond to new problems, often perceived as so dire and widespread that only the federal government could address them. However, such growth has generated the bureaucratic complexity that makes it so difficult for presidents to act as chief executives.

The national security bureaucracy's tremendous expansion took place over two decades in response to two major conflicts, World War II and the Cold War. The key law that was the basis for the permanent expansion of the foreign policy bureaucracy was the **National Security Act of 1947**. It was one of the most important acts ever passed by Congress and signed by the president, because it laid the foundation for the modern foreign policy bureaucracy. This restructuring was intended to produce a more efficient national security process that would be more valuable to the president in his conduct of foreign policy. The act restructured the national security process in three major areas:

- The military, by creating the National Military Establishment (forerunner to the DOD), consisting of the secretary of defense, the Joint Chiefs of Staff, and the Departments of Army, Navy, and Air Force

- Intelligence, by creating the CIA and the director of central intelligence

- National security advice to the president, by creating the National Security Council

The most recent expansion of the national security bureaucracy came in response to the September 11, 2001, terrorist attacks. In addition to providing large budgetary increases for the military and the intelligence community, President George W. Bush first created the Office of Homeland Security by executive order to coordinate the government's counterterrorist efforts. In 2002, Congress, over the initial objections of President Bush and his advisers, turned the office into a full-fledged Department of Homeland Security in order to reorganize numerous executive branch agencies involved in counterterrorism and give it greater stature to help coordinate and lead the counterterrorism effort. Additionally, following the recommendation of a commission that studied the September 11 attacks, the Bush administration also lobbied successfully for a new Office of the Director of National Intelligence (ODNI), created by the Intelligence Reform and Prevention of Terrorism Act of 2004 (P.L. 108-458), which removed the coordinating role from the director of the CIA and provided the new director of national intelligence with some expanded powers to coordinate the decentralized intelligence community. (Chapter 6 discusses both the Department of Homeland Security and ODNI in greater detail.) In spite of both changes, much of the intelligence community, especially the FBI and the CIA, remained largely untouched, and many relevant agencies—including many situated in the Department of Defense—remained outside the direct control of either of the new organizations. The foreign economic bureaucracy has also been expanding since the Bill Clinton administration, as the global economy has become more and more important to both foreign affairs and to national prosperity (discussed in Chapter 7).

The foreign policy bureaucracy reflects these bureaucratic characteristics and challenges and problems. Hence, as we discussed in Chapter 3, the bureaucracy is both a source of and a constraint on presidential power. White House leadership requires it to engage with, manage, and coordinate the foreign policy bureaucracy to harness its resources and activities. But the nature, roles, and processes of these complex agencies and organizations often constrain presidential leadership. In this chapter, and each of the next three, we examine the core members of the foreign policy bureaucracy to understand their nature, structures and processes, and policymaking roles and influence. We begin with the US Department of State.

THE DEPARTMENT OF STATE AT HOME AND ABROAD

The US Department of State is a main component of the foreign policy bureaucracy and an important executive branch organization. One of four original cabinet departments created as part of the new government of the United States in 1789, the State Department was the lead organization responsible for the conduct of US foreign policy throughout most of American history. However, with the rise of the Cold War, the containment strategy, and the president's effort to manage foreign policy, the State Department's influence declined. Nevertheless, although the policymaking process is no longer centered in the State Department, it remains an important bureaucratic institution involved in foreign policy.

The Functions of the Department of State

Within the foreign policy bureaucracy, the Department of State emphasizes five major purposes or missions for which it was originally created (e.g., Campbell 1971; Rubin 1985). We'll look at each in turn.

First, an important function of the State Department is to *represent the US government overseas*, usually to foreign governments. The members of the State Department who are part of the foreign service (known as **foreign service officers**, or FSOs) serve abroad in embassies in the capital cities of foreign countries, in consulates in major cities of foreign countries, in other missions abroad, and in international governmental organizations such as the United Nations. In this role, the US ambassador and the FSO act in the name of the US government and communicate the official foreign policy of the United States to people abroad. Given the primitive nature of transportation and communications until the 1970s or so, this was a crucial role because the foreign service was the principal channel through which governments communicated. Today, with more and more organizations of the US government employing official representatives overseas, this unique role of the foreign service has declined in importance. Also, with the technological revolution in transportation and instant communications, the US president and foreign leaders no longer are dependent on FSOs to communicate official governmental policy.

The second major State Department purpose is to *represent the views of foreigners, usually foreign governments, to the US government*. An important job of the foreign service is to interact with foreign government officials in the United States and abroad, learn their official positions on international issues, and communicate their views to other parts of the US government. Although other bureaucratic agencies represent the views of a certain constituency, the fact that the State Department represents the views of foreign governments, as opposed to organized domestic interests, is unique within the bureaucracy. It also contributes heavily to charges of **clientelism** aimed at State Department officers, who are regularly accused of weighing the interests and concerns of their assigned countries more heavily than those of the United States. Also, with the rise of other bureaucratic agencies and the mass media, contemporary presidents are no longer as dependent on the State Department for learning the foreign policies of other governments.

The third major purpose of the State Department is *to conduct diplomacy and negotiations abroad*. In the past, if the president wanted to conclude a treaty or come to some common understanding with an adversary or friend, he had to rely on ambassadors and FSOs to negotiate in the name of the US government. Communications were so slow that the president had little choice but to entrust considerable authority to his ambassadors and subordinates abroad. This is no longer the case. The speed of communications now gives presidents the ability to control negotiations on those issues they deem most important. In addition to engaging in substantially more diplomacy themselves, such as through summitry, presidents have also increasingly turned to special envoys and others outside the State Department for their diplomatic initiatives. For example, President Nixon believed that opening relations with the People's Republic of China and concluding the first SALT treaty with the Soviet Union were too important to entrust to the bureaucracy, so he relied instead on the personal diplomacy of national security adviser Henry Kissinger. Currently, Donald Trump's administration leans heavily on White House adviser (and Trump's son-in-law) Jared Kushner for sensitive negotiations in the Middle East with Israel, Saudi Arabia, and other countries. Nor is it unusual for presidents or their closest advisers to pick up the phone and communicate directly with international leaders, or for presidents to appoint special envoys to represent the US government in the president's name for a particular foreign policy issue. Examples include Ronald Reagan's appointment of former diplomat Philip Habib to lead US efforts on Lebanon in the early 1980s, Barack Obama's appointment of former senator George Mitchell as special envoy for the Middle East, and Trump's appointment of Stephen Biegun as special envoy for North Korea.

The State Department's fourth major purpose is *to analyze and report on foreign events*. Most FSOs located abroad spend the bulk of their time analyzing events and transmitting these analyses through cables back to the State Department in Washington, DC. Many of the FSOs in Washington spend their time reading the cables, using them as the principal source of information for communicating with their superiors—ultimately the secretary of state—and fulfilling their foreign policy functions. Decisions and directions for implementing and representing US foreign policy abroad are subsequently communicated via cable to the embassies, consulates, and missions in the field. In some ways, the **cable traffic** remains the heart and soul of the contemporary State Department—consisting of more than 2.5 million cables and 25 million e-mail messages a year (Zimmerman 1997). Yet, where past presidents may have relied on reports and analyses of foreign events provided by the State Department, since the 1960s they have turned increasingly to their national security advisers and their own staff, other parts of the bureaucracy (e.g., the Department of Defense and the intelligence community), and even the media to keep informed about world politics.

State's final major function is *to provide policy advice to the president*. No department function has suffered more than this one. Before World War II, the foreign policy process tended to be centered in the State Department, but since then it has shifted increasingly to the White House. Now, the State Department generally must work through the National Security Council system and process and compete with many more bureaucratic rivals such as Defense, Treasury, the intelligence community, and others. In recent decades, new White House–based structures for homeland security and economics have further diffused State's role and access. The president also tends to rely on a small informal circle of major advisers, only one of whom may be the secretary of state. Thus, the overall policy influence of State depends heavily on both the working relationship between the president and the secretary of state, and the way the secretary of state works with the department itself.

Bureaucratic Structure and Process

The State Department began in 1789 with a staff of six, a budget of $7,961, and two diplomatic missions. By 2019, the State Department had a budget of about $55 billion (including US Agency for International Development funds and other international programming) and operated more than 300 embassies, consulates, and diplomatic missions around the world. However, although the Department of State is a complex organization with a broad mandate that operates as if it were a large bureaucratic organization, compared to most bureaucracies within the US government, the State Department is relatively small. Of its approximately 75,000 employees, about 13,000 are foreign service officers who have primary responsibility for fulfilling the State Department's major functions. Another 11,000 civil service officers and thousands of other employees are basically support personnel: doctors, security officers, secretaries, drivers, other workers, and many foreign nationals employed by the overseas diplomatic missions. Roughly two thirds of all department employees are located in State's home office in the Foggy Bottom neighborhood of Washington, D.C., and the remaining third are located abroad. For FSOs within the department, the reverse is true; roughly one third of all FSOs are located in Washington, DC, while the other two thirds are located at missions abroad.

At Home. The State Department shares the common elements found in any government or private-sector bureaucracy: hierarchy, specialization, and routinization. Figure 4.1 shows that there are five major hierarchical levels within the State Department: the secretary of state, deputy secretary of state, undersecretaries of state, assistant secretaries of state, and deputy assistant secretaries of state. The top three levels of officials are referred to as the "seventh-floor principals" because their offices are on the top floor of the State Department building in Washington, DC. The **secretary of state** is the chief officer responsible for governing and managing the State Department for the president. There are now two **deputy secretaries** of state—one is the principal adviser to the secretary and one serves as the chief operating officer of the agency. The department was reorganized in 1999 and again in 2010, so that now the secretaries and deputy secretary have the support of six (up from

FIGURE 4.1

Overview of State Department Organization, 2019

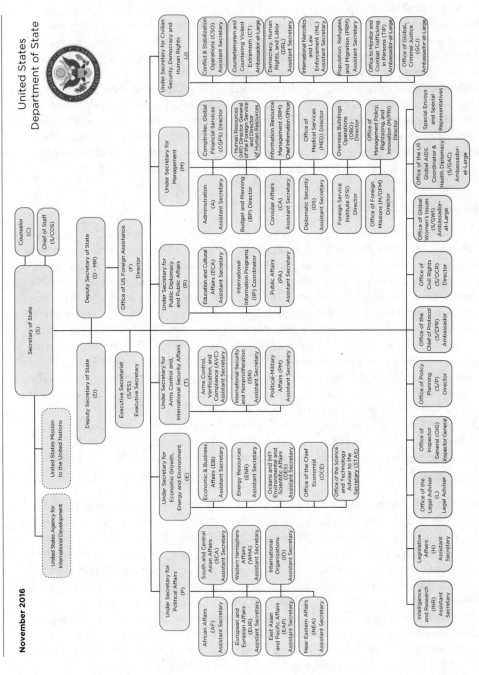

Source: US Department of State (https://www.state.gov/documents/organization/263637.pdf).

four) **undersecretaries**, each responsible for supervising one of the following broad areas: political affairs; economic growth, energy and environment; arms control and international security affairs; civilian security, democracy, and human rights; public diplomacy and public affairs; and management (including budget and personnel). A counselor and other units that report directly to the secretary, such as the Policy Planning Staff and the Bureau of Intelligence and Research, play significant roles at times as well.

As the highest-ranking officials in the State Department, the seventh-floor principals tend to be generalists and are responsible for the department's overall conduct. Most of the specialized work of the department, however, occurs at the **bureau** level. Like most foreign policy bureaucracies, the State Department is organized into both geographic and issue-oriented bureaus. There are six geographic bureaus, often referred to as the "baronies" because of their centrality to the State Department's functions: African Affairs, East Asian and Pacific Affairs, European and Eurasian Affairs (including Russia), Near Eastern Affairs, South and Central Asian Affairs, and Western Hemisphere Affairs. The bureaus are run by **assistant secretaries** with **deputy assistant secretaries** (or directors and deputy directors)—referred to as "bureau principals"—(see the example from the Bureau of African Affairs in Figure 4.2).

Within a geographic bureau, the assistant secretary has one or more deputies, and the bureau's area focus is subdivided into regions, and then countries. For example, as Figure 4.2 shows, the Bureau of African Affairs is divided into west, central and east, and southern African affairs, each of which then includes country subdivisions. Each country, in turn, is managed by a **country director**—or desk officer—who reports to one of the

FIGURE 4.2

Organization of the Bureau of African Affairs

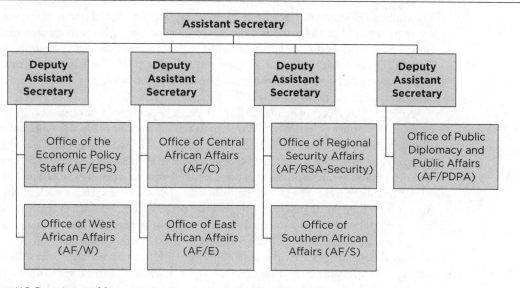

Source: U.S. Department of State.

deputy assistant secretaries responsible for that part of the region, who in turn reports to the assistant secretary. Thus, the assistant secretary and the deputy assistant secretaries develop expertise and have responsibilities at the regional level. The assistant secretary for African Affairs, for example, is likely to be a principal advisor to the undersecretary of state for political affairs and possibly the secretary of state (and his or her deputy) on African issues. The country director for South Africa within the bureau is the specialist and expert on the current situation in that particular country and the key link in all of the information and decisions communicated—through the cable traffic—between his or her superiors at home and those in the field.

Abroad. Overseas, the State Department operates more than 300 embassies, consulates, and diplomatic missions. About 170 of these are embassy missions (usually called **embassies**) in countries with which the United States maintains official diplomatic relations. The remaining missions are other consulates or diplomatic missions, many of which provide various services for Americans and issue visas to foreigners for travel to the United States, support the main embassy in larger metropolitan areas, and maintain other permanent missions, such as to international organizations like the United Nations or the Organization of American States. In a few special cases, the United States does not have full diplomatic relations with a country (such as Cuba, Iran, North Korea, and Bhutan). In such cases, the United States is usually represented by a US Liaison Office or US Interests Section. The size and complexity of embassies vary enormously, though they are all organized in a similar bureaucratic fashion. For a long time, the largest embassy was in London with a staff approaching 300; today the embassy in Iraq is the largest as a result of the war—with dozens of buildings and thousands of staff. Smaller embassies such as many in Africa often have staffs of only a few people.

Figure 4.3 gives an idea of how an overseas mission, such as an embassy, is organized. The common bureaucratic elements of hierarchy, specialization, and routinization are evident here as well. The **ambassador** is the chief of mission, the highest representative of the United States stationed abroad, with responsibility over those individuals employed by the embassy. The ambassador has the assistance of a **deputy chief of mission** and a **country team**, composed of FSOs from the State Department and other governmental agencies with more specific areas of responsibility (Dorman 2011).

An interesting aspect of Figure 4.3 is the presence of personnel from agencies other than the State Department. Until World War II, most officials stationed abroad as representatives of the US government were from the State Department. This is no longer the case. The US government now has more than 30,000 employees abroad (not counting CIA personnel or American troops in military bases). Of these, State Department personnel make up roughly 30 percent of the total. The rest come from other bureaucratic agencies such as the US Agency for International Development (about 20 percent), the Defense Department (about 25 percent, excluding troops), and the Peace Corps (about 20 percent). The presence of some of these agencies is so large that they may have their own facilities separate from the main embassy, although the ambassador remains the senior US governmental official within the country. Indeed, almost every department and agency within the executive branch is internationally involved in some way and has representatives overseas. So, the State Department's dominance has diminished steadily as other agencies and their personnel have increased.

FIGURE 4.3

An Embassy Organizational Chart

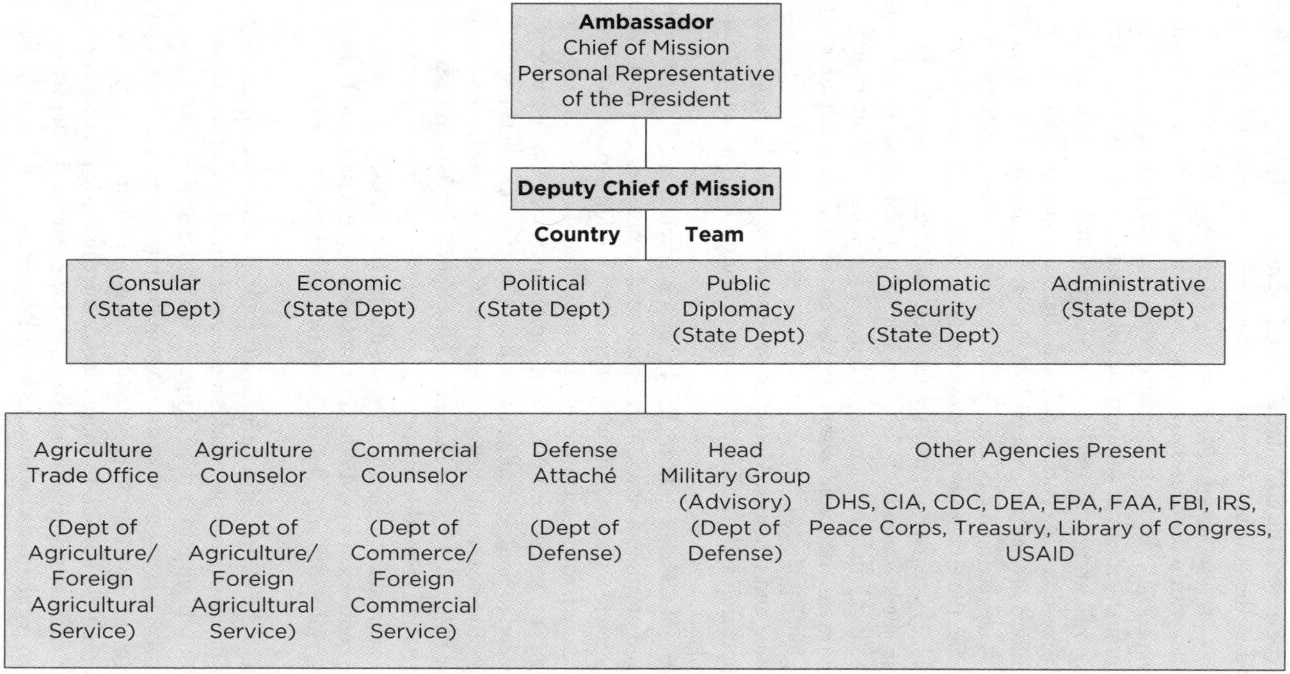

Ambassador
Chief of Mission
Personal Representative
of the President

Deputy Chief of Mission

Country Team

| Consular (State Dept) | Economic (State Dept) | Political (State Dept) | Public Diplomacy (State Dept) | Diplomatic Security (State Dept) | Administrative (State Dept) |

| Agriculture Trade Office (Dept of Agriculture/ Foreign Agricultural Service) | Agriculture Counselor (Dept of Agriculture/ Foreign Agricultural Service) | Commercial Counselor (Dept of Commerce/ Foreign Commercial Service) | Defense Attaché (Dept of Defense) | Head Military Group (Advisory) (Dept of Defense) | Other Agencies Present DHS, CIA, CDC, DEA, EPA, FAA, FBI, IRS, Peace Corps, Treasury, Library of Congress, USAID |

DHS – Department of Homeland Security
CIA – Central Intelligence Agency
CDC – Centers for Disease Control
DEA – Drug Enforcement Administration
EPA – Environmental Protection Agency

FAA – Federal Aviation Administration
FBI – Federal Bureau of Investigation
IRS – Internal Revenue Service
USAID – US Agency for International Development

Source: Shawn Dorman, ed., *Inside a U.S. Embassy: How the Foreign Service Works for America, Third Edition* (Washington, DC: American Foreign Service Association, 2011).

One agency not depicted in Figure 4.3 is the CIA. It does have a major presence abroad but is officially kept secret. The **CIA station chief**, for instance, is likely to have an official position attached to the embassy in order to provide "cover" and diplomatic immunity. Other intelligence personnel and operatives will either be attached to the embassy or occupy private roles within the country (such as working for a multinational corporation).

Like all bureaucracies, the State Department is organized hierarchically. Not only is there a top-to-bottom hierarchy of authority and labor, but a pecking order also exists within each level. For example, at the undersecretary level, management is considered the least significant of the six positions. In contrast, political affairs is considered the most prestigious, especially by members of the foreign service. A similar pecking order exists at the bureau level and abroad. The geographic bureaus—the baronies—are considered more important and prestigious than those that involve crosscutting or functional issues. Historically, the European bureau has been the most prestigious, while the African bureau has been the least, reflecting its generally low priority in US foreign policy. The issue-oriented bureaus that are involved in political matters, such as the bureaus for political-military affairs and for international security and nonproliferation, are also considered more important than those concerned with global affairs, such as oceans and the environment, democracy and human rights, or population and refugees. Moreover, these specializations by region and function often create competition and "turf" issues among the bureaus, as well as coordination and efficiency challenges.

Abroad, large embassies in industrialized countries, such as the London embassy, are more desirable and prestigious assignments than small embassies in Third World countries, such as Brazzaville, Congo. Likewise, within the foreign service, five "career cones" are similarly structured, with a hierarchy placing the political cone ahead of the economic, consular, management, and, since 1999, public diplomacy cones. These patterns of hierarchy and prestige tend to hold generally, but the rise of "hot" issues will temporarily enhance one bureau or position over another, as when the Vietnam War increased the importance of the East Asian and Pacific Bureau and the Southeast Asia embassies during the 1960s; the conflicts in El Salvador and Nicaragua increased the importance of the Western Hemisphere Bureau and the regional embassies during the 1980s; and since 2001, the war on terrorism and conflicts in the Middle East and between Pakistan and India have made the Near Eastern and South and Central Asian Bureaus more prominent.

Process. Because the State Department is a complex bureaucracy that addresses many issues, its policy process is complex and issue dependent. The secretary of state, like the president, is most influential for those issues in which he or she is most interested and involved. Yet most issues are routine, day-to-day matters (involving visas, a report, or a local incident abroad) and can be handled by a few people in the appropriate bureau at home and in the field abroad. In these cases, a **bureaucratic process** exists in which information and decisions routinely flow up and down within the department at home as well as through regularized channels between Washington, DC, and the field offices.

Those issues perceived to be more significant for US foreign policy involve a much larger process, including higher level officials within and beyond the State Department. This can be illustrated by the US government's repeated efforts over many decades to further a comprehensive settlement of the Arab-Israeli conflict. The issue falls within the immediate jurisdiction of the Bureau of Near Eastern Affairs and involves the most relevant assistant secretary and country directors (for Israel, Jordan, Egypt, Syria, and Lebanon) and relevant embassies in the field. But the importance of the issue often increases the scope of the participants. The bureau principals and many of the seventh-floor principals, possibly including the secretary of state, are likely to be involved and kept abreast of matters. Currently, the Middle East has important implications for other country directors within the bureau and for other bureaus—such as European Affairs (given their dependency on Arab oil); Political-Military Affairs (since it is the site of a major military conflict); Democracy, Human Rights, and Labor; and Population, Refugees, and Migration (given the Palestinian refugee status and violence in the West Bank and Gaza Strip); Legal Affairs (for questions involving international law); Legislative Affairs (given the interest of certain members and committees of Congress); and Public Affairs (given the interest of the media and the public).

Nor is the issue restricted to the State Department. As events in the Trump administration nicely illustrate, presidential envoys (e.g., Brett McGurk, former special envoy for the Global Coalition to Defeat the Islamic State), officials from other foreign policy agencies such as the Defense Department, and White House officials such as national security adviser John Bolton or top presidential adviser Jared Kushner) are likely to be involved. Indeed, as the current example of Kushner demonstrates, the White House is likely to desire policy control, often bypassing the State Department, and presidents themselves may prioritize the issue and place themselves at the forefront when important issues occur. When this happens, high-profile diplomatic efforts and even trips to the region such as those of President Obama in June 2009 and President Trump in 2017 and 2018 may ensue. In short, the more an issue is perceived as significant, the more likely a variety of bureaus will be involved, the higher up the issue will go within the department, and the more likely that other elements of the foreign policy bureaucracy and the White House will also be involved, resulting in a larger, more complex policy process full of opportunities for bureaucratic conflict and coordination problems.

Appointments. The president technically appoints all ambassadors and major officials within the State Department down to the deputy assistant secretary. Since presidents are not likely to have much foreign policy expertise, they typically rely on personal staff and the secretary of state to select appropriate people. Remaining policy positions, such as country directors at home or members of the embassies abroad, are staffed by FSOs who are placed through an established personnel system administered by the director general of the foreign service under the undersecretary for management. As with the civil and military services, the president has very little, if any, influence over personnel decisions within the foreign service.

Controversy has always surrounded presidential appointments. Members of the foreign service believe that appointments to ambassadorships and high-level positions below the secretary of state should generally go to FSOs because of their expertise and understanding of the workings of the State Department. Some presidents have appointed more FSOs to important policy positions than others, but non-FSOs have been increasingly appointed at the assistant secretary and deputy assistant secretary levels as well as to ambassadorships. Over time, FSOs have been getting fewer significant appointments at home and often become ambassadors to smaller, less important countries. Outside appointees tend to be from business, academia and research institutes, or government, and they may be knowledgeable about foreign affairs but not about the foreign service or the operations of the department.

Particularly irksome to the foreign service are presidential **political appointments**. This refers to those individuals, such as ambassadors, who are basically unqualified for the job—they are friends or, more often, major contributors to the president's campaign who possess little foreign policy interest or knowledge. In these cases, the prestige of being appointed ambassador, a title that reverts to the individual for life, is thought to be a personal thank you for friendship and political support, not a request for commitment and hard work. Although political appointees can sometimes cause controversy and diplomatic faux pas abroad, they can breathe fresh air into the US embassy and form a strong team with a capable FSO as the deputy chief of mission. Such appointees can also make constructive use of their personal connections with the president.

Continuing a tradition that extended back to President Andrew Jackson in the early nineteenth century, under President George H. W. Bush, roughly one third of the ambassadors were non-foreign-service-career appointees, and more than 50 percent of those ambassadorships were considered political appointments. Presidents Clinton, George W. Bush, and Obama continued this practice—with the regular blessing of the US Senate, which usually approves presidential appointments with little or no dissent (see Lacey and Bonner 2001; Sciolino 1989; US Congress, Senate Committee on Foreign Relations 1981).

A few recent examples illustrate the more controversial ambassadorial appointments by a president: In 1989, Peter Secchia, a multimillionaire lumber tycoon who was crucial in the elder Bush's victory in the Michigan Republican Party caucus over presidential challenger Pat Robertson, was appointed ambassador to Italy. Ambassador Secchia created constant controversy in Italy by his tendency to use profanity and make sexist remarks in public. In 2009, President Obama named attorney John Roos as ambassador to Japan despite the fact that he had almost no experience in the region, no diplomatic background, and few political credentials other than having raised more than half a million dollars for Obama's political campaign. Major fundraisers were also appointed as ambassadors to the United Kingdom (a former vice president of Citibank) and France (the former president of the Jim Henson Company—of the "Muppets" fame).

For President Trump, the controversy has only heightened. Trump's ambassador appointments contributed about the same amount to his presidential campaign as all the ambassadors from Reagan, both Bushes, Clinton, and Obama *combined* (Chapman 2019). More than 40 percent of the Trump administration's appointments have no foreign service experience, the highest level of political appointments in decades. More than half of them cannot speak the language of the country to which they are assigned, the lowest level since the 1980s. Many others—such as ambassador to Israel David Friedman, a significant donor and adviser to the 2016 Trump campaign, and Gordon Sondland, a businessman (hotels) and Trump campaign donor named ambassador to the European Union who became embroiled in the controversy over President Trump's efforts to enlist Ukrainian aid for his 2020 election—proved very controversial. Moreover, the Trump administration left many key posts unfilled, limiting the ability of the United States to conduct relations with key countries. As one report noted, "[T]he Trump administration appears to hold a modern record for the slows. At the end of 2017, Trump's first year in office, only 64 new ambassadors had been confirmed, filling about one-third of 188 posts" (McManus 2018). In the late spring of its third year, the Trump administration still had no ambassadors to Australia, Brazil, Chile, Saudi Arabia, Turkey, Egypt, Mexico, Honduras, Panama, Pakistan, Jordan, South Africa, Singapore, several Central Asian countries, and others.

Bureaucracies like the State Department are complex institutions of hierarchy, specialization, and routinization in which the policymaking process is affected by the nature of the issue. This often produces **careerist-appointee issues**—political tension between career members of the permanent bureaucracy versus presidential appointees, who are often referred to as "in-outers" since they tend to go back and forth between the government and private sectors and from one government position to another. Careerists, such as the foreign service in the State Department, tend to be part of a particular subculture and loyal to the institution where they have worked for years. Appointees, or in-outers, tend to have little understanding of or allegiance to the particular bureaucracy for which they work. How this careerist-appointee tension between insiders and in-outers plays itself out has important ramifications for the policymaking process in general, including the particular role of the State Department and the foreign service, but it is also a general feature of the structures and processes of the foreign policy bureaucracy that affects all agencies and the White House in some important ways, as we will see in subsequent chapters (Halperin 1974; Heclo 1988; Rockman 1981).

Foreign Aid and Public Diplomacy

The US Agency for International Development. Ever since the Foreign Affairs Reform and Restructuring Act of 1998, the **US Agency for International Development (USAID)** has been housed within the Department of State, and its director reports to the secretary of state. However, USAID remains largely autonomous and was, from its 1961 inception until 1998, separate from the department. Indeed, it still maintains separate offices, with State in the complex at Foggy Bottom, and USAID in the Ronald Reagan Building. However, in recent years, greater effort to coordinate the goals and purposes of the two organizations has occurred. For example, since 2003, State and USAID have collaborated to produce a single, integrated strategic plan to better coordinate foreign policy and development programs.

The agency was established in 1961 by President Kennedy (along with the Peace Corps) to help Third World countries develop and to counter the expansion of Soviet influence around the world. Since then, USAID has provided loans, grants, and technical assistance to developing countries to spur economic and political development, with priority targets shifting with the context of the times (see Kirschten 1993; USAID 2004). Since 1961, USAID has been responsible for most US economic assistance programs, administering well over $500 billion in such aid during that period. The agency administers its bilateral assistance programs through a central headquarters and overseas offices, with a workforce composed of direct hires and personal services contractors (both US and foreign national personnel). As discussed earlier, USAID often has a larger overseas presence than the foreign service in a developing country (see "A Closer Look: US Foreign Assistance and Nation-Building" for an overview of US foreign assistance).

A Closer Look

US FOREIGN ASSISTANCE AND NATION-BUILDING

Foreign assistance involves a variety of aid programs and government agencies. Security-related assistance—that is, programs that are targeted to stabilize foreign governments and strengthen police and military forces—is provided covertly by the CIA and, principally, by the DOD. Economic developmental assistance—programs to promote human welfare, economic development, and political stability in other societies—is provided by the Department of Agriculture (Food for Peace Program); the Department of the Treasury (through multilateral assistance to international governmental organizations, such as the World Bank, African Development Bank, Asian Development Bank, Inter-American Development Bank, and other United Nations agencies); the **Peace Corps** (created by President Kennedy to help people in developing countries—with over 6,000 volunteers today in more than seventy countries—meet basic needs for health, food, shelter, and education); and, most importantly, USAID.

Following World War II, the US government began to engage in the practice of **foreign assistance**. Most of this assistance in the postwar years went to Western Europe in the form of the **Marshall Plan** to help those countries reconstruct their economies and stabilize their political systems. As Western Europe recovered from the war and the Cold War began, more and more American foreign assistance was directed to other areas of the world as part of the United States's larger strategy to contain the Soviet Union and communism. Since the 1990s, foreign assistance—broadly defined—has fluctuated between $15 billion and $50 billion a year, with security-related and developmental aid to other countries making up around two thirds and one third of the total, respectively. The largest recipients over the past two decades have been Egypt, Israel, Iraq, and Afghanistan.

In the Cold War era, foreign aid was partly justified as a way to counter Soviet influence. Since the end of the Cold War, other priorities, including sustainable development, transnational and humanitarian issues, and democracy and "transformational aid" for nation-building, have been central. Interventions in Panama, Somalia, Haiti, Afghanistan, and Iraq illustrate nation-building and other purposes, while also showing the challenges facing American efforts to build stable and modernizing nations.

However, foreign aid is a particularly difficult sell in today's political environment. Questions continue to be raised about the effectiveness and purpose of foreign assistance. Most recently, each of the first three budget proposals of the Trump administration included reductions to the foreign aid budget of about one third. Although the US Congress, which heavily influences foreign assistance legislation and budgets, rejected the proposed cuts and maintained—even increased—foreign aid funds, many members are unsupportive and do not believe that foreign aid is a salient issue with voters. Public opinion on foreign aid often gives policymakers contradictory signals: Americans believe in helping those in need but are much more concerned with the needs of American society at home than of societies abroad. In fact, most Americans tend to greatly overestimate the amount the United States spends on foreign assistance. They would be surprised to know that the total foreign assistance budget—including all economic, military, agricultural, and humanitarian aid—is only about 1 percent of the total federal budget (see Ruttan 1996; Tarnoff and Lawson 2018; USAID 2004).

What challenges do these characteristics of US foreign assistance pose to presidential leadership and policies?

Public Diplomacy. For most of the past sixty years, the US government has been involved in disseminating information about the United States and in promoting US cultural activities abroad. Until 1999, the responsibility for these activities rested in the **United States Information Agency (USIA)**, a small yet significant agency administering a worldwide network of international broadcasting, film, and videotape/DVD programs; magazines and other print media; and a variety of informational, educational, and cultural activities, including the maintenance of libraries and book programs, lectures and cultural presentations, and English instruction. USIA also administered a number of **international exchange programs**, such as the Fulbright program, involving more than 20,000 students, scholars, and practitioners from America and abroad. (This is actually one large part of more than seventy international exchange and training programs administered in more than fifteen federal departments and agencies involving over 60,000 people.) The purpose behind USIA's activities was to promote cross-cultural knowledge and understanding to foster a more supportive environment for US foreign policy (Hansen 1984; US Congress, General Accounting Office 1993).

As a consequence of the Foreign Affairs Reform and Restructuring Act, in 1998 the USIA was abolished and its programs dispersed. The broadcast elements were housed under the Broadcasting Board of Governors in the International Broadcast Bureau (IBB), which continued to administer such entities as the well-known Voice of America (VOA), the major broadcasting arm and official voice of the US government. Begun during World War II as part of the war effort, VOA broadcasts a mixture of general news, public affairs programs, music, and entertainment throughout the world in more than forty languages on radio, satellite television, and the Internet to an estimated audience of over 100 million people. It is currently staffed by approximately 1,100 individuals, most of whom work in the United States. In addition to the VOA, the IBB administers a range of additional operations, including Radio Free Europe/Radio Liberty; Radio Free Asia; Radio/Television Marti, created by the Reagan administration to propagandize the virtues of the American way of life to the people of Cuba; and Alhurra Television and Radio Sawa, created under President George W. Bush to broadcast in the Middle East after the September 11, 2001, events.

Such programs have always been controversial. Some believe the operations should serve purely as a propaganda outlet in which the United States is portrayed in a positive light while American adversaries are portrayed negatively; others believe that they should operate more subtly, reflecting some of the norms of the journalism profession and the American national media. Hence, it is not surprising that programming has fluctuated under different administrations. Of course, the collapse of the communist regimes in the Soviet Union and Eastern Europe deeply affected all the broadcast programs, but especially Radio Liberty and Radio Free Europe, raising questions concerning their future and ultimate purpose and forcing serious downsizing until the post-9/11 environment prompted modest increases. More recently, George W. Bush's administration attempted to use the VOA and new outlets like Radio Sawa and Alhurra Television to improve the image of the United States around the world, especially in the Middle East, as part of a broader campaign to reduce anti-Americanism in the region (LaFranchi 2001; Ungar 2005).

The remaining parts of the old USIA mission—**public diplomacy** and **cultural exchanges**—were integrated into the Department of State. First, a new undersecretary of public diplomacy and public affairs was established, with bureaus for educational and cultural affairs (now housing the Fulbright and cultural exchange programs), international information programs (now managing the production of media and information packages), and traditional public affairs. Additionally, public diplomacy officers were assigned to each regional and functional bureau of the department; in 2005, these officers were upgraded to deputy assistant rank to improve their performance and influence. These steps were designed to overcome the fundamental tension that exists within the department between the policy-oriented foreign service and the program-oriented public diplomacy people, which has resulted in the marginalization of the public diplomacy personnel who fit rather uneasily in the dominant subculture of the department.

Although some efforts were made to enhance the role of public diplomacy as a tool in the post-9/11 campaign against terrorism and anti-American sentiments, the operation continued to struggle. George W. Bush attempted to improve the profile and activities of public diplomacy, even naming longtime confidante Karen Hughes to the role of undersecretary for public diplomacy and public affairs. However, even these actions had limited effects. President Obama had three undersecretaries of public diplomacy (including the former president and CEO of Discovery Communications), none of whom made it to three years in office. President Trump waited until the end of his first year to appoint Irwin Steven Goldstein (who ran global communications for the *Wall Street Journal* and Dow Jones), but he lasted only three months in office before the president fired him for public comments defending Rex Tillerson, Trump's first Secretary of State, who had just been fired. With his third year in office almost over, Trump had not nominated a replacement.

THE FOREIGN SERVICE SUBCULTURE

One of the key results of bureaucratic organization and, especially, specialization is the role of **organizational subculture**. Every organization or bureaucracy eventually develops a subculture, or a number of subcultures: a common set of goals and norms acquired by individuals within a group or organization. Subculture is essential to the organization's identity and actions. These beliefs and norms result in certain incentives and disincentives that influence the behavior of individuals within the organization, and the organization's overall behavior as well. According to James Q. Wilson (1989:91), writing in *Bureaucracy*, subculture produces "a persistent, patterned way of thinking about the central tasks of and human relationships within an organization. Culture is to an organization what personality is to an individual. Like human culture generally, it is passed on from one generation to the next. It changes slowly, if at all" (see also Scott 1969; Whyte 1956).

New members quickly discover they are expected to learn and absorb the rules and norms that pervade the organization. These rules and norms are formally or officially communicated and enforced (e.g., by disseminating departmental guidelines on appropriate "professional" behavior or by affecting career advancement through the personnel evaluation and promotion system) and informally enforced (e.g., through peer interaction). People quickly learn to play by the rules of the game if they want to be accepted by their peers and be professionally successful within the organization. This produces conformity in the behavior of most individuals, thereby reinforcing and promoting the organizational subculture. Understanding the role and behavior of a bureaucracy like the State Department depends on understanding the core subculture of its most important employees: the foreign service.

Identifying and describing a subculture is no simple feat. Discussing the major beliefs and norms that prevail in a group or organization necessarily results in broad generalizations that oversimplify the organization's complexity and are unlikely to apply perfectly to any one individual. Despite these complications, much work has been done on the subculture of the foreign service, and a strong consensus exists on its major attributes (see also Clarke 1987; Crosby 1991; Rockman 1981; Rubin 1985; US Department of State 1992). The subculture of the foreign service is particularly strong because of its small size—only 13,000 FSOs—relative to other bureaucratic organizations. Together, the structure and subculture of the State Department bureaucracy determine how well the department fulfills its primary functions and influences the overall policymaking process (see Kopp and Gillespie 2008; Schake 2012). The foreign service subculture has five key characteristics:

- A tendency to be elitist or exclusivist

- A preference for overseas experience and to identify with foreign viewpoints

- An emphasis on the policy instruments of diplomacy and negotiation

- A tendency to be generalists

- A tendency to be loyal and cautious

The foreign service is commonly considered an **elitist** or exclusivist group. This elitism takes two forms. First, the foreign service is elitist in the sense that it is difficult to become an FSO and FSOs consider themselves to be the crème de la crème of the government in foreign policy expertise. There is much truth to this, for the demand to join the foreign service is extraordinarily high and the job openings are few. The Foreign Service Exam is also extremely demanding. Few applicants do well, and those who score high have no guarantee that a position will be found for them.

The foreign service is also considered elitist in another sense: Throughout most of its history, membership in the foreign service consisted of men who were White Anglo-Saxon Protestants (WASPs) from wealthy, urbane families who often attended Ivy League schools. In other words, the foreign service consisted of a very exclusive **old boy network**. Entrance into the foreign service was based on anything but merit. Instead, the key was an individual's "pedigree"—family, background, education—and his connections. This exclusiveness resulted in an air of superiority among FSOs relative to other government employees, especially as other foreign policy bureaucracies expanded during World War II and the Cold War (Weil 1978).

Much has changed within the State Department, especially since the 1980s. The old boy system has opened up to new entrants. Connections and pedigrees have been replaced by a more demanding merit system based on the Foreign Service Exam. Women, minorities, and individuals who are not from the Northeast, not Protestant, and not upper or upper-middle class, have become part of the foreign service. Nonetheless, the process of change has been a slow one, and the foreign service—especially its upper levels—continues to be dominated by white men from affluent segments of society. (See "A Different Perspective: Gender and Race Discrimination in Hiring and Personnel Systems.")

A Different Perspective

GENDER AND RACE DISCRIMINATION IN HIRING AND PERSONNEL SYSTEMS

Historically, being a woman in the world of US diplomacy has involved vastly different experiences and perspectives than has been the case for men, and considerable controversy has existed over the composition of the foreign service. Even though personnel selection and promotion is currently based on a merit system, most FSOs are white men from more privileged backgrounds. More women and minorities have gained entry to the foreign service in the past few decades, but they remain underrepresented in comparison to their numbers in society. This pattern becomes even more noticeable as one moves up the career ladder to more senior positions in the foreign service. In fact, prior to 1980, no woman had ever been put in charge of any of the major regional bureaus.

In a 1989 class action suit, a US Court of Appeals found the State Department guilty of **sex discrimination** against women in its hiring and promotion practices. The court ordered that such promotion practices be remedied and the Foreign Service Exam revised. Subsequently, in the George H. W. Bush administration, women were named to 23.2 percent of the appointments at the top six levels of the department. Under Bill Clinton, that figure rose to 28.2 percent. Yet some people remain frustrated with the gradual nature of the changing composition and emphasize the need to make the foreign service

more democratic and more representative, arguing that diversity can be a source of strength to the department's international efforts in a world of great heterogeneity.

Although slow to change, the State Department's personnel system is becoming more merit oriented. Yet because the Foreign Service Exam is so demanding, those from more privileged backgrounds are likely to perform better. Also, because of the foreign service's small size, job openings are few and the rate of turnover is slow. New personnel problems are also arising. Whereas once the spouse (and children) accompanied the FSO from post to post and played the important role of host, the rise of professional careers for both the husband and the wife has generated much frustration with the rotation tradition of "worldwide availability." As always, controversies over personnel are likely to plague the State Department, and other governmental organizations, into the future (see Olmstead, Baer, Joyce, and Prince 1984; Scott and Rexford 1997; US Congress 1989b).

In a society where women are highly underrepresented throughout government, particularly at the higher levels, even the image of breaking into top positions offers encouragement to the ranks of women and minorities hoping to garner employment in foreign policy. In the Department of State, three of the past seven (but none of the past three) secretaries of state have been women, appearing to signal a major shift from the history of male dominance in that position: Madeleine Albright (Clinton), Condoleezza Rice (George W. Bush), and Hillary Clinton (Obama) (see Cooper and Liu 1997; Duffy and Shannon 2005; Gibbs 1997; Isaacson 1999; Keating 2009; Ratnesar et al. 2005). In the Trump administration, however, aside from Nikki Haley, the US ambassador to the United Nations for Trump's first two years, only one woman occupied a position in the top three tiers of the department (Andrea Thompson, the undersecretary for arms control and international security).

What do you think is the impact of greater numbers, roles, and authority for women in the diplomatic corps for US foreign policy and policymaking?

A second characteristic of the foreign service subculture is that FSOs usually prefer to be stationed abroad and tend to identify with foreign viewpoints. For an FSO, to be abroad rather than in Washington, DC, is to be where the action and excitement is—in the field. It is also a way to see and experience the world, often a key motivating factor among foreign service applicants (e.g., Kopp and Gillespie 2008). This is reinforced by an FSO's privileged lifestyle abroad and constant interaction with foreign elites. The preference is not only for overseas experience but also for choice assignments such as London, Paris, and Rome. This orientation toward overseas experience and identifying with foreign countries is reinforced by the foreign service personnel system, in which career advancement is based on service abroad. To be posted in Washington, DC, too often or too long may hurt career opportunities. In fact, the typical career goal of an FSO is to become an ambassador, not secretary of state or another major policymaking official close to the president.

This emphasis on overseas experience and identifying with foreign viewpoints often is detrimental to the ability of FSOs to operate successfully in the foreign policy maze at home. Because FSOs are more interested in and knowledgeable about what is happening abroad than at home, they may not be motivated or equipped to influence the policy-making process outside the State Department. Often, they are accused of allowing the interests of the countries in which they serve to trump US interests, to the frustration of the White House and senior appointees. For example, objections by Arab leaders led officers in State's Middle East bureau to water down ambitious proposals for a US democracy promotion plan in the region, while a number of FSOs serving as ambassadors in the region refused to use White House–approved talking points explaining and defending the US position on Iraq for fear of offending their hosts (Kaplan 2004). In the first month of the Trump administration, roughly 1,000 State Department personnel signed a sharply worded memo criticizing the White House effort to institute a travel ban on people from a handful of Muslim-majority countries, prompting the White House to condemn these "career bureaucrats" and call for them to quit if they would not support the policy.

Such behavior frequently results in accusations that members of the foreign service so identify with foreign viewpoints that they have "gone native," and other officials in the policymaking process may therefore not take an FSO's policy positions seriously.

These subcultural traits make it difficult for the State Department as an organization to have a strong influence on the foreign policymaking process (Kaplan 1994).

The third major characteristic of the foreign service is its emphasis on diplomacy as the principal tool of US foreign policy. FSOs see themselves as **diplomats**—a long-honored profession in the history of world politics. And the ability to engage in diplomacy and conduct negotiations is an art—mastery of which is not learned in a book but through field experience overseas (in earlier times, it was part of an elitist subculture into which one was born). The problem with the foreign service's focus on diplomacy is that, with the rise of the Cold War, that approach was superseded by increased reliance on the military, economic, and cultural instruments of foreign policy: force, covert operations, assistance, trade, economic sanctions, cultural programs, and international broadcasting. Even after the end of the Cold War, as the instruments to support America's global policy have multiplied, the foreign service's emphasis on the role of diplomacy has contributed to the decline of the State Department.

The fourth characteristic of FSOs is their tendency to be generalists. Although the foreign service prides itself on its foreign policy expertise, most FSOs are not specialists. This is a function of the **foreign service personnel system**. Not only is there an emphasis on overseas service, as discussed, but a rotation system operates based usually on three-year tours. This means that every three years an FSO is stationed in a new post abroad (though every third or fourth tour may be at home), often in a new region of the world. It is not unusual, for example, to find a new FSO with a degree in East Asian studies posted first in Haiti, then maybe in Somalia, then in Washington, DC, in the Western Hemisphere bureau, abroad again in Cameroon, and so on, maybe never getting the opportunity to use his or her original East Asian training. The little specialized training that does take place occurs within the State Department (no bureaucratic incentives exist to obtain graduate degrees) and in the Foreign Service Institute. The emphasis, rather, is to produce well-rounded experts with wide-ranging experience and intuitive understanding, able to fulfill any foreign policy position. Those individuals who prefer to stay within a region and specialize do so at the risk of career advancement. The major exception to this pattern is when an FSO begins to gain considerable seniority; at that point an area of specialization may be carved out (Ayres 1983a; Bacchus 1983).

This emphasis on the creation of well-rounded, generalist diplomats runs counter to the expansion of bureaucracy, which emphasizes the development of specialists. On the one hand, the development of personnel with general knowledge and a broader perspective allows for the integration of context and history in policy analysis, something that has eroded with the growth of specialization on top of specialization. On the other hand, FSOs are often at a disadvantage with their counterparts from other bureaucracies because they may lack detailed knowledge vital to an issue making its way through the policy process. When coupled with the other characteristics, it also helps to explain why governmental politics tends to be an FSO's weakest suit. Their elitism, parochialism, emphasis on diplomacy, and generalist training frequently hamstring their participation in interagency processes, as does their frequently aggressive resistance to ideas and information that originate outside their particular spheres. The rotation system also provides little incentive for learning the local language and culture, since each posting tends to be a temporary stop.

The fifth characteristic common to FSOs is their tendency to be loyal and cautious. FSOs are loyal to the foreign service and identify closely with the State Department as an institution. Such loyalty is easy to understand, for most FSOs spend their adult careers within the foreign service and the State Department. Given the limited number of FSOs, an FSO ends up working and interacting with familiar colleagues over fifteen or twenty years. Informal networks of relationships that build up with time are reinforced by the formal personnel process in which one's immediate superiors regularly evaluate one's performance. In addition, FSOs are also known for being cautious. They are hesitant about bucking the dominant beliefs and norms of the foreign service, and they also often provide "low-risk" advice and are reluctant to take individual policy initiatives. For example, before a request or decision is cabled abroad, the desk officer with primary jurisdiction must make sure it has been cleared (approved) by all other officials interested in the issue. If an issue triggers the participation of officials from seven or eight bureaus, no matter how distant their involvement, all the participants are kept apprised of the process and sign off on any decisions, no matter how minor. The result tends to be a cautious, cumbersome process built around compromise and consensus.

Such caution and loyalty can be found in the history of the State Department from its beginning, and the evaluation and promotion procedures of the department are partly to blame as well. However, the traits intensified after World War II and the coming of the Cold War, which ushered in the rise of anti-communism and **McCarthyism** in the country and the government, especially in Congress. The State Department, especially the offices focusing on Asia, was badly damaged.

This portrait of the foreign service subculture is not particularly complimentary. Many FSOs are likely to disagree with what they might consider to be a caricature of the foreign service. However, this is the consensus position within the foreign policy literature, and this perspective also tends to be shared by other members of the foreign policy bureaucracy, including the White House, as we discuss in the next section.

ROLE AND INFLUENCE: THE DECLINE OF STATE

For more than 150 years the State Department was the major organization responsible for foreign affairs. US foreign policy was made within the State Department, managed by its members, and carried out by ambassadors and other department members abroad. Other organizations within the government, such as the Treasury Department and especially the military, were involved in the conduct of US foreign policy, but the State Department was the dominant agency. Since World War II, however, influence began to flow to other agencies in the governmental bureaucracy and to the White House. Thus, the State Department has experienced a real decline in its overall role in the conduct of US foreign policy. What factors account for the department's diminished role?

Increasing Importance of International Affairs

The first key cause of the decline in the State Department's role in US foreign policy-making is the *growing importance of international affairs* for the United States. During the twentieth century, international affairs became increasingly important for the United States as it rose to global power and leadership (see Chapter 2). With World War I, the global depression of the 1930s, the global war of the 1940s, the Cold War after World War II, the increasing interdependence of the international political economy, and the rise of transnational threats such as terrorism, disease, global environmental issues, events far beyond American borders became increasingly important. The US government, including the president, can no longer afford to concentrate on domestic affairs and be unresponsive to the international scene.

Rise of American Power

The second cause of the decline in the State Department's role in US foreign policymaking is *the rise of American power* in the twentieth century. By World War II, the United States was the most powerful country in the history of the world. Therefore, not only was the United States increasingly impacted by the international system, but US foreign policy also increasingly affected the workings of that system. America's growing global role during World War II and the Cold War increased presidential power in the making of foreign policy. The global power and role of the United States was so large that the conduct of foreign policy could no longer be left to the State Department.

Expansion of the Foreign Policy Bureaucracy

A third major factor driving the decline of the State Department's influence in foreign policy is *the expansion of the players with foreign policy roles in the US bureaucracy*. Immediately after World War II, the 1947 National Security Act established the National Security Council (NSC), Department of Defense, and Central Intelligence Agency. Over time, the intelligence community expanded to introduce new agencies, and other foreign affairs agencies were created. Other bureaucracies such as the Department of the Treasury and the Department of Commerce expanded their roles in foreign affairs, and new organizations such as the Department of Homeland Security were created to address emerging problems. Indeed, the foreign policy bureaucracy has grown in size and complexity, and, since the 1950s, presidents have increasingly decided to lead foreign policy directly and to manage the growing foreign policy bureaucracy through a White House–centered system using the national security adviser and NSC staff. Consequently, the State Department is no longer the only organization within the executive branch with major responsibilities for the conduct of foreign affairs.

The Global Communications Revolution

The fourth major reason for the decline in the influence of the State Department was *the communications revolution*. Before the existence of the airplane and telephone, it took months for American officials in different parts of the world to travel or to communicate with each other via diplomatic pouch. The president was dependent on the State Department and its members located abroad to officially represent the US government. American ambassadors and other State Department employees consequently had wide latitude in influencing negotiating positions or other important aspects of US foreign policy. Changes in technology and the development of instant communications have allowed the president and the White House to communicate directly and instantly with the leaders of other countries and their foreign policy officials, so the White House has become far less dependent on the State Department in the day-to-day management of foreign policy (see Dizard 2001).

Increasing Reliance on Force

A fifth reason for the State Department's fall from its leading position in the policymaking process has been *the reliance on force as a major instrument in US foreign policy*. With the rise of the Cold War, US foreign policy focused on the need to contain the threat of Soviet communism throughout the globe. The basis of the containment strategy—the effort to confine the Soviet empire to Eastern Europe and China—was to deter or reverse a Soviet challenge to the international status quo through the threat and use of force. The containment policy resulted in the expansion of America's military capabilities through the development of nuclear weapons, a large standing conventional military force, counterinsurgency forces, and covert operations. This meant not only the growth of the military and the CIA but also the president's increasing use of these organizations as the means of conducting US foreign policy. Similarly, in the twenty-first century, the centrality of the global war on terror also contributed to State's waning influence in much the same way. After 9/11, for example, it was the military and intelligence agencies that received most of the budget increases and new policy authority. Most recently, the Trump administration's $4.75 trillion budget proposal for fiscal 2020 included not only a 5 percent increase to the Defense Department (to about $750 billion) but also a steep, 23 percent cut to the foreign affairs budget (to about $40 billion). Hence, diplomacy, the strength of the State Department, was superseded by the threat and use of force in the post–World War II period, and these newly formed bureaucratic organizations also became serious rivals in the policy process, especially in competition for budget resources.

Increasing Importance of International Economics

Finally, as the forces of economic globalization have accelerated, especially over the past several decades, the State Department has faced *challenges from the foreign economic bureaucracy* as those agencies have played a more central role in policy deliberation and implementation. This has resulted in more salient foreign policy roles for treasury secretaries and other economic policy advisers and agencies, especially in the past two decades. Moreover, new structures for White House coordination in this issue area—such as the National Economic Council, which was established in the Clinton administration—have also forced State to contend with a more diverse range of rivals.

Consequences for Presidential Reliance on State

Since the 1950s, presidents and their closest advisers have generally had a negative perception of the State Department's performance. John Kennedy, for example, referred to the State Department as a "bowl of jelly." Lyndon Johnson considered members of the foreign service to be "sissies, snobs, and lightweights who sacrificed too little and thought themselves better than their country." Richard Nixon declared in his 1968 campaign that "I want a secretary of state who will join me in cleaning house in the State Department" (Halberstam 1969:299); and Condoleezza Rice's appointment as secretary of state in George W. Bush's second term prompted a former adviser to note, "You can't be true to the president's foreign policy and be 'nice' to the Foreign Service" (Kaplan 2004). These negative images of and experiences in working with the State Department have contributed to presidents' increasing reliance on a White House–centered policymaking process.

Although Barack Obama relied more heavily on diplomacy in his first term, and Hillary Clinton worked strenuously to elevate the role of the State Department and its FSOs in the policy process, the department remains just one voice among many in the widening foreign policy bureaucracy. With the victory of Donald Trump in the 2016 election, the more familiar antagonism has returned. As Ron Neumann, a retired foreign service officer with thirty-seven years of experience, said, "The Trump administration appears to have a unique 'contempt' for the career workforce . . . prompting many top policy experts to leave the government's diplomatic arm, whether they want to or not" (Corrigan and Government Executive 2018). Consequently, the department has not escaped or overcome the persistent problems it has faced as its influence and role eroded after World War II.

The nature and performance of the State Department and the shift in its role since World War II have been accompanied by a cluster of common complaints from the White House, which have both stemmed from and contributed to its declining influence. It has often been argued that the State Department is *inefficient and slow*. As discussed earlier, the State Department operates as a very large, cumbersome bureaucracy with an extended clearance procedure that involves numerous officials and bureaus for any issue. The president and other major foreign policy officials have often complained that the State Department moves too slowly, especially if there is a pressing issue at hand. When the State Department does respond, another complaint is that *the staff work is often poor*. National Security Adviser Kissinger, after issuing a National Security Study Memorandum directing the bureaucracy to provide information, analyses, and policy alternatives, was often frustrated with the work produced by the State Department and frequently forced the department to prepare new studies.

Most presidents have complained that the State Department is *unresponsive* to the president and often refuses to follow orders. Given the foreign service's particular subculture, FSOs often seem to act as if they know what is best for US foreign policy. The department is perceived as being unresponsive since FSOs are career members of the bureaucracy who will outlive the short political life of any president. Some presidents, including Donald Trump, appear to believe that career bureaucrats who have served other administrations, especially of the other political party, are insufficiently loyal and cannot be trusted. A closely related complaint often heard is that the State Department *resists change* (e.g., Schake 2012). Bureaucratic resistance to change is not unique to the State Department; all bureaucracies develop patterns and policies over time, making them resistant to changes the president may want to initiate. However, the cautious, incremental approach to foreign policy is often frustrating to a new administration seeking innovation and change.

Another common complaint is that the State Department is *incapable of putting its own house in order*. In other words, the State Department has not been successful in reforming its structure and subculture so that it operates more efficiently, produces higher quality staff work, and is more responsive to presidential orders and initiatives (e.g., Schake 2012). Endless studies of the operations of the State Department have been conducted, and a number of efforts at reorganization have occurred since World War II. Under Hillary Clinton, for example, another round of shuffling occurred at State. Among other things, energy and the environment were moved from Global Affairs and into Economic and Business Affairs (newly named Economic Growth, Energy, and the Environment). Global Affairs, in turn, was reorganized to include a greater focus on human rights and human security. Donald Trump's approach was more draconian—his administration simply sought to reduce the size and role of the department, reducing personnel, freezing hiring, and leaving positions unfilled.

In general, the net result has been superficial change in the formal organizational chart, and even what one account called the "hollowing out" of the department (Corrigan and Government Executive 2018), while the foreign service subculture and day-to-day bureaucratic operations of the State Department remain largely intact. Of course, the difficulty in changing a bureaucratic organization, from without or within, is not limited to the State Department. The subculture of any organization tends to produce bureaucrats—FSOs, in the case of the State Department—who believe that they are performing their jobs properly, helping to fulfill the functions of the organization, and making a contribution to the public policy of the US government.

Considering these complaints, it is not surprising that presidents have found the State Department *unable to lead US foreign policy*—the final complaint commonly heard. No matter how much presidents may want to rely on the State Department for the conduct of US foreign policy, they soon conclude that State has resisted change in the internal workings of the department and is unable to lead. This is why the roles of the national security adviser and staff have grown tremendously over time to the detriment of the State Department (see Chapter 9). Indeed, reflecting on foreign policymaking, a group of NSC staffers from George H. W. Bush's administration observed that interagency groups chaired by State were more often ineffective than those chaired by NSC staff (National Security Council Project 1999a). In the Obama administration, NSC officials chaired all the coordinating committees of the National Security Council's interagency processes (Presidential Policy Directive 1, February 13, 2009). President Trump continued this practice, but, as we discuss in more detail in Chapter 8, also sharply curtailed the interagency processes themselves, reducing the access of the State Department (as well as other bureaucratic agencies) to the foreign policymaking process and further limiting its policy role.

Such perceptions quite naturally have serious policymaking consequences. One relatively recent example will suffice to highlight not only the bureaucratic divisions that often stymie American foreign policy but also the deterioration of State's influence resulting from the combination of its behavior and perceptions of it by others. Not long after the Bush administration was wrapping up its military campaign in Afghanistan, top foreign policy officials began to target Iraq for subsequent military operations to remove Saddam Hussein from power. Consequently, in the Department of State, Thomas Warrick, a careerist working in the Middle East bureau, headed a **Future of Iraq Project** designed to consider the issues and challenges of a post-Hussein Iraq (Fallows 2004; Rieff 2003). Wide-ranging—and drawing on experts at State, USAID, and other agencies; representatives of NGOs (nongovernmental organizations); as well as many Iraqi exiles representing a broad range of views—the project consisted of numerous working groups on just about every aspect of the issue. Both the CIA and the Defense Department were also involved. Eventually, under Warrick's direction, the many working groups of the project produced thirteen volumes—thousands of pages—of material that explored "almost everything, good and bad, that has happened in Iraq since the fall of Saddam Hussein," but well before the US military operation ever began (Fallows 2004:52).

However, Secretary of Defense Donald Rumsfeld and his subordinates completely ignored the need for postwar planning, even when the Defense Department was charged with the responsibility. Finally, in late January 2003, DOD formed the Office of Reconstruction and Humanitarian Assistance just two months before the war would begin. General Jay Garner, tapped to lead the effort, immediately asked for Thomas Warrick to be named to his team. He was turned down by the Office of the Secretary of Defense. When he requested information from the Future of Iraq Project, again, according to Garner, his superiors refused, telling him to ignore the work. Why? "The Pentagon didn't want to touch anything connected to the Department of State" (Rieff 2003:32). State was apparently simply frozen out of the policymaking loop, in large measure because its conclusions did not match those of the civilian leadership in the DOD. Consequently, as one observer glibly characterized it, "Donald Rumsfeld's Defense Department ended up administering postwar Iraq but being surprised by the electricity problems, while Colin Powell's State Department was marginalized but fully aware of it" (Drezner 2003:2). Of course, the consequences were far more serious, as the rushed planning led by Garner and the military precipitated myriad postwar failures and contributed to increased instability, a rising insurgency, and a continuing Iraq War (see Chapter 10 for more on the decision-making dynamics in Iraq's postwar reconstruction efforts).

THE SECRETARY OF STATE

Despite the decline of the State Department as an institution, individual State Department officials have played influential roles in the making of US foreign policy for the president and within the policymaking process. Secretaries of state often act as major spokespersons for the administration in foreign policy and major advisers to the president, even if the agency itself is left out or marginalized. Sometimes, lower level State Department officials may also play important roles, depending on the people involved and the issue.

Table 4.2 details the secretaries of state since the Roosevelt years. Many of the people who have served as secretary of state have been consequential in the making of US foreign policy. Henry Kissinger, Cyrus Vance, George Shultz, James Baker, Warren Christopher, Madeleine Albright, Condoleezza Rice, Hillary Clinton, John Kerry, and Mike Pompeo are all examples of strong and powerful secretaries of state in US foreign policy who have had good relationships with the president since the ascendancy of a White House–centered system.

TABLE 4.2

Secretaries of State

Name	Year	President	Background
Edward R. Stettinius	1944	Truman	Business and government
James F. Byrnes	1945	Truman	Law, Congress, and the Supreme Court
George C. Marshall	1947	Truman	Army
Dean Acheson	1949	Truman	Law and government
John Foster Dulles	1953	Eisenhower	Law and government
Christian A. Herter	1959	Eisenhower	Congress and government
Dean Rusk	1961	Kennedy	Foundation and government
William P. Rogers	1969	Nixon	Law and government
Henry Kissinger	1973	Nixon	Academia and government
Cyrus R. Vance	1977	Carter	Law and government
Edmund S. Muskie	1980	Carter	Law, Congress, and government
Alexander M. Haig	1981	Reagan	Army and government
George P. Shultz	1982	Reagan	Academia, business, and government
James A. Baker, III	1989	George H. W. Bush	Law and government
Lawrence S. Eagleburger	1992	George H. W. Bush	Government
Warren M. Christopher	1993	Clinton	Law and government
Madeleine K. Albright	1997	Clinton	Academia and government
Colin Powell	2001	George W. Bush	Army and government
Condoleezza Rice	2005	George W. Bush	Academia and government
Hillary Clinton	2009	Obama	Government and law
John Kerry	2013	Obama	Government
Rex Tillerson	2017	Trump	Oil industry
Mike Pompeo	2018	Trump	Business and government

Strong and powerful secretaries of state, in turn, can rely heavily on many officials within the State Department (some of whom are appointees) for information and advice in formulating their policy positions. They may also opt to work with and empower the careerists within the department. Hence, the decline of the State Department as an institution in the formal policymaking process has not foreclosed key State Department officials from exercising influence in the foreign policymaking process. However, since World War II, and especially since the Kennedy administration and the rise of White House–centered policymaking, secretaries of state have faced a fundamental choice. On the one hand, they can stress their role as adviser and spokesperson for the president, and thus preserve policy influence. On the other hand, they can emphasize their role as manager of the department, advocating for and relying on the resources, recommendations, and personnel of the department. Over the past five decades or so, this **inside-outside dilemma** has challenged all who have held the position.

The most recent occupants of the position illustrate the dilemma nicely. When George W. Bush nominated Colin Powell to serve as secretary of state, the outpouring of praise was instant. Almost from the start, Powell sought to empower the department and its personnel, and to rally morale among its careerists (McGeary 2001:24–32). He also emphasized career personnel in mid-level and ambassadorial appointments and other responsibilities. Moreover, he sought to inject State Department analyses into policy discussions. The consequence was that "State Department officials . . . love Powell" (Kessler and Ricks 2004:A7). Indeed, in 2008, career State Department employees told the authors that the mere mention of Powell in an audience of FSOs prompts an outpouring of praise. However, in contrast to these positive views within the agency, Powell was cynically regarded as "Foreign Service Officer-in-chief" outside the department (Kaplan 2004). Consequently, Powell soon found himself on the losing end of the contest for policy influence with the president (see Kitfield 2001; also Daalder and Lindsay 2003; Woodward 2004, 2007). After the presidential election of 2004, Powell resigned and was replaced by Condoleezza Rice as secretary of state.

Powell's successor, Condoleezza Rice, followed Madeleine Albright as the second woman to hold the post of secretary of state. Rice moved to State from her role as national security adviser, a position she gained largely by virtue of her role as a key foreign policy adviser to George W. Bush during the 2000 campaign. In stark contrast to Powell, however, Rice leaned heavily on her extraordinarily close relationship with the president, which led one observer to characterize her as the president's "alter ego" (Kaplan 2004). To be sure, Rice made efforts to signal to State Department employees that she would be their secretary of state (see Diehl 2005; Duffy and Shannon 2005; Ratnesar et al. 2005), but her overall orientation, and the most significant element of her influence, remained her connection to the White House.

Barack Obama's first secretary of state was Hillary Clinton, President Obama's main rival for the presidential nomination in 2008. As secretary of state, Clinton took up a central role in policy formulation by walking a fine line between the two ends of the inside-outside dilemma. Given substantial autonomy by President Obama in her role as secretary of state, Clinton drew on her substantial political capital and skills to emerge as the president's leading foreign policy voice, aided in part by the ineffectiveness of Obama's first national security adviser, Jim Jones, and later by her good relationship with Jones's replacement, Tom Donilon. According to one account, she managed this by deftly combining a mix of outsiders and career diplomats throughout the upper and middle levels of the department and effectively engaging in the advisory process (Keating 2009).

From the start, Clinton assiduously advanced the president's agenda and kept close to him as she assumed the leading role on foreign policy. One of her key policy deputies—James Steinberg (who served as deputy national security adviser in the Clinton administration, and as a foreign policy adviser to the Obama campaign)—worked closely with Donilon, who was first deputy national security adviser and then national security adviser (Donilon also served in the Clinton administration's State Department) to improve State–White House collaboration (Rothkopf 2009). Also, her first deputy secretary of state, Jacob Lew, was well respected by the White House (he became the director of the Office of Management and Budget in 2010, and White House chief of staff in 2012).

Within the agency, Clinton "made a vigorous effort to widen her circle, wooing and pulling into her orbit the agency's Foreign Service and civil service officials, many of whom said in interviews that she . . . brought a new energy to the building" (Romano 2010). According to a number of State Department employees at various levels, Clinton had success "heading off the historical tensions between career employees and quadrennial political newcomers by relying on the counsel of senior Foreign Service operatives and reaching out in general" (Romano 2010). As one colorful account notes:

> She . . . walked the halls and popped into offices unexpectedly, created an
> electronic "sounding board," and held seven internal town hall meetings to
> listen to gripes about everything from policy to cafeteria food to bullying in the
> workplace. She installed six new showers that joggers requested, [took] steps to
> remedy overseas pay inequities and instituted a policy that allows partners of gay
> diplomats to receive benefits. She became a heroine to the Foreign Service when
> she went to bat to get funding for 3,000 new Foreign Service positions for State
> operations and the U.S. Agency for International Development—the first boost
> of this magnitude in two decades. (Romano 2010)

Hillary Clinton is not the first secretary of state to try to thread the needle on the inside-outside dilemma. However, by the end of 2012, she had managed to walk that line at least as effectively as anyone before her, and better than most.

In 2012, Clinton announced her plans to step down as secretary of state after President Obama's first term. Her successor, John Kerry, a former senator from Massachusetts and the 2004 democratic candidate for the presidency, followed Clinton's lead, seeking to balance the inside-outside dilemma by emphasizing his role as adviser and diplomat, working closely with the national security adviser (Susan Rice) and the secretary of defense (Robert Gates). According to O'Hanlon (2016), Kerry sought this balance by demonstrating his "relative preference for diplomacy over either grand strategy or security policy. He really is a diplomat, more than a strategist or a wartime officeholder."

Since assuming the office of the presidency in January 2017, Donald Trump has already had two secretaries of state. Their experiences reveal other aspects of the inside-outside dilemma, although to be fair, both had to contend with a chaotic and dysfunctional NSC process that complicated all advisory relationships (see Chapter 8). President Trump's first choice to lead the State Department was former Exxon oil executive Rex Tillerson, an accomplished businessman with no government experience. While Tillerson attempted to focus on diplomacy and on downsizing the State Department to create greater efficiency, his experience in the year or so of his tenure demonstrates what happens when the secretary is neither inside nor outside. Within the State Department, Tillerson's emphasis on downsizing, cutting personnel and budget, and centralizing decision making alienated him from the agency. According to Farrow (2018), Tillerson was "aloof and insulated from the Department" and made almost no effort to engage with its members. Over his time in office, he was increasingly isolated from the career professionals, who left the State Department in record numbers, especially at the senior level. Those who remained suffered from low morale, and recruiting and hiring of new personnel stagnated as hiring was frozen. By the end of 2017, Tillerson had assembled only ten of the forty-four top appointees in the department, severely hampering his ability to work within the agency (Gardiner 2017).

But Tillerson never managed to position himself well on the outside either. In his relationship with the White House, Tillerson was never embraced as a member of the president's inner circle. According to many reports, Tillerson frequently disagreed with President Trump and sought to steer him away from his preferred courses of action. He often took public positions that contradicted the president's preferences and, at times, the president's Twitter statements. He also clashed repeatedly with Jared Kushner, the president's son-in-law, who was assigned key diplomatic duties normally entrusted to the secretary of state, and with others in the White House, including John Kelly, the president's chief of staff (Farrow 2018). Tillerson's already-tense relationship with Trump worsened after a contentious meeting held in the Pentagon in July 2017, which was geared at providing a tutorial on foreign policy and national security matters to the inexperienced president (Liptak et al. 2017). According to many press reports, Tillerson was frustrated and dismissive and, afterward, referred to President Trump as a "[expletive deleted] moron" and threatened to resign (Liptak et al. 2017; Lee et al. 2017). In March 2018, Trump fired Tillerson, who was traveling in Africa at the time. He did so by Twitter, leaving then–Chief of Staff John Kelly to alert Tillerson of the impending tweet. Apparently intended to be insulting,

> Tillerson was the first Cabinet official ever to be fired on social media; Trump only got around to calling him some three hours later. The sequence appeared to be a calculated snub: Trump had come to dislike Tillerson, who'd called him a "moron." John Kelly, then the president's chief of staff, later made a point of noting that Tillerson had been on the toilet when Kelly had phoned him in advance of Trump's tweet to tell him that his dismissal was likely imminent. (Bayoumy 2019)

In the tweet that publicly announced Tillerson's dismissal, President Trump identified Mike Pompeo, his first CIA director, as Tillerson's replacement. Although Pompeo took some initial steps to improve morale in the department, lifting the hiring freeze, using his more constructive relationship with the White House to get key positions filled, and engaging more openly and effectively with its personnel, his approach to the role chiefly emphasized the outsider orientation (Ignatius 2018). Pompeo carefully cultivated his relationship with the president and took care to represent him in the most positive light in his public comments. According to Schwartz (2019), "Pompeo was the first secretary in many years who seemed to have a bond with the president comparable to Kissinger's with Nixon." As Pompeo himself characterized his approach:

> I've spent a lot of time building an understanding of what President Trump's mission statement is . . . [a]nd therefore, what my mission statement is. Commander's intent. What is it that we are trying to accomplish, and how is it that we're going to deliver that for the American people? (Schwartz 2019)

However, by 2019 Pompeo had severely alienated the career professionals in the department. In part, this occurred because of his role in controversial efforts to enlist foreign interference in the 2020 US election, which led a number of State Department employees to defy Pompeo and testify in the House impeachment process.

THE FUTURE?

With the end of the Cold War, the State Department appeared poised to play a more prominent role in the making of US foreign policy. However, negative perceptions of the department's competency shared by political leaders, along with persistent conflicts—such as the Persian Gulf, Kosovo, Afghanistan, and Iraq wars and the global war on terrorism—and the increasingly significant global economic challenges suggest that the department's status is not likely to change dramatically.

This is the conclusion of a task force commissioned by the Department of State almost thirty years ago to examine its own role and needs into the future given the collapse of the Cold War. Entitled *State 2000: A New Model for Managing Foreign Affairs*, the study also acknowledged that it will be "a difficult adaptation for an institution bound in tradition" and "there are, of course, limits to what the leadership of the Department can do about the culture of the institution" (US Department of State 1992:79–80). Unfortunately, most observers would say that too little has changed in the nearly three decades since the publication of report.

It should no longer be surprising that, although the State Department remains a key agency in the foreign policy bureaucracy and individual officials within the department will continue to play significant roles, the president has turned to other agencies within the government for information, advice, and management of the national security process, such as the Department of Defense and the intelligence community, in addition to the National Security Council. Yet, as we will see in Chapters 5 and 6, the president has had problems in managing these bureaucratic organizations as well.

THINK ABOUT THIS

The Trump administration's second secretary of state—Mike Pompeo—took on the role promising to restore the "diplomatic swagger" of the department. Think about the nature of the foreign policy bureaucracy and the role of the State Department discussed in this chapter.

What are the implications of bureaucratic structures and personnel issues for US foreign policymaking?

KEY TERMS

ambassador   102

assistant secretaries   101

bureau   101

bureaucracy   92

bureaucratic process   104

cable traffic   98

careerist-appointee issues   107

CIA station chief   104

clientelism   98

coordination issues   92

country director   101

country team   102

Visit **edge.sagepub.com/scottrosati7e** to help you accomplish your coursework goals in an easy-to-use learning environment.

Understanding the Foreign Policy Bureaucracy

THE DEPARTMENT OF DEFENSE

PHOTO 5.1 U.S. military personnel in Romania in February 2017.

DANIEL MIHAILESCU/AFP/Getty Images

LEARNING OBJECTIVES

1. Know the functions and features of the modern military establishment.

2. Understand the structures and processes of the US Department of Defense.

3. Identify the Defense Department subcultures and their consequences.

4. Describe the nature and dynamics of the use of force in US foreign policymaking.

5. Assess and explain the nature and challenges related to the role and influence of the Department of Defense in US foreign policymaking.

INTRODUCTION: THE DEPARTMENT OF DEFENSE

Before World War II, the United States generally maintained only a small career military. During times of conflict—such as the War of 1812, the Mexican-American War, the Civil War, and World War I—the US government recruited a "citizen militia" to form a large military to fight the war and then quickly demobilized it when hostilities ceased. Much of this can be explained by the advantages of the geographic location of the United States between two oceans and the relative weakness of its two neighbors. This policy was reinforced by a popular distrust of the large, professional military establishments that existed in the Old (European) World. The military was also decentralized during this period: Instead of a unified department with specific services responsible for different missions, the United States maintained a Department of the Navy (including the Marines) and a

War Department (consisting of the army and later an army air corps—from which today's separate air force emerged). Overall direction and coordination were the responsibility of the civilian commander in chief, the president of the United States.

As we stated in Chapter 4, since World War II the military has grown to be an especially powerful force, not only in its global reach and coercive might but also with its major role in US foreign policymaking. In this chapter, we continue our examination of the key players of the foreign policy bureaucracy by focusing on the basic functions (or missions), structure and process, and subcultures of the military establishment. We also discuss the use of force in the conduct of US foreign policy and the military's effects on the policymaking process.

THE NATURE OF THE MODERN MILITARY ESTABLISHMENT

In the Global Era, America's entry into World War II and its efforts to contain the threat of Soviet communism during the subsequent Cold War resulted in enormous changes that transformed the old military into the modern military establishment. Not only was the modern military establishment reorganized for greater centralization and specialization into the Department of Defense, but it was also expanded dramatically to include a large, permanent professional military situated in a heavyweight player in the foreign policy bureaucracy with great size and scope.

The Defense Department: Functions over Time

Although the US military has developed into a large, permanent, professional force during peacetime and has grown enormously in size and scope since the early twentieth century, its basic functions or purposes have remained consistent. Today, as throughout US history, the central purpose of the military is to "defend and protect" the United States. Related to that central function, the US military conducts military operations at the direction of the political and civilian leadership, as stipulated in the US Constitution, engaging in fighting to support the country (and, for the individual soldier, being willing to give up one's life).

Prior to the twentieth century, the US military establishment played a relatively minor role in the making of US foreign policy. Limits on its deployment and use also existed, stemming from its relatively small size and resources. However, in addition to its activities on the North American continent related to the westward expansion of the United States and, of course, the American Civil War from 1861 to 1865, the military was used more than 100 times in foreign operations in Central and Latin America, the Caribbean, Asia and the Pacific, Africa, and the Middle East (Salazar Torreon and Plagakis 2018). After World War II, the use of military force, or hard power, by a permanent, large bureaucracy became the foundation of the US policy of containment during the Cold War, which tended to revolve around a "threat-oriented" foreign policy. From 1946 to the end of 2018, American policymakers used the armed forces almost 700 times as a "political" instrument to influence the actions of other countries (Blechman and Kaplan 1978; Salazar Torreon and Plagakis 2018; Fordham 1998), and the threat and use of military force continues to the present day.

Greater Military Unification and Specialization

The experience of World War II generated a desire to create unity of effort within the military, as well as to establish a more centralized source of military counsel and advice. With the passage of the landmark **National Security Act of 1947,** American leaders were concerned not only about the policymaking process (which, as we will see in Chapter 8, led to the creation of the National Security Council) but also about the fragmentation, lack of coordination, and infighting among the different armed services supporting the war effort during World War II. Nowhere was this more noticeable than in the Pacific theater, where jurisdiction was divided between the Army and the Navy. General Douglas MacArthur was in charge of American forces in the Southeastern Asian theater (with General Joseph W. Stilwell in charge of the China-Burma-India theater), while Admiral Chester Nimitz was responsible for military operations throughout the northern and central Pacific. This division of authority resulted in competing, and not always complementary, military strategies being implemented by the United States in the Pacific.

Following World War II, a major debate ensued in which the Army favored a highly integrated military system, which the Navy strongly opposed. The National Security Act reflected a compromise: The old War and Navy Departments were replaced by a single **Department of Defense,** composed of a loose confederation of three military departments: the Army, Navy (including the Marines), and Air Force. Coordination of service activities was to be accomplished by the Joint Chiefs of Staff, which was also to be the central locus of military advice, and the Office of the Secretary of Defense was created to make the military more responsive to the president as the commander in chief (Zegart 1999).

Large, Permanent Military

The reorganization and centralization were accompanied by the development of a large, permanent military, replacing the small career force that grew in size temporarily during wartime. Although the US military initially began to demobilize after World War II, the rise of the Cold War resulted in reinstitution of the draft in 1947 in order to maintain a large military force that received extensive training even in peacetime (i.e., when a major "hot war" did not exist). This change occurred because, really for the first time since 1812, most Americans feared for the security of their country and believed that the threat of communism required the development of a large, permanent, professional military to defend the country and keep the peace. This revolutionary transformation in the US military did not come easily and was bitterly fought over in Congress during the late 1940s, until the Korean War resulted in US military intervention (Halberstam 2007).

Expansion in Bureaucratic Size and Scope

In the Cold War environment, the Department of Defense (DOD) became the largest bureaucracy in the US government and American society. By 1989—the year the Berlin Wall came down—the DOD spent almost $300 billion per year and employed well over 4 million people: about 2 million full-time soldiers, 1.5 million troops in the reserves and National Guard, and 1 million civilians (plus contractors). Military spending represented roughly 30 percent of total expenditures by the US government (as high as 50 percent during the 1950s). The DOD also employed roughly 60 percent of all full-time US government employees (not including members of the reserves and the National Guard) and one third of all federal civil servants. Defense Department personnel were located on more than 1,000 military bases and other properties in every state in the nation. Some 500,000 troops were permanently stationed throughout the world in more than 3,000 installations, including over 330 major military bases in over twenty countries and twenty-five US overseas territories (such as the Panama Canal Zone), predominantly in Europe, Asia, and the Pacific. With military personnel in more than 130 countries, the United States provided military training, in one form or another, to 75 percent of the world's armed forces (US Senate, Committee on Foreign Relations 1989).

After the collapse of the Soviet Union and the Cold War, the DOD experienced some downsizing, but following the events of September 11, 2001, it increased in size again, as did its budget. Today, the US military has about 1.3 million troops on active duty, with another 865,000 in the reserves. Its defense budget is nearly $750 billion, and it deploys approximately 200,000 troops across 175 different countries, with more than 800 military bases, large and small, in over 70 countries. The Trump administration requested increases in the Defense Department budget each year and has proposed increases to the number of active-duty soldiers in the Army and Marines, expansion of aircraft in the Air Force, and growth in the number of Navy vessels by more than 25 percent, including additional aircraft carriers and carrier group vessels.

In many ways, the military exists as a society within American society. It has its own system of laws, courts, and military police (MP), and most military bases are relatively large, urban complexes that maintain barracks and residential facilities for families. They also have medical (e.g., hospitals) and educational facilities (from kindergarten to adult extension college classes), commissaries (military supermarkets and department stores), and recreational facilities (bowling alleys, movie theaters, and country clubs). The military has made an effort to provide its personnel with every amenity of modern life, at least in terms of material comfort, at home as well as abroad, including in war zones such as Iraq and Afghanistan.

In addition to the Army, Navy, and Air Force academies, the military operates its own system of graduate colleges and universities to prepare its middle officers for senior staff and command positions. These include the Army War College, Naval War College, Air University, Armed Forces Staff College, Defense Systems Management School, and National Defense University, which consists of the National War College and Industrial College of the Armed Forces. The military services, individually and jointly, also maintain a number of colleges and research institutes in the health sciences as well as Reserve Officer Training Corps (ROTC) programs located in most public colleges and universities in the country. DOD also owns more than seventy industrial plants and facilities, many dating back to World War II.

Furthermore, today's military is considerably more than just the Department of Defense. For example, the Department of Homeland Security includes the Coast Guard (with more than 35,000 personnel), which has important military functions. The Department of Veterans Affairs (VA) was created to assist wounded war veterans and maintains an extensive system of VA hospitals throughout the country.

The space program within the National Aeronautics and Space Administration (NASA), originally a civilian-run organization to promote a nonmilitary space mission, supports more military than civilian missions today. The Department of Energy oversees about twenty government-owned energy facilities, privately operated by industry and universities (such as the Savannah River Plant in South Carolina) responsible for the design, manufacturing, testing, and retirement of nuclear weapons going back to the Manhattan Project. From its height of more than 140,000 workers in the 1980s, the nuclear weapons production process has shrunk, but the Department of Energy remains responsible for storage of vast hazardous substances and environmental cleanup (Cochran et al. 1987; US Congress 1994).

ORGANIZATIONAL STRUCTURE AND PROCESS

The DOD expanded into an enormous national and global bureaucracy during the Cold War, and it is characterized by the hierarchy, specialization, and routinization (or standard operating procedures) common to all bureaucracies, as discussed in Chapter 4. However, despite the fact that it is clearly more centralized than the military establishment before World War II, its size and complexity create issues and challenges that persist, despite efforts to address them. To better understand the dynamics of the defense process, we have to compare the formal organizational model to political reality.

According to the formal organization chart and the ideal bureaucratic model, the DOD operates very rationally within a pyramid-like structure composed of three levels. The individual services implement and carry out the plans and policies of their superiors—the Joint Chiefs of Staff, which consists of the senior military officers, and the Office of the Secretary of Defense, which represents the president and the civilian control dictated by the Constitution. Unfortunately, the political reality of the policymaking process within the Defense Department is far removed from the ideal and among the most complex of any governmental bureaucracy (see Figure 5.1).

Indeed, despite its reorganization and its formal structures, the military became so enormous and remained so decentralized during the Cold War that each of the military services possessed its own mission, standard operating procedures, and subcultures over which the president has been able to exercise only limited control. This is better understood by considering the role of the services, the Joint Chiefs of Staff, and the Office of the Secretary of Defense (see Coates and Kilian 1985; Luttwak 1985; Perry 1989).

The military **services** were created to implement US defense policy. The Army, Navy, Marines, and Air Force each have specialized responsibilities in preparing for and engaging in war. During much of the Cold War, the Army was primarily responsible for land warfare. The Navy maintained more than 500 ships, including twelve aircraft carriers with hundreds of aircraft, for sea and coastal warfare. The Marine Corps was an assault force, maintaining its own air and landing craft. The Air Force operated more than 2,000 aircraft in support of its air warfare mission. Day-to-day military operations were based on clearly defined divisions of labor (between and within services) and rank (from general down to army private) during the Cold War.

FIGURE 5.1
The Department of Defense Organizational Dynamics

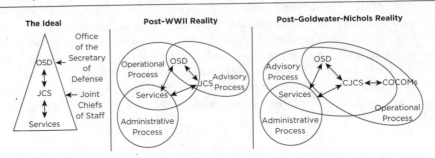

Note: CJCS, chair of the Joint Chiefs of Staff; COCOMs, combatant commanders; JCS, Joint Chiefs of Staff; OSD, Office of the Secretary of Defense.

The **Joint Chiefs of Staff (JCS)** was created after World War II to coordinate military strategy among the services and represented the entire military in advising the secretary of defense and the president. The JCS originally consisted of the four highest military officers: the chair, chief of staff of the Army, chief of naval operations, and chief of staff of the Air Force (the commandant of the Marine Corps was added in 1958). The **chair of the JCS (CJCS)** was appointed by the president for up to four years, while the other positions were a function of the personnel systems within the individual services. A joint staff, no larger than a few hundred military officers on loan from the individual services for a limited term, existed to support the JCS's work and mission.

Over its first four decades, the JCS was a weak body, unable to enforce a coherent military policy and coordinate the individual services. The CJCS, the only presidential appointment representing the entire military, had only one vote and no real power to represent or force support from the other members (until the Goldwater-Nichols Act of 1986). Each of the other four members represented the interests of the individual services. Decisions over issues tended to produce competing interests that were resolved through compromise and consensus within the JCS, and each service tended to get most but not all of its demands met. In this way, the JCS was able to symbolically present a unified military position that the civilians in the Office of the Secretary of Defense and the president found difficult to combat.

The **Office of the Secretary of Defense (OSD)** was created to provide better civilian control of the military and to advise the president. The OSD is the predominantly civilian side of the DOD, where the political appointees generally reside. The major hierarchy of administrative officers are the secretary of defense, a deputy secretary, undersecretaries, assistant secretaries, and deputy assistant secretaries, all nominated by the president and confirmed by the US Senate. Most of the routine day-to-day activity within the OSD takes place in organizational units or bureaus that specialize in certain defense subjects and issues.

In practice, the OSD had little legal authority (until Goldwater-Nichols) to influence the operations of the JCS or the individual services. One simple illustration of the fragmentation within the DOD and the independent autonomy of the individual services can be found in official US governmental publications such as the *Congressional Directory*. Even today, this publication lists the Army, Navy, and Air Force as separate "departments" within the executive branch (the Marine Corps is an autonomous part of the Navy), even though they are officially a part of the DOD, indicative of their autonomous power (US Congress, n.d.).

The Goldwater-Nichols Reforms

Concerns about the decentralized nature of the DOD and its implications for policy formulation and implementation spurred debate on reform of the DOD, especially the military and the JCS. In the 1980s the debate and calls for reform were taken up by Congress and eventually resulted in the Goldwater-Nichols Act of 1986 (Roman and Tarr 1998).

The **Goldwater-Nichols Act** addressed three general issues within the military establishment and had a major impact on the military and its role in US foreign policy, especially in the advisory and operational arenas (Kitfield 1995; Locker 2002). First, the act made the CJCS the sole adviser to the president, redefining the role of the position. This removed the old corporate system of advisory consensus, allowing the strengthened CJCS to provide advice, while informing the president of dissenting service chief opinion. The act also provided the CJCS with a vice chair and a joint staff, further centralizing the role and authority as the preeminent adviser to the president on military affairs. General Colin Powell was the first CJCS to really reap the harvest of this expanded role (e.g., Roman and Tarr 1998). The appointment of Powell as CJCS in 1989 increased the power of the JCS chair because of his considerable political skills in operating within the military and as a presidential adviser. This has made the presidential appointment of the CJCS even more important and "politicized," and the appointment of the CJCS now tends to represent the presidential desires of the time rather than seniority and JCS successor norms.

The Goldwater-Nichols reforms had other effects as well. The act clarified the operational chain of command of the regional commanders, establishing a system of unified **combatant commands (COCOMs)** under combatant commanders (CCDRs) who are directly responsible to the secretary of defense and the president. The reform also better integrated the JCS into the process and reduced service competition and duplication of effort in a theater of operation. Last, the act made joint service mandatory for all officers who wished to be promoted to general, thus removing any stigma associated with service on the joint staff. Officers now seek out joint staff service, with only the "best and the brightest" receiving such assignments, which mark them for continued service and potential to rise to the very top of the military hierarchy.

A More Efficient but Complex Organizational Process

Understanding the services, the JCS, the OSD, and the reforms of the Goldwater-Nichols Act helps to shed light on the complexity of the DOD's structure and process. Even after the 1986 reforms, rather than the simple centralized, civilian-controlled process implied by the formal hierarchical structure, three independent but overlapping systems or processes are at work in the DOD: *administration* (involving the military's basic infrastructure), *advice* about the use of force, and *operations* and military conduct on the ground (the meat of the military). Although even this depiction simplifies the complex policy process within the department, it more accurately reflects the basic operating patterns and it has important implications for the foreign policymaking process and White House leadership (see Figure 5.1).

The Administrative Process. The least exciting but very important process within the DOD is the *administrative process*. This involves day-to-day management of the military and remains pretty much controlled by the individual services. Personnel decisions about recruiting, training, tours (including joint tours of duty), and promotion are individual service affairs, as are the daily routines and activities concerning health, schooling, provisions, recreation, security, and so on. Requests for weaponry are also heavily influenced within each of the services, ultimately through the chief of staff and the JCS.

In many ways, the key to understanding the decentralized process of the DOD in the post–World War II era is to examine who controls the **budget and personnel systems**, since these administrative roles tend to determine how any organization actually operates. Decisions about the military budget (how to spend the money available) and military personnel (tours of duty and promotions) have been made within each of the services. Furthermore, the budgetary and personnel practices within each service have become institutionalized and standardized, making them very resistant to change. As General David C. Jones (1982:79), former CJCS, stated, "He who controls dollars, promotions, and assignments controls the organization—and the services so control, especially with regard to personnel actions."

Decisions over which weapons to build, where to deploy them, and how to use them in combat are typically made within an individual service, validated by the JCS, and usually approved by the OSD—all within the constraints of the overall military budget. The president and the secretary of defense might exercise influence on the issues in which they are most interested and to which they are most attentive—and occasionally they force compliance on particular weapons development and acquisition—but otherwise they have limited impact on the actual operations of the services—the heart and soul of the military.

The Advisory Process. Many Americans do not realize that since the Korean War the civilian leadership, including the secretary of defense and the president, have often been skeptical of military advice. The president is the commander in chief and determines when and where to use armed force abroad. Most presidents rely on their most trusted foreign policy advisers, including the national security adviser and the secretary of defense, when it comes to such important decisions. Since Goldwater-Nichols and the increased prominence of the CJCS and the relevant COCOMs, the credibility of military advice has improved, although tensions and contradictions continue to affect the process.

The conventional stereotype (especially in movies) portrays the military as always recommending the use of force to deal with international crises. In fact, studies of military advice during crises suggest that the military tends to be reluctant to initiate the use of force. Through most of the Cold War years, in fact, civilians tended to be much more "hard-line" and quicker to recommend force (see Halberstam 1969). In *Soldiers, Statesmen, and Cold War Crises*, Richard Betts (1977) found the Army to be the most cautious in recommending force (since it takes the brunt of the casualties), while the Air Force tends to be most optimistic about force, especially the use of air power. He also found that the military has its greatest impact on civilian leadership when military advice "opposes" the use of force (since this is the unexpected position), while it is least credible when it recommends force. Especially since Vietnam, the military may be eager to expand its capabilities through more sophisticated weaponry and more personnel, but it tends to be reluctant to put them at risk. However, once a decision to use force has been made, the military aggressively argues for more dominating uses of force and prefers that civilians should stand aside and allow the military to do whatever is necessary to succeed, which may require escalation.

A few examples illustrate this tension. During the Reagan administration, Secretary of State Alexander Haig and then George Shultz were the major advocates of military force, while Secretary of Defense Caspar Weinberger, representing the military, was reluctant to use force unless it had the full support of the American public. Likewise, President George H. W. Bush and National Security Adviser Brent Scowcroft were the most vehement in support of a major military response to the Iraqi invasion of Kuwait and the need to take Saddam Hussein to the brink of war to compel his withdrawal, while Secretary of State James Baker and CJCS Colin Powell were much more cautious, preferring economic sanctions over force. A similar situation arose between military and civilian leaders (such as Secretary of State Madeleine Albright) over Bosnia and Kosovo during the Clinton administration (see Halberstam 2001; Woodward 1991). After the September 11, 2001, terrorist attacks, the US military was much more cautious about using force, especially in Iraq, than its civilian leaders and top White House advisers, leading to open conflict between the OSD and the uniformed military. Tensions between the uniformed military and the civilian advisers in the Obama administration also affected policymaking, including over questions of deployment and operations in Iraq and Afghanistan. The more cautious military served as a brake and ballast point on a number of matters in the first years of the Trump administration as well.

Indeed, military failures in Vietnam, Beirut (1982), and Grenada (1983) led to what is commonly referred to as the **Weinberger-Powell Doctrine**, which became the popular military paradigm until September 11, 2001. The keys to this doctrine were spelled out first by Secretary of Defense Caspar Weinberger in Washington, DC, on November 28, 1984, at an address to the Washington Press Club in which he defined six criteria for the use of force:

(1) The United States should not commit forces to combat overseas unless the particular engagement or occasion is deemed vital to its national interests or its allies' interests, and the conflict should be declared before the United States takes action.

(2) Once ground troops are committed, they should be supported wholeheartedly.

(3) If the United States decides to commit forces overseas, it should have clearly defined political and military objectives.

(4) The relationship between US objectives and the forces committed must be continually reassessed and adjusted if necessary.

(5) Before the United States commits forces to combat abroad, support must be assured by the American people and Congress.

(6) The commitment of US forces should be a last resort.

These criteria were aimed at defining the role of the US military in the future to ensure that another Vietnam did not occur.

In 1992, then-CJCS Colin Powell wrote an article in *Foreign Affairs* titled "U.S. Forces and the Challenges Ahead" in which he redefined the checklist approach to committing US troops, citing the success of US forces in Panama and the Gulf War, which were tailored in both cases to meet the threats presented. He emphasized that Weinberger's six points should be used only as a guide to the commitment of troops. Overall, he espoused the use of decisive force to overcome a threat, clearly defined rules of engagement, and an exit strategy to avoid mission creep (i.e., the adding of extra tasks and goals) and excessive casualties. In short, the military should not be placed in a situation where it cannot utilize overwhelming force, win, and come home swiftly with strong public support (see also Halberstam 2001). Clearly, one of the major lessons learned by the military from the Vietnam War, especially within the Army, was to avoid the use of troops unless overwhelming force will be used and there is strong and visible public backing. As Eliot Cohen (1984:165) concluded, "The most substantial constraints on America's ability to conduct small wars result from the resistance of the American defense establishment to the very notion of engaging in such conflicts, and from the unsuitability of that establishment for fighting such wars."

In sum, decisions to use American armed forces are dominated by the civilian leadership, while decisions concerning administration and basic military operations of the armed forces tend to be made within the military. This is the kind of division of labor that is preferred by most within the military but that often frustrates presidents who want to control US foreign policy.

In terms of policy advice and participation in the policymaking process, before we leave this topic we want to call attention to two additional features. First, the complex structures of the services, the JCS, and the OSD create parochial perspectives that often compete and conflict with each other. A key aspect of this is the careerist-appointee divide, which has been highlighted in clashes between the OSD and uniformed military in the past four or five administrations. Second, the structures and processes of the DOD also help to explain part of its bureaucratic clout in the foreign policy process. In effect, the DOD has two voices in many policymaking deliberations—one from the uniformed military and one from the OSD. In the National Security Council itself, for example, both the secretary of defense and the CJCS are statutory members. No other agency of the foreign policy bureaucracy has this advantage.

The Operational Process. The operational process includes the military strategy and tactics employed by the armed forces and involves the individual services, the OSD, and, since the Goldwater-Nichols Act, the CJCS and the relevant combat commander. The secretary of defense and the OSD clearly have their greatest independent impact, when they have any impact at all, at the strategic level. A president may be able to affect war preparations, national military strategy, and overall force structure (and the development of large weapons systems), depending on the level of interest and attention displayed by the president, the secretary of defense, the secretary's immediate subordinates (as well as their working relationship with the JCS, especially the chair), and, naturally, Congress.

At the tactical level, the president usually has little control over the existing command structure and set of bureaucratic standard operating procedures for operations and military conduct on the ground. Since Goldwater-Nichols, usually the regional combat commander is the main military official responsible for employing the forces of the different services and has considerable leeway in doing so through use of his or her subordinate officers. Presidents, through the secretary of defense and the OSD and the advice of the CJCS, may be able to fine-tune specific military tactics, but more than this is usually beyond their competence and control.

At the operational level, the services used to dominate military operations through the so-called unified commands. Unified commands contain forces from two or more services (the Navy and Marine Corps are considered within the same department) and are regional or functional in orientation. However, with the Goldwater-Nichols reforms, the new unified COCOMs (formerly called commanders in chief) are no longer responsible to the heads of their services (e.g., the Army chief of staff or the chief of naval operations). Goldwater-Nichols changed the operational chain of command so that COCOMs report directly to the secretary of defense and the president, usually through the CJCS. This not only has increased the power of the civilians and the CJCS but also has made each COCOM extremely powerful.

In conducting military operations, the DOD divides the world into six major regions and four major functional areas, each led by a COCOM (see Table 5.1 for an overview of the unified commands and how the military divides the world geographically). The newest of the commands is the Cyber Command, established during the Obama administration to engage in both offensive and defensive cyberwar activities. In December 2018, the Trump administration proposed the creation of an eleventh command—Space Command—which would house a new "space force" (situated in the US Air Force and called for by the administration earlier in the year) and integrate planning and operations across services. This command was established in August 2019, with Air Force General John W. Raymond as its head.

Procedural and Structural Challenges

With the dramatic expansion, enormous bureaucratic size at home and abroad, and relative decentralization of the military establishment brought about by the rise of the Cold War, numerous organizational and political trends that were often problematic developed, including information problems, duplication and overlapping of activities, and difficulty of military coordination. These are three major problems common to all complex bureaucracies, but they are especially important in the DOD, given its role and functions in national defense. Overall, the US military "war machine" has been big and powerful since World War II, yet a close examination demonstrates that it was not nearly as effective a fighting force or as finely tuned an organization during war or peace as many Americans commonly believed.

TABLE 5.1
The Military's Unified Command Structure

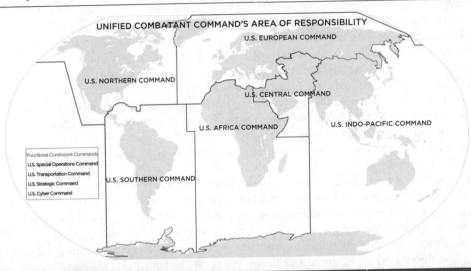

UNIFIED COMBATANT COMMAND'S AREA OF RESPONSIBILITY

U.S. EUROPEAN COMMAND

U.S. NORTHERN COMMAND

U.S. CENTRAL COMMAND

U.S. AFRICA COMMAND

U.S. INDO-PACIFIC COMMAND

Functional Combatant Commands
U.S. Special Operations Command
U.S. Transportation Command
U.S. Strategic Command
U.S. Cyber Command

U.S. SOUTHERN COMMAND

Commands	Area of Responsibility	Traditional Combat Commander
Regional		
Africa Command (AFRICOM)	African continent with the exception of Egypt	Army general
European Command (EUCOM)	Europe and Israel	Army or Air Force general
Indo-Pacific Command (INDOPACOM)	The Pacific, Asia, and the Indian Ocean	Navy admiral
Central Command (CENTCOM)	Mideast and Egypt	Army or Marine general
Southern Command (SOUTHCOM)	Central and South America	Army general
Northern Command (NORTHCOM)	North America, the Caribbean, and coastal waters	Marine general or Navy admiral
Functional		
Strategic Command (STRATCOM)	Nuclear forces, space operations, and satellites	Air Force general
Transportation Command (TRANSCOM)	Movement of forces and material	Air Force general
Special Operations Command (SOCOM)	Special-purpose forces of all services	Army general
Cyber Command (CYBERCOM)	Direct, synchronize, and coordinate cyberspace planning and operations	Army or Air Force general
Space Command (SPACECOM)	Organize, direct, and coordinate space operations	Air Force general

Source: US Department of Defense. Updater Private [CC BY-SA 4.0 (https://creativecommons.org/licenses/by-sa/4.0.

Problems of Information. Beyond the difficulty of communicating within such an enormous bureaucracy, other information problems plagued the military. The first was a heavy reliance on obtaining measurable indicators of military capabilities and operations, while deemphasizing the more intangible or human dimensions of warfare. Second was a tendency to inflate or deflate the information in accordance with service "political" interests. Not surprisingly, one of the major lessons of the Vietnam War that continues to have a major impact is that, during wartime, information needs to be closely controlled by the military and the DOD.

In Vietnam, for example, under General William Westmoreland and Secretary of Defense Robert McNamara, body counts became the ultimate "objective" indicator of how well or poorly the United States was performing in the war. Thus, if enemy body counts went up, this was used as an indication to the DOD and the country that the United States was winning. Not surprisingly, after a firefight soldiers on the ground made estimates of body counts from a distance (as opposed to risking ambush) and learned to err on the side of higher body counts to please their superiors and advance their careers, resulting in the overreporting of enemy-killed-in-action figures. At the same time, there were also incentives to deflate the number of North Vietnamese Army troops coming down the Ho Chi Minh Trail into South Vietnam.

Political battles were also fought over the "order of battle"—that is, the size of enemy forces in South Vietnam—with CIA estimates much higher than those of the MACV (Military Assistance Command in Vietnam), especially throughout 1967. The military won the political fight in Washington, but historical hindsight supports the CIA position. Ironically, the military leadership (including General Westmoreland and the JCS) and the civilian leadership (including President Johnson) were aware of the accuracy of the larger enemy numbers. They simply found the lower estimates more politically appealing for boosting public optimism and combating the antiwar demonstrations that were increasing on the home front, giving a false impression to the American people of "light at the end of the tunnel" that was overwhelmed by the Tet Offensive (Berman 1989).

Duplication and Overlap of Activities. Given the size and autonomy of and competition between the services, considerable duplication and overlap of activities have resulted. Although most Americans believe that there is one Air Force, the US military actually has four major air forces: the Air Force itself; the Army Air Force (consisting primarily of helicopters to support the Army's land mission), which maintains more aircraft than the Air Force; the naval air arm, involving a large carrier air force to defend the Navy fleet and undertake air strikes; and the Marine Air Force to support its own mission. Why has each service had its own air force and flown its own missions? The absence of dependable support from the other services—such as air support from the Air Force for Army troops—forced each service to fend for itself, promoting duplication. Some duplication may be helpful to ensure the success of a mission, but the military services have been so decentralized and autonomous that excessive duplication became the norm.

Coordination Problems. During the Cold War, lack of coordination among the services often made it difficult to develop truly unified and mutually reinforcing military activities and operations. Each service tended to pursue its own mission and tactical orientation largely independent of the others, resulting in a patchwork military strategy, which together may or may not have promoted the overriding goals of US foreign policy.

Why? The tremendous size, decentralization, specialization, and strength of the service subcultures allowed minimal military as well as civilian control, which often led to considerable **interservice rivalry**. Even though the military enjoyed substantial political and financial support from the president, Congress, and the public at large, the Army, Navy, Marines, and Air Force competed intensely with each other for resources, control, and preeminence—the ultimate indicators of success and the main tools for building a modern force (see Halperin and Halperin 1984). The same lack of real coordination often existed in military operations. Once American forces were engaged in combat abroad, every service expected to get a piece of the action.

In addition to the strong interservice rivalries, much **intraservice rivalry** (i.e., rivalry within a service) existed as well, and these rivalries also complicated coordination. Each service is organized into different branches and commands (such as infantry, armor, and artillery within the Army) that develop particular subcultures, with which personnel tend to identify strongly and compete for resources. As another example drawn from the Vietnam War, this intraservice rivalry impeded the Army's ability to conduct war successfully in Vietnam. Under President Kennedy most of the 18,000 troops sent were Army Special Forces (or Green Berets). Although originally organized in the late 1950s to conduct behind-the-lines training of partisan forces against Cold War enemies of the United States, during the early 1960s Green Berets became specially trained to perform **counterinsurgency** (and antiguerilla) operations—which required certain political, economic, and cultural skills (such as language training), in addition to military skills, to help the population defend itself. However, by the mid-1960s, more and more conventionally trained soldiers were sent to Vietnam, pushing counterinsurgency into the background. This was reinforced by the dominant Army view that Green Berets, though held in high regard for their prowess, were not trained to do things the conventional Army way. Hence, as the war became Americanized, the conventional Army came to rely on the helicopter and the air cavalry—the latest technologies for concentrating firepower by quickly moving personnel and equipment in support of "search and destroy" operations (Betts 1977).

THE MODERN MILITARY SUBCULTURE(S)

Examining the department's organizational subcultures helps explain the workings of the military and civil-military relations within the DOD, as well as shed light on the department's engagement in the foreign policymaking process. With both civilian and military personnel (the basis of the DOD's version of the careerist-appointee divide), different services, and differences between officers and enlisted personnel, the DOD bureaucracy is not only enormous but also diverse, composed of many different elements. Consequently, the department does not have a single subculture. However, a number of general characteristics have pervaded the military since World War II. Most members of the military, especially career officers, tend to share six characteristics:

- A managerial style
- Pursuit of procurement and high technology
- Preoccupation with careerism
- Belief in the separation of politics and military combat

- Promotion of the principle of concentration in warfare strategy

- An emerging commitment to "jointness"

First, it is commonly argued that the military not only produces warriors but especially *emphasizes a "managerial class"* of military leaders. The primary purpose of the military is to prepare and engage in war and, historically, carrying out this function required the development of a warrior class in society. In the United States, the military has been the institution where this warrior tradition was fostered. However, the **manager** has become increasingly important since modern bureaucratic warfare demands the ability of officers to become "managers of violence." Or maybe to be more accurate, officers are now expected to be both warriors and administrators. Given the enormous expansion of the military bureaucracy in size, scope, and complexity, this is a natural development and has been reinforced by the civilian leadership since Secretary of Defense McNamara in the 1960s.

McNamara entered office committed to seizing control of the DOD and making it more efficient and responsive to the president. McNamara's background was in the corporate world, and he had gained a reputation as an excellent manager while chief executive officer of the Ford Motor Company. During the Kennedy and Johnson administrations, McNamara appointed numerous "whiz kids" to positions in the OSD in his effort to restructure the department as well as streamline and improve the flow of information and the budgetary process. Although the basic military missions of the services continued, McNamara was successful in spreading his managerial approach throughout the military during the Vietnam War. For a modern-day consequence of this managerial subculture, see "A Closer Look: Death by PowerPoint."

A Closer Look

DEATH BY POWERPOINT

In 2005, General H. R. McMaster, who was commanding US troops in their efforts to take the northern Iraqi city of Tal Afar, directed his attention to an unusual step: banning the use of PowerPoint presentations. About a decade later, Secretary of Defense Ashton Carter took a similar step, banning PowerPoint in a critical meeting on US security policy in the Middle East. Why? Part of the explanation rests on the excessive dependence on highly complicated presentation slides and the inordinate amount of time US military planners devote to their construction. This illustration of the managerial subculture and its implications is well captured in this excerpt from a *New York Times* article:

Gen. Stanley A. McChrystal, the leader of American and NATO forces in Afghanistan, was shown a PowerPoint slide in Kabul last summer that was meant to portray the complexity of American military strategy, but looked more like a bowl of spaghetti.

"When we understand that slide, we'll have won the war," General McChrystal dryly remarked, one of his advisers recalled, as the room erupted in laughter.

The slide has since bounced around the Internet as an example of a military tool that has spun out of control. Like an insurgency,

(Continued)

(Continued)

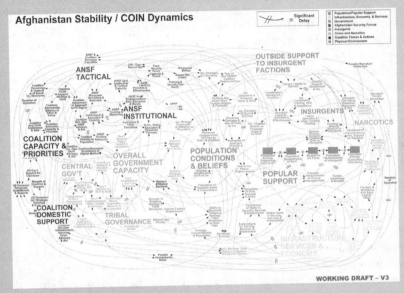

PowerPoint has crept into the daily lives of military commanders and reached the level of near obsession. The amount of time expended on PowerPoint, the Microsoft presentation program of computer-generated charts, graphs and bullet points, has made it a running joke in the Pentagon and in Iraq and Afghanistan.

"PowerPoint makes us stupid," Gen. James N. Mattis of the Marine Corps, the Joint Forces commander, said this month at a military conference in North Carolina. (He spoke without PowerPoint.) . . .

. . . Commanders say that behind all the PowerPoint jokes are serious concerns that the program stifles discussion, critical thinking and thoughtful decision-making. Not least, it ties up junior officers—referred to as PowerPoint Rangers—in the daily preparation of slides, be it for a Joint Staff meeting in Washington or for a platoon leader's pre-mission combat briefing in a remote pocket of Afghanistan.

Last year when a military Web site, Company Command, asked an Army platoon leader in Iraq, Lt. Sam Nuxoll, how he spent most of his time, he responded, "Making PowerPoint slides." When pressed, he said he was serious. . . .

Despite such tales, "death by PowerPoint," the phrase used to described the numbing sensation that accompanies a 30-slide briefing, seems here to stay. The program, which first went on sale in 1987 and was acquired by Microsoft soon afterward, is deeply embedded in a military culture that has come to rely on PowerPoint's hierarchical ordering of a confused world.

How does this example illustrate the managerial emphasis in the DOD's subculture? What are its implications?

Source: Elisabeth Bumiller, "We Have Met the Enemy and He Is PowerPoint," *New York Times*, April 27, 2010 (https://www.nytimes.com/2010/04/27/world/27power point.html).

The most successful military officers became those with administrative skills. Symptomatic of this change were the postgraduate degrees and curricula pursued by senior officers. Where history and military strategy were once the norm, the emphasis became business administration, public administration, and engineering. Even at US military colleges, knowledge of military history, international conflict, and military strategy no longer became dominant (except at the "war colleges" for senior officers). The emphasis has not been on the art of war but on learning how to administer a large bureaucracy. This has been accompanied by the rise of "bureaucratese" within the military—the development of a technical language among a select group of professionals and bureaucrats (including academics). Acronyms and jargon, such as MAD (mutual assured destruction), KIA (killed in action), and "collateral damage" (civilian injuries and fatalities and property damage), have proliferated, distancing the military and civilian managers from the brutality of war (see US Congress, Department of Defense 1991; Van Creveld 1989).

The rise of "managerialism" has been reinforced by a second characteristic of the military subculture, the *quest for more procurement and high technology*. A strong norm developed that a modern military requires advanced and expensive "hardware" (weaponry and support facilities). This "materialist" bias for more weapons—particularly those that are state-of-the-art—required more expert personnel to maintain and administer the hardware, and somewhat reduced the importance of intangibles such as leadership and will, during times of conflict. It also led the upper echelons of the military to take a much more active political role in civil-military relations: influencing the president, lobbying Congress, using the media, and campaigning to build public support for more procurement and high technology. Thus, the military, along with its supporters, became a potent force in the politics of national defense, reducing military accountability to civilian leadership and exacerbating the difficulties the president faced as commander in chief.

A third characteristic of the military subculture is the rise of *careerism*. A personnel system developed within each of the services that promotes individual conformity to the dominant norms and status quo and places a premium on individual preoccupation with career advancement. There has been an "**up or out**" expectation according to which either an officer is regularly promoted within the service, requiring high evaluations from his or her superiors, or the officer's career will suffer. Furthermore, officers have been expected to "**punch their tickets**"—that is, serve in a variety of specified positions and roles throughout their service. This normally includes a combat record, which is usually crucial to high career advancement. As many observers have pointed out, the military career ladder has become little different from the governmental or corporate career ladder, typical of any large bureaucracy. In each of the services, the end product became an "organization man or woman" who learned organizational norms and was able to contribute to the performance of the individual services' missions.

The fourth characteristic of the military's subculture is a belief in the *separation of politics and military combat*. The military perspective has been that the civilian leadership, symbolized by the president and Congress, decides when and where to go to war; but once the decision has been made, it is time for the politicians and civilians to stand aside and let the military do what it does best: fight wars. Most presidents and civilian leaders see the nature of civil-military relations quite differently—that the president is the commander in chief before, during, and after a war, as stipulated in the US Constitution (see Huntington 1957).

Given such differing interpretations, the military and civilian leadership often have found themselves in political battles during times of peace and war. For example, during the Korean War, President Truman relieved General MacArthur from his command of the United Nations forces for insubordination, triggering a national controversy over the conduct of the war and the containment policy (see Halberstam 2007). The American failure in the Vietnam War fueled a similar debate, for many attributed the loss of the war to civilian interference with the military's ability to perform its mission, while others blamed the military's inability to succeed within the appropriately described limitations set by the civilian leadership. More recently, the uniformed military and its civilian managers clashed over planning and preparation for the 2003 Iraq War, with Secretary of Defense Donald Rumsfeld and his OSD intervening directly in operational matters. We will discuss this more in the next section of this chapter.

The fifth characteristic that is part of the socialization or conditioning of military personnel is the belief in the principle of *concentration of forces and firepower* (or attrition warfare) as the most effective strategy to deter, weaken, exhaust, and ultimately defeat the enemy. This is what the conventional US military has been fundamentally organized, equipped, and trained to do. Given the different responsibilities and missions of each service, this emphasis has resulted in the historical development of three different warfare strategies. The Army emphasizes control of land through the destruction of the enemy's army and occupation of its territory (for the Marines, preferably through amphibious landings); the Navy emphasizes a maritime strategy of control of the sea by decisive defeat of the enemy's fleet; and the Air Force asserts the primacy of airpower over every other form of combat for defeating the enemy (see Davis 1967; Wylie 1966).

In responding to the challenges of the 1990s and the new century, the military also has placed a somewhat greater emphasis on money, resources, personnel, and training for **unconventional war**—low-intensity conflict, guerrilla warfare, civil war, and counterterrorism. Such operations focus on less conventional military/civilian operations, including humanitarian, peacekeeping, peace enforcement missions, and nation-building, which have increased since the end of the Cold War. At home, this might include disaster relief activities such as after Hurricane Katrina in 2005, or border security operations such as those authorized by the Trump administration as part of its approach to the "national emergency" caused by asylum seekers and illegal immigration.

Finally, the last (and newest) characteristic of the overall military subculture has been emerging since the Goldwater-Nichols Act. Although the rivalry between and within the services has continued since the Goldwater Nichols reforms, a new military emphasis on "*jointness*" has developed. This is especially the case at the operational level, with stronger unified commands and a stronger chair of the JCS providing military advice. The military subculture also is incorporating more of a joint orientation, especially at the more senior levels. All senior officers are now expected to complete at least two years of joint duty, those who get the opportunity attend a war college of another service, and the joint staff of the JCS is now considered a significant duty and an important stepping stone to career advancement.

THE DOD AND THE USE OF FORCE

The basic functions of the modern military establishment, its organizational reality and complexity, and its dominant military subculture have produced a military paradox: The US military has become a powerful force over time, yet it has faced limits on the range of foreign and national security policy applications to which that power has been targeted. The military has been organized and trained primarily to fight nuclear and conventional wars—the American way of war. In many ways, however, the military's performance in warfare since World War II and the quality of its performance prior to Goldwater-Nichols has been unimpressive except for those few occasions involving more classic conventional warfare.

Warfare Before and After World War II

Throughout its history, the US military has been organized and trained for classic **conventional warfare** with other states, usually powerful ones. The great military strategies and wars that have influenced the US military historically have been European—the British military being the main model for emulation. World Wars I and II, the greatest conventional military clashes in world history, demonstrated the need to organize and train for massive, general conventional war and called for a strategy of concentration of forces and attrition to defeat the enemy.

This was reinforced by the Korean War, the first major military conflict of the Cold War. The Korean War of 1950 was a "limited" war where the US military was successful in stopping the North Korean invasion of South Korea after the peninsula was divided following World War II, but General MacArthur was unsuccessful in his determination to reunify the entire peninsula, only to trigger Chinese military intervention that produced prolonged military stalemate until the cease fire in 1953 (and led to MacArthur's firing by President Truman; see Halberstam 2007).

Although nuclear weapons were not used in the Korean War, initially they were part of the general arsenal in support of the conventional strategy of attrition. The increasing destructiveness of nuclear weapons and advances in missile technology during the 1950s resulted in the military also being organized and trained for a new, nuclear form of war. Therefore, following World War II, the US military was prepared to fight principally two types of wars: a conventional war and a nuclear war.

For forty years, the US military plans focused on conventional and nuclear war with the Soviet Union. This preparation was the foundation of containment and the **deterrence strategy,** to stop Soviet expansionism through the threat and use of military force. Such a strategy presupposed a conventional war most likely occurring in central Europe and then on the Korean Peninsula in Asia. It also was based on the likelihood of a nuclear battle predominantly fought in the territories of the United States and the Soviet Union. Refinements were made to these general strategies, such as a concern with limited nuclear war and limited conventional war directed predominantly at the Soviet Union and its surrogates (see Brodie 1973).

Historically, reliance on a conventionally trained military did not pose a problem for dealing with uprisings or guerrilla war. Such conflicts were not widespread and were often subdued by sending American Marines to restore stability in places like Nicaragua, as was often done during the early part of the twentieth century. However, in the years following World War II, the explosion of nationalism, the increase in new state and nonstate actors, and the proliferation of weaponry throughout the globe had major implications for contemporary warfare. First, developing countries became better able to resist the projection of great-power military force abroad. Second, most of the low-intensity conflicts throughout the world—such as civil wars, guerrilla wars, and terrorism—began to involve the great powers directly. This meant that use of conventional force became less appropriate with time and has had greater difficulty succeeding, as the America experience in Vietnam and the Soviet experience in Afghanistan illustrate.

The Vietnam War. The United States first faced this new environment in Vietnam. Most American leaders, and the public, operated under the assumption that the projection of US military force into Vietnam would quickly contain the enemy and stabilize the situation. Yet the United States and the US military were poorly prepared for a war without front lines and where distinguishing between friend and foe was nearly impossible. Thus, a conventionally trained military of more than 550,000 troops by 1966 was thrown into a most unconventional war. In part because the enemy's will to resist was greater than the American will to win, the US military suffered its first major defeat in war (see Map 5.1).

The military lessons of Vietnam have been hotly debated. Some, like Harry Summers (1982), a retired colonel in the US Army, argued for a more organized conventional approach to the war. Others, such as retired military officers Andrew Krepinevich (1986) and Mark Clodfelter (1989), argued that the US military was ill equipped and ill trained to counter the enemy's unconventional strategy. As one Army general quoted by Krepinevich commented:

> "[I]f you really want to be cost-effective, you have to fight the war the way the VC [Vietcong] fought it. You have to fight it down in the muck and in the mud and at night, and on a day-to-day basis." Yet, the general told the correspondent, "that's not the American way, and you are not going to get the American soldier to fight that way." (Krepinevich 1986:171; see also Shafer 1988)

From the perspective of the US military, the restrictions and limitations imposed by the president and the secretary of defense hamstrung the military's efforts. For example, similar to limits imposed by Truman in Korea when American troops pushed up the Korean Peninsula approaching the Chinese border, President Johnson made certain operations off-limits, such as attacking Cambodia, Laos, or North Vietnam, for fear of triggering the military intervention of the People's Republic of China.

MAP 5.1

Vietnam War

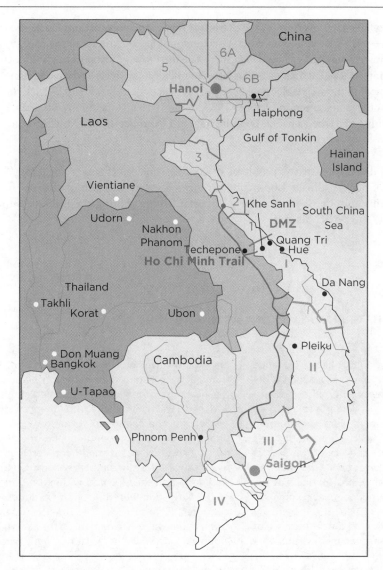

Source: The United States Air Force in Southeast Asia, 1963-1971. Carl Berger, Editor. Office of Air Force History. US Government Publishing Office.

After Vietnam. The failure of the US effort in Vietnam reinforced the bureaucratic structure and subculture of the military against unconventional warfare and in continuing support of the principle of concentration—to overwhelm the enemy with a quick delivery of massive firepower—along with a new interest in force mobility. Yet, military performance since Vietnam throughout the 1970s and 1980s was often found lacking. As military strategist Edward Luttwak (1985:17) concluded:

> Irrefutable facts overwhelm the patriotic impulse to overlook our failures in war—from Vietnam in its most varied and prolonged entirety; to the clumsy Mayaguez raid of 1975, in which forty-one died to save forty; to the Iran rescue attempt in 1980, which ended in bitter humiliation, with eight dead and none rescued; to the avoidable tragedy of Beirut, which took the lives of 241 Marines and other servicemen in October 1983; to the Grenada operation of the same month . . . ; to the Lebanon bombing raid of December 4, 1983, in which the Navy lost two costly aircraft.

A good illustration of the problems of coordination and focus is the 1983 Grenada invasion. See "A Closer Look: The Grenada Victory as Military Fiasco" for more detail; this episode was particularly important in prompting the military reforms of the Goldwater-Nichols Act.

A Closer Look

THE GRENADA VICTORY AS MILITARY FIASCO

What should have been a quick military advance and mopping-up exercise became an incredibly slow, cumbersome, and inefficient military operation. Consider the mission: to defeat a token force of 679 Cubans, most of whom were construction workers, and a few Grenadians on an island that was only 133 square miles (twice the size of the District of Columbia). Yet *Operation Urgent Fury* required three days and more than 7,000 Marines, Army rangers, paratroopers, and independent commando teams from all the services to subdue the enemy and occupy the island—all for the official purpose of rescuing predominantly American medical students who were never in danger.

The problems were endless. First, intelligence was poor. The intelligence community did not know the number of enemy troops or how well they were equipped. When the military operations bogged down after the first day, estimates escalated to as high as several thousand Cuban troops. In fact, the military did not have maps of the island, requiring many of the invading troops to rely on tourist maps from Michelin during the three-day operation. And the invading troops were never briefed about a second medical school campus with American students.

Second, the command structure was inappropriate for the task. Although a land operation, the military strategy was planned and commanded by naval officers for the simple reason that Grenada was geographically located within the boundaries of the Navy-dominated Atlantic Command headquartered in Norfolk, Virginia. Thus, the operational commander was a vice admiral on the aircraft carrier *Independence*, while there was never any agreement concerning the existence of a single commander for the ground forces and every service naturally had to play a role in the invasion.

Third, the military operations were slow and inefficient. The rangers (the Army's elite conventional troops) invaded from the north, while the Marines invaded from the south. Yet, advances were repeatedly stalled by sporadic enemy fire and inflated reports of enemy strength where rangers and Marines had to be reinforced by paratroopers from the Army's 82nd Airborne Division on the second and third days. A team of the Navy's elite troops, the SEALs, not only failed to rescue the governor-general of Grenada but became trapped with the governor and his family in the governor's residence. A secret Delta Force of elite army commandos failed in its mission to rescue political prisoners. Both the SEALs and the Delta Force eventually were rescued by the Marines.

Fourth, units from the various services had difficulty communicating with one another. In one case, it was reported that a ranger unit was unable to call in an air strike to the Navy command. To overcome this obstacle an ingenious soldier slipped into a nearby phone booth and used his AT&T long-distance card to reach Fort Bragg, North Carolina, which relayed the request through the Pentagon to the *Independence* for the air strike.

In the end, US forces suffered eighteen killed and 116 wounded (as opposed to twenty-five Cubans killed), many due to accidents and friendly fire. The operation was so slow in rescuing the 224 American medical students (which was the official justification for the invasion following a successful military coup) that many of them may have been placed at greater risk by the operation itself since they were completely at the mercy of the Cubans and Grenadians. However sloppy the operation, the Reagan administration's response was to issue more than 1,600 medals for meritorious service and heroism, even though only 7,000 American troops set foot on the island and a much smaller number were actually involved in combat.

How do the reforms of Goldwater-Nichols make a military fiasco like Grenada less likely?

Source: Adkin (1989), Ayres (1983b), and Taylor (1983).

After Goldwater-Nichols

Goldwater-Nichols had a major impact on the military's conduct, helping to alleviate (but not eliminate) coordination, information, and duplication problems and making the military more successful during the use of force and the deployment of troops. Since 1986, the US military has experienced important successes in Panama (1989), the Gulf War (1991), and Kosovo (1999), although key challenges related to the structure, process, and subculture of the DOD have remained.

The December 1989 invasion of Panama was successful in overthrowing General Manuel Noriega. Much of this success was due to the fact that "the main part of the Panama attack was a virtual replay of a World War II battle, with paratroops dropping from the sky and tanks blasting through a city to overwhelm the opposition" (Trainor 1989:1). The victory came at great cost. Twenty-five American soldiers were killed and hundreds wounded (many due to friendly fire), and there were thousands of Panamanian civilian casualties (and displaced persons) through bombing and shelling. In addition, the United States maintained a large military occupation force; provided millions of dollars in reconstruction aid to the new government, which quickly resorted to old, corrupt ways; and faced significant global criticism for American gunboat diplomacy, especially given its twelve previous invasions of Panama.

The **Persian Gulf War** was a tremendous military success that also used a major military innovation. The Army adopted the "air-land battle doctrine," which emphasized mobility and flexibility in the concentration and application of firepower on the ground with the support of the other services in the air to attack the enemy where they might be most vulnerable. This stunning success was notable in light of past performances. Why did the US military perform so successfully in the Persian Gulf War? A key reason is that this was the kind of conventional war (or battle) that the US military is best trained and equipped to fight. According to military strategist Eliot Cohen (1991:22):

> The United States fought in a theater ideally suited to our military strengths, an empty desert. . . . We had half a year to mass and train troops, and to prepare elaborate plans to attack. . . . We also had the luxury of one of the best port, road, and air base networks in the world, including military facilities built by our engineers, and the support of a wealthy and cooperative host nation [that is, Saudi Arabia].

Also, with Iraq facing global economic sanctions, the United States "could bring to bear the weight of our cold war–rich armed forces without fear of Soviet opposition in the theater or aggression elsewhere." The Persian Gulf War, in other words, represented a classic conventional confrontation.

The successful Kosovo War under President Clinton had many similarities. Although the physical environment of the former Yugoslavia was not nearly as ideal as the desert, Serbia was a weaker (and more overextended) conventional military adversary than Iraq. Regardless, the American-led NATO attack and massive bombing of Kosovo and Serbia, reinforced by the threat of a ground invasion, persuaded Serbia's leadership to capitulate and withdraw its forces within weeks. What makes this victory particularly unique is that it was accomplished purely through an air war without the use of any ground troops—a military first.

The Military Since 9/11

Since September 11, 2001, the US military has been involved in two major military wars in Afghanistan and Iraq, as well as other uses of force. Throughout, these experiences illustrate the DOD's efforts to adapt to a changing environment, but they also reveal key features and tensions in the foreign policymaking process, both within the DOD, and between the DOD, the White House, and other players in the foreign policy process.

Military Transformation, Rumsfeld, and Iraq and Afghanistan after 9/11. Under President George W. Bush, Donald Rumsfeld became the most powerful (and controversial) secretary of defense since Robert McNamara, and probably since World War II. Rumsfeld attempted to make major and controversial changes in promoting a smaller, more mobile, and more technologically advanced conventional military force structure, strategy, and set of tactics, which triggered considerable resentment and pushback from the uniformed military. After 9/11, the civilian leadership—especially Secretary of Defense Rumsfeld, Vice President Cheney, and President Bush—was the most vocal for a quick military response and unhappy with the initial conventional, "preponderant force" war plans for Afghanistan and Iraq provided by the military. Their persistence and decisions contributed to the initial success of the Afghanistan and Iraq Wars, as well as their unraveling, with important military implications.

Rumsfeld's aggressive approach to his role as secretary of defense rested on several factors. First, Rumsfeld had more than three decades of experience as a prominent Washington insider, occupying important positions of power within Republican administrations going back to President Nixon. Second, Rumsfeld had a strong and domineering personality, along with being a tough "hands-on" manager and a fierce bureaucratic infighter. Third, Rumsfeld was loyal to President Bush and had strong support from the president until 2006. Fourth, Rumsfeld had strong and forceful civilian officials within the OSD, most notably Deputy Secretary of Defense Paul Wolfowitz and Undersecretary of Defense Douglas Feith. Fifth, Rumsfeld also had a very strong relationship with Cheney (who was selected by Rumsfeld as his deputy chief of staff under President Ford more than thirty-five years earlier). Sixth, Rumsfeld became secretary of defense at a time when the chair of the JCS was not as strong or visible as it was under CJCS Crowe and Powell. Finally, Condoleezza Rice, Bush's first-term national security adviser, was not a strong manager of the national security process, and President Bush embraced a tendency to delegate important responsibilities to key individuals and organizations outside the White House, allowing significant space for Rumsfeld to operate (see Mann 2004; Packer 2005; Woodward 2002, 2004).

Rumsfeld began his tenure as secretary of defense with a belief in the need to transform the US military into a leaner, swifter, high-tech, more effective fighting force. Despite considerable military resistance, Rumsfeld was convinced that there should be much greater emphasis on newer military technologies, smaller numbers of "boots (troops) on the ground," precision bombing and the use of special forces, and "command and control" in linking combat operations together as a unified whole. This would allow for smaller and faster military strikes, throwing the enemy off balance and ultimately resulting in greater military success—with fewer American casualties (see Boot 2003; Kaplan 2005).

The terrorist attacks of September 11, 2001, changed Rumsfeld's strategy. Rather than focusing on trying to alter and transform the organizational structures and subcultures within the military in accordance with this vision (in the face of tremendous institutional resistance), Rumsfeld and his DOD team had to conduct a global war on terrorism. This meant that Rumsfeld's focus was to attempt to transform actual combat operations, which historically had been dominated either by the different military services or, after Goldwater-Nichols, by the combat commander(s) and the chair of the JCS. In some ways Rumsfeld was successful: The military operations in Afghanistan in 2001 and Iraq in 2003 reflected his perspective and his dominance of the planning. However, the initial military success in the wars in Afghanistan and, especially, Iraq was not followed by relative peace, stability, and reconstruction in either of the countries in the more unconventional conflict that followed (see Biddle 2003; Boot 2005).

In Iraq, Rumsfeld, with the support of the president, opposed the initial Iraqi War plan by CENTCOM, which called for roughly 400,000 troops (for the war and especially for postwar reconstruction). Rumsfeld aggressively forced the invasion plan to be trimmed and streamlined down to around 160,000 troops, with a heavy reliance on speed and special forces consistent with his vision of military transformation. The initial military operations were incredibly successful: The US invasion quickly overwhelmed the Iraqi army, captured Baghdad, deposed Saddam Hussein, and occupied Iraq.

MAP 5.2

Iraq

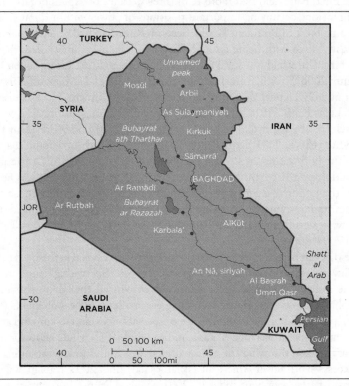

Rumsfeld also succeeded in persuading the president to delegate the "post-reconstruction" Phase IV stage of the war to DOD, giving the OSD and Rumsfeld the authority and responsibility. Here, success was elusive. Not only did the emphasis on Iraq lead to a deemphasis on the war in Afghanistan, which began to unravel in the second Bush term, but Rumsfeld and his deputies had incredibly optimistic assumptions about how the Americans would be treated as liberators in Iraq. This led them to pay little attention to postwar reconstruction planning and to assume that almost all American troops could return home within three months after the end of the actual (Phase III) war. Rumsfeld also marginalized or ignored bureaucratic rivals—led by the State Department—who had developed extensive reconstruction plans based on much more pessimistic assumptions about postwar security and stability.

On the ground, the lean approach to the invasion forced by Rumsfeld also resulted in much confusion between the civilians in the OSD, the military, and the civilians in the Civil Provisional Authority (CPA)—the initial governing body led by Paul Bremer, a foreign service officer in the Department of State—which was responsible for reconstruction and the transfer of power to a new Iraqi government. The CPA made numerous decisions that inadvertently contributed to the rise of the insurgency (such as the decision to disband the Iraqi army completely as opposed to only its leadership). This was reinforced by the relative isolation of the CPA within the so-called Green Zone (a relatively secure area in Baghdad that was formerly the seat of the Hussein regime), in which the soldiers who fought throughout Iraq often referred to the CPA as "Can't Provide Anything" (Hammer 2004; Packer 2005) (see Map 5.2).

Finally, with the insurgency steadily increasing its attacks and the general situation in Iraq steadily deteriorating, by 2004 the military found itself increasingly fighting a guerilla war. The military attempted to fight and adapt as best it could to its changing political-military environment, but the troops had little knowledge of the culture or language of the insurgents, and almost no intelligence about the insurgency. This led to a number of controversial decisions in Washington, DC, and in Iraq, where large numbers of Iraqis were detained, imprisoned, and often tortured in prisons such as Abu Ghraib in order to gain desperately needed intelligence (Hersh 2004; more about this in Chapter 6, on intelligence). As the insurgency in Iraq grew, the unanticipated second war with Iraq that ensued led to a major political backlash and a semi-military revolt against the civilian leadership of Rumsfeld, who was fired in November 2004. Although the Bush administration's military surge and new tactics and strategies employed by new Secretary of Defense Robert Gates and General David Petraeus, the new commander in Iraq, helped to stabilize the situation, the American public and political system turned against the Iraq War and the Bush administration (see Ricks 2009).

Obama's Wars. The Obama administration inherited a hornet's nest in Afghanistan and Iraq. In Afghanistan, faced with the resurgence of the Taliban and the deterioration of the "long war," President Obama made important decisions to escalate the American presence. With the growing number of US troops alongside NATO forces, and increased numbers of civilian embassy personnel and contractors, it became "Obama's War" (see Figure 5.2). With respect to Iraq, in accordance with Obama's campaign pledge, the strategy was to increasingly turn over the war to the Iraqis with the number of American troops steadily declining in the hope that sufficient stability could be maintained throughout Iraq—a type of "Iraqification" similar to "Vietnamization" over a generation earlier. President Obama officially declared that US combat troops were completely withdrawn in 2011 (despite the presence of thousands of so-called military advisers). However, with the emergence of the Islamic State and its success gaining control of territory in Iraq and Syria after 2011, Obama again escalated US military activities and presence in both countries in 2014 and after. Both of these instances illustrate important elements of the advisory and operational role and influence of the DOD in US foreign policymaking.

In the first year of the Obama administration, the president and his advisers decided to "surge" US forces to meet the challenges of the deteriorating situation. Although media coverage fueled a public perception of a collegial inner circle, tensions and conflict grew between the Pentagon (Secretary of Defense Robert Gates; General David Petraeus, then the combat commander for CENTCOM; and CJCS Admiral Michael Mullen), other presidential advisers, and the White House staff, specifically over escalation decisions for the AfPak (Afghanistan-Pakistan) War (see Map 5.3). In March 2009, President Obama, who was heavily focused on the state of the economy, relied largely on the judgment of Mullins and especially Gates (supported by Secretary of State Hillary Clinton) and

FIGURE 5.2

Boots on the Ground in Afghanistan and Iraq

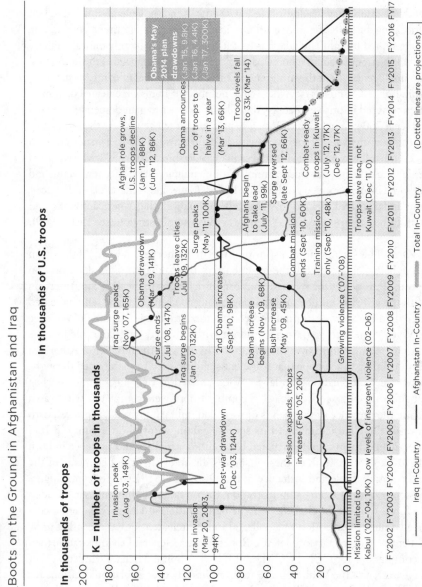

Source: Amy Belasco, *The Cost of Iraq, Afghanistan, and Other Global War on Terror Operations Since 9/11,* Congressional Research Service RL33110, December 8, 2014 (https://fas.org/sgp/crs/natsec/RL33110.pdf), p. 9

approved a Pentagon request for an additional 30,000 troops, which President Bush had deferred to his successor. Five months later, Gates, Mullen, and Petraeus came back with a request for an additional 40,000 troops and the implementation of a full-spectrum **counterinsurgency** strategy in a report written by General McChrystal (the US commander in Afghanistan), which was leaked to the press ahead of the policy discussions.

The leaked McChrystal report constrained the president and his advisers. President Obama and his White House staff felt "blindsided" by the Pentagon's second large request, which came even before the full implementation and review of the March decision. The ensuing deliberative process reflected significant policy disagreements. The war of leaks that ensued showed the military's push for a second surge in troops countered by a White

MAP 5.3

Afghanistan with Its Neighboring Countries

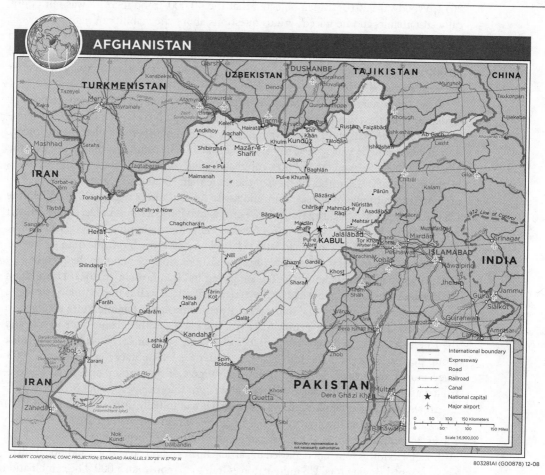

LAMBERT CONFORMAL CONIC PROJECTION; STANDARD PARALLELS 30°25' N 37°10' N

803281AI (G00878) 12-08

Source: Courtesy of the University of Texas Libraries, The University of Texas at Austin.

House staff position claiming that the military was trying to box the president in on the troop deployment issue. The four-month decision process produced a "centrist" compromise announced at West Point in December 2009. The framing context of the so-called centrist option is key to understanding the policy process and outcome. The options presented to the president included an unrealistic high option of 85,000 troops, a low estimate of 20,000, and the remaining two estimates of 40,000 and 30,000–35,000, respectively, which were too similar to differentiate. Vice President Joe Biden and the White House staff were the major proponents of limited escalation and a counterterrorism strategy focusing on al-Qaeda, while the Pentagon argued for 40,000 more troops and a strategy of counterinsurgency.

Obama complained that he had been given just one real option and felt he was being manipulated to accept the hybrid recommendation. However, the behavior and action of the major civilian and military players within the DOD, especially Gates, Petraeus, and Mullin, proved difficult to overcome due to their united position (Garrison et al. 2014; Woodward 2010). Biden objected that the 40,000-troop increase was not politically sustainable, and he raised serious questions about the viability of many aspects of the counterinsurgency policy piece. Clinton, however, endorsed the plan with Gates and Mullen. Eventually, Obama reluctantly agreed to a compromise decision: a "surge" of 30,000 troops, and a hybrid counterinsurgency and counterterrorism strategy to go after the Taliban and al-Qaeda.

After three more years of fighting and after a two-day summit in Chicago attended by leaders of more than fifty countries, including twenty-eight NATO countries and the presidents of Afghanistan and Pakistan (but not the Taliban or other so-called enemy forces), a final communiqué was agreed to on May 21, 2012. According to the agreement, the US-NATO alliance would hand over command of all combat missions to Afghan forces by the middle of 2013; withdraw most of the more than 100,000 foreign troops by the end of 2014; and continue to advise, train, and assist Afghan forces beyond 2014. When the US-led International Security Assistance Force ended its operations in December 2014, it was immediately replaced by *Operation Resolute Hope*, in which some 13,000 NATO military advisers (including more than 8,000 US military personnel) provide training, advice, and assistance to the Afghan security forces. This operation continues to the present.

In Iraq, the Obama administration completed its "Iraqification" in 2011. However, in the chaos and instability generated by the Syrian civil war, as well as the continued struggles of the new Iraqi regime to maintain security and control, the **Islamic State** emerged to present new challenges. The Islamic State (IS, also known as the Islamic State in Iraq and the Levant, or ISIL, and the Islamic State in Iraq and Syria, or ISIS) is a Salafist jihadist group that participated in the Iraq insurgency after the US military intervention in 2003. Even more radical than al-Qaeda, IS took advantage of the turmoil and, by 2015, controlled a large swath of territory in Syria and western Iraq, even capturing Mosul.

In response, the Obama administration, which had initially dismissed the threat from IS, escalated American involvement, supplying increased aid and advice to Iraqi and Kurdish forces and engaging in an extensive campaign of airstrikes beginning in August 2014. Although US forces were not deployed to participate in ground operations, additional advisers were sent, bringing total US military forces in Iraq to more than 5,000. The combination of aggressive airstrikes and ground operations by Iraqi and Kurdish forces killed thousands of IS fighters and, by the end of 2017, IS no longer held territory in Iraq (see Map 5.4).

MAP 5.4

Territory Lost by the Islamic State

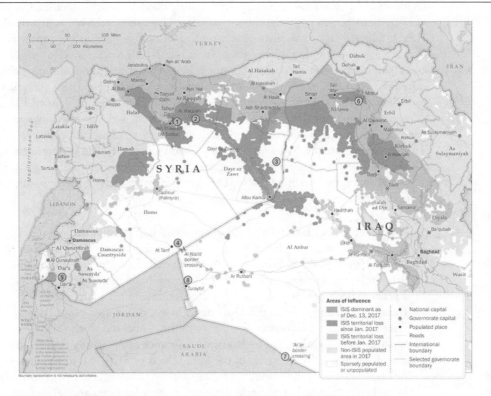

Source: U.S. Department of State.

In Syria, IS control was harder to combat, in part because of the complicated political and strategic landscape that involved IS, al-Qaeda, and Syrian rebels resisting both IS and the Assad regime, as well as involvement by the United States and allies including the United Kingdom, Canada, Australia, Turkey, Jordan and other Middle Eastern partners, and Russia. The Obama administration began efforts to aid the Syrian opposition in 2011 and expanded those efforts to support attacks on IS in 2014. That year, the United States led a multinational coalition to target and attack IS forces, chiefly from the air, although several thousand US troops were also deployed. The combination of these attacks began to roll back IS control by the end of the Obama administration, but the challenge persisted and the Trump administration inherited it in January 2017.

The Trump Tightrope. Donald Trump assumed office in January 2017 facing not only the challenges of ongoing US military operations in several countries but also those of his contradictory preferences and approaches to US military power and operations. On the one hand, Trump had campaigned in 2016 calling for less US military intervention, especially in the Middle East. In the campaign and in office, Trump also regularly questioned US military commitments, deployments, and operations in numerous US alliances, including NATO and South Korea. On the other hand, he sought significant expansion of US military power, pushing substantial budget increases in each of his first three years. He also adopted aggressive rhetoric and confrontational steps signaling a more bellicose US response to a number of situations, including North Korean nuclear proliferation and US opposition to the Maduro regime in Venezuela. The Trump administration also exited the 2015 agreement designed to control Iran's nuclear programs (completed by the Obama administration, Germany, France, Russia, China, and the United Kingdom). A more confrontational approach to Iran soon emerged, with hawkish advisers such as Secretary of State Mike Pompeo and National Security Adviser John Bolton pushing Trump to designate the Iran Revolutionary Guard Corps (IRGC) as a terrorist organization, while playing up connections between Iran and al-Qaeda.

These moves on Iran came despite Defense Department advice and opposition to the more confrontational approach. According to one account,

> "Like most things Iran-related, DoD opposed," said a senior defense official, speaking on condition of anonymity to describe ongoing tensions between the White House National Security Council, which has mounted a "maximum pressure" campaign against Iran, and a Pentagon brass that has cautioned against unnecessary provocations. . . . "It was pretty much a fait accompli from Pompeo and Bolton, and DoD basically got rolled over," added a former administration official familiar with the deliberations who also insisted on anonymity. . . . The Pentagon resistance came mainly from Gen. Joseph Dunford, the chairman of the Joint Chiefs of Staff, and top civilian officials including John Rood, the Pentagon's top policy official, and Kathryn Wheelbarger, the acting assistant defense secretary for international security affairs. (Morgan and Toosi 2019)

As this episode suggests, the role of the DOD and its functions in the advisory and planning processes continue to be dynamic.

Consider several examples. On Syria, President Trump inherited the challenge of countering IS, while addressing the broader crisis generated by the Syrian civil war and the atrocities of the Assad regime. In response, the administration initially adopted its predecessor's approach, and then expanded US military operations to target the Syrian regime for the first time in the spring of 2017. As in Iraq, US operations resulted in the steady reduction of IS forces and control over territory, such that the last IS stronghold was defeated by US-backed Kurdish forces on the ground in early 2019. However, between 2017 and 2019, the president vacillated on what to do in Syria. In January and September 2018, the president supported expanded US operations, in-country deployments—which reached about 2,000 forces in 2018—and long-term commitments of US forces and support. Then, in December, in defiance of advice from Secretary of Defense James Mattis and CJCS General Joseph Dunford, the president unilaterally announced (via Twitter) that he was ordering the withdrawal of US forces by early 2019, since IS had been defeated on the ground. This decision led Mattis to resign in protest. Subsequently, while US forces were reduced, the White House again reversed itself to embrace a more open-ended commitment of hundreds of US troops, which both the DOD and the national security adviser preferred. However, in the fall of 2019, after Bolton was fired by Trump, the president again reversed course and ordered the withdrawal of most US troops, abandoning America's Kurdish partners to Turkey and Syria.

As this example illustrates, the relationship between the president and his secretary of defense was often tense. Initially, Secretary of Defense Mattis developed a positive relationship with Trump, taking care not to challenge him publicly or confront him over his inexperience or lack of understanding of national security matters. However, by 2018, Mattis's ability to persuade the president and resist what he regarded as reckless and unproductive actions deteriorated. Through the summer of 2018, significant disagreements emerged over NATO policy, US military commitment to and cooperation with South Korea, the decision to withdraw the United States from the Iran nuclear deal, the creation of a new "space force," and other matters (Schmitt et al. 2018; Woodward 2018). Mattis also used his position to "slow-walk" requests and orders from the president with which he disagreed, intending to delay and derail them. When Trump announced the decision to withdraw from Syria, Mattis finally had enough and resigned. He was replaced by Patrick Shanahan, a former Boeing executive, who served as acting secretary of defense until June 2019. At that time, Mark Esper (who had been secretary of the Army from January 2017 until June 2019) replaced Shanahan as acting secretary of defense and was then nominated and confirmed as secretary of defense in July 2019.

DOD AND THE NATURE OF THE MODERN MILITARY ESTABLISHMENT

The role and influence of the military establishment in US foreign policymaking has grown since World War II, and it is shaped by the structures, processes, and subcultures of the DOD, as well as by the relationships between the uniformed military (careerists) and civilian members (appointees) of the department, between the DOD and other agencies of the foreign policy bureaucracy, and between the OSD and military advisers on the one hand and the White House on the other. Significant variations in the dynamics exist, and challenges in coordination and cooperation are persistent. In the more recent environment, the military has become even more active in a variety of missions and has seen its budget increase substantially. As Dana Priest (2003:11) argued, "U.S. leaders have been turning more and more to the military to solve problems that are often, at their root, political and economic. This has become the U.S. military's mission and it has been going on for more than a decade without much public discussion or debate."

At the same time, critical questions remain that will shape the role and influence of the DOD in US foreign policy going forward. Some of these involve the policymaking process in the executive branch, and between the executive branch and Congress, which we will take up in Chapters 7 and 9. Others have to do with key questions about the nature and purposes of the military establishment. Let's address several of those matters here before we move on to discuss other parts of the foreign policy bureaucracy and the overall policymaking process

First, one key question that continues to generate debate concerns the budget of the Defense Department. When it comes to budget, how much is enough? The US DOD budget reached about $750 billion in 2019, and this excludes military spending for such departments as Energy, the Coast Guard, NASA, and the Veterans Administration. After a short period of reduction after the end of the Cold War, the budget has been increasing at a time when no major adversary such as the Soviet Union directly challenges the United States. To place this in comparative context, the US government accounts for almost half

FIGURE 5.3
Comparative Defense Spending

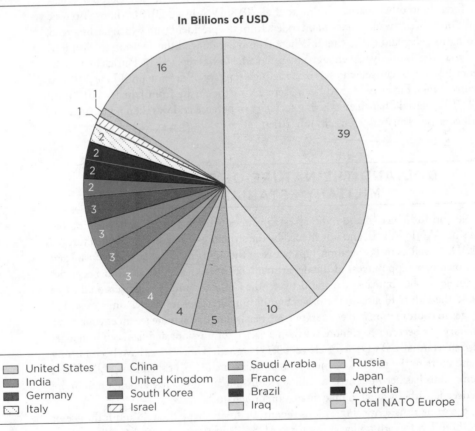

In Billions of USD

- United States
- India
- Germany
- Italy
- China
- United Kingdom
- South Korea
- Israel
- Saudi Arabia
- France
- Brazil
- Iraq
- Russia
- Japan
- Australia
- Total NATO Europe

Source: Adapted from the International Institute of Strategic Studies, 2018.

TABLE 5.2

US Total Military Force Structure (in thousands)

	Total Personnel	Army	Navy	Marine Corps	Air Force
Active	1314	476	327.9	185	325.1
Reserves	366.3	199	59	38.5	69.8
Guard	449.6	343	0	0	106.6
Total	2129.9	1018	386.9	223.5	501.5

Source: US Congress, *National Defense Authorization Act for Fiscal Year 2018,* CRS Report (https://www.congress.gov/115/crpt/hrpt404/CRPT-115hrpt404.pdf).

of the world's military expenditures (see Figure 5.3). Members of NATO, including the United States, account for almost 80 percent of the world's military expenditures, while China spends about 10 percent. And then there are traditional US allies that are not part of NATO—such as Japan, Taiwan, South Korea, and Australia. Throwing money to the military to address the complexity of the post–Cold War environment and the war on terrorism appears to be a major part of US foreign policy. But how much is enough? And what are the implications of devoting such a major part of the US budget to military spending?

Then there is the question of how much is enough in terms of military personnel in the current environment. Many argue that the military does not have sufficient manpower to perform all these missions and that constant activation has hurt military readiness. There are currently around 1.3 million active full-time soldiers. What is less well known is that since the Persian Gulf War the reserves and the National Guard have constantly been activated and engaged in a variety of military missions abroad. Unlike the Vietnam War, joining the reserves and National Guard is no longer a way to avoid the active military; they are an integral part of the overall military that is on constant call and is regularly activated, as is commonly the case in Afghanistan and Iraq (and at a lower cost, since reserve and Guard members are employed only part time until activated). Currently, there are also almost 400,000 personnel in the reserves and about 450,000 in the National Guard. Together, the active military, the reserves, and the National Guard make up a total force structure of more than 2.1 million.

In addition, there are questions about how much of a permanent military presence the United States should have abroad. The number of military bases in the United States and abroad has also been reduced somewhat, but almost 200,000 active-duty personnel remain stationed abroad in 800 bases and deployments, big and small, scattered across about 175 countries (see Map 5.5). According to the Fiscal Year 2018 Base Structure Report from the US Defense Department, the US operates more than 500 significant installations across more than 160 countries. Furthermore, about 50,000 active-duty military are regularly stationed "afloat" (such as on aircraft carriers).

How much is enough depends considerably on the national military strategy agreed to by civilians and the military. The assumption that drove the official pre-9/11 national

MAP 5.5

US Military Deployments around the World

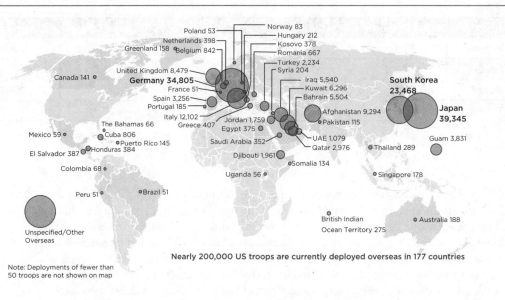

Nearly 200,000 US troops are currently deployed overseas in 177 countries

Note: Deployments of fewer than 50 troops are not shown on map

Source: Data from Department of Defense, Sstockholm International Peace Research Institute (2015 data), *Politico.*

military strategy was to be prepared for engaging simultaneously in "two major regional conflicts" (such as in the Persian Gulf and the Korean Peninsula) contemplated in the *2001 Quadrennial Defense Review* (QDR, conducted every four years until 2014, when it was replaced by the *National Defense Strategy*). The QDR and the overall national military strategy have since been dramatically amended in light of 9/11, and the Iraq and Afghan Wars. The QDR from 2008 (US Department of Defense 2009: 1) states,

> The United States, our allies, and our partners face a spectrum of challenges, including violent transnational extremist networks, hostile states armed with weapons of mass destruction, rising regional powers, emerging space and cyber threats, natural and pandemic disasters, and a growing competition for resources.

This quite expansive and enormous undertaking now incorporates asymmetrical along with conventional and nuclear war. In 2018, the *National Defense Strategy* directed attention to five central external threats to the United States: China, Russia, North Korea, Iran, and terrorist groups with global reach. According to this most recent document, meeting the challenges from China and Russia have priority over others matters, including terrorism. (See "A Different Perspective: Competing Visions of Military Strategy" for more on these matters.)

A Different Perspective

COMPETING VISIONS OF MILITARY STRATEGY

US military strategy was long dominated by a focus on conventional war. During the Cold War, strategy centered on countering the Soviet Union and engaging in major and regional conflicts. Beginning in Vietnam, the US began to develop other approaches centered on low-intensity conflict, but these tended to be peripheral to the main US efforts. In fact, despite its reluctance, the US military has always fought "small wars," that is, unconventional forms of warfare that have, in recent history, gone by such names as "counterinsurgencies," "low-intensity conflicts," "stability and reconstruction operations," and **asymmetrical warfare**.

After the Cold War, and especially in the post-9/11 context, the DOD devoted greater attention to developing a counterinsurgency (or COIN) strategy, which has been very controversial within the military, especially within the Army and the Marines. As the military effort in Iraq deteriorated, a network of individuals within the Army (sometimes labeled "COINdinistas") gained in credibility and in 2006 produced the first *Counterinsurgency Field Manual* since the Vietnam War. And they began to implement it, first in Iraq in 2007 with the surge and then in Afghanistan by the summer of 2009, with General Petraeus playing a critical role in each stage. Counterinsurgency emphasizes not the killing of the enemy, but the protection of the population and promotion of a stable, legitimate government. Such unconventional operations were increasingly integrated into US national military strategy and doctrine, as well as military education and training.

In 2017, the DOD moved to circle US strategy back. The *National Defense Strategy* emphasized a focus on China and Russia, as well as other states, while deemphasizing unconventional operations.

As Secretary of Defense Mattis stated in January 2018, "Great power competition—not terrorism—is now the primary focus of U.S. national security" (quoted in Denison 2019). Such a shift in strategy involves efforts to reduce the US role in peripheral areas and low-intensity conflicts but also requires major shifts in the DOD's approach and a redirection of resources to more conventional force modernization. Even while it moved to expand US defense spending, the Trump administration also proposed reductions in spending on areas related to peripheral and COIN targets. Nevertheless, as one recent analysis put it:

> The Defense Department has been resistant to actually allocate the funding required to meet the needs of crucial programs . . . that they identify as crucial to combatting growing Chinese threats and influence in an era of great power competition.

> Hence, the eagerness by some drafters of the *National Defense Strategy* to remove funding for America's enduring peripheral conflict clashes with a resistance in other parts of the organization to end these missions. The result is an inability to fully commit to the culture change needed for a robust overhaul of American defense priorities away from the post-9/11 war on terror. (Denison 2019)

To what extent should the US military be oriented to fight nuclear, conventional, and/or asymmetrical/low-intensity wars?

Source: Cordesman (2012), Davidson (2010), Denison (2019), Hastings (2011), Kilcullen (2009), and US Department of the Army (2006).

Finally, how should the DOD (and the United States in general) address new threats and challenges? One of the most problematic of these is the arena of cyberwarfare. In the high-speed, interconnected world of the digital age, a new form of warfare has emerged. **Cyberwarfare** is the attempt by one state or nation to cause disruption, discord, damage, death, or destruction by using computers and other digital devices for digital attacks on the computer systems of another. Hacking and hackers are at the core of cyberwarfare, but the concept refers to the actions of states/nations, or directed by states/nations, rather than those in which individual hackers or criminal groups might engage. However, nonstate actors such as terrorist groups may engage in cyberwarfare.

Most experts regard cyberwarfare as a highly likely component of future conflicts. Such attacks may be directed at government information systems; military and industrial targets; commercial networks and institutions; universities and hospitals—which are especially vulnerable; and infrastructure such as power/electricity, water, and gas. As you might already conclude, most developed and developing economies depend on information systems, computers, and computer networks for everything from governing and infrastructure to transportation and communications, and so are very vulnerable to cyberwarfare.

The weapons of cyberwarfare are quite sophisticated. They include such things as phishing attacks and ransomware designed to gain access to computer hardware, accounts, and information systems; viruses and malware designed to corrupt and control computer systems and networks; denial-of-service attacks that make computers/networks unavailable to users; and what are known as "zero-day" vulnerabilities or exploits, which are bugs or flaws in software (such as Microsoft's Windows operating system or Office software, or Adobe's Flash software) that are unknown to the manufacturer and/or public and are thus open for exploitation because they have not been patched. The intelligence agencies of many countries amass an evolving suite of such weapons and employ them in what seems to be constantly evolving, adapting, and sophisticated ways.

As many as thirty to sixty countries are currently developing cyberwarfare capabilities, according to the US intelligence community. Currently, the leading players in the cyberwarfare arena include the United States and its friends and allies such as the United Kingdom and Israel, as well as Russia, China, Iran, and North Korea. The US Defense Department has annually identified China's increasing defense spending on cyberwar capabilities as a point of great concern, while Iran and North Korea have developed significant cyberwar capabilities and have launched disruptive attacks against such targets as the US financial system (Iran, in 2012–2013) and Sony (North Korea, in 2014). In fall of 2017, the US Department of Homeland Security and the Federal Bureau of Investigation warned of a serious and expansive North Korean cyber campaign they called HIDDEN COBRA, through which North Korea was targeting the US aerospace, telecommunications, and finance industries through malware attacks designed to penetrate computer networks and exploit access (US-CERT 2017).

Russia is a major player as well, with a highly advanced cyberwarfare strategy and capabilities that it has deployed aggressively against its neighbors, European countries, and the United States (see Map 5.6). For example, one of the earliest cyberattacks came in 2007 when Estonia announced its plans to remove a Soviet-era monument to Red Army troops from the center of the capital city to a cemetery on the outskirts of town. As anti-Estonian protests ignited, fueled by false information disseminated by the

Russian media, Russia launched cyberattacks against Estonia that interrupted banks, disabled ATMs, shut down e-mail, and disrupted government and private communications networks through denial-of-service attacks in which websites and networks were overwhelmed by the volume of phishing attempts and other attacks by large numbers of botnets (McGuinness 2017). More recently, the US intelligence community confidently concluded that Russia organized and directed cyberattacks and cyberwarfare against the United States in its attempts to sow chaos and to influence the 2016 election. Indeed, as

MAP 5.6

Russian Meddling in Europe

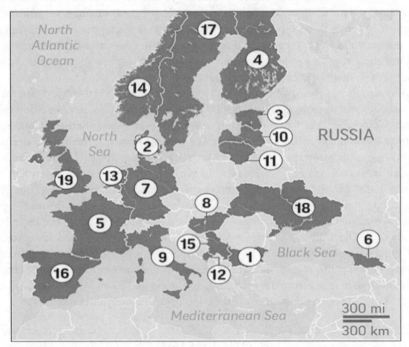

Countries that Russia has targeted with methods that could include cyberattacks, disinformation, covert social media plans, corruption or other means to destabilize democratic governments, according to a U.S. Senate Democratic report:

1. Bulgaria	6. Georgia	11. Lithuania	16. Spain
2. Denmark	7. Germany	12. Montenegro	17. Sweden
3. Estonia	8. Hungary	13. Netherlands	18. Ukraine
4. Finland	9. Italy	14. Norway	19. United
5. France	10. Latvia	15. Serbia	Kingdom

SOURCES: Maps4News/HERE; Senate Foreign Relations Committee

Source: Maps4News/HERE, Senate Foreign Relations Committee.

the *Report on the Investigation Into Russian Interference in the 2016 Presidential Election* from Special Counsel Robert Mueller (former director of the FBI) carefully detailed and forcefully concluded, "The Russian government interfered in the 2016 Presidential election in sweeping and systematic fashion."

For the United States, as we noted earlier, cyberwarfare is a growing priority. Indeed, one of the earliest instances of cyberwarfare involved the United States. In 2010, as Iran pursued its covert nuclear weapons campaign programs, its facilities, especially the Natanz uranium enrichment plant, began experiencing widespread and unusual failures in the centrifuges used to enrich uranium for weapons development. Not long after, other computer networks in Iran began experiencing strange patterns of failure and unexplained shutdowns. Soon, signs of malicious files began to appear on computers around the world. Ultimately, these problems were attributed to a computer worm called Stuxnet, developed by the United States and Israel as apparently the world's first digital weapon and unleashed against the Iranian industrial targets to disrupt and impede Iran's nuclear weapons program. Taking advantage of a flaw in the Windows operating system, the worm penetrated the computers controlling the operations and caused Iranian centrifuges to malfunction. Unfortunately, Stuxnet soon spread outside its targeted range and was identified on many computer networks around the world, although its harmful operations were narrowly targeted to a precise set of computer software and hardware configurations and it did little damage outside its Iranian targets (see Zetter 2014).

Cyberwarfare has recently been elevated to the status of a special Unified Combatant Command, to take its place alongside similar commands for regions like the Middle East (Central Command), Pacific (Pacific Command), the Americas (Southern Command), Europe (European Command), and others. The leading agency in the intelligence community responsible for much of the cyberwarfare capabilities in the United States is the National Security Agency (NSA), located in Fort Meade, Maryland. Currently, Cyber Command, the theater command for US cyberwarfare, is housed on the top floor of the NSA, and the director of the NSA also serves as the head of Cyber Command to ensure that the operational role of the command is closely connected to the technical capabilities of the NSA. In the middle of 2018, the Trump administration released National Security Presidential Memorandum 13 (NSPM 13) and quietly expanded the scope and freedom of Cyber Command to engage in more aggressive and proactive cyberwarfare activities, with fewer steps in and restrictions on the approval process. This new freedom has already been used in cyber operations against Russia, Iran, North Korea, and others.

CONCLUSION

The Department of Defense is a key agency in the foreign policy bureaucracy. Its main components—the military services, the JCS, and the OSD—play important roles in the foreign policymaking process, in both formulation and implementation. Its size, command of budgetary resources, and control over a central instrument of foreign policy have ensured it clout in policy process, while its structures, processes, and subcultures have combined to create challenges for its functions and operations. We now turn to the intelligence community, a third major component of the foreign policy bureaucracy.

THINK ABOUT THIS

The Department of Defense is often regarded as the 800-pound gorilla of the foreign policy bureaucracy. Think about the characteristics and roles of the Defense Department discussed in this chapter.

What factors contribute to and detract from the role and influence of the Department of Defense in US foreign policymaking?

KEY TERMS

Visit **edge.sagepub.com/scottrosati7e** to help you accomplish your coursework goals in an easy-to-use learning environment.

Understanding the Foreign Policy Bureaucracy

THE INTELLIGENCE COMMUNITY

PHOTO 6.1 A Central Intelligence Agency video conference.

LEARNING OBJECTIVES

1. Know the purposes and activities of the intelligence community.

2. Identify the major agencies of the intelligence community and their responsibilities.

3. Understand the structures and processes of the US intelligence community and the challenges they generate for foreign policymaking.

4. Describe the nature and dynamics of the use of covert operations in US foreign policymaking.

After World War II, the United States developed an extensive intelligence community within the executive branch, which has had important effects on the process and content of US foreign policy. The intelligence community plays important roles as part of the "eyes and ears" of the foreign policy bureaucracy, gathering and analyzing information to help policymakers make decisions, and as part of the "sword and shield" of US foreign policy, protecting communication and security and carrying out operations. The seventeen components scattered across many bureaucratic agencies each reflect the core characteristics of bureaucracy. But, collectively speaking, the intelligence community is the most decentralized component of the foreign policy bureaucracy. This has presented unique challenges for management and coordination in the foreign policy process. In this chapter, we continue our examination of the key players of the foreign policy bureaucracy by focusing on the major functions and components of the intelligence community. We then discuss some key aspects of the intelligence community's structure and processes, and the challenges they pose for the foreign policymaking process. We also discuss important activities of the intelligence community in the conduct of US foreign policy, especially covert operations.

THE PURPOSES AND ACTIVITIES OF INTELLIGENCE

Most European states developed intelligence functions during the 1920s and 1930s, but in the United States, modern intelligence developed more slowly. The US government had a very limited intelligence capability during the nineteenth century, relying on the Secret Service, the military, and the State Department. American intelligence became more professional and grew during the first half of the twentieth century with the establishment of military intelligence, the Federal Bureau of Investigation (FBI), and, during World War II, the Office of Strategic Services (OSS), the precursor to the Central Intelligence Agency (CIA).

With the Cold War and the passage of the National Security Act of 1947, the intelligence community expanded into large, complex, modern bureaucracies. After the collapse of the Soviet Union, the intelligence budget and staff experienced some downsizing, followed by a significant increase due to the September 11 attacks and the subsequent war on terrorism. Although the exact amount the United States spends on intelligence remains classified, in 1998 then–director of central intelligence (DCI) George Tenet publicly revealed the intelligence budget at $26.7 billion (Shane 2004). Today, the Office of the Director of National Intelligence (2019a, 2019b) estimates the intelligence budget at more than $60 billion (which does not include the military intelligence program, estimated at another $21 billion).

In the early twentieth century, **intelligence** simply referred to information or news. Since the 1950s, however, intelligence has come to include three broad sets of activities: data collection and analysis; counterintelligence; and political and paramilitary intervention. After World War II, the intelligence community expanded—in size, resources, and activities—in each of these areas.

Eyes and Ears: Collecting and Analyzing Information

The primary purpose of the intelligence community is to collect and analyze information for military and civilian policymakers in the executive branch. This activity is referred to as the **intelligence cycle** or process. Most intelligence organizations are engaged in collecting and analyzing information for policymakers (see Johnson and Wirtz 2004; Lowenthal 2011).

The intelligence cycle has five phases that generate a continuous process of interaction between those who collect and analyze information and those who make policy decisions: (1) planning and direction, (2) collection, (3) processing, (4) analysis and production, and (5) dissemination (see Figure 6.1). The intelligence process begins with planning, direction, and "tasking," which usually responds to the climate of the times (e.g., strategic intelligence about the Soviet Union during the Cold War or, in recent times, about terrorism). In 2005, for example, the country's first *National Intelligence Strategy* emphasized as central priorities the need to focus on terrorism, the proliferation of weapons of mass destruction (WMDs), democratization, the ability to penetrate difficult organizations and closed societies, and other objectives. After taking office in 2009, the Obama administration shifted focus to some new or revised tasks, including combating violent extremism,

FIGURE 6.1
The Intelligence Cycle

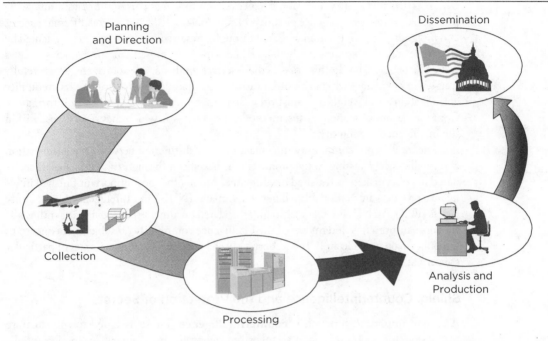

Planning and Direction

Collection

Processing

Analysis and Production

Dissemination

Source: Adapted from Central Intelligence Agency Office of Public Affairs, *Fact Book on Intelligence* (2005).

providing strategic intelligence and warning, integrating counterintelligence capabilities, and enhancing cybersecurity, the latter two of which received heightened attention and their own offices and coordinators. In 2019, the *National Intelligence Strategy* of the Trump administration stressed targeting traditional adversaries (e.g., Russia, China, North Korea, Iran), emphasizing cyberthreats, counterterrorism, counterproliferation, and better integration of counterintelligence. In its *Worldwide Threat Assessment of the US Intelligence Community* in early 2019, the Office of the Director of National Intelligence (ODNI) placed cybersecurity at the top of the list of concerns, while also stressing aspects of human security such as global health, climate change, and population displacement as important threats (Coats 2019).

Once requirements are received, collection techniques are allocated to gather the data. The United States has developed a large array of methods for collecting intelligence, ranging from the simple to the extremely complex. Four of the most common collection methods are (1) electronic signals (SIGINT); (2) photography (PHOTINT or IMINT); (3) human sources (HUMINT); and (4) "open sources" that are publicly available (such as radio, television, newspapers, and the Internet).

Once collected, the raw information is processed. Because raw information from the collection stage is almost never useful, processing is required to render complex data into an intelligence picture. During the analysis and production stage, pieces of information from various sources are pulled together to paint this intelligence picture. This process may occur within a particular agency of the intelligence community or as part of the community-wide process. A complete intelligence picture is ideally constructed from several different sources and methods (e.g., information gathered through human sources is confirmed or denied by electronic and photography methods), and perhaps from more than one agency source as well. The people who do this are called **all-source analysts**. All-source analysts carefully weigh the raw data—which can often prove to be inaccurate—to evaluate its credibility and reliability and weigh it against other information, and they synthesize information from the various collection means, methods, and sources to which they have access within the intelligence community.

The intelligence community thus makes a clear distinction between raw information and intelligence, referring to the products that have been through this cycle and disseminated to policymakers as **finished intelligence**. Among the most important finished intelligence products are National Intelligence Estimates (NIEs) and Intelligence Community Briefs (ICB). An NIE is a relatively regular, updated document that provides a synthesis of the most authoritative judgments of the intelligence community on subjects of concern to US policymakers, while an ICB is a shorter, special document on urgent issues of particular concern at a given time.

Shield: Counterintelligence and the Protection of Secrets

A second important function is **counterintelligence**. Those assigned to this area are responsible for the protection of secrets from the prying eyes and ears of foreign intelligence agencies, both at home and abroad. For forty years, American counterintelligence focused on protecting the national security bureaucracy from penetration by the Soviet Union and its allies. As Dan Coats (2019:12), then the US director of national intelligence, warned:

> Penetrating the US national decision-making apparatus and the Intelligence Community will remain a key objective for numerous foreign intelligence services [such as Russia, China, Iran, and Cuba] and other entities. In addition, targeting of national security information and proprietary technology from US companies and research institutions will remain a sophisticated and persistent threat . . . . We [also] assess that nonstate actors—including hacktivist groups, transnational criminals, and terrorist groups—will attempt to gain access to classified information to support their objectives. They are likely to improve their intelligence capabilities—to include recruiting sources and performing physical and technical surveillance—and they will use human, technical, and cyber means to perform their illicit activities and avoid detection and capture.

The duties of the men and women who work in counterintelligence range widely and include the prevention and investigation of espionage, subversion, and sabotage against American targets. The functions performed by counterintelligence are of the highest priority, for they are intended to protect American secrets from those who would use such information to harm the United States.

Sword: Covert Operations

In addition to the traditional intelligence functions of data collection and analysis, and counterintelligence, American intelligence agencies are also tasked with **covert political and paramilitary operations** in support of US foreign policy. These involve governmental acts, such as propaganda campaigns, psychological warfare, secret financial assistance, destabilization and subversion campaigns, support for partisan resistance movements, assassinations and other "direct action," and coups d'état. The CIA, the organization most (but not exclusively) involved in this area, has developed a certain notoriety for its covert operations over the years, as we discuss later in the chapter.

THE MAJOR INTELLIGENCE ORGANIZATIONS

Although the public generally thinks of the CIA, the intelligence community is much larger than one agency and has been expanding since the 1940s. Its sprawling size and challenges have prompted regular calls to reform or restructure its organization to improve its coordination and activities. These calls produced few results until 2001, but the intelligence failures surrounding the 9/11 attacks and Iraq finally led to some structural and procedural changes, although their impact has been relatively limited to date.

As Figure 6.2 shows, the **intelligence community** includes all or parts of seventeen different federal organizations. The major components are (1) the National Security Agency (NSA); (2) intelligence units within each of the military services; (3) the National Reconnaissance Office (NRO) and the National Geospatial-Intelligence Agency (NGA); (4) the Defense Intelligence Agency (DIA); (5) the State Department's Bureau of Intelligence and Research (INR); (6) the FBI; (7) other agencies in the executive branch that are engaged in intelligence activities, such as the Departments of Energy, the Treasury, and Homeland Security, and the Drug Enforcement Administration (DEA); (8) the CIA; and (9) the most recent addition, the ODNI, which now has the daunting task of coordinating this sprawling community.

The organizations listed fall within three general categories based on their principal function in the intelligence process. First, the producers are those who analyze and disseminate finished intelligence products to consumers. These products take many forms, from daily summaries to detailed research studies, but it is primarily through these products that the intelligence community interacts with policymakers. Second are the organizations that focus on collection and processing. This is the largest grouping, where most of the growth in the intelligence community has taken place. Third, some organizations also conduct an additional function in the research and development of equipment (or collection platforms). For example, the NRO, while producing imagery products, is also engaged in the development of new, more technologically advanced imagery systems. In addition, some of these organizations may also have counterintelligence and political and paramilitary intervention missions.

FIGURE 6.2

The Members of the Intelligence Community: An Organizational Overview

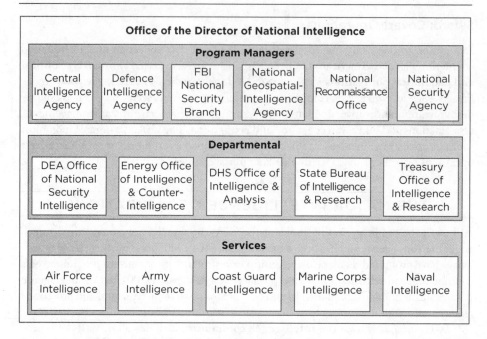

Office of the Director of National Intelligence

Program Managers

| Central Intelligence Agency | Defence Intelligence Agency | FBI National Security Branch | National Geospatial-Intelligence Agency | National Reconnaissance Office | National Security Agency |

Departmental

| DEA Office of National Security Intelligence | Energy Office of Intelligence & Counter-Intelligence | DHS Office of Intelligence & Analysis | State Bureau of Intelligence & Research | Treasury Office of Intelligence & Research |

Services

| Air Force Intelligence | Army Intelligence | Coast Guard Intelligence | Marine Corps Intelligence | Naval Intelligence |

Source: Adapted from http://www.intelligence.gov/, https://www.dni.gov/index.php/what-we-do/members-of-the-ic, and https://www.intelligencecareers.gov/icmembers.html.

For most of the post–World War II period, these agencies were only loosely coordinated by the director of central intelligence, who also served as the director of the CIA. Always in a weak position, without the power over budgets, tasking, or hiring and firing in any of the agencies other than the CIA, the DCI rarely succeeded in imposing much order on the intelligence community. In 2004, the Intelligence Reform and Prevention of Terrorism Act created the new ODNI, and the director of national intelligence (DNI) was provided with increased powers to coordinate the activities of the rest of the intelligence community.

Intelligence Organizations of the Defense Department

Most of the US intelligence organizations, including personnel and budget, are officially a part of the Department of Defense. The Pentagon spends about eighty cents of every intelligence dollar, with the big accounts being those of the NSA and NRO, America's technical collection services.

The National Security Agency (NSA). The highly secretive NSA was created in 1952 within the DOD, though its origins go back to World War I and the army's Signal Corps.

It has grown to become the largest and, along with the CIA, most important intelligence agency. Until relatively recently, the NSA was so secretive that for decades its acronym was said to stand for "No Such Agency" (Bamford 1982, 2001). The major function of the NSA is the collection and exploitation of SIGINT (communications, radar, and telemetry intelligence). The NSA maintains "listening posts" located in US governmental facilities abroad, including US embassies and particularly American military bases around the world, equipped with sophisticated electronics for intercepting communications messages. The intercepted messages are relayed to the NSA's headquarters in Fort Meade, Maryland, where an extensive and sophisticated array of computers process the information. It was, for example, the NSA that intercepted a 2010 cell phone call to one of Osama bin Laden's most trusted couriers that enabled the intelligence community to track the courier to the compound in Pakistan where bin Laden was hiding. This key piece of information was essential to the subsequent 2011 raid on the compound that killed bin Laden.

NSA also has special responsibility in **cryptology**, the study of making and breaking codes. The NSA devises the codes for the US government, performing an important counterintelligence function by helping to keep communications secret. Since much of the information that the NSA intercepts is in code, efforts are made to break the codes of other countries and decipher the messages, unbeknownst to the original source. For example, this proved critical to the success of the Allies in World War II. More recently, the NSA was able to provide good information on Iran's diplomatic, military, and security plans because it had broken that country's codes; US intelligence suffered when this capability was revealed to Iran and then made public in 2004 (Wright and Ricks 2004).

The National Reconnaissance Office (NRO) and the National Geospatial-Intelligence Agency (NGA). Although the NRO and NGA are not well known to the American public, both are involved in the imagery subfield of intelligence. This area of intelligence collection has experienced tremendous growth in techniques and sophistication since the end of World War II. In the 1960s, the National Photographic Interpretation Center and the Defense Mapping Agency worked on imagery. In 1996, these agencies and others were merged into the National Imagery and Mapping Agency, which was then renamed in 2004 to bear its current NGA designation.

The NRO was created during the Cold War to help centralize the management of reconnaissance flights. In the late 1950s, the United States developed the U-2 spy plane, a fast, high-altitude jet aircraft designed to fly long distances. The U-2 was equipped with photographic equipment for taking detailed ground pictures and became an important source of early information on Soviet military forces. U-2 flights by the CIA and Air Force intelligence also helped to verify the existence of Soviet intermediate-range missiles in Cuba during the early days of the Cuban Missile Crisis in 1962. After the U-2 pilot Francis Gary Powers was shot down and captured by the Soviet Union in 1960, the NRO was created to better coordinate aerial reconnaissance. Later, as the U-2 and its successor—the Lockheed Blackbird—became increasingly vulnerable to surface-to-air missiles, the NRO began to rely on the use of satellites such as the KH-11 and its successors to obtain military information about the Soviet Union, intelligence for the war on terror, and other data. The most recent versions of these satellites began launching in 2018, and the United States currently plans a new generation of reconnaissance satellites—currently called Blackjack—for 2021.

Today, the NRO is responsible for the development and supervision (via the Air Force and NASA) of high-altitude surveillance mechanisms (e.g., imagery-based intelligence, or IMINT). NGA then processes the raw data acquired from the airborne platforms into imagery products used by the all-source analysts. In recent years, however, reliance on imagery has been called into question. Over the years, flight paths and orbits of satellites have been compromised. As a result, it is not too difficult for those wishing to keep their activities secret to limit their activities when imagery assets are known to be overhead.

The Defense Intelligence Agency (DIA). The DIA was created in 1961 in response to the Bay of Pigs fiasco, where the CIA trained Cuban expatriates to invade Cuba and overthrow Fidel Castro—an operation that failed miserably and led to global condemnation of the United States. The DIA's purpose is to better coordinate the many intelligence activities undertaken by the DOD in the hope of giving the military a single and more influential voice in the government's intelligence process. However, many of the problems that afflict the military establishment also plague the DIA. Staff consist of military and civilian analysts drawn from the individual services and the Office of the Secretary of Defense, requiring that the different subcultures and divided loyalties within the organizations be overcome. The DIA provides the military services and the regional combat commanders (COCOMs) with finished intelligence products focused on their requirements. These requirements are usually tactical in nature, focusing on the composition, disposition, and capabilities of potential military adversaries.

The Military Services. Each of the military services maintains its own intelligence capability. American **military intelligence** consists primarily of service efforts to collect and process tactical military information, including the force structures, tactics employed, and operational capabilities of other military forces—especially those of the Soviet Union after World War II. These include Army Intelligence (G-2), one of the nation's oldest intelligence operations; Air Force intelligence; the Office of Naval Intelligence; the Intelligence Department of the Marine Corps, and Coast Guard intelligence. Recently, the Army and Air Force have developed unmanned aerial vehicles (UAVs), or drones, which now play a more important role in intelligence collection and have been very active in post-9/11 operations in Afghanistan, Iraq, Syria, and elsewhere. Army intelligence has also had a counterintelligence function and an extensive history of involvement in preventing treason, espionage, sabotage, gambling, prostitution, and black marketeering at home and abroad. As discussed in Chapter 5, the Goldwater-Nichols Defense Reorganization Act of 1986 forced the services into a joint operational environment. As a result, the primary customers of military intelligence are currently the COCOMs of the various regional and functional commands. Each COCOM has its own **joint intelligence center** (JIC) that responds to the commander's own needs and makes requests for particular intelligence collection, usually through the DIA.

Non-DOD Organizations

Other cabinet-level departments have their own intelligence activities. Although the most important are under the Departments of State (the Bureau of Intelligence and Research, or INR) and Justice (the FBI and the DEA), other executive branch agencies, such as the Departments of Energy, the Treasury, and Homeland Security (see our discussion later in the chapter), also conduct intelligence activities related to their own areas of interest and are part of the seventeen agencies under the ODNI. Other departments and agencies throughout the executive branch, such as the Department of Commerce, also have intelligence units and engage in intelligence activities in a world of globalization.

The Bureau of Intelligence and Research (INR). The State Department is involved in intelligence work, predominantly in analysis, through its INR. The INR analyzes the department's cable traffic from abroad and information from other agencies in the intelligence community. As one of the producers of finished intelligence, it is actively involved in the process that produces community-wide intelligence estimates (NIEs) and provides advice to the secretary of state and State Department personnel on intelligence matters. Because the INR is so much smaller than the other two producers of finished intelligence (the CIA and the DIA), it is often thought to be the weakest. However, the INR's influence is often a function of the secretary of state. For example, during the Reagan administration, Secretary of State George Shultz (1982–1989) met regularly with the assistant secretary who ran the bureau, but James Baker (1989–1992) rarely did. In 2019, Secretary of State Mike Pompeo also signaled plans to expand State's intelligence analysis by creating a new "cyberbureau" to focus on cybersecurity and cyberattacks.

The Federal Bureau of Investigation (FBI). The FBI is a part of the Department of Justice. It began as the Bureau of Investigation in 1908 and is the oldest governmental organization developed for the purpose of intelligence. It is the intelligence organization with primary responsibility for US domestic counterintelligence and internal security. The FBI is unique not only in its geographic focus on the United States but also in its performance of both domestic-oriented and foreign policy functions, including federal law enforcement, foreign counterintelligence, and internal security against threats to the US government. Long driven by a law enforcement and anti-communist counterintelligence orientation fostered by J. Edgar Hoover, who served as its director from 1924 to 1972 (see Kessler 1994), the FBI underwent a major reorganization after the September 11, 2001, terrorist attacks on the United States to improve its antiterrorism activities. Its intelligence and terrorism elements were reorganized into a National Security division, answerable to both the ODNI and the FBI director. Moreover, the FBI has been working to streamline and better coordinate its own information-sharing procedures, including establishing a unified computer system to collect, manage, and share information on its case files.

The Departments of Energy and the Treasury and the Drug Enforcement Administration (DEA). The Departments of Energy and the Treasury, and the DEA, control intelligence activities focused on their needs. The Department of Energy's Office of Intelligence and Counterintelligence provides technical intelligence analyses on all aspects of nuclear weapons, nuclear materials, and energy issues worldwide. The Department of the Treasury's Office of Intelligence and Analysis was created in 2004 to help safeguard the financial system against illicit use and to combat rogue nations, terrorist facilitators, WMD proliferators, money launderers, drug kingpins, and other national security threats. The DEA's Office of National Security Intelligence provides intelligence on controlled substances laws and regulations of the United States, focusing on illicit traffic and reducing the availability of illicit controlled substances on the domestic and international markets.

The CIA, the ODNI, and Intelligence Coordination since World War II

Since World War II, the CIA has been the principal intelligence organization responsible for national or strategic needs. Until 2005, the CIA was also supposed to coordinate the whole intelligence community, with "**tasking authority**" over intelligence-collecting assets of the entire community to meet national security needs. These coordination and tasking roles have become the responsibility of the DNI since 2004. Now, the CIA's main customers are the DNI, the National Security Council (NSC), and the president, with State, Defense, and other agencies as important consumers as well.

The Central Intelligence Agency (CIA). Created by the National Security Act of 1947, the CIA soon became the best known and most important agency of the foreign policy bureaucracy responsible for intelligence. The CIA has played an important role in the collection and analysis of data, is the primary intelligence organization responsible for counterintelligence outside the United States, and has been the major intelligence organization engaged in political and paramilitary action abroad. Until 2005, in addition to these three intelligence functions, the CIA director was also the DCI—a situation called "**dual-hatting**"—and thus responsible for coordinating the entire intelligence community for the president of the United States (Turner 2005). Since the 2004 intelligence reform law, the DCI position no longer exists: The CIA director is now responsible only for the CIA, while the coordination and tasking roles have passed to the ODNI and its head, the DNI.

The CIA is composed of several main divisions or directorates, which have carried various names over the years. Currently, the main directorates are Analysis (formerly Intelligence), Science and Technology, and Operations (formerly the National Clandestine Service). In 2015, then–CIA director John Brennan reorganized the agency to establish a new directorate—the Directorate for Digital Innovation—to improve strategic and anticipatory intelligence. Among its functions, the new directorate had primary responsibility for cyberespionage. Brennan also reorganized the agency to establish a series of new "mission centers" (Africa, East Asia/Pacific, Europe/Eurasia, Near East, South/Central Asia, Western Hemisphere, Counterintelligence, Counterterrorism, Global Issues, Weapons/Counterproliferation, and, since 2017, a special Korea mission center), each headed by an assistant director. The mission centers integrate the agency's efforts across the directorates. These new centers were modeled after the CIA's Counterterrorism Center, which was established after the 9/11 attacks.

Most current CIA personnel are involved in the Directorate of Analysis. This directorate is principally responsible for producing the CIA's intelligence assessments for the policymaking community and participating in the development of NIEs, which are a product of the entire intelligence community (coordinated by the ODNI). The Directorate of Science and Technology is responsible for developing mechanisms and gadgets used in the type of intelligence activities made most famous in the 007 James Bond movies (though these have always been more science fiction than reality; Richelson 2002). The personnel within the Directorate of Operations are involved in HUMINT and covert operations. The last directorate—the Directorate of Support—assists the other agency directorates in their operations, providing security, supply chains, facilities, financial and medical services, business systems, human resources, logistics, and other areas of support.

The Office of the Director of National Intelligence (ODNI). The newest element of the US intelligence community is the **Office of the Director of National Intelligence (ODNI),** which was established in December 2004 with the passage of the Intelligence Reform and Prevention of Terrorism Act. Headed up by the **director of national intelligence (DNI),** this office was created to establish a central authority for coordination of the seventeen agencies that make up the intelligence community.

The DNI replaces the DCI (director of central intelligence) position, whose occupant is no longer "dual-hatted" and serves only as the director of the CIA. The 2004 reform legislation provided the new DNI with increased authority (compared to the DCI) to coordinate the intelligence community, including greater budgetary control (the DNI prepares a community-wide budget) and enhanced authority over personnel. However, the reform stopped short of providing the new office with complete or exclusive authority over the intelligence agencies of the Defense, State, Justice, Energy, and Commerce Departments, and the relationship between the DNI and the CIA is ambiguous and contentious (Pillar 2010). The ODNI has a staff (which has grown to about 2,000 people) and deputies to assist the DNI (the principal deputy DNI) and to head each of its four directorates (Enterprise Capacity, Mission Integration, National Security Partnerships, and Strategy and Engagement). The DNI also supervises the work of the National Intelligence Council (which produces NIEs) and a number of intelligence centers, including the National Counterterrorism Center, the National Counterintelligence and Security Center, the National Counterproliferation Center, and the Cyber Threat Intelligence Integration Center (Office of the Director of National Intelligence, 2019a; Zegart 2005).

PATTERNS IN THE INTELLIGENCE PROCESS

The rise of a large and complex intelligence community has affected both the intelligence cycle and the intelligence product. As we noted earlier, until 2005, the DCI was responsible for coordination of the entire community as well as the direction of the CIA, but in reality the DCI had direct control only over a small element of the intelligence agencies. In 2003 congressional hearings were held and a "national commission" was created to examine the workings (and failures) of the intelligence community prior to the September 11, 2001, terrorist attacks. The political results of the hearings and the so-called 9/11 Commission report (US National Commission on Terrorist Attacks 2003) was the passage of the **Intelligence Reform and Prevention of Terrorism Act of 2004**

FIGURE 6.3

Intelligence Community after 2005: An Organizational View

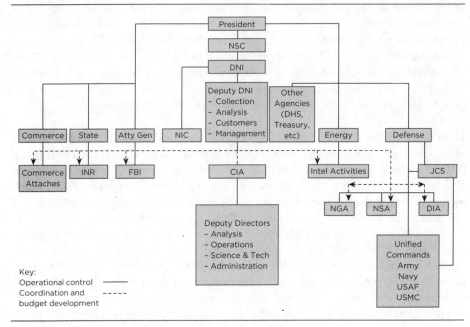

Key:
Operational control ———
Coordination and - - - - -
budget development

(P.L. 108-458), which restructured the intelligence community. Although the consequences of the relatively recent reforms are still evolving, the newly restructured formal
relationships are represented in Figure 6.3.

Several elements of the new structure are particularly important to understand. First, the
ODNI and its director are more central to the intelligence community, with greater budgetary and tasking authority than was provided to the DCI prior to 2005. Second, the director
of the CIA has a diminished role, limited mostly to running a single agency. Additionally,
the CIA director no longer participates in the NSC or its interagency groups unless invited
by the president; that role now goes to the DNI. (President Obama did not make the CIA
director a regular member of the NSC or its interagency subgroups, but President Trump
named both the CIA director and the DNI to his.) Finally, although the 2004 reforms
increase the potential for central coordination, the new structure still clearly reveals the continuing challenges of a sprawling intelligence community. In particular, just like before 2004,
the DNI has continued to face serious challenges in bringing the fragmented intelligence
community together to perform its roles in the policymaking process successfully (Pillar
2010). Three challenges are especially noteworthy: (1) difficulties in achieving coordination,
(2) producer-consumer problems, and (3) variations in intelligence success.

Coordination Problems

The intelligence community has become so large and complex that coordinating the work of
various intelligence organizations in support of the president's foreign policy is very difficult.

As we have seen, this is a recurring theme in the foreign policy bureaucracy. Indeed, calls for reform—and greater centralization—of the intelligence community go back at least to the Nixon administration (Zegart 2005).

The major problem has been a lack of central authority—despite the existence of a formal DCI after World War II. With so much of the intelligence community operating under the DOD, it was inevitable that the people executing the missions within the intelligence community would be more responsive to the DOD's institutional incentives and pressures. The NSA; Army, Navy, and Air Force intelligence; the NRO and NGA; and the DIA are part of the DOD and most of the personnel operate within the military chain of command. As you might already anticipate, this is true for many of the other intelligence agencies: The INR is responsive to the structure and norms of the State Department; the FBI is a semiautonomous agency within the Department of Justice; Homeland Security has its own emphasis, processes, and budget; and so on.

These separate organizations and agencies all have their own reporting lines or channels through their own agency heads, which establishes **stovepipes** between the agencies and top-level policymakers—direct channels from those involved in collection and analysis to high-level policymakers. Hence, rather than bringing different means of collection together and having a coherent and centralized intelligence cycle—in part to ensure that all the relevant information from all the relevant agencies is weighed and finished—each stovepipe allows intelligence to pass through various agencies, depending on the stage of the intelligence process and the particular means of collecting information. So, for example, the Office of the Secretary of Defense can inject intelligence from the DIA or the service intelligence offices directly into policy discussions. It is also possible for the White House to reach directly into one or more intelligence collection/analysis agencies and pull information into policy discussions, avoiding the intelligence community (or even agency) processes.

The 9/11 attacks changed the context substantially, however, and in 2004 the US Congress enacted legislation to try to improve centralization and coordination. As we noted earlier, the principal change instituted by the 2004 reform act was the creation of the ODNI, and the position of the DNI, with greater authority to coordinate the intelligence community. The first DNI—longtime diplomat John Negroponte, who served as UN ambassador for President George W. Bush in his first term—was confirmed in April 2005. He was followed by former NSA director Admiral Mike McConnell in 2007, Admiral Dennis Blair in 2009, and Lt. General James R. Clapper in 2010. Donald Trump named former senator Dan Coats in 2017, who served until August 2019 when he and his principal deputy director, Sue Gordon, were forced out of office by Trump, who grew frustrated with what he regarded as Coats's independence and lack of loyalty to the president. Trump's initial choice to replace Coats—Rep. John Ratcliffe of Texas—withdrew under controversy, and a new nominee had not been named as of the fall. Instead, as the president did in many other cases, an acting DNI was named—Joseph McGuire, who had previously headed the National Counterterrorism Center.

The DNI has the authority to develop the intelligence budget for most of the community (covering about 80 percent of the spending, including that of the Defense Department elements), as well as to transfer funds among agencies to meet priorities. The DNI was also assigned direct control of the National Intelligence Council and the ODNI staff, which play important roles in the coordination of collection and processing of intelligence. Moreover, as we noted earlier, centers on counterterrorism, counterproliferation, and others were established, all of which are under the DNI's authority, even though they are staffed by representatives of the other agencies. Finally, although the DNI has no role in determining the heads of the other agencies, he or she has the authority to approve or disapprove the hiring of key deputy positions across the intelligence community.

Thus, the fallout from the September 11 attacks prompted key structural and procedural changes. However, long-standing bureaucratic practices and the continued fragmentation of separate agencies has complicated this effort at improved coordination. While the new DNI has increased authority and control over some of these subcommunities—especially in wielding budgetary power—change has not been as dramatic as the initial reform legislation might have indicated (Pillar 2010).

For example, because the 2004 intelligence reform act included language confirming the authority of cabinet officials in the intelligence community, the DNI has faced continued challenges. For one, the defense secretary's statutory authority continues to include control over the DIA, NSA, NRO, and NGA, and so represents a major challenge for coordination (Fessenden 2005). Additionally, tensions between the DNI and the CIA also exist. Indeed, in 2006, CIA director Porter Goss was forced out, in large part because of feuding between his office and the DNI (Ackerman 2006). Similarly, in 2009, DNI Dennis Blair and CIA director Leon Panetta clashed over who had the authority to appoint "station chiefs" for coordinating intelligence activities in foreign countries (Baer 2009; Mazzetti 2009).

The successful raid that killed Osama bin Laden in 2011 suggests there are times when intelligence coordination does occur. This operation involved coordination across the intelligence community, including intercepts by the NSA, tracking and imagery analysis by the NGA, and aggressive efforts by the CIA. The actual raid on Abbottabad, Pakistan, involved an elite Navy SEALs team from the Defense Department's Joint Special Operations Command (JSOC), which carried out the ground operation, under the direction of the CIA. As a former CIA official noted, "The Abbottabad raid amounted to 'a complete incorporation of JSOC into a C.I.A. operation'" (Schmidle 2011). However, the ODNI was almost invisible in this effort, which was managed principally by Leon Panetta, who was then director of the CIA. In contrast, the 2019 raid that killed Islamic State leader Abu Bakr al-Baghdadi was led by the Defense Department and its special forces, which coordinated with the CIA and other intelligence agencies to establish and run the successful operation.

The **National Intelligence Council (NIC)** is one of the principal tools through which the DCI, and now the DNI, coordinates the community. The NIC is supposed to assist in the dissemination stage of the intelligence process. The NIC is an interagency organization composed of senior analysts from the various members of the intelligence community. The NIC produces the **National Intelligence Estimates (NIEs)**, intended to be an important product of the intelligence community. The NIEs are one of the few products the intelligence community produces jointly. Yet policymakers often criticize NIEs because they are said to reflect the lowest common denominators agreed upon by the various members of the community. Such compromised intelligence assessments tend to be the order of the day, given the intelligence agencies' different subcultures and perspectives. Originally, under the direction of the DCI, the NIC was transferred to the DNI's office in the 2004 intelligence reform.

The most significant challenge is that the decentralized bureaucratic nature of the intelligence community means considerable independent action is performed by the various intelligence agencies, regardless of coordination efforts at the top. When they do interact, the policymaking process often involves infighting and compromise. During the Cuban Missile Crisis, for example, when the president was trying to verify whether intermediate-range strategic missiles capable of delivering nuclear warheads to the United States were stationed in Cuba, the NRO and the CIA were feuding over which bureaucracy had responsibility for the U-2 flights. U-2 flights were deferred for two days until the NRO and the CIA agreed that they would each be responsible for alternate flights. Thus, crucial information was delayed during a period when the United States and the Soviet Union faced their greatest crisis (Allison 1971).

Historically, coordination in counterintelligence has been an area of particular contention between the FBI and the CIA (Riebling 2002). The cultures of intelligence and law enforcement are vastly different. For the intelligence-oriented CIA, the purpose is policy. For the law enforcement–oriented FBI, the purpose is to convict criminals. Various spy cases have highlighted the lack of coordination between the two organizations. For example, the lack of coordination probably delayed the detection and arrest of CIA double agent Aldrich Ames for years until 1995. In the aftermath of the Ames case, the FBI and the CIA created a jointly staffed counterintelligence office to try to correct the mistakes.

The events of September 11, 2001, however, show there is still much to be worked out. Despite the initial emphasis by the Bush administration and the media on the lack of warning and complete surprise of the terrorist attacks, it is now known that the intelligence community actually had many different pieces of information, but there was poor communication, coordination, and cooperation among a variety of intelligence organizations, especially within the FBI. Subsequent intelligence failures regarding the prewar assessments of Iraq's WMD capabilities also highlighted serious deficiencies in intelligence structures and processes. These problems led directly to congressional hearings and to the 2004 intelligence reform legislation (see "A Closer Look: Intelligence Community Coordination Problems before September 11, 2001").

A Closer Look

INTELLIGENCE COMMUNITY COORDINATION PROBLEMS BEFORE SEPTEMBER 11, 2001

The sprawling intelligence community poses many coordination problems. Consider the following two excerpts about recent events before September 11. They demonstrate the impact of diverging departmental missions, policy preferences and cultures, and coordination challenges that led to demands for reform:

[W]hile the issue of terrorism was rising in importance in every agency with a role to play in guarding against the threat, terrorism remained just one among their many concerns. For the Pentagon, preparing to fight two major theater wars remained the

(Continued)

(Continued)

priority—and in the distance loomed the rise of China and the acquisition of long-range missiles by nuclear-armed rogue states. The customs agents searched luggage and shipments coming across borders—to sniff out illegal drug shipments more than germ weapons. Foreign service officers working their first tour of duty in consular sections of US embassies abroad, and Immigration and Naturalization Services personnel at US ports of entry worried more about preventing entry to people who wished to stay for good than keeping out people who wished to do the United States harm. The FBI tracked federal criminals at home and sought to garner evidence that could stand up in US courts against terrorists abroad, but did not take the initiative to track people who might terrorize our nation. And the list goes on. In each and every case other critical agency functions were, for very understandable reasons, given priority over countering the terrorism threat. (Daalder and Destler 2001)

Looking back on it now, it is difficult to choose the precise moment when US government officials—hobbled by old-fashioned rules, saddled with ancient computers that could not talk to one another and driven by silly bureaucratic rivalries—missed their best chance to thwart the plot by 19 hijackers to take over four airplanes, turn them into flying missiles, and kill almost 3,000 people on September 11, 2001. Was it in early 1999, when the National Security Agency, eavesdropping on a suspected terrorist facility in the Middle East, first learned (but kept to itself) that a 25-year-old Saudi named Nawaf Alhazmi had links to Osama bin Laden? Or was it in March 2000, when the CIA heard from its spies overseas (but did not tell the FBI) that Alhazmi had flown to Los Angeles a few weeks before? Then there was the bungled meeting between the CIA and the FBI in June 2001, when the CIA hinted at Alhazmi's role but would not put everything it knew on the table. Washington may have had one more chance to change history in late August 2001, when FBI headquarters finally heard that Alhazmi and other bin Laden operatives were loose in the United States. But against the advice of detectives in the field, agents at FBI headquarters assigned the case a low priority, and nearly two weeks passed before the bureau asked its Los Angeles field office to track down the suspects. That last e-mail was dated Sept. 11, 2001.

Apart from the terrorists, the biggest enemy the government faced before 9/11 was itself. Agents at both the FBI and the CIA had a longtime habit of stovepiping—keeping information to themselves or sharing it with only a handful of people. That made for good secret-keeping but discouraged critical thinking by the people on the front lines. When an FBI agent in Phoenix, Arizona noticed two months before the attacks that Middle Eastern men were taking flying lessons in his backyard and alerted headquarters that something ghastly might be in the offing, agents in Washington took no action. And a month later, when a group of agents in Minnesota warned that a French-born Moroccan named Zacarias Moussaoui was in the area illegally and trying to learn how to fly a commercial jet, officials at FBI headquarters never put the two warnings together. In the culture of the FBI, agents were not champions at imagining crimes that had not been committed; they were simply supposed to investigate crimes after they occurred. (Duffy 2003)

How does the creation of the ODNI, led by the DNI, help to address these coordination problems, and how does it fail to do so, or even make them worse?

Another consequence of the September 11 attacks was the creation of the Department of Homeland Security. Initially, an Office of Homeland Security (OHS) within the Executive Office of the President was created by President Bush's executive order, with former Pennsylvania governor Tom Ridge as its first director. Planned almost entirely within the White House, "no department heads were asked to join the clique of senior White House aides who planned the redesign. Cabinet secretaries didn't know about the plan until the last minute," including most major foreign policy advisers (Lizza 2002:10–12). The purpose of the OHS was to coordinate and centralize intelligence among the numerous organizations involved (which include dozens of different governmental departments and agencies, plus their interaction with state and local governments) to prevent and respond to security threats against the United States. Despite the authority given to Director Ridge and his ability to report directly to the president, the OHS struggled to gain control over the agencies it was to coordinate. As former national security adviser Anthony Lake noted, to do so, it had to "take powers away from various different agencies that now have them. There is nothing harder in the federal government than doing that" (quoted in Nakashima and Graham 2001:A1).

In June 2002, President Bush asked Congress (at the urging of many members) to increase the prestige and visibility of the OHS by approving its change to a Department of Homeland Security (DHS)—giving it cabinet-level status. Ultimately, the White House and Congress consolidated twenty-two federal agencies and 177,000 employees to form a new department—absorbing the independent Federal Emergency Management Agency (FEMA) and transferring the Customs Service from Treasury, most of the Immigration and Naturalization Service (INS) from Justice, the Transportation Security Administration from Transportation, the Coast Guard from Transportation, and the US Secret Service from Treasury (along with smaller agencies from other departments).

Yet, the DHS has been far from successful. Unlike the OHS, which was part of the Executive Office of the President, the DHS is part of the larger executive branch bureaucracy. In one sense, moving out of a White House office actually dampened the new department's ability to persuade other agencies to participate and collaborate in its efforts. Under the legislation, despite the reorganization and transfer of some agencies to the new department, the most important intelligence agencies involved in antiterrorism—the FBI and the CIA, as well as those in the DOD—maintained their independence and jurisdictional autonomy. By late 2005, observers were calling the DHS experiment a story of "haphazard design, bureaucratic warfare, and unfulfilled promises" and a "bureaucratic Frankenstein" (Crowley 2004; Glasser and Grunwald 2005). Indeed, Michael Chertoff, Ridge's successor as head of the DHS, initiated a sweeping review of the department because of its failures to make progress. More recently, the intense controversy over the DHS response to border security and immigration elevated the criticism of the agency even further, while the inability or unwillingness of the department to address problems of election security and foreign interference fueled concern that the department was less effective than needed.

Furthermore, almost from the outset, former national security adviser Condoleezza Rice (with President Bush's approval) made it clear that the national security adviser and NSC staff (and interagency process) would not report to the homeland security secretary, and in response to 9/11, she beefed up the NSC's antiterrorism unit and staff. President

Obama's first national security adviser, Jim Jones, further "integrated" homeland security functions into the NSC system (DeYoung 2009). Moreover, the 2004 reform act created a new National Counterterrorism Center under the direction of the DNI, further eroding the reach of the DHS. However, in 2011, the Obama administration strengthened the DHS role and autonomy on cybersecurity issues, providing it with the central responsibility and enhanced authority to protect the country's federal civilian electronic networks. Overall, then, although some improvement in cooperation may eventually develop from the creation of the DHS, the reality is that there is now another large bureaucratic organization and layer, as well as additional (and even more complicated) stovepipes within the intelligence process.

In sum, across the intelligence community, decentralization and coordination problems persist in spite of recent reform efforts. Several examples illustrate the continuing problem. First, the new National Counterterrorism Center in the ODNI must contend with the CIA's own counterterrorism mission center, which retains primary responsibility for disrupting terrorist plots and organizations. Second, while the FBI's intelligence and terrorism elements have been reorganized into a National Security division and placed under the authority of the DNI, the new division remains a part of the FBI, and the DNI shares authority with the FBI director, not to mention the attorney general. Third, control and coordination over human intelligence and covert operations have been placed in the hands of the deputy director of operations within the CIA. This individual not only controls the CIA's intelligence operations but also coordinates uniform practices, training, and operations of all human intelligence across the community. This deputy director also reports to both the CIA director and the DNI. Fourth, the Defense Department continues to expand its intelligence activities and has strengthened the role of the Office of the Secretary of Defense in coordinating and directing those activities. Finally, CIA station chiefs in foreign countries are required to report to both the CIA director and the DNI. In short, while the DNI was developed in part to end the practice of "dual-hatting" the CIA director, the new structures and procedures create a number of new "dual-hat" situations that generate additional coordination problems. As an example, Table 6.1 gives an overview of the elaborate bureaucratic war on terrorism. The war on terrorism, especially at home, involves more than forty federal agencies as well as fifty states and hundreds of local governments (and their corresponding officials and agencies). The official list of involved agencies is classified, but the table presents a sample of the major national bureaucratic players and their roles.

Producer-Consumer Problems

The vast array of increasingly effective intelligence-gathering methods has resulted in an explosion of data available to the consumer (i.e., the policymaker). The community now has the ability to easily overwhelm consumers with reams of information. The current challenge posed by the technology and information age is to sort through the volumes of information to produce the relevant finished products to be disseminated to policymakers in various forms. Table 6.2 offers a sample of the voluminous amount of information produced by the intelligence community, providing an overview of the types of products provided to the customers that the intelligence community serves. The problem is not a shortage of assessments but their production and consumption.

TABLE 6.1

Major Federal Agencies Involved in the War on Terrorism

Area	Agency and Functions
National Policy	National Security Council (White House)—coordinates foreign strategy
	Department of Homeland Security—coordinates domestic defense
	Council of Economic Advisers (White House)—coordinates economic recovery
Intelligence	Office of the Director of National Intelligence—coordinates all foreign intelligence
	Central Intelligence Agency—coordinates all human intelligence; deploys spies
	National Security Agency (Defense)—intercepts foreign communications
	National Reconnaissance Office (Defense)—runs spy satellites
	Defense Intelligence Agency (Defense)—coordinates military intelligence
	Special Operations Command (Defense)—scouts hostile territory
	State Department—negotiates with foreign governments
	Federal Bureau of Investigation (Justice)—investigates attacks
	Treasury Department—monitors suspicious financial activity
	Securities and Exchange Commission—monitors suspicious trades
Preemption and Retaliation	Defense Department—stages military strikes
	FBI—arrests terrorists
	Drug Enforcement Administration (Justice)—attacks, e.g., Afghan opium trade
	Treasury Department—freezes terrorist accounts
Border Security	Coast Guard (DHS in peacetime, Defense in wartime)—patrols coasts and waterways
	Immigration and Naturalization Service (DHS)—monitors people entering the United States
	Customs Service (DHS)—monitors goods entering the United States
	North American Aerospace Defense Command (Defense/Canada)—monitors aircraft and missiles
Disaster Preparedness and Response	FBI—coordinates crisis response
	Office for Domestic Preparedness (Justice)—trains and equips local agencies
	Federal Emergency Management Agency—supports, trains, and equips local fire, medical personnel
	Bureau of Alcohol, Tobacco, and Firearms (Treasury)—trains locals in explosives handling
	National Guard (Defense)—provides disaster relief, security
	Joint Task Force, Civil Support (Defense)—coordinates other military assistance
	Health and Human Services Department (DHHS)—assists locals with bioterrorism, mass casualties

(Continued)

TABLE 6.1

(Continued)

Area	Agency and Functions
	Centers for Disease Control and Prevention (DHHS)—detects disease outbreaks
	Environmental Protection Agency—responds to chemical attacks
	Energy Department—responds to radioactive and nuclear attacks
	Agriculture Department—responds to attacks on food supply, crops, and livestock
	Food and Drug Administration—monitors food supply
	Veterans Affairs Department—provides extra hospital space
	Transportation Department—protects transportation infrastructure
	National Infrastructure Protection Center (FBI)—protects computer networks
	Critical Infrastructure Assurance Office (Commerce)—protects computer networks

Source: Sydney Freedberg, Jr. "Shoring Up America," *National Journal*, October 20, 2001, p. 3243; U.S. General Accounting Office, *Combating Terrorism: Intergovernmental Partnership in a National Strategy and Local Preparedness* (March 22, 2002).

There are often serious problems between intelligence "producers"—analysts within the intelligence community—and "consumers"—the policymakers, especially the president and other high-level officials, who use this information to make decisions and justify their policies. From the perspective of the president and other senior officials, the problem is that the intelligence community frequently does not provide actionable intelligence. For the members of the intelligence community, the problem is the ambiguous and contradictory guidelines and expectations of superiors and the president. The president and other policymakers and members of the intelligence bureaucracy occupy different roles, and different motivations influence their behavior.

Consequently, it should not be too surprising that a **producer-consumer problem** is a common part of the intelligence process. Presidents are always sensitive to the domestic political implications of their policies as they try to gain control of the bureaucracy, govern foreign policy, and lead the country. Sometimes, individual presidents and other top advisers are simply not interested in intelligence that challenges strongly held views. According to many public reports, for example, President Trump infrequently participated in daily intelligence briefings in person, did not often read the reports, preferred short bulleted summaries and graphics to longer written content, and frequently disagreed publicly (often on Twitter) with his intelligence advisers and their analyses/information (e.g., Perlmutter-Gumbiner, Dilanian, and Kube 2019; Walcott 2019).

When consumers have not already made up their minds or when they are not strongly leaning in a particular direction, they want relevant information and honest intelligence appraisals to better understand the issue and arrive at an optimal decision. However, when a course of action already has been decided or if consumers are ideologically predisposed, they are likely to want information that reinforces their views. Under either

TABLE 6.2

Selected Products of the Intelligence Community

Category	Product
Current Intelligence Products	*President's Daily Brief* (CIA)
	Secretary's Morning Summary (INR)
	World Intelligence Review (CIA)
	Economic Intelligence Brief (CIA)
	Military Intelligence Digest (DIA)
	Executive Highlights (DIA/NSA)
	Defense Intelligence Terrorism Summary (DIA)
Weeklies/Periodicals/Ad Hoc Publications	*Defense Intelligence Report* (DIA)
	Intelligence Assessment (CIA)
	Terrorist Threat Report (CIA)
	Peacekeeping Perspectives (INR)
Estimative Intelligence Products	*National Intelligence Estimates* (ODNI)
	Intelligence Community Briefs (ODNI)
	Defense Intelligence Assessment (DIA)
	Worldwide Threat Assessment of US Intelligence Community (ODNI)
	National Intelligence Strategy (ODNI)
	Global Trends (NIC)
Warning Intelligence	*Warning Watchlist* (NIC)
	Warning Memoranda (NIC)
	Defense Warning System Reports and Watch Condition Changes (DIA)
Research and Scientific and Technological Intelligence	*The World Factbook* (CIA)
	Handbook of Economic Statistics (CIA)

Source: US Director of Central Intelligence, *A Consumer's Guide to Intelligence*; Intel.gov, "How the IC Works" (https://www.intelligence.gov/how-the-ic-works#key-products-carousel).

of these circumstances, a president or other top adviser may become frustrated with the intelligence product, especially if it is a result of infighting and compromise.

In the bureaucratic and political environment in which the intelligence community operates, it is easy to see how producers can also become frustrated with the intelligence process. The ideal mission of intelligence officers involved in data collection and analysis is to provide a comprehensive and honest assessment of available information. Yet they operate within a bureaucratic setting and must be cognizant of how their work affects their careers. Furthermore, they have to be carefully attuned to the policy inclinations and personal perspectives of higher level officials, such as presidents and their political appointees. CIA director Gina Haspell applied this insight to her interactions with President Trump, attempting to tailor her style and delivery, and even her words, to improve their impact on the president (e.g., Barnes and Goldman 2019). While in principle intelligence analysis should provide policymakers with what they need to make good decisions, not what they want to hear, in many ways

> the analyst is the modern messenger whose penalty for bringing bad news might not be so severe as in ancient times, but who does risk "banishment" of sorts if his conclusions fail to serve a policymaker's need to appear in control of events.... [T]he first commandment for the analyst ... is (and has to be) "Thou Shalt Not Lose Thy Audience." (US National Intelligence Council 2005: xx, xxxvi)

One of the problems analysts face is that they and their consumers may have different priorities as to what issues are important. For example, antiterrorism was not a relatively high foreign policy priority before 9/11, despite the warnings of many analysts. Producers had a difficult time, for instance, getting warnings about the possibility of al-Qaeda attacks into policy discussions at the highest level prior to September 11, 2001. In the current context, producers have struggled to generate attention from the highest levels—especially the president—about the threats to election security from Russia and others. Highly sensitive to the implication that Russian interference affected the 2016 presidential election, President Trump has been unreceptive to such discussions, and the interagency groups of the NSC have barely addressed the issue, despite the consensus in the intelligence community about the seriousness of the problem and its ongoing threat to future US elections. Indeed, although Kirstjen Nielsen (then secretary of homeland security) and other intelligence community leaders sought to bring the issue to the table, public reports from 2019 indicated that Nielsen was told by acting White House chief of staff Mick Mulvaney that it "wasn't a great subject and should be kept below [the president's level" because the president "equated any public discussion of malign Russian election activity with questions about the legitimacy of his victory" (Tapper and Acosta 2019).

Even when producers and consumers share similar priorities, their different perspectives can lead to the **politicization of intelligence**, which occurs when intelligence is slanted to fit the policy preferences or assumptions of key officials. In practice, politicization can occur in at least two ways: (1) when policymakers exert pressure on the intelligence community to produce evidence or finished intelligence that suits their preferences and (2) when policymakers "cherry-pick" from raw intelligence or reports only those pieces of evidence or conclusions with which they agree. In either form, the result is a corruption of intelligence.

As a facet of the producer-consumer problem, politicization has been a long-standing concern, made especially problematic when key intelligence officials such as the DCI are too heavily engaged in policy advocacy, or when policymakers exert too much pressure in favor of policy positions they hold strongly. For example, politicization affected intelligence estimates in Vietnam. According to John Huizenga, chief of intelligence estimates for Soviet affairs during the Johnson administration, "In doing estimates about Vietnam, the problem was that if you believed that the policy being pursued was going to be a flat failure, and you said so, you were going to be out of business" (Ranelagh 1986:455).

The same pattern of the politicization of intelligence plagued the process in the Reagan administration. For instance, Reagan officials pressured the CIA to produce studies concluding that El Salvadoran guerrillas and the Nicaraguan government posed a threat to US security, and compelled the CIA to bring its estimates of Soviet military expenditures and production into accordance with the more pessimistic assessments made by military intelligence. DCI William Casey was especially demanding. Not only was Casey given cabinet rank, but he also was a policy adviser with strongly held policy preferences. According to many, the combination led Casey and others to pressure the CIA to produce evidence in support of Casey's views. For example, Casey exerted considerable pressure on intelligence analysts to conclude that the Soviet Union had been behind the assassination attempt on the Pope in 1981 and equally powerful pressure to conclude that the Soviet Union was a major sponsor and coordinator of terrorism. In the latter instance, Casey eventually demanded a report that reviewed only the evidence in favor of that view and then circulated it as the judgment of his agency (Jeffreys-Jones 1989).

Similar concerns were expressed about pressure from President George W. Bush's administration on the prewar intelligence on Iraq and its possession of WMDs. A leading expert on intelligence, Thomas Powers (2003:12), concludes that "the invasion and conquest of Iraq by the United States" in spring 2002 "was the result of what is probably the least ambiguous case of the misreading of secret intelligence information in American history" by both producers (including the role of DCI George Tenet) and, in particular, by the consumers.

According to Kenneth Pollack (2004:78), who served the United States in the CIA and on the NSC staff for the Reagan, George H. W. Bush, and Clinton administrations, "The intelligence community did overestimate the scope and progress of Iraq's WMD programs, although not to the extent that many people believe. The administration stretched those estimates to make a case not only for going to war but for doing so at once." As Pollack (2004:78–92), whose account is worthy of quoting at length, described it:

> [M]any administration officials reacted strongly, negatively, and aggressively when presented with information or analyses that contradicted what they already believed about Iraq .... Intelligence officers who presented analyses that were at odds with the preexisting views of senior administration officials were subjected to barrages of questions and requests for additional information. They were asked to justify their work sentence by sentence ....
>
> Bush administration officials also ... set up their own shop in the Pentagon, called the Office of Special Plans [OSP], in order to sift through the information on Iraq themselves. To a great extent, OSP personnel "cherry-picked" the intelligence they passed on, selecting reports that supported the administration's preexisting position and ignoring all the rest.
>
> Most problematic of all, the OSP often chose to believe reports that trained intelligence officers considered unreliable or downright false. In particular, it gave great credence to reports from the Iraqi National Congress, whose leader was the administration-backed Ahmed Chalabi ....

[Administration officials were also guilty of] distortion of intelligence estimates when making the public case for war. As best as I can tell, these officials were guilty not of lying, but of creative omission. They discussed only those elements of intelligence estimates that served their cause . . . time after time senior administration officials discussed only the worst-case, and least likely, scenario, and failed to mention the intelligence community's most likely scenario.

The current administration faced similar charges of politicization in a number of areas. One, which we already noted, concerned information about Russian interference in US elections. Another involved reports on the threat of migration and asylum seekers, which appeared to exaggerate connections between immigration and violence/terrorism, despite information from the Departments of Homeland Security and Justice that indicated otherwise. This controversy prompted calls for the public report to be withdrawn (Tatum and Jarrett 2019).

In effect, in these instances, intense preconceptions of senior administration officials were said to have slanted and tainted the honesty of the process responsible for intelligence information and assessments. Clearly, members of the intelligence community often must respond to cross-cutting pressures, and this affects the intelligence process and often contributes to producer-consumer problems (Goodman 1997).

Variation in Intelligence Success

In an ideal setting, the intelligence community is engaged in a precarious business. Even without problems in the producer-consumer relationship and coördination difficulties due to the intelligence community's large size, bureaucratic nature, and complexity, the success of intelligence is not guaranteed. The world is simply too big, too complex, and constantly evolving for information ever to be complete or adequate, while predictions about future behavior and trends can never be more than probabilities.

In fact, ever since the surprise attack on Pearl Harbor in 1941, scholars and analysts have pointed out that there will always be a major **signal-to-noise problem**—in other words, given the vast amount of stimuli and potential information available, it is difficult to sort out the truly relevant information and signals that need to be highlighted, collected, processed, and analyzed. And the environmental and noise problems have grown tremendously over the years. According to Lt. General Michael V. Hayden, who served as director of NSA before becoming the deputy DNI and then the CIA director, "Forty years ago there were 5,000 standalone computers, no fax machines and not one cellular phone. Today there are over 180 million computers—most of them networked. There are roughly 14 million fax machines and 40 million cellphones, and those numbers continue to grow" (quoted in Bamford 2002:5). Of course, the world today is marked by exponentially greater numbers of all these devices!

When one adds the size and complexity of the intelligence community, difficulties in coordination, and producer-consumer problems, a considerable amount of intelligence failure is inevitable in actual practice. The ambiguity of the phenomena to be explained and predicted, the intelligence community's bureaucratic structure, and major policymakers' personalities and beliefs together determine the nature of the intelligence process and the value of the end product. Along with intelligence successes, such as the Cuban Missile Crisis, there will be intelligence failures (Betts 1978; Westerfield 1995).

Critics of the intelligence community's record argue that there have been many major errors. When North Korea invaded South Korea in 1950, it did so with no warning from the intelligence community. Nor did the community warn of the likelihood of Chinese intervention a short time later. A decade later, no systematic warning of the Soviet's move to place missiles in Cuba came before the U-2 over-flights provided photographic evidence in October 1962. During the Vietnam War, key questions involved the strength of the enemy's forces and the ability of the US military to weaken enemy will by destroying enemy personnel and supplies getting into South Vietnam. As noted in Chapter 5, the military and the CIA constantly fought over these intelligence estimates during the mid-1960s, while President Johnson and his closest military and civilian advisers supported the more optimistic military assessments.

In the 1970s, the intelligence community gave no warning of the Egyptian attack on Israel in 1973. Moreover, the size and scope of the Iranian Revolution against the shah of Iran in 1979, as well as the failure of the shah to repress it, was a surprise to members of the government. One reason was the dependence of the intelligence community on official Iranian sources and Savak, Iran's intelligence agency, for information about Iran's domestic situation. The information Savak provided portrayed a stable and vibrant shah regime, even though the domestic opposition was building slowly over the years (Sick 1985).

Critics also argue that the intelligence failed to predict the collapse of the Soviet Union in the late 1980s and early 1990s, while Iraq's attack on Kuwait on August 2, 1990, represented both intelligence failure and success. First, the US intelligence community and policymakers showed little foresight concerning any threat that Iraq posed to American interests. On the contrary, after the rise of Ayatollah Khomeini in Iran, the Reagan and elder Bush administrations supported and sided with Saddam Hussein in the 1980s. Second, as Saddam Hussein's threats against Kuwait increased and he began to mass Iraqi troops along the Kuwaiti border in July 1990, the CIA warned administration policymakers of a possible invasion and predicted that one was imminent twenty-four to forty-eight hours before it occurred. Third, despite this warning, President Bush and his close advisers chose to discount and ignore the warning as unlikely—a classic example of the producer-consumer problem with intelligence estimates. Hence, when the Iraqi invasion occurred, President Bush and his advisers were initially shocked and caught by surprise (Wines 1990).

About a year later, on August 18, 1991, President Bush and other high-level officials of his administration were shocked to learn of the overthrow of Mikhail Gorbachev, the president of the Soviet Union. Yet, according to *Newsweek* (1991:44), "For nearly a year the CIA and the Pentagon's DIA had peppered the Bush administration with a series of increasingly dire warnings that Mikhail Gorbachev's days were numbered. The problem was getting anyone to pay attention." In fact, on August 17, the day before the coup, "the CIA's *National Intelligence Daily* (NID), which circulates among top administration officials, said Kremlin conservatives were prepared to move against the Soviet president." Nevertheless, "until tanks rolled in the streets of Moscow, the White House and the State Department insisted that Gorbachev could weather any challenge." One of the problems was that the State Department's INR maintained that Gorbachev's future was safe. More important, however, it appears that President Bush's commitment to and reliance on Gorbachev in American-Soviet relations, shared by his senior advisers, colored his optimism. Thus, what could have been a great intelligence success ended in an intelligence failure.

Even more recently, the intelligence community's well-publicized failures prior to the 9/11 attacks exposed an unimaginative and uncoordinated counterterrorist program excessively reliant on technical sources. Intelligence and law enforcement officials were tantalizingly close to uncovering the al-Qaeda plot but failed to share information or act aggressively to pursue leads. At the same time, the president and his senior advisers were largely inattentive to repeated warnings issued by the CIA and the NSC's Counterterrorism Strategy Group (Clarke 2004; Eichenwald 2012; Parker and Stern 2005). Subsequently, the failures to provide accurate and reliable assessments of Iraq's programs and capabilities for WMDs further exposed weaknesses in the intelligence process. While senior officials were responsible for politicizing intelligence, and bear some responsibility for the failure, the intelligence community also failed to provide good assessments, basing many of its conclusions on sketchy, controversial evidence. At times, other evidence or points of view were insufficiently weighed or incorporated into the finished products, or raw intelligence was stovepiped into the highest levels without adequate vetting. In the end, as countless postwar reports on the weapons indicate, the prewar claims were almost entirely wrong.

With the advantage of hindsight, it is clear that "the CIA, FBI, and other agencies had significant fragments of information that, under ideal circumstances, could have provided some warning if they had all been pieced together and shared rapidly" (Risen 2001). The **9/11 Commission** investigating the matter details a number of important facts that demonstrate this, including the following: After tracking two identified terrorists abroad and then while they were living in the United States for one year and nine months, the CIA did not notify other government agencies until August 23, 2001. After one of the terrorists' visas expired, the State Department, not knowing any better, issued a new one. In another instance, after being warned by the CIA, the FBI lost track of two suspected terrorists after their arrival in the country and processing by the INS. In January 2001, the Federal Aviation Administration (FAA) issued fifteen memos to the aviation industry warning of possibly imminent hijacking of airliners inside the United States, with two naming Osama bin Laden as a suspect. In a July 5 White House meeting, counterterrorism officials warned the FBI, FAA, INS, and other agencies that a major attack on the United States was coming soon. On July 10, the FBI's Phoenix office warned that an unusual number of Middle Eastern men were enrolling in US flight schools and speculated that they may have been part of an Osama bin Laden plot—but the report was ignored at FBI headquarters. On August 6, President Bush was warned in a *President's Daily Brief* entitled "Bin Laden Determined to Strike in US" about the possibility of al-Qaeda strikes, including the hijacking of airplanes. On August 17, an FBI field office in Minnesota warned that Zacarias Moussaoui might be planning to "fly something into the World Trade Center"—he was arrested, but there was no follow-up FBI investigation. On the day before September 11, the NSA intercepted two cryptic communications that referred to a major event scheduled for the next day, but analysts at the secret eavesdropping agency did not read the messages until September 12 (National Commission on Terrorist Attacks 2003). Recognition of these problems were behind the major shake-up of the intelligence community and other governmental organizations, first in the Homeland Security reorganization, and then in the broader intelligence reforms of 2004.

Within the past few years, other failures have had major consequences. For example, both the CIA and the NSA suffered serious security breaches that resulted in the penetration of some computers and the theft of many of their cyberweapons, which hacking groups then released to the public (Shane, Perlroth, and Sanger 2017). On the NSA side, the penetration was later traced to NSA contractors and their computers, while a CIA employee was behind the breach of the CIA's Center for Cyber Intelligence (Goldman 2018).

Another failure also had far-reaching consequences. According to the March 2019 report of Robert Mueller, the special counsel charged with investigating Russian and US activities surrounding the 2016 election:

> At the same time that the [Internet Research Agency, a Kremlin-linked organization] operation began to focus on supporting candidate Trump in early 2016, the Russian government employed a second form of interference: cyber intrusions (hacking) and releases of hacked materials damaging to the Clinton Campaign. The Russian intelligence service known as the Main Intelligence Directorate of the General Staff of the Russian Army (GRU) carried out these operations.
>
> In March 2016, the GRU began hacking the email accounts of Clinton Campaign volunteers and employees, including campaign chairman John Podesta. In April 2016, the GRU hacked into the computer networks of the Democratic Congressional Campaign Committee (DCCC) and the Democratic National Committee (DNC). The GRU stole hundreds of thousands of documents from the compromised email accounts and networks. Around the time that the DNC announced in mid-June 2016 the Russian government's role in hacking its network, the GRU began disseminating stolen materials through the fictitious online personas "DCLeaks" and "Guccifer 2.0." The GRU later released additional materials through the organization WikiLeaks. (Mueller et al. 2019)

As Amy Zegart, an accomplished analyst of intelligence and national security policy, and Michael Morell, a former deputy director and acting director of the CIA, describe it:

> Russia's multifaceted "active measures" campaign ahead of the 2016 election was designed to undermine public faith in the U.S. democratic process, sow divisions in American society, and boost public support for one presidential candidate over another. Much of this effort did not go undetected for long . . . . But although U.S. intelligence officials knew that Russia had used social media as a propaganda tool against its own citizens and its neighbors, particularly Ukraine, it took them at least two years to realize that similar efforts were being made in the United States. This lapse deprived the president of valuable time to fully understand Moscow's intentions and develop policy options before the election ever began.

[Jeh] Johnson [the secretary of homeland security] later stated that Russia's social media operation "was something . . . that we were just beginning to see." Likewise, [James] Clapper [the director of national intelligence] wrote in his memoir that "in the summer of 2015, it would never have occurred to us that low-level Russian intelligence operatives might be posing as Americans on social media." Indeed, the intelligence community did not understand the magnitude of the attack, which reached more than 120 million U.S. citizens, until well after the election. The Senate Intelligence Committee noted in 2018 that its own bipartisan investigation "exposed a far more extensive Russian effort to manipulate social media outlets to sow discord and to interfere in the 2016 election and American society" than the U.S. intelligence community had found even as late as 2017. (Zegart and Morell 2019)

Given the nature of the intelligence community's structure and processes, the patterns of coordination problems, producer-consumer problems, and variations in intelligence success are likely to continue. "A Closer Look: Intelligence and the Cyber Threat" considers some important challenges facing the intelligence community in the current and future context that are closely related to the matters we have just discussed.

A Closer Look

INTELLIGENCE AND THE CYBER THREAT

Being relevant, timely, and effective, both in operations and in policy roles, is a matter of concern for all parts of the foreign policy bureaucracy. Some analysts and practitioners worry about the capacity of the US intelligence community to meet its current challenges. According to Amy Zegart and Michael Morell (2019), a "moment of reckoning" confronts the US intelligence community as it faces the challenges of dramatic technological changes. In particular, cyber threats are increasingly serious. Barely mentioned before 2012, then–Secretary of Defense Leon Panetta "warned that a 'cyber–Pearl Harbor' could devastate the United States' critical infrastructure without warning" (Zegart and Morell 2019).

And yet, according to Zegart, well-known scholar of the intelligence community, and Morell, former deputy director and twice acting director of the CIA, the most recent National Intelligence Strategy fails to meet these challenges (Zegart and Morell 2019). These observers note that the 2019 strategy strikes "a decidedly complacent tone and contain[s] vague exhortations to 'increase integration and coordination,' 'better leverage partnerships,' and 'increase transparency while protecting national security information.' Much more is needed."

However, Zegart and Morell also stress an important element of continuity:

For all that needs to change, even more important is what should not. The first priority of any transformation effort should be to do no harm to the intelligence community's most valuable asset: its commitment to objectivity, no matter the policy or political consequences . . . .

This core principle is being tested by a president who publicly disparages his intelligence officers and disagrees openly with their agencies' assessments. Such behavior puts pressure on the intelligence community to "call it" the president's way rather than going where the evidence leads. So far, under [former] Director of National Intelligence Dan Coats, the intelligence community [held] firm to its ethos. But the risks are high. The U.S. intelligence community can develop the best strategy for intelligence in a new technological era, but if it ever loses its reputation for objectivity, nonpartisanship, and professionalism, it will lose its value to the nation.

How do the structure, processes, and roles of the intelligence community complicate attempts to adapt and innovate to meet current challenges?

Source: Zegart and Morell (2019).

THE CIA AND COVERT OPERATIONS

The origins of the CIA lie with the operations of the **Office of Strategic Services (OSS)** in World War II. Although the OSS is often remembered for daring operations behind enemy lines under Director William "Wild Bill" Donovan, the office was also engaged in analyzing the enemy using bright, young minds of all ages and diverse backgrounds. The OSS was disbanded following the war, and many of its intelligence activities and personnel were lodged temporarily with the Central Intelligence Group until the passage of the National Security Act of 1947, which created the CIA.

The National Security Act, which made the CIA the major agency responsible for intelligence abroad, was the product of political compromise. Many perceived a need for a foreign intelligence capability during peacetime and supported an agency that could centralize the intelligence process. Others, however, argued against the rise of a super spy agency and saw the centralization as a threat to agencies already involved in intelligence. Therefore, a new intelligence agency was created, but at least one of the two leadership positions, the DCI and deputy director, had to be occupied by a civilian. Both positions had to be confirmed by the Senate, and the DCI reported directly to the president. And, as we have already discussed, although the DCI was given the responsibility for coordinating the intelligence process throughout the government and to act as the major adviser to the president on intelligence matters, the other intelligence agencies retained their autonomy. The act also attempted to clarify jurisdictional boundaries and disputes, restricting the FBI to domestic activities and limiting the CIA's legal role to areas outside US borders.

Although the CIA is heavily involved in all three basic intelligence functions and had the additional responsibility of coordinating the intelligence community until 2005, when most people think of the CIA, they think of spies, covert action, and "dirty tricks." Within the CIA, the **Directorate of Operations** is responsible for the CIA's most renowned activities—covert operations. Operations actually involve two types of activities: espionage and political and paramilitary covert intervention. **Espionage** involves human intelligence and counterintelligence, such as running spies and double agents abroad in order to access information and preventing foreign intelligence agencies from penetrating the CIA. This type of operation received unusual publicity in 2019 when press reports revealed that the CIA had been forced to exfiltrate a source highly placed in the Kremlin who had been providing invaluable intelligence on Russian President Vladimer Putin for a decade or more. This source had provided key intelligence linking Putin himself to the decision to interfere in the 2016 US elections, and the CIA feared that heightened scrutiny and the Trump administration's mishandling of intelligence information might result in the source's exposure (e.g., Barnes, Goldman, and Sanger 2019; Harris and Nakashima 2019). Political and paramilitary **covert intervention** involves a variety of operations, where so-called dirty tricks and coercive force are most commonly practiced.

The division of the CIA into analysis and operations sections involves different—and sometimes competing—subcultures within the agency. The Directorate of Analysis and the Directorate of Science and Technology tend to employ analysts and scientists who often hold doctorates and are research and scholarship oriented. Operations, in contrast, are composed of two different subcultures because espionage and political-paramilitary intervention are two different activities and require different kinds of skills. As one analysis puts it

> On the one hand, the [Directorate of Analysis] is inhabited by well-educated professionals who value academic knowledge and believe the agency's primary role should be to warn, monitor, and forecast through careful research and analysis. On the other hand, the secretive and patriotic members of the Directorate of Operations see risky endeavors like spying and covert action as the CIA's real contribution to national security. This second subculture is so exclusive, however, it has been characterized as a "fraternity of old boys" that is often too accepting of its own members and too intolerant of oversight. (Jones 1998:72)

Indeed, in December 2018, Beth Kimber, a thirty-four-year veteran of the CIA, was named as the first woman to head the Directorate of Operations. (Gina Haspell had been nominated by the Obama administration but her nomination was withdrawn under pressure from the US Senate—she later became the CIA director.)

In fact, even the operations subculture is complicated. Espionage agents act as spies and tend to be secretive, cautious, and loyal. CIA operatives involved in political and paramilitary activities tend to be much more action oriented, adventuristic, bold, and often flamboyant (Hersh 1992). Operations and action types—often referred to as "cowboys"—have dominated CIA leadership through most of its history. For a long time, directors of central intelligence, for example, have tended to come from the operations side of intelligence within the government and military (many of the earlier DCIs were originally with the OSS). For example, the current CIA director—Gina Haspell, the first woman to lead the agency—served in the Directorate of Operations throughout her career, holding positions such as CIA "station chief" in a number of countries and playing a key role in counterterrorism operations after the 9/11 attacks.

American policymakers have relied on CIA covert action as a major US foreign policy instrument since World War II. Since its creation, the CIA and its covert operations evolved through four stages: (1) the "good ol' days," 1947 through the early 1970s; (2) the "fall" and reform, early 1970s to 1979; (3) the resurgence, during the 1980s; and (4) the adjustment, in the post–Cold War and post-9/11 periods (Johnson 2004).

The "Good Ol' Days"

Initially, extensive covert operations were not envisioned. The CIA was created to provide the president with an intelligence capability to engage in data collection and analysis as well as to coordinate the larger intelligence community existing at the time. In fact, "nobody mentioned the Soviet Union or its clandestine services in the congressional debate on the CIA provision of the National Security Act. Congressmen were introspectively concerned with Gestapo-like tendencies at home" (Jeffreys-Jones 1989:41). However, one clause of the CIA charter allowed it to "perform such other functions and duties related to intelligence affecting the national security as the National Security Council may from time to time direct," which provided the later legal justification for involving the CIA in cloak-and-dagger operations.

Soon, presidential directives such as NSC 5412/I on March 12, 1955, called for covert operations "so planned and executed that any U.S. Government responsibility for them is not evident to unauthorized persons and that if uncovered the U.S. Government can plausibly disclaim any responsibility for them" (Jeffreys-Jones 1989:83). As NSC 5412/I stipulated, everything and anything was allowed:

> Propaganda; political action; economic warfare; escape and evasion and evacuation measures; subversion against hostile states or groups including assistance to underground movements, guerrillas and refugee liberation groups; support of indigenous and anticommunist elements in threatened countries of the free world; deception plans and operations; and all activities compatible with this directive necessary to accomplish the foregoing. (quoted in Jeffreys-Jones 1989:83)

Such measures were justified in terms of an anti-communist philosophy and a power-politics, ends-justify-the-means strategy that became the basis of a national security ethos that pervaded American policymaking during the Cold War Consensus.

The top-secret report of the General James Doolittle Committee to the 1954 Hoover Commission on government organization further explained:

> It is now clear that we are facing an implacable enemy whose avowed objective is world domination by whatever means at whatever cost. There are no rules in such a game. Hitherto acceptable norms of human conduct do not apply. If the U.S. is to survive, long-standing American concepts of "fair play" must be reconsidered. We must develop effective espionage and counterespionage services. We must learn to subvert, sabotage and destroy our enemies by more clever, more sophisticated and more effective methods than those used against us. It may become necessary that the American people will be made acquainted with, understand and support this fundamentally repugnant philosophy. (US Congress 1976:9)

Many of these covert operations were so incompatible with the American political culture of liberal democracy that secrecy was of the essence. Often the goal was not really to maintain secrets from enemies abroad; the existence of an operation was often exposed, sometimes deliberately, on the assumption that knowledge of a CIA operation invoked sufficient fear to promote its success. Instead, it was imperative to maintain secrecy at home for fear that leaks would trigger domestic opposition that would place the future of covert operations at risk.

The heyday of covert operations occurred under Director Allen Dulles from 1952 to 1961, a time when his brother, John Foster Dulles, also served as secretary of state (Grose 1995). Even though the president often remained distant from the details of an operation, the DCI responded to presidential initiative and choice. Also, no real oversight existed outside the executive branch, as Congress generally preferred to remain on the sidelines in deference to presidential leadership and the Cold War Consensus (Barrett 2005). It has been reported that, by 1953, the CIA had major covert operations in progress in forty-eight countries, while three fourths of the agency's budget and two thirds of its employees were devoted to espionage and political intervention (Ransom 1983:303). A US Senate select committee investigating foreign and military intelligence in 1975 found that the CIA had "conducted some 900 major or sensitive covert action projects plus several thousand smaller projects since 1961" (US Congress 1976:445). In other words, the CIA, in its heyday, was engaged in covert operations all over the world, with as much as one third of its interventions taking place in "pro-Western" democracies (Jeffreys-Jones 1989:51). Table 6.3 highlights some of the major covert operations during the "good ol' days" that have come to light, although much CIA covert activity remains unknown.

The examples of CIA covert operations in Table 6.3, along with other covert activities in which the United States engaged, generally fall into seven categories:

- *Manipulating foreign democratic elections*. In both Italy and France in 1948, for example, the United States worried that the economic and political instability after World War II, which strengthened legal communist parties in those countries, would eventually result in electoral victories for those parties. Consequently, the CIA engaged in a variety of efforts to undermine the communists and strengthen the centrist parties.

- *Organizing partisan resistance movements*. In the late 1940s and 1950s, the CIA also supported partisan resistance movements in communist countries to promote internal instability and domestic uprisings. For example, the CIA trained emigrés and secretly transported them into Albania, Poland, Yugoslavia, the Baltic states, Soviet Georgia, and the Ukraine.

- *Overthrowing foreign governments*. Under President Eisenhower, the CIA became involved in a series of efforts to overthrow foreign governments. Such efforts include the Iranian coup of 1953 to overthrow the Iranian nationalist leader Mohammad Mossadegh and restore the Pahlavi dynasty, headed by the shah (Bill 1988) and the 1954 coup in Guatemala to overthrow democratically elected President Jacobo Arbenz and replace him with a military dictator, General Castillo de Armas (Immerman 1982; Schlesinger and Kinzer 1982).

TABLE 6.3

Major CIA Covert Operations During the "Good Ol' Days"

Year	Operation
1947–1948	Propaganda campaign during the 1948 Italian national elections
1947–1948	Propaganda campaign during the 1948 French national elections
1948–1952	Partisan resistance movements in Eastern Europe and Soviet Union
1949	Anglo-American effort to overthrow the Albanian government
1950–1970s	Propaganda campaigns through Radio Liberty and Radio Free Europe
1952–1960	Kuomintang (KMT) Chinese partisan resistance movement on Sino-Burmese border
1953	Anglo-American overthrow of Prime Minister Mohammed Mossadegh of Iran
1953–1954	Campaign to support Ramon Magsaysay's presidential candidacy and counter Huk insurgency in Philippines
1954	Overthrow of democratic President Jacobo Arbenz of Guatemala
1950s–1970s	Subsidization of domestic and foreign groups and publications
1953–1970s	Drug testing and mind-control program
1954–1970s	Effort to overthrow leader Ho Chi Minh and the North Vietnamese government
1955	Effort to destabilize President José Figueres's government of Costa Rica
1958	Support of Tibetan partisan resistance movement in China
1958–1965	Effort to destabilize President Sukarno of Indonesia
1960	Alleged effort to assassinate General Abdul Kassem, leader of Iraq
1961	Alleged effort to assassinate President Abdul Nasser of Egypt
1960s	Alleged effort to assassinate political leader Patrice Lumumba of Congo
1962–1963	Effort to overthrow Fidel Castro, leader of Cuba
1963	Effort to assassinate Rafael Trujillo, leader of Dominican Republic
1964	Effort to destabilize President Kwame Nkrumah of Ghana
1967	Effort to assassinate Fidel Castro of Cuba
1967–1970s	Fought secret war in Laos
	Conducted pacification and Phoenix programs in Vietnam
	Destabilized the Ecuadorean governments of Ibarra and Arosemena
	Destabilized Prime Minister Cheddi Jagan's government of British Guiana
	Supported overthrow of President Ngo Dinh Diem of South Vietnam
	Campaign in support of President Eduardo Frei in 1964 Chilean elections
	Supported military coup against President Joao Goulart of Brazil
	Supported military coup in Greece
	Domestic campaign against antiwar movement and political dissent
1970–1973	Destabilized democratic Chilean government of President Salvador Allende

Source: Jeffreys-Jones (1989); Kwitny (1984); Powers (1979); Prados (1986); Ranelagh (1986); Wise and Ross (1990); US Congress, Senate, *Alleged Assassination Plots Involving Foreign Leaders,* Congressional Report (94th Cong., 1st sess., November 18, 1975); and US Congress, Senate, *Final Report of the Select Committee to Study Governmental Operations with Respect to Intelligence Activities,* Books 1–6, Congressional Report (94th Cong., 2nd sess., April 14, 1976).

- *Participating in foreign assassinations.* During this period, the CIA engaged in plans to assassinate foreign leaders. Later investigations revealed efforts to kill such leaders as Patrice Lumumba, prime minister and national leader of the Congo (Zaire); Fidel Castro in Cuba; and the democratically elected socialist president Salvador Allende in Chile. With respect to Castro, for example, most were hair-brained schemes that only James Bond could have pulled off, such as attempts to slip Castro the hallucinogen LSD via a cigar, to give him a pen with a poison tip, to explode clamshells while he dove in the Caribbean, and to sprinkle his shoes with an agent to make his beard fall out and with it, according to the psychological warfare experts, his Latin machismo (Jeffreys-Jones 1989:132). The CIA even went so far as to turn to the Mafia for assistance to kill him. Most of these assassination efforts were unsuccessful, although Lumumba was assassinated eventually, clearing the way for the US-backed dictator—Mobutu Sese Seko—who ruled a corrupt regime for thirty years and impoverished the country (Kalb 1981), and Allende was eventually removed from power three years after one of his top supporters in the military, General Rene Schneider, was assassinated. The CIA also conducted the infamous **Phoenix program**, during the Vietnam War, which targeted thousands of suspected Vietcong and communist supporters for "neutralization." Not only were many innocent individuals jailed, but torture, terrorism, and assassination were also used as part of the Phoenix operation.

- *Supporting friendly, often authoritarian, governments.* The CIA also supported foreign governments allied to the United States in such places as Iran, Cuba (before Fidel), Nicaragua, and elsewhere, often participating in an allied government's violent repression of its own people. For example, in Indonesia, after actively destabilizing President Sukarno (like many Indonesians, he had only one name), a prominent leader of the Third World nonaligned movement beginning in 1958, the CIA then actively supported his successor after Sukarno's ouster. The CIA then assisted the new government of General Suharto in eliminating Indonesian Communist Party members and repressing all internal dissent, which included providing the Indonesian army with lists of people to be arrested and killed—estimated as high as 2 to 3 million people (Bleifuss 1990; Smith 1976). In South Africa, the CIA supported the "White" apartheid regime, even providing the regime with a tip from a "deep cover" CIA agent that led to the August 5, 1962, arrest of Nelson Mandela, the underground leader of the African National Congress (ANC), the major force opposing the Afrikaner government and the system of apartheid (Albright and Kunstel 1990).

- *Training foreign military, intelligence, and police personnel.* The CIA also frequently offered "retainers" to foreign leaders, putting them on the CIA payroll, and the CIA frequently engaged in training of foreign intelligence personnel, including those engaged in covert operations. The armed forces and the national police of many governments allied with the United States also were trained by US military and government personnel.

- *Pursuing various covert actions at home against American citizens.* The CIA spent millions of dollars funding hundreds of private individuals and groups active in business, labor, journalism, education, philanthropy, religion, and the arts as a means to promote the anti-communist message and stifle dissent against the US policy of containment (US Congress 1976:179–204). In domestic covert operations, the CIA opened the mail of American citizens, kept more than 1.5 million names on file, and infiltrated religious, media-related, and academic organizations; the FBI carried out more than 500,000 investigations of so-called subversives without a single court conviction and created files on more than 1 million Americans; the NSA monitored cables sent overseas or received by Americans from 1947 to 1975; Army intelligence investigated more than 100,000 American citizens during the Vietnam War era; and the Internal Revenue Service allowed tax information to be misused by intelligence agencies for political purposes. Paranoia about threats to security in the late 1950s was so great that Project MKULTRA (pronounced "m-k-ultra") was created to explore "brainwashing" techniques that involved mind-control experiments on human beings (Donner 1981).

The "Fall" and Reform during the 1970s

The failure of Vietnam politicized segments of American society and contributed to the collapse of the anti-communist consensus. The domestic political environment became even more critical when the revelations of Watergate uncovered abuses of presidential power. A period of intense scrutiny ensued. President Ford appointed the Rockefeller Commission in 1975 to investigate the intelligence community and recommend reforms. However, while the Rockefeller Commission was operating, President Ford and Secretary of State Henry Kissinger were supervising a major CIA covert operation in Angola. Ford and Kissinger tried to keep the operation secret from Congress at a time when members of Congress were reasserting their authority in foreign affairs. When word of the Angolan operation leaked, Congress voted to abort it and began its own investigation of intelligence (Stockwell 1978).

The House and the Senate each conducted major investigations of the intelligence community and covert operations. The Pike Committee and Church Committee investigations (named after the chairman of each chamber's Foreign Relations Committee) led to the first public knowledge of the scale of covert operations conducted by the CIA. In this political climate, the intelligence community, especially the CIA and covert operations, experienced a major decline. During this time, more than 1,800 covert operatives were fired or forced to take early retirement, and most covert operations were cut, including major political and paramilitary programs. Congress also asserted itself in oversight. For example, in the 1980 Intelligence Oversight Act, it established new, permanent **intelligence committees** in both chambers and required the submission to Congress of a **presidential finding**, explaining the need for and nature of any covert actions. Presidential executive orders were issued that limited the kinds of covert operations the CIA could conduct, such as forbidding US governmental personnel from becoming involved in political assassinations. The net impact was that the use of covert operations as a tool of US foreign policy, and morale among covert operatives, reached its nadir by the end of the 1970s (Johnson 1989, 2005).

Resurgence in the 1980s

Beginning in 1980, the CIA and covert operations got a new lease on life. The resurgence of the CIA began during the last year of the Carter administration, when President Carter approved a major covert operation to send money and arms to the Afghan resistance forces fighting the Soviet occupation through US-controlled sources and agents in Pakistan and Saudi Arabia (Coll 2004). It was under the Reagan administration, however, that the CIA and the use of covert operations became a major force in US foreign policy, reminiscent of the Cold War days. Under William Casey, a strident anti-communist and former member of the OSS during World War II, the CIA rejuvenated its operations division and rehired many former covert operatives. Although the CIA's budget remained secret, experts believe that it may have grown more than 20 percent a year during this time—a faster rate of growth than that experienced by the military in its buildup and at a time when efforts were made to impose domestic spending cuts (Taubman 1983).

Under Casey, the CIA launched over a dozen "major" covert operations (defined by the congressional intelligence committees as an operation costing more than $5 million or designed to overthrow a foreign government) in places such as Central America, Angola, Libya, Ethiopia, Mauritius, Cambodia, Afghanistan, and Iran. Major operations included a huge CIA Afghanistan operation to support insurgents—known as the *mujahideen*— against the invading Soviet military, and a campaign to destabilize and overthrow the new Nicaraguan Sandinista regime. In Nicaragua, the covert Contra war was eventually outlawed by Congress in 1985 and 1986. Nevertheless, the Reagan administration circumvented the law by pursuing the Contra operation through the NSC staff and relying on private operatives and groups, triggering a crisis of governance for the Reagan presidency when the true nature of the Contra covert operations became exposed (Kagan 1996; Scott 1996). In Afghanistan, through Pakistan and Saudi Arabia, the CIA provided billions in support for arms and training, and played an important role in helping the insurgents force the Soviets to withdraw and the Taliban regime to take power, although it also inadvertently helped to create the al-Qaeda network that would plague the United States later (Coll 2004; Scott 1996).

Adjusting to the Post–Cold War and Post-9/11 Era

According to Theodore Draper (1997:18),

> Of all the organizations that miss having the Soviet Union as an enemy, the CIA has undoubtedly been hit the hardest. The reason is that the CIA was specifically established in 1947 to struggle with the Soviet enemy . . . . But now the enemy has vanished. Its most dedicated American antagonist has been deprived of its mission . . . . [Now], the CIA wanders about in a wilderness of self-doubt and recrimination.

Recent years have not been much kinder, as the spectacular failures of September 11 and Iraq left the CIA reeling. One analysis concluded that the CIA has "lost its place and standing in Washington," while a CIA veteran reacted to the 2004 intelligence reforms by saying, "The agency, as we know it, is gone" (Gorman 2005; Risen 2006:220). Yet in late 2005, the CIA's central role in collecting human intelligence and carrying out and coordinating covert operations was confirmed with the strengthening of the Directorate of Operations. And, since 9/11, the agency's covert antiterrorist programs have grown into the largest covert action program since the height of the Cold War.

In the Post–Cold War Years. The Cold War's end ushered in a set of challenges for the CIA and its covert action mission, which appeared much less central to US foreign policy without the Cold War's context. Consequently, while the CIA sought new missions in the post–Cold War context, its budget growth first slowed under George H. W. Bush and then began to decline under Bill Clinton. At the same time, challenges to CIA activities began. Congress attempted to enact tighter controls over covert action, but the elder Bush vetoed the legislation in 1992. Not long after, New York senator Daniel Patrick Moynihan sponsored legislation to eliminate the CIA entirely. Between 1990 and 2001, a spate of studies—some from Congress, some from special commissions, and some from policy think-tanks—all recommended reforms of the intelligence community (Commission on the Roles and Capabilities of the United States Intelligence Community 1996; Council on Foreign Relations 1996; US House of Representatives, Permanent Select Committee on Intelligence 1996).

In the midst of this turmoil, the CIA continued some traditional covert operations and added some new actions as well. For example, the CIA applied its traditional instruments in the 1990s against Iraq and Kosovo. In Iraq, starting with a Bush administration finding that authorized efforts to destabilize the Iraqi economy in 1990 (after the Iran-Iraq War), the CIA engaged in a series of efforts to undermine Saddam Hussein, none of which was particularly effective. Under President Clinton, for example, the CIA supported the "Iraqi National Congress," spending about $120 million seeking Hussein's assassination or overthrow. These operations collapsed when the resistance was infiltrated by Hussein's forces, although the United States committed itself to "regime change" in Iraq again in 1998. In Kosovo in 1999, the CIA launched a campaign against Serbia and Slobodan Milošević that combined propaganda, destabilization, support of opposition groups, and other methods to undermine the regime (Godson 2000; Johnson 2000; Risen 2000).

At the same time, the CIA took up a role in new areas as well, including drug trafficking, economic intelligence, and counterterrorism. On the drug war, the CIA began to cooperate with other agencies, including the FBI and the DEA, to break up drug rings. The CIA also increased its activities in the highly controversial arena of economic espionage, not only collecting information on trade practices but even attempting to steal trade secrets. Finally, with rising concerns about terrorism after the 1993 World Trade Center bombing, the CIA accelerated its counterterrorism operations as well. Although some success occurred, the attacks in 1998 on US embassies in Kenya and Tanzania, the 2000 bombing of the *USS Cole* in Yemen, and, of course, the September 11 attacks amply demonstrate the limits of these efforts (Baer 2002; Naftali 2005).

After September 11, 2001. The attacks of 9/11 initiated a new season for the CIA and its covert operations mission. Just a few days after the attack, George W. Bush signed a presidential finding starting what has grown into the largest covert operation since the heyday of the Cold War, dwarfing even the decade-long Afghanistan operations of the 1980s. In addition to activities in advance and support of US operations in Afghanistan and Iraq, the CIA began a host of interrelated programs to break up terror cells, assassinate terrorists, capture and interrogate al-Qaeda suspects, gain access to and disrupt financial networks, eavesdrop, and engage in a variety of other activities (Clarke 2004; Risen 2005; Schroen 2005). The CIA budget for covert operations was nearly doubled to almost $50 billion and, for the first time in a decade, the CIA began to expand its operations directorate as well. The counterterrorism center at the CIA more than doubled in size, becoming the epicenter of covert actions against terrorism (Pincus 2001).

The administration sought and received broad grants of authority to conduct its war on terrorism, and it authorized even broader activities by the intelligence community. The administration and Congress rushed the **USA Patriot Act** through and dramatically expanded the intelligence and investigative powers of the government. Little congressional oversight occurred either, as Congress deferred to the administration in the atmosphere of national security urgency. This began to change in 2003 and 2004 when certain intelligence practices were revealed and became politicized, such as US involvement with torture.

The year 2004 saw renewed concern for democratic norms due to a series of revelations stemming from several highly controversial programs intended to thwart the growing insurgency in Iraq and engage in the war on terror. These revelations included (1) decisions about the treatment of prisoners, which allowed harsh treatment, even torture, in US facilities in Guantanamo Bay, Iraq, Afghanistan, and elsewhere in violation of both domestic and international laws as described earlier; (2) the establishment and operations of secret CIA-run prisons in other countries; and (3) most controversial of all, spying activities at home that impact American citizens' civil liberties, including intrusive information gathering, "fishing expedition" investigations by the FBI and Army intelligence, and extensive eavesdropping by the NSA (Baker 2005; Gellman and Linzer 2005; Isikoff 2006; Risen 2005).

At the same time, however, the CIA came under criticism for its failures to prevent the September 11 attacks and then, later, for its role in the prewar Iraq intelligence fiasco. A number of investigations issued scathing reports of CIA failures. Additionally, as some of the covert actions become public—especially the CIA programs for assassination, capture, and interrogation, and its secret "rendition" prison system abroad—heightened scrutiny occurred. Hence, by 2006, a number of developments combined to reverse the initial exuberance: major intelligence reform weakening the CIA's role; sagging morale from the failures of the previous five years; leadership turnover and infighting among careerists and appointees; new organizational rivalries between the CIA and the ODNI; and new challenges from the Defense Department for roles in covert operations. Indeed, the revelations of controversial torture, assassination, and surveillance programs that were deliberately concealed from Congress and the American people generated outcries and calls for full investigations (Kane and Pershing 2009). See "A Different Perspective: Checks and Balances and the Intelligence Community—A View from Congress" for the viewpoint of one member on these matters.

A Different Perspective

CHECKS AND BALANCES AND THE INTELLIGENCE COMMUNITY: A VIEW FROM CONGRESS

Congresswoman Jane Harman (D-CA), former chair of the House Intelligence Committee, shared her concerns about encroachments on the congressional oversight role of the intelligence community in a 2009 opinion piece in the *Los Angeles Time* (Harman 2009). Harman was the ranking member on the House Intelligence Committee from 2003 to 2006 and thus part of the "Gang of Eight"—the House and Senate leaders required by law to receive information about CIA covert actions.

According to Harman, the briefings on a highly secretive program known as the "Terrorist Surveillance Program" were held about four times a year in the White House Situation Room and delivered by Michael Hayden, former director of the NSA and the CIA, along with other CIA officials and Alberto R. Gonzales, who was the White House counsel at the time. However, far from thorough and accurate, the briefings Harman described were quite limited, even misleading,

and the Justice Department did not participate. As Harman (2009) put it, "It is now clear to me that we learned only what the briefers wanted to tell us—even though they were required by law to keep us 'fully and currently informed.'" Harman concluded forcefully:

> Security and liberty are not a zero-sum game. Our Constitution protects both. Members of each branch of government take an oath to uphold the Constitution. Bipartisan oversight by Congress to assure that the laws we pass are faithfully executed is an indispensable part of that equation.

How much should the US Congress be involved in such intelligence policy matters in order to maintain democratic accountability?

Source: Jane Harman, "What the CIA Hid from Congress." *Los Angeles Times,* July 25, 2009.

However, under President Obama, the CIA continued a variety of covert actions in the war on terror. As we discussed earlier, aggressive efforts were made to locate Osama bin Laden and other al-Qaeda leaders, including the highly publicized and successful May 2011 raid in Pakistan that resulted in bin Laden's death. Additionally, under CIA director Leon Panetta and his successors, the CIA expanded its use of drones to strike terrorist targets. This program was first expanded in Pakistan and involved what the CIA called "profile" strikes (involving drone attacks on a specific individual) and "signature" strikes (involving more general targeting of groups and suspicious activities). For example, while a profile attack might kill an al-Qaeda leader traveling in a vehicle, a signature attack might target a funeral of a known al-Qaeda leader, "on the grounds that attending an al-Qaeda funeral is evidence of hostile intentions toward the United States .... [I]f the US slaughters a particular crowd of people at an al-Qaeda funeral, they are sure to kill men plotting to attack the United States" (Morley 2012). Highly controversial within US interagency discussions, and with US allies such as Pakistan, **drone strikes** were soon expanded into

Yemen, and then to other places. For example, the United States carried out drone strikes in Syria as US activities against the Islamic State and in the Syrian civil war expanded, especially after 2014. However, the administration later took steps to curtail drone strikes elsewhere when reports of civilian casualties increased. The Obama administration also initiated a program to arm and train Syrian rebels to fight against the Assad regime.

Although the Trump administration developed a tense relationship with the US intelligence community, in particular because of the community's role in exposing Russian interference in the 2016 US elections, the administration continued to rely on covert operations as part of its counterterrorism strategy. The Trump administration canceled the covert operation to arm and support Syrian rebels, but it dramatically expanded the strategy of drone strikes, accelerating their use in the Middle East and extending them to countries in Africa as well (Penney et al. 2018). The Trump administration also expanded "direct action" by the CIA and the US military as part of its counterterrorism policies (Tankel, 2018).

THE INTELLIGENCE COMMUNITY AND US FOREIGN POLICYMAKING

The intelligence community plays a significant role in the formulation and implementation of US foreign policy. At the same time, it remains heavily influenced by powerful bureaucratic functions, structures, and subcultures that have developed over time, and problems of coordination, producer-consumer challenges, and intelligence failures continue to plague it. The collapse of the Soviet Union and the end of the Cold War in 1989, and the subsequent challenges generated by the post-9/11 war on terrorism, represented a historic opportunity for some serious rethinking of the role of intelligence in American society and US foreign policy. For example, how large and what kind of an intelligence community is required in the complex environment of the twenty-first century? What type of intelligence and counterintelligence activities does the government require? How much accountability and independence (and secrecy) should be required or allowed? How can the sprawling intelligence community be better organized and coordinated to improve its ability to provide essential information to policymakers? Adapting the intelligence community and its activity to the demands of the twenty-first century remains difficult and elusive. Areas of progress and success continue to be matched by shortcomings. Given the long tension between intelligence needs and intelligence capabilities, these dilemmas are not likely to disappear, and the role and influence of the intelligence community as a key part of the foreign policy bureaucracy remains a key question in US foreign policymaking.

THINK ABOUT THIS

The sprawling intelligence community is often characterized as the "eyes and ears" and "sword and shield" of the foreign policy bureaucracy. Think about the nature of the intelligence community and its role in US foreign policymaking.

What are the central challenges of coordination and decentralization in the intelligence community and what are their implications and consequences?

KEY TERMS

Visit **edge.sagepub.com/scottrosati7e** to help you accomplish your coursework goals in an easy-to-use learning environment.

Managing the Foreign Policy Bureaucracy

THE NATIONAL SECURITY COUNCIL SYSTEM

7

PHOTO 7.1 Then–national security adviser John Bolton meeting with President Donald Trump and Secretary of State Mike Pompeo.

Andrew Harrer/Bloomberg/Getty Images

LEARNING OBJECTIVES

1. Know the importance of organization and management for the foreign policy process

2. Identify the features and components of the National Security Council system

3. Understand the key patterns in the evolution of the NSC system.

4. Describe the nature and role of the national security adviser in the NSC system.

The nature of the presidency and size and complexity of the foreign policy bureaucracy present challenges for White House leadership in the foreign policymaking process. The nature and roles of the foreign policy bureaucracy we detailed in the previous three chapters make presidential management particularly important. Setting the general direction and tone of an administration, however, does not guarantee that a president's vision and priorities will prevail. In fact, much of the government's foreign policy is made and carried out by the bureaucracy. So, White House leadership in foreign policy depends in part on management and coordination of the foreign policy bureaucracy. Indeed, a central lesson of the post–World War II foreign policy process involves the need for active and organized management. But, how can a president manage the sprawling and decentralized bureaucracy with all its parts and perspectives in order to provide direction and leadership?

Since World War II, the principal instrument for organizing and managing the foreign policy process has been the National Security Council (NSC) system. Moreover, as the foreign policy bureaucracy has grown over the decades since World War II, presidents increasingly have concluded that the NSC system itself requires active White House leadership.

ORGANIZING AND MANAGING THE POLICY PROCESS

Let's begin with a simple starting point for understanding the importance of the NSC system to the management of executive branch foreign policymaking. As Robert Cutler (1956), national security adviser to President Eisenhower, once put it, it's useful to think of the policy process as a "policy hill." Moving up the hill on the left side, information is gathered and weighed, and options are formulated. At the top of the hill, options are considered, and decisions are made. Moving down the hill on the right side, those decisions are implemented and monitored, with evaluation and problem identification linking back to the left side of the hill, where the process might start again.

At each of these stages, organization and management is necessary for effective foreign policymaking. As we have seen in the past three chapters, the agencies of the foreign policy bureaucracy are central to the formulation and implementation sides of the hill. Their roles and contributions at the top of the policy hill are also significant, as they shape information and options, and many of the core advisers to the president represent and lead the bureaucratic agencies. Because of the complex and far-flung foreign policy bureaucracy and its specialization and (often) competing subcultures and roles, coordination and cooperation is not the default. As a result, active efforts are needed to overcome the bureaucratic "pathologies" we discussed in Chapter 4.

Since the 1947 National Security Act, the NSC system has been the focal point for the management of executive branch foreign policymaking. Within the NSC system, a president's success in managing the foreign policy bureaucracy is very much a function of (1) the president's foreign policy orientation, agenda, and level of involvement and (2) the organization of the foreign policymaking process (Edwards and Wayne 2005).

The President's Orientation, Agenda, and Level of Involvement

The president's beliefs and worldview set the general direction and foreign policy orientation for the administration. Presidents try to set goals and promote policies that reflect their foreign policy orientation and agenda. This is critical because the role of the bureaucracy is too important to be left to chance; presidents must be attentive to and actively involved in the bureaucracy's operations to ensure that US foreign policy during their administration accords with their preferences. As Brent Scowcroft, who served as national security adviser to both President Ford and the first President Bush, suggested, "The NSC system was really developed to serve an activist president in foreign policy" (National Security Council Project 1999a:35). The more a president is attentive to and involved in what goes on throughout the executive branch, the better the chance for effective management and direction of the bureaucracy.

As we saw in Chapter 3, presidents have varying styles, with some more hands-on and attentive to details, and others more disengaged and focused on the "big picture." Presidents with very different styles may each be successful leaders, but active management of and involvement in the policy process is necessary for effective foreign policymaking. So, less engaged presidents need staff and structures that provide the attentiveness and involvement, while more engaged presidents need staff and structures that facilitate timely decision-making. As one observer summarized, "The purpose of the NSC is not to make the president conform to the NSC, but to make the federal government enhance the way a president gets to good decisions" (James Carafano, quoted in Toosi 2019).

Because the bureaucracy is so large and complex, a president must be selective, setting agendas and prioritizing issues, given time and information constraints. The president must understand that the bureaucracy will be most responsive to those issues and agenda items that matter most to—and get the most attention from—the White House. General "policy reviews," especially at the beginning of a new administration; involvement in the policy-making process; and "presidential speeches" offer unique opportunities for the president to gain control over the bureaucracy and foreign policy (Goldgeier 2000).

Organization of the Policymaking Process

Ultimately, the president must rely on others to exercise presidential leadership and manage the bureaucracy. Hence, the choice of presidential staff and advisers and their roles and behavior in the policymaking process are absolutely critical. The president must decide who will staff the administration and how they will interact. This is important to keeping the president informed, enabling the president to make decisions, and making sure that those decisions are faithfully implemented. The president cannot assume when taking office that the policymaking system in place will automatically do these things or manage the bureaucracy effectively. On the contrary, presidents who want to manage the bureaucracy, as opposed to responding to bureaucratic momentum, must establish an effective structure and policy process that fits their personal style and responds to their own priorities. As President Obama advised President-elect Donald Trump in November 2016, "How you set up a process and a system to surface information, generate options for the president, understanding that ultimately the president is going to be the final decision maker, . . . that's something that's going to have to be attended to right away" (quoted in Beutler 2016).

While organizing the policymaking process, the president must make a number of important decisions about structure and process. A key choice is whether to rely on the White House or a lead agency (e.g., the State Department) to be responsible for coordinating the foreign policy process. Another important choice is whether to have only a few individuals who are allowed to act in the president's name responsible for the overall conduct of foreign policy or to have power more decentralized throughout the foreign policy bureaucracy. Finally, presidents also choose what level of access to the Oval Office different policymaking officials in the process should have.

Decisions about these issues determine how the foreign policymaking process will operate. If the president, or the president's personal staff, is reluctant to be involved in influencing the policymaking process, policies will soon develop by fait accompli without presidential input, thereby weakening the president's ability to manage the foreign policy bureaucracy. As Richard Neustadt (1960) would say, unless presidents are willing and able to make hard choices, they are more likely to act as a "clerk" than a leader. These are crucial decisions, because how the policy process operates determines the extent to which information and policy alternatives flow to the president, whether the bureaucracy is responsive to the presidential agenda, and whether policies are implemented in accordance with presidential decisions—each of the points on the policy hill illustration we used earlier to understand the process.

It is not unusual for presidents to enter office claiming that they will rely on **cabinet government** as their principal means of managing the bureaucracy. This means that the president plans to rely heavily on cabinet secretaries and departments for information and advice. Such a policymaking process tends to be highly decentralized and open, often allowing the State Department to act as the lead agency responsible for coordinating the conduct of US foreign policy. In this scenario, the secretary of state is typically the principal spokesperson for US foreign policy, acting as the major adviser to the president, and the State Department is responsible for coordinating the interagency policy process within the rest of the foreign policy bureaucracy (Destler 1972).

Cabinet government and a **State Department–centered system** constitute the popular perception of presidential power and executive branch operation. Unfortunately, a president who attempts to operate this way quickly discovers that the bureaucracy, including the cabinet departments and many of the cabinet secretaries, may often be unresponsive to the White House. Although some presidents—Eisenhower and Reagan come to mind—have embraced this approach, it has become increasingly less appealing. Recent presidents who were initially disposed to it—including Reagan and George W. Bush—abandoned cabinet government in favor of greater White House control and direction. Most presidents learn quickly that it is not a good approach to effective management of the foreign policy bureaucracy or presidential leadership.

Instead, since World War II, presidents have tended to adopt three related approaches to the organization and process of foreign policymaking: (1) a White House–centered system, (2) an increasingly centralized policymaking process, and (3) an increasingly narrow and closed level of participation in the process. First, in managing the foreign policymaking process, presidents have increasingly relied on a **White House–centered NSC system**, revolving around the national security adviser and the NSC staff. Unlike much of the established and entrenched bureaucracy, including the Department of State and the DOD, these staff members are most responsive to the president. Because they work for the president directly, they tend to reflect a White House (rather than agency) perspective. Moreover, with a White House–centered approach, only presidential authority can resolve disagreements among bureaucratic agencies. For example, comparably ranked members of State and Defense who participate in interagency discussions are equal to each other and neither has inherent authority over the other, so when they disagree, resolving differences in difficult. By contrast, in a White House–centered system, interagency discussions are chaired and directed by presidential staff, who carry White House authority and can thus manage agency disagreements more effectively.

Presidents quickly turn to those they trust most, who tend to be the White House staff and agencies within the Executive Office of the President (EOP), and the number of such advisers tends to shrink. This occurs because of time constraints on the president and increasing familiarity among presidents and advisers. As presidents begin to interact with their advisers, they learn more about their advisers' policy views, personalities, and operating styles and make judgments about the value of their advice, trust, and friendship. With time, presidents tend to become more selective as to whom they interact with and rely on for advice. This often tends to "close" the policymaking process and narrow the range of information and opinions that come before the president, because the presidency is such an "awesome office . . . where no one really stands up to the president, where there is no equality, where no one tells the president he is wrong." In other words, inevitably the office "tends by its nature to inhibit dissent and opposition" (Halberstam 1969:456). The experiences of the Trump administration illustrate this, as the president replaced numerous advisers, sometimes multiple times, over his first three years, steadily narrowing the circle of those on whom he relied.

To sum up, the key to presidential management of the foreign policy bureaucracy involves the choices the president makes about foreign policy orientation and agenda, level of involvement, and the dynamics of the policymaking process. These presidential choices determine the extent to which the president will manage the bureaucracy and make it responsive. However, what works for one president may not work for others. These presidential choices are very much a function of a president's personal characteristics—beliefs, personality, and operating style (George 1980b). Therefore, it is not surprising that presidential management of foreign policy tends to revolve around a White House–centered system that becomes more centralized and closed over time, for it is most responsive to presidents and their personal characteristics. These basic choices provide the foundations for understanding the nature and role of the NSC system as the focal point for presidential management of the foreign policy bureaucracy and the foreign policymaking process.

THE NATIONAL SECURITY COUNCIL SYSTEM

Since its creation in the 1947 National Security Act, the **National Security Council (NSC)** has evolved into an **NSC system** that bears little resemblance to the original council itself. The NSC was once an important advisory and decision-making body, but it subsequently declined in importance. Today the NSC is largely a pro forma or ceremonial part of an NSC system that consists of four components: (1) the NSC; (2) the special assistant to the president for national security affairs (better known as the national security adviser or NSC adviser); (3) the NSC staff; and (4) the **NSC interagency process** by which national policy is formulated, implemented, and evaluated.

The NSC, within the EOP, is the key agency or organization on which presidents have relied since World War II. Its chief director—the national security adviser—is often regarded as the single most important appointment the president makes because that person usually becomes the most important policy adviser to the president and is responsible for coordinating the foreign policymaking process within the larger executive branch. The NSC staff serves the national security adviser and, therefore, works directly for the president as his or her personal foreign policy staff. Since World War II, the NSC staff has grown from a handful of members in low-key roles to hundreds of staff drawn from think tanks, the policy community, academia, and the foreign policy bureaucracy who play a much more central role in the structure and process of the NSC system. Typically, the national security adviser and the NSC staff are at the heart of the NSC interagency process, which brings together representatives of the agencies of the foreign policy bureaucracy to engage in policy formulation, advice, and monitoring/evaluation. To understand how the president uses the NSC system to manage US foreign policy, we discuss the origins, evolution, and operations of the NSC system, first by considering the NSC and the national security adviser, and then turning to the NSC staff and NSC interagency structures in more detail later in the chapter.

The Origins of the NSC System

The NSC came into existence in 1947 with the passage of the National Security Act, which restructured the policy process in the areas of defense, intelligence, and national security advice to the president. As part of the National Security Act, the NSC was created to advise the president, act as a vehicle for long-range planning, and promote the coordination and integration of the national security process. To do so, the structure of the NSC originally consisted of (1) a formal advisory council composed of high-level foreign policy officials and (2) a small support staff headed by an executive secretary.

Although the membership list was soon revised, the "original statutory members" of the NSC included the president, secretary of state, secretary of defense, secretary of the Army, secretary of the Navy, secretary of the Air Force, and the chair of the National Security Resources Board (NSRB; responsible for emergency planning and civil defense), but the president could also invite others to attend the meetings. Congress amended the act in 1949 to add the vice president, eliminate the service secretaries and the chair of the NSRB, and include the director of central intelligence and the chair of the Joint Chiefs of Staff as intelligence and military advisers to the council, respectively. A small staff, headed by a civilian executive secretary, provided support for the formal council advisory meetings, helped coordinate the policy process, and conducted long-range planning.

The purpose of the National Security Act was to rationalize the national security process and force the president to be more responsive to formal lines of authority in the foreign policy bureaucracy, especially within the military. The act's formulation and passage was a response to what many people in Congress and the executive branch thought was a chaotic national security policymaking process during World War II. In addition, many people were unhappy with President Roosevelt's management style. Roosevelt avoided formal channels of communication and instead relied on an informal, ad hoc managerial style. He oversaw the bureaucracy and made policy by relying on a variety of individuals of different ranks located throughout the bureaucracy. This managerial style served Roosevelt well as president, but it concerned many, especially the high-level officials and agencies who were often circumvented. Such concerns heightened with the rise to the presidency of Harry Truman, who lacked experience in foreign policy.

Hence, the desire to provide the US government with a policymaking apparatus that would promote greater staffing, advice, and coordination—and force the president to comply with a more formal process and structured participation of the foreign policy bureaucracy—led to the establishment of the NSC and its advice, long-term planning, and coordination functions. Modeled after the British war cabinet, it was a means of imposing a cabinet government on the president when national security decisions were involved. The only legal flexibility that the original act gave the president was the ability to invite officials to NSC meetings in addition to the statutory members.

Changing Patterns in the NSC

Presidents have found the NSC, as originally designed, to be both a potentially useful tool and a source of frustration in managing foreign policy. It should not be surprising to learn that presidents have used those aspects of the NSC they have found useful while ignoring or circumventing those aspects they have found constraining. As the original NSC developed, two major adaptations occurred. First, providing policy advice and coordinating the policy process for the president became the NSC's two major functions, while long-term planning was almost never implemented. A notable exception involved the Truman administration and the development of **NSC-68**. NSC memorandum 68 was a staff document approved by the president in 1950. It represented a concerted effort by members of the NSC staff to predict US-Soviet relations into the 1950s and recommend US foreign policy alternatives for presidential consideration. NSC-68 provided the official justification for the policy of global containment of Soviet communism and, through the institutionalization of this policy due to the Korean War, influenced the foreign policies of subsequent administrations during the Cold War.

Second, the NSC staff (and the national security adviser role, which was not created until 1957) became more significant over time, while the NSC as a decision-making body has declined in importance. The 1947 National Security Act legally defined who the president must accept as major foreign advisers. Clearly, this is not acceptable to most presidents. If a president wants to do more than act as a clerk, he or she must be allowed to decide who to rely on for foreign policy advice. Changes in the law have been made over the years reflecting this concern: As noted, since 1949 the NSC now formally includes the president, vice president, secretary of state, and secretary of defense as statutory members, with the chair of the Joint Chiefs of Staff and the director of national intelligence (director of central intelligence prior to 2005) as advisory members. However, as has always been the case, presidents can invite other individuals to participate as they see fit. Very simply, presidents will interact with those policymakers they trust the most and will avoid officials with whom they have policy disagreements or personality conflicts. Presidents have used—or not used—the NSC as it has suited them.

This has ultimately resulted in the decline of the NSC itself as a formal advisory and decision-making body, and the rise of the NSC *system* as the foreign policy process has gradually become White House centered. Presidents have increasingly relied on the national security adviser and the NSC staff to manage the process and provide an independent source of information and advice (see Table 7.1 for a list of national security advisers and their backgrounds). Accordingly, the role of the national security adviser has evolved considerably. Henry Kissinger, who served as Nixon's national security adviser, probably elevated the role more than anyone. However, the centrality of the position had been growing steadily over the previous decade, from little more than an executive secretary under

TABLE 7.1

National Security Advisers

Name	Year	President	Background
Sidney W. Souers	1947	Truman	Business, Navy
James S. Lay Jr.	1950	Truman	Business, Army
Robert Cutler	1953	Eisenhower	Law, Army
Dillon Anderson	1955	Eisenhower	Law, Army
William Jackson	1956	Eisenhower	Law, business, Army
Robert Cutler	1957	Eisenhower	Law, Army
Gordon Gray	1958	Eisenhower	Law, Army
McGeorge Bundy	1961	Johnson	Law, Army, journalism
Walt W. Rostow	1966	Johnson	Academia
Henry A. Kissinger	1969	Nixon	Academia, government
Brent Scowcroft	1975	Ford	Academia, Air Force
Zbigniew Brzezinski	1977	Carter	Academia
Richard V. Allen	1981	Reagan	Academia, government
William P. Clark	1982	Reagan	Law
Robert C. McFarlane	1983	Reagan	Army, government
John M. Poindexter	1985	Reagan	Navy
Frank C. Carlucci	1987	Reagan	Business, government
Colin L. Powell	1987	Reagan	Army
Brent Scowcroft	1989	George H. W. Bush	Air Force, academia
Anthony Lake	1993	Clinton	Academia, government
Samuel "Sandy" Berger	1997	Clinton	Law, government
Condoleezza Rice	2001	George W. Bush	Academia, government
Stephen Hadley	2005	George W. Bush	Law, government
James Jones	2009	Obama	Military, government
Thomas Donilon	2010	Obama	Government, law
Susan Rice	2013	Obama	Government, policy, think tanks
Michael Flynn	2017	Trump	Military
H. R. McMaster	2017	Trump	Military
John Bolton	2018	Trump	Law, government
Robert O'Brien	2019	Trump	Law, government

Source: United States Government Manual.

Truman and Eisenhower to increasingly central advisers and process managers. Kissinger thrust the position into prominence during the Nixon administration and, by the time George H. W. Bush appointed Brent Scowcroft as his national security adviser, a kind of consensus had emerged on the importance of the holder of the position as a central process manager, an honest broker, and a policy adviser. Scowcroft's successors in subsequent administrations largely modeled their behavior after him (Burke 2009b; National Security Council Project 1999a), at least until the Trump administration, whose approach was a dramatic departure from this consensus.

There is obviously variation in the behavior of national security advisers over time, which is largely attributable to presidential style and preferences. However, with the first six years of the Reagan administration as the exception, there has been a general trend toward relying on the national security adviser to exercise institutional control over the foreign policy bureaucracy and process. In this trend, the role of the adviser as a central player is generally accepted. For example, an extensive 1999 discussion with nine previous national security advisers (Allen, Berger, Carlucci, Lake, MacFarlane, Powell, Poindexter, Rostow, and Scowcroft) revealed substantial consensus on the mix of **honest broker**, process manager, and personal adviser while emphasizing the need for the national security adviser to be the central manager of the policy process. As Powell summarized:

> It is the role of the national security advisor to get it all out—all the agendas, all the facts, all the opinions, all of the gray and white and black areas written down—and use a highly qualified staff, the National Security Council staff, to put all of these agreements and disagreements into a form that can be sent back to . . . however many people are debating the issue, and say: "this is the issue as we understand it. These are the points of agreement and disagreement. We agree and disagree. So, let's have a meeting. Let's fight it out." And at some point it's up to the national security advisor to take all of those points, do an integral calculus of the whole thing . . . and to say to the president: "Mr. President, we have heard all these points of view and . . . this is what I think and this is my recommendation to you." You make that recommendation, with both the secretaries of state and defense and all the other cabinet officers and agencies involved knowing what you're going to recommend. And then the president decides. (National Security Council Project 2000:51)

This is ideally how the national security adviser and the NSC system should work, but much depends on a president's management style.

THE EVOLVING NATURE AND ROLE OF THE NSC SYSTEM

Presidential management styles have differed with each president and have evolved over time. It should therefore be no surprise that the NSC system has also evolved and varied. As Colin Powell observed, "The duty of the National Security Council staff and the [national security adviser] is to mold themselves to the personality of the president . . . . [T]he NSC has to mold itself to the will and desire and feelings of the president" (National Security Council Project 2000:52). Overall, the NSC system tends to have two overlapping levels: (1) an informal process (face-to-face meetings or private phone calls) among the president's closest advisers and (2) a formal NSC interagency process through use of the national security adviser and the NSC staff.

To better understand how contemporary presidents have managed the executive branch, a more detailed look at the operation of the general foreign policymaking process and the NSC system is needed. According to I. M. Destler, Leslie H. Gelb, and Anthony Lake (1984), there have been three major stages in the evolution of the NSC system and the foreign policy process at the presidential level: (1) Presidents Truman and Eisenhower used the NSC as an advisory body with a staff to support their reliance on cabinet secretaries and their departments; (2) under Presidents Kennedy and Johnson, the NSC was eclipsed, and the traditional role of the cabinet, especially the State Department, was challenged by the rise of the national security adviser and staff; and (3) beginning with President Nixon, the national security adviser and staff became ascendant in the policymaking process. Since Ronald Reagan, a fourth stage emerged, with a contemporary consensus model first established by George H. W. Bush and then adopted by each subsequent president, until Donald Trump.

The Early NSC as Advisory Body, 1947–1960

During the 1950s, the NSC was used as an advisory body to assist the president in making foreign policy. Even though the NSC provided information and advice to the president, the secretary of state remained the chief foreign policy spokesperson and adviser to the president, and the State Department often acted as the lead organization in formulating and implementing foreign policy. Both Presidents Truman and Eisenhower relied on strong cabinet officers, such as the secretary of state, for information and advice. Truman relied on the secretary of state, Dean Acheson, and the secretary of defense, George C. Marshall, for counsel and to carry out presidential policy. Along with Clark Clifford, the White House counsel, an informal advisory process developed between President Truman and these officials. Truman was also hesitant to compromise his independence by relying on the NSC, initially refusing to attend its meetings, but following the North Korean attack on South Korea in 1950, it became a regular forum for discussion. The NSC staff was kept very small, consisting of roughly twenty people under an executive director who organized and provided support for the council meetings.

President Eisenhower relied heavily on the formal NSC as an advisory body. In eight years, the NSC held 346 meetings, roughly one each week, as compared to 128 meetings in more than five years under President Truman. Most of the meetings lasted two and a half hours, with President Eisenhower usually presiding (Destler et al. 1984:172). President Eisenhower also established the position of **national security adviser** (formally titled the special assistant to the president for national security affairs) to supervise the staff. Two interagency committees, both managed by the national security adviser, were created to assist in the preparation of the formal meetings and to oversee policy implementation. The NSC staff tripled in size and became the major vehicle for coordinating the information and advice provided to the president by the national security departments and agencies. John Foster Dulles, the secretary of state, was the major foreign policy spokesperson throughout the administration and acted as a major adviser to the president. Furthermore, Eisenhower also relied on more informal channels of interaction, especially when it came to fast-moving developments and crises.

The Rise of the NSC Adviser and Staff, 1961–1968

Beginning with the Kennedy administration, the NSC declined as a formal advisory body, while the national security adviser and staff grew as independent sources of information and advice for the president. By the early 1960s, the modern NSC system and process was in place and presidential management of the foreign policymaking process came to rely increasingly on a White House–centered system that emphasized the use of the national security adviser, staff, and interagency groups (Rockman 1981). In this system, the formal NSC as an advisory body was replaced by interagency groups whose membership was determined by the president. The NSC staff also grew in importance to become the personal staff to the president for foreign policy and key players in the foreign policy process. Finally, the national security adviser became the key official responsible for managing the interagency groups and coordinating the policy process, as well as for providing information and advice to the president.

Kennedy entered office with a personal management style that tended to be very informal. He quickly scrapped Eisenhower's formal foreign policy apparatus, but his failure to develop an alternative decision-making structure resulted in ad hoc structures, processes, and interactions among his foreign policy advisers. This approach lasted only a few months—until the **Bay of Pigs** fiasco. The covert effort to train a Cuban military force and overthrow Castro by invading Cuba, which began under President Eisenhower, failed miserably in large measure because of the decentralized and chaotic nature of the decision-making process. To address the problem, Kennedy moved to centralize the decision-making process in the White House, using his national security adviser, McGeorge Bundy, to manage the working groups and ensure that information and advice reached the president.

In this climate, Bundy—and his successors—increasingly came to act as a personal adviser to the president as well as a manager. This advisory role was reinforced by the substantial growth in foreign policy expertise and specialization in the NSC staff, providing the president with an independent source of information and advice (Daalder and Destler 2009). Such White House activism was reinforced by Kennedy's low regard for the competence of the State Department and his growing frustration with Dean Rusk as secretary of state. A "situation room" for crisis management was also set up in the White House basement, enabling the president to receive and transmit international communications as well as hold meetings and manage interagency coordination.

President Johnson initially decided to work with Kennedy's appointees to maintain continuity and promote legitimacy for his presidency. However, with time, Johnson came to rely on his own group of loyal, supportive advisers and replaced Bundy with Walt Rostow as national security adviser in March 1966. Johnson preferred to delegate authority to people such as Robert McNamara at the Defense Department and Dean Rusk at the State Department. When he wanted additional advice, he did not turn to his staff, as Kennedy had, but rather to those senior political figures he knew well, such as former advisers Dean Acheson and Clark Clifford. When he did get highly involved, he tended to dominate the policy process. Although interagency groups operated through the NSC, key presidential decisions were made in informal sessions with his closest advisers (Daalder and Destler 2009; Rothkopf 2005). Many of Johnson's most important decisions involving Vietnam, for instance, were made during his **Tuesday Lunch group**, composed of senior advisers Clifford, McNamara, Rostow, and Rusk.

The NSC Adviser and Staff Ascendant, 1969–1988

Beginning with President Nixon, the national security adviser and staff became ascendant over the cabinet officers and departments for information, advice, and management of the foreign policy process for the president. The adviser also began to act as a spokesperson for the president and became active in the actual operations and conduct of US foreign policy. To assist the national security adviser, the staff grew in size and influence as well.

Nixon came to the presidency with a strong interest in foreign affairs and a great distrust of the bureaucracy, which he felt tended to limit information and options available to the president. Nixon's management strategy was to use the White House to control or circumvent the bureaucracy, establishing a centralized decision-making structure that relied on the national security adviser, Henry Kissinger, and his NSC staff (Hersh 1983; Morris 1977). The Nixon-Kissinger NSC system created numerous interagency committees, chaired by Kissinger, or his deputy, designed to provide information and options to the president. Nixon, always the loner, rarely attended NSC meetings, preferring to consider the products of the committees by himself and personally consult with his closest advisers, especially Kissinger (Daalder and Destler 2009).

Nixon and Kissinger activated the bureaucracy by issuing national security study memoranda (NSSMs), which laid out the issues to be addressed and the agencies involved, and presented deadlines for agency submission of policy recommendations. Subsequent interagency meetings chaired by Kissinger or his deputies considered options and made recommendations for the president. Once the president decided on a particular course of action, often in consultation with Kissinger, a national security decision memorandum (NSDM) would be issued by Kissinger and his staff to instruct the bureaucracy on the policy's implementation. Soon, Kissinger became the president's manager, major adviser, spokesman, and, in some cases, implementer of foreign policy. Kissinger's power was symbolized by his movement from the basement of the White House to a prestigious office on the main floor of the West Wing, down the hall from the Oval Office. The policy process became so centralized in Kissinger's hands, usually with Nixon's blessing, that the ability of many traditional foreign policy agencies and high-level officials to influence the process dwindled. Kissinger and his staff, nevertheless, did develop important contacts and networks with trusted lower level officials throughout the bureaucracy. Given Kissinger's crucial role, the size of the NSC staff increased to more than 100 staffers during this period.

As national security adviser, Kissinger reached a pinnacle of power under President Nixon that no single presidential adviser experienced before or since. When William Rogers eventually resigned in 1973, Nixon appointed Kissinger as secretary of state as well, and one man held the two most important foreign policy positions in the US government.

Such a centralized policy process was clearly responsive to Nixon and Kissinger, but few policy alternatives tended to be considered, and there was considerable internal dissent—even outright rebellion—throughout the executive branch at their heavy-handed approach.

This White House–centered system under Kissinger continued to operate after Nixon's resignation because of President Ford's management style, though with some modifications. In 1975, Brent Scowcroft, Kissinger's deputy national security assistant since 1973, became the national security adviser and managed the day-to-day NSC process. Scowcroft emphasized his role as process manager (and honest broker) more than Kissinger did, and opened the policy process to other officials such as Donald Rumsfeld as secretary of defense. Nonetheless, Ford, who had minimal exposure to foreign affairs, developed a close working relationship with Kissinger and remained dependent on his secretary of state throughout his term of office.

In many respects, the Carter and Reagan administrations that followed Nixon and Ford represented reactions to the highly centralized Nixon-Kissinger system. President Carter adopted a similar foreign policymaking apparatus but sought to reduce its centralization enough to remain relatively open to input by cabinet officials and departments (Moens 1990; Rosati 1987). Eschewing the approach of his recent predecessors, Carter relied on two formal interagency groups within the NSC system, which became primarily responsible for the working operations of the foreign policy process. The Policy Review Committee (PRC) was established to develop policy at the secretarial level on issues for which one department had been designated as the lead agency by the president. The Special Coordinating Committee (SCC) was established to deal with cross-cutting issues, such as arms control and crisis management, and was chaired by National Security Adviser Zbigniew Brzezinski. At the lowest level of the NSC system were two working groups at the assistant secretary level that did much of the legwork for the PRC and SCC and were also responsible for issues of lesser significance.

Carter relied principally on Brzezinski and Secretary of State Cyrus Vance. Brzezinski, as national security adviser and head of the NSC staff, was primarily responsible for coordinating the interagency operations of the NSC system, while Vance was the chief negotiator and major spokesperson for the president. However, this arrangement soon began to suffer. Brzezinski and Vance increasingly differed over policy, and their diverging personal styles exacerbated the situation. The growing conflict resulted in considerable bureaucratic infighting, especially between the staffs of Brzezinski and Vance (Rosati 1987). With the taking of American hostages in Iran and the Soviet intervention in Afghanistan in late 1979, Carter supported Brzezinski over Vance, reinstating containment as the cornerstone of US foreign policy. Carter also decided to attempt a military rescue of the hostages, a decision arrived at while Vance, the lone dissenter, was vacationing in Florida. Increasingly isolated within the administration, Vance soon resigned, convinced that he no longer enjoyed the president's support. He was replaced by Edmund Muskie, but Brzezinski and his NSC staff had clearly become ascendant within the foreign policy process by the end of Carter's term of office.

President Reagan preferred to delegate authority, tended to remain uninvolved in daily operations, and lacked considerable experience and knowledge of foreign affairs. He entered office committed to reversing the Nixon-Kissinger and Carter trend toward a strong national security adviser and NSC staff. Reagan preferred to set the broad principles and directions of policy, rely on his foreign policy officials and their agencies for information and advice, and delegate to his advisers. Unlike his recent predecessors, Reagan's initial preference was for his national security adviser and staff to act as little more than clerks responsible for coordinating the process, reminiscent of their role during the early NSC days (Daalder and Destler 2009). The national security adviser's job was to supervise the staff and provide support for the formal NSC process. Unlike Kissinger, who chaired all the interagency committees, or Brzezinski, who chaired some, the national security adviser in the Reagan administration initially chaired no committees.

Unlike his predecessors, Reagan initially had the national security adviser (and other foreign policy advisers) report to him through the White House staff rather than directly. This placed the "troika" of James Baker as chief of staff, Michael Deaver as deputy chief of staff, and Edwin Meese as political counselor during his first term—with Baker replaced by Donald Regan and then Howard Baker during Reagan's second term—in important gatekeeping roles vis-à-vis the national security adviser. As a further indication of the reduction in the national security adviser's stature and influence, his office was moved away from the president into the White House basement.

From the beginning, however, the foreign policymaking process failed to function smoothly. First, the initial secretary of state, Alexander Haig, thought that he was going to be the "vicar" of the Reagan administration's foreign policy, responsible for developing a State Department–centered system for the president. Haig could not understand that, even though Reagan had deemphasized the role of the national security adviser and staff, he preferred a White House–centered system that relied on his personal staff. The result was constant political infighting between Haig and the White House staff until Reagan finally accepted Haig's resignation in 1982. Second, key personnel changed frequently. Reagan had six national security advisers, each one lasting little more than a year. Richard Allen was replaced by William Clark, then by Robert McFarlane, John Poindexter, Frank Carlucci, and finally Colin Powell. These constant changes of crucial personnel reduced the national security adviser's clout within the executive branch even further than originally intended by President Reagan.

There was so little management of the policy process by the middle years of the Reagan administration that informal coalitions between officials and groups developed over different issues. For example, despite a consensus within the administration in support of the Contras and their effort to overthrow the Sandinistas in Nicaragua, even after American assistance was banned by Congress, there was considerable disagreement among Reagan's advisers over exchanging arms for hostages with Iran. Secretary of State George Shultz and Secretary of Defense Caspar Weinberger fought the initiative. Reagan, however, was committed to the Iran venture, and, consequently, the circle of participants within the policy process narrowed: The White House, the NSC, and the CIA remained involved, while the secretary of state and the secretary of defense were eliminated or circumvented. NSC staff implemented both of these initiatives. Thus, rather than ensuring a thorough interagency process, the NSC staff became more like just another bureaucratic voice contending for a role and influence and helped produce the Iran-Contra affair.

For a number of reasons, management of the bureaucracy improved in the latter years of the Reagan administration. First, Frank Carlucci and then Colin Powell were brought in as national security adviser, restoring the stature of the position and reorienting the role of the NSC staff. Two of the dominant personalities in the Reagan administration foreign policy team also departed—Secretary of Defense Weinberger returned to private life and Director of Central Intelligence Casey died in office—leaving George Shultz in a strengthened position. Finally, former senator Howard Baker replaced the ineffective Donald Regan as chief of staff, helping to make the policy process work more efficiently for the president. When Reagan left office, his NSC system was in considerably better shape than at any other time in his two terms, and it functioned more along the lines of his predecessors' White House–centered approach to management.

The Contemporary NSC Model, 1989–Present

When George H. W. Bush took office in 1989, he and his national security adviser, Brent Scowcroft, established an NSC system and process that reflected an emerging consensus on the role of the national security adviser (see "A Different Perspective: The Contemporary Role of the NSC Adviser and Staff"), and the negative lessons of both the Nixon-Kissinger system and those Bush learned as Reagan's vice president. In a sense, the learning curve of the previous eight administrations and four decades or so led to the Bush-Scowcroft approach. With minor variations, the structures and processes were adopted by all subsequent presidents—until Donald Trump took office in 2017.

A Different Perspective

THE CONTEMPORARY ROLE OF THE NSC ADVISER AND STAFF

Despite all the public attention focused on the national security adviser as a consequence of assertive individuals in that position (Kissinger, Brzezinski) and controversies over their behavior (McFarlane, Poindexter), the view from the inside has evolved. According to Brent Scowcroft, the central architect of the modern-day NSC system—the national security adviser has two central roles: "The first was to run the system, to make the process work and work efficiently, and provide the president with the perspectives he needed. . . . [The] second role was to provide a source of advice to [the president] that was unalloyed by departmental responsibilities and interests." The "honest broker" task of the first role was most important. As two long-time practitioners/analysts of the policy process summarize:

A consensus has emerged on the importance of the position as predominantly central process manager and honest broker—as a means to promote and protect the president. . . . [T]here are some tasks that the NSC advisor and staff are uniquely placed to undertake, and it is their responsibility to make sure that they do so. These include:

- Staffing the president's daily foreign policy activity: his communications with foreign leaders and the preparation and conduct of his trips overseas;
- Managing the process of making decisions on major foreign and national security issues;

(Continued)

- Driving the policymaking process to make real choices, in a timely manner; [and]
- Overseeing the full implementation of the decisions the president has made.

All of these tasks are important—and none can be left to others. (Daalder and Destler 2009:318-319)

Given this insider view, consider our description of the evolution of the national security adviser and NSC system.

What essential characteristics are necessary for the person holding the national security adviser position?

George H. W. Bush's NSC System. President Bush established a White House–centered system revolving around an NSC process in which cabinet officials and departments played a prominent role. President Bush was comfortable with such a White House–centered policymaking process because of the foreign policy expertise and policymaking experience he acquired during the Nixon, Ford, and Reagan years, especially as director of central intelligence, US ambassador to the United Nations, and vice president (Mulcahy 1991). Highly regarded by virtually all those who observed or participated, the NSC system the elder Bush and Scowcroft constructed become the model on which all subsequent administrations have depended (Burke 2009b), until the Trump administration, that is.

George H. W. Bush established a three-tiered formal interagency policy process dependent on the NSC staff and the coordination of the national security adviser. At the top, Scowcroft and his deputy national security adviser served as chairs of the two key NSC committees coordinating the Bush administration's foreign policy machinery—the NSC **Principals Committee** (PC, a secretary-level group) and the NSC **Deputies Committee** (DC, a deputy secretary–level group). Below these committees, the Bush White House established a series of NSC interagency working groups. In the Bush administration's system, these working groups, or "policy coordinating committees," as the Bush administration labeled them, did most of the work to formulate policy options for higher level consideration and also to supervise and coordinate the implementation of policy choices. Organized into various regional (e.g., Europe, Soviet Union, Latin America) and functional units (e.g., arms control, defense, intelligence), these working groups were chaired by assistant secretaries of state for the regional units, and assistant secretaries (or their equivalents) from Defense, Treasury, the CIA, and elsewhere for functional units. However, an NSC staff member served as executive secretary for each working group so as to increase White House control and policy coordination (see Figure 7.1 for an overview of the structure and process of the elder Bush's NSC system).

The PC-DC process helped to further centralize policy control by the White House, national security adviser, and NSC staff. The DC, through the deputy national security adviser and the NSC staff, reviewed all work from the coordinating committees and

FIGURE 7.1

George H. W. Bush's Foreign Policy System

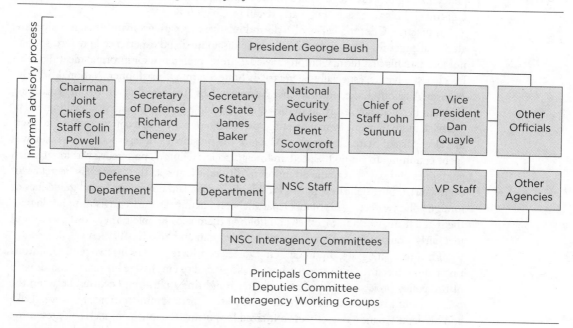

made recommendations to the PC, under the leadership of the national security adviser. Effectively, the PC served as a White House–led center for considering all national security questions. President Bush attended most of the PC meetings himself (National Security Council Project 1999b). Bush supplemented this formal structure and process with an informal advisory process that usually included National Security Adviser Scowcroft, the White House chief of staff (initially John Sununu, then Samuel Skinner), Secretary of State James Baker, Secretary of Defense Dick Cheney, and Chair of the Joint Chiefs of Staff Colin Powell. Emphasis was on loyalty and quiet teamwork, "in marked contrast to the public feuds over policy and bureaucratic turf in previous administrations—the Shultz-Weinberger, Vance-Brzezinski, or Rogers-Kissinger battles" (Deibel 1991:5).

Bill Clinton's NSC System. President Clinton recognized the merits of his predecessor's approach and adopted it for his own administration. The basic structure remained three-tiered, although Clinton broadened the circle of PC members to include the secretary of the treasury, the US ambassador to the United Nations, the special assistant to the president for economic policy, and the White House chief of staff, in part reflecting the importance of economic issues and the changing political context of the post–Cold War world. The national security adviser and his deputy chaired the PC and DC, while assistant secretaries from State and Defense generally chaired the working groups, which prepared policy studies and facilitated implementation of decisions. Clinton was also determined to improve the coordination and centralization of economic policy, both foreign and domestic, and therefore created the National Economic Council (NEC), modeled on the NSC. We discuss the role of the foreign economic bureaucracy and policymaking process, in general, and the NEC and the national economic adviser under Clinton and his successors in greater detail in Chapter 8.

In practice, Clinton's personal style and relative inexperience with foreign policy created challenges for this system that his more disciplined and experienced predecessor had not faced. In his first term, Clinton showed a strong preference for informal meetings with his closest advisers, especially Secretary of State Warren Christopher, National Security Adviser Anthony Lake, and Defense Secretary Les Aspin and, later, Aspin's successor, William Perry. In fact, early on in the administration, Clinton's apparent unwillingness to establish more frequent formal meetings on foreign policy created concern among advisers like Secretary of State Christopher. Much of the president's time, especially early on, was spent cramming to get up to speed on foreign policy. Clinton's preference was to set broad guidelines and pay spasmodic attention to different issues as they arose. As Secretary of State Christopher delicately put it, President Clinton laid down "the broad guidelines of foreign policy, expecting his State Department and national security advisors to implement them as a team, working together, and holding them accountable if they don't carry it out in a fairly straightforward way" (quoted in Friedman and Sciolino 1993:A3).

The functioning of Clinton's system evolved considerably over his two terms. Clinton's first national security adviser—Anthony Lake—tried to emphasize his role as coordinator of the policy process and prevent the bitter infighting that often occurred between the occupants of his position and secretaries of state in past administrations. However, Lake and his deputy, Sandy Berger, were criticized for putting too much emphasis on presenting consensus positions to the president and for not being proactive enough in the important tasks of managing the NSC staff and interagency process and bringing the president's attention to focus on national security. Many of these problems were most visible in the Clinton administration's policy toward the former Yugoslavia (Daalder and Destler 2009; Rothkopf 2005). Policymaking improved in 1995, when Leon Panetta took over as chief of staff from Clinton's friend Thomas "Mack" McClarty and imposed more structure and a more orderly process on the White House.

In the second term, things improved even more when Sandy Berger (who had a much closer relationship with President Clinton than Lake and was a more aggressive manager of the process) became national security adviser; Madeleine Albright, former ambassador to the United Nations, became secretary of state; and William Cohen (a former senator from Maine and the only major Clinton appointee from the Republican Party) became secretary of defense. Clinton's increasing comfort with and interest in foreign policy led him to pay more attention to national security issues, and many of the early problems largely disappeared (Daalder and Destler 2009; National Security Council Project 2000).

George W. Bush's NSC System. George W. Bush continued to use the formal three-tiered NSC interagency process established by his father, while supplementing it with a heavy reliance on informal meetings among his principal foreign policy advisers, especially after the attacks of September 11. Throughout his administration, these advisers included Condoleezza Rice, first as national security adviser and then as secretary of state; Colin Powell as secretary of state; Donald Rumsfeld as secretary of defense; Richard Myers as chair of the Joint Chiefs of Staff, and Dick Cheney as vice president. Until his resignation, CIA Director George Tenet was also a member of this inner circle, while White House staff including Andrew Card (chief of staff), Karl Rove (senior adviser), and Karen Hughes (White House counselor and director of communications) were also key members of the informal advisory system.

Although the younger Bush's foreign policy structure resembled that of his father, the results were very different, demonstrating that getting the structure "right" is only part of the battle for an effective foreign policy process. This was due to a combination of several factors. First, while the younger Bush drew wide praise for assembling a strong team of advisers such as Powell, Rumsfeld, and Cheney, among these heavyweights there were significant policy differences, especially between Rumsfeld and Cheney on the one hand, and Colin Powell on the other. Rumsfeld, an experienced secretary of defense known for his skills as a bureaucratic infighter, favored a strong assertive nationalism—or hegemonist approach in one formulation—to the US role abroad, a perspective shared by his key ally, Vice President Cheney (Daalder and Lindsay 2003). Powell reflected a more selective and pragmatic realist orientation. These differences surfaced on a variety of issues both before and after the September 11 attacks, including how to deal with North Korea, Iran, the war on terrorism, and Iraq, to name a few. Nor were these rifts contained to the top-level advisers. In fact, they extended to the mid and lower levels as well, with tensions between State and Defense appointees, Defense appointees and the uniformed military, and Defense and the CIA. One critical aspect of these disputes pitted the administration's neoconservatives, or "neocons," against other more traditional conservative nationalists and internationalists. For example, Deputy Secretary of Defense Paul Wolfowitz, a neocon, and Deputy Secretary of State Richard Armitage, a more pragmatic conservative, clashed regularly on a wide variety of issues. As one observation noted, "The Bush administration had trouble singing from the same foreign policy hymnal" (Walcott and Holt 2003). Powell's isolation, in particular, probably contributed to his decision to resign his post at the end of Bush's first term (Duffy and Shannon 2005:36).

Second, disagreements among Bush's advisers were exacerbated by the performance of **Condoleezza Rice** as national security adviser, who proved considerably less effective than her mentor, Brent Scowcroft. Many observers of the foreign policy process "consider her one of the weakest national security advisors in recent history in terms of managing interagency conflicts" (Kessler and Ricks 2004:7). She was relatively unsuccessful in her role as central manager of the NSC system and the NSC interagency process, instead emphasizing her close personal relationship with the president over her role as honest broker (Baker 2008; Burke 2005; Daalder and Destler 2009; Packer 2005). From the start, Rice failed to drive the foreign policy process effectively. For example, Richard Clarke, an NSC staff member in charge of counterterrorism for Clinton and Bush until 2003, pressed Rice to hold early, high-level NSC interagency meetings on the threat posed by al-Qaeda, but Rice failed to respond to his requests and a series of increasingly urgent warnings throughout the summer of 2001, waiting until September 4, 2001, to hold the first Principals Committee meeting (Clarke 2004). Similarly, critics argue that disputes over issues such as North Korea and Iran were never resolved through the NSC interagency process (Kessler and Ricks 2004), and Colin Powell asserts that the formal NSC never consistently met formally to consider, debate, and decide the alternatives that resulted in the 2003 military invasion of Iraq (Powell 2012).

Third, even a more experienced and aggressive national security adviser would have struggled to contend with the administration's foreign policy heavyweights. But Rice and her successor, Stephen Hadley, faced the problem of the unprecedented role of Vice President Cheney in the foreign policy process. As we discussed in "A Closer Look" in Chapter 3, Cheney first assembled a mini-NSC staff in his own office, pressed hard—ultimately unsuccessfully—to chair the PC, and then ensconced himself on that committee and salted the other interagency groups with members of his staff. Moreover, he worked closely with ally Donald Rumsfeld to press their more assertive positions (as well as to undermine Powell), ignoring Rice's attempts at control. Both Cheney and Rumsfeld conducted significant portions of their foreign policy discussions and advising outside the structures of the NSC system, making it even more difficult for Rice (Elliott and Calabresi 2004; see also "A Closer Look: Dealing with Terrorists, Circumventing the Process . . . and the Law?").

A Closer Look

DEALING WITH TERRORISTS, CIRCUMVENTING THE PROCESS . . . AND THE LAW?

Barton Gellman (2008:162–168) provides this revealing account of Vice President Dick Cheney's willingness to circumvent the NSC system and process, raising important questions about the tension between national security needs and the rule of law:

Just past the Oval Office, in the private dining room overlooking the South Lawn, Cheney joined Bush for lunch on November 13, 2001 . . . . Cheney brought a four-page text. David Addington, his lawyer, had drafted it in strict secrecy.

The United States was at war in Afghanistan, Osama bin Laden's base of operations. It was the first substantial response to September 11. Now U.S. troops faced a question: What should they do with a captured fighter from al Qaeda or the Taliban?

Questions like that nearly always get scrubbed in an "interagency review." Secretary of State Colin Powell appointed Pierre Prosper, ambassador-at-large for war crimes to lead a working group . . . . Prosper convened representatives from Justice, Defense and the Joint Chiefs of Staff. Condi Rice and Alberto Gonzales sent lawyers . . . . Cheney's staff did not show up. Addington knew what his client wanted, and the "interagency was just constipated," said Jim Haynes, his ally at the Pentagon.

Addington typed out an order that stripped foreign terrorist suspects of access to any court—civilian or military, domestic or foreign. They could be confined indefinitely, without charge. They would be tried, if at all, in closed "military commissions," modeled on the ones Franklin Roosevelt set up for Nazi saboteurs in World War II . . . . By relying on Roosevelt's model and on the 1942 Supreme Court case upholding it, Addington discarded six decades of intervening laws and treaties. Since then, the

United States had led the world in creating. . . international institutions and international law, some of it enacted into U.S. statutes . . . .

It was difficult to tell what the president knew, if anything, about the military order now heading toward his lunch table. Certainly he approved the idea that this was going to be a new kind of war, without a lot of lawyerly coddling for terrorists. When details became important, someone was supposed to tell him. Was he aware of [the Attorney General's] objections? Had anyone offered a heads-up on the legal risks, or the likely reaction of allies? Did Bush intend to keep his national security advisor and secretary of state out of the loop?

. . . Three days later, Cheney brought the order to lunch with the president. No one told Colin Powell or Condi Rice. No one told their lawyers, William H. Taft IV and John Bellinger. No one told Pierre Prosper, who was waiting for a reply to the option paper he sent the White House. Jim Haynes, the Pentagon lawyer, said the order "was very closely held because it was coming right from the top."

Cheney emerged from lunch with a thumbs up from the president . . . . The vice president chanced no last-minute protest. He sent the order on a swift path to execution, leaving no trace of his touch. In less than an hour the document traversed a West Wing circuit that gave its words the power of command . . . . Bush was standing, ready to depart, when [deputy staff secretary Stuart] Bowen arrived in the Oval Office. Addington's words were now bound in a blue portfolio, embossed with the presidential seal . . . . Bush pulled out a Sharpie from his breast pocket and signed . . . .

Bush was airborne for Crawford when CNN broke into its broadcast with the news. Condi Rice, furious, sent [senior national security lawyer] John Bellinger to complain. Colin Powell had the television going in his office. He picked up the phone to Pierre Prosper.

"What the hell just happened?" he asked.

How was the vice president able to accomplish this, and what are the implications for the presidential management of the foreign policy process?

Finally, the NSC process and the role of the national security adviser as coordinator were downplayed and kept at a very low profile by the president and his management style. Initially, Bush adopted a less engaged and less collegial "**CEO style.**" After September 11, the Bush system became more informal and ad hoc in nature (Milbank and Graham 2001; Thomas 2002a). President Bush, however, became so engaged and forceful once he had made up his mind to take the nation into a war on terrorism, that the policymaking process at the presidential level became increasingly closed and the range of views expressed was very narrow, such as over the invasion of Iraq (see Badie 2010; Woodward 2002, 2004, 2007). The net result, in the words of some observers, is "not that he is a socially awkward loner or a paranoid. He can charm and joke like the frat president he was. Still, beneath a hail-fellow manner, Bush has a defensive edge, a don't-tread-on-me prickliness. . . . In the Bush White House, disagreement is often equated with disloyalty" (Thomas 2005:33,34). This weakened Secretary of State Powell and strengthened the influence of Vice President Cheney and Secretary of Defense Rumsfeld within these informal group sessions, and it gave them greater leeway to circumvent the NSC system altogether.

Bush's second term saw some of these problems reduced. Ironically, with Powell's resignation and Rice's move to the State Department, the NSC system in the second term appeared in some ways to be in better shape than in the first term. For one, Rice retained her close personal relationship with President Bush, an advantage Powell never had in attempting to press his policy positions. Also, with her former deputy national security adviser, Stephen Hadley, becoming national security adviser, Rice had an ally in the policymaking process, enabling her to balance more effectively the views of other participants (Allen 2004; Ratnesar 2005). Further, because Hadley lacked Rice's close relationship with the president, he focused more on the process manager side of the national security adviser role (Daalder and Destler 2009). Finally, persistent criticism of Cheney for his role in the prewar intelligence fiasco and in the leaking of a CIA operative's name, among other things, coupled with Bush's greater confidence in his own foreign policy judgments, combined to reduce the overpowering impact of the vice president on the administration's foreign policy.

Barack Obama's NSC System. President Obama quickly established a formal NSC system that reflected the Bush-Scowcroft model. The same three tiers remained, with the same basic responsibilities: a Principals Committee at the top, a Deputies Committee in the middle, and a series of "interagency policy committees" at the bottom (Presidential Policy Directive 1, February 13, 2009). President Obama added the secretaries of energy, treasury, and homeland security; the attorney general; the White House chief of staff; and the UN ambassador to the Principals Committee; as well as the director of national intelligence, the chair of the Joint Chiefs of Staff, and the director of the Office of Management and Budget as advisory members. The counsel to the president, the vice president's personal national security adviser, and the deputies to the national security adviser and the secretary of state were invited to attend any meeting, while other individuals were included according to the issue at hand.

In a signal of his determination to establish a strongly centralized White House–dominated structure and process, Obama designated his first national security adviser (former Marine general James Jones), deputy national security adviser (Thomas Donilon, a former State Department appointee), and NSC staff members as chairs of all the relevant committees from the PC to the policy committees. This move was also viewed as part of an effort by Obama and his national security adviser to correct the problems of his predecessor. According to one account, "Jones, a retired Marine general, made it clear that he will run the process and be the primary conduit of national security advice to Obama, eliminating the 'back channels' that at times in the Bush administration allowed Cabinet secretaries and the vice president's office to unilaterally influence and make policy out of view of the others" (DeYoung 2009:A1). As one official stated, "We have reenergized the interagency process and are aggressively putting together new policy on a range of issues. The NSC should be at the center of that process: coordinating, making sure everyone with equities is engaged and is heard. It is working as it should" (Rozen 2009).

Second, Obama continued the trend of the past two decades of integrating a wider array of agencies and issues into the NSC system. Spurred by a complex issue agenda that included traditional national security issues, such as the ongoing wars in Afghanistan and Iraq, the global economic crisis, and a host of additional issues ranging from counterterrorism to the global environment, Obama's NSC system included "new NSC directorates [to deal with] such department-spanning 21st-century issues as cybersecurity, energy, climate change, nation-building and infrastructure" and, perhaps most broadly, global engagement (DeYoung 2009:A1).

Finally, Obama's White House staff played a more important role in the NSC process, including chiefs of staff Rahm Emanuel, William Daley, and then Jacob Lew; counselor to the president David Axelrod; and other personal aides (Hoagland 2009). Stemming from the continued need for presidents to maintain White House leadership of an increasingly sprawling foreign policy bureaucracy, this trend also suggests the extent to which political calculations and "message cohesion and control" increasingly influence policymaking.

Despite these adjustments, the NSC system under Obama reflected more continuity than change (Burke 2009a). Not surprisingly, some of the problems that emerged were similar to those of the past as well. For one, Obama's first national security adviser—James Jones—was relatively ineffective. Not only was he a relatively passive manager of the process, but his style also did not mesh well with the president's "informal, substantively intense" approach (Destler 2009), and he approached his role with considerably less energy than most of his predecessors (Lee and Lubold 2010).

Because of these and other concerns, Obama replaced Jones with Thomas Donilon in October 2010. In contrast to Jones, Donilon was more seasoned in the ways of the bureaucracy, and he was more energetic and focused on the management of the process and the provision of advice to the president. He also enjoyed a close personal relationship with the president, who trusted him (Garrison, Rosati, and Scott 2012). Donilon's approach as process manager had a positive effect. According to one observer:

> The NSC became more organized and disciplined, with effective paper trails being created, and a network of effective oral communications between members being instituted. . . . [D]uring the Libyan crisis of 2011, Donilon did what he was expected to do by Obama. He set up decision-making and policy-making processes for the president to make his choices and in ways that would allow his orders to be properly implemented. (Jackson 2012)

Obama's style also affected the way the system functioned. On the one hand, the president approached the process with discipline and engagement. As some observers noted, Obama relied on and valued the NSC machinery, insisted on a regular process in an effort to try to avoid back-channel end runs, and actively participated in the discussions and decisions (Jackson 2012). However, the president also tended to put himself at the center of the discussions and deliberations, often trying to play the role of his own honest broker. Given Obama's limited experience and knowledge, this sometimes backfired.

In particular, during the 2009 debate about whether to employ a military "surge" in Afghanistan, for example, Obama was proactive, but he had difficulty in getting the military and Secretary of Defense Gates to cooperate and avoid end runs. He even tried to prepare his own memos outlining his thinking and seeking a greater range of options—the job of the national security adviser—reflecting his frustration with Jones. According to one report, the president instructed, "Get me some other people's opinions on this. . . . I want more than what's in this room" (Rudalevige 2009).

There are benefits from such engagement, but there are also costs, as presidents can easily lose control of the process by becoming their own national security adviser and/or come to dominate the process and stifle discussion and debate if their preferences are too obvious (Alter 2010; Garrison et al. 2012; Jackson 2012; Woodward 2010). After 2010, although Obama remained an active and assertive participant, with the change from Jones to Donilon, the tendency for the president to act as his own national security adviser was reduced, largely because Donilon managed the process better than Jones, served as a better honest broker, and enjoyed the president's trust.

After his reelection in 2012, Obama faced the task of replacing key personnel in his NSC system. Key advisers such as Donilon, Secretary of State Hillary Clinton, Defense Secretary Leon Panetta, and Treasury Secretary Timothy Geithner stepped down. The president replaced Donilon with Susan Rice, who had served as ambassador to the United Nations during the first term. The overall structure and operation of the NSC system remained largely consistent, and Rice emphasized her role as the central custodian and coordinator of the process. By the time she took over in mid-2013, her NSC staff had grown to almost 400 members and were integrally involved in all levels of the interagency process.

Although Rice took on a variety of higher profile public roles, she emphasized her process manager role. Benefiting from a close relationship of trust with Obama, Rice drew on her positions in the president's inner circle and at the center of the NSC system. According to White House officials who worked with her, Rice "purposely tried to be less of an advocate for her own positions and more of an honest broker in representing to the president a range of available options" (Pace 2014). Rice herself "compared her [national security adviser] role to that of a basketball point guard—the position she played on her high school basketball team and the code name assigned to her by the Secret Service. 'I'm setting up the play,' Rice said. 'I have to see the whole court. I'm usually running the play but passing it to somebody else'" (quoted in Pace 2014).

However, criticism of the centralized White House–oriented approach grew. Advisers from the foreign policy bureaucracy—such as Chuck Hagel, the defense secretary who served from February 2013 to November 2014—complained after his resignation that the White House was excessively micromanaging the foreign policy process. Congress even got involved in 2016, introducing legislation to limit the size of the NSC staff and/or require congressional confirmation if it exceeded a certain size (see Senate National Defense Authorization Act 2017 S.2943, Section 1089). Rice herself responded to these concerns by trimming the size of the NSC staff after 2015, taking it back down to about 180 members by the time Obama left office, close to 90 percent of whom were career professionals in the foreign policy bureaucracy. Nevertheless, as she left office with the outgoing Obama administration, Rice (2017) defended the White House–centered structure and process:

> The NSC staff should be focused on advising the President, and coordinating
> strategy and policy, while departments and agencies should focus on
> implementation. . . . [However], the buck still stops at the White House.
> Especially in the face of polarized politics and a relentless, 24-hour news cycle.
> It falls to the NSC staff to frame for the President the toughest national security

decisions, weighing disparate and sometimes competing information and equities from across our government. And it falls to the NSC staff to ensure the President is fully briefed on the costs, trade-offs, and risks associated with any major decision, ensuring prioritization and discipline in the face of complex, interrelated threats as well as demands for fiscal responsibility.

The Trump NSC System: Correction or Confusion? The Trump administration took office apparently determined to ignore almost three decades of consensus—and more than six decades of learning and adaptation—about the role and functions of the NSC system in the foreign policy process. According to the Trump White House, its approach constituted a much-needed correction. In 2019, for example, White House spokesperson Hogan Gidley defended the Trump administration's sharp deviation from the past practices of both Republican and Democratic presidents, arguing that Trump

> inherited a bloated, dysfunctional NSC from the Obama administration that had grossly distorted the balance between agencies and the White House . . . . President Trump recognized these issues immediately and corrected them with, among other things, an executive order that restructured and reorganized the NSC so it would better serve the president and the American people. (quoted in Toosi 2019)

The Trump administration's approach also reflected the preferences of the president, whose unstructured and undisciplined style and preferences led him to dislike process, and whose "outsider" mentality led him to value personal relationships and loyalty and to deeply distrust career professionals from the foreign policy bureaucracy.

Formally, the Trump administration's National Security Policy Memorandum (NSPM) 2 largely adopted the consensus structures and processes first established by the Bush administration in 1989 with its three-tiered structures. Although NSPM 2 mostly copied previous presidential memoranda on the NSC system, several interesting deviations were present. First, this initial memorandum gave the national security adviser *and* a new homeland security adviser coordinating authority over the NSC system. Moreover, the initial memo stipulated that the White House chief strategist—controversial figure Steve Bannon—was a regular member of the NSC Principals Committee, while the director of national intelligence and the chair of the Joint Chiefs of Staff were not, a highly unusual departure from past practice and one that elevated the political side of the White House in the NSC system. Finally, the White House also established a Strategic Initiatives Group alongside its formal NSC system, placing Bannon and the president's son-in-law, Jared Kushner (whose official title is senior adviser to the president), outside the coordinating structures and processes of the NSC system.

Significant criticism of these steps—along with early upheaval in staffing, including the firing of Trump's first national security adviser, Michael Flynn, after only twenty-four days in the position—led the Trump administration to undo each of them in NSPM 4 in early April. In the revised structure, the homeland security adviser and council were returned to a status subordinate to the national security adviser and NSC system, Bannon was removed from the PC, and the director of national intelligence and chair of the Joint Chiefs of Staff were restored as members. The Strategic Initiatives Group was also deemphasized and eventually dismantled.

Formal structure and organization notwithstanding, virtually nothing in the operations of the NSC system in the Trump administration resembled past practices. The role and performance of the national security adviser also departed from the norm and contributed to the unevenness of the Trump administration's foreign policy. Indeed, most analysts pointed to the highly aberrant approach as a central factor behind the inconsistency and ineffectiveness of foreign policymaking and White House leadership. The lack of effective structure and process was evident from the start, with a disorganized presidential transition in which Trump officials interacted with the Obama NSC staff in episodic and limited ways. Once in office, the Trump administration moved very slowly to organize, staff, and use the NSC system. According to one recent account from staffers involved,

> Traditional NSC staffers believe deeply in what they call the "policy process," a time-tested way of conducting the foreign and national security policy of the world's most powerful country. It involves a proper set of meetings, a chance for every agency to weigh in, and a rigorous legal review before the president makes a major decision. The early Trump days had virtually none of that, and the subject matter experts who make up much of the NSC career staff were largely ignored, even shunned. (Toosi 2019)

Michael Flynn, the president's first national security adviser, failed to engage and use the NSC system as well. Although many NSC staff members tried to sustain the traditional process, Flynn largely ignored them and the policy papers they generated, while the president and select advisers took decisions and actions without involving the NSC process. After Flynn was fired, eventually pleading guilty to lying to the FBI, the new national security adviser—H. R. McMaster—attempted to restore a more traditional structure and process to the NSC system, but he was unable to reign in Trump's unstructured approach to decision making or prevent the president's close advisers from circumventing the process. The president himself became increasingly unhappy with McMaster and his attempt to impose a more coherent organizational structure and process and forced his resignation in March 2018 (Perry 2018).

John Bolton, a rigid unilateralist whose emphasis on US sovereignty, independence, and power appealed to Trump, replaced McMaster in April 2018. Bolton quickly abandoned McMaster's approach and returned to the less structured process, orienting himself almost exclusively to the president as a personal adviser. According to reports, Bolton "told the NSC directorates that his job was to be a senior adviser to the president. Rather than overseeing meetings and policy discussions among principals, he told them, he planned to spend as much time as he could at Trump's side" (DeYoung et al. 2019). While the familiar three-tiered system and interagency process remained in place formally, virtually no concerted use occurred. Little coordination of policy debates at the DC or PC levels occurred, and the PC rarely met at all, leading Secretary of Defense James Mattis to write to Bolton just before Mattis resigned in December 2018 complaining about the harm the lack of meetings and coordination was causing to foreign policymaking (DeYoung et al. 2019). Bolton also replaced some NSC staff members who, as career professionals, had subject area expertise with outsider appointees who had more obvious ideological congruity with Bolton (and the president).

Perhaps unsurprisingly, Bolton soon ran into problems as well. Having abandoned the process manager and honest broker roles, Bolton relied almost exclusively on his role as adviser to Trump, which soon deteriorated as well (e.g., Glasser 2019; Rothkopf 2019). Bolton "saw his role as advisory, but Trump thinks he's his own adviser" (Parker and Rucker 2019). Tensions and disagreements between Bolton and the president on issues such as Ukraine, North Korea, Syria, Iran, Russia, and Afghanistan became increasingly sharp and pronounced, and by the summer of 2019, Bolton was increasingly cut out of the policy process (e.g., Bender and Salama 2019; DeYoung 2019; Parker and Rucker 2019). Acting chief of staff Mick Mulvaney began taking up some of Bolton's role and had his own national security adviser (Rob Blair)—an unusual position and practice for a chief of staff—play an increasingly prominent role (Bender and Salama 2019). Moreover, the rift between Bolton and Pompeo was, if anything, even more stark, and Pompeo's better relationship with Trump played a role in his ouster as well (DeYoung 2019). As the disagreements among Bolton, Pompeo, and Trump grew, the president became increasingly unhappy with Bolton and abruptly announced his departure (on Twitter) on September 9, 2019, catching advisers and staff across the administration by surprise.

A few examples illustrate the unstructured national security process under the Trump administration. No interagency review process occurred prior to the early announcement of the ban on travel and immigration from a number of countries—mostly Muslim—despite the obvious policy and legal implications for the Departments of Justice and Homeland Security, which were not even consulted (see "A Closer Look: Deciding on a Travel Ban") (Toosi 2019). Similarly, the NSC system was not involved in the decision process leading to Trump's controversial—and ultimately largely unsuccessful—meetings with North Korean tyrant Kim Jong Un. The president also decided to withdraw from the Intermediate-Range Nuclear Forces Treaty with Russia without a single PC meeting (DeYoung et al. 2019). No thorough NSC process led to Trump's on-again, off-again decisions to withdraw US troops from Syria in late 2018 and early 2019, and reports of an early decision to expand US operations in Yemen further illustrate the administration's casual and haphazard approach to the policy process:

> One morning during the first full week of the Trump presidency, an NSC staffer says he received a call from a friend who dealt with military issues, asking him if he knew that the president had given the Pentagon the go-ahead to pursue more raids against terrorists in Yemen. The staffer was confused—the topic was under discussion at the NSC, having been passed on from the Obama administration. But when had the idea of raids in Yemen reached the president? Soon, he found out: Flynn, Defense Secretary Jim Mattis and a handful of other officials had raised the subject directly with Trump over a dinner that week and the president had green-lit their plans.

Flynn and other officials, according to reports at the time, felt it was fine to do this because Trump wanted a faster decision-making process when it came to such military strikes. And former and current U.S. officials stress that if Trump, or any president, wants to make a decision this way, it's largely his prerogative. But later that week, NSC staffers and U.S. officials from other agencies were surprised when they were summoned to a deputies committee meeting on the same topic. "I wondered to myself, 'Why exactly are we meeting? What are we doing here?'" one attendee recalled. "The decision was kind of made and at the same time these meetings were being had" (Toosi 2019).

In mid-2019, the NSC process was not involved in efforts to open communication with Iranian leaders and was largely circumvented in the administration's efforts to negotiate with the Afghan government and representatives of the Taliban to end US involvement in Afghanistan (DeYoung 2019).

In the fall of 2019, President Trump named his fourth national security adviser in less than three years. After consideration of a variety of options, the president turned to Robert O'Brien, who served previously as special presidential envoy for hostage affairs, to fill the position. O'Brien faced similar challenges as his predecessors in the administration: how to build and operate a structure and process and how to play process manager, honest broker, and policy adviser roles for a president without real interest in the structure and process of foreign policy advising and decision making. However, among O'Brien's first actions was a plan to reduce the size and role of the NSC staff even further, suggesting that little had been learned from the experience of the first three years.

A Closer Look

DECIDING ON A TRAVEL BAN

According to the reports based on extensive interviews with current and former NSC staff members, the Trump administration decision process largely ignored the structures and process of the NSC system right from the start. One account described an early situation:

New presidents often issue a flurry of executive orders upon taking office—Obama did it—but those actions tend to be about reversing previous orders or otherwise fairly simple directives with long time frames for implementation. By contrast, some of the orders Trump aides sought to push through his first few days were complex, legally murky policy measures affecting numerous constituencies, and they were supposed to take effect rapidly.

On Monday evening, Jan. 23, 2017, the first full business day of the Trump administration, a batch of draft executive orders landed in the inboxes of several NSC career staffers. They included the infamous travel ban, which, among other things, barred from U.S. soil the citizens of seven majority-Muslim countries and temporarily stopped the United States from accepting refugees. That order was a lengthy document, around

3,000 words, with many national security implications. It had clearly been written by a handful of Trump political appointees, some of whom had worked as congressional staffers, and was apparently inspired by Trump's campaign promise to bar Muslims from the United States.

Typically, an executive order of such immense impact would have undergone weeks, if not months, of NSC-coordinated interagency review. Instead, on that Monday night, former NSC staffers say they were asked to review the travel ban and about half a dozen other draft executive orders in less than a day.

NSC staffers scrambled to slow things down, warning Trump aides that the executive orders could harm U.S. national security. For example, the travel ban covered Iraqis, a move likely to infuriate Iraq's government, one of America's top counterterrorism partners. The ban also cast the U.S. refugee resettlement program as a potential terrorist threat, despite next-to-no factual evidence. And it appeared to give preference to non-Muslim refugees, hinting at a potentially illegal religious test.

The political appointees brushed off the warnings, so NSC staffers alerted colleagues in other agencies in hopes that they would speak up and change the debate. They urged that government lawyers get time to weigh the consequences, and they quietly hoped that news of the ban would reach human rights activists and reporters (it did). None of it mattered. Trump signed the travel ban that Friday, spurring nationwide protests and court rulings against it.

How might such an unstructured process affect the ability of the White House to exercise leadership and coordination of the foreign policy bureaucracy?

Source: Toosi (2019).

Ultimately, the shortcomings of the Trump administration's foreign policy rest on three factors. First, the structures and processes of the NSC system failed to manage the policy process and harness the foreign policy bureaucracy to effective presidential decision-making. Second, personnel matters severely hindered the effective management of foreign policy. Not only did the administration struggle to place experienced foreign policy professionals in key appointed positions, but serious conflict between career personnel and appointees also hampered the process, and the national security advisers selected by the president were largely unsuccessful in playing the key roles of the job. Finally, and most important, the NSC system and its operations reflected the style and approach of the president himself. Simply put, President Trump was not interested or engaged in a deliberative process and did not welcome information and advice, preferring to make his own decisions. According to Parker and Rucker (2019), a Republican close to the president said "He really doesn't believe in advisers...He really just has people around him he asks questions of." When it comes to foreign policy, another former senior adviser to Trump told Parker and Rucker (2019) "There is no person that is part of the daily Trump decision-making process that can survive long term." With no sign of correction, and many of the most respected advisers already departed, the unstructured and disorganized management of the foreign policy process appeared likely to continue throughout the administration's time in office.

THE NSC SYSTEM AND PRESIDENTIAL MANAGEMENT IN PERSPECTIVE

All post–World War II presidents have had mixed success in managing the foreign policy bureaucracy. Presidential management depends on the important choices presidents make about their foreign policy orientation, their political agenda and level of involvement therein, their presidential appointments, and the organization of the decision-making process. As the bureaucracy has grown in size and complexity, the NSC has come to be the major institution involved in managing the foreign policy bureaucracy, though not as originally intended. The president has come to rely increasingly on a White House–centered foreign policy process managed by the national security adviser and staff.

From the perspective of the years since World War II, there has been both continuity and change in the overall making of US foreign policy. There has been considerable continuity in the national security process and reliance on the NSC. Several major changes are worth noting, however. One such change has been in the issues that presidents must manage. For example, foreign economic policymaking no longer takes a backseat to national security policymaking, as it did during the Cold War. A second change has been the rise of the White House staff as participants in the NSC system and process. Presidents want their most trusted staff and advisers to assist them, so it is no surprise that, as the players and agencies involved in the process expand, presidents turn to White House staff to help them manage the increasingly complicated process.

Ultimately, the NSC system exists for presidential management. It is meant to provide structure and process for presidents to receive the best information, make the best decisions, and ensure that those decisions are carried out. Because, as we have seen, presidential styles vary, the NSC system is meant to support presidents' strengths and minimize their weaknesses, while helping them to meet the challenges of foreign policymaking in an increasingly complex world. As the US role in the world has grown, so too has the "footprint" of the foreign policy bureaucracy, which has helped speed the development of a White House–centered system. As the Brownlow Commission concluded in the 1930s, "the President needs help." Since World War II, presidents have increasingly turned to the national security adviser and staff and the NSC system to provide that help. The approaches and results of the past three decades, including the deviation of the Trump administration from the consensus approach, show the centrality and importance of well-organized and effective structures and processes of that system.

THINK ABOUT THIS

In late 2016, President Barack Obama advised President-elect Donald Trump on the importance of establishing a structured and effective "process and a system to surface information [and] generate options for the president" through the National Security Council system. Think about the discussion of the NSC system and its roles and functions in US foreign policymaking.

What features and functions of the NSC system contribute to successful presidential leadership in foreign policymaking?

KEY TERMS

Bay of Pigs   221
cabinet government   214
CEO style   231
Deputies Committee   226
honest broker   219
national security adviser   220

National Security Council
   (NSC)   215
NSC interagency
   process   215
NSC-68   217
NSC system   215

Principals Committee   226
State Department–centered
   system   214
Tuesday Lunch group   222
White House–centered
   NSC system   214

Visit **edge.sagepub.com/scottrosati7e** to help you accomplish your coursework goals in an easy-to-use learning environment.

The Foreign Economic Bureaucracy and the National Economic Council

8

PHOTO 8.1 President Donald Trump at the 2018 G-7 summit meeting.

Jesco Denzel/Bundesregierung/Getty Images

LEARNING OBJECTIVES

1. Know the context of US foreign economic policy.

2. Identify the major agencies and organizations of the foreign economic bureaucracy.

3. Understand the background of modern approaches to managing and coordinating foreign economic policymaking.

4. Describe the nature, role, and challenges of the National Economic Council in foreign economic policymaking.

In 1944 the United States convened a meeting in Bretton Woods, New Hampshire, to help ensure that countries would not engage in another trade war like the one precipitating the Great Depression and World War II. The result was the establishment of what is often referred to as the **Liberal International Economic Order (LIEO),** which combined commitments to the ideas of free trade and free market economics with the construction of international institutions to help countries coordinate and cooperate in their pursuit of economic security. The LIEO promoted and spread free trade and encouraged market economies that worked together, and it established international institutions to tie states together and help them cooperate. Its establishment after World War II contributed to the development of the global economy.

In this context, the US foreign economic bureaucracy expanded in the post–World War II years and, especially since the early 1970s, its role in foreign policy has expanded as foreign economics has become more important to the United States. In many ways, foreign economic policy has increasingly become "high policy" since the collapse of the Bretton Woods system in the early 1970s. In this chapter, we provide an overview of the foreign economic bureaucracy and the president's approach and ability to manage the policymaking process—especially the key governmental institutions involved and presidential efforts at coordination.

US FOREIGN ECONOMIC POLICY IN CONTEXT

Let's begin by discussing the historical context of US foreign economic policy. For much of America's history, foreign and national security policy revolved around foreign economic policy—especially involving trade. In fact, trade policy played an important role in the movement for independence from Britain, and America's first attempts to project military power beyond its shores were motivated by the high costs of sailing the Mediterranean Sea because of attacks on commercial shipping by the Barbary pirates. Even after World War I, Americans believed that their interests in the rest of the world were largely commercial. American foreign economic policy since the founding has focused on internal economic development; the protection of domestic industry from foreign competition and investment; and the expansion of American commerce abroad, especially in Latin America and Asia.

This pattern in US foreign economic policy was deeply affected by the collapse of the international economy accompanying the **Great Depression** and the onset of World War II. After the war with Germany and Japan, Americans realized that "open door" policies, "dollar diplomacy," and world trade depended on global peace and stability, which in turn depended on international leadership to establish and maintain an international order. With the rise of US power, this eventually resulted in active efforts to restore a new stability and prosperity to the international political economy by the creation of the Bretton Woods system. The **Bretton Woods** international economic system was founded by the United States and its major allies, including the United Kingdom, premised on the principles of free trade, international cooperation, and the development of international economic organizations (such as the General Agreement on Tariffs and Trade, the International Monetary Fund, and the World Bank).

Because the US economy was so dominant in the world—with a relatively low proportion tied to international trade—until the 1970s, foreign economic policy generally took a back seat to the so-called high politics of national security and the Cold War. This meant that there was much delegation of responsibility to senior and lower level officials within the bureaucratic agencies involved in foreign economics. However, such delegation and subordination proved to be temporary. Beginning in the 1960s, the international economic system experienced increasing instability. American economic strength declined dramatically relative to others, and connections to international trade and investment grew more important. By 1971, the Bretton Woods system no longer could be sustained: President Nixon removed a weakened dollar from the gold standard and allowed its value to float relative to other major currencies; a surcharge was placed on Japanese imports to offset growing deficits in the balance of payments and the rise of protectionist sentiment at home; and "wage and price controls" were imposed on the American economy to arrest the growth of domestic inflation. Beginning in 1973, America's energy costs also increased dramatically with the rise of the ability of the **Organization of Petroleum Exporting Countries (OPEC)** to influence the supply of foreign oil, on which the US economy became increasingly dependent.

These changes in the international economic environment intensified many of the problems of inflation, unemployment, and deficits experienced by the US economy and Americans beginning in the late 1960s at all levels—national, state, and local. Such conditions forced international economic issues onto the government and public agendas, making foreign economic policy and the foreign economic bureaucracy part of high US foreign policy, especially after the Cold War (see Figure 8.1). The signing and passage of the North American Free Trade Agreement (NAFTA), as well as the creation of the World Trade Organization (WTO) with American participation under the elder Bush and Clinton, are indicative of the high priority of US foreign economic policy in recent years. The consequences of the global economic crisis from 2008 to 2010 prompted significant

FIGURE 8.1

The Growth in US Trade (data from US Census Bureau)

Source: Adapted from US Bureau of Economic Analysis, Net Exports of Goods and Services [NETEXP], retrieved from FRED, Federal Reserve Bank of St. Louis (https://fred.stlouisfed.org/series/NETEXP); and US Bureau of Economic Analysis, Real Exports of Goods and Services [EXPGSC1], retrieved from FRED, Federal Reserve Bank of St. Louis (https://fred.stlouisfed.org/series/EXPGSC1), July 17, 2019.

attention from the Bush and Obama administrations to the high policy of economics (see Madrick 2009; Roubini and Mihm 2010; Spero and Hart 2009). More recently, the tensions and consequences of globalization have prompted the Trump administration to pay great attention to foreign economic policy.

Although there were many factors behind Donald Trump's election in 2016 (such as disaffection with the Democratic candidate Hillary Clinton, Russian meddling in the election, a cultural backlash, and a general desire by some voters to shake things up in Washington), one factor was clearly economic. Historically most Republicans favored free trade and market-based capitalism, but a key part of Trump's political base rejected free trade as they saw themselves as its victims. Many of these voters found themselves poorly paid, underemployed, or unemployed, as their former jobs could now be done more cheaply by foreign workers (or even robots). This populist, or nativist, set of voters found their voice in candidate Trump, who called for NAFTA to be renegotiated and questioned the assumptions behind free trade's appeal. Almost immediately after his inauguration, Trump took action on his more protectionist preferences. Among other things, the Trump administration (1) withdrew the United States from the Trans-Pacific Partnership, which had been negotiated between the United States and eleven Pacific Rim partners to counter China's growing economic might; (2) forced the renegotiation of NAFTA with Mexico and Canada (now called the US-Mexico-Canada Agreement, or USMCA); (3) threatened and/or implemented a series of tariffs against major American trade partners in North America, Europe, and Asia—most notably China—in an attempt to reduce US trade deficits; and (4) weakened global economic institutions such as the WTO. See "A Different Perspective: Free Trade and Economic Security" for more on this change.

A Different Perspective

FREE TRADE AND ECONOMIC SECURITY

In the foreign economic policy realm, post–World War II American policymakers have long embraced the fundamental principles of liberal economics, with its emphasis on the benefits and advantages of free trade for countries and individuals. A cornerstone of US foreign economic policy since World War II has been to work toward the reduction of trade barriers, the establishment of international institutions to promote cooperation, and increasing engagement and integration of the United States and other economies into an open trading zone with few formal barriers to trade, especially those generated by policy decisions such as tariff and nontariff barriers.

Advocates stress the merits of openness for the *aggregate* economic growth of the United States and its trade partners, as well as the political benefits of international cooperation that economic interdependence and integration fosters. They often point to the historical lessons derived from periods of relatively free trade versus those in which protectionism was more common and aggressive—with the 1920s–1930s interwar experience of the Great Depression and global conflict as key examples. As the undersecretary for commerce for George W. Bush's administration summarized in 2001: "Open markets . . . lead to more jobs, higher revenues, more profits, and overall economic growth."

But in the recent context, some US policymakers have taken a different perspective. Critics argue that free trade can have important negative consequences for economic security. For one, skeptics point to the harsh impact of free trade on specific sectors of the economy and workforce, with the loss of jobs in sectors such as the auto industry and other manufacturing sectors. Moreover, some stress the potential consequences of free trade for strategic industries, arguing that sectors vital to national security must be maintained—the US steel industry and other high-tech sectors vital for the defense industry come to mind. Many critics further highlight that freer markets tend to become more unstable at times and produce gross inequalities. Finally, critics also argue that the expanding reach of economic interactions fostered by globalization and free trade are at the heart of the cultural clashes between the United States and other parts of the world, contributing to the anti-Americanism and hostility that can lead to violence such as terrorism.

Today, this perspective has reached the White House. Breaking with decades of bipartisan commitments and support, President Trump has adopted an economic nationalist approach. As like-minded advisers gained influence in his administration, in his first two years President Trump embraced criticisms of free trade. Among other things, his version of economic security led him to

- Withdraw the United States from the Trans-Pacific Partnership

- Renegotiate some elements of NAFTA (now the USMCA)

- Threaten to withdraw from the WTO

- Threaten to impose a tax on US companies moving their factories abroad

- Threaten to impose tariffs on foreign corporations exporting to the United States from third countries (especially developing countries like Mexico)

- Enact tariffs

  - On solar panels and washing machines (30 to 50 percent).

  - On steel (25 percent) and aluminum (10 percent) from most countries, including the European Union, Canada, and Mexico (while exempting South Korea, Brazil, Australia, and Argentina), though he later lifted the tariffs against Canada and Mexico after negotiating the USMCA.

  - On $250 billion of goods from China, initially, with another $300 billion in tariffs proposed in 2019.

Perhaps most surprisingly, members of the Republican Party in Congress, long stalwart advocates of free trade, have gone along with Trump, while members of the Democratic Party, often critical of free trade for its effects on labor and the environment, have opposed these moves. Thus, the tension between free trade and economic security is on full display.

What do you think is the proper balance between the principles of liberal trade and the need for economic and human security given increasing globalization?

In sum, since World War II, the US economy has become more intertwined with the workings of the international economy. American economic transactions have proliferated abroad and, at the same time, economic transactions emanating from abroad have increasingly penetrated the US economy. Thus, the US economy has become a larger part of, and more dependent on, the global political economy. These trends highlight the increasing importance of the international economy to American economic performance as well as to the standard of living and quality of life in the United States. They also indicate why foreign economic policy has grown in importance. With that increasing importance, it should be no surprise that the foreign economic bureaucracy has both expanded and become more influential in US foreign policy. How is the US government organized for foreign economic policymaking?

RELEVANT GOVERNMENTAL AGENCIES

As the global political economy grew in importance for the national economy, US foreign economic policy broadened, and the bureaucratic structures involved in this arena expanded. Since the 1950s, small departmental advisory staffs with international responsibilities have turned into full-fledged bureaus, while agencies within the Executive Office of the President (EOP) have become more active in international economic matters. Furthermore, the jurisdictional lines between those governmental institutions that have primary responsibility for domestic economic policy, as opposed to foreign economic policy, have become blurred, in large part because domestic and international economics have become much more intertwined.

Today, numerous governmental institutions and agencies play a role—large or small—in the making of US foreign economic policy. Several are located within the EOP and occupy more of a consultative or coordinating role, as indicated in Table 8.1. The following review highlights key agencies and their roles and interaction in foreign economic policy, with attention to areas of continuity and change in order to better understand presidential efforts to manage and coordinate them (see Cohen 2000; Destler 2005; Goddard 1993).

Executive Departments

Treasury Department. The **Treasury Department** is probably the most important agency in areas of international economics, such as trade and monetary issues, and it has often taken the lead on questions of foreign economic policy in general. The **secretary of the treasury** acts as a major policy adviser to the president, with responsibilities involving domestic and international financial, economic, and tax policy. The treasury secretary

TABLE 8.1

Executive Branch Organizations Shaping Economic Policy Today

Organization	Offices, Bureaus, and Agencies
EOP Agencies	Council of Economic Advisers
	National Economic Council
	Office of Management and Budget
	Office of the US Trade Representative

Organization	Offices, Bureaus, and Agencies
Executive Departments	Agriculture Department
	Commodity Credit Corporation
	Foreign Agriculture Service
	Commerce Department
	Bureau of Industry and Security
	Foreign Commercial Service
	International Trade Administration
	US Travel and Tourism Office
	Energy Department
	Office of International Affairs
	Labor Department
	Bureau of International Labor Affairs
	State Department
	Bureau of Economic and Business Affairs
	Bureau of International Organization Affairs
	Bureau of Oceans and International Environmental and Scientific Affairs
	US Agency for International Development
	Treasury Department
	Office of International Affairs
	Homeland Security
	Customs and Border Protection
	Immigration and Customs Enforcement
Other Agencies	Commodity Futures Trading Commission
	Export-Import Bank
	Federal Deposit Insurance Corporation (FDIC)
	Federal Reserve Board (the Fed)
	Federal Trade Commission
	Overseas Private Investment Corporation
	Securities and Exchange Commission
	US International Trade Commission
	US Trade and Development Agency

Source: The US Government Manual.

also officially represents the US government in key international economic organizations such as the International Monetary Fund (IMF), the World Bank, the WTO, the Inter-American Development Bank, and the African Development Bank.

The secretary heads a large, complex bureaucratic department of which the undersecretary for international economic affairs and several assistant secretaries have primary departmental responsibility over international monetary, financial, commercial, energy, and trade policies and programs. The office plays an important role in diplomatic negotiations concerning international economic matters and oversees US participation in the multilateral development banks such as the World Bank, to which the US government contributes more than $9 billion in grants and credits on an annual basis. This helps to explain why the United States has such a major voice in the World Bank and the IMF.

Department of State. The Department of State also plays a prominent role in all areas of US foreign economic policy. Although the State Department has had a long history of managing US external relations, it has declined relative to the Treasury Department in influence on US international economic policy. At the senior official level, the undersecretary for economic growth, energy, and environment acts as principal adviser to the secretary concerning international trade, agriculture, energy, finance, and transportation and relations with developing countries. Further down the hierarchy, the Bureau for Economic and Business Affairs has primary day-to-day departmental responsibility for formulating and implementing policy with regard to foreign economic matters. Other bureaus also share some major responsibilities in international economic issues. As we discussed in Chapter 5, the State Department is also home to the US Agency for International Development (USAID), which is principally responsible for administering economic assistance and supervising economic development policy abroad.

Department of Agriculture. The Department of Agriculture plays a major role in the area of agricultural trade. The Foreign Agricultural Service was created in 1953 to stimulate overseas markets for US agricultural products, principally through its network of agricultural counselors, attachés, and trade officers stationed overseas and reinforced by a support staff abroad and at home. The Foreign Agricultural Service maintains a worldwide agricultural intelligence and reporting system and plays an active role in US governmental trade policy and trade negotiations. The Foreign Agricultural Service also supervises and participates in the Food for Peace Program (Public Law 480 Program) and the Commodity Credit Corporation, which provides grants and credits to foreign governments and purchasers both as economic assistance and to encourage the development and expansion of overseas markets for US agricultural commodities. In 2017, the Trump administration reorganized the department to establish an undersecretary for trade and foreign agricultural affairs to better focus its activities in support of agricultural trade. Ted McKinney, a former agriculture industry businessman and state of Indiana Department of Agriculture official was named to the post in mid-2017.

Department of Commerce. The Department of Commerce has important international responsibilities in the area of trade. The department's International Trade Administration has the primary responsibility for the importation of foreign products, international economic policy, and trade promotion, especially nonagricultural. The Foreign Commercial Service is stationed overseas to provide services to the US exporting and international business community. The US Tourism and Travel Office (within the International Trade Administration) is the bureaucratic agency within the Commerce Department that attempts to promote foreign tourism in the United States. The Bureau of Industry and Security (formerly the Bureau of Export Administration), headed by an undersecretary for industry and security, directs the government's export control policy, which includes processing license applications and enforcing US export control laws (including high-technology items). Assistant secretaries for export administration and export enforcement head the central arms of the bureau.

Department of Energy. The Department of Energy has the major responsibility for energy policies, plans, and programs. The Office of the Assistant Secretary for International Affairs manages programs and activities relating to the international aspects of overall energy policy. These activities include energy preparedness and plans in case of national emergency, involvement in international energy negotiations, and coordination of international energy programs with foreign governments and such international organizations as the International Energy Agency and the International Atomic Energy Agency.

Department of Labor. The Department of Labor handles questions concerning domestic and international labor. The department's Bureau of International Labor Affairs assists in formulating international economic and trade policies that affect American workers; represents the United States in international bodies such as the International Labor Organization; and engages in technical assistance abroad and trade union exchange programs. Its central emphases include promoting a fair global playing field for US workers; strengthening labor standards and enforcing trade commitments; and combating international child labor, forced labor, and human trafficking.

Other Agencies

Other agencies have missions that affect US foreign economic policy. In the sections that follow, we highlight the most important agencies and discuss them briefly.

The Fed. Similar to other agencies with specialized missions, the involvement of the **Federal Reserve Board (the Fed)** in the international economic sphere flows from its monetary management within the domestic (and international) economy. The Fed is an independent agency that determines and executes the general monetary, credit, and operating principles of the US Federal Reserve System (consisting of twelve Federal Reserve Banks), serving as the government's central bank. It is headed by a seven-member Board of Governors and a twelve-member Federal Open Market Committee (FOMC) that makes the key financial decisions and oversees the Fed system as a whole. Although the president appoints the seven members of the Fed's Board of Governors and most of the members of the FOMC (with the advice and consent of the Senate) and designates the chair, as an independent agency the Fed is not "officially" under presidential control.

The chair of the Fed is the single most important official as the chair of the Board of Governors and the FOMC. The president of the New York Fed is the vice chair of the FOMC and is the next most consequential official, given the New York Fed's strategic location in the financial center of the United States. By influencing the lending and invest-ing activities of American commercial banks, such as the cost and availability of money and credit, the Fed affects not only the state of the American economy but also the country's international balance-of-payments position and the government's foreign economic policy. Fed policies also influence the activities of other major banking systems, such as in Europe and Japan—giving it a critical economic role (see Greider 1987).

The US International Trade Commission. The US International Trade Commission (ITC) is an independent agency with broad powers of investigation relating to customs laws, export and import trade, and foreign competition. For example, the commission often adjudicates disputes between American industry and international corporations within the United States over charges of unfair trading practices. The ITC also provides analysis and maintains tariffs and the US tariff schedule. The ITC is made up of six commissioners appointed for nine-year terms by the president with the advice and consent of the Senate.

The Export-Import Bank. The **Export-Import Bank (EXIM)** is a government cor-poration that subsidizes American company exports abroad. Although established in 1934 to promote trade only with the Soviet Union, during most of its history it has provided grants and credits to aid the export financing of US goods and services abroad in general. However, it is prohibited from competing with private financing. The EXIM also guaran-tees the Foreign Credit Insurance Association, an association of US insurance companies organized by the bank in 1961 to ensure export transactions against risk of default.

The Overseas Private Investment Corporation. The Overseas Private Investment Corporation (OPIC) is an independent agency that stimulates foreign investment, pre-dominantly in developing countries. It offers US exporters assistance in finding invest-ment opportunities, insurance to protect their investments, and loans and loan guarantees to help finance their projects. OPIC insures American companies against the political risks of foreign investment, such as expropriation and damage from war, revolution, insur-rection, or civil strife. With the collapse of communist regimes, OPIC began to support American investment in the economies of Eastern Europe in the 1990s.

US Trade and Development Agency. The US Trade and Development Agency became an independent entity in 1992. It was designed to assist in the creation of jobs for Americans by helping US companies export and pursue overseas business opportunities, especially in development projects in emerging economies.

EOP Agencies

Agencies within the EOP also have become more active in the making of US foreign economic policy. The Office of Management and Budget, the Office of the United States Trade Representative, and the National Economic Council have major responsibilities concerning budgetary and trade matters and play important roles in the president's effort to coordinate and manage US foreign economic policy. We discuss these important players in greater detail later in this chapter. The **Council of Economic Advisers (CEA)**, with three members and a small staff, was created in 1946 to assess the state of the American economy and advise the president on economic matters. One of the three CEA members is assigned international responsibilities and participates in official delegations to the Organization for Economic Cooperation and Development (OECD) countries—Western Europe, Canada, and Japan. CEA members are usually academics in economics and often do not have much of a role in day-to-day economic advice, although occasionally they may depend on their particular relationship to the president.

MANAGING THE FOREIGN ECONOMIC BUREAUCRACY

By now, the landscape of the foreign economic bureaucracy should look familiar. Like the foreign policy bureaucracy, many agencies are involved, and their roles and jurisdictions are both specialized and overlapping. Thus, it should not be a surprise that, just as it is with the foreign policy bureaucracy, major challenges and problems of management and coordination face the executive branch. How has the White House addressed these policymaking challenges?

Presidential Attention and Knowledge

As we have seen in our discussion of the National Security Council system and the foreign policy bureaucracy, presidential style and orientation are central to the organization and process of foreign policymaking, and foreign economic policymaking is no exception. Thus, part of the challenge in coordinating the foreign economic bureaucracy involves the lack of presidential attention to and knowledge of international economic affairs. Indeed, as a general rule, since the Cold War, most presidents and their closest foreign policy advisers have been more knowledgeable and comfortable dealing with traditional political and military issues associated with national security policy. Paul Volcker, former chair of the Fed, has commented that American presidents "have not in my experience wanted to spend much time on the complexities of international finance" (quoted in Goddard 1993:176). For the most part, during the Cold War, foreign economics was not considered high policy and, hence, did not attract much presidential attention.

Not surprisingly, the "low" priority of international economics during the Cold War left a strong legacy in the making of US foreign policy: a foreign economic bureaucracy expanding in size and power but enjoying considerable freedom from presidential supervision and control. As I. M. Destler (1994) put it, the net result has been a divided governmental policymaking process with a relatively centralized "security complex" and a decentralized "economic complex." The overall result for the making of foreign economic policy, according to Harald Malmgren (1972:42), a former deputy special representative for trade negotiations for the president, is that "widespread confusion exists as to who is responsible for what. Both policy and daily decisions seem to be aimed in several different directions simultaneously."

For certain policy areas, appropriate lead agencies are readily identifiable: the Department of Treasury for monetary matters, the Office of the US Trade Representative for most trade issues, the Department of Agriculture for food, the Department of Energy for issues within its sphere, and the Department of State for matters concerning assistance and many Third World issues. "But it is much harder, of course, to assure that [these agencies] will keep their parochialism in check. And no single department or cabinet member can exercise effective oversight of overall foreign economic policy" (Destler 2005:215). Many of these agencies have also tended to be very sensitive and responsive to Congress and business/trade-oriented interest groups.

Foreign Economic Policy Coordination during the Cold War

Historically, the State Department was the lead agency responsible for coordinating US foreign economic policy (except during war, when the White House usually became more prominent), while the foreign economic bureaucracy was much smaller and less complex and bureaucratic. This began to change during the twentieth century, especially after World War II, when the foreign economic bureaucracy expanded in size and complexity. The main result is that the Treasury Department grew in prominence, becoming "a first among equals," with the secretary of the treasury usually serving as the president's official economic spokesperson, but not to the point of being powerful enough to coordinate foreign economic policy across the competing bureaucratic agencies. As a consequence, as the foreign economic bureaucracy expanded, power effectively decentralized, making it very difficult for the president to manage economic aspects of foreign policy. To try to meet this challenge, during the Cold War, presidents used different strategies to coordinate the foreign economic policymaking process, with three main approaches involving the Office of Management and Budget, the Office of the US Trade Representative, and, most often, interagency committees usually coordinated within the EOP (see Cohen 2000; Destler 1996, 2005; Dolan 2001; Juster and Lazarus 1997; and Malmgren 1972).

An early effort at coordination involved the government's budgetary process. The Bureau of the Budget was created in 1921 and placed within the EOP by President Franklin Roosevelt in 1939 in order to coordinate and streamline the budgetary process of an expanding government. The Bureau of the Budget was the precursor to the **Office of Management and Budget (OMB)**, created in 1970 to coordinate and supervise the government's budget and fiscal program for the president. The formulation of the budget of the US government is of great importance because it affects the activities of all bureaucratic agencies and represents the fiscal and spending policies of the federal government, currently to the tune of more than $3 trillion per year. As one analyst has stated, "Although the politics of the budget is often considered an internal concern, no external issue is as critical to foreign and national security strategy" (Deibel 1991:15). However, even the assistance of the OMB and a sizable staff have not allowed the president to develop a coherent governmental policy with respect to issues involving international monetary matters, trade, investment, energy, and assistance.

The late 1970s witnessed the growing prominence of the **Office of the US Trade Representative (USTR)** as a coordinator of US trade policy. Created by Congress in 1962 as part of the EOP, since President Carter, the USTR, a cabinet-level official with the rank of ambassador, has acted as a major presidential adviser, public spokesperson, and often the chief representative of the US government on trade matters. Nevertheless, the USTR has had limited success in directing and managing US trade policy for the president. Much depends on the individual trade representative, his or her relationship with the president, and the quality of the USTR staff.

Most presidents have come to rely on the third strategy—the creation of different interagency committees at the cabinet and subcabinet levels to promote interaction and coordination of foreign economic policy. These agencies are often coordinated within the EOP or are chaired by a lead agency, most often the Treasury Department. These efforts have had mixed success, and none of the interagency groups has gained the kind of permanence and prestige that the National Security Council (NSC) system has come to enjoy in national security policy. On the whole, US policymakers found it very difficult to pursue a steady economic policy, and presidents failed to establish consistency in their organization of economic issues and the policymaking process. The interagency process varied under each president and sometimes within the same administration. Foreign and domestic economics were sometimes integrated, sometimes kept distinct.

THE NATIONAL ECONOMIC COUNCIL AND THE HIGH POLITICS OF INTERNATIONAL ECONOMICS

Throughout the 1970s and 1980s, plans to reform and reorganize the foreign economic policymaking process to promote greater policy coordination and coherence arose from many quarters. Little came of these recommendations until Bill Clinton became president. Although Clinton was relatively inexperienced in national security policy, he was deeply interested and knowledgeable about issues of economics, both domestic and international. As one Clinton adviser stated, "Unlike his predecessors, he doesn't see the distinction between economics and politics or between the domestic economy and the international economy" (Stokes 1993:615). This interest led Clinton to try to better organize and coordinate the (foreign) economic bureaucracy by issuing a 1993 executive order to establish a new structure within the EOP—the **National Economic Council (NEC)** (Destler 1996; Dolan and Rosati 2006; Juster and Lazarus 1997).

The new NEC—like the National Security Council, after which it was modeled—is a formal mechanism led by the **national economic director (or NEC director)**—and a small staff (of a few dozen people). Its main functions are (1) to coordinate the economic policymaking process with respect to domestic and international economic issues; (2) to coordinate economic policy advice to the president; (3) to ensure that economic policy decisions and programs are consistent with the president's stated goals and to ensure that those goals are effectively pursued; and (4) to monitor implementation of the president's economic policy agenda.

During his two terms of office, Clinton relied on three NEC directors to help him manage the bureaucracy and make economic policy at home and abroad. Along with the secretary of the treasury, the new NEC director clearly became one of the president's most prominent advisers in the making of US economic policy (Table 8.2 lists those who have served as NEC directors).

TABLE 8.2

National Economic Council Directors

Name	Year	President	Background
Robert Rubin	1993	Clinton	Law, Wall Street
Laura D. Tyson	1995	Clinton	Academia
Gene Sperling	1997	Clinton	Law, government
Lawrence Lindsey	2001	Bush	Academia
Stephen Friedman	2003	Bush	Business, Wall Street
Allan B. Hubbard	2005	Bush	Business
Keith Hennessey	2007	Bush	Business, government
Lawrence Summers	2009	Obama	Academia, business, government
Gene Sperling	2011	Obama	Law, government
Jeffrey Zients	2014	Obama	Business, government
Gary Cohn	2017	Trump	Business, finance
Larry Kudlow	2018	Trump	Finance, government, media

The NEC was designed to function as an honest broker, coordinating the formation and implementation of economic policy by the major policymakers and the variety of executive agencies involved. It has been described as a "low-profile but powerful institutional mechanism created to coordinate the Administration's Cabinet-level economic policymaking. The goal was to do for economic policy what the National Security Council (NSC) has done for national security policy" (Wildavsky 1996:1417). Much like the 1947 creation of the NSC, the creation of the NEC was a revolutionary institutional change in the making of US economic policy. Let's consider the origins, development, and operation of the NEC to highlight the challenges of managing the foreign economic policy bureaucracy.

Origins

Clinton's NEC was based on a notion that had bounced around Congress, universities, and think tanks for years. Despite previous presidential efforts and failures at coordination from the White House, especially by presidents Nixon and Ford, Clinton was determined to try to create an "Economic Security Council, similar in status to the NSC, with responsibility for coordinating America's international economic policy" (Clinton and Gore 1992:131–132). Despite the misgivings of some advisers, President-elect Bill Clinton pushed his economic team to develop a plan. His team embraced the concept, as reflected in a "Memorandum to the President-Elect":

> [T]he combination of Cold War victory and deep economic difficulties allows—and indeed, demands—a shift of priority and resources away from national

security as traditionally defined, toward the broader problems of making America competitive in a fiercely competitive world .... [T]he Economic Council and its staff would be your instrument for assuring that economic policy gets attention equal to traditional national security, working extremely closely with the NSC and its staff when international economic issues are under consideration, and with the domestic policy Council and its staff on domestic policy matters. (quoted in Juster and Lazarus 1997:8)

Reflecting the priority he placed on this issue, Clinton announced his economic team even before his team of national security advisers.

Clinton's choice to head the new council was Wall Street financier Robert Rubin, whom he asked to "replicate on the economic side what George Bush had done on the foreign-policy side" ("In Bob We Trust" 1994:28). Clinton chose Rubin to reassure Wall Street and because of his ability to create an atmosphere of collegiality among a group of smart, aggressive personalities as a partner of Goldman Sachs—Rubin's Wall Street firm. Rubin took the job only after Clinton assured him that the NEC's role would be taken seriously.

Robert Rubin and the Transition

As the first special assistant to the president for economic policy, Robert Rubin (who later became treasury secretary) was consequential in defining the initial role of the position and the council operations. The NEC director position was created to serve as "senior economic advisor—chairing senior staff meetings and conferring with the president privately" (Judis 1993:25). In this context, Rubin "conceived his role as honest broker, organizing options for the president, but he [was] not ... hesitant about articulating his own views" as well (Judis 1993:21). For the most part the national economic director and the NEC were able to minimize conflict that its creation engendered with the economic bureaucracy while promoting a relatively open and collegial process. Rubin's role demonstrates the importance that individuals and personalities play in influencing the organization and dynamics of the policy process.

Rubin molded the NEC into the center of White House economic policymaking, blending and balancing the roles of the other important economic agencies such as the Office of the USTR, the OMB, and the Department of Treasury, along with the NSC itself. As his deputies, Rubin chose Gene Sperling, an economic director on the campaign, and Bowman Cutter, a former management consultant at the OMB under President Carter. The remainder of the NEC staff included lawyers, political activists, professors, Congressional Budget Office analysts, congressional aides, and former lobbyists. Together, this small group—in consultation with Clinton's economic principals—planned the NEC's jurisdiction processes, including its linkages to the NSC system. For example, the NEC and the NSC maintained a joint international economics staff within the NSC—a strategy that had been worked out by Rubin and Anthony Lake, Clinton's national security adviser, over coffee in late 1992.

As Rubin explained: "We had to define [the NEC], we had to create its acceptance within the government process, and then we had to staff it, all at the same time that we were working on the economic plan" (quoted in Ifill 1993:22). Forming a team that reflected Clinton's broad ideology but without "sharp elbows" or big egos was difficult enough; Rubin also faced the challenge of harnessing the numerous departments and agencies into the yoke of a new formal structure responsible for policy coordination. The NEC had to be powerful enough to coordinate policy, while managing the almost inevitable bureaucratic turf wars. The most important of these involved the administration's treasury secretary, Lloyd Bentsen, and secretary of state, Warren Christopher. The State Department was accustomed to policy coordination through the NSC and had steadily become less influential in the making of foreign economic policy. Treasury, however, was a different matter. Not only was Bentsen regarded as one of the most prominent and powerful cabinet members, but the Treasury Department also had little experience with policy coordination and was considered the most resistant to NEC management.

With Bentsen and the other principal participants, Rubin succeeded largely because he had the support of the president, and because he nurtured the view of the NEC as an honest broker of each agency's policy input. Still, the task of integrating a broad range of policy preferences from more than sixteen cabinet members with a variety of bureaucratic, constituency, and political agendas was difficult. As Rubin characterized the situation:

> Almost all issues have cross-agency ramifications, so you have to have some mechanism for getting the views of the different agencies, or you wind up with the President making a decision based on the perspective of one agency and not knowing what six other agencies might think about it . . . . You have to make sure that you are dealing with the President—and with everybody else in the economic team and in the Administration—in a totally neutral way . . . that you express the pluses and minuses, and then totally separate that from the expression of your opinion. (quoted in Ifill 1993:22)

The NEC in Operation

From its inception, the NEC has been structured very much like the NSC, with two important exceptions: First, the NEC coordinates domestic, intermestic, and international economic policy (with two deputy directors, one for international economics and the other for domestic economics). Second, the NEC's staff is considerably smaller—a few dozen members within the NEC versus as many as ten times that number within the NSC. Like the NSC, the NEC consists of three basic interagency committees and a formal interagency process, along with informal interaction among prominent officials. First, a "core group" of senior officials—the Principals Committee—met for the most prominent issues, usually led by the NEC director. Second, a Deputies Committee was created of senior subcabinet officials. Finally, at the lowest level, other interagency working groups were created on an ad hoc basis, made up of various officials and chaired by key NEC aides (see Figure 8.2).

The Principals Committee was NEC's power base. Here Rubin and subsequent directors used their management skills while demonstrating their influence with

FIGURE 8.2

Organizational Structure of the NEC Policymaking System

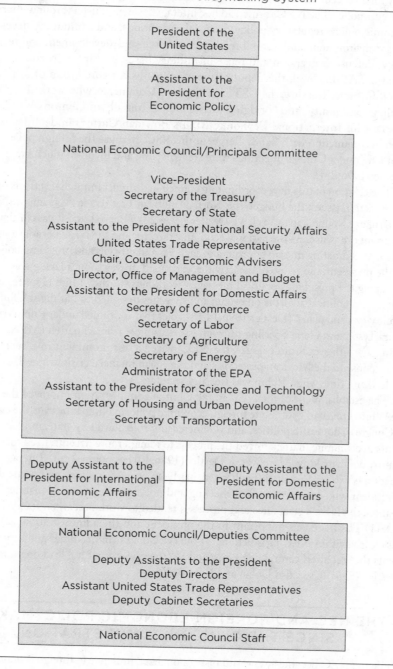

the president. The principals usually discussed only urgent issues and proposals that were ready for an executive decision. At the Deputies Committee level, the NEC met regularly to discuss policy. The NEC formed ad hoc interagency issue clusters around international economic policy; regulatory policy, financial institutions, and community development; energy, environment, and natural resources; research-and-development and technology policy; defense conversion and reuse of military bases; and infrastructure and transportation. At this level, the deputies' meeting involved a core group of officials from the NSC, State, Treasury, the USTR's office, and Commerce, who worked on "building a policy community" and "bridging jurisdictions." Initially in Clinton's NEC, Deputy Assistant for International Economic Affairs Bowman Cutter ran deputies' meetings, often in conjunction with Sandy Berger at the NSC. Because the foreign policy deputies "bonded," under Clinton, meetings were freewheeling and involved much brainstorming (Destler 1996:28).

The creation of this new coordinating council had almost immediate effects on "front-burner action issues: the budget, the North American Free Trade Agreement (NAFTA), the Uruguay Round, Japan," as I. M. Destler (1996:28) observed, and it has continued to be important ever since. As the national economic director and the NEC became a significant force in coordinating myriad bureaucratic agencies and officials and providing policy advice for the president, the scope of its activities expanded. It was soon "playing a growing role in shaping the president's political messages, working with the White House's communications and political advisors on events and speeches designed to highlight Clinton's economic views and plans" (Destler 1996:14,18), roles that continued under Rubin's successors Laura Tyson and Gene Sperling for such issues as most favored nation (MFN) status for China. For other economic issues, the NEC played a less prominent role, such as in the US response to the Mexican peso crisis and the Asian financial crisis, where Treasury took the lead at a time when Rubin was treasury secretary.

The establishment of the NEC in the Clinton administration improved the ability of the White House to coordinate foreign economic policymaking. However, the critical role of Congress, domestic politics, and the increasing role played by state and local governments in economic matters forced the process to remain more decentralized than national security policymaking. Moreover, as Destler (1996:40) has pointed out, "Interagency coordination is extraordinarily difficult, particularly on economic issues, and particularly with a president who engages in a freewheeling and not always predictable manner." Since its creation, the NEC's structures and processes tended to work best when four criteria were met: (1) The issue was important to the president and the administration, (2) the issue was clearly within NEC jurisdiction, (3) the NEC had firm deadlines and action-forcing events that required central decisions, and (4) there was a natural lead operating agency (Destler 1996:36; see also Dolan and Rosati 2006).

THE NEC AND FOREIGN ECONOMIC POLICYMAKING SINCE THE CLINTON ADMINISTRATION

While the NEC became a powerful institutionalized presence in foreign economic policy, its continued role depended greatly on presidential interest in international economics.

The NEC under George W. Bush

Under President George W. Bush, the NEC continued to play an important role in coordinating foreign economic policy. Bush decided to keep and even strengthen the NEC, but he had a difficult time staffing his economic team, especially the national economic director role. Attesting to the challenges of coordinating the decentralized foreign economic bureaucracy, some of the power behind President Bush's economic policies came from outside of the NEC (Dolan and Rosati 2006; Sanger 2001) and, once the global economic crisis began in 2008, the president increasingly relied on the leadership of the Treasury Department under Secretary Henry Paulsen to respond.

President Bush continued to institutionalize the NEC. With respect to the nexus between security and economic issues, Bush enacted some major changes in the relationship between the NSC and the NEC in the policymaking process. In particular, Bush ordered the national security adviser and the NEC director to "share a foreign policy desk to more effectively integrate economics with security issues in America's post–cold war foreign policy objectives" (Sanger 2001). Bush stated that the move was designed to "make sure the economic people don't run off with foreign policy and vice versa." He justified his moves by referring to the major role the Treasury Department had in the Clinton administration in setting foreign policy toward East Asia, Latin America, and Russia. "Globalization has altered the dynamics in the White House, as well as between the White House and the Treasury. We have to respond to that" (Sanger 2001). Bush also added foreign economics experts to the joint NSC/NEC international economics staff. The staff dealt with two sorts of issues: setting general international economic policy and coordinating White House responses to regional and international financial crises. Initially, under Condoleezza Rice, the staff was physically located within the NSC structure but reported both to her and to the NEC director through a newly created deputy assistant for international economic policy.

However, the Bush administration had considerable turnover in its senior foreign economic policy officials, especially the Secretary of Treasury and the NEC director. In economic policy, Bush originally appeared to be comfortable with Lawrence Lindsey heading the NEC. Lindsey brought to the NEC years of experience as a member of the Federal Reserve Board of Governors, as a professor of economics at Harvard, and as a staff member on Reagan's CEA. He was chosen to head the NEC over others in part because of his friendship with the president and his ability to explain complex economic issues to Bush in simple terms. For treasury secretary, Bush initially selected Paul O'Neill, former CEO of Alcoa. O'Neill had a reputation as a deficit hawk and had little experience in international economic policymaking. O'Neill was never seen as effective and was often off-message with the White House. Lindsey, in contrast, was a Reagan-style tax cutter and ardent free trader and his role as go-to-guy in both domestic and foreign economic policy was seen in Bush's commitment to following through with the $1.6 trillion tax cut he had proposed during the campaign and his willingness to go ahead with American participation in the Free Trade Area of the Americas (FTAA).

With the lackluster performance of the American economy, Bush changed his major economic team following the 2002 congressional elections. Treasury Secretary O'Neill was replaced by business executive Jack Snow, and NEC director Lindsey was replaced by Stephen Friedman. However positive Lindsey's relationship with Bush, he was asked to resign because he was seen as an ineffective policy coordinator and manager. Moreover, and most damaging to his career, was his public estimate that the war in Iraq might cost more than $200 billion, which was seen as an act of disloyalty and drew the ire of Vice President Cheney and the president.

Friedman, a former partner of Robert Rubin at Goldman Sachs and an adviser to the Clinton administration, replaced Lindsey and was expected to bring more centrist support to the president's economic plans. However, Friedman was staunchly opposed to the ballooning deficit and never really asserted himself on other issues. He was replaced in 2005 by the third NEC director, Allan B. Hubbard, who aligned himself well with the president based in part on their past friendship; Bush and Hubbard were classmates at Harvard Business School. Being a close friend of the president increased Hubbard's ability to get the president's economic advisers to work together, something that did not occur smoothly under the two previous NEC directors. However, Hubbard lasted only two years in the position, replaced by Keith Hennessey, who had served as a staff member on the NEC since 2002 and remained as NEC director until Bush's second term ended.

Finally, the economic crisis that hit full force in 2008 put the Bush administration in crisis management mode. Very simply, the financial system and the US economy had "derailed" off the tracks of conventional free market thought. President Bush turned to Treasury Secretary Paulsen, who soon eclipsed the NEC director in role and influence. Paulsen asked for massive government intervention in the economy, including the $700 billion TARP (Troubled Asset Relief Program) to restore liquidity (i.e., money) and lending to the financial-banking sector. As part of the Emergency Economic Stabilization Act of 2008, commonly referred to as a "bailout" of the US financial system, Congress quickly enacted a law proposed by Paulsen in October 2008 for the US government to purchase distressed assets, especially mortgage-backed securities, and make capital injections into banks—both foreign and domestic.

Foreign Economic Policymaking and the Obama NEC

Barack Obama inherited this dramatic economic crisis when he was inaugurated in January 2009. To head off what appeared to be a looming global catastrophe and promote recovery, Obama enlisted a proactive team of strong personalities with often differing economic philosophies. Obama assembled his first economic team from a group of individuals renowned for their experience, intellect, and ability to deconstruct the most challenging economic problems, while trying to create an atmosphere of consensus through open discussion.

Foreign economic policymaking emerged from the interaction of three sources: (1) the NEC and NEC Director Lawrence Summers and his successors, Gene Sperling and Jeffrey Zients; (2) the Treasury Department and Treasury Secretary Timothy Geithner and his successor, Jacob Lew; and (3) the Federal Reserve Board and

Fed chief Ben Bernanke and his successor, Janet Yellen. As Simon Johnson (2009), a former chief economist at the IMF, described the new economic team:

> In the configuration of responsibility for economic strategy in the current administration, the NEC, led by Lawrence Summers, has a broad mandate—covering essentially all issues to some degree. But the Treasury Secretary Timothy F. Geithner has enormous authority and discretion with regard to the financial sector. The CEA plays a supportive analytical role, which can matter on particular points, and other departments or agencies tend to have a more limited scope. For major economic policy initiatives, the most important drivers within the administration are the views of Mr. Summers, Mr. Geithner and their respective staffs. These obviously interact with—and bump up against—the Federal Reserve on many technical issues and Congress on everything political. There are also increasing indications that Mr. Summers's economic council and Mr. Geithner's Treasury are not exactly on convergent paths.

Not surprisingly, there appeared to be tremendous overlap in the minds and thinking of the principal advisers on whom President Obama initially relied. They also appeared to have a complementary working relationship with each other and the president despite differences in personality, temperament, and policy views. At the same time, there were reports that the forceful and experienced personalities that Obama assembled also clashed under the stress of their work. According to Jackie Calmes (2009):

> Underlying tensions have gripped Mr. Obama's economic advisors as they . . . struggled with the gravest financial crisis since the Depression. By all accounts, much of the tension derive[d] from the president's choice of the brilliant but sometimes supercilious Mr. Summers to be the director of the National Economic Council, making him the policy impresario of the team . . . . Along the way, Mr. Summers . . . forcefully debated the Treasury secretary, his onetime protégé Timothy F. Geithner, over what to do with troubled banks. He . . . clashed with Peter R. Orszag, the budget director, over fiscal and health policy issues. He . . . collided with Austin Goolsbee, an economist on the Council of Economic Advisors, over whether to rescue Chrysler. And he and Mrs. Romer [CEA chair] have squabbled over how best to make the economic case for overhauling health care.

What was particularly unique was the close and overt working relationship between Fed chair Ben Bernanke and the rest of the Obama economic team—especially given the Fed's traditional independence within the executive branch and from the president. Clearly, the necessity to work together on the very serious crisis overrode some of the bureaucratic autonomy and protectiveness (see "A Closer Look: President Obama's First Economic Team").

A Closer Look

PRESIDENT OBAMA'S FIRST ECONOMIC TEAM

NEC Director Lawrence Summers was the only Obama top economic director with a West Wing office. He had daily access to the president and saw the president more than his other advisers, and Summers also controlled the daily economic briefings. "As the Obama team has coalesced, Summers, who leads a daily economic briefing for the president, has seemed to emerge as the strategic mastermind of the administration's macroeconomic response to the biggest crisis since the Depression" (Freeland 2009). He outlined his responsibilities as National Economic Council director:

> My role is to make sure the president gets access to the best economic thinking he can on everything that touches the economy. That means making sure that no arguments go scrutinized . . . and it means helping everyone on the president's economic team make the best case for whatever policies they prefer. It is certainly incredible, as intellectually challenging as anything I've ever done. . . . What makes it so challenging and exciting, as well as exhausting, is the range of subjects. (quoted in Freeland 2009)

And Summers was impressed with "Obama's determination to use his presidency to effect long-term change—no matter how pressing the immediate problems" (quoted in Freeland 2009).

Timothy Geithner, Obama's secretary of the treasury, was the president of the Federal Reserve Bank of New York and intimately involved during the start of the banking crisis in the fall of 2008. As one commentator observed, "Mr. Geithner has been the most prominent administration spokesman on all matters financial and fiscal" (Johnson 2009). As Geithner (2009) himself explained it,

> Although this crisis in some ways started in the United States, it is a global crisis . . . . The rest of the world needs the US economy and financial system to recover in order for it to revive. We remain at the center of global economic activity with financial and trade ties to every region of the globe. Just as importantly, we need the rest of the world to recover if we are to prosper again here at home. As a consequence, the community of nations must work together . . . to revive economies around the world and to lay the groundwork for a new, more stable and more sustainable pattern of growth in the future. This crisis is not simply a more severe version of the usual business cycle recession, the typical downturn in which economies ultimately adjust and stabilize. Instead, it is an abrupt correction of financial excesses that has overwhelmed economies' and markets' self-correcting mechanisms, and so can only be ended by extraordinary policy responses.

Ben Bernanke was chair of the Federal Reserve Board of Governors from 2006 to 2014. According to one analysis,

> The Fed has never wielded as much power as it does right now, but the very expansion of its mission has exposed it to more second-guessing and more challenges to its political independence than ever before. . . . The Fed chairman and the central bank are also caught in a political cross fire over how to overhaul the nation's system of financial regulation.

> President Obama has proposed a sweeping plan that would make the Fed more powerful in some respects and less powerful in others. Mr. Obama's plan would put the Fed in charge of regulating systemic risk, like the buildup of dangerous mortgages during the housing bubble and would give the Fed

power to impose tougher regulation over financial institutions deemed too big to fail. (Andrews 2009)

As Bernanke (2009) saw it, it was the "perfect storm," of economic misfortune in which "housing, credit and financial problems converged into a major crisis the likes of which haven't been seen since the 1930s." Therefore, they needed to think "outside the box."

Richard Wolffe (2010) argued that the economic team saw it as their patriotic duty to govern and save the economy first and foremost. If that meant compromise and bending to Washington's and Wall Street's political realities, that was the cost of doing the country's business. Most importantly, Bernanke set an unprecedented role for working and cooperating with Treasury and the NEC, rather than its more passive or invisible, and definitely independent, role historically. In practice, Bernanke minimized the political independence of the Fed because of his real fear that the loss in "confidence" and the economic meltdown would snowball into a real global depression.

Does it really matter which individuals occupy the positions of the NEC director, treasury secretary, and chair of the Fed?

Confident but inexperienced, Obama had the enthusiasm to transform economic policy as he proposed to do in his 2008 campaign, but he did not exert a proactive "process" role (as opposed to policy) in economic issues, given the nature of his economic team. This was reinforced by his limited experience and knowledge of the international economy. Obama understandably wanted "results" and proved more pragmatic in practice that his populist and idealistic rhetoric during the campaign suggested (see Alter 2010; Calmes 2009; Green 2010; Johnson 2009; Lizza 2010; Suskind 2011).

Ultimately, Obama was successful in restoring confidence in the financial system, getting his stimulus package passed, arresting the economic decline in 2009, and passing his major health care legislation. After this flurry of activity in the first eighteen months of the administration, the president made some changes in his economic team. The most notable of these was the replacement of Larry Summers as NEC director with Gene Sperling—who had previously occupied the same role under President Clinton—in early 2011. Sperling was a central figure in the administration's struggle with the Republican-controlled house over the US budget and was central to other administration initiatives such as the American Jobs Act, the extension of the Transition Adjustment Assistance program, the universal dislocated worker plan, the small business tax credit, manufacturing policy, housing initiatives, and economic assistance for veterans. As NEC director, Sperling continued the central coordinating efforts established by his predecessors.

The policies that began under George W. Bush and were passed in 2009–2010 by Obama became controversial and helped to intensify the partisanship that was already pervasive in Washington, DC, politics. Criticized on the right for being too liberal, and by the left for falling under Wall Street's spell, Obama managed to make both sides unhappy. With the significant gains by the Republicans during the 2010 election, especially in Congress, gridlock became the norm in the nation's capital relative to the economy.

Nevertheless, amid signs of economic improvement throughout the summer and fall of 2012, Obama won reelection in a campaign in which economic issues—including the federal budget and debt, jobs and growth, trade and investment—dominated. Immediately after the November 2012 election, Obama and his economic team moved to address efforts to sustain and accelerate the slow economic recovery at home and abroad. Jeffrey Zients replaced Sperling as NEC director, and Jack Lew replaced Geithner as treasury secretary. Under Zients, the NEC led the Obama administration's efforts to negotiate with the increasingly assertive Congress over tax and budget plans. Zients was also central to the Obama administration's successful efforts to gain trade promotion authority to negotiate a Trans-Pacific Partnership and take other steps to provide support to US workers and strengthen US trade policy enforcement measures. Lew, who had been Obama's second director of the OMB (following Peter Orszag) and third chief of staff (following Rahm Emmanuel and William Daley), was central to the budget impasse and efforts to avoid a default on US debts.

The Trump Administration and (Lack of) Coordination in Foreign Economic Policymaking

Donald Trump took office in January 2017, bringing a decidedly different set of preferences on foreign economic policy. Driven by a more nationalist approach, the president embraced protectionism and displayed suspicion, if not outright hostility, toward many of the trade policies, partners, and multilateral institutions his predecessors had worked to establish. Such strong views and preferences combined with inexperience and surprising unfamiliarity with many of the empirical foundations of the global economy and international economic policy. The same failure to establish an effective organization, structure, and process in foreign policymaking hampered the administration's effectiveness in foreign economic policymaking.

Trump brought a set of odd bedfellows to his foreign economic policy team. At Treasury, he appointed Steven Mnuchin, an investment banker (Goldman Sachs), hedge fund manager, and sometime film industry executive. Trump's first national economic director was Gary Cohn, another Goldman Sachs executive, who played a powerful role in the year he held the position. Known as a "globalist" who advocated for free trade, Cohn faced the challenge of managing the president's antipathy toward both trade and the global economy.

Cohn was also challenged by Trump's appointment of Peter Navarro to the newly established White House **National Trade Council (NTC)**, which the president announced in December 2016 as a new player in the foreign economic policymaking arena. Navarro and the new council took a much more aggressively nationalist approach to foreign economic policy. According to press reports, Navarro "pulled the president so far right on trade that more moderate aides [worried] his proposals could launch a global trade war if Trump [took] them too seriously, according to a dozen interviews with White House officials, close advisers, and Republican congressional aides" (Cook and Restuccia 2017). However, under Cohn's pressure, the new council (which originally appeared to be independent from, and rival to, the NEC) was folded into the less significant Office of Trade and Manufacturing Policy in April 2017, and then both were consolidated under the NEC in September 2017 by new White House Chief of Staff John Kelly (Restuccia, Toosi, and Palmeri 2017).

Other important voices on the Trump foreign economic policy team included USTR Robert Lighthizer, Secretary of Agriculture Sonny Perdue, and Secretary of Commerce Wilbur Ross. Early press reports indicated that these advisers had "been jockeying for influence for months, with Ross, Navarro and Lighthizer fighting to protect their central role in the process" (Cook and Restuccia 2017). Navarro, in particular, "earned a reputation for stalking the halls of the West Wing at night and on the weekends to find a moment to slip into the Oval Office to privately discuss trade with the president, according to one White House official and a close adviser to the administration. It's his way of maintaining influence through proximity" (Cook and Restuccia 2017). Cohn and the NEC initially emerged as the lead voice, especially once Navarro and his office were integrated into the NEC and Navarro was made to report to Cohn (Restuccia et al. 2017).

The process, however, was far from organized. As was the case with President Trump's NSC system, the president's unstructured style and mercurial views combined with adviser differences, inefficient structure and process, and bureaucratic complexities to generate a chaotic policymaking environment. There is little evidence that the formal structure of the NEC, which embraced the familiar three tiers of its predecessors, functioned any more seriously or regularly than the Trump administration's NSC system. Also, the tension between the more free trade–oriented advisers like Cohn and the more protectionist officials like Navarro and President Trump himself contributed to a fractured process. Prior to his departure in February 2018, White House staff secretary and key Cohn ally Rob Porter described the process as one in which some advisers worked to head off what they regarded as the president's more extreme ideas through persuasion, control of paperwork, and "slow-walking things or not taking things up to him" (Woodward 2018:2–4; see "A Closer Look: Cohn, Coordination, or Confusion?" for an example). In early February, however, after Porter's resignation, Navarro and the Office of Trade and Manufacturing Policy were moved back out of the NEC, and the president decided to implement an extensive set of tariffs against China, as well as American allies and friends in Europe, North America, and Asia. Cohn resigned soon thereafter, replaced by Larry Kudlow, whose most recent role was as a financial commentator on networks such as CNBC. Although Kudlow was known as a free trade advocate prior to his appointment, he pivoted to embrace Trump's positions on tariffs when he was named to the position.

A Closer Look

COHN, COORDINATION, OR CONFUSION?

As we saw in Chapter 7, the Trump National Security Council system struggled to be effective in its policy coordination role. The National Economic Council system in the Trump White House was similarly challenged. Journalist Bob Woodward (2018) recounts a telling episode from September 2017.

The Trump administration had been wrestling with the president's desire to confront American trade deficits with many of its key trading partners. Gary Cohn, the administration's first director of the National Economic Council, visited the Oval Office and found a draft letter to South Korea announcing the termination of the United States-Korea Free Trade Agreement (KORUS). According to Woodward, Cohn was "appalled," even though the agreement was "one of the foundations of an economic relationship,

(Continued)

(Continued)

a military alliance and, most important, top secret intelligence operations and capabilities" that were vital to the United States, especially in its efforts to counter North Korea and monitor its nuclear weapons and missile programs (Woodward 2018:1–2). As Woodward (p. 2) put it, the arrangement with South Korea "enabled the United States to detect an ICBM launch in North Korea within seven seconds . . . [which] would give the United States military the time to shoot down a North Korean missile. It is perhaps the most important and most secret operation in the United States government."

Cohn's concerns were therefore well founded, as ending the trade agreement risked jeopardizing the overall US–South Korean relationship, including critical national security interests. Woodward (pp. 2–3) described the situation and subsequent actions:

> Despite almost daily reports of chaos and discord in the White House, the public did not know how bad the internal situation actually was. Trump was always shifting, rarely fixed, erratic. He would get in a bad mood, something large or small would infuriate him, and he would say about the KORUS trade agreement, "We're withdrawing today."

> But now there was the letter, dated September 5, 2017, a potential trigger to a national security catastrophe. Cohn was worried Trump would sign the letter if he saw it.

> Cohn removed the letter draft from the Resolute Desk. He placed it in a blue folder marked "KEEP."

> "I stole it off his desk," he later told an associate. "I wouldn't let him see it. He's never going to see that document. Got to protect the country."

> In the anarchy and disorder of the White House, and Trump's mind, the president never noticed the missing letter.

> Ordinarily Rob Porter, the staff secretary and organizer of presidential paperwork, would have been responsible for producing letters like this to the South Korean president. But this time, alarmingly, the letter draft had come to Trump through an unknown channel.

What does this episode suggest about the interactions between presidential style and orientation, advisory roles, and foreign economic policy structure and process?

Source: Woodward (2018).

FOREIGN ECONOMICS AND THE UNCERTAIN FUTURE OF PRESIDENTIAL POWER

Presidents face real challenges in the making of economic policy. For one, domestic and international economics are classic intermestic issues, which heighten the paradox of presidential power. The politics and the nature of the US economy often drives much of the life cycle that presidents experience and the frustrations of exercising leadership in a political environment with so many constraints and uncertainties, as we discussed in Chapter 3. Moreover, as we have seen in this chapter, the foreign economic bureaucracy is large and complicated, and it generates complex politics and policymaking, with serious challenges for management and coordination.

In addition, the US government is heavily involved in the "politics of the international political economy." The United States is not all-powerful and is increasingly enmeshed in a global interdependent world. As depicted in Figure 8.3, the US president and the foreign economic bureaucracy must also interact with other governments—especially in developed countries such as Canada, Europe, and Japan (often referred to as the G-7, or G-8 if Russia is included) and other strongly emerging markets such as Australia, Brazil, China, India, and South Korea (the G-20)—in efforts to minimize global economic instability and downturns as well as to promote economic growth and prosperity. US foreign economic policy must also contend with other important governmental and nongovernmental organizations (NGOs), such as the IMF, the World Bank, the WTO, multinational corporations, and private volunteer organizations.

The good news is that presidents finally have some improved opportunities to manage and coordinate economic policymaking process with the creation of and reliance on the NEC. Although the Treasury Department and the treasury secretary have traditionally taken the international lead, the NEC has become institutionalized and a prominent

FIGURE 8.3

The United States and the International Political Economy

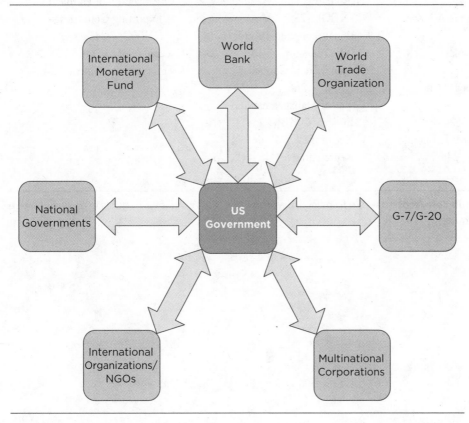

part of the policymaking landscape. Even so, the foreign economic policymaking process remains an incredible challenge for any US president, given the complexity of the domestic and international political economy. It symbolizes the continued trend toward White House–centered policymaking in response to challenging presidential efforts to better manage and govern foreign policy in general.

THINK ABOUT THIS

In his 1992 presidential election campaign, Bill Clinton and his campaign advisers repeatedly stated, "It's the economy, stupid" to emphasize the central importance of economic issues in the campaign. Similarly, international economic issues have grown in importance and priority in US foreign policy since World War II.

What challenges do the rising importance of international economics and the foreign economic bureaucracy present for US foreign policymaking?

KEY TERMS

Bretton Woods   244

Council of Economic Advisers (CEA)   252

Export-Import Bank (EXIM)   252

Federal Reserve Board (the Fed)   251

Great Depression   244

Liberal International Economic Order (LIEO)   243

National Economic Council (NEC)   255

national economic director (or NEC director)   255

National Trade Council (NTC)   266

Office of Management and Budget (OMB)   254

Office of the US Trade Representative (USTR)   254

Organization of Petroleum Exporting Countries (OPEC)   245

secretary of the treasury   248

Treasury Department   248

Visit **edge.sagepub.com/scottrosati7e** to help you accomplish your coursework goals in an easy-to-use learning environment.

Congress and Interbranch Politics

9

Win McNamee/Getty Images

PHOTO 9.1 Senate Foreign Relations Committee Chairman Senator Bob Corker (R-TN) gavels the start of a markup meeting on the proposed nuclear agreement with Iran.

LEARNING OBJECTIVES

1. Know the constitutional and institutional context of congressional foreign policymaking.

2. Identify the major historical patterns of interbranch relations in US foreign policy.

3. Understand the context of post–Cold War congressional foreign policymaking.

4. Describe the congressional foreign policy activity in key foreign policy issue areas.

Congress plays a significant and often misunderstood role in the making of US foreign policy, one that presents significant challenges for White House leadership. Conventional wisdom often dismisses Congress and its role, preferring to emphasize the president as "the decider" and casting Congress as some combination of uninterested, inactive, compliant, and deferential. However, for decades presidents and their high-level advisers have seen it differently, regularly complaining about congressional influence. The US Constitution provides Congress and its members with a seemingly impressive array of foreign policy powers, so the institution and its members are capable of playing a formidable role. However, just like presidents, whose leadership in US foreign policymaking is a variable rather than a constant, Congress has, in practice, not been consistent in applying those powers to shape foreign policy, and its engagement and influence also vary.

Nevertheless, understanding the patterns and dynamics of US foreign policymaking requires attention to Congress and its members as part of the governmental circle, interacting with the White House and the foreign policy bureaucracy. In this chapter, we complete our examination of the key governmental institutions and players in foreign policy by considering the context, historical patterns, and policy behavior of Congress. We examine the constitutional foundation of Congress's power in foreign policy; the ways the institution and its members influence foreign policy; and the patterns of legislative-executive relations and congressional influence since World War II in areas such as the war powers, advice and consent, the power of legislation, and the power of investigations.

THE CONTEXT OF CONGRESSIONAL FOREIGN POLICYMAKING

Since World War II, Congress has alternatively been characterized as acquiescent, resurgent, deferent, assertive, subservient, coequal, and imperial. As we will see, each of these characterizations has sometimes been accurate. As Rebecca Hersman (2000:105) suggests, "The complex and often troubled relationship between Congress and the executive branch over foreign policy defies simple explanations and convenient caricatures." In fact, congressional foreign policy behavior is highly context dependent, which will be readily apparent by the end of this chapter. We begin by discussing the constitutional and institutional context of interbranch politics in the making of US foreign policy.

The Constitutional Foundation of Foreign Policy

Just a few pages in length, and more than 200 years old, the Constitution is a short, ambiguous document arrived at by negotiation and compromise. Nowhere is this more evident than with respect to its treatment of foreign affairs: The document does not even mention or refer to "the foreign affairs power." Instead, as we discussed in Chapter 3, Article II of the Constitution enumerates the powers of the president. Placing the general executive power in the president, the Constitution also specifies certain foreign policy powers, including commander in chief, treaty-making and the appointment of ambassadors and cabinet heads (with the advice and consent of the Senate), receiving foreign dignitaries, commissioning military officers, the general executive power, and the power of the veto.

Article I of the Constitution enumerates the powers of the legislative branch. It places the general legislative power in the Congress and stipulates important foreign policy powers by stating that Congress shall

> provide for the common Defense and general Welfare; ... regulate commerce with foreign nations, and among the several States, and with the Indian tribes; ... define and punish piracies and felonies committed on the high seas, and offenses against the law of nations; ... declare war, grant letters of marque and reprisal, and make rules concerning captures on land and water; ... raise and support armies; ... provide and maintain a navy; ... make rules for the government and regulation of the land and naval forces; [and] provide for calling forth the militia to execute the laws of the Union, suppress insurrections, and repel invasions.

Further, key diplomatic powers of the president are subject to the advice and consent of the Senate, as noted previously. Finally, Congress has the power "to make all laws which shall be necessary and proper for carrying into execution the foregoing powers, and all other powers vested by this Constitution in the government of the United States, or in any department or officer thereof."

Hence, the Constitution clearly gives Congress a broad range of powers in the area of foreign policy. There is, in fact, no foreign policy power provided to the president that is not shared by Congress. Although Americans typically understand the distribution of power between Congress and the president as a "separation of powers," the Constitution actually establishes **separate institutions sharing power** (Corwin 1957)—which is what is meant by "checks and balances." For example, while the Congress provides military funding and declares war, the president is the commander in chief. Congress may pass bills, but the president may veto them, and Congress may then override the veto. The president is able to make treaties and appointments, but the Senate must provide its advice and consent. As students of the Constitution such as Edwin Corwin (1957) have indicated, the result is an **invitation to struggle**, which has fostered recurring conflicts between Congress and the president in the making of foreign policy throughout American history (see also Crabb and Holt 1992).

The Courts, the Congress, and the Presidency

Because of the ambiguity in this invitation to struggle, the power of **judicial review** (determining the constitutionality of a law or action) has often required the third branch of the US government to play a role in US foreign policy. Generally speaking, in foreign policy, the Supreme Court has tended to rule that the office of the president predominates, especially when the use of force abroad is involved (Fisher 2004a; Henkin 1996). Let us consider a number of key areas in which the courts have shaped the sharing of power among the separate institutions of the US government.

The parameters of the courts' views are summarized nicely in two key cases. In *United States v. Curtiss-Wright Export Corp.* (1936), the Supreme Court not only upheld a congressional grant of authority to the president to prevent the sale of arms to belligerents (which the Curtiss-Wright Corporation had violated in a war involving Bolivia and Paraguay), but it also ruled generally in favor of national governmental and presidential supremacy in foreign policy. The famous majority opinion by Justice George Sutherland asserted that the president's "very delicate, plenary and exclusive power . . . as the sole organ of the federal government in the field of international relations . . . does not require as a basis for its exercise an act of Congress."

In contrast, *Youngstown Sheet & Tube Co. v. Sawyer* (1952) resulted in the Supreme Court invalidating President Truman's attempt to invoke national security emergency powers during the Korean War to seize domestic steel mills that were under nationwide strike. The Supreme Court concluded that the president's steel seizure was not authorized by Congress, so the president had violated Congress's lawmaking authority. The famous concurring opinion by Justice Robert Jackson established a three-tiered hierarchy of legitimate presidential actions. First, "when the President acts pursuant to an express or implied authorization of Congress, his authority is at its maximum, for it includes all that he possesses in his own right plus all that Congress can delegate." Second, "when the President acts in absence of either a congressional grant or denial of authority, he can only rely upon his own independent powers, but there is a **zone of twilight** in which he and Congress may have concurrent authority, or in which its distribution is uncertain." The third level occurs "when the President takes measures incompatible with the express or implied will of Congress, his power is at its lowest ebb, for then he can rely only upon his own constitutional powers minus any constitutional powers of Congress over the matter." The combination of these cases displays the parameters of the "invitation to struggle." Louis Henkin (1987:285) has observed, "Important foreign affairs powers lie in [Justice Jackson's] twilight zone."

The courts have affected many specific areas of foreign policy. For example, in the area of treaties and executive agreements, the courts have consistently strengthened the power of the president, in part by determining that executive agreements, which are not subject to ratification by the Senate (as formal treaties are), nevertheless have the same force as treaties (see, e.g., *US v. Belmont* [1937] and *US v. Pink* [1942]). With respect to the war powers, the courts have struck a delicate balance that also tends to favor the executive branch.

In many instances, the courts have evaded weighing in on such disputes by characterizing them as **political questions** or by relying on doctrines such as "ripeness" and "implied consent." Good examples of this practice include the court's decisions in *Crockett v. Reagan* (1981), in which some members of Congress challenged the Reagan administration's power to send military advisors into El Salvador, and *Lowry v. Reagan* (1987), in which some members of Congress asked the court to require the Reagan administration to comply with the War Powers Act. Similarly, in *Dellums v. Bush* (1990) and again in *Campbell v. Clinton* (1999), the courts rejected claims by some members of Congress that George H. W. Bush and Bill Clinton had violated the Constitution either by not consulting adequately with Congress (Bush) or by using force in Kosovo without a congressional authorization (Clinton).

In both cases, the courts referred to an **implied consent** doctrine that held that Congress had to try to stop the action before resort to the courts was appropriate. However, in both the *Dellums* and *Campbell* cases, the courts rejected broad administration claims that sole authority to determine uses of force rested with the executive branch. In *Dellums v. Bush*, for example, the court ruled that the administration's claim that it had sole power to decide whether to use force "evaded[d] the plain language of the Constitution and it cannot stand."

Court decisions have affected some congressional foreign policy tools as well, including the use of the "**legislative veto**" and access to information. In a 1983 decision, the Supreme Court ruled in *Immigration and Naturalization Service v. Chadha* that the legislative veto, here involving immigration, was unconstitutional because it violated the separation of powers. The decision called into question Congress's ability to veto presidential decisions— that is, to pass a concurrent resolution without the president's signature—concerning, for example, the use of force abroad under the War Powers Act, sales of major weapons systems to foreign governments under the International Security Assistance and Arms Export Control Act, and the export of nuclear fuel and facilities to foreign countries under the Nonproliferation Act (Destler 2005).

The courts have also ruled on issues related to claims of **executive privilege**, or the right of the executive branch to withhold information from Congress and the public. In the main, the courts have rejected broad claims of this sort and placed restrictions on such privileges. For example, in *New York Times v. United States* (1971) and *US v. Nixon* (1974), the courts denied the executive the power to withhold information or prevent the publication of the *Pentagon Papers* by the press. Similarly, in the 1990s, cases involving Bill Clinton and the Whitewater corruption scandal, the Paula Jones sexual harassment case, and the Monica Lewinsky affair all weakened the president's powers to exert executive privilege and confidentiality. George W. Bush's administration challenged such limits in several instances, including a 2001 case when the General Accounting Office (now the Governmental Accountability Office) on behalf of Congress sued Vice President Dick Cheney (who led the energy interagency task force) to release classified information that led to the Bush administration's energy policy. The court ultimately decided for the administration in this case (Fisher 2004b). In its third year, the Trump administration also advanced aggressive claims of executive power and privilege, triggering legal fights over a variety of matters. The Trump administration even sought to challenge the right of Congress to exercise oversight hearings and subpoena witnesses at all.

Congressional Actors and Avenues of Influence

Congress has been disadvantaged by the combination of the practices and precedents of executive action and some court decisions. Even its own structural characteristics can also be an impediment to policy influence and leadership. For example, the sheer size of Congress—with its 535 members—makes efficient, coherent foreign policy action by Congress difficult. Nevertheless, the institution is still a formidable player in foreign affairs for several reasons. First, and perhaps most important, speaking of Congress as "a player" in foreign policy is inaccurate. In fact, Congress is composed of many players and each is capable of influencing foreign policy. As Rudalevige (2005:428) argues, "Congress is not truly an 'it' but a 'they.'"

At the heart of congressional foreign policymaking are individual members of Congress, especially those who elect to commit themselves and their time to foreign policy matters, who some refer to as "congressional foreign policy entrepreneurs" (e.g., Carter and Scott 2009, 2010; Lantis 2019). As Howell and Pevehouse (2007:34) note, "Congress does not check presidential power, individuals within it do," and individuals have many routes available to shape foreign policy (e.g., Carter and Scott 2009; Kriner 2010; Lantis 2019). Indeed, as one analyst notes (Tama 2018b), in the current context, both junior and senior members of Congress are engaged in the key areas of congressional activity:

> Relatively junior members of Congress are driving or shaping many activist foreign policy initiatives today. This pattern is evident in the ongoing debate over military aid to Saudi Arabia, which has been led in part by first-term Republican Senator Todd Young and second-term Democratic Senator Jeanne Shaheen. Similarly, two first-term senators—Democrat Tim Kaine and Republican Jeff Flake—have spearheaded efforts to pass legislation that would replace the 2001

law authorizing the use of military force against the perpetrators of the 9/11 terrorist attacks with legislation better-suited to current U.S. counterterrorism operations. Other relatively junior senators who have become leading voices on foreign policy include first-term Democrat Chris Murphy and second-term Republican Marco Rubio . . . . But, in addition to junior members who are becoming active on international issues, Congress retains a considerable number of experienced lawmakers with a strong track record in foreign policy. Such members include Representatives Eliot Engel, Kay Granger, Steny Hoyer, Jim McGovern, Chris Smith, and Mac Thornberry, and Senators Ben Cardin, Lindsay Graham, Pat Leahy, Bob Menendez, and Jack Reed.

In addition to this important understanding, the multiple actors in Congress include the collective institution, each individual chamber, the many committees and subcommittees in which the work of Congress is done, congressional caucuses, the congressional leadership, and the professional staff and support organizations of Congress. This means that we must be careful to distinguish between "activity" and "influence" when we discuss Congress, as there is more to congressional foreign policy behavior than formal outputs such as legislation (Carter and Scott 2009; Lindsay 1994; Martin 2000).

Members of Congress have a wide range of congressional **avenues of influence** on which to rely. According to Scott (1997), we should distinguish between two dimensions, along which four congressional avenues of influence can be differentiated (see Figure 9.1). Avenues can be either legislative or nonlegislative. Legislative actions involve those most formal things that Congress does to pass laws, approve treaties, and authorize and appropriate funds. By contrast, nonlegislative actions include congressional activities not related to specific legislative documents. Moreover, there are both direct and indirect avenues.

FIGURE 9.1

Congressional Paths to Foreign Policy Influence

Path	Direct	Indirect
Legislative	Issue-specific legislation Treaties (Senate) War powers Appropriations Foreign commerce	Nonbinding legislation Appointments (Senate) Procedural legislation
Nonlegislative	Informal advice/letters Consultations Oversight/hearings Use of courts	Framing opinion Foreign contacts

Source: Adapted from James M. Scott, "In the Loop: Congressional Influence in American Foreign Policy," *Journal of Political and Military Sociology* 25 (Summer 1997): 61.

When members take direct action, they target specific foreign policy issues and problems, but when they take indirect action, they typically take aim at the broader context, policy process, or policy climate to signal preferences or condition policy. If we focus only on the direct-legislative avenue, it is easy to understand why so many observers downplay the importance of Congress and its members, since outright legislating of foreign policy is relatively rare (e.g., Hinckley 1994). Our more nuanced distinction helps us to understand that there are many ways that members can influence foreign policy other than by simply trying to make laws. The four quadrants of Figure 9.1 identify key examples of congressional foreign policy activity in each of the four avenues.

As Congress has become increasingly polarized over the past couple decades, it has become even more difficult to assemble majorities to pass legislation. Nevertheless, members of Congress can, if enough votes can be mustered, directly influence policy by legislating action. Also, they can link their efforts across these different paths to maximize their potential impact. Just as important, though, they can also shape decision making—in the executive branch—by triggering **anticipated reactions**. Essentially, this aspect of congressional influence refers to the threat of congressional legislative action, and the use of that threat as leverage by members to bring administration proposals or actions into line with their preferences. Such congressional signaling or conditioning can play an important role in foreign policy decisions, even without formal legislative actions by the institution (Howell and Pevehouse 2007; Kriner 2010; Lindsay 1994).

HISTORICAL PATTERNS OF INTERBRANCH RELATIONS ON FOREIGN POLICY

In spite of the opportunities, members of Congress have not always availed themselves of these congressional paths of influence. Historically, the distribution of foreign policymaking power between Congress and the president has been fluid and dynamic, with neither Congress nor the president always predominant.

We begin by considering broad patterns of congressional assertiveness on foreign policy, in which we clearly see the dynamic nature of interbranch politics. Figure 9.2 presents evidence from one analysis of four different types of **congressional foreign policy activity** and their variance from 1945 to 1997. According to Scott and Carter (2002), when members of Congress accede to the administration's request, their behavior is "compliant." When members modify the administration's request, delivering a result either more or less than the administration desired, their behavior is "resistant." "Rejection" behavior is when Congress flatly refuses to enact the administration's desires. Finally, when members of Congress go beyond reacting to the administration's policy requests and proposals and choose to enact their own foreign policy agenda, their behavior is "independent" (Scott and Carter 2002:128–129). When these activities are separated into Cold War, post-Vietnam, and post–Cold War periods, they show two characteristics: (1) variance over time and (2) increasingly assertive behavior by Congress across the three time periods.

As Figure 9.2 shows, during the Cold War years presidential leadership was common (almost half of congressional action complied with presidential preferences). After Vietnam, congressional compliance with presidential leadership sharply fell,

FIGURE 9.2

Congressional Foreign Policy Actions and Assertiveness over Time

Behavior	Time Periods		
	Cold War (1946–1967)	Post-Vietnam (1968–1988)	Post–Cold War (1989–1997)
Compliant	42.4%	22.6%	23.7%
Resistant	28.4%	38.4%	47.4%
Rejection	8.2%	14.6%	2.6%
Independent	21.1%	24.4%	26.3%

Source: Adapted from James M. Scott and Ralph G. Carter, "Acting on the Hill: Congressional Assertiveness in U.S. Foreign Policy," *Congress and the Presidency* 29 (Autumn 2002): 159.

while resistant, rejection, and independent behavior all increased substantially. In the post–Cold War period, Congress continued to challenge presidential leadership, becoming more likely to take its own independent foreign policy actions rather than just comply with presidential leadership. Now, think about the more than twenty years that have passed since the end of the data in Figure 9.2: What might you expect the breakdown of congressional activity to look like since then?

The evidence in Figure 9.2 strongly suggests a Cold War period in which presidential dominance and congressional deference prevailed, followed by a post-Vietnam period of congressional reassertiveness. Since then, we might well expect evidence from the most recent two decades to show a similar pattern, with a period of presidential dominance during the crisis atmosphere surrounding 9/11 giving way to a period of congressional reassertiveness not long after. We might also expect differences in party control of Congress and the White House to cause periods of more activity and assertiveness, while periods when the same party controlled both branches exhibit less. Let's consider these periods and patterns of behavior in more detail to gain a better understanding of their nature and dynamics and the factors shaping them.

Presidential Leadership in the Cold War Era

Congress was most compliant with presidential leadership during the Cold War. However, the congressional role was more complex than a simple "presidential dominance" story, even during this time. In fact, legislative-executive relations evolved through four phases or periods during the height of the Cold War: (1) accommodation, 1944–1950; (2) antagonism, 1951–1955; (3) acquiescence, 1955–1965; and (4) awakening, 1966–1969 (Bax 1977).

Congressional Accommodation, 1944-1950. Initial signs of reassertiveness by Congress after World War II quickly gave way to accommodation as members of Congress collaborated with the administration to counter the Soviet threat. For example, Congress initially resisted Truman's proposal of the Marshall Plan to counter the devastation suffered by Europe in the war—isolationist sentiment was still strong among members of Congress, especially Republicans. This resistance eventually gave way to support as Truman convinced Congress and the American public of the grave political instability that most European states faced from their economic situation and from the growing threat of Soviet communism. Bipartisan, collaborative efforts between Congress and the president resulted in American participation in the United Nations, the International Bank for Reconstruction and Development (World Bank), the International Monetary Fund (IMF), and the General Agreement on Tariffs and Trade (GATT). Congress also supported the National Security Act of 1947, foreign assistance to Greece and Turkey as part of the Truman Doctrine, remobilization of the military, the establishment of the North Atlantic Treaty Organization (NATO), and the permanent stationing of American troops in Europe—a peacetime American military commitment unprecedented in the nation's history.

Congressional Antagonism, 1951–1955. Despite the broad Cold War Consensus, conservative members of Congress were increasingly concerned that the United States was not doing enough to "win" the Cold War. As the Republican Party gained control of Congress, these concerns and the virulent anti-communism underlying them led to sweeping congressional investigations of communist threats at home, as well as growing political attacks against the Truman administration and the Democratic Party. The political right was motivated by the suspicion that communists and their liberal-left supporters had penetrated the major institutions of American society, including the executive branch, and were aiding and abetting the enemy. Conservative members of Congress accused the executive branch of allowing communists to occupy important positions, and attacked high-level administration officials such as Dean Acheson (who served as secretary of state) and General George Marshall (who served as secretary of state and secretary of defense) as a "criminal crowd of traitors and appeasers." It was in this political climate that Senator Joseph McCarthy of Wisconsin thrived. Before its demise in 1954, **McCarthyism** traded on and fueled the anti-communism of the time to investigate alleged communist infiltration and treasonous behavior in the State Department, the United Nations, other parts of the federal government, the Truman administration, the Democratic Party, academia, Hollywood, and even the Eisenhower administration after the 1952 elections.

Congressional Acquiescence, 1955–1965. With the decline of McCarthyism, the ensuing decade constituted the height of **bipartisanship** and congressional compliance with presidential leadership. While pockets and episodes of congressional criticism remained (usually over not doing enough to fight the Cold War), this period was the heyday of presidential power and the president's ability to exercise prerogative government in order to fight the Cold War in the name of national security. The president's foreign policies rarely encountered serious challenges. Although Congress seldom gave the president all that he wanted in important areas such as defense and foreign assistance, members of Congress generally complied with presidential leadership and the growing independence of the executive branch in the making of US foreign policy. Thus, the demands of national security took precedence over all other concerns, and, according to Frans Bax (1977:887), "the chief function of Congress became the legitimizing of presidential decisions" and the legislative-executive relationship of this period spawned the "two presidencies thesis" we discussed in Chapter 3 (Wildavsky 1966).

The Cold War Consensus and bipartisanship of this period were so strong that, in many cases, foreign policy decisions were made without consulting Congress or getting its formal approval; at best, congressional leaders might be informed after the fact. Presidential supremacy and the assumption of congressional support reached its height under Presidents Kennedy and Johnson. Not surprisingly, the fateful decisions to fully Americanize the Vietnam War were made with virtually no input from Congress. The Cold War Consensus often prevented questions from being asked about whether the United States should or should not commit itself to defend South Vietnam from communism. Rather, the questions always revolved only around how much American involvement it would take to contain communist aggression and prevent the downfall of an ally. For example, after the Gulf of Tonkin incident in August 1964, members of Congress rushed the Gulf of Tonkin Resolution through rather than seriously debating the pros and cons of the resolution submitted by President Johnson. The vote was unanimous: 416–0 in the House of Representatives and 88–2 in the Senate.

Congressional Awakening, 1966–1969. Congressional uneasiness with Cold War policies and presidential leadership began to emerge even before the escalation of American involvement in Vietnam. According to Johnson (2006) and Carter and Scott (2009), in the early 1960s key individuals in Congress such as J. William Fulbright, Wayne Morse, Ernest Gruening, and Stuart Symington led a "foreign aid revolt" that challenged the amounts, priorities, and purposes of US assistance. These "entrepreneurs" challenged the White House in an effort to recast foreign aid (away from military aid) and place restrictions on it (especially to dictators). Such efforts paid off and, by the mid-1960s, the Johnson administration had been forced to accept a variety of restrictions. As one scholar commented, "The foreign aid revolt had succeeded beyond anything [its initiators] could have imagined. In the process a new era in executive-legislative relations was inaugurated" (Johnson 2006:104).

By 1966, such uneasiness had spread to US foreign policy in Vietnam. Total troop levels exceeded 550,000, but there still seemed to be no "light at the end of the tunnel" (a phrase that came to be associated with President Johnson's and General William Westmoreland's optimistic spin on how the war effort was going). As a result, some members of Congress began to criticize the administration's lack of restraint in and overemphasis on the use of force. Determined to inject a different point of view into the decision-making process, the leading critics in Congress began a series of congressional investigations of American policy in Vietnam.

These efforts to broaden the debate and scrutinize administration decisions were best symbolized by the hearings convened by the Senate Foreign Relations Committee under the chairmanship of J. William Fulbright (D-AR). Once a "Cold Warrior" in support of administration policy, Fulbright moved steadily from private to public dissent in the 1960s over the Vietnam War. As President Johnson's perspective narrowed and groupthink among his advisers prevailed (see Chapter 10), Fulbright moved from private objections to outright dissent by 1965. As he characterized it (Fulbright 1966:28–29):

Since 1961, when the Democrats came back to power, I have made recommendations to the President on a number of occasions through confidential memorandums. In April, 1965, I sent President Johnson a note containing certain recommendations of the war in Vietnam, recommendations which I reiterated thereafter in private conversations with high Administration officials. When it became very clear that the Administration did not find my ideas persuasive, I began to make my views known publicly in the hope, if not of bringing about a change in Administration policy, then at least of opening up a debate on that policy.

On April 5, 1965, Fulbright sent a memorandum to President Johnson challenging the intervention. When that failed to change the president's course, Fulbright then became more public in 1966 when he began "televised" Foreign Relations Committee hearings to focus on the shortcomings of US policy in Vietnam and expanded his public critique of Vietnam policy. While members continued to appropriate funds to support the troops in Vietnam, more and more members became uncomfortable with—and willing to challenge the president over—the lack of progress in the war effort and the administration's failure to consult with them on crucial questions of war and peace. Members also began to question the logic of key foreign policy strategies such as containment, and the Cold War Consensus that had muted foreign policy competition began to fracture. This congressional awakening set the stage for the congressional reassertion in legislative-executive relations that dominated the post–Vietnam War years.

The Post-Vietnam Congressional Resurgence

In the late 1960s, with the Cold War Consensus a casualty of the Vietnam War, Congress began to reassert its constitutional authority in the making of US foreign policy. This reassertion occurred for a number of complementary reasons, many of which had to do with the Vietnam War. First, the war was not going well. Over half a million American troops and $30 billion a year were not producing the light at the end of the tunnel that President Johnson and General Westmoreland were proclaiming. In fact, with what became known as the Tet Offensive in early 1968, the North Vietnamese successfully contested most of South Vietnam for a short time, occupying major cities and even the American embassy in Saigon before being defeated. Second, growing segments of the American public began to question President Johnson's handling of the unsuccessful war. Third, US policy in Vietnam was increasingly criticized by other countries, including the United Kingdom, France, and other American allies in Europe. Fourth, Republican Richard Nixon's victory over Democrat Hubert Humphrey in the election of 1968 resulted in divided government and added a more partisan dimension to legislative-executive relations. Finally, although Nixon began to withdraw US troops as part of a strategy of Vietnamization (to turn the war over to the South Vietnamese), he also escalated the levels of military conflict and bombing to achieve "peace with honor"—which increasingly politicized everything.

A classic struggle between the legislative and executive branches ensued. Members of Congress became increasingly active in the making of US foreign policy, demanding from the president and the executive branch more information, consultation, and participation in policymaking. In fact, by 1973, Congress cut off all funding of direct American military involvement in the Vietnam War; and with the end of the war, congressional reassertion intensified. In 1973, the War Powers Act was passed over President Nixon's veto, followed shortly by the Budget and Impoundment Control Act of 1974, and a series of additional direct and indirect legislative efforts to rein in the White House and reassert congressional foreign policy influence.

Not surprisingly, President Nixon resisted congressional reassertion every step of the way. But the end of the Vietnam War, the Watergate affair, and concerns over controversial Cold War policies released a flood of congressional involvement in foreign policy. In addition to efforts to end the Vietnam War, over the ensuing fifteen years or so, Congress inserted itself into practically every corner of US foreign policy. For example, Congress asserted itself in the diplomatic arena, requiring that executive agreements be reported to Congress for review. Congress also tackled military aid, foreign aid, and arms sales policies and processes, giving itself greater control in both areas. Substantively, Congress tackled US policies toward many different countries, required human rights and democracy to be considered in US assistance and diplomacy, resisted a variety of arms control and other treaties, and became increasingly involved in defense policy. On intelligence, Congress strengthened legislative oversight in a series of actions between 1975 and 1980, while also establishing new procedures, requirements, and restrictions on nuclear export laws. In the 1980s, Congress continued to assert itself, resisting the Reagan administration's policies on arms control and Central America, and, in the case of South Africa, applying sanctions against the apartheid regime over administration resistance and, ultimately, a presidential veto.

Understanding Congressional Reassertiveness

After Vietnam, all presidents faced a more powerful, less compliant Congress. Presidential leadership faced new challenges as changes in the post-Vietnam political environment resulted in the relative decline of presidential power and the rise of congressional involvement. A number of factors explain both the efforts to reassert congressional influence and the success in doing so. First, and probably most important, congressional deference and support was in large part a consequence of the Cold War Consensus, or shared views about the US role in the world and the strategies to follow to pursue US interests (Melanson 2005). With Vietnam, Watergate, and other changes in the 1960s and 1970s, the Cold War Consensus that provided for presidential dominance eroded, paving the way for greater congressional activism.

Second, the level of congressional activism on foreign policy depends, at least in part, on the international context, especially the level of threat facing the country, and on the success of presidential policies (Lindsay 2003). As one observer argues, after Vietnam "many Americans became convinced that communist revolutions in the third world posed no direct threat to core U.S. security interests, just as détente persuaded many that Leonid Brezhnev's Soviet Union posed less of a threat to core U.S. security interests" (Lindsay 2003:533). Moreover, Vietnam, intelligence abuses, the excesses of the Nixon administration, and other issues convinced many observers that Cold War policies were anything but successful.

Third, Congress enacted a number of major institutional changes that led to a more diverse, representative, decentralized, open, informed, and independent Congress, contributing to its post-Vietnam reassertion (Crabb and Holt 1992; Ripley 1988). Four of these changes are most important.

Membership. Congress experienced a major turnover in its membership beginning in the 1970s. Changes occurred in region, party, and ideology. Throughout the Cold War years of the 1950s and 1960s, both the House and the Senate were dominated by southerners, members of the Democratic Party, and political conservatives. The situation changed during the early 1970s. By this time, many of the more powerful southern Democrats were replaced by younger members of Congress who still tended to be Democrats but were less conservative. This situation resulted in a new Democratic leadership that was much more liberal, much less southern, and much more willing to be assertive in foreign policy. The rise of the new leadership was reinforced by the 1974 post–Vietnam War and post-Watergate congressional elections, in which Republicans faced major losses, resulting in a large influx of new liberal Democrats into Congress. The new Democratic leadership, in coalition with the new members of Congress, took a more activist congressional role in US foreign policy (Bernstein and Freudenberg 1977). In the late 1970s and early 1980s, when Republicans gained seats in Congress (including a majority in the Senate from 1981 to 1987), the new members tended to be more conservative. The overall result of these changes in membership has been a more diverse, representative, polarized, and politicized Congress that contains very active liberal and conservative members.

Committees. Not only did the change in congressional membership during the 1970s produce changes in the distribution and exercise of power within Congress, but the new Democratic liberal leadership also changed the congressional committee rules of the game. Power was stripped from committees and in particular from committee chairs. Every committee was now required to have multiple subcommittees, subdividing both issues and committee membership, and no committee member could be chair of more than one of its subcommittees. Thus, power moved from committees and committee chairs to subcommittees and subcommittee chairs. More committees (and subcommittees) also gained jurisdiction over foreign policy issues. For example, new committees covering intelligence and the budget were created, and many other committees have become more active in foreign policy. This has been especially the case for other types of international (and intermestic) issues, such as trade, finance, energy, transportation, communications, tourism, technology and space, immigration, and the environment—all of which have grown in importance in foreign policy. These changes have resulted in greater committee and congressional involvement in the making of US foreign policy. (See Tables 9.1 and 9.2 for lists of relevant committees in the current Congress.)

Congressional Norms and Procedures. Structural and procedural changes reduced (but did not eliminate) the importance of seniority, reciprocity, public collegiality, and other norms, contributing to an increase in the number of members seeking to put their stamp on policy. Moreover, congressional reforms during the 1970s resulted in a much more open and democratic process instead of committee activity occurring behind

TABLE 9.1

Senate Committees with Jurisdiction over Foreign Policy (116th Congress, 2019–2020)

Relevant Committees (Total Subcommittees)
Agriculture, Nutrition, and Forestry (5)
Appropriations (12)
Armed Services (7)
Banking, Housing, and Urban Affairs (5)
Budget (0)
Commerce, Science, and Transportation (6)
Energy and Natural Resources (4)
Environment and Public Works (4)
Finance (5)
Foreign Relations (7)
Homeland Security and Governmental Affairs (3)
Intelligence
Judiciary (6)
Veterans' Affairs (0)

Source: US Senate (http://senate.gov).

closed doors. Most formal committee activity is now open to the media and the public. Furthermore, **voice votes** (the option to vote as a group and thus remain unaccountable) have been mostly replaced by **roll call votes,** in which each member must take an independent public stand on the issue. While informal interaction, bargaining, and highly sensitive work such as intelligence continue to occur behind the scenes, congressional procedures are more open today than in the past (as reflected in C-SPAN television coverage of House and Senate hearings and proceedings in the two chambers).

Staffing. Congressional reformers in the 1970s realized that the small legislative support staffs made Congress dependent on the executive branch for information. Consequently, they expanded congressional staffs tremendously during and after Vietnam. Individual representatives and senators began to enjoy the presence of large **personal staffs.** **Committee staffs** for both the majority and minority parties, such as for the Senate Committee on Foreign Relations, also expanded tremendously. Congress also increased the size of its support agencies and began using them consistently. For example, the Government Accountability Office (GAO), the largest support agency, employing almost 20,000 people, is the investigative arm of Congress and engages in oversight of the executive branch. The Congressional Research Service (CRS) provides research and analysis on issues of importance to congressional committees and individual members of Congress.

TABLE 9.2

House Committees with Jurisdiction over Foreign Policy (116th Congress, 2019–2020)

Relevant Committees (Total Subcommittees)
Agriculture (6)
Appropriations (12)
Armed Services (6)
Budget (0)
Climate Crisis (0)
Education and Labor (5)
Energy and Commerce (6)
Financial Services (6)
Foreign Affairs (6)
Homeland Security (6)
Intelligence (4)
Judiciary (5)
Natural Resources (5)
Oversight and Government Reform (5)
Science, Space, and Technology (5)
Small Business (5)
Transportation and Infrastructure (6)
Veterans' Affairs (5)
Ways and Means (6)

Source: US House of Representatives (http://house.gov).

Finally, the Congressional Budget Office (CBO), created in 1974 to provide financial and budgetary information and assessments, gives Congress an alternative to reliance on the executive's Office of Management and Budget.

Overall, these changes provided the foundation for members of Congress to become more active in the making of foreign policy. These changes greatly complicated the White House's ability to control the agenda and enact the president's preferred policies, as they empowered a wider range of members within committees and on the chamber floors.

CONGRESS AFTER THE COLD WAR

The end of the Cold War in 1989 provided further incentives for congressional engagement on foreign policy. The collapse of the Soviet Union and the decline of communism dramatically reduced the level of threat facing the country. As one observer aptly commented, "It's like Las Vegas; when you reduce the size of the ante, more people come to the table" (quoted in CQ Press 1999:9). Moreover, intermestic issues and increasing constituency pressures have led to greater congressional challenges to presidential leadership on a variety of issues. Also, the cost or risk of challenging the president diminished because of a decline in public interest in international matters (Lindsay 2000). Consequently, not only have presidents had greater difficulty enacting their priorities, but the changed issue agenda also increased the willingness of members of Congress to challenge the president on foreign affairs (Marshall and Prins 2002). Three features of the two decades of the post–Cold War years are especially important for understanding Congress and its role and influence in the politics of US foreign policy.

Polarization and Partisanship.

When it comes to Congress, the post–Cold War environment is one of increasing ideological **polarization** and **partisanship** (Jeong and Quirk 2017; Jochim and Jones 2012; Martini 2015; Milner and Tingley 2015; Peake 2017). Since the end of the Cold War, these ideological and partisan divides affect virtually every congressional arena: party leaders, the

FIGURE 9.3

Mean Ideology Scores by Party, 102nd–113th Congresses

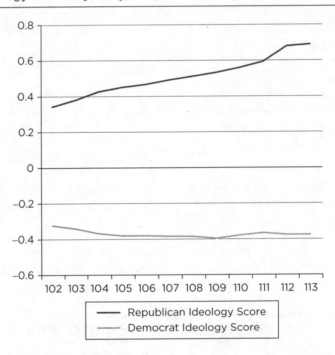

Source: Data from DW-Nominate (https://www.voteview.com/about).

voting of rank-and-file members on foreign and defense policy issues, and the behavior of individual members of Congress who are especially attentive to foreign policy (e.g., Carter & Scott 2009, 2010; DeLaet & Scott 2006; Lantis 2019; Marsh & Lantis 2018; McCormick, Wittkopf, & Danna 1997; Rohde 1994; Sinclair 1993; Smith 1994; Wittkopf & McCormick 1998).

Figure 9.3 shows the growing ideological gap between Republicans and Democrats in Congress from 1991 to 2014. The gap has only widened since then. With ideological polarization almost doubling since the end of the Cold War, manifestations of the growing partisanship also increased. For example, in terms of party unity voting—where members vote with their own party—according to the *Washington Post*'s "Congress Votes Database," members voted with their respective parties about 80–85 percent of the time at the end of the Cold War, but 90–95 percent of the time by 2015. Members also became increasingly supportive of presidents of their own party, and increasingly resistant to those of the other party after the Cold War, according to presidential support scores from the Texas A&M Presidential Data Archive (but see "A Different Perspective: Is Bipartisanship Really Dead?").

A Different Perspective

IS BIPARTISANSHIP REALLY DEAD?

Many politicians and academic studies lament the demise of bipartisan cooperation in US foreign policy, and evidence of the partisan rancor on Capitol Hill and between Congress and the president is not hard to find. However, in the changing international and domestic environment of the past decade or so, some evidence suggests that rumors of the death of bipartisanship have been exaggerated, to paraphrase Mark Twain.

In late 2018, the Center for Strategic and International Studies released *Beyond the Water's Edge: Measuring the Internationalism of Congress*, a report on the foreign policy views of members of Congress. According to this report, in contrast to simpler, Cold War–era ideological positions ranging from right to left, conservative to liberal, or isolationist to internationalist, today members of Congress tend to hold one of three foreign policy orientations. These orientations are *order-driven members*, who emphasize preservation of the post–World War II liberal international order; *values-driven members*, who ground their calls for US engagement in statements of guiding values embracing human rights, religious values, or democracy promotion; and *limits-driven members*, who desire to minimize the risks and costs associated with US international engagement. According to the report, Republicans and Democrats can be found in each of these orientations, which suggests good prospects for cooperation across party lines on issues such as foreign aid, countering cybersecurity threats and challenges from Russia and China, trade, oversight and limits on the use of force, countering global authoritarianism, and others.

According to recent research by Jordan Tama, an associate professor in the School of

(Continued)

(Continued)

International Service at American University, cooperation across party lines is still alive and well. As Tama (2018a) puts it:

First, bipartisanship still occurs on a number of key US foreign policy issues, despite the severe overall polarization of US politics. Second, contemporary foreign policy bipartisanship often deviates from the standard image of bipartisanship, in which the president gains the support of lawmakers in both parties. This political alignment, which I label "classic bipartisanship," is reflected in the common saying that politics should stop at the water's edge. But today's foreign policy debates frequently involve both parties in Congress working together to challenge the president or feature alliances between Democrats and Republicans that are generated by intra-party splits. I call the former alignment "anti-presidential bipartisanship," and follow other scholars in calling the latter alignment "cross-partisanship."

Tama's evidence indicates foreign policy voting by Congress shows high percentages of classic bipartisanship, anti-presidential bipartisanship, and cross-partisanship. His insights also mesh well with the Center for Strategic and International Studies report (see Tama 2018b), and his perspective is supported by the research of others (e.g., Chaudoin et al. 2010; Jochim and Jones 2012; Trubowitz and Mello 2011).

What does this different perspective on foreign policy orientations and the nature of cross-party cooperation suggest for the effect of the legislative-executive relationship on foreign policy?

Sources: Policy Items: Insights from the Social Sciences (Social Science Research Council); Jordan Tama. "Congress, Trump, and Internationalism in U.S. Foreign Policy"; Stephen Chaudoin, Helen V. Milner and Dustin H. Tingley. "The Center Still Holds: Liberal Internationalism Survives." *International Security*. Volume 35: Issue: Summer 2010 p.75–94; Peter Trubowitz and Nicole Mellow, "Foreign Policy, Bipartisanship and the Paradox of Post-September 11 America," *International Politics* 48 (2011): 164–87.

Studies show that congressional partisanship and polarization have affected general levels of congressional activity and assertiveness in the post–World War II era; and they have had an impact on presidential decisions to use force, negotiate executive agreements and treaties, enact economic sanctions, and provide food assistance, among other things (e.g., Carter and Scott 2009; DeLaet and Scott 2006; Howell and Pevehouse 2007; Martin 2000; Scott and Carter 2002; Smith 1994). As David Rohde (1994:99) has argued, "Congress has grown increasingly assertive in foreign and defense policy and . . . conflict over these issues has grown increasingly partisan." Which party controls Congress and the White House is more significant than ever, as both partisanship and the lack of consensus make foreign policy more like politics as usual.

Divided Government

As we first discussed in Chapter 3, **divided government** has become the norm for Washington, DC. Increasingly, Congress and the presidency are led by members of the opposing political parties. From the 59th Congress to the 88th Congress (1905–1965), the White House and at least one chamber of Congress were controlled by different parties in just seven congresses. From the 89th Congress to the 100th Congress (1965–1989), government was divided eight times; and since 1989 (101st–116th Congresses), the White House and at least one chamber of Congress have been controlled by different parties ten times.

The existence of divided government is consequential because members of the party in opposition to the president can exercise greater control within Congress as a result of their majority status. This gives the opposition party the ability to dominate the organization of Congress—in leadership positions (such as Speaker of the House and Senate majority leader), as chairs of committees and subcommittees, and with majority representation on each and every committee and subcommittee. Hence, President Clinton, a Democrat, had to deal with a Congress that was dominated by Republicans; President George W. Bush had to deal with divided government in the first two and last two years of his presidency; President Obama faced a House of Representatives in Republican hands after the 2010 midterm elections, and a Republican-led Congress after 2014; and President Trump faced a partially divided government when Democrats won majority control of the House of Representatives in the 2018 midterm elections.

With divided government, political incentives for congressional activity and assertiveness increase, making White House leadership on foreign policy more complicated. Moreover, in four of the ten congresses since 2001, Congress itself has been divided, with different parties controlling each chamber. Although a divided Congress gives the White House political allies controlling one chamber on Capitol Hill, it also introduces the added complication of partisan strife between the chambers, which may make leadership from both Congress and the White House more difficult.

The Politics of Threat

In the post–Cold War context, a third important feature has been the salience of the **politics of threat**. As Howell, Jackman, and Rogowski (2013) conclude in *The Wartime President: Executive Influence and the Nationalizing Politics of Threat*, when political debates focus on national threats and priorities, Congress is more likely to defer to the president's policy preferences. When the threat context is amplified in the national debate, power tends to flow toward the president and the executive branch. During times of peace, or when the political debate over threat is less salient, power tends to flow back to Congress, as Schlesinger (1989) argued in *The Imperial Presidency*. In periods of perceived national emergency, Americans in government and society are also likely to turn to the president and rally behind him or her and the exercise of "prerogative power" (see Chapter 3) to address the situation.

As we noted, with the end of the Cold War, the focal point of more than four decades of US foreign policy disappeared and, along with it, the clarity of the Soviet threat as a peer competitor to the United States. In the more benign but complicated environment of the post–Cold War world, presidents have found that the threat environment has played a significant role in the interactions between the legislative and executive branches. Not surprisingly, when threat—and thus interests—are clearest, congressional assertiveness tends to be muted and White House foreign policy leadership enhanced, as was the case in the high-threat environment during the height of the Cold War. This has led to a "politics of threat," in which variation in the clarity of threat and interests—and the claims of these things by presidents and members of Congress—have affected levels of congressional assertiveness or support toward the White House, especially by the party opposite the president. Thus, in the post–Cold War context, as Howell et al. (2013) argue, the perceived threat of terrorism and wars in Afghanistan and Iraq expanded presidential power and leadership.

Impact on Congressional Foreign Policymaking

In the post–Cold War context, these three factors have combined to shape congressional foreign policy activity and legislative-executive relations. Throughout the past two decades, the White House has faced a series of congressional challenges across a whole host of foreign policy issue areas, major and minor. For example, in the face of divided government, the Clinton administration watched four major international agreements fall to congressional, mostly partisan, opposition (the comprehensive test ban, land mines, global warming, and international criminal court agreements). Similarly, Congress dismantled both the administration's attempts to prioritize democracy promotion and sustainable development as foreign policy goals and its strategy for coping with ethnic conflict and instability. Efforts to strengthen the ability of international organizations such as the United Nations and the International Monetary Fund to respond to global problems were resisted and restricted, and the administration was forced to accept, despite its strenuous opposition, the restructuring of the foreign agencies, increased defense spending, covert assistance to promote regime change in Iraq, strengthened primary and secondary sanctions on Cuba, and a host of other issues driven by Congress (e.g., Scott 1998).

Prior to September 11, 2001, Congress appeared poised to provide the administration of George W. Bush with similar challenges on issues ranging from the United Nations to defense strategy and spending to national missile defense and arms control to trade, especially after Vermont Senator Jim Jeffords left the Republican Party, giving the Democrats the majority in the Senate. Then terrorists struck New York City and Washington, DC, and the ensuing state of emergency generated a dramatic shift, and the level of threat and public concern with international affairs surged. Congress almost immediately rallied behind the White House in the face of this crisis. For example, as James Lindsay (2003) describes, members of the president's party dropped their opposition to repaying American dues to the United Nations, while Democrats gave in to the president's position on national missile defense without a fight. Congress also cooperated or acquiesced in granting sweeping new powers for homeland security and intelligence operations and a series of additional issues. Most important, Congress granted broad authorization to the president to use force, first in Afghanistan in 2001 and then, in a 2002 vote, in Iraq as well. These two congressional authorizations were not as sweeping as the original administration requests, but they were as much "blank checks" as the 1964 Gulf of Tonkin Resolution (Kassop 2003).

However, as the 9/11 attacks receded into the past, and as the costly American military intervention into Iraq ground on with little sign of ending, the state of emergency and concomitant threat context relaxed, and the increasingly polarized and partisan Congress grew restless on a variety of international issues, including homeland security, intelligence reform, and trade. In 2005 and 2006, congressional Democrats were increasingly bold in their opposition to the administration, and even some Republicans began to join in as the public's discontent with President George W. Bush and the war in Iraq grew (e.g., John Warner and Richard Lugar on new strategies and benchmarks for the Iraq war; John McCain on a ban on torture; see Broder 2005; Hulse 2005). Other challenges on issues such as immigration also ensued, leading one observer to flatly declare the "the Bush era . . . isn't over. . . . But the 9–11 era is" (Rozen 2005). Such assertiveness across a whole range of foreign policy issues grew significantly stronger when the Democratic Party won majorities in both chambers of Congress in the 2006 midterm elections in what was widely understood as a referendum on the Bush administration's foreign policy.

These patterns continued into the Obama and Trump administrations as well. Divided government and partisanship proved good predictors of legislative-executive relations as Democrats in Congress adopted a more supportive approach to the Obama administration, and Republicans in Congress were substantially more supportive of the Trump administration, even despite its highly volatile and controversial foreign policy positions.

During the 111th Congress (2009–2010), Republicans in the minority in Congress seemingly took every opportunity to criticize and attack the democratic administration's foreign policy. After the November 2010 elections, the Republicans gained the majority in the House of Representatives and reduced the Democratic majority to a 53–47 advantage. In the ensuing 112th Congress, foreign policy challenges from Congress, especially the House, ramped up. For example, Obama was only narrowly able to secure approval of his New START nuclear arms control treaty with Russia by a 71–26 vote (67 votes were required) and then only after a lengthy debate and the addition of amendments to placate Republicans. The economy clearly dominated the agenda. Obama, the Democrats, and the Republicans fought constant partisan battles and were in continual "gridlock" over issues such as the economic recovery, the budget, and the debt—leading the government to almost shut down at one point (see Bohan, Sullivan, and Ferraro 2011). The partisanship was intensified by divided government, ideological differences, and political one-upmanship.

The 2012 elections returned Obama to a second term, extended the Democratic majority in the Senate by two seats to fifty-five, and narrowed the Republican majority in the House by eight seats (234–201). However, the 2014 midterms put Republican majorities in control of both chambers, and congressional activism and opposition to administration foreign policy accelerated. Indeed, with no prospects for legislative support, Obama turned to executive orders and executive agreements to address immigration, improve relations with Cuba, conclude a multilateral agreement to control Iran's pursuit of nuclear weapons, and join a global accord to combat climate change. The Republican-led Congress opposed each of these actions and, when the Trump administration succeeded the Obama administration in 2017, the more tenuous nature of each of these presidential steps led to the new administration's ability to undo each of them, also by executive order.

The Republican-led Congress proved much more supportive of the Trump administration than its predecessor, but even so, it took action to address concerns about the Trump approach. For example, the Trump administration proposed steep cuts to the US foreign aid budget and State Department funding in each of its first three years. In foreign aid, these cuts ranged from 25 percent to 35 percent of the budget. Even with Republicans in control of both branches, these proposals failed in Congress. Republican leaders simply refused to support the president's requests. Similarly, despite strong opposition from the White House, the Republican Congress legislated a strong sanctions bill against Russia in response to its attacks on the US elections, interference in European politics, and aggression in Ukraine. The veto-proof majorities in both chambers forced the administration to sign the legislation into law and, although President Trump delayed implementing the sanctions for as long as possible, the administration was forced to begin applying them in the spring of 2019.

In November 2018, Democrats swept into the majority in the House of Representatives and immediately ramped up challenges to the Trump administration. In 2019, legislative efforts on foreign aid, the use of military force, countering Russian election interference, trade, human rights, and other matters took shape in the House. Many of these efforts resulted in bills that passed the lower chamber. Committee hearings and oversight activities on a variety of subjects also increased in the House, including the start of the impeachment process in the fall of 2019 over President Trump's efforts to force Ukraine to interfere in the 2020 US election. Even the Republican-controlled Senate got in on the act on key issues such as the use of force in Yemen and Iran (Mascaro 2019). As one observer summarized,

> So what's the common theme among these signs of Congress' reasserting itself in foreign policy? . . . It's precisely Congress' growing frustration with Trump's foreign policy that appears to be motivating this reemergence. (Geltzer 2019)

And President Trump's response? The White House ramped up its own partisan attacks on Democrats in Congress, engaged in partisan pressure on its Republican allies, and cast key foreign policy priorities in terms of crisis and national emergency to gain advantage in the politics of threat.

CONGRESSIONAL BEHAVIOR IN FOUR POLICY AREAS

Now that we have examined the context, multiple congressional actors and paths of influence, and overall patterns of legislative-executive relations in foreign policy, let's finish by considering congressional activity and influence in four general issue areas: (1) the war powers, (2) advice and consent, (3) the power to appropriate funds and to make laws, and (4) the power of oversight and investigation.

The War Powers

The use of American armed forces abroad has been the factor most responsible for the growth of presidential power and the straining of relations between Congress and the president. According to Louis Henkin (1987:290), "There is no evidence that the framers contemplated any significant independent role—or authority—for the President as the Commander in chief when there was no war." Yet Congress has declared war just five times in American history, while presidents have committed military forces abroad in more than 200 instances. Therefore, as discussed earlier, the president's power over questions of war has grown remarkably over time. Only after the bitter experience with the Vietnam War did Congress attempt to redress the imbalance, eventually overriding a veto by President Nixon to enact the **War Powers Act**.

The War Powers Act was designed "to fulfill the intent of the framers of the Constitution of the United States and ensure that the collective judgment of both the Congress and the President will apply to the introduction of United States Armed Forces" into conflict situations abroad. The act has three central requirements:

1. Presidential Consultation: According to the War Powers Act, "the President in every possible instance shall consult with Congress before introducing United States Armed Forces" into situations of conflict abroad and "after such introduction shall consult regularly with the Congress until" they have been removed from such situations.

2. Presidential Reporting: According to subsection 4(a) of the act, the president shall submit a report to Congress within forty-eight hours if, in the absence of a declaration of war, US armed forces are introduced abroad under the following three situations:

   a. "into hostilities or into situations where imminent involvement in hostilities is clearly indicated by the circumstances"

   b. "into the territory, airspace or waters of a foreign nation, while equipped for combat, except for deployments which relate solely to supply, replacement, repair, or training of such forces"

   c. "in numbers which substantially enlarge United States Armed Forces equipped for combat already located in a foreign nation"

   A report is required to describe the circumstances, the president's constitutional and legislative authority, and the estimated scope and duration of involvement. If US armed forces remain in a situation of hostilities in accordance with subsection 4(a)(1), the president must continue to report to Congress at least every six months.

3. Congressional Action: If US armed forces are introduced into a situation of hostilities as stipulated in subsection 4(a)(1), the president must terminate their involvement within sixty days unless Congress extends the deadline. The president can extend the deadline for an additional thirty days, if deemed necessary for the safe withdrawal of American troops. Congress may pass a "concurrent resolution" to terminate the military intervention earlier; this requires a simple majority in both chambers and is not subject to presidential veto. Second, Congress may pass a "joint resolution," signed by the president, to extend the deadline. Finally, Congress may do nothing, allowing the time limitation to take effect.

The War Powers Act represented a major effort at congressional reassertion and complicates the president's ability to use force abroad. On the surface, the act may not appear much more than symbolic. Since 1973, presidents have used US armed forces abroad in numerous situations involving the War Powers Act. In each case, the president initiated, formulated, and approved the use of force with little or no consultation—informing members of Congress only after a decision had been made given his role as commander in chief.

However, the War Powers Act does enable Congress to influence the president's decision to use troops abroad through the reporting requirement and its ability to terminate, modify, or approve military action if US troops are committed. As Kriner (2010) shows, individual members of Congress engage in a variety of activities—public framing, hearings, proposing legislation, and others across the range of the avenues of influence we described—before, during, and after uses of force that influence such decisions. Since the War Powers Act was passed, presidents must be cautious in deciding when, where, and how US troops are to be committed. Indeed, studies by Howell and Pevehouse (2007) and Auerswald and Cowhey (1997) show that the act changed the decision-making environment and made presidents much more selective in their decision to use force.

The first major test of the War Powers Act occurred when President Reagan deployed 1,500 American troops in Beirut from September 1982 to March 1984 to promote stability in Lebanon. When Reagan sent US troops (along with British, French, and Italian troops) to Beirut, he reported to Congress in accordance with the act. However, he also stated that there was no intention or expectation that US armed forces would become involved in hostilities, thereby circumventing the time limitation and Congress's further participation. (US Congress, House Committee on Foreign Affairs 1982). As the conflict in Beirut escalated and American troops were fired upon, a major debate ensued and members of Congress and the president appeared to be heading toward a constitutional crisis over the war-making power. But a legislative-executive compromise was negotiated in which Congress agreed to activate subsection 4(a)(1), indicating a situation of hostilities, by passing a joint resolution that the president would acknowledge by signing. In return, the president received congressional support to use military troops in Lebanon for up to eighteen months. However, President Reagan issued a statement to accompany the signing of the resolution that effectively rejected the legitimacy of the War Powers Act, which has become the norm.

The recent cases of Afghanistan and Iraq are also instructive. First, in both cases, the George W. Bush administration decided to use force with little involvement or consultation with Congress. In fact, in the Iraq case, the administration made the decision much earlier than it was publicly acknowledged and made a number of efforts to conceal the choice from Congress and the public. Nevertheless, in both cases the president received broad congressional authorization for the use of force (although not as broad as the president wanted), nor was the War Powers Act acknowledged or invoked (Kassop 2003; Packer 2005; Woodward 2004).

Within three days of 9/11, on September 14, the House voted 420–1 and the Senate voted 98–0 in support of a 9/11 military force resolution, initially submitted by President Bush, that the president is authorized to use all necessary and appropriate force against those nations, organizations or persons he determines planned, authorized, committed or aided the terrorist attacks that occurred on Sept. 11 or harbored such organizations or persons, in order to prevent any future acts of international terrorism against the United States by such nations, organizations or persons.

In the more specific Iraqi resolution, Congress authorized the president to "use the Armed Forces of the United States as he determines to be necessary and appropriate to (1) defend the national security of the United States against the continuing threat posed by Iraq; and (2) enforce all relevant United Nations Security Council Resolutions." This resolution passed the House 296–133 and the Senate 77–23.

In Obama's 2011 decision to use force against Libya in support of the resistance to Moammar Ghaddafi's rule, the administration did not bother to consult prior to the introduction of US forces, maintaining that its briefings of members on the operations were sufficient given Obama's role as commander in chief. In fact, the administration maintained that the War Powers Act did not even apply because "U.S. operations do not involve sustained fighting or active exchanges of fire with hostile forces, nor do they involve U.S. ground troops" (Savage and Landler 2011). Despite complaints and efforts by Congress to force the administration to adhere to the ninety-day clock and seek congressional approval, including a bipartisan resolution condemning the action passed by the House of Representatives, the administration continued its use of force. Even a lawsuit by Dennis Kucinich (D-OH) and nine other members did not succeed in persuading the administration to observe the War Powers Act, but the context of the act's constraints contributed to limits on the nature and duration of the US action, and the furor died down as the US role shifted to less active efforts in the late summer of 2011.

Most recently, in 2019, Congress responded to concerns about the Trump administration's involvement in the conflict in Yemen (alongside Saudi Arabia) and the potential for military conflict in Iran. As a consequence, in April both the House and the Senate passed bipartisan legislation calling for an end to US military support and involvement in the conflict in Yemen, invoking the War Powers Act and relying on it to do so. However, President Trump vetoed the measure and, though a substantial number of Republicans in both chambers supported it, Congress lacked the votes needed to override the veto (Benen 2019; Golshan 2019). As concerns over the administration's intentions toward Iran grew, members of the House began efforts to repeal the 2001 Authorization for Use of Military Force to which the Bush, Obama, and Trump administrations all referred in support of their decisions involving the use of the American military. Barbara Lee, a Democrat from Texas who was the only member of Congress against the 2001 authorization, took the lead in the effort, introducing new legislation to limit President Trump.

In sum, the War Powers Act has given Congress the potential to play a more active role in the use of force abroad. The act has been of major symbolic importance in promoting congressional reassertion in foreign policy and has served as a model for other legislation. The act is indicative of a more assertive Congress and a transformed political environment since Vietnam. It may even have changed the environment and influenced future decisions to use force. However, members of Congress have been cautious in challenging presidential initiatives in so vital a matter even though presidents must be much more cautious today than in the Cold War years. The typical response to hostilities by most members of Congress and the public is to "rally round the flag" in support of the president—the September 11 attacks being the most obvious recent example.

Advice on and Consent to Appointments and Treaties

The Senate has the constitutional authority to advise presidents on and consent to their appointments and treaties. These are two areas in which senators possess power in foreign policy matters that members of the House of Representatives do not share, helping to account for the Senate's greater prestige and power within Congress. These powers also give individual members opportunities to shape policy by giving them some influence over personnel, as well as opportunities to link **advice and consent** on appointments and treaties to other policy concerns.

With respect to presidential **appointments**, since World War II members of the Senate have tended to be hesitant to exercise this power too aggressively (Franck and Weisband 1979; Johnson 1985, US Congress, House Committee on Foreign Affairs 1982). Indeed, the Senate has tended to rubberstamp ambassadorships and presidential appointments to the executive branch, especially for lower level appointments. However, as we discussed in Chapter 3, presidents have taken longer to appoint personnel—with President Trump failing to fill a remarkably high number of positions and leaving others to "acting" personnel. The Senate confirmation process has also become slower and more cumbersome over the years, often taking months (Ornstein and Donilon 2000). Moreover, partisanship has increasingly impacted the appointment process, so that some appointments (especially to the Supreme Court) result in serious political fights. According to Stack and Campbell (2003:29),

> Some senators routinely take advantage of their leverage to foil presidential nominations if they consider the nominees are out of step with existing congressional majorities. Others regard advice and consent not as a mere formality but as an important constitutional weapon guarding the independence of Congress from the executive branch.

It is not unusual for at least one major presidential appointment to draw a great deal of attention and political controversy—and even fail or have to be withdrawn—during a president's term of office. Examples can be found in every presidency. Congressional impact can occur at different, and sometimes less visible, levels as well. The late Jesse Helms, a Republican senator from North Carolina, was particularly active in the appointment process. As a member of the Committee on Foreign Relations, he held up and criticized many appointments made by Reagan and the elder Bush for holding insufficiently conservative views. When Helms became chair of the Foreign Relations Committee in 1994, he successfully blocked several of President Clinton's appointments, engaging in "hostage-taking" by blocking an appointment "in order to extract concessions from the president" (Stack and Campbell 2003:29; see also Carter and Scott 2009) (see "A Closer Look: Jesse Helms Tackles the Foreign Affairs Agencies"). Hence, whether members object to a particular individual, or seek to link appointments to other issues to gain leverage, the appointment process ensures the potential for their influence.

A Closer Look

JESSE HELMS TACKLES THE FOREIGN AFFAIRS AGENCIES

In 1995, Senator Jesse Helms (R-NC) became chair of the Foreign Relations Committee and initiated a campaign to restructure the foreign affairs agencies of the US government. Helms first raised the restructuring initiative in 1994, demanding the abolition of the US Agency for International Development (USAID), the Arms Control and Disarmament Agency (ACDA), and the US Information Agency (USIA). That same year he also tried to freeze all assistant secretary of state nominations pending reorganization. Helms's campaign centered on a legislative proposal that called for the elimination of the three agencies just noted (whose functions would be merged into the State Department) and changes to streamline and centralize the State Department. His committee completed its work on his Foreign Relations Revitalization Act of 1995 in May, and it was ready for the Senate floor in July 1995.

However, Helms's reform initiative met with opposition from the Clinton White House and the foreign policy agencies themselves. Faced with this determined resistance, Helms escalated his efforts. He halted business meetings of the Senate Foreign Relations Committee, blocked more than a dozen treaties and other international agreements, including the second Strategic Arms Reduction Treaty and the Chemical Weapons Convention (CWC), so that they could not be voted on by the full Senate. Helms also froze State Department promotions and held up thirty ambassadorial nominations and one assistant secretary of state nomination.

A stalemate ensued. Lacking sixty votes to overcome a filibuster, Helms could not take his bill to the floor for a vote. The administration could not get its personnel confirmed or its international agreements ratified because Helms would not allow them out of his committee. Months of bargaining followed. In August, Helms managed to obtain a personal meeting with the president, and he released a group of the nominees and a handful of minor treaties to the Senate floor in response. In December, a deal was reached in which Helms agreed to release eighteen ambassadorial nominations, several minor tax treaties, and both the START II arms control treaty and the CWC in return for action on his restructuring initiative. This deal collapsed in 1996 when the House of Representatives tried to link payment of American UN arrears to international family planning issues, prompting President Clinton to veto the bill in April.

After the 1996 election, Helms revived the initiative, offering the **Foreign Affairs Reform and Restructuring Act of 1997** and informing his colleagues and the administration that ambassadorial appointments and the CWC) would remain locked up in the Foreign Relations Committee until action on his bill was completed. As Helms later described it in a hearing on the initiative:

> I discussed this matter with the distinguished Ranking Member, Senator Biden, who readily agreed that it was essential that this be a bipartisan project. Thereby, we together sent the administration a clear message that there must be no repeat of the unsuccessful battles waged in 1995 and 1996 and to the credit of both the President and the Secretary of State, the administration came forward with a reform plan addressing many, though not all of my key concerns, and in the ensuing months Senator Biden and I, along with our respective staffs, devoted dozens of hours to hammering out the final package. (US Senate, Committee on Foreign Relations 1997:265–66).

In April 1997, the Senate ratified the CWC and the Clinton administration released a plan supporting the restructuring of the agencies. However,

(Continued)

due to the linkage between the restructuring bill, the UN payments, and the family planning issue (driven chiefly by the House of Representatives), the Foreign Affairs Reform and Restructuring Act was placed on the back-burner until the fall of 1998. In October of that year, the final version of the legislation was finally signed by President Clinton. The bill eliminated the ACDA and the USIA, merging their operations into the State Department. USAID survived but was placed under the direct control of the secretary of state. Helms had achieved some but not all of his restructuring.

How do Jesse Helms's efforts illustrate the avenues open to members of Congress to try to influence foreign policy, and what are the consequences of such efforts?

Source: Ralph G. Carter and James M. Scott, *Choosing to Lead: Understanding Congressional Foreign Policy Entrepreneurs* (Durham, NC: Duke University Press 2009).

The general structure of international agreements has tended to provide advantages to the president. Since World War II, a large number of overseas commitments have been made by the United States—approximately 1,800 such agreements from 1789 to 2000—the vast majority of which came after 1945. Although almost 2,000 such agreements were in the form of formal **treaties**, subject to the advice and consent of the Senate, most of these commitments were **executive agreements**—not requiring senatorial advice and consent. In fact, by the end of the century, more than 90 percent of the international agreements of the United States were in the form of executive agreements (O'Brien 2003). About the time of the Vietnam War, members of Congress became concerned with the proliferation of executive agreements.

In response, Congress has tried four techniques in attempting to restore its advice and consent role in the agreement-making process. First, Congress passed the 1969 National Commitments Act and the 1972 Case Act and required the president to report all agreements within sixty days of their completion to ensure that Congress was aware of the commitment and had a chance to review or even reject it. Second, members of Congress have also tried—mostly unsuccessfully—to force the president to submit executive agreements to the Senate as treaties. Third, Congress has used the power of the purse in some cases, withholding funds necessary to implement executive agreements. Finally, Congress has tried to subject executive agreements to disapproval or approval, with limited success and the likelihood that such requirements may be unconstitutional.

When international agreements are negotiated as treaties, the Senate's role and influence has been much more significant. The Senate may amend a treaty, which requires it to be renegotiated, or it may attach "reservations," "understandings," and "policy declarations" to guide future US practices, both on the treaty and, in increasingly more cases, on other issues. Since the Vietnam War and the end of the Cold War, members of the Senate have been increasingly likely to use treaty processes to shape policy in these ways (Auerswald and Maltzman 2003). For example, to gain passage of the Panama Canal treaties in 1978, President Carter was forced to accept two controversial reservations that emphasized American security concerns to protect the canal. Moreover, Senate opposition can be exercised simply by keeping treaties from coming to the floor for a final vote, which has been done repeatedly with international human rights covenants. As well, individual members in key positions can hold treaties hostage, just as they do appointments. Presidents are aware of these possibilities and usually attempt to incorporate congressional preferences during the negotiations to such actions. As Martin (2000) argues, the Senate thus influences treaties in ways other than with up-or-down votes.

Three recent examples provide good illustrations. The Clinton administration gained ratification of the 1997 Chemical Weapons Convention but only after a difficult and highly charged political fight within the Senate. First, the treaty was bottled up in the Senate Foreign Relations Committee by Chairman Jesse Helms (see "A Closer Look"). Then, the White House had to reach out to Republican Majority Leader Trent Lott of Missouri. In exchange for his support, Lott demanded changes in the Conventional Forces in Europe and Anti-Ballistic Missile treaties, while Helms continued to hold the treaty in the Foreign Relations Committee. To get the treaty to a vote, the Clinton administration granted virtually everything that Lott and Helms had demanded.

Just two years later, the administration had its Comprehensive Test Ban Treaty rejected outright, with Republicans uniting in opposition to the treaty. As Helms refused to release the treaty from committee, fellow Republican senators Jon Kyl of Arizona and Paul Coverdell of Georgia worked to build opposition to the treaty. By October, confident that he had the votes to defeat the treaty, Lott decided it was time to give supporters a vote. Seeing that they lacked the necessary votes, Democrats, including Clinton, pleaded for a delay but were ignored. On October 13, the treaty was defeated 51–48 (DeLaet, Rowling, and Scott 2007).

More recently, Obama had to work hard to secure Senate approval of his New START nuclear arms control treaty with Russia. Negotiated over the first sixteen months of his presidency as part of the effort to "reset" US-Russian relations, the treaty, which proposed to slash the two sides' nuclear arsenals by about 30 percent, stalled in the Senate after its completion. Opposition from Republican members blocked ratification until just before Christmas, when the administration and its supporters gained just enough Republican support to ensure ratification by agreeing to two amendments to the ratifying document (not the treaty itself) that stated the administration's support of a limited missile-defense program and continued funding of nuclear weapons modernization programs (Sheridan and Branigin 2010).

The difficulty in securing Senate approval of treaties, complicated by the increasingly polarized and partisan environment, led Obama to resort to executive agreements to complete major multilateral diplomatic initiatives: the 2015 Joint Comprehensive Plan of Action to control Iran's pursuit of nuclear weapons (concluded between Iran, the five permanent members of the UN Security Council, and the European Union) and the 2015 Paris Agreement on climate change (which currently has 196 signatories, representing all countries of the world except the United States). President Obama was able to conclude these agreements without Senate ratification because they were executive agreements, but President Trump was therefore able to reverse these US commitments without congressional approval, which he did in 2018.

The recent context also demonstrates other actions that members of Congress can take to try to shape policy where agreements and treaties are concerned. Of course, members can try to frame the public debate and thus bring political pressure to bear on the White

House. For example, in 2015 Senator Tom Cotton (R-AR) and forty-six Republican senators prepared and sent a controversial open letter to Iran seeking to undermine the Obama administration's nuclear talks with Iran. In it, Cotton warned Iranian leaders that Congress and future Republican administrations would likely alter or even revoke the deal—which is, of course, exactly what the Trump administration did. Similarly, Republican leaders in Congress invited Israeli president Benjamin Netanyahu to deliver an address to a joint session of Congress in 2015 to argue against the US-Iran nuclear talks and urge the imposition of new sanctions against Iran instead. Finally, after more than two years in which the Trump administration took a variety of actions to undermine the US commitment to the NATO alliance, Congress took action to shore up support for the alliance and reassure American allies. In March 2019, Senate Majority Leader Mitch McConnell (R-KY) and House Speaker Nancy Pelosi (D-CA) invited NATO General Secretary Jens Stoltenberg to address Congress, which he did on April 3, 2019, calling for increased alliance unity and efforts to counter increasingly aggressive Russian efforts to undermine it. Later in 2019, the Senate Armed Services Committee took further steps to signal strong bipartisan support for NATO and make it difficult for President Trump to withdraw from the alliance agreement, adopting an amendment to the defense spending bill (Gould 2019).

The Senate has also been active in the area of foreign economics and trade policy, often through its treaty powers, as these areas are more controversial and often have direct economic implications for constituents (Destler 1994; Nollen and Quinn 1994). Since the creation of the original Bretton Woods system during World War II, Congress has mostly delegated authority on regular rounds of negotiations to open trade, including the agreements to create the North American Free Trade Agreement (NAFTA) and the World Trade Organization (WTO) in 1994. In both cases, the Senate agreed to provide the executive branch and the president with what is referred to as **fast-track authority** to negotiate such international economic agreements, promising an up-or-down vote on the agreements. President Clinton obtained ratification for both NAFTA and the WTO, but with free trade becoming increasingly controversial in the globalizing economy, he was unsuccessful in getting congressional support for additional fast-track authority for future international economic and trade agreements.

George W. Bush finally succeeded in 2002—after the 9/11 attacks—in getting compromise legislation giving him fast-track authority, which he used to negotiate the Central American Free Trade Agreement, signed and ratified in August 2005. In October 2011, Barack Obama gained congressional approval of long-delayed free trade agreements with South Korea, Colombia, and Panama. He also gained congressional authority to negotiate the Trans-Pacific Partnership (TPP), a trade agreement with partners in the Pacific Rim to improve those countries' ability to counter China's growing economic might. However, the TPP proved controversial and President Trump withdrew the United States from the agreement almost immediately after taking office in January 2017.

The Power of the Purse and the Power to Make Laws

Congress is also a force to be reckoned with in foreign policy because of its control of the purse and its ability to make laws. This has always been the greatest strength of the legislative branch, guaranteeing it a role in the policymaking process for most foreign policy issues, especially in economics and other intermestic issues. The main vehicles by which members of Congress access their legislative and spending powers are the legislative process and annual budget cycle. These complex procedures "hard-wire" Congress into policymaking, providing regular opportunities for members to initiate action on their preferences. Ultimately, since presidents cannot do what is not funded, they must eventually come to Congress.

No simplified summaries of the legislative and budget processes do justice to the complexity they exhibit. Legislation must wind its way from introduction through (often multiple) committees and subcommittees for hearings and markup, the floors of both chambers, and conference committees to reconcile the differences between the House and Senate versions. Ample access points exist for members to engage in the legislative process, but that also means there are many chokepoints where legislation can fail or be amended by another member with a different idea. The **legislative process** is also divided between an **authorization process**, based in substantive committees that "authorize government programs" and their general amounts; and an **appropriation process**, based in the appropriations committees that actually provide "money" for programs. For example, the foreign relations committees play the central role in authorizing the annual foreign aid and foreign operations bills, which fund the foreign affairs agencies and international assistance programs, but the appropriations committees engage in a second process to allocate funds to be spent. Both bills must make it through both processes. The legislative process is thus not only incredibly complex but also very political. Ultimately, bargaining and compromise are the keys to legislative success (Oleszek 2003; Sinclair 2000).

A good illustration of the opportunities provided by the legislative and budget processes is foreign assistance. Congressional involvement in foreign assistance policy has often been used by members of Congress to influence US foreign policy. Members can (1) "earmark" foreign aid funds for specific countries or purposes (e.g., specifying a certain amount of aid to Pakistan, or to combat the global HIV/AIDS crisis); (2) attach conditions that govern the allocation of funds (e.g., progress on human rights); or (3) attach reporting or certification requirements, forcing the executive branch to provide information to Congress. Congress has also leveraged its role in foreign assistance—as well as the broader **power of the purse**—to make occasional inroads on presidential dominance of the war-making power. For example, Congress cut off all US military assistance to South Vietnam and Cambodia in February 1975, thereby accelerating the end of the war in April of that year.

At times, Congress has taken the initiative through its power of the purse in setting the public agenda and steering foreign policy. For example, US government human rights policy is commonly attributed to the initiative taken by President Carter, who was a major advocate of international human rights. However, US support for human rights actually was initiated within Congress following Watergate and was manifested primarily through US foreign assistance policy. Foreign assistance legislation was amended to prohibit security and developmental assistance to any country engaging in a consistent pattern of gross violations of internationally recognized human rights. Likewise, Congress's threatened passage of the 1985 anti-apartheid bill over President Reagan's veto forced him to issue an executive order imposing sanctions on South Africa. In 1986, unsatisfied with the administration's half-measures, Congress enacted the Comprehensive Anti-Apartheid Act over the president's veto.

The terrorist attacks of 9/11 initially increased congressional and bipartisan support for the president's foreign policy in general and antiterrorist policies in particular. Among other things, Congress was quick to pass legislation to authorize the war on terrorism, as discussed earlier, as well as to appropriate funds; to provide additional foreign assistance to countries supporting the antiterrorism war; and to pass an antiterrorism bill—called the USA Patriot Act—that expanded the government's ability to engage in domestic intelligence surveillance, detain suspects, and penetrate the banking and financial systems. Congress also dramatically increased spending on homeland security, defense, and intelligence.

During the Trump administration, Congress asserted itself on foreign aid as well, using its power of the purse to reverse or reject White House policy proposals. Although President Trump proposed to slash foreign aid spending by about 30 percent in each of his first three budget proposals, the Republican-led Congress refused to go along. Instead, under the leadership of key individuals, Congress restored, and even increased, foreign aid in the first two budget cycles and was poised to do the same in 2019.

The same patterns that have evolved with congressional involvement in foreign assistance also operate in other areas of foreign policy, such as national defense, energy, immigration, the environmental, and especially economics. First, members of Congress have taken a renewed interest in foreign policy issues since the Vietnam War. Second, while the president usually initiates policy and proposes legislation, the Congress shapes it. Sometimes major presidential initiatives are rejected outright; more often they are modified or fine-tuned by Congress. Third, Congress can take the initiative or replace a presidential initiative with one of its own. Fourth, Congress has become increasingly involved in the details of the defense budget. Fifth, the more an issue is divorced from national security affairs or the use of force—such as economics—the greater the congressional attention, involvement, and influence (Manning 1977).

The Power of Oversight and Investigation

Congress also has the power to oversee and investigate public policy matters. As former House member Lee Hamilton, a Republican from Indiana and his coauthor noted, "Congress must do more than write the laws; it must make sure that the administration is carrying out those laws the way Congress intended" (Hamilton and Tama 2003:56). Linked directly to the legislative process, **congressional oversight** to ensure that the president and the executive branch implement policies in accordance with the letter and intent of legislation can powerfully restrain presidential power and the foreign policy bureaucracy. This right represents, in fact, the ultimate means by which Congress may exercise its constitutional role. Ultimately, if sufficient abuse of power is determined by Congress, the president may be "removed from office on impeachment for, and on conviction of, treason, bribery, or other high crimes and misdemeanors."

Since World War II, how has Congress employed its oversight powers? With respect to legislative oversight in foreign policy, we can identify three main approaches by which Congress oversees the executive branch: (1) regular oversight tied to the authorization and appropriation cycles, (2) event-driven oversight triggered by policy agendas and issues, and (3) crisis-driven oversight prompted by major policy failures and/or scandals. Together, these approaches may result in a proactive, continuous supervision of the executive branch versus a more reactive, crisis-driven approach (Aberbach 1990; Deering 2003). Over time, members have relied on a mix of each kind, although there has been variation.

With each year's budget cycle, the foreign affairs committees and subcommittees in Congress engage in "regular oversight," holding hearings on agency programs and activities, considering agency budget requests, and collecting information from the executive branch and others. Greatly assisted by personal and committee staff, this oversight provides numerous opportunities for "**watchdog**" activities. It also leads members to support, revise, or oppose policy activities across a wide range of organizations. (See "A Closer Look: Pushing the President" for some additional insights.) More episodically, a particular member of Congress in a key position might organize an oversight hearing on an issue of particular interest, or one driven by current developments. In these instances of oversight, Congress gathers information on policy problems and administration responses or policies (or the lack thereof), which may lead to further action. For example, Pennsylvania Senator Arlen Specter, while still a Republican, promised to hold hearings on the controversial issue of domestic spying in 2006 as chair of the Senate Judiciary Committee. Such "event-driven oversight" is especially important to congressional foreign policy agendas.

A Closer Look

PUSHING THE PRESIDENT

The high-stakes territorial disputes in the South China Sea and China's increasingly assertive claims pose challenges for its neighbors in the region and for the United States. Since 2014, the Obama administration, followed by the Trump administration, has had to take actions to address US concerns in the region. However, these efforts to respond to the South China Sea challenge are shaped by more than the executive branch. Making sense of US diplomacy and its policy approach to this potentially volatile territorial issue requires attention not only to the presidency but also to members of Congress. The most recent context provides an instructive example of the steps and sequences of congressional activities to shape foreign policy.

After the 2016 elections and the change in administration, members of Congress initially waited to see what the new administration's approach would be.

They were encouraged by Secretary of State nominee Rex Tillerson's firm and assertive statements at his confirmation hearings, during which he called for confrontation. However, assertiveness receded as the new administration sought cooperation with China to address North Korea's nuclear weapons program.

As a consequence, members of Congress took action to prod the reluctant administration forward, combining signals, hearings, and the introduction of legislation to press their preferences for a different, more assertive approach. For example, seven senators wrote to the White House urging more aggressive action, including the resumption of naval patrols in the South China Sea. According to one congressional aide, "We thought it was important to weigh in and also to try to help shake things loose in the administration on this" (DeLuce 2017). Bob Corker (R-TN), chair

(Continued)

(Continued)

of the Senate Foreign Relations Committee, joined with Senators Marco Rubio (R-FL), Cory Gardner (R-CO), Benjamin Cardin (D-MD), Jack Reed (D-RI), Edward Markey (D-MA), and Brian Schatz (D-HI) on the letter. In addition, Rubio introduced the South China Sea and East China Sea Sanctions Act of 2017 in March, legislation that would escalate US responses to include entry and property sanctions (currently pending in committee at this writing). In response, the administration ended its freeze of naval operations in the region (it had denied several requests from the Defense Department for such operations) and, in May 2017, authorized the first such action of its tenure in office. Administration officials including Secretary of State Tillerson and Secretary of Defense James Mattis also delivered more assertive warnings to China in public statements made during travel in the region in June 2017, and the administration increasingly embraced an approach similar to that of its predecessor, with somewhat more emphasis on shows of force.

What does this example suggest about congressional foreign policy activity and influence?

Source: Adapted from James M. Scott, "The Challenge of the South China Sea: Congressional Engagement and the U.S. Policy Response," *All Azimuth* 7 (Summer 2018): 1-26.

When policy failures and/or scandals hit, Congress typically responds retrospectively by organizing hearings to investigate the causes of the failures. Such "crisis-driven oversight" occasionally leads to future legislative efforts to correct the problems identified. The most well-known examples of crisis-driven oversight include the internal security investigations of the late 1940s and early 1950s, when a number of congressional committees were active in investigating communist influence in government, academia and education, the media, Hollywood, and other walks of American life. Following this, during the height of the Cold War Consensus, oversight lapsed. The general attitude toward oversight of the national security bureaucracy at the time was expressed by Senator Leverett Saltonstall, the ranking Republican on the Armed Services Committee: "It is not a question of reluctance on the part of the CIA officials to speak to us. Instead, it is a question of our reluctance, if you will, to seek information and knowledge on subjects which I personally, as a member of Congress and as a citizen, would rather not have" (quoted in Treverton 1990:74).

With the Vietnam War, crisis-driven investigative oversight increased. A major entry was the Watergate hearings—the congressional investigation of Nixon's presidential conduct, which eventually produced three impeachment counts by the House Judiciary Committee and forced Nixon's resignation. Additional investigations included two detailed House and Senate investigations of the intelligence community by the Pike and Church Committees in 1975, which stimulated the creation of intelligence oversight committees within each chamber and triggered efforts at intelligence reform (Johnson 2005; Smist 1994). A decade later, the Reagan administration's efforts to covertly exchange arms for hostages with Iran and to fight a secret war to overthrow the Sandinista government in Nicaragua produced the Iran-Contra affair, which led to major investigations—the Tower Commission, consisting of John Tower, Brent Scowcroft, and Edmund Muskie; then initial closed-door congressional investigations by the intelligence committees; and then a joint House and Senate congressional investigation that led to the Iran-Contra hearings and subsequent report by the joint congressional committee.

After the Cold War, Congress investigated the US relationship with Iraq during George H. W. Bush's administration. Later, President Clinton experienced a number of congressional investigations during his time in office, including those of Whitewater, Clinton and Gore's 1996 presidential campaign and fund-raising efforts, and the Monica Lewinsky affair. The last of these resulted in Clinton's impeachment and subsequent trial in the Senate, in which the articles of impeachment were voted down. Like investigations of the past, the Clinton investigations were heavily partisan as a result of divided government—led by Republican members of Congress after the 1994 elections to damage a sitting Democrat in the White House.

Most recently, in the aftermath of the 9/11 attacks, the House and Senate intelligence committees held a joint investigation of the intelligence community's mistakes leading to the attacks, releasing a scathing report in December 2002 (US Congress 2002). After it became clear that prewar claims of Iraq's possession of weapons of mass destruction were almost completely wrong, the Senate intelligence committee held another investigation, releasing its highly critical assessment in July 2004 (US Senate, Select Committee on Intelligence 2004). Further revelations of controversial activities by the intelligence community as part of the war on terror, including torture and an alleged secret assassination program, led to additional investigations in 2009 (Isenstadt 2009). The Obama administration faced congressional scrutiny in the wake of the 2012 Benghazi episode in which Libyan terrorists attacked US facilities, with six congressional committees conducting ten investigations over the next four years. And, following the 2018 midterm elections that put Democrats in the majority in the House of Representatives, the House began numerous oversight hearings investigating various aspects of the Trump administration's activities and processes, including those related to the 2016 election, Russian interference, security procedures for personnel, and others. Following whistleblower revelations of illegal efforts by the Trump administration to enlist foreign interference in the 2020 election, the House turned to its most powerful oversight tool, beginning impeachment proceedings against President Trump in the fall of 2019.

Two additional characteristics of oversight bear noting at this point: (1) reporting requirements and (2) the increasingly common use of special commissions to conduct investigations. **Reporting requirements** are a congressional mechanism that fuels oversight. As we noted earlier, such requirements extract information from the executive branch through regular reports and notifications as well as through special reports. Congress and the president increasingly collaborate to delegate oversight and investigative responsibilities to special, so-called blue-ribbon **commissions**, generally drawn from key experts and former policymakers from both political parties (Campbell 2001). Examples include the Rockefeller Commission, appointed by President Ford to investigate the intelligence community in the mid-1970s; the previously mentioned Tower Commission; the Aspin-Brown Commission, appointed in 1995 to investigate the intelligence community; the Hart-Rudman Commission, appointed in 1999 to study US national security; and the Kean and Silberman-Robb commissions, appointed after 9/11 to investigate the attacks and the intelligence on weapons of mass destruction in Iraq, respectively.

CONGRESS AND THE POLITICS
OF FOREIGN POLICY

To what extent is Congress a force to be reckoned with in the making of contemporary US foreign policy? No simple answer or single relationship prevails today between the legislative and executive branches in the making of US foreign policy. Clearly, as we discussed earlier in the chapter, interbranch politics in foreign policy have been fluid and dynamic, with neither Congress nor the president always predominant, especially since the collapse of the Cold War Consensus.

How might the complex politics of legislative-executive relations evolve in the future? Three principal elements support the continuation of an active, though sporadic, congressional role in the foreign policymaking process. First, Congress has experienced institutional changes that were instrumental in allowing its reassertion of influence in foreign policy. These changes are not temporary but have been institutionalized in a more bureaucratic environment. Furthermore, major membership turnover—which has the potential to alter Congress as an institution—is difficult to achieve in a short period of time, given the high reelection rates of incumbents and the large number of "safe seats." Moreover, the differences in the strength of each major party in each chamber is so small that the switch of only a few seats from one party to another following an election can produce different party control in the House and/or the Senate, creating considerable uncertainty for the future of divided government, presidential power, and majority coalitions. In this sense, the outcome of future congressional elections is both uncertain and likely to be potentially quite significant.

Second, changes in the domestic environment since the Cold War have prompted and reinforced congressional activism in foreign affairs. The Cold War Consensus that fueled bipartisanship and the imperial presidency has been replaced by competing policy perspectives and greater diversity in domestic politics, which constrains presidential power while strengthening Congress's role in foreign policy. The 9/11 attacks and the war on terrorism do not seem to have produced a new foreign policy consensus to replace the anti-communist consensus of the Cold War years, nor did the Great Recession reinforce the simple free market and free trade orientation for promoting economic recovery and growth.

Finally, changes in the international environment have affected the foreign policy agenda in ways that should ensure congressional involvement. The international system has become more complex since the 1950s, when most Americans saw the world divided between two superpowers and their opposing forces. A more complex international environment has provided the setting for America's failure in Vietnam and the shattering of the Cold War Consensus in domestic politics. This has been reinforced by the demise of the Soviet empire and the changes taking place in Eastern Europe. What were once considered "low" policy issues, such as international economics, have been elevated to the top of the contemporary foreign policy agenda—intermestic issues that members of Congress traditionally influence—even with the growing importance of terrorism as an issue.

Although institutional changes in Congress, changes in the domestic environment, and changes in the international environment and foreign policy agenda combine to ensure a prominent role for Congress in the future conduct of US foreign policy, congressional dominance is unlikely. At the same time, however, the days of presidential supremacy in most areas of foreign policy have passed. Unless a global calamity occurs that creates the perception of a chronic state of national emergency for the United States and ushers in a new period of legislative-executive relations, considerable congressional involvement and influence will continue for the foreseeable future regardless of who is president and what party is in power.

THINK ABOUT THIS

Senator John McCain, who passed away in 2018, once said of Congress and its foreign policy, "Whether we are of the same party, we are not the president's subordinates. We are his equal!" Think about the discussion of Congress and foreign policy in this chapter.

What characteristics and conditions shape congressional engagement, activity, and influence in US foreign policymaking?

KEY TERMS

advice and consent   296
anticipated reactions   277
appointments   296
appropriation process   301
authorization process   301
avenues of influence   276
bipartisanship   279
commissions   305
committee staffs   284
congressional foreign policy
   activity   277
congressional oversight   302
divided government   288

executive agreements   298
executive privilege   275
fast-track authority   300
implied consent   274
invitation to struggle   273
judicial review   273
legislative process   301
legislative veto   274
McCarthyism   279
partisanship   286
personal staffs   284
polarization   286
political questions   274

politics of threat   289
power of the purse   301
reporting requirements   305
roll call votes   284
separate institutions
   sharing power   273
treaties   298
voice votes   284
War Powers Act   293
watchdog   303
zone of twilight   274

Visit **edge.sagepub.com/scottrosati7e** to help you accomplish your coursework goals in an easy-to-use learning environment.

Explaining the Politics and Processes of Foreign Policymaking

LEARNING OBJECTIVES

1. Understand the nature of the policymaking process.

2. Identify the major models of US foreign policymaking.

3. Explain the patterns of US foreign policymaking.

PHOTO 10.1 President Barack Obama meeting with advisers; President Donald Trump meeting with his national security advisers; President George W. Bush meeting with US Senators Hillary Clinton, George Allen, John Warner, and White House aides.

Now that we have examined the president, the foreign policy and foreign economic bureaucracies, the National Security Council (NSC) system and the National Economic Council (NEC), and Congress, let's finish this second major section of our text by thinking about ways to understand and explain the broad patterns and dynamics in the politics and processes of foreign policymaking. In this chapter, we conceptualize, synthesize, and better understand the complexity and dominant patterns of the policymaking process within the White House, in the executive branch, and between the executive and legislative branches. We first review the different stages of policymaking and models of policymaking. Then we discuss major approaches to explain the foreign policymaking process and proceed to highlight three major policymaking levels, moving from the role of presidential politics (including individual beliefs and personality) to broader interbranch politics, before concluding the chapter.

CONTEXT: THE POLICYMAKING PROCESS

Given our discussion of all the players, perspectives, and processes of the past seven chapters, it will probably not surprise you to know that the policymaking process is complex and not always linear. Nevertheless, it helps to think of it as a series of steps or stages through which decisions are made and implemented. Although there are a number of ways to lay out these steps, most scholars of foreign policy emphasize three general stages in the policymaking or decision-making process: agenda setting, policy formulation, and policy implementation.

The initial stage of policymaking is **agenda setting**, during which a problem or issue is defined and must get the attention of governmental officials and organizations if policy is eventually to be produced. Problems and issues become part of the government's agenda in a variety of ways (Kingdon 1984; Rochefort and Cobb 1993). First, issues get on the agenda as a result of initiatives taken by officials, including the president, key advisers, and members of Congress. Hedrick Smith (1988:93) points out in *The Power Game* the importance of defining and manipulating an issue to affect the "power loop"—that is, to affect which participants are involved and the circulation of information in order to control the policymaking process: "Those who are in control of policy, whether the president and his top advisers or bureaucrats buried in the bowels of government, will try desperately to keep the information loop small, no matter what the issue; those who are on the losing side internally will try to widen the circle." Moreover, issues that the government has considered important in the past tend to remain on the agenda. Continuing agenda status explains much governmental behavior: The hundreds of issues that the bureaucracy considers daily are usually of this type. This also accounts for the difficulty presidents have managing the bureaucracy, since so much of what the government does involves refining and implementing existing policies. Many of these policies become so institutionalized and routinized that careerists can "control policy by keeping the power loop small" (Smith 1988:80).

Finally, issues are placed on the agenda as a result of domestic and international events such as crises. The terrorist attacks of September 11, Hurricane Katrina demolishing New Orleans and impacting the price of oil, the collapse of the financial markets in 2008, the so-called Arab Spring and subsequent violence in the Middle East since 2010, and the Russian aggression in Crimea and Ukraine are examples of such events and crises that triggered foreign policy attention.

Once an issue makes it on the governmental agenda, the second stage—**policy formulation**—begins. This stage is what most people think of when it comes to policymaking—the process of identifying and weighing goals and options and the interaction of policymakers as they arrive at a decision. Once a policy is identified and selected, the final stage begins: In this **policy implementation** stage, the decision is carried out by members or agents of the government.

The distinctions among agenda setting, policy formulation, and policy implementation are not as clear-cut as described, since policymaking is usually a complex, political, and messy process. For example, once an issue is on the governmental agenda, its level of importance may change due to events at home or abroad. Issues and policies are not formulated solely at one point in time but often involve a series of decisions over time.

Furthermore, the implementation of policy does not necessarily end the policymaking process for any one issue, given that its success or failure often affects future agenda setting and formulation, which may produce changes in policy. In other words, the agenda-setting, policy formulation, and policy implementation stages affect each other, overlap, and proceed in cycles. Nevertheless, the three stages serve as useful analytical tools for making sense of the nature of policymaking within the executive branch.

EXPLAINING POLICYMAKING

Scholars of US foreign policy have developed and applied many approaches to explain the foreign policymaking process. We want to highlight five of these: (1) rational actor, (2) groupthink, (3) governmental politics, (4) organizational process, and (5) interbranch politics. These models provide five alternative perspectives on presidential power, the nature of the policymaking process, and the politics of US foreign policy. As "models," they represent simplifications of reality that call our attention to the most significant, consequential players and processes to explain why the United States takes particular foreign policy actions.

We begin with the rational actor model because it involves the most simplistic version and "ideal" process that most people envision when they think of foreign policymaking. This model assumes that the very complex field of players, organizations, and institutions can be boiled down to the presumption of a single decision-maker who arrives at decisions through a very rational process. The alternative models are presented from the most centralized to the most decentralized—groupthink, then governmental politics, organizational process, and interbranch politics models—and they assume a less rational, more political process in which the beliefs, personalities, and roles of officials within and outside the Oval Office are consequential in affecting the outcomes. Whereas groupthink portrays a centralized policymaking process under presidential control, governmental politics, organizational process, and interbranch politics portray a decentralized policymaking process with much less control exercised by the president. (Table 10.1 provides an overview of each model.)

The Rational Actor Ideal

On Tuesday, October 16, 1962, the intelligence community informed President John Kennedy that the Soviet Union was transporting and deploying to Cuba medium- and intermediate-range ballistic missiles with nuclear warheads that could strike much of the continental United States. This triggered what became known as the Cuban Missile Crisis. The president assembled a group of his most trusted advisers to consider the American response. The group included Attorney General Robert Kennedy, Secretary of State Dean Rusk, Secretary of Defense Robert McNamara, Director of Central Intelligence John McCone, Secretary of the Treasury Douglas Dillon, Special Assistant for National Security Affairs McGeorge Bundy, Special Counsel Theodore Sorensen, Undersecretary of State George Ball, and Chair of the Joint Chiefs of Staff (CJCS) Maxwell Taylor. For five days they met secretly and virtually round the clock, discussing and debating the information available, goals, and possible policy options. Then on Saturday, October 20,

TABLE 10.1

Policymaking Models

The Model	Decision Structure and Process	Key Explanatory Concepts
Rational Actor	Centralized Rational	Presidential goals and beliefs
Groupthink	Centralized Irrational	Beliefs of leader(s) Personality of leader(s) Group norms and dynamics
Governmental Politics	Pluralistic Political	Policymaker beliefs and personality Policymaker roles and power
Organizational Process	Decentralized Relatively autonomous bureaucracies Dynamic	Organizational structures and roles Organizational subcultures Organizational programs and routines
Interbranch Politics	Decentralized Political	Legislative and executive branch players Policymaker and elected official roles and power Political calculations Interbranch bargaining

Kennedy decided to blockade Cuba, while privately offering Nikita Khrushchev, chair of the Communist Party of the Soviet Union, a political solution (withdrawal of Soviet missiles in Cuba for withdrawal of American missiles in Turkey and a US pledge not to invade Cuba). By the following Sunday, October 28, the Soviet leader had agreed, and the Cuban Missile Crisis was history.

As Graham Allison suggested in *Essence of Decision: Explaining the Cuban Missile Crisis*, most people assume that the policymaking process operates according to what scholars have referred to as the **rational actor model** (see Figure 10.1). In fact, many scholars have concluded that Kennedy's decision approximated a rational and optimal process under presidential control, contributing to the prompt resolution of the crisis (for other viewpoints, see Lebow 1981; Nathan 1975; Snyder 1978). This is the ideal type that is consistent with the formal organizational charts that portray the government as extremely hierarchical.

In the rational actor model, the decision maker moves through a clear process, from identifying problems and the goals/interests of a country to developing and evaluating options, making the choice of the "best" one, and implementing it faithfully and consistently. In terms of US foreign policy, this conception rests on several key assumptions: (1) Ultimately the government operates according to a pyramid of authority; (2) the president is on top and exercises power over foreign policy; (3) advice and information

FIGURE 10.1

The Rational Actor Model

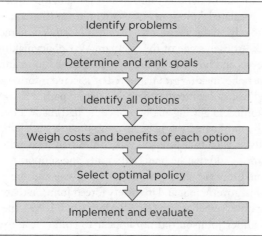

from advisers and the bureaucracy flow to the president; (4) the president makes policy choices based on this advice and information; and (5) the president uses staff within the Executive Office of the President, such as the NSC or NEC, and cabinet appointees to manage and coordinate the vast bureaucracy. In this scenario, the president governs foreign policy and the bureaucracy serves and responds to presidential interests—consistent with the popular image of policymaking.

This perspective assumes not only that the president is ultimately in charge but also that the policymaking process proceeds in accordance with a rational or open process responsive to presidential beliefs and wishes. That is, once an issue gets on the governmental agenda, the president relies on formal policymaking channels (such as the NSC interagency process) for information and advice and informally consults trusted governmental policymakers. Then, the president determines the foreign policy goals to be achieved, considers a wide assortment of policy options, and selects the policy alternative that will best fulfill those objectives. Once the president makes a decision, the bureaucracy faithfully implements the policy in accordance with the president's wishes.

Thus, the rational actor model depicts a policymaking process that is both centralized and rational. At times, the very complex policymaking process may, in fact, operate in a way that justifies the assumptions and simplifications of the rational actor model. In crises like the Cuban Missile Crisis, for instance, the policymaking process may approximate a rational process in which a variety of goals, information, and policy alternatives are considered by the president, who chooses a course of action that is implemented through established bureaucratic procedures or through trusted advisers. In any event, whatever the "reality," the result is that the actual process performs "as if" the rational actor model assumptions apply, and the details of what actually occurs in deliberations within the "black box" of government are just not important enough for attention.

Groupthink

From 1964 to 1968, President Lyndon Johnson and a small group of advisers made a number of decisions that escalated American involvement in the Vietnam War. Once the initial decision was taken to rely on the use of force to defeat North Vietnamese aggression, there was no turning back. At each stage of the Vietnam War policymaking process, decisions centered on force levels and how much force should be used to maintain an independent South Vietnam. The policymaking group ignored or rejected information and policy alternatives that diverged from, or contradicted, the escalatory path. This was primarily because Johnson was accustomed to getting his way once he had made a decision. Through his strong personality, he dominated the policymaking process on Vietnam. Administration policymakers quickly learned that Johnson was committed to avoiding the loss of South Vietnam to communism and that he preferred loyalty and support for his Vietnam policy over open discussion. Only the shock of the Tet Offensive and the collapse of the Cold War Consensus within government and in society forced Johnson to reconsider his policies.

Although some observers disagree (e.g., Barrett 1988, 1989), the Vietnam War policymaking process under Johnson did not appear to come close to the simplifications and assumptions of the rational actor model. Instead, it reflected **groupthink**, a concept developed by Irving Janis (1982) as a result of his work in social psychology. Janis argued that the adage "two minds are better than one" often is not borne out by the dynamics of small-group behavior. Instead, high cohesiveness and *esprit de corps* often develop among members of a group. This is true especially when members have similar backgrounds and beliefs, a strong leader emerges within the group, and the group faces a stressful situation. Under these circumstances, the group develops a strong concurrence-seeking tendency, and members tend to conform to group norms or decisions.

Both the rational actor model and groupthink presume a centralized policymaking structure under presidential control, but groupthink describes a different policymaking process. Instead of deliberating the relevant goals, searching for information, considering alternatives, and selecting the policy option that maximizes goals, as the rational actor model depicts, groupthink often results in a nonrational process. **Symptoms of groupthink** include an overestimation of the competency and inherent morality of the group; a tendency to stereotype out-groups and rationalize decisions; and the tendency to pressure members toward uniformity (usually through self-censorship), providing the illusion of unanimity. Groupthink—having members of a group think alike—is often promoted and maintained because of a strong domineering leader within the group.

Janis predicts that the more that groupthink characterizes a policymaking process, the less likely it is that decisions will have a successful outcome. Failure results because the policymaking group is not open to new information and resists considering alternative policy options. These deficiencies prevent adjustments in policy that may maximize the chances of success, as prescribed by the rational actor model. Under groupthink, the group is committed to a particular policy regardless of changes or developments. Groupthink characteristics help to explain the rigidity and ultimate failure of Johnson's Vietnam policy.

A similar situation occurred in the Iran-Contra affair during the Reagan administration, especially the Iranian element of the initiative. Throughout 1985 and 1986, a number of decisions were made by President Reagan that led to selling arms to Iran in exchange for the release of American hostages held in the Middle East, the profits of which were diverted to support the Nicaraguan Contras (in violation of a law prohibiting such assistance). Once it became public, the Iranian initiative led to an outcry against Reagan and triggered the Iran-Contra affair. The failure of this initiative appears to have been heavily a function of the groupthink process.

While the Reagan administration's foreign policy officials fully supported and actively engaged in efforts to support the Contras and overthrow the Nicaraguan Sandinistas, a major policy split developed within the administration over the Iranian initiative. During the initial policymaking meetings, Secretary of State George Shultz and Secretary of Defense Caspar Weinberger were strongly opposed to the Iranian initiative on both moral and practical grounds. In fact, on two different occasions, Shultz and Weinberger believed they had convinced Reagan to abandon the policy. However, Reagan was personally interested in the fate of the hostages, and the national security adviser (first Robert McFarlane and then John Poindexter) and Director of Central Intelligence William Casey were strong advocates of the initiative. With Reagan committed to the Iranian initiative, the policymaking circle narrowed to include only those who supported the initiative. Thus, dissenters within the administration (i.e., Shultz and Weinberger) were circumvented, and a small group of like-minded individuals implemented US foreign policy that was committed to the release of the hostages (Tower Commission 1987; Woodward 1987).

A similar groupthink process appears to have prevailed following the attacks of September 11, 2001. Like his father, President George W. Bush wanted a strong reaction to the attacks. Unlike the 1991 situation, however, virtually all of Bush's senior advisers also seemed to favor a relatively strong political and military reaction that quickly became a global war on terrorism from the very beginning. But Bush was very much the driving force. According to Dan Balz and Bob Woodward (2002:A1) of the *Washington Post*, within just thirteen hours after the attacks, Bush met with his senior foreign policy aides and told them, "This is the time for self-defense. We have made the decision to punish whoever harbors terrorists, not just the perpetrators." Their job, the president said, "was to figure out how to do it." In other words, "the president and his advisers started America on the road to war that night without a map. They had only a vague sense of how to respond, based largely on the visceral reactions of the president." Not surprisingly, within forty-eight to seventy-two hours of September 11, more formal decisions were made and a general strategy was laid out to fight the war on terrorism, beginning with going after al-Qaeda and the Taliban in Afghanistan and then eventually going after Saddam Hussein in Iraq (see also Elliott 2002; Thomas 2002b; Woodward 2002).

After September 11, George W. Bush dominated his meetings with his senior foreign policy advisers. According to Woodward (2002):

When the meeting began in the White House Situation Room, Bush decided to let the meeting proceed with its routine presentations and updates before getting to the point. "I just want to make sure that all of us did agree on this plan, right?" he said after the reports. He looked around the table from face to face. There is an aspect of . . . urgency in Bush at such moments. He leans his head forward and holds it still, makes eye contact, maintains it, saying, in effect: You're on board, you're with me, right? Are we right, the president was asking. Are we still confident? He wanted a precise affirmation from each one [of his advisers] . . . . He was almost demanding they take an oath.

As Woodward explained, "In fact, the president had not really opened the door a crack for anyone to raise concerns or deal with any second thoughts. He was not really listening. He wanted to talk" (Woodward 2002). Even President Bush admitted, "[T]hat is not a good habit at times. It is very important to create an environment in which people feel comfortable about speaking their minds" (quoted Woodward 2002).

The younger Bush also relied on a small group of advisers and a closed process when it came to the critical decision to invade Iraq in 2003. In this case, not only did President Bush play a forceful role, but Secretary of Defense Donald Rumsfeld and Vice President Dick Cheney in particular were very powerful advocates for war. Secretary of State Colin Powell was the major advocate for moving more deliberately, relying on diplomacy, and, most importantly, advocating the building of a strong multilateral coalition and gaining international support before going to war. Powell tended to be the lone voice, with Condoleezza Rice being relatively passive as national security adviser. Over time, Powell found himself more and more isolated, ignored, and even unwelcome in policy discussions. Ultimately, the most hard-line and war prone dominated the proceedings and carried the day, usually led by President Bush himself (see Badie 2010).

Governmental Politics

In a speech before the United Nations on May 20, 1968, the Russians signaled that they were interested in responding to the Johnson administration's overtures to reach an agreement on arms limitations. This was the beginning of the Strategic Arms Limitations Talks, known as SALT I. Although President Johnson wanted a US SALT position ready by late summer, he refused to involve the White House in the policymaking process. Instead, he wanted to present the USSR with a consensus SALT position that reflected bureaucratic concerns:

> Neither Johnson nor his staff would take part in bureaucracy's epic struggle to produce not just a simple, clear proposal, but one that would actually make a serious matter of SALT. In Johnson's day there was no Henry Kissinger to hold the bureaucracy in line and to force up presidential options, as distinct from the preferences of the various parts of the government. Unlike Nixon, Johnson—as everyone in government knew—wanted agreement, not options. This meant that the Joint Chiefs had to be on board. (Newhouse 1973:108)

Accordingly, the national security bureaucracy—the Defense Department, the State Department, the Arms Control and Disarmament Agency, and the Central Intelligence Agency—was left on its own to interact, bargain, and agree on a consensus SALT position (Newhouse 1973; Rosati 1981).

The formulation of the US government's first SALT position resulted from a policymaking process that did not reflect the rational actor or groupthink model. It reflected a policymaking process that Graham Allison (1971) has called "governmental politics" (see also Halperin 1974; Halperin and Kanter 1973). **Governmental politics** describes a policymaking process that is neither centralized under the president nor rational but, rather, is based on a pluralistic policymaking environment in which power is diffused and the process revolves around political competition and compromise among the policymakers.

Under governmental politics, an issue is likely to trigger involvement of individuals from a variety of bureaucratic organizations, each differing in goals and objectives. However, no policymaker or organization is predominant. The president (or the White House), if involved, is merely one participant, although his influence may be the most powerful. In this "pluralistic structure" within the policymaking process, different policymakers tend to provide information and advocate different policy alternatives. Given the competition and advocacy among the participants, none of whom can dominate the process, decisions emerge from political bargaining, coalition building, and compromise. Nor does the policymaking process necessarily cease once a decision is made. Policymakers and bureaucratic organizations least satisfied by the decision may continue the fight, trying to reverse or modify the decision and its implementation. As an old Washington cliché states, "the only decision that is final is the one you agree with."

A governmental politics process is likely to prevail for agenda issues that are important enough to trigger the involvement of a number of policymakers and bureaucratic organizations, but not important enough to engage the dominant interest and involvement of the president (or a personal adviser acting in the president's name). The process is particularly useful for understanding the interagency processes we described in Chapters 7 and 8. First, presidents and their closest advisers must be selective as to which issues to emphasize, leaving governmental politics to prevail for most other issues. Second, the president's management style may reinforce the practice of governmental politics. For instance, President Reagan downplayed the role of the national security adviser and staff, preferring to delegate authority and remain removed from most foreign policy issues. This management style intensified the political infighting among policymakers that tends to occur in the foreign policy bureaucracy. As Hedrick Smith (1988:561) describes it , "The skirmishes of the Reagan period . . . fit a pattern of bureaucratic tribal warfare—institutional conflict fired by the pride, interests, loyalties, and jealousies of large bureaucratic clans, protecting their policy turf and using guile as well as argument to prevail in the battle over policy." In this context, even when presidents, or their closest advisers, become heavily involved, they may be unable to dominate policymaking.

Recent evidence of the power of governmental politics comes from the Obama administration. From well before he assumed office in January 2009, President Obama welcomed the input of multiple advisers and a variety of perspectives and sought to establish a collegial process for advice and decision making. However, despite this preference for a diverse and collegial inner circle, bureaucratic tensions escalated and strongly influenced the escalation decisions for military operations in Afghanistan-Pakistan. In March 2009, Obama approved a Pentagon request for an additional 30,000 troops that President Bush had deferred to his successor. At the time, Obama relied heavily on the judgment of CJCS Michael Mullins and especially Secretary of Defense Robert Gates (supported by Secretary of State Hillary Clinton), in part because of his lack of knowledge about national security, because he was preoccupied with the state of the economy, and because his national security adviser did not play a central role.

Less than half a year later, the Pentagon returned to request an additional 40,000 troops and a broad "counterinsurgency" strategy. General Stanley McChrystal (the US Commander in Afghanistan) released a report initiated by Gates, Mullen, and General David Petraeus (the combat commander for CENTCOM). The president and his White House staff reportedly felt manipulated by the Pentagon's public leak of the report and request for additional troops before policy deliberation and the evaluation of the still-incomplete deployment of the previously authorized troops (Alter 2010; Hastings 2010; Woodward 2010).

What followed was a complicated and contentious process that led to a compromise decision (or a **"political resultant"** in the language of Allison 1971), which was announced in a speech at West Point in December 2009: a "surge" of an additional 40,000 troops, a hybrid "counterinsurgency" strategy with a "covert counterterrorism" element to pursue the Taliban and al-Qaeda, and an agreement to bolster the Afghan government and train the Afghan military/police. The president and his personal staff had to struggle to persuade the McChrystal report advocates to agree to a full review in early 2011, and the beginning of the withdrawal of US military forces in July 2011 "depending on the conditions" (ultimately the withdrawal began in the summer of 2011 and proceeded slowly through the end of 2016, but 8,400 US troops remained at the end of the Obama administration). Although Vice President Joe Biden and White House staffers opposed the troop escalation, the aggressive efforts of the Defense Department faction and their bureaucratic alliance with Hillary Clinton at State prevailed. Hence, despite the effort by the president to promote a deliberative process with numerous meetings over four months, the process exhibited all the major characteristics of the governmental politics model, with the resulting political compromise producing a tentative consensus for the surge (Alter 2010; Kornblut, Wilson, and DeYoung 2009:A1; Woodward 2010).

In sum, governmental politics describes policymaking as extremely political. Unlike the rational actor model or groupthink, governmental politics describes the president as not ultimately controlling the policymaking process. Instead, policymaking is more pluralistic, involving a variety of policymakers and bureaucratic organizations, each exercising some political clout. When no one actor is able to dominate the policymaking process, competitive politics usually prevail, and decisions become a function of bargaining, infighting, pulling and hauling, coalition building, and possibly compromise.

Organizational Process

On January 28, 1986, the military's ability to place reconnaissance satellites in orbit and the National Aeronautics and Space Administration (NASA) space program came to an abrupt halt when the *Challenger* space shuttle exploded shortly after liftoff, killing the astronauts. Americans were shocked by the tragedy and tried to understand who was to blame for what went wrong. Efforts to locate the responsible parties were based on the assumption that the government operated according to the rational actor model and that particular individuals were in charge. But this is not how the policymaking process for the space shuttle program operated. Nor do the policymaking models of groupthink or governmental politics enlighten us in this case.

To really understand what happened to the *Challenger*, one has to look at the organizational routines within the bureaucracies involved, principally NASA, the Department of Defense (DOD), and their corporate suppliers. NASA's major mission by the 1980s had become the space shuttle. Following repeated delays in the *Challenger*'s expected launch, NASA's mission and **standard operating procedures** resulted in a tendency to deemphasize equipment deficiencies and overlook safety precautions to expedite the launch. The DOD was under pressure to replace aging military reconnaissance satellites with newer, more sophisticated versions. The major mission of Morton Thiokol, Inc., the manufacturer of the rocket boosters, was to make money and maintain its production schedule without damaging the overall reliability of the equipment vital for the space shuttle launchings (including the defective O-rings ultimately found to be at fault). Therefore, the power of the different bureaucratic missions and routines resulted in each of the organizational units, especially within NASA, ignoring warnings about equipment defects and deficiencies. This situation prevailed because all of the organizations involved had played their respective roles for years and enjoyed a string of successful shuttle launches. However, on the day the shuttle exploded, the flaws produced by the **organizational routines** and standard operating procedures came together, surpassing a critical threshold and resulting in tragedy.

Was any particular individual or set of individuals to blame? Fault actually lay with a bureaucratic system of numerous organizations and with the structures and subcultures prevailing within those organizations. US space policy and the *Challenger* tragedy were a function of the different behaviors produced by the organizations involved in the shuttle program. In *Essence of Decision*, Graham Allison (1971) describes this situation as the **organizational process model** of policymaking. This model emerged from the study of bureaucracy and organizational behavior that has prevailed within the fields of economics and public administration.

The organizational process model depicts a decentralized government in which the key actors are bureaucratic organizations rather than the president or a group of policymakers. Policymaking tends to be feudal, with most bureaucratic organizations relatively autonomous from the political leadership and each other. In this process, US foreign policy consists of the sum of the various foreign policies produced by the organizations comprising the foreign policy bureaucracy. In other words, the bureaucracy has become so large and complex that it is an independent driving force behind policy, and the president, more often than not, is only the symbolic leader.

A policymaking process dominated by the bureaucracy not only may prevent foreign policy coherence, but it also may produce contradictory policies. This helps to explain why the State Department can be negotiating peace between warring factions while the CIA is supporting one side or the other at the very same time. It also may help to explain why the CIA's covert national security operations often involve individuals and groups within the criminal underworld, including those involved in the drug trade, even though the government has been fighting a long-standing war on drugs. These contradictions are one of the by-products of the president's limited ability to control the immense bureaucracy and promote a rational policymaking process throughout the executive branch.

Each bureaucracy develops its own organizational missions, occupational roles, and standard operating procedures. As discussed in Chapter 5 and subsequent chapters, each bureaucracy is based on hierarchy, specialization, and routinization. These characteristics are reflected in the bureaucratic structures and subcultures that develop over time. Hence, organizational behavior tends to be **incremental** in nature, where members of organizations act very similarly from one day to the next. Behavior also reflects established bureaucratic repertoires and routines, with standard operating procedures for addressing a set of issues.

An organizational process model is most helpful in understanding policy formulation for agenda issues that are not important enough to gain presidential attention. Much of the day-to-day policy set by the executive branch involves minor issues that are the domain of bureaucratic organizations. These issues do not typically move up the bureaucratic hierarchy; if they do, they are routinely rubber-stamped by superiors. Such issues turn bureaucrats into policymakers by allowing them to make and implement policies usually in accordance with their organization's norms and routines. But, even for those issues that do gain the attention of high-level officials, policymakers are still dependent on the bureaucracy for information, policy alternatives, and policy implementation. These organizational programs and routines often constrain what policymakers can do in the future and determine how their decisions will be carried out.

It is the implementation stage of policymaking that the organizational process model describes most powerfully. For example, although President Reagan made the decision to invade Grenada in 1983, the military bureaucracy was responsible for the operation that—however bungled—eventually succeeded in occupying the island. Likewise, that same military bureaucracy was responsible for the tremendous success of Operation Desert Storm once President George H. W. Bush officially decided to go to war with Iraq in January 1991.

The bureaucracy, especially the CIA, also appears to have played a crucial role in setting the policy agenda and options for what would become President George W. Bush's response to the September 11 attacks. According to Balz and Woodward (2002:A1), on the morning of September 13, two days after the attack, Bush met with his so-called war cabinet in the White House Situation Room. CIA Director George J. Tenet, a holdover from the Clinton administration, "and several other agency officials described in more detail the ideas Tenet had outlined the previous day. This was the second presentation in what became an increasingly detailed set of CIA proposals for expanding its war on terrorism." The CIA plan "called for bringing together expanded intelligence-gathering resources, covert action, sophisticated technology, agency paramilitary teams and opposition forces in Afghanistan. They would then be combined with US military power and Special Forces into an elaborate and lethal package designed to destroy the shadowy terrorist networks." As Balz and Woodward (2002:A1) report,

It was a memorable performance, and it had a huge effect on the president, according to his advisors. For two days Bush had expressed in the most direct way possible his determination to track down and destroy the terrorists responsible for the attacks of Sept. 11. Now, for the first time, he was being told without reservation that there was a way to do this, that he did not have to wait indefinitely, that the agency had a plan . . . . It was a detailed master plan for covert war in Afghanistan and a top secret "Worldwide Attack Matrix."

As powerful as bureaucracies are, they do not always dominate the implementation process nor are they always devoid of presidential control. In the case of the war in Iraq, the organizational process model did not reflect the final invasion plan. Although conducted by the military, it was not dominated by the military. The actual war plan that the military had "on the shelf" was revised again and again by the civilian leadership, especially within the Office of the Secretary of Defense (OSD) under Donald Rumsfeld, apparently with the president's strong support. The civilian leadership also ignored the many studies and recommendations that were made by various parts of the bureaucracy regarding the difficulty of Iraq's postwar reconstruction phase if the president chose to go to war with Iraq. But, consistent with the organizational process model, DOD control over the policy ensured that its processes heavily influenced policy implementation (see "A Closer Look: Bureaucratic Planning for Postwar Reconstruction in Iraq").

A Closer Look

BUREAUCRATIC PLANNING FOR POSTWAR RECONSTRUCTION IN IRAQ

When President Bush decided to increase the military force presence and troop buildup in the Middle East in order to coerce Saddam Hussein and possibly invade Iraq beginning in the fall of 2002, this triggered considerable bureaucratic involvement. Much of the bureaucracy, in fact, became heavily engaged in postwar reconstruction plans—in particular, the State Department, the Army, the CIA, and the US Agency for International Development. See Table 10.2 for the numerous governmental (and nongovernmental) bureaucratic agencies that became involved and the nature of their involvement before the invasion.

In an exhaustive review entitled "Blind into Baghdad," James Fallows (2004:54) found that

almost everything, good and bad, that has happened in Iraq since the fall of Saddam Hussein's regime was the subject of extensive pre-war discussion and analysis. This

is particularly true of what proved to be the harshest realities for the United States since the fall of Baghdad: that occupying the country is much more difficult than conquering it.

The bureaucratic studies and recommendations that were produced were relatively clairvoyant about the difficulty of postwar reconstruction; the importance of establishing immediate security and stability; and the need for a large presence on the ground, including military and civilian components of the government, private voluntary organizations, and international organizations with experience in postwar stability and reconstruction efforts such as in Bosnia and Kosovo. As Fallows (2004:54) summarized, US bureaucratic "predictions about postwar Iraq's problems have proved as accurate as the assessments of pre-war Iraq's strategic threat have proved flawed."

(Continued)

(Continued)

TABLE 10.2

Bureaucratic Involvement in Iraq Post-Conflict Reconstruction

---

1. State Department's "Future of Iraq Project"
   - Began October 2001
   - Seventeen working groups

2. CIA War-Gaming Exercises
   - Final report consisted of thirteen volumes, plus a one-volume summary
   - Began May 2002

3. US Agency for International Development's "Iraq Working Group"
   - Highlighted risk of civil disorder
   - Began September 2002
   - Heavily involved the nongovernmental organization and private volunteer organization community

4. Army War College, Strategic Studies Institute "Postwar Planning Exercises"
   - Began October 2002
   - December report titled "Reconstructing Iraq: Insights, Challenges, and Missions for Military Forces in a Post-Conflict Scenario"

5. Army and Pentagon's Joint Staff "Original Invasion Plan"

6. Senate Foreign Relations Committee Hearings
   - Projected need for very high troop levels, especially for "after" the war
   - On July 31, 2002

7. Council on Foreign Relations
   - Emphasized the importance and difficulty of postwar security
   - Created working group on "Guiding Principles for US Post–Cold War Conflict in Iraq"

8. DOD's study by Sam Gardiner, retired Air Force colonel, "Net Assessment for Iraq"
   - Began on December 2002
   - Report in January 2003

Timeline:
   - January 19, 2003 report
   - January 29, 2003—Jay M. Garner, retired three-star Army general appointed to head all postwar efforts in Iraq
   - Office in Pentagon
   - Started from scratch
   - March 19, 2003—Iraq War Begins

In this case, the DOD and the civilian leadership in the OSD under Rumsfeld were able to gain control of what the military calls "Phase IV" of the war, ignoring the reports and input of other agencies. Instead Rumsfeld, Deputy Secretary of Defense Paul Wolfowitz, and Undersecretary of Defense Douglas Feith within the OSD, with the strong support of the Office of the Vice President under Dick Cheney and his chief of staff, Scooter Libby, relied on extremely optimistic assumptions about the postwar environment on the ground in Iraq once the American liberators had arrived and overthrown Saddam Hussein.

The Iraq invasion plan and the subsequent lack of plans or preparedness for postwar reconstruction raise some serious questions about presidential management of the bureaucracy. Why did President Bush not rely on the NSC interagency process for coordinating postwar reconstruction as would normally have been the case? Why did National Security Adviser Rice allow this crucial stage to be delegated outside the White House and to the DOD? Why was one part of the bureaucracy—the OSD—given so much power and control? Why were other parts of the foreign policy bureaucracy virtually excluded or ignored in the final analysis? As former national security advisers Brent Scowcroft and Samuel R. Berger (2005:51) argue, "Given the stakes, the complexity and the interagency nature of policy decisions associated with stabilization and reconstruction, the National Security Council should have responsibility for overarching policy in this area" (see also Gordon 2004).

Fallows (2004:73) drew a harsh picture: "None of the government working groups that had seriously looked into the question had simply 'imagined' that occupying Iraq would be more difficult than defeating it. They had presented years' worth of experience suggesting that this would be the central reality of the undertaking." Yet they were ignored and dismissed. Therefore, Fallows (2004:73) concluded, "What David Halberstam said of Robert McNamara in *The Best and the Brightest* [for the Vietnam War] is true of those at OSD as well: they were brilliant, and they were fools."

What does the Iraq postwar planning fiasco reveal about the nature of bureaucratic politics and the importance of presidential management?

Interbranch Politics

The central premise of the **interbranch politics model** of US foreign policymaking stems principally from the insights of Chapter 9 and its emphasis on the members of Congress, their multiple avenues of influence, and the political factors the prompt their engagement or compliance in US foreign policy. As Robert Pastor (1981, 1992) put it, the best way to understand foreign policy is to focus on the relationship between Congress and the executive. This perspective is similar to the "political process" approach described by Roger Hilsman (1993), whose book *The Politics of Policymaking in Defense and Foreign Affairs* emphasizes the large number of actors from both the executive and legislative branches who are involved in the foreign policy decision-making process. Hilsman's perspective emphasizes politics, bargaining, and the presence of various power centers across the branches of government, each seeking to achieve their respective goals. As much or more than any of these players, members of Congress are "political animals" who are preoccupied with their institutional status and power, their electoral security, and how they are perceived within and beyond the Washington Beltway. They tend to be driven by electoral concerns and are continually soliciting funds from private contributors for reelection campaigns (Fenno 1978; Mayhew 1974).

As Bruce Jentleson (1990) suggested, interbranch policymaking may take one of at least four strains: *cooperation*, in which the policymakers from both branches work together to make policy; *constructive compromise*, in which policymakers from the two branches devise solutions that garner enough support from each side for policy to proceed, although these sometimes satisfy no group completely and contain inherent contradictions;

institutional competition, involving legislative-executive or interagency contention (actors may pursue parallel policymaking, seeking to act independently of one another to make policy fit the preferences of the dominant view, or the members of each circle may forge alliances with like-minded members of the other circles to compete over policy); *confrontation and stalemate*, in which each circle, endowed with some "negative power," blocks the preferences of the others. Chapter 9 is full of examples of each of these variants.

Summary: Understanding Foreign Policy Decisions

All five models highlight different concepts to explain the policymaking process in US foreign policy: The rational actor model emphasizes the beliefs and calculations of presidents (and their closest advisers); groupthink focuses on the beliefs and personalities of the leaders within the group and the norms that prevail for the group; governmental politics emphasizes the varying beliefs, personalities, roles, and positions of power that policymakers occupy; the organizational process model emphasizes organizational missions, bureaucratic structures and subcultures, roles, and standard operating procedures; interbranch politics focuses on the political process by which policymakers and elected officials from Congress and the executive branch pursue their institutional, personal, political, and policy goals (review Table 10.1).

The models have different implications for the possibilities of change in US foreign policy, for government learning, and for democratic accountability (Etheredge 1985; Levy 1994). The rational actor model suggests that presidents and other government officials are receptive to new information and readily adapt to changes in the environment in order to maximize the opportunity to promote appropriate and successful policies. In other words, such rationality provides optimism about the ability of governments to "learn" and change their foreign policy. It also allows the president to be accountable for the decisions made. This explains why the rational actor model is considered the ideal type (George 1980b; George and Stern 2001, Steiner 1983).

In contrast, groupthink, governmental politics, organizational process, and interbranch politics are much more pessimistic about the government's ability to learn and change its foreign policy. These models suggest that there are considerable psychological, social, political, bureaucratic, and institutional obstacles to governmental learning and that continuity, compromise, and incrementalism are likely to prevail in US foreign policy over time until crises and failure occur (Krasner 1972; Rosati 1981; Snyder 1978).

Finally, these models also highlight the possibility that different models or processes are likely to occur in different contexts. In the next section, we discuss three major policymaking patterns that are most likely to occur in the actual practice of US foreign policy.

PATTERNS OF FOREIGN POLICYMAKING

Since the 1970s, the groupthink, governmental politics, organizational process, and interbranch politics models gained popularity relative to the rational actor model as alternative and superior ways of understanding the policymaking process. Yet these models were also criticized on a number of grounds. Analysts and scholars argued that it was not clear when these models actually explained policymaking. Discussions of the models were often too rigid, for they specified a particular policymaking structure and process, thereby precluding the variety and complexity of political possibilities. The models also were often treated in isolation from one another when, in fact, they overlapped, and more than one model was often involved for any particular policymaking process. In other words, it was argued that these models also oversimplified the political messiness and complexity of the policymaking process in US foreign policy.

This point has probably best been made in a volume entitled *Beyond Groupthink: Political Group Dynamics and Foreign Policymaking,* edited by Paul 't Hart, Eric K. Stern, and Bengt Sundelius (1997:5), who contend that most foreign policy decisions are shaped by small groups and are therefore not well explained by rational actor, organizational process, or bureaucratic politics models. However, they also argue that group decision-making is more varied and complex than just groupthink. As they state:

> It seems eminently reasonable, therefore, to treat groupthink as a contingent phenomenon, rather than as a general property of foreign policy decisionmaking in high-level groups . . . . A cursory look at the standard textbooks on foreign policymaking will reveal that if they deal with small group decisionmaking at all, the presentation is likely to be dominated by the groupthink phenomenon, inadvertently equating "group decisionmaking" with "groupthink." This is a gross simplification, betraying the enormous variety of groups and group processes that play a part in foreign policymaking which, ironically, had been recognized by early analysts not infatuated with the powerful groupthink heuristic. ('t Hart et al. 1997:11–12)

Similarly, Thomas Preston and Paul 't Hart (1999; also Preston 2001) argue that bureaucratic politics should also be seen as a variable rather than a constant. These authors contend that "bureaucratic politics manifests itself more and differently in some issues [and] policy domains . . . than in others" and that the key factor accounting for this variance is "the role played by political leaders in shaping the structures and processes involved in governmental decision-making." In short, presidential style and attention is a critical determinant of the nature of policymaking.

Finally, a substantial body of literature since the end of the Cold War has stressed the variable—but important—role of Congress and legislative-executive interactions in foreign policymaking (e.g., Carter and Scott 2009; Howell and Pevehouse 2007; Kriner 2010; Lantis 2019; Lindsay 1994; Milner and Tingley 2015). In this perspective, the "invitation to struggle" to two separate institutions sharing power establishes a political process in which the individuals and institutions of both branches shape foreign policy. Ultimately, these models—especially groupthink, governmental politics, organization processes, and interbranch politics—indicate that there needs to be a recognition of a certain amount of decision-making variety—"a multilevel approach" that highlights the interplay among individual, group, and institutional factors and takes into consideration complexity and context. Although there are situations in which one of the models may be particularly applicable, to maximize their strengths, it is probably useful to think in terms of three general types or patterns for understanding policymaking within the executive branch: presidential politics, bureaucratic politics, and interbranch politics.

Presidential Politics

Presidential politics operates when the president becomes interested and active in an issue, through direct personal involvement or indirectly when staff and advisers act in the president's name. As discussed in Chapters 7 and 8, presidents rely both on informal channels of communication with close advisers and on a more formal process, usually under the supervision of the NSC adviser (or NEC director) and staff. When an issue is of sufficient importance to gain the attention and interest of the president (or the president's surrogates), the policymaking process is also likely to involve other high-level policymakers from executive branch bureaucratic organizations and agencies. Such was the case, for example, during the Cuban Missile Crisis, in decisions leading to the escalation of the war in Vietnam, during the Iran hostage crisis, during the Persian Gulf crisis of 1990–1991, and after the September 11, 2001, terrorist attacks. For example, President Obama clearly embraced a "top-down" approach in responding to many major issues, such as addressing the severe economic recession and developing the New START nuclear arms treaty with Russia in 2009–2010, among others.

The notion of presidential politics makes it clear that the president's involvement is crucial. Presidential politics also indicates that the policymaking process is very political without precluding any possibilities about the particular dynamics of the process. A relatively open policymaking process may occur in which there is a broad search for information and policy views and alternatives are aired as suggested by the rational actor model. Alternatively, presidential politics may result in a relatively closed process more akin to groupthink. Other patterns may operate, as well, creating situations in which participants may be dissatisfied with presidential decisions and attempt to get them reversed or modified. In all cases, policymaking and politics are inseparable since prominent individuals are likely to be involved, issues in question affect the future of US foreign policy, and the stakes tend to be high. In the final analysis, how the politics of the policymaking process actually proceed depends on the beliefs, personalities, and roles of the participants and the nature of their interaction.

When presidential politics is most applicable, the role and importance of personality and beliefs—especially (but not necessarily exclusively) of the president—are at their highest. Presidential politics is heavily a function of the personality and beliefs of the president and his or her closest advisers, because most of the other policymakers involved take their cues from the president, who ultimately makes the decision. Certainly, bureaucratic politics (discussed later in the chapter) are also heavily influenced by the personalities and beliefs of the individuals involved, but organizational factors balance and constrain them in important ways.

Cognition and Images. It is relatively well known, especially within the study of psychology, that people construct their own reality to a considerable extent. Such is the nature of human **cognition and perception**, that is, how people perceive and process the world around them. According to John Steinbruner (1974:12–13,112), "The mind of man [sic], for all its marvels, is a limited instrument." Given the complexity of the world and the limitations of the mind, the mind "constantly struggles to impose clear, coherent meaning on events." Therefore, Alexander George (1980b:57) concludes:

> Every individual acquires during the course of development a set of beliefs and personal constructs about the physical and social environment. These beliefs provide him with a relatively coherent way of organizing and making sense of what would otherwise be a confusing and overwhelming array of signals and cues picked up from the environment from his senses .... These beliefs and constructs necessarily simplify and structure the external world.

Basically, the mind imposes clarity and tries to make sense of reality through reliance on a few common cognitive principles (see Rosati 2000, 2010a, 2010b). These include (1) the principle of cognitive structures of belief (that the human mind tends to consist of a vast assortment of beliefs that are organized and internally structured, especially around more central beliefs); (2) the principle of selective memory (that people tend to remember certain things better than others, especially the general picture or concept, and be loose with the details); (3) the principle of selective attention and perception (that, although the mind can perceive stable, significant features of the environment, it tends to be selective and incomplete in its attention); (4) the principle of causal inference (that people tend to make inferences about what happened and why based on their beliefs); and (5) the principle of cognitive stability (that the mind tends to keep internal belief relationships stable once formed, especially in the core structure of beliefs).

Two dominant theoretical approaches in cognitive psychology—cognitive consistency theory and schema theory—agree that central beliefs are most consequential but differ regarding the level of coherence and interconnectedness between beliefs. During the 1950s and 1960s, it was popular to view the individual as a "consistency seeker"—motivated to maintain consistency and reduce discrepancies among beliefs. The assumption behind **cognitive consistency** is that "individuals do not merely subscribe to a random collection of beliefs" but make sense of the world by acquiring and maintaining "coherent systems of beliefs which are internally consistent" (Bern 1970:13). Therefore, individuals attempt to avoid the acquisition of information that is inconsistent or incompatible with their belief systems, especially their central beliefs.

A second generation of scholarship emerged in the 1970s describing a more complex cognitive process based on developments in social cognition and schema theory, viewing the individual as a "cognitive miser." According to this view, the minds of individuals are limited in their capacity to process information, so they tend to rely on schemas, shortcuts, or simplifications. **Schemas** are mental constructs that represent different clumps of knowledge (or comprehension) about various facets of the environment. They necessarily simplify and structure the external environment, enabling individuals to absorb new information and make sense of the world around them. The more complex and uncertain the environment, the more likely individuals are to rely on schemas and cognitive heuristics—shortcuts in information processing—to make sense of the world and the situation at hand. Very simply, the mind relies on common patterns of perception and misperception, such as a tendency to categorize and stereotype, to simplify causal inferences, and to use historical analogies.

The human mind perceives the world and processes information by compartmentalizing and sorting things into categories. This necessarily simplifies and often leads to a certain amount of stereotyping. One common tendency in world politics, in this respect, is for the mind to form beliefs and schemas of the "other." The **enemy image**—according to which "we are good" and "they are bad"—may be the most simpleminded image of all. Such is the image of the Soviet Union and communism that most Americans acquired during the Cold War. Once formed, such an image of the enemy tends to be rigid and resistant to change. For example, in a classic work, Ole Holsti (1967) found that during the 1950s Secretary of State John Foster Dulles held an enemy image of the Soviet Union and resisted new information inconsistent with this image by engaging in a variety of psychological processes: discrediting (the information), searching (for other consistent information), reinterpreting (the information), differentiating (between different aspects of the information), engaging in wishful thinking, and refusing to think about it.

In fact, conflict situations often result in **mirror images**: Each party holds an image that is diametrically opposite the other. In other words, each party has a positive and benevolent self-image, while holding a negative and malevolent image of the enemy. As Ralph White (1968) found in *Nobody Wanted War*, an analysis of the two world wars and the Vietnam War revealed that each party tends to hold a "diabolical enemy-image" and a "virile and moral self-image that becomes the source of mutual selective attention, absence of empathy (for the other), and insecurity." Such black-and-white thinking contributes to misperception, escalation, intervention, and war—or a Cold War in the case of the United States and the Soviet Union.

Given the mind's need for certainty and clarity and the tendency to categorize and stereotype, there will also be a corresponding tendency to simplify inferences about causality. As Jervis (1976) put it, "People want to be able to explain as much as possible of what goes on around them. To admit that a phenomenon cannot be explained, or at least cannot be explained without adding numerous and complex exceptions to our beliefs, is both psychologically uncomfortable and intellectually unsatisfying."

Such simplifying tendencies heavily reinforce people's perceptions, especially in the case of enemy images. For example, it was virtually inconceivable in the minds of most Americans that the United States could "lose" the war in Vietnam, yet they could not allow South Vietnam to fall to communism given the devastating international and domestic consequences that they feared would result. In fact, American (especially civilian) policymakers oscillated continually between optimistic and pessimistic assessments in the early 1960s, immediately preceding the fateful decisions to militarily intervene and Americanize the war.

The third perceptual tendency is to use **historical analogies** in making sense of the present. According to Jervis (1976:217), "Previous international events provide the statesman with a range of imaginable situations and allow him to detect patterns and causal links that can help him understand his world" since "we cannot make sense out of our environment without assuming that, in some sense, the future will resemble the past." But "a too narrow conception of the past and a failure to appreciate the impact of changed circumstances also result in 'the tyranny of the past' upon the imagination."

In his examination of analogies and the Vietnam War, Yuen Foong Khong (1992) concluded that the lessons President Johnson and his advisers drew from Munich, Dien Bien Phu, and, most important, the Korean War had a powerful influence on the decision-making process. The use of these historical analogies helped to reinforce the enemy image and predispose the United States toward military intervention. It also helps to explain how the domino theory became a powerful metaphor in the minds of Americans—that the lessons of the past made clear that anything short of a policy of global containment would result in one country after another falling like dominoes to communist expansion.

The enemy image of Soviet communism, and the cognitive dynamics behind it, was the basis of the consensus in the making of US foreign policy during the Cold War. It laid the foundation for the rise of the president and the national security state and American intervention (overt and covert) throughout the world. Such an enemy image revolving around Soviet communism would not survive the Vietnam War and the collapse of the Soviet Union. But the enemy image of communism was a powerful cognitive force in the making of US foreign policy following World War II and continues to have a powerful legacy, even well after the end of the Cold War.

As a result of 9/11, such powerful enemy images appear to have heavily influenced President George W. Bush, as he declared and conducted a global war on terrorism. According to the Bush administration, Osama bin Laden, terrorists in general, Saddam Hussein, and other "axis of evil" states supporting terrorism became the new enemy (replacing the Soviet Union and communism). According to Balz and Woodward (2002), "Bush fashioned a war of absolutes: good vs. evil, with us or against us. He brought a black-and-white mind-set" to the problem at hand (see also Kessler 2003; Thomas 2002b).

Such images were reinforced by Bush's national security team. According to George Packer (2005:64–65) in *The Assassin's Gate*, "They entered government in the aftermath of the trauma in Vietnam, and they were forged as Cold War hawks. They devoted their career to restoring American military power and its projection around the world." And "when September 11 forced the imagination to grapple with something radically new, the president's foreign policy advisers reached for what they had always known. The threat, as they saw it, lay in well-armed enemy states. The answer, as ever, was military power and the will to use it."

In sum, the cognitive approach and the cognitive patterns of perception and misperception identified here have a profound effect on decision making as some of the examples illustrate. The conceptual baggage, the worldviews, and the cognitive dynamics of policymakers play a powerful role. This means that individuals and policymakers rarely formulate decisions through an open intellectual process where goals (and preferences) are clearly ordered, a strong search is made for relevant information, a variety of different alternatives are considered, and the option that maximizes benefits while minimizing costs is selected. Usually this is simply too demanding and too time consuming a process for human beings and the human mind (e.g., Tetlock 2006).

Personality. In addition to the study of cognition and images, one must integrate the role of personality and motivation. Increasingly, an individual, including a policymaker, should be viewed as a **motivated tactician**, or "a fully engaged thinker who has multiple cognitive strategies available and chooses among them based on goals, motives, and needs. Sometimes the motivated tactician chooses wisely, in the interests of adaptability and accuracy, and sometimes the motivated tactician chooses defensively, in the interests of speed or self-esteem" (Fiske and Taylor 1999:13).

The role of **personality** and motivation was initially popularized by psychoanalytic theorists such as Sigmund Freud and the political scientist Harold Lasswell and later culminated in *The Authoritarian Personality*, which argued that beliefs were dependent on ego-defensive needs. Developmental psychologists and other scholars such as Jean Piaget, Eric Erikson, and Abraham Maslow have emphasized that beliefs also fulfill individuals' more positive needs. The classic work highlighting the motivational foundation of political beliefs and behavior is *Woodrow Wilson and Colonel House: A Personality Study* by Alexander George and Juliette George (1956), which distinguished between the "power-seeker" and "power-holder." In Wilson's efforts to gain power in order to overcome his low self-esteem from his childhood days, he conformed to the dominant beliefs of individuals who could significantly influence his rise. However, once Wilson gained a position of power, he would demonstrate incredible rigidity and closed-mindedness after he took a stand.

Holsti (1967:13) also integrated the role of personality in examining John Foster Dulles's rigid enemy image of the Soviet Union, recognizing that "certain personality types can be more easily persuaded than others to change their attitudes." Individuals "also appear to differ in their tolerance for dissonance and tend to use different means to re-establish stable attitudes." As Vamik Volkan (1988) discusses, the need to have enemies and allies appears to be quite powerful among the human species.

The case of Lyndon Johnson, while not unique, demonstrates the impact of an individual's personality and beliefs on the foreign policymaking process and US foreign policy. According to Doris Kearns Goodwin (1991), in *Lyndon Johnson and the American Dream*, one must delve into Johnson's childhood and personal development in the context of the times to understand his decisions and actions as president. Johnson, the eldest of five children, was born in 1908 in Stonewall, Blanco County, Texas, a small rural community. His mother came from a relatively wealthy and well-respected family, but his father was a small-time farmer, heavily involved in local Democratic politics, crude and vulgar, and a hard drinker. According to Goodwin (1991:385), "The picture of Johnson's early life suggests a childhood torn between the irreconcilable demands of his mother—who hoped to find in his intellectual and cultural achievement a recompense of her dead father, unhappy marriage, and thwarted ambition—and those of his father—who considered intellect and culture unmanly pursuits." In this environment, Johnson did not feel loved for who he was and seemed unable to please his parents. The only time he felt comfortable and secure was with his grandfather, who would reminisce and romanticize about the glory days of the intrepid cowboy and the reformism of the Populist Party. The situation worsened as Johnson grew older, for when his grandfather died, he drew closer to his father, to the disapproval of his mother.

According to Goodwin's account, to overcome the terrible fear of rejection that resulted from his upbringing, Johnson developed a desperate and insatiable need to be loved. His tremendous drive to "acquire power and achieve good works" was an attempt to fulfill this need. His boundless energy was directed into politics, initially as a staff aide to a congressman, then as a participant in Franklin Roosevelt's New Deal, later as a member of the House of Representatives, then as a senator (becoming the youngest majority leader in history), and finally in the White House, first as vice president and then president. The consummate political animal, Johnson lived and breathed politics, and bargained and compromised to make deals and policy. Yet, given his family and his rural Texan roots during the first half of the twentieth century, he also strived to achieve "great works," to help people as he understood them. This is best embodied in his commitment to eliminate poverty through his Great Society programs, which Goodwin argues acted as a vehicle to attract the admiration and love of Americans, fellow Texans, and, ultimately, his parents.

Johnson's personality helps to explain his "particular management style" as president. He could not bear to be alone and always had to be in control. He was constantly in motion, on the phone, with the radio or television always on around him. The Johnson White House revolved around his need for people to love, support, and be loyal to him. He often challenged his aides to acts of manhood in order for them to display this loyalty. Once Johnson made up his mind, he wanted consensus and support behind his position. As Johnson himself could so graphically state, "I don't want loyalty. I want *loyalty*. I want him to kiss my ass in Macy's window at high noon and tell me it smells like roses. I want his pecker in my pocket" (Halberstam 1973:434).

Johnson was also overly defensive and sensitive to criticism. Those who were skeptical or didn't go along often received the famous "Johnson treatment"—the use of friendship, intimacy, bargaining, horse-trading, gifts, and anything else it might take to get them on board. Continued criticism or disagreement represented disloyalty, and those involved would eventually be completely frozen out of the power loop and Johnson's life. He was so sensitive to what was said about him, for example, "that it was not unusual for him to watch the evening news on all three networks at the same time, all the while paying attention to how they reported 'his' presidency" (Goodwin 1991:268).

Although Johnson was primarily interested in and comfortable dealing with domestic issues and politics, "in dealing with foreign policy . . . he was insecure, fearful, his touch unsure . . . . As a result, his greatest anxiety—unlike his attitude toward domestic affairs—was to avoid making a serious error rather than to achieve great things" (Goodwin 1991:268). Johnson tended to be heavily dependent on his advisers for information and understanding about world politics. The experience of World War II and Korea—the need to avoid appeasement at all costs—made a far-reaching and decisive impression on Johnson, as it did for many of the Cold War leadership. According to Goodwin (1991:100–101), Johnson believed that

> the way to prevent conflict was to stop aggressors at the start—the lesson of Munich. In every war, Johnson believed, the enemy is an alien force that 'invades' the allies' house . . . . America alone, our attitudes and behavior, were the key to war and peace. Nor was this mode of thought unique to Lyndon Johnson. On the contrary, it was deeply rooted in the American experience.

These beliefs were the foundation for the global policy of containment that, in failing to discriminate between different situations at different times, led Johnson to Americanize the war in Vietnam.

Although Johnson delegated much authority in foreign policy, he was a domineering leader on those issues in which he was interested. Whereas in domestic affairs Johnson was sophisticated and pragmatic, he operated as much more the "idealist and ideologue" in foreign affairs and for Vietnam. With regard to the deteriorating situation in Vietnam, once the decision to escalate US involvement was made early in his administration, the decision process was then closed. Future decisions never involved a serious consideration of deescalation or withdrawal—the choices were always between more or less and different types of escalation as a means of finding light at the end of the tunnel. As David Halberstam (1973:456) concluded, "The Presidency is an awesome office, even with a mild inhabitant. It tends by its nature to inhibit dissent and opposition, and with a man like Johnson it was simply too much, too powerful an office occupied by too forceful a man."

The advisers Johnson came to rely on, Walt Rostow and Dean Rusk, shared his anti-communist philosophy and belief in the "utility of force." When one of his advisers, Robert McNamara, came to reconsider and question the policies in Vietnam, he was shunned and eventually forced to resign. As Goodwin (1991:418) relates,

> The President's will, once expressed, was not challenged . . . . Advisors began to anticipate his reactions before they said or did anything . . . . The more Johnson's energies turned to his critics, the more obsessed he became with the need to discredit his opponents, the less anyone tried to stop him.

Hence, as the consensus behind Vietnam within Johnson's administration and the country began to break, a type of "siege mentality" developed, and the president began to insulate himself, finding comfort in his small group of loyal advisers. Only when many of his advisers and much of the country turned against the American war in Vietnam was Johnson able to realize the tragedy he faced. The Tet Offensive and the growing challenges by Eugene McCarthy and Johnson's archrival, Robert Kennedy, in the presidential primaries were clear indicators that Johnson had lost control of his presidency and the country. Although he had risen to the top, the love and admiration he so needed to receive from the American people had been denied him, and he withdrew from public life.

Many additional illustrations can be provided concerning the powerful impact of an individual's personality on decision making. For example, the events of September 11, 2001, had a profound effect on George W. Bush personally and gave him a new national security focus preoccupied with the war on terrorism. According to Woodward (2002),

> Reflecting on his own personality, [Bush] described himself at various points as "fiery," "impatient," "a gut player" who liked to "provoke" people around him and someone who likes to talk—perhaps too much—in meetings. He admitted that first lady Laura Bush had told him to tone down the 'tough guy' rhetoric on terrorism.

According to Evan Thomas (2005:33,34,37),

> Bush may be the most isolated president in modern history, at least since the late-stage Richard Nixon. It's not that he is a socially awkward loner or a paranoid. He can charm and joke like the frat president he was. Still, beneath a hail-fellow manner, Bush has a defensive edge, a don't tread-on-me prickliness.

In fact, "in the Bush White House, disagreement is often equated with disloyalty . . . . In subtle ways, Bush does not encourage truth-telling or at least a full exploration of all that could go wrong . . . . Bush generally prefers short conversations—long on conclusion, short on reasoning." Clearly, given President Bush's personality, he became much more active and domineering, which contributed to the nature of the national security process over questions of how to respond to September 11 and about going to war with Afghanistan and Iraq (see also Badie 2010).

The forty-fourth president of the United States, Barack Obama, presented interesting contrasts to some of the style and personality characteristics of Johnson and George W. Bush. For one, Obama was more comfortable with argument, disagreement, and complex information than many of his predecessors. Obama's style and personality appeared to emphasize collaboration and deliberation, and he enjoyed a self-confidence (Drew 2009) that enabled him to pay attention to what other people thought while being at ease in an environment in which others had a voice. An interesting indicator of this style was his avid embrace of *A Team of Rivals* by Doris Kearns Goodwin (2006), a book about Abraham Lincoln's strong-minded and independent advisers and the way the president selected, worked with, and managed them. Obama's deliberative nature and comfort with debate and disagreement also fostered his penchant for good listening, his emphasis on inclusiveness (even with those who disagreed), and his self-confidence to serve as a "benevolent referee" by not taking sides in a discussion before a decision was needed. Finally, apparently motivated by achievement rather than power per se (Drew 2009), Obama preferred to work for consensus while serving as a catalyst (see Drew 2009; Lawrence 2008; Walsh 2008; Yoffe 2008).

In contrast to the previous examples, these traits in Obama produced a less domineering or consensus-forcing president (like Johnson or the younger Bush), and one who did not personalize challenges or challengers (like the elder Bush) or decide rashly, without deliberation (like the younger Bush). Such traits can be linked to Obama's policy preferences as president (e.g., for diplomacy) and the policymaking processes he fostered (deliberative, open, and mostly collegial). These traits also helped to minimize groupthink, even while they generated vigorous policy debate and, sometimes, contentious bureaucratic politics.

What about the forty-fifth president? Donald Trump's volatile and domineering style and approach to politics has generated a great deal of attention. Sympathetic observers applaud his blunt and unconventional approach, while critics highlight his impetuousness, thin skin, and grandiose sense of his own importance. In a recent analysis, Allesandro Nai, Ferran Martinez i Coma, and Jurgen Maier (2019) assessed Trump's personality in the context of more than 100 other political leaders around the world. According to their personality assessment, Trump is extremely extraverted; extremely low on agreeableness; extremely low on conscientiousness; extremely neurotic (low emotional stability); and extremely high on narcissism, psychopathy, and Machiavellianism. Compared to the scores of other leaders in the study, Trump's scores on agreeableness, conscientiousness, and emotional stability were the lowest, and his scores for narcissism and Machiavellianism were the highest. The authors also concluded that Trump's negative tone and appeals to fear were comparatively high. As they summarize, "Trump's off-the-charts personality and campaigning style suggest that even when compared with other abrasive, narcissistic, and confrontational political figures, he stands out as an outlier among the outliers." This assessment is broadly consistent with those of other analysts (e.g., Immelman, 2017; McAdams 2016; Sherman 2015). What do you think these personality traits might mean for foreign policymaking?

Bureaucratic Politics

Bureaucratic politics prevail when presidents and their closest advisers remain relatively uninvolved or are unable to dominate the policymaking process (see Figure 10.2). Under these circumstances, other policymakers and bureaucratic organizations become the key determinants of policymaking and the interagency process. This perspective is described powerfully by Charles Maechling, Jr. (1976:18):

> The principal actors represent giant departments and agencies, each with its own constellation of vested interests and statutory responsibilities . . . . Behind the confident facade that each actor presents to his colleagues and to the outside world lurks a morbid compulsion to protect himself from the unexpected, to make the weight of one's agency count and to appear effective in the eyes of superiors.

FIGURE 10.2
Bureaucratic Politics

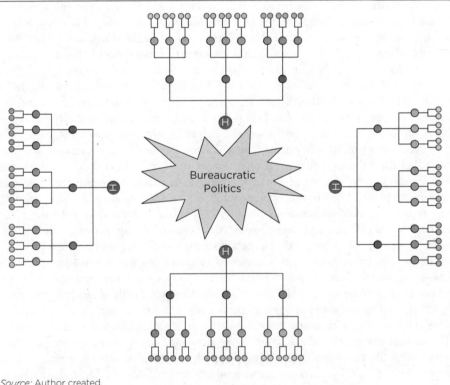

Source: Author created.

American foreign policy concerning Japan, for example, is often dominated by competing bureaucratic interests. According to Robert Pear (1989:1), "the State Department, the Pentagon, and the NSC emphasize Japan's value as a geopolitical and strategic asset and are seen by officials in other agencies as overly protective of Japan." The Department of Commerce and the Office of the US Trade Representative usually "worry about the health of the American economy and favor a tougher attitude." The Department of the Treasury, the Office of Management and Budget, and the Council of Economic Advisers usually "adhere to free market principles and have generally opposed any government intervention to help American businesses compete with the Japanese." Not surprisingly, the US government struggles to pursue a coherent policy toward Japan because of the series of turf wars among federal agencies that limit communication and coordination, even with the existence of the NEC.

According to Howard Wiarda, a similar phenomenon occurs in US foreign policy toward Mexico, where dozens of agencies play a role in some aspect of policy. As Wiarda (2000:176) puts it,

> Not only is there often rivalry and bureaucratic politics between cabinet departments, but there are other rivalries within departments—for instance, between the Army and Navy within Defense, between Customs and INS within Treasury, between FBI and DEA within Justice. To say these agencies are not always on the same wavelength would be an understatement.

Similar problems plagued US policy toward China over the past two decades or so as well, as a result of what seem to be competing US national security interests with interests about economic relations and human rights. These illustrations demonstrate the difficulty of making foreign policy when national security and foreign economic (and other) interests intersect.

Such bureaucratic politics may reflect the bargaining, coalition building, and compromise described by the governmental politics model. Or officials may pursue independent policies based on organizational missions, structures and subcultures, routines, and standard operating procedures as suggested by the organizational process model (Allison and Halperin 1972). Other possibilities, however, cannot be ruled out. For example, bureaucratic and personal infighting could be so intense that compromise among the participants is not possible—instead, political winners and losers result. Regardless of the particular policymaking process, bureaucratic politics always involve a political process reflecting the interactions between the officials, organizations, and political environment prevailing at the time. The beliefs, personalities, and roles of the individuals involved, often reflecting the bureaucratic structures and subcultures of their respective organizations, determine the nature of bureaucratic policymaking.

Since presidents and their closest advisers are involved for only selective issues, bureaucratic politics tend to prevail for most issues in US foreign policy. A minor issue is likely to attract the attention of very few officials and agencies. Minor issues do not cross over many organization jurisdictions, and the stakes are not high enough to concern many officials (Rosati 1981). More important issues will attract the attention of many more officials and bureaucratic organizations. Ultimately, as Charles Maechling, Jr. (1976:3) states,

For every publicized decision [the president] makes, this second echelon of decision makers makes a hundred equally important ones. And it is this steady stream of less conspicuous decisions, building on and interlocking with their predecessors, that fixes the direction and contours of foreign policy, just as effectively as the few spectacular decisions that are the result of conscious deliberation at the top.

The implementation stage of the policy process is usually dominated by the bureaucracy because it usually reflects the bureaucratic structures and subcultures of the organizations involved, thus resembling the organizational process model. Presidential politics may intrude occasionally, as with President Kennedy's efforts to influence policy implementation during the Cuban Missile Crisis. In some instances, presidential politics may be consequential, as was the case with Secretary of State Henry Kissinger's use of back channels to the People's Republic of China and the Soviet Union under President Nixon. And there is the case of Secretary of Defense Rumsfeld (the civilian leader representing the president) successfully cutting and trimming the military's and CENTCOM's invasion plans for Iraq during 2002 and early 2003. However, most presidential decisions that require implementation are dependent on the bureaucracy.

As Morton Halperin (1974:290) puts it in *Bureaucratic Politics and Foreign Policy*,

At one extreme, if an action is a simple one capable of being carried out by a single individual in Washington without detailed technical expertise or training, presidential influence is likely to be overwhelming. To the degree that an action is a complicated one, requiring the cooperation of large numbers of people, many of them stationed outside of Washington, presidential influence on implementation fades.

Therefore, the most effective way a president can control the policy implementation stage is to decide against any action or policy initiative, thereby circumventing the need for bureaucratic implementation altogether. See "A Closer Look: Decisions and Donald Trump."

A Closer Look

DECISIONS AND DONALD TRUMP

Part of the explanation for how and when presidential politics and bureaucratic politics dominate turns on issues related to individual characteristics of presidents and advisers. Tyler Jost and Robert Schub, two scholars of US foreign policymaking, recently assessed the Trump administration's decision-making dynamics. As Jost and Schub (2019) note, two key factors are foundational to good decisions: (1) securing information from all relevant parts of the bureaucracy and (2) conducting an orderly and systematic process that brings the bureaucratic players into discussion and deliberation with each other and the White House.

Jost and Schub identify a number of key problems in the Trump administration that complicate and detract from these two factors. For one, the president himself resists advice. As Jost and Schub put it, despite his lack of experience in foreign policy and politics in general, "the president has indicated that he's already an expert on complex topics, despite having little experience, and . . . it's unclear whether the president is sufficiently inquisitive and willing to dedicate time to internalize new information . . . . Trump is also prone to making sudden policy changes that unexpectedly override his advisers."

Another problem is the nature of the White House relationship with the State Department. As we saw in Chapter 4, the role and influence of the State Department has suffered a long-term decline. This situation appears even worse in the Trump administration. According to Jost and Schub (2019):

> Trump entered office with a distrust of the State Department. Under Secretary of State Rex Tillerson, insiders described a "parallel department" that effectively segregated Trump's senior diplomatic adviser from the experienced strategists in the State Department. While the state of State seems to have improved since Tillerson's departure, diplomatic posts remain vacant and officials still describe "chaotic decision-making" processes. This spring, the administration proposed cuts to the department's budget. Given these problems, it's unclear whether [Secretary of State Mike] Pompeo can offer the president the full benefit of his department's expertise.

Finally, the linchpin of the structures and processes that typically promote the two key factors—the national security adviser and the National Security Council system—appear unlikely to do what is necessary to mitigate the problems and ensure thorough information-gathering and broad policy deliberations. As Jost and Schub (2019) put it:

> As adviser to President George H. W. Bush, Brent Scowcroft played the role of an "honest broker," providing airtime to leaders from each bureaucracy to help the president make informed decisions. John Bolton is an unlikely candidate to adopt Scowcroft's model. Formal meetings of senior officials reportedly dwindled after the transition from H. R. McMaster to Bolton. Bolton didn't convene a single "principals committee" meeting on exiting the Intermediate-Range Nuclear Forces Treaty. Instead, Bolton's deeply hawkish beliefs likely incline him toward advocating specific policies—much as Henry Kissinger did—rather than ensuring the president hears all U.S. government views.

Bolton himself became increasingly ineffective in the foreign policy process—even to the point of being cut out of the advisory process himself—before he was fired abruptly on September 9, 2019. These developments only heighten concerns that decisions in the Trump administration will be made with a dysfunctional process (e.g., Bender and Salama 2019; Collins, Liptak, and Cohen 2019; DeYoung 2019; Parker and Rucker 2019).

What are the implications for quality of foreign policy decisions and the patterns of foreign policy-making in the Trump administration?

Interbranch Politics

As a pattern of policymaking, interbranch politics captures the broader institutional dynamic involving legislative-executive relations. Although the first two patterns stress the White House and the foreign policy bureaucracy, this perspective incorporates Congress and its variable role and influence as well.

As Scott and Carter (2002) and Carter and Scott (2009) stress, incorporating Congress into our understanding of the patterns of foreign policymaking is improved by differentiating between two important dimensions that characterize congressional foreign policy behavior: (1) Congress can be more or less active, engaging in much or little foreign policy–related activity; and (2) Congress can be more or less assertive, supporting or opposing a president's foreign policy and leadership. As Scott and Carter (2002:158–159) show, such a two-dimensional activity-assertiveness framework posits four models of congressional foreign policy behavior, as shown in Figure 10.3:

1. A *competitive Congress* whose greater levels of both activity and assertiveness lead it to challenge the president for foreign policy influence, a pattern of behavior reflective of the idea of a resurgent Congress

2. A *disengaged Congress* whose relative inactivity and compliance with presidential preferences reflect the acquiescent Congress more involved in domestic policy than foreign policy and more likely to defer to and support the president

3. A *supportive Congress* whose greater activity is combined with less assertive behavior, indicating a Congress cooperating with the president to achieve foreign policy goals over which there is substantial consensus

4. A *strategic Congress* whose combination of less activity but greater assertiveness suggest a Congress that selects its battles carefully but is willing to challenge the president when it is interested

These four models reflect the range of congressional foreign policy behavior that we discussed in Chapter 9. In the context of that discussion, this two-dimensional conception suggests that Congress has rarely been disengaged or acquiescent in the strict sense of being inactive and compliant, nor has it often been competitive or resurgent in the strict sense of being both active and assertive after Vietnam and especially in the post–Cold War world. Instead, Congress has shifted from a Cold War model of a supportive Congress (that is, more active but less assertive) to a post-Vietnam competitive Congress (that is, active and assertive) to a post–Cold War strategic Congress (that is, less active but more assertive)—for national security and especially economic (and other intermestic) policies.

FIGURE 10.3

Models of Congressional Foreign Policy Behavior

		ACTIVITY	
		More Active	Less Active
ASSERTIVENESS	More Assertive	Competitive Congress	Strategic Congress
	Less Assertive	Supportive Congress	Disengaged Congress

Source: Adapted from James M. Scott and Ralph G. Carter, "Acting on the Hill: Congressional Assertiveness in U.S. Foreign Policy," *Congress and the Presidency*, 29 (Autumn 2002): 165.

Since interbranch politics depend on how Congress influences foreign policy (see Chapter 9) and *when* members choose to engage in efforts to do so, understanding interbranch politics requires addressing the cues and conditions that motivate congressional foreign policy behavior, because, as Figure 10.3 indicates, members do not engage in the same way in all situations. Congress may be compliant, competitive, or confrontational, and no single form or sequence prevails. Members of Congress are motivated by a wide variety of cues (factors that members consider) and conditions (situational characteristics) of the policy context/structure. As Carter and Scott (2009), Scott and Carter (2014), and Scott (2018) note, among the most significant of these cues and conditions are public opinion, policy preferences, partisanship, the nature of the policy process, differences in policy type and issue, and policy instruments. Particular configurations of these factors help to explain the patterns of interbranch politics:

- *Public Opinion:* As we noted earlier, members of Congress are powerfully driven by political calculations related to public opinion and reelection concerns. With respect to foreign policy, these concerns have several dimensions. First, members are attentive to broad public opinion regarding the president, with popular presidents and popular policies more likely to receive support than unpopular ones. Moreover, policies regarded by the public as failures are likely targets for congressional activity and assertiveness. Second, members are attuned to constituency opinion and tend not to stray far from the broad preferences of their districts or states (or the preferences of those who fund their campaigns).

- *Policy Preferences:* Members are also motivated by their own preferences and ideology, which are in turn shaped by their personal experiences and values. Member policy preferences, as typically measured by ideological predisposition and their personal interest in creating good public policy, are central to congressional behavior in foreign policy. Moreover, situations of broad policy consensus or agreement—such as at the height of the Cold War—contribute to more supportive and disengaged Congresses.

- *Partisanship:* Foreign policy is an increasingly partisan process, and partisan calculations provide significant motives for interbranch politics. While partisanship is not necessarily the driving force behind all congressional activism and assertiveness in US foreign policy, its impact has expanded since the Vietnam War. Of course, as we discussed in Chapter 9, this means that situations of divided government increase the salience of interbranch politics and the prospects of competitive and strategic Congresses.

- *Policy Process and Timing:* The foreign policy process is cyclical. While the initial cycle of policymaking is often dominated by the executive branch, subsequent cycles often trigger interbranch politics because they afford members of Congress opportunities to play a significant role through annual budget authorization/appropriation cycles and oversight responsibilities.

- *Policy Context:* As others have argued (e.g., Ripley and Franklin 1990; Ripley and Lindsay 1993), different foreign policy contexts tend to involve distinct legislative-executive orientations. By their nature, crises—or even high-stakes or high-threat issues—favor the executive and push Congress to the background, *at least for a time.* In a crisis, the need for a speedy response often leads presidents to keep the decision unit as small as possible; members of Congress are rarely invited to participate (Hermann 1972, 2011). Members either rally in support of the president's response to the crisis, arguing that the country needs to present a united front to the provocateur, or defer to the president for a time. Yet extended crisis decision-making tends to invite congressional second-guessing and invites later involvement by members (e.g., Schraeder 1994). Noncrisis foreign policy can be divided in two types: **structural foreign policy** and **strategic foreign policy** (e.g., Ripley and Lindsay 1993). The conventional wisdom long held that the presidency dominates strategic decisions—those involving the basic ends of foreign policy— while Congress was more comfortable in making structural foreign policy—as it dealt with the means to implement those ends. However, numerous studies suggest members are increasingly likely to address strategic issues since the early Cold War years (e.g., Carter and Scott 2009; Howell and Pevehouse 2007; Kriner 2010). Indeed, many members seek out strategic foreign policy issues whenever they see a policy vacuum or a need for a policy correction (see the next point).

- *Policy Structure:* As just noted, differences between *policy corrections* and *policy vacuums* are also significant for interbranch politics. In **policy corrections**, members need to overcome the inertia of existing policy, persuading the president to change course. But, policy failures are especially inviting targets for correction, especially when public opinion is activated. In contrast, **policy vacuums**—when problems are identified but policy actions have not been taken—present members with opportunities to act in contexts less dominated by other stakeholders, especially in the executive branch. Members identifying such vacuums relevant to problems that matter to them engage in activities to convince the administration to address the problem in ways that conform to member preferences, and/or to convince enough other members to act through legislative avenues to persuade or force the president to respond (e.g., Carter and Scott 2009; Wawro 2001).

- *Policy Instrument:* It is also helpful to distinguish between **executive-dominated instruments** and **legislative-dominated instruments** (Pastor 1992). Policies relying on the use of force, diplomacy, and intelligence activities are usually initiated by the executive branch, with Congress generally playing a more reactive role. Other policies, such as those relying on aid and tied more closely to the annual authorization/appropriation cycle, are more amenable to congressional initiative and thus typically involve interbranch politics more extensively.

See "A Different Perspective: From Presidential Preeminence to Interbranch Politics" for further insights on the patterns of interbranch politics based on these factors.

A Different Perspective

The presidential politics and bureaucratic politics patterns place the president and the foreign policy bureaucracy at the center of US foreign policymaking and highlight key processes through which they shape decisions. However, the interbranch politics model introduces a different perspective. Two recent studies by Scott and Carter (2014) and Scott (2018) offer an alternative viewpoint that captures the complex playing field and policymaking process, examining policymaking patterns in the war on terror in the George W. Bush administration and the South China Sea challenge in the Obama and Trump administrations. Together, these studies suggest that the roles of the legislative and executive branches are partially contingent on the cyclical nature of policymaking:

- *Initial Cycle:* Initial foreign policymaking phases begin with problem recognition and response. In this initial cycle, the executive branch is most likely to take the initiative, while members of Congress typically respond with substantial deference to presidential leadership. Compliance with presidential initiatives is common at the outset, especially in crisis or potential crisis situations. Individual members often engage in basic framing activities that reflect problem recognition and signal their concerns, but most members take a wait-and-see approach, leaving more extensive attention to the handful of individual members with particular interests in the problem (entrepreneurs).

- *Subsequent Cycles:* As the initial response of the president and foreign policy bureaucracy unfolds, members of Congress react, and congressional engagement increases in later process cycles. In some circumstances, member engagement is essentially supportive. This is particularly likely with policy success, with relatively high public approval of the policy and/or president, and with co-partisans. In such success situations, members may engage in "band-wagoning" or bidding wars to out-do a president in responding to a situation, effectively proposing increased efforts in line with the general administration policy response. However, with unsuccessful policy, lack of policy response, and/or low public approval, congressional engagement is generally more competitive, especially among partisan opponents of the president. Members are more likely to make "balancing" or "prodding" efforts to resist or redirect administration initiatives. Individual members with relatively high levels of attention, interest, and engagement (entrepreneurs) typically take the lead. Congressional activity and assertiveness is likely to begin in nonlegislative and indirect avenues (oversight, framing, signaling) and then extend to more direct and legislative approaches (procedural and/or substantive legislation), focusing on legislative-dominated instruments

(Continued)

(Continued)

(e.g., budgets), before extending to executive-dominated instruments (e.g., strategy statements, use of military). Changes in the partisan balance in Congress are likely to lead to greater or lesser assertiveness (depending on the direction of the shift vis-à-vis the party of the president).

- *Extended Cycles:* The role and activity of Congress in extended cycles may escalate to legislative-executive confrontation. The first contingency is the problem development itself. Some developments defuse the issue and reduce interbranch politics (e.g., a crisis is averted or resolved). Also, administrations that respond to

congressional activity by adjusting policy may increase congressional compliance, pending further developments, while nonresponsiveness—rejection of congressional preferences/proposals (defiance) or failure to act (policy vacuums)—invites more confrontational interbranch politics. In either case, both public opinion and partisanship continue to play a role, with unpopular presidents and policies inviting more confrontational efforts, and partisan divisions generating more policy challenges.

How does this alternative perspective contribute to our understanding of the complex politics of US foreign policy?

A Note on Crises

As we have suggested, numerous scholars have also found that the decision-making context—that is, the environment in which decisions are made—has an important influence on individual behavior and the policymaking process. Crises are particularly important decision contexts. A foreign policy **crisis** (commonly defined in terms of surprise, a threat to values, and little time to respond)—Holsti's major concern—involves periods of high stress and decisions concerning complex and ambiguous issues (Hermann 1969). Crises such as the 1979 Soviet invasion of Afghanistan, the Iraqi invasion of Kuwait in 1990, and the September 11 terrorist attacks are times that typically catapult an issue onto the agenda and trigger presidential politics. As President George W. Bush acknowledged, the crisis of 9/11 had a profound effect on him personally and gave him a new presidential focus and mission revolving around the threat of terrorism. According to National Security Adviser Condoleezza Rice, "The president really had the sense here that this was a historic moment, that he had been cast into a historic moment" (Balz and Woodward 2002).

Times of crisis, in fact, tend to produce considerable emotional and psychological stress on policymakers, often intensifying individual images and personalities, which often inhibit an open and rational decision-making process. Scholars such as Holsti (1990) have reviewed the literature on the relationships among crisis, stress, and decision making and concluded that situations perceived to be crises produced individual stress and affected the nature of decision making for individuals and policymaking groups (see also Lebow 1981; Oneal 1988; Snyder 1978). Holsti found two patterns, based on experimental work in psychology. On the one hand, low and moderate levels of stress were often conducive to rational decision-making, because individuals became more attentive and motivated to find a solution to the problem at hand. In some cases, high levels of stress may increase performance for elementary tasks over limited periods of time.

On the other hand, prolonged periods of high stress tend to result in defective decision-making, especially for tasks that are complex, are ambiguous, and involve uncertainty. During such crises, "lack of rest and diversion, combined with excessively long working hours, are likely to magnify the stresses in the situation" (Holsti 1990:124). According to Holsti (1990:124), the preponderance of evidence from psychological experiments, psychological field research (e.g., studies of individual behavior during natural disasters and combat), and historical studies of international crises indicated "that intense and protracted stress erodes rather than enhances the ability of individuals to cope with complex problems."

Holsti (1990) further identified a number of patterns associated with high stress and its impact on individual and group decision-making. Specifically, high stress tends to (1) heighten the salience of time by distorting judgment, usually leading to a significant overestimation of how fast time is passing; (2) reduce the size of the policymaking group; (3) reduce tolerance for ambiguity and increase the tendency to stereotype and rationalize; (4) increase cognitive rigidity, reliance on familiar decision rules, and the use of basic beliefs and metaphorical thinking; (5) encourage random and selective searches for information; (6) produce concern for the present and immediate future; (7) minimize communication with potential adversaries; (8) increase the use of ad hoc communication channels; (9) limit the search for and assessment of alternatives, often to one approach; (10) increase the likelihood of a polarized choice, favoring positions of overcautiousness or greater risk-taking; and (11) disrupt complex learning and the reexamination of decisions. The stress produced by foreign policy crises, in other words, often contributes to poor policymaking performance and maladaptive behavior.

Although international crises usually inhibit rational decision-making, Holsti (1990:117,127,131) recognizes that "not all crises spin out of control owing to misperceptions, miscalculations, or other cognitive malfunctions." Therefore, "just as we cannot assume that 'good' processes will ensure high-quality decisions, we cannot assume that erratic processes will always result in low-quality decisions" or end up in fiascoes. Nevertheless, theories of deterrence and compellence (and coercive diplomacy), which have been so central to great-power politics and US foreign policy, "presuppose rational and predictable decision processes," and "scholars and policymakers tend to be sanguine about the ability of policymakers to be creative when the situation requires it." In short, periods of intense crisis and stress may inhibit and overwhelm rationality during times when it is most needed.

THE COMPLEX REALITY OF POLICYMAKING

We have examined the complexity of how policymaking operates within the executive branch. We have seen that policymaking involves three stages: agenda setting, policy formulation, and policy implementation. We reviewed key policymaking models and highlighted three general policymaking patterns—presidential politics, bureaucratic politics, and interbranch politics. We now have a better understanding of the varying roles of key players and varying patterns in the dynamics of the policymaking process.

Although our discussion helps to highlight some of the salient features and patterns of the complex politics of US foreign policy—and some of the reasons presidential and White House leadership is a variable and not a constant—even our more complicated picture actually oversimplifies policymaking. First, the government does not consider one issue at a time but hundreds of foreign policy issues simultaneously. In other words, numerous policymaking processes operate within the executive branch at the same time. Nor are agenda-setting, policy formation, and policy implementation processes clearly separated—they often overlap and have an impact on one another. Ultimately, policymaking efforts to address the dozens of issues that arise involve the input of the beliefs, personalities, and roles of hundreds of individuals from numerous organizations and institutions across the legislative and executive branches. These interactions and dynamic processes represent the complex politics of US foreign policy as it occurs in the executive branch.

THINK ABOUT THIS

As Roger Hilsman once described, when it comes to US foreign policymaking, the simplification of reality known as the rational actor model assumes centralized and orderly procedures for making national decisions. Think about the discussion of the policymaking process in this chapter.

Why is the rational actor model insufficient for understanding and explaining US foreign policymaking?

KEY TERMS

agenda setting 310
bureaucratic politics 334
cognition and perception 326
cognitive consistency 327
crisis 342
enemy image 328
executive-dominated
   instruments 340
governmental politics 317
groupthink 314
historical analogies 328
incremental 320

interbranch politics
   model 323
legislative-dominated
   instruments 340
mirror images 328
motivated tactician 329
organizational process
   model 319
organizational
   routines 319
personality 330
policy corrections 340

policy formulation 310
policy implementation 310
policy vacuums 340
political resultant 318
presidential politics 326
rational actor model 312
schemas 327
standard operating
   procedures 319
strategic foreign policy 340
structural foreign policy 340
symptoms of groupthink 314

Visit **edge.sagepub.com/scottrosati7e** to help you accomplish your coursework goals in an easy-to-use learning environment.

The Society and Domestic Politics

In Part III, we examine the societal context and the effects of three key components of domestic politics on the politics of US foreign policy. Chapter 11 discusses the role of public opinion in foreign policy. Chapter 12 discusses political participation and group politics. Chapter 13 discusses the role of the media and the communications process.

The Public and Foreign Policy

PHOTO 11.1 American protestors making their voices heard.

11

LEARNING OBJECTIVES

1. Identify the differences between the traditional wisdom and the new consensus about public opinion and its impact.

2. Understand the major features of the public, its views and opinions, and their influence.

3. Explain the patterns of public opinion in the mass public.

4. Compare the nature and dynamics of political ideologies and foreign policy orientations.

5. Describe the nature and influence of political culture and American national style.

More than thirty years ago, Edward Djerejian, a State Department employee assigned to the White House, "expressed surprise at the interaction of domestic politics and foreign policy. . . . At the State Department you make the best judgments on the foreign policy interests of the United States. Here you have to be abundantly aware, and put in the equation, domestic political considerations. That's new for me" (quoted in Weinraub 1985). In the decades since Djerejian made this comment, the role and impact of societal forces have certainly not diminished. Quite the contrary, they have grown increasingly important to the politics of US foreign policy since the end of the Cold War. The foreign policy context has become more like the domestic political context, which no longer stops "at the water's edge."

Now that we have examined the international context and players and institutions of the US government and foreign policymaking process, we turn to the societal context to examine three major components: public opinion, interest groups, and the media. In this chapter, our focus is on public opinion—the public's beliefs about the world—and its significance in foreign policy, while Chapters 12 and 13 concentrate on the public's participation in the political process through group politics and the role of the media in the politics of foreign policy. Conventional wisdom tends to dismiss the public and its beliefs when it comes to influence on US foreign policy and policymakers. Ultimately, however, what the American people believe and how they behave sets the social context and domestic political boundaries within which the government and the policymaking process must operate. As Farnham (2004) has argued, foreign policy decision-makers are aware of the constraints and opportunities in the domestic political environment, which affect their calculations of what can and cannot be done.

THE IMPACT OF PUBLIC OPINION

Until relatively recently, policymakers, observers, and academics shared a consensus or conventional wisdom on the role of public opinion that tended to minimize its importance. However, after the Vietnam War a new consensus began to form that afforded more importance and attention to the role of public opinion.

The Traditional Wisdom

According to the traditional wisdom, it does not matter what the public thinks about foreign policy issues, because it has little impact on the government and the policymaking process. This provides political leaders, especially the president, a great degree of freedom of action in foreign policymaking. Often characterized as the "Almond-Lippman consensus," after Gabriel Almond and Walter Lippman, two early advocates of this view, this conventional wisdom allowed most observers of US foreign policy to focus on government policymakers and institutions in explaining how US foreign policy is made, while ignoring the public and much of society (Almond 1960; Cohen 1973; Lippmann 1922).

The **Almond-Lippmann consensus** concluded that public opinion was volatile, unstructured, and of little significance to foreign policy. As Ole Holsti (1992:442) summarized, the consensus view centered on three major propositions:

- Because the public is uninterested and uninformed about foreign affairs, public opinion is highly volatile and thus it provides dubious foundations for a sound foreign policy.

- Public attitudes on foreign affairs are so lacking in structure and coherence that they might best be described as "non-attitudes."

- Public opinion has a very limited impact on the conduct of foreign policy, as policymakers regard it as something to be shaped, not something to be followed.

Growing out of the height of the Cold War, this view continues to be held by many observers of US foreign policy, as well as by parts of the general public.

This traditional view leads to a harsh conclusion about American democracy, and about the tension between the demands of national security and democratic practice. If the public role is minimal and the public is responsive to and easily manipulated by political leaders, then US foreign policymaking is not as democratic as it may seem. Many observers and policymakers throughout American history, in fact, have held an **elitist view of the public** and foreign policymaking, arguing that policymakers should be distanced from the public.

As with any stereotype, this traditional picture of the public holds some truth. Much of the public is uninformed, fickle, and responsive to established leaders. Indeed, in the current context, with the spread of social media and the opportunities for leaders such as President Trump to use Facebook and Twitter to push their perspectives and arguments, however inaccurate, the manipulability of the public is even more problematic. These characteristics often have given leaders great flexibility in pursuing their foreign policy perspectives, at least in terms of public opinion and public support. However, since the Vietnam War, this conventional wisdom has proved less accurate.

The New Consensus: A More Complex and Consequential Public

Henry Kissinger once argued that public support is "the acid test of foreign policy": Without it, foreign policy is not sustainable (quoted in Gelb 1972:459). As Leslie Gelb (1972:461) argued,

> Academicians and public-opinion experts have helped to perpetuate the myth in their own way by "demonstrating" that foreign policy simply is not a salient issue to the voter and that whatever the president says and does goes, [while] official silence on the subject prevails. [But presidents have] known better. Citizens may not single out national security affairs as the basis for their votes—although war and peace issues often are so mentioned—but the security area inevitably plays an important part in determining their overall impression of how the President is doing his job. Moreover, communication leaders and "elites" judge the President's performance with regard to foreign policy, and the mood which they convey to the public affects public appraisals of the man in the White House.

Hence, for Gelb, "American public opinion was the essential domino" affecting US foreign policy in Vietnam.

Spurred by views such as these, a growing number of observers of US foreign policy have challenged the conventional wisdom of the Almond-Lippmann consensus. For example, some studies have indicated that the opinions of the mass public on foreign policy are more stable and structured than the Almond-Lippman consensus suggested, especially when it comes to more general foreign policy opinion (such as preferences for internationalism or opinions on the appropriate uses of force) rather than views on very specific issues that require detailed information. Other studies have concluded that policy generally falls in line with broad public views and that it typically shifts in the direction of changes in public views; thus, policy is more responsive to opinion than the Almond-Lippmann consensus indicated. Also, increasingly broad agreement exists that public opinion generates powerful constraints on the range of policy options available to decision makers.

Finally, studies indicate that greater intensity of opinion leads to tighter links between opinion and specific policy choices (see Holsti, 2004; Jentleson 1992; Page and Shapiro 1992; Popkin 1991).

Unraveling the role of the public and its beliefs in the making of US foreign policy is not a simple task. Nevertheless, three major points lend support to the **new consensus** and indicate that the traditional wisdom is simplistic and incomplete. First, the public holds different types of beliefs, which include public opinion (the most specific), political ideology (broader values and ideas), and political culture (the broadest orientations about values and norms about society, government, American self-image, and national style abroad). Second, different types of "publics" exist: The most common breakdown is among the elite, attentive, and mass publics. Finally, the public exercises influence directly through polls, through participation in elections and group politics, and, most indirectly, through **political socialization** (the informal process of human interaction by which Americans acquire their political beliefs, for example, from parents, schools, peers, and media).

The traditional wisdom tends to focus predominantly on public opinion. This emphasis places attention on the level of influence that the specific opinions of the mass public have directly on policymakers, predominantly through the impact of polls. Yet the traditional view typically ignores the important role of the elite and attentive publics, political ideology and culture, and the other ways in which the public influences national politics and the governmental policymaking process. American political culture sets the broad context within which the politics of US foreign policy operates. The ideological beliefs of Americans further narrow what is possible and probable within domestic politics and the policymaking process. Finally, public opinion affects the foreign policy process as it fluctuates within the confines of American political culture and ideology.

UNDERSTANDING PUBLIC OPINION

The new consensus rests on several key corrections to the relatively simple understanding of the public and its opinions. First, there are several different "publics" whose interest in and engagement on foreign policy matters vary. Moreover, there are different types of opinions or beliefs, which have varying characteristics and impact. Finally, there are varying kinds of influence that public opinion may have. Being clear—and more nuanced—on these factors makes for a better assessment and understanding of the role of public opinion in the politics of US foreign policy.

Elite, Attentive, and Mass Publics

Typically, when people discuss the public, they are referring to all Americans. It is easy to dismiss the public as an inconsequential actor in foreign policy at this level. The traditional wisdom, however, is misleading when it treats the public as a single, homogeneous entity. The United States is a complex and diverse society of more than 325 million people. Certainly, not all Americans are inconsequential in American politics and the making of US foreign policy. There are, in fact, at least three types of publics: the elite public, the attentive public, the mass public (see Figure 11.1).

FIGURE 11.1

The Publics

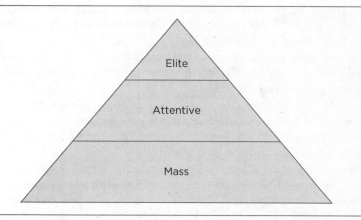

The **elite public** is a small portion of the population with the means and the interest to participate in and shape politics. These **opinion leaders** are "all members of the society who occupy positions which enable them regularly to transmit, either locally or nationally, opinions about any issue to unknown persons outside of their occupational field or about more than one class of issues to unknown professional colleagues" (Rosenau 1961:45). Opinion leaders generally are the people who are most informed about national and international affairs and whose ideas and views tend to be communicated broadly. Although a very small percentage of the population (depending on the issue), opinion leaders consist of people in various leadership positions, such as major governmental and business leaders, well-known journalists, established professors and professionals, and other prominent individuals from different walks of life. This is not to say that the information and views they hold are correct; rather, it is that their understanding of the world tends to be communicated more readily to other members of society. In other words, opinion leaders tend to have great visibility in American society, and both government officials and members of society usually consider their views to be more credible and legitimate than those of the mass public.

The **attentive public** includes people who are also relatively attentive and informed about national and international affairs but whose views are not disseminated as widely as those of opinion leaders. The size of the attentive public varies from issue to issue. For the most visible issues, the attentive public may be as large as one fourth of the entire public. For most issues that do not receive wide media coverage, the attentive public may represent less than 10 percent of the population. The attentive public tends to be invisible at the national and community levels, but among their peers they may act as opinion leaders. Thus, it is often said that the attentive public acts as local mediators between opinion leaders and the mass public. As Adler (1984:143) noted, "The opinions of the attentive public are often better informed and more predictive of policy trends than are the views of the general [or mass] public."

Most Americans are not part of the elite or attentive publics. The majority forms the **mass public**, the segment of the American population emphasized by the traditional wisdom. Although the proportion varies, at least two thirds to three fourths of Americans form the mass public for most issues. Those within the mass public tend to have little interest in national and international affairs. Only those issues that make it to the front page of the newspaper and receive considerable media play gain the attention of the mass public, and then usually only briefly. Therefore, the mass public tends to be poorly informed about national and international affairs.

Because the mass public includes most Americans, there is obviously tremendous variation in the level of interest and information within this segment of the population. Some Americans, maybe as many as 20 percent, have virtually no interest in public affairs or limited access to information and have been labeled "chronic know-nothings." Others may be more attentive and somewhat better informed about foreign policy issues. Between these two ends of the mass public spectrum are most Americans, who generally demonstrate little interest but acquire some information about national and international affairs through upbringing, education, and the media (Bennett 1996; Neumann 1986).

Two key characteristics account for the differing levels of interest in and information about national and international affairs between the elite and the mass publics. First, the more educated an individual, the more likely that he or she will be interested in and informed about national and international affairs. Second, individuals raised in upper-middle-class or upper-class families and environments are the people most likely to become interested in and informed about national and international affairs. Clearly, socioeconomic class and level of education are closely related. The higher the class background, the more likely one will go to college and pursue a graduate degree; moreover, the higher the level of education achieved, the more likely one will acquire more wealth, a professional occupation, and higher status within society. High levels of socioeconomic status and education not only reinforce each other and produce individuals with high levels of interest in and information about national and international affairs, but they also help to provide the analytical and communication skills that tend to separate the elite and attentive publics from the mass public.

A Range of "Opinion"

A second correction on which the new consensus rests is that "public opinion" actually involves multiple parts or components. Strictly speaking, **public opinion** refers to the attitudes held by Americans generally toward *specific* issues and topics, expressed primarily through polls and periodically through voting, and generally reflecting the mass public. In this component, the views of the public most closely represent the characterization of the Almond-Lippman consensus. However, we may also identify **public attitudes** or values, which represent broader viewpoints held by the public that do not require specific knowledge of the world or current events. These broader attitudes generally prove more structured and stable, even among the mass public.

Even more broadly, **political ideology** refers to beliefs about the preferred ends and means of a society (e.g., liberty, equality, representative government, market-oriented economy). In this respect, we are also interested in the **foreign policy orientations** permeating

American society—that is, how Americans see the world and the preferred role the United States should play in international relations. Together, the ideological and foreign policy orientations prevailing in American society set the broad boundaries of legitimate political discourse and agenda setting within which public opinion operates to influence domestic politics, the policymaking process, and the country's national interests.

Finally, political culture plays the broadest, most subtle role of all. **Political culture** refers to "self-identity" and how people see themselves and their country relative to the rest of the world. This level of public opinion is on those cultural assumptions that Americans have about what it means to be an "American." Not only does this suggest the existence of an **American national style**, but such nationalistic beliefs are also particularly evident and powerful forces in the politics of US foreign policy in times of crisis and war.

Impact on Foreign Policy

Public opinion, broadly defined to include these multiple types and levels, also has a range of effects and influence on US foreign policy. Within this context, we can distinguish between two major paths of influence: (1) directly on policymakers within the government and (2) much more indirectly by influencing the general domestic political process.

Direct and Immediate Impact. In terms of direct and immediate impact on policymakers within the government, there are two contradictory consequences. The most obvious is that inattentive, uninformed, and erratic public opinion on specific issues (among the mass public) gives policymakers great leeway in acting on most issues. The content of public opinion serves as a poor guide for policymakers, especially given its fluctuating nature, and political leaders are often able to lead public opinion—that is, educate and manipulate the public—to support and follow their policies. Moreover, during crisis periods, such as when troops are deployed abroad, the public tends to **rally around the flag** by supporting presidents and their policies. As the traditional wisdom argues, public opinion often reinforces and strengthens presidential power because the president is the most visible political figure in the United States, especially with respect to foreign policy, in determining which issues are before the public and how they are discussed.

A second consequence, usually ignored by those who hold to the traditional wisdom, is that for some issues, especially those that are most salient, public opinion may act as an immediate and direct constraint on political officials in the policymaking process. No matter how inattentive, uninformed, and erratic public opinion is, the public votes political leaders in and out of office, so elected officials are particularly sensitive to public opinion. Within the White House, it is not uncommon to hear people say that "compared with analysts, presidents and potential presidents themselves see a close link between stands in foreign policy and the outcomes of presidential elections" (Halperin 1974:67). Even a casual review of the past two decades reveals extensive efforts by each administration to shape and cultivate public opinion and support (see Heilemann and Halperin [2010] on the 2008 presidential election).

Furthermore, if public feeling becomes intense concerning a particularly salient issue, it severely constrains the choices available within the policymaking process. For example, once the public was educated and led on the issue of anti-communism, American leaders began to feel constrained by public opinion, as Cold War lessons—for instance, that the United States should take a hard-line approach and never appease aggressors—were internalized by Americans. The last remnant of this anti-communist legacy in the present era can still be seen in aspects of US foreign policy toward North Korea and Cuba.

In addition, public support for a policy may turn rapidly into public disapproval. Although the public tends to rally around the flag and the president during a crisis such as war, public support for presidential policies tends to dwindle over time. Studies, such as John Mueller's (1973) classic, *War, Presidents, and Public Opinion*, demonstrate that the longer a war lasts (and the greater the casualties), the more public support will erode. Quick and successful operations, as in Grenada, Panama, the Persian Gulf, and Kosovo, maximize support; lengthy and unsuccessful conflicts, as in Korea, Vietnam, Lebanon, and Iraq, bring public disapproval (see Gelpi, Feaver, and Reifler 2005/2006). George W. Bush learned how quickly **public approval** can pivot as support changed to opposition as time, cost, and casualties mounted in Iraq after 2003, and Barack Obama watched public support evaporate for his initial economic policies as well as military action in Afghanistan.

The impact of public opinion fluctuated dramatically for President George H. W. Bush during and after the 1990–1991 Persian Gulf crisis (see Figures 11.2 and 11.3). Three stages occurred: Public opinion was supportive during August and September 1990—the initial stage of the crisis; it became divided from October 1990 to early January 1991, as the use of force became more likely; and once the war began, public opinion became

FIGURE 11.2

President George Bush's Public Approval During the 1990–1991 Persian Gulf Crisis

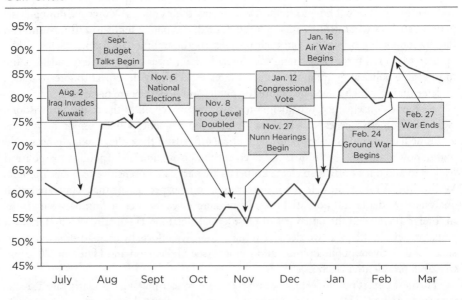

Source: Data from The Gallup Organization.

FIGURE 11.3

President George W. Bush's Public Approval after 9/11

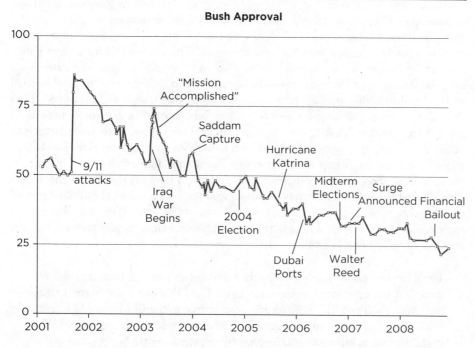

Bush Approval

Source: Pew Research Center, "Bush and Public Opinion: Reviewing the Bush Years and the Public's Final Verdict," December 18, 2008 (https://www.people-press.org/2008/12/18/bush-and-public-opinion/).

highly supportive and reinforced presidential power once again. Following the dramatic success of the Persian Gulf War, Bush's reelection appeared to be assured. Unfortunately for Bush, his high public approval dropped dramatically following the war, especially over economic and domestic concerns, and the public voted Bill Clinton in and Bush out in 1992. Ten years later, despite all-time public approval ratings following 9/11, President George W. Bush saw his approval decline steadily in the face of continued violence in Iraq and economic and political troubles at home, which helped to flip Congress to Democratic Party control in 2006 and contributed to Barack Obama's 2008 presidential election victory as well.

Barack Obama faced a similar pattern. As we discussed in Chapter 3, his public approval began in the high 60s and even 70s but declined steadily in 2009 and early 2010 to reach the mid-40s, where it hovered until the 2012 election (see Figure 3.5). As his successful campaign for reelection in 2012 unfolded, Obama's approval rating crept slowly higher, to the point where it exceeded 50 percent in the fall. His handling of national security was a major element of this increase, as the public consistently approved of his foreign policy leadership (and favored it over that of his rival, Mitt Romney) throughout the election campaign. In Obama's second term, his public approval remained relatively steady between

45 percent and 50 percent. Since the 2016 presidential election, Obama's approval rating has climbed even higher, to levels above 50 percent.

Recent research also indicates that public attitudes may well be more consistent and influential than the more uninformed and volatile public opinion on specific issues. For example, Bruce Jentleson (1992:72) found that public opinion "varies according to the 'principal policy objective' for which force is used." The tendency is for greater public support for the use of force in order to "contain" and "restrain" an aggressor state—such as in the Persian Gulf War—as opposed to using force to "initiate" and "impose" internal political change within another state—such as within Nicaragua, Somalia, or Haiti. Thus the public tends to discriminate over the use of force more than is commonly thought and is "pretty prudent." Asking the American public if the United States should intervene militarily in Iran, or Venezuela, or the South China Sea—to mention three hot-button issues for the current Trump administration—may not produce much helpful insights, as the answers to those questions suppose a relatively high level of information and under- standing that the mass public rarely displays. However, asking the more attitude-oriented question about "principal policy objective," as Jentleson suggests, is more likely to reveal more consistent views that do not depend on high information requirements. There are important implications, as Jentleson (1992:72) concludes:

> The American public is less gun shy than during the Vietnam trauma period of
> the 1970s, but more cautious than during the Cold War consensus of the 1950s
> and 1960s . . . . Presidents who contemplate getting militarily involved in internal
> political conflicts—of which there may well be even more in the post–Cold War
> world than when bipolarity had its constraining effects—had better get in and
> out quickly and successfully. Otherwise, the public is strongly disposed to oppose
> the policy.

As can be seen in the war in Iraq, from overwhelming support in early 2003 at the beginning of the invasion, public support dwindled steadily—with temporary interrup- tions for such events as the capture of Saddam Hussein or the Iraqi elections in 2005—to the point where more than half of the public regarded the action as a mistake by early 2005. Similarly, the public's preference for withdrawal also increased steadily as casual- ties mounted (Mueller 2005). In late 2005, for example, polls showed that, even though most Americans embraced democracy promotion as a foreign policy goal, a majority of Americans opposed the use of military force (either directly or via threats) to promote democracy and believed that the goal of establishing democracy in Iraq did not warrant going to war.

More recent polling shows a similar pattern. For example, in 2019, 60 percent of the public opposed a US attack on Iran, but almost 80 percent supported military action in the event of Iranian military attacks on the United States (Kahn 2019). Even more broadly, a 2018 survey of Americans that focused on attitudes rather than specific situa- tions suggested similar views, finding "a national voter population that is largely skeptical of the practicality or benefits of military intervention overseas, including both the physical involvement of the US military and also extending to military aid in the form of funds or equipment as well" (Carden 2018). In this survey, 86 percent of respondents said the American military should be used only as a last resort, and almost 60 percent believed military aid to most foreign countries was counterproductive.

Finally, the collapse of the Cold War Consensus has made public opinion somewhat less responsive to the president. During the 1950s, most American leaders and members of the elite public shared a similar Cold War view of the world that the mass public tended to follow. Since the Vietnam War, however, differing views of the world and US foreign policy have arisen, leading to greater diversity and volatility in public opinion. This has made it more difficult for presidents to rally and maintain public support—especially beyond their base—for particular policies in an environment in which opinion leaders with different foreign policy views now compete with each other for public support.

In sum, the influence of public opinion on the foreign policy process has contradictory consequences and is more complex than the traditional wisdom suggests. For many issues, public opinion has limited immediate and direct impact on the policymaking process. However, for other issues high in salience, public opinion has an immediate and direct effect on policymakers within the government, including the president and members of Congress. The common denominators in these two contradictory patterns are (1) the level of salience and the politicization of issues and (2) the level of success or failure perceived among a public that tends to be pragmatic and impatient.

Indirect and Longer-Term Influence. There are also important, but more indirect and longer term influences of public opinion. First, the public elects major governmental officials. Whether or not Americans are interested or informed about foreign policy, the public chooses who becomes president and who runs Congress. Although individuals with high levels of education and socioeconomic class are usually more interested in and informed about national and international affairs, members of the elite and the mass public ultimately determine who becomes president and sets the country's foreign policy direction.

Second, the ability of political leaders to influence the policymaking process during their tenure is heavily a function of their public prestige. Take another look at Figure 3.5, which clearly illustrates that public approval of presidential performance over time not only fluctuates dramatically but also tends to decrease for each president. This accounts for the presidential life cycle, during which presidents tend to enter office with highly favorable public opinion only to see it diminish with time, weakening their ability to govern.

President Trump faced problems in this regard, with persistently low public approval, which limited his ability to persuade Congress to follow his lead on many controversial legislative matters. As the Pew Research Center concluded, Trump's public support was consistently lower than that of any of his recent predecessors (see Figure 11.4). The popular public opinion polling site FiveThirtyEight.com noted that "Trump's approval rating is 22 percentage points lower than the average modern president's. Meanwhile, his net approval rating (approval rating minus disapproval rating), −15 percentage points, makes him the only president in negative territory one year through his first term" (Enten 2018). Moreover, in a sign of the increasingly partisan and polarized political context we have discussed previously, public opinion is more polarized on Trump than it has been for any previous president, extending a trend seen since the end of the Cold War (see Figure 11.5).

FIGURE 11.4

Job Approval in the Third Year, Reagan to Trump

At start of Trump's third year in office, his job approval lags most of his recent predecessors
Presidential job approval at beginning of third year in office (%)

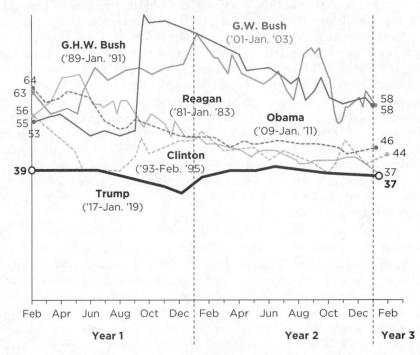

Source: Pew Research Center, "Trump Begins Third Year with Low Job Approval and Doubts about His Honesty," January 18, 2019 (https://www.people-press.org/2019/01/18/trump-begins-third-year-with-low-job-approval-and-doubts-about-his-honesty/).

MAJOR PATTERNS IN PUBLIC OPINION

The views of the elite and attentive publics are more stable and structured, and their values are more coherent and consistent, than are those of the mass public, but one of the reasons public opinion and its influence is so complicated is because of the mass public's inattentiveness. When it comes to the vast majority of the public, three major patterns characterize American public opinion. With respect to particular issues and developments in international affairs, mass public opinion tends to be inattentive, uninformed, and volatile. These traits support the traditional understanding of the nature of public opinion. They are also a key reason policymakers enjoy significant leeway from the constraints and parameters of public opinion and are able to shape opinion through their own efforts. However, this fact does not prevent public opinion from influencing domestic politics and the policymaking process.

FIGURE 11.5

Partisanship in Presidential Approval Ratings

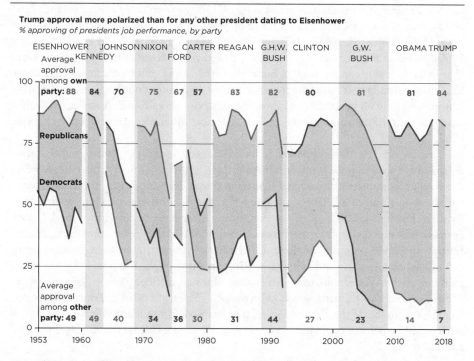

Trump approval more polarized than for any other president dating to Eisenhower
% approving of presidents job performance, by party

Source: Pew Research Center, "Trump's Approval Ratings So Far Are Unusually Stable and Deeply Partisan," August 1, 2018 (https://www.pewresearch.org/fact-tank/2018/08/01/trumps-approval-ratings-so-far-are-unusually-stable-and-deeply-partisan/ft_18-08-01_trumpapproval_more-polarized/).

First, public opinion represents views expressed by Americans who, for the most part, are inattentive—that is, they have little interest in the details of national and international affairs. Although most Americans are exposed to a great deal of information about national and international affairs through the mass media, few Americans take advantage of the available information. For example, only three of the fifty best-selling magazines—*Time, Newsweek,* and *US News & World Report*—emphasize national and/or international affairs. Clearly, most Americans who try to acquire information beyond television, radio, and the local newspaper by subscribing to magazines are interested in things other than politics: entertainment, travel, home life, fashion, sex, sports and recreation, mechanics, family matters, and more. The availability and increasing use of the Internet has reinforced these trends for the most part.

This limited interest in national and international affairs produces and reinforces the second major pattern: Most Americans are relatively uninformed about national and international affairs. The mass public acquires little information about the political world, and much of the information it does acquire tends to be simplistic and often inaccurate.

For example, a poll taken in 1964 revealed that 25 percent of all Americans had never heard of the war in Vietnam; 28 percent did not know that mainland China was communist; 29 percent were unaware that another Chinese government existed on the island of Taiwan; and 54 percent had never heard of Mao Zedong, chairman of the Communist Party of the People's Republic of China. During the height of the Cold War in the early 1960s, barely more than half of Americans polled could describe the meaning of Cold War in a reasonably correct fashion. Surveys of Americans' geographic knowledge at the time demonstrated that only 65 percent of people could point out England on a map of Europe and only 60 percent could show Brazil's position in South America, while less than one third of the respondents could locate most other countries correctly (Erskine 1962, 1963).

Two decades later, little appeared to have changed. A survey in 1988 found that with regard to US foreign policy in Central America—a salient national security issue when the Reagan administration's secret Contra war was exposed during the Iran-Contra episode—only half of all Americans knew that the Sandinistas and Contras had been fighting. Furthermore, a majority of Americans incorrectly believed that the US government was supporting the guerrillas in El Salvador and the government in Nicaragua. During the same year, one in three Americans could not name a single member of NATO, whereas—it is hard to believe—16 percent thought the Soviet Union was a member of the Western alliance. Americans also had difficulty identifying countries and regions on a world map, as was shown when 75 percent of adult Americans polled were unable to locate the Persian Gulf, 50 percent could not identify Japan and South Africa, and 14 percent could not even correctly locate the United States (Delli Carpini and Keeter 1997).

Nor is the current context much different. According to a 2002 survey of Americans between the ages of 18 and 24 by the National Geographic Society, one in ten could not locate the United States on a blank map of the world, only one in seven could identify Iraq, one in four could find Saudi Arabia, and 30 percent could not locate the Pacific Ocean, the world's largest body of water (Recer 2002). According to a March 2011 *Newsweek* survey, an astonishing 73 percent of Americans (of all ages) could not accurately identify the reasons for the Cold War. The Pew Research Center (2011) found that 43 percent of Americans could not identify the state of Israel—a major ally and the top recipient of US foreign aid—on a map of the eastern Mediterranean (even when given the names of four countries to choose from). Moreover, almost one in five Americans could not identify Hillary Clinton as the US Secretary of State when pictures of her, Joe Biden, Bill Richardson, and Condoleezza Rice were provided, despite her prominence. Similarly, in late 2010 the Program on International Policy Attitudes found that the median estimate among Americans was that the United States devoted 25 percent of its budget to foreign aid; their preferred amount was 10 percent (WorldPublicOpinion.org 2010). The actual amount is less than 1 percent.

When we consider the historical context of these low levels of interest and information, we can identify three general trends. First, the level of interest and attention accorded to politics by most Americans has probably declined over the past decades. One hundred years ago, politics and election campaigns were one of the few major forms of entertainment for many Americans; today, so many things compete with politics for people's attention—such as television, music, professional and college sports, Hollywood and movies, the shopping mall and mass consumerism—that a low level of political interest is only natural.

Second, although the mass public tends to be poorly informed overall, Americans today are exposed to more information and are likely to have less simplistic images of the United States and the world than they held during periods such as the Cold War. Much of this is due to rising enrollments in higher education over the past three decades and improved news coverage by the mass media and through the Internet. The final trend is that the size of the elite public has grown over time as a result of increases in higher education since the 1960s (Delli Carpini and Keeter 1991).

Low levels of attention and information produce a third pattern in public opinion—its tendency to be volatile and to fluctuate over time. Since most Americans are uninterested and ill informed, their opinions about national and international issues tend to be very "soft" and open to change. Most Americans give little thought to most issues and are not committed to particular positions. Still, they have opinions and readily offer them when solicited by a public opinion poll—no more than a general snapshot of what the mass public may think at that brief moment (Bardes and Oldendick 2002). Not surprisingly, as an issue gets more media coverage, public attention increases for a while, members of the mass public acquire more information, and individual opinions change and harden.

The volatility has an interesting and consequential political component as well. The mass public is prone to embrace views and accept information from their political "teams," whether or not it is accurate. A few examples from recent years illustrate this nicely and suggest that Americans believe what they want to believe politically. For instance, "when Gallup polled Americans the week before and the week after the [2016] presidential election, Democrats and Republicans flipped their perceptions of the economy, even though nothing had actually changed about the economy. What changed was which team was winning" (Resnick 2019). In addition to illustrating volatility and fluctuation, this phenomenon also demonstrates "motivated reasoning" on the part of the public, as "rooting for a team changes your perception of the world" (Resnick 2019).

Similarly, leaders like Donald Trump have learned that they have significant power to move and shape the fickle views of the mass public. For instance, Gallup surveys show that Republicans viewed Russia's Vladimir Putin quite unfavorably in 2015, with just 12 percent of Republicans having a favorable view of him at that time. Yet, by early 2017, despite clear and mounting evidence of Russia's attacks on and subversion of the 2016 elections, along with continued interference in European politics and intervention in Ukraine, 32 percent of Republicans held a favorable view (Swift 2017). Free trade is another example. For the whole post–World War II period, conservatives have favored free trade and free trade agreements. However, the Pew Research Center (2017) found that, in the two-year period from 2015 to 2017, support for free trade among Republicans fell from 56 percent to 36 percent. This shift, of course, coincides with Donald Trump's political campaign and his early months as president, during which time he regularly decried the merits of free trade, in part through his controversial use of Twitter.

POLITICAL IDEOLOGY AND FOREIGN
POLICY ORIENTATIONS

Moving more broadly from public opinion and political attitudes to the broader layer of the ideological and foreign policy orientations of Americans, let's begin with two points about the types of publics and the nature of public beliefs in mind. First, a discussion of ideological and foreign policy views must focus on the elite public and the extent to which foreign policy is supported by the mass public because the elite public tends to have stronger and more influential ideological and foreign policy beliefs than the mass public. Second, the ideological and foreign policy orientations of Americans tend to be more stable as compared to their expressions of public opinion. Ideological beliefs do not fluctuate readily; they tend to resist change because they are formed early in life through the process of political socialization. This is especially true among members of the elite public, who tend to be more attentive to national and international affairs and have more knowledge and greater emotional commitment to their views. The mass public tends to have less sophisticated or consistent views in comparison to the elite public while remaining more open and responsive to the ideological and foreign policy appeals of the elite public.

Ideological and foreign policy orientations in American society affect public opinion, influence the electoral process and voters' choices, affect the activity of groups and social movements in domestic politics, and are passed on to newer generations of Americans through the socialization process. In short, they are the field in which public opinion develops and they set the broad boundaries within which the complex politics of US foreign policy operates and the nation's interests are defined.

According to Ole Holsti and James Rosenau (1984), the ideological and foreign policy orientations of Americans have gone through two major phases since the end of World War II: (1) an ideological and foreign policy consensus, which prevailed during the Cold War years; and (2) an increase in ideological and foreign policy diversity, which has occurred since Vietnam and the end of the Cold War.

The Cold War Years of Anti-communism and the Liberal-Conservative Consensus

Holsti and Rosenau (1984) argue that most Americans in government and society shared a similar foreign policy orientation during the Cold War years, which they call **Cold War internationalism**. Cold War internationalists saw a conflict-ridden, bipolar world that pitted the Soviet Union and communism against the United States and democracy. The Soviet Union was seen as an ambitious, aggressive, expansionist empire, leading a strong and patient group of communist allies toward a revolutionary goal: imposing a Moscow-dominated imperial system throughout the world. The United States, in contrast, was seen as the civilized and benevolent leader of democracy and prosperity throughout the so-called "free world." In a world where victory for one side was seen as defeat for the other, the assumed threat to American national security posed by the Soviet Union and communism became the predominant concern of American policymakers. It was this view of the world that laid the basis for the national security ethos to thrive during the Cold

War years in which US foreign policy revolved around a strategy of containment of Soviet expansionism through the development, threat, and use of force around the world.

The Cold War years led to the development of an ideological and foreign policy consensus throughout American society and government, an extraordinary time in American history. As Thomas Mann (1990a:11) explains,

> The bipartisan foreign policy consensus that prevailed for almost two decades after World War II was sustained by a leadership stratum that shared an internationalist and interventionist view of the U.S. role in world affairs, an attentive and educated group of citizens who followed and supported this leadership, and a poorly informed and largely inert mass public that tolerated official policy as long as it appeared to be working.

This societal consensus fostered the rise of presidential power, the expansion of the foreign policy bureaucracy, the development of an acquiescent Congress, and the rise of a national security ethos and free market ethos in government and society. It also set the context for understanding the reinforcing role that public opinion and domestic politics played throughout the Cold War years in the making of US foreign policy.

The growing anti-communist foreign policy consensus reflected a larger set of ideological patterns that evolved in American society. During the Cold War years, according to Godfrey Hodgson (1976:73), "a strange hybrid, liberal conservatism, blanketed the scene and muffled debate." The two major aspects of the **liberal-conservative consensus** were beliefs in a democratic-capitalist political economy based on private enterprise and the idea that the main threat to this beneficent system was communism.

By the mid-1950s, most Americans within the mass and elite publics were part of this liberal-conservative ideological consensus. This consensus became possible during the 1950s because most conservatives accepted the legitimacy of the limited welfare state created by the New Deal under Franklin Roosevelt, while most liberals adopted the anti-communist stance in vogue following World War II. Therefore, the liberal-conservative consensus represented neither liberalism nor conservatism but was a hybrid or amalgamation of the two ideologies. Differences did exist among members of the consensus. Liberals were more favorable toward welfare and government intervention in the economy, while conservatives generally were opposed to such policies. Conservatives were more prone to rely on force to respond to instability in the Third World, while liberals were more sympathetic to the need to promote Third World economic and political development. However, such differences were overshadowed by agreement on the promise of the American private market system and the threat of communism.

During the anti-communist consensus years of the late 1940s and 1950s, most liberals became strong advocates of anti-communism and containment, while conservatives increasingly accepted the notion of a limited welfare state in the domestic economy, especially during the Eisenhower administration. Those further to the left, who were critical of an aggressive US policy of global containment abroad and believed in greater restructuring of American society at home, lost credibility and were effectively silenced throughout the Cold War with the rise of McCarthyism. But the far right failed to persuade either the Truman or the Eisenhower administration (and most Americans) to reorient foreign policies beyond containment.

In short, a consensus developed within the United States during the 1950s that the world was divided between two hostile forces: communism led by the Soviet Union, and democracy and free markets led by the United States. Despite disagreements over tactics (How much force? Where should it be applied?), most Americans agreed on the source of the threat—communism—and the necessity of using force to counter its expansion throughout the world. Ideological anti-communism thus became the glue that bound the consensus among liberals, moderates, and conservatives, especially within the elite public. It also limited political choices available to policymakers. In the words of David Halberstam (1969:108), "It was an ideological and bipartisan movement; it enjoyed the support of the press, of the churches, of Hollywood. There was stunningly little debate or sophistication of the levels of anticommunism. It was totally centrist and politically very safe; anything else was politically dangerous."

The Post-Vietnam Fragmentation and Dissensus

Events of the 1960s and early 1970s, such as the civil rights movement, the war on poverty, and Watergate, led many Americans to question the ideological and foreign policy beliefs that were the basis of the consensus during the Cold War years. But the Vietnam War had the most traumatic impact on Americans, leading to the collapse of the ideological and foreign policy consensus that prevailed throughout the Cold War. The "failure" of Vietnam undermined many of these beliefs. Americans seemed to be dying for a lost cause—more than 58,000 Americans died in Vietnam, with over 350,000 other Americans wounded. For what? This tragic loss led people to raise questions about US foreign policy. Members of the mass public, on the one hand, came to critique the Vietnam War and US foreign policy predominantly from a pragmatic perspective—they emphasized the limited importance of Vietnam and questioned the US failure to win the war. Members of the elite public, on the other hand, were more likely to debate the goals and virtue of US foreign policy.

By the late 1960s, a substantial number of average Americans had also turned against the government and its policies in Vietnam; some wanted out through victory and military escalation, but most wanted out via withdrawal. Ultimately, this divide led to increasing political fragmentation in the decades after Vietnam. The American society became more ideologically diverse with competing foreign policy orientations. The 1960s and early 1970s resulted in a resurgence of liberalism and the rise of the new left, while the 1970s and 1980s witnessed the rise of modern conservatism and the political right. Second, greater ideological diversity led to three competing foreign policy views or schools of thought during the 1970s and 1980s: conservative internationalism, liberal internationalism, and non-internationalism (Schneider 1983; see also Holsti and Rosenau 1984). With the collapse of the Soviet Union, the war on terrorism following the 9/11 attacks, and the global recession, a great debate prevailed over national security policy that created even more conflict and confusion for the politics of US foreign policy, with the proliferation of additional orientations (e.g., Dolan 2008; Posen and Ross 1996; Rosati and Creed 1997).

Growth of the Left and Liberal Internationalism. The events of the1960s resulted in the growth of the political left in the United States and an alternative understanding of American society. Although anti-communism and McCarthyism had silenced most liberals and leftists by the early 1950s, the "new left" entered the political scene in the late 1950s with the rise of the civil rights movement and grew dramatically as the Vietnam War intensified. Members of the new left and the counterculture dissented and rebelled against the liberal-conservative ideological and anti-communist consensus of mainstream society, which they held responsible for Vietnam.

With the rise of the new left, liberalism once again began to emphasize the values of freedom and equality and turned away from the importance of anti-communism abroad and at home. Liberals were more likely to promote active governmental intervention in the economy and to support needy individuals. Moreover, the Vietnam War and events of the 1960s prompted most liberals to become supportive of greater individualism in American life. Thus, liberalism became quite distinct from conservatism in the post-Vietnam years.

Liberals and those on the political left saw a much more complex and interdependent world, composed of many important countries, global actors, and issues—a position that Schneider (1983) refers to as **liberal internationalism** (and Holsti and Rosenau [1984] refer to as post–Cold War internationalism). Liberals now were opposed to anti-communism as the driving force in US foreign policy. They believed it was important to address not only the East-West conflict (and the possibilities for cooperation) but also West-West issues (especially economic), involving relations between the United States and its allies, and North-South issues, focusing on the relationships among industrialized nations, international organizations, and the Third World. Such a liberal internationalist orientation tended to have a strong association with members of the Democratic Party, and it influenced the Democratic administrations of Carter, Clinton, and Obama.

Growth of the Right and Conservative Internationalism. At the same time, many Americans continued to hold a more conservative understanding of America and the world, emphasizing the threat of communism abroad and the importance of the private market at home—the same values that had once been the basis of the ideological consensus during the Cold War. In fact, the late 1970s and 1980s witnessed the resurgence of conservatism and the right, best associated with Ronald Reagan and the Republican Party, in reaction to the perceived excesses of liberalism and the left during the 1960s and 1970s. Conservatives were particularly critical of the insufficient concern with the communist threat abroad and the moral decay they believed prevailed at home. These concerns account not only for the rise of conservatism but also for the growth of ultraconservatism and the political right, including the religious fundamentalist right.

These Americans, especially conservatives and those on the political right, continued to believe in **conservative internationalism** (or Cold War internationalism) after the Vietnam War, especially during the 1970s and 1980s. In other words, they believed that the major global threat to the security of the United States and global order was communism directed by the Soviet Union, requiring a strong American military presence in much of the world. Yet disagreement among conservatives existed concerning the severity of the Soviet threat and the appropriate foreign policy strategy.

Concerns over the Soviet threat also led to the development of another conservative orientation in foreign policy: **neo-conservatives**. A strange hybrid of disaffected liberal, "Cold Warriors," neocons (as they also came to be known) broke with the Democratic Party over what they perceived as its dovish retreat from assertive foreign policies. Although Reagan's "crusade for freedom," the Reagan Doctrine, and other policies met with their approval, the neocons never achieved the influence they sought within the administration. The neocons stressed the preeminence and (benevolent) hegemony of the United States as the world's dominant power, including the need to wield American power—especially military power—to promote American democracy and capitalism abroad, unilaterally if necessary. Many of these neocons found a home in George W. Bush's administration and played an instrumental role in shaping the administration's response to the 9/11 attacks, until the Iraq War shifted from what seemed like a success to a failed policy (Ehrman 1995; Mann 2004).

The Rise of Non-internationalism. Proponents of the third popular orientation, which spanned the political spectrum, recognized the increasing complexity of the world and the difficulty the United States had in affecting it and advocated a type of **non-internationalism** (or semi-isolationism). Some non-internationalists argued that the United States needed to limit its involvement to those areas of the world where it really has vital interests—primarily Western Europe and Japan. Other non-internationalists believed that the United States should deescalate its overseas military commitments and presence— in other words, "strategically disengage"—and concentrate on improving its international commercial and economic position. Whatever the particular position, non-internationalists were likely to believe that the highest priority of American society and the US government should be to avoid entanglements abroad and address domestic issues and problems at home. Non-internationalists also tended to be more supportive of protecting American industry and jobs in the international political economy. Such a non-internationalist perspective was most prevalent among the mass public (in comparison to the elite public), among whom isolationist sentiment has historically been strong.

Fragmentation, Confusion, and Reorientation?

The momentous events surrounding the end of the Cold War, including the collapse of communism in Eastern Europe and of the Soviet Union from 1989 to 1991, raised the possibility of profound changes in American foreign policy orientations. The liberal and conservative internationalist orientations became less well defined. In fact, right after the collapse of the Soviet Union, there was an initial outpouring of optimism across the political spectrum that "peace was at hand" and it was "the end of history" in which democratic liberalism would prevail globally (see Fukuyama 1989).

This outlook was short lived after the September 11, 2001, attacks, the war on terrorism, and the Iraq War. Indeed, another great debate has been generated over the nature of the world and the proper role of the United States abroad since the 1990s. This debate does not fit neatly into liberal, conservative, or non-internationalist orientations, especially in the area of national security policy. Initially, foreign economic policy was less affected, but with the uneven costs of the globalizing world economy, growing inequality at home, and the major economic collapse beginning in 2008, pressure grew on the commitment to free trade and the liberal international economic order. The net result is that the ideological and foreign policy orientations are more fragmented than ever, there is less consistency and coherence of thought, and presidents find it more difficult to find lasting political support and legitimacy for their policies (see "A Different Perspective: Changing Orientations toward US Foreign Policy").

A Different Perspective

CHANGING ORIENTATIONS TOWARD US FOREIGN POLICY

For much of the post–World War II period, discussion of the foreign policy orientations of the American public, elites and masses, turned on variants of the isolationism-internationalism debate. Holsti (1979) characterized this in terms of a "three-headed eagle": Cold War internationalism, post–Cold War internationalism, and semi-isolationism. Holsti and Rosenau (1984) later developed four orientations: hard-liners, internationalists, isolationists, and accommodationists. Eugene Wittkopf (1990) described foreign policy orientations based on their militant and cooperative elements, identifying four orientations: internationalists (supporting both cooperative and militant internationalism), accommodationists (supporting cooperative internationalism), hard-liners (supporting militant internationalism), and isolationists (supporting neither).

As the Cold War receded, signs that these traditional orientations were changing emerged. In response, Rosati and Creed (1997) moved somewhat past the underlying emphasis on isolationism and internationalism but still built on the work of Holsti, Rosenau, and Wittkopf to outline six orientations: global crusaders, global containers, selective containers, global reformers, global transformers, and selective engagers. Just over a decade later, in the wake of the changes of the twenty-first century and the global war on terror, Dolan (2008) further expanded the arena, identifying nine competing orientations: missionaries, hegemonists, globalizers, global capitalists, narrow realists, progressive internationalists, anti-imperialists, neighbors, and disengagers.

Enter the Center for Strategic and International Studies (CSIS), with its 2018 analysis entitled *Beyond the Water's Edge: Measuring the Internationalism of Congress* (Hicks et al. 2018). According to the CSIS, for elite opinion, at least, as reflected by members of Congress, the landscape of foreign policy orientations is shifting. The CSIS identifies three archetypal foreign policy orientations or worldviews (Hicks et al. 2018:2):

- *Order-Driven:* "Defending and leading the liberal international order is the core foreign policy preference driver for the first and largest grouping of members identified by this analysis. Viewing the set of alliances and international institutions developed after World War II as pillars of U.S. national interest, adherents to this viewpoint tend to be the most supportive among the archetypes of employing military force

(Continued)

(Continued)

in defense of the international order. These members tend to view Russia (especially) and China as threats and seek to confront their policies on the global stage. Strengthening alliances was also a driving motivation for these members."

- *Values-Driven:* "Promoting U.S. values abroad was the core motivation of the second major grouping identified. Members in this group do not necessarily share the same values. For example, human rights took center stage for some; others were motivated by democracy promotion. Religious views appeared formative for some but not for all. What they share, however, is the grounding of calls for U.S. international engagement in statements of guiding values and principles. These members tended to be foremost advocates for U.S. foreign aid programs, including humanitarian, development and global health assistance, and working through multilateral

institutions. In addition, while these members tended to be skeptical of the use of U.S. military force, some supported military operations in service of humanitarian goals."

- *Limits-Driven:* "The final grouping of members was defined by a relatively circumscribed assessment of national interests and a desire to minimize the risks and costs associated with U.S. international engagement. Although members in this grouping may support elements of the post–World War II international order and may desire to spread U.S. values in some contexts, their core foreign policy motivation is to limit potential costs and entanglements abroad. Therefore, they tend to oppose the use of military force and foreign assistance and can be particularly critical of alliances and multilateral institutions."

What do these changing foreign policy orientations mean for US foreign policymaking?

As Richard Melanson (1990:17) aptly suggested at the start of these shifts, "In sum, a **fragmentation/swing model** has replaced that of [a] Cold War **followership model** as the most accurate depiction of foreign policy attitudes, . . . and its emergence has surely complicated the efforts of presidents to win and keep public support for their foreign policies." Where once public opinion fluctuated within only a narrow range consistent with the liberal-conservative and Cold War internationalist consensus during the Cold War years, public opinion is now much more open to greater fluctuation, reflecting the breakdown of the Cold War Consensus. Members of the mass public are more likely to change their opinion and be open to "populist" appeals. Sometimes they are responsive to a more conservative internationalist position while at other times they are more receptive to a liberal internationalist position or some hybrid orientation. Sometimes they are more responsive to Democratic Party candidates and policies; sometimes they are more receptive to Republican Party candidates and policies. And, as the past several years indicate, a significant portion of the mass public is also open to non-internationalist appeals such as those advanced by Donald Trump in his political campaign and first three years in the White House.

Hence, the post–Vietnam War years have produced a much more complex and messy political process in which public opinion is more volatile than during the Cold War years of consensus. As William Schneider (1987:51) pointed out, when a foreign policy issue gets on the political agenda and is framed in terms of security and "military strength," the conservative internationalist orientation tends to win the political debate—such as immediately following the 9/11 attacks. However, if it is framed in terms of "peace," then the liberal internationalist perspective tends to prevail. "Instead of elite consensus and mass followership, what emerged was an unstable system of competing coalitions in which the mass public swings left or right unpredictably in response to its current fears and concerns." There are also times when an issue such as trade may trigger a strong non-internationalist orientation among the public such as over issues concerning jobs and the economy.

Members of the elite public tend to be more committed to some variant of conservative or liberal internationalism, but they usually are opposed to non-internationalism, although Trump's success suggests some limits to that observation. Members of the mass public tend to be more moderate and pragmatic in their beliefs, demonstrating both liberal and conservative elements, and a segment of them are often thought to be more receptive to the non-internationalist orientation (Wittkopf 1990) (but see "A Closer Look: Is the American Public Really Flirting with Isolationism?"). And now there are differences not only between these internationalist orientations but also increasingly within them, reflecting this more complex and confused world reality.

A Closer Look

IS THE AMERICAN PUBLIC REALLY FLIRTING WITH ISOLATIONISM?

For many observers, the 2016 election victory of Donald Trump provided further indication of a shift toward isolationism—or a version of non-internationalism in our terms. From anti-immigration and aggressively nationalist policy preferences—including hostility to free trade, international organizations, and allies—to other aspects of his "America First" approach, Trump seemed to play to an increasingly important segment of the Republican base that leaned toward disengagement. The Pew Research Center (2013, 2016) found one indicator of this trend away from internationalism, reporting that the percentage of the American population taking the position that the United States should "mind its own business" and let others take care of themselves grew from 20 percent in 1984 to 57 percent in 2016.

Popular accounts and reporting seem to reinforce this perspective, and some scholars have also sounded the alarm . . . or even made the appeal.

(Continued)

(Continued)

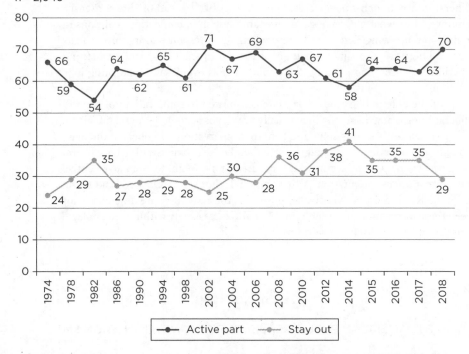

FIGURE 11.6

Opinions about the Preferred US Role in World Affairs

Do you think it will be best for the future of the country if we take an active part in world affairs or if we stay out of world affairs? (%)
n = 2,046

Source: Figure 1 in Dina Smeltz, Ivo Daalder, Karl Friedhoff, Craig Kafura, and Lily Wojtowicz, *America Engaged: American Public Opinion and US Foreign Policy,* Chicago Council on Global Affairs, 2018 (https://digital.thechicago council.org/america-engaged).

But is this accurate? More than a year into the Trump administration, the Chicago Council on Global Affairs (Smeltz et al. 2018) reported that the percentage of Americans who think the United States should take an active role in world affairs was at its highest point since 1974 (with the exception of a short spike immediately after 9/11) (see Figure 11.6).

Furthermore, more than 90 percent of Americans surveyed supported international cooperation with allies and others, with about two thirds supporting

Opinions about Working through the United Nations

When dealing with international problems, the United States should be more willing to make decisions within the United Nations even if this means that the United States will sometimes have to go along with a policy that is not its first choice. (%)
n = 1,008

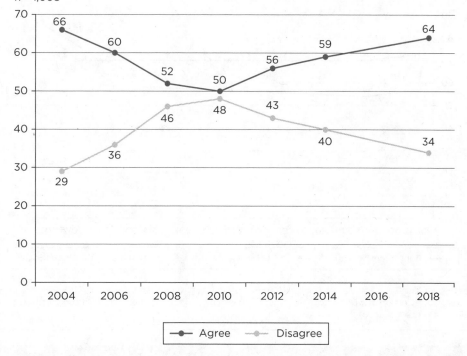

Source: Figure 4 in Dina Smeltz, Ivo Daalder, Karl Friedhoff, Craig Kafura, and Lily Wojtowicz, *America Engaged: American Public Opinion and US Foreign Policy,* Chicago Council on Global Affairs, 2018 (https://digital.thechicago council.org/america-engaged).

doing so even if it meant that the United States had to go along with policies it did not prefer. Nearly two thirds of respondents preferred working through the United Nations as well (see Figure 11.7).

Perhaps most surprisingly, this same survey showed increasing support for free trade, despite the hostile rhetoric from the Trump campaign and the White House (see Figure 11.8).

(Continued)

(Continued)

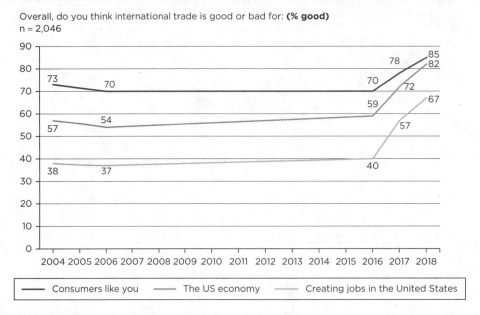

FIGURE 11.8
Opinions about World Trade

Overall, do you think international trade is good or bad for: **(% good)**
n = 2,046

Legend: Consumers like you — The US economy — Creating jobs in the United States

Source: Figure 10 in Dina Smeltz, Ivo Daalder, Karl Friedhoff, Craig Kafura, and Lily Wojtowicz, *America Engaged: American Public Opinion and US Foreign Policy,* Chicago Council on Global Affairs, 2018 (https://digital.thechicago council.org/america-engaged).

Just one year later, the 2019 Chicago Council on Foreign Relations survey concluded that these trends persisted, with the American public "rejecting retreat" and supporting continued—even expanded—US engagement in world affairs.

Does this seem like an American public shifting toward isolationism or non-internationalism?

Foreign economic policy orientations and the free market ethos were much less affected by the Vietnam War, the collapse of the Cold War Consensus, the collapse of the Soviet Union, and the 9/11 attacks, but the Great Recession challenged these shared views. Internationalists still tend to sympathize with a free market ethos. Conservative internationalists are the strongest believers and advocates of an unregulated international political economy based on a free market (except for using coercion and embargoes, for example, against perceived enemies such as Cuba). Liberal internationalists, for the most part, also believe in a market-oriented international political economy but argue for the need for more international multilateral cooperation, management, and regulation. Both conservative and liberal internationalists, for the most part, believe that US foreign policy overall must support, for example, NAFTA, the World Trade Organization (WTO), and trade with China despite different views about that nation's growing great power status. It is the non-internationalists who are the least receptive to the free market ethos and most willing to advocate protectionism for local industry and labor, especially for people who have been, are, or might in the future be directly affected. However, as conservative and liberal internationalists fragment, protectionist sentiments have emerged in both camps.

The fragmentation of public ideological and foreign policy beliefs gives a president great opportunity but also creates great risks. Presidents are no longer driven to pursue only an anti-communist containment policy or economic policies that rely principally on market and nongovernmental forces. Yet it is unclear how far presidents may go in pursuing any policy before losing public support in either national security or economic affairs. Presidents no longer come to office with automatic majorities behind their policies. No matter what presidents and their advisers believe, a substantial number of Americans—in the mass public and especially the elite public—disagree, or are open to disagreement, with presidential policy. Hence, there is a continual presidential search for, and frustration in obtaining, consensus and "policy legitimation" (see Destler, Gelb and Lake 1984; George 1980a; Rosati 1997).

All post–Vietnam War presidents have discovered that most Americans expect presidential promises to be fulfilled, but it has become increasingly difficult for presidents to deliver. Differences in the ideological and foreign policy beliefs among the elite public, coupled with a pragmatic but volatile mass public, have provided a new set of domestic boundaries and possibilities for the making of US foreign policy since Vietnam. Indeed, foreign policy orientations continue to be fragmented, the temporary period of consensus immediately after the 9/11 attacks notwithstanding. Complicating efforts to generate broad agreement are signs of isolationism in the mass public and the elites; growing rifts within both parties about how to contend with terrorism and other conflicts; the ongoing conflicts in Iraq, Afghanistan, and Syria; a so-called human security agenda involving the global environment and human rights; and an increasingly interdependent and globalized political economy. As always, much depends on the extent to which Americans consider their individual security and the nation's security to be threatened, whether by terrorism, the global economy, or other countries and issues. Whatever the case, foreign policy orientations are likely to remain highly diverse, making it difficult for any president from either party to govern.

AMERICAN POLITICAL CULTURE AND NATIONAL STYLE

Moving out to the broadest, and most subtle, layer, we now turn to context of American political culture and national style, in which the previous aspects of public perspectives and view are embedded. Culture and style influence "the manner in which members of society, including the state elite, define themselves and their place in the larger global setting" (Deudney and Ikenberry 1992:111), giving shape to the arena of possible and preferable actions and the perceptual maps of the policymakers themselves.

Innocence, Benevolence, and Exceptionalism

Studies of American political culture typically portray Americans as a confident and optimistic people who have a special sense of destiny about the future of their country and its place in the world. In *Backfire*, for example, Loren Baritz (1985) argues that Americans see themselves as an example for the rest of the world—a "city on a hill"—and hold an idealistic and missionary spirit. This translates into a sense of American innocence, benevolence, and exceptionalism. Together, these beliefs contribute powerfully to the sense of an American mission to lead the world, which runs deep within the political culture of the United States. While substantial differences exist over how to do so (e.g., through international engagement or by remaining aloof and setting an example), the sense of purpose and destiny is pervasive.

Americans tend to see the United States as innocent in world affairs: benign and defensive rather than manipulative and aggressive. This sense of **American innocence** is consistent with the isolationist sentiments that have played such a dominant role in US foreign policy, especially before the Cold War. According to this view, Americans have not been introspective and concerned with nation-building and with serving as a "city on a hill" for other people and countries to emulate (promoting and reinforcing the myth of American isolation historically). Over the years, necessity, events, and other countries have forced the United States to become actively involved in war and world politics. Thus, German disregard for American neutrality forced the United States to fight in World War I, while the Japanese bombing of Pearl Harbor forced American entry into World War II. The 9/11 attacks have reinforced this, with popular analogies to Pearl Harbor, even though the United States has been a target of terrorists (both at home and abroad) for some time now. Thus, Americans tend to see themselves and their country as the innocent victims of the acts of others.

When the United States does become involved abroad, American behavior is perceived as benevolent. The premise of **American benevolence** means that Americans do not become involved in war, for example, solely to defend themselves. Instead, the United States enters wars to rid the world of evil and promote peace and freedom for all. So, World War I represented the "war to end all wars," in which European realpolitik would be replaced by American idealism. In World War II, the United States and its allies were dedicated to ridding the world of fascism and constructing a world based on a liberal political and economic order as represented by the United Nations. Likewise, the public goal of the war on terrorism is to defeat al-Qaeda and other terrorist networks, while in Iraq and Afghanistan the United States sought to bring the benefits of freedom and democracy to a region in which those principles have not flourished.

Finally, Americans have a strong sense of **American exceptionalism** as well. American history is perceived as one success story after another, from westward expansion to economic development to the rise of the United States as a global power. This reflects an American sense of "manifest destiny"—a belief in the superiority of American culture and way of life that goes back to the early nineteenth century. American exceptionalism implies a special role and even divine purpose for the United States, along with the conviction that America represents progress and the best social model for the future of the world. This sense of exceptionalism also translates into a powerful sense of efficacy—"that Americans can do anything they desire, can build nations or rebuild societies, can speed progress, bring freedom and democracy to the world" (Robertson 1980:349).

Such American innocence, benevolence, and exceptionalism strongly support the conviction of a uniquely **American mission** in world affairs (e.g. Burns 1957). Based on the combination of the political values of the United States (e.g., liberalism, democracy, egalitarianism) and the broad belief that they are universal, the sense of mission is a sort of messianism—a "missionary urge to remake the world in the American image" in order to "save" it (Rourke, Carter, and Boyer 1996:102). It thus involves a sense of duty and destiny stemming from the view that the United States is "the custodian of the future of humanity" (Walt Whitman, quoted in Crabb 1982:378).

Thus, for example, in the Cold War, Soviet aggression forced the United States to take an active global leadership role, build up its military to contain aggression, and intervene throughout the world, but not simply as a struggle for power between two great powers. Instead, it represented a "messianic" struggle between good and evil—the forces of democracy versus totalitarianism, capitalism versus communism, Christianity versus atheism. Thus, the globe was seen to be divided into two hostile blocs: the "evil" communist world led by the Soviet Union versus the "free world" led by the United States. In addition, the United States had not only rescued Western Europe through its generosity with the Marshall Plan but also promoted liberal societies in Third World countries and assisted their nation-building efforts based on the American model. Americans, therefore, saw themselves not as imperialistic or even self-interested during the Cold War but as an innocent society composed of benevolent and exceptional people who symbolized progress and a hopeful future for the world. And, at the Cold War's end, according to Richard Betts (2002:20),

> the novelty of complete primacy may account for the thoughtless, indeed
> innocently arrogant way in which many Americans took its benefits for granted.
> Most who gave any thought to foreign policy came implicitly to regard the
> entire world after 1989 as they had regarded Western Europe and Japan during
> the past half-century: partners in principle but vassals in practice. The United
> States would lead the civilized community of nations in the expansion and
> consolidation of a liberal world order.

Innocence, benevolence, and exceptionalism are not uniquely American beliefs but to some degree are common cultural and national values within all societies. Groups and societies often see themselves as a superior and chosen people. This is typical of all great powers in world history. As Godfrey Hodgson (1976:6) has observed, "All nations live by myths. Any nation is the sum of the consciousness of its people: the chaotic infinitude of the experience and perceptions of millions alive and dead."

Although a strong sense of nationalism is not a uniquely American trait, what may be somewhat unique to the United States is the strong belief in "freedom" (and "liberty")—the key value that unifies and defines Americans as Alexis de Tocqueville (1945) so aptly described it in his masterpiece, *Democracy in America*, in 1835. This may help to explain why phrases such as "the free world," "democracy," "the free market," and "free trade" have been used with great regularity since World War II and resonate throughout the body politic. Furthermore, given America's short history, the rapid changes experienced with industrialization and modernization, and its ethnic diversity, American nationalism is as powerful a cultural force for most Americans as for any people throughout history.

According to Richard Barnet (1972:251), "All nations preach the ethic of national superiority, but the United States has made a religion of it." Niall Ferguson (2004:viii)—a sympathetic observer of the exercise of American power—highlights how the United States acts as an "empire in denial," that Americans could somehow be a great power without, at the same time, behaving like previous great powers and engaging in imperialism (what he calls the "imperialism of anti-imperialism").

Foreign Policy Implications

American political culture and national style have at least six important implications for US foreign policy. First, they contribute to the tendency of Americans to oversimplify, with a naive and rose-colored view, the history of the United States and its role in world affairs. Implicit in the previous section, concepts such as "freedom," "democracy," "the free market," and "free trade" have become sacrosanct in the American mind and interwoven with the "United States of America." Westward expansion, for example, is fondly recalled in terms of the frontier spirit, individualism, and ruggedness represented by the farmer and gunslinger (reflected in numerous movies and stars such as John Wayne), ignoring alternative interpretations that emphasize the ruthlessness of westward expansion and the taking of Native American and Mexican land and lives.

Not only had the United States won the Cold War, but it also appeared that peace was at hand, and, for some, it was "the end of history." However, "September 11 reminded those Americans with a rosy view that not all the world sees U.S. primacy as benign" (Betts 2002:465), and yet it also contributed to the oversimplification of good and evil in the world once again. Such simple and naive images make it difficult for Americans to tolerate and accept historical facts or political realities that are inconsistent with their optimistic images.

Second, America's national style has often embodied a nationalist and idealistic yearning that has turned the United States into a **moral crusader**. This is probably best associated with the presidency of Woodrow Wilson and the coining of the term "Wilsonianism." As summed up by Robert Nisbet (1988:32), "From Wilson's day to ours the embedded purpose—sometimes articulated in words, more often not—of American foreign policy, under Democrats and Republicans alike oftentimes, has boiled down to America-on-a-Permanent-Mission; a mission to make the rest of the world a little more like America the Beautiful" (see "A Closer Look: Moralism and America's View of the World").

A Closer Look

MORALISM AND AMERICA'S VIEW OF THE WORLD

Moralism/idealism has three components. First, it means that the United States involves itself in international affairs "only for sufficient ethical reasons" (i.e., that foreign policy "should be motivated by moral principles"). Second, moralism/idealism signifies the belief that a peaceful and prosperous world can be created according to universal (i.e., US) moral principles. Third, it rests on the presumption of the benevolence and moral superiority of US purposes and values. Moralism/idealism therefore constitutes the impulse to promote certain values in foreign policy, rather than to defend various interests, and it involves the "forceful assertion of society's ideological principles" (Crabb 1982:377).

The moralization of foreign policy has been a major pattern throughout US history—including Wilsonianism; US Cold War policies; Carter's human rights campaign; Reagan's battle against the "evil empire"; George W. Bush's effort to rid the world of all terrorists, whether "dead or alive"; and Bush's "with-us-or-against-us" approach to international affairs. According to Howard Fineman (2003:25), "Every president invokes God and asks his blessing. Every president promises, though not always in so many words, to lead according to moral principles rooted in biblical tradition." Furthermore, as Stanley Hoffmann (1968:194) has observed,

> There is a parallel here: like the ideological tenets of communism, American principles—those of a deeply Christian, liberal society, a

kind of synthesis or smorgasbord of Locke, Paine, and Kant—are universal and equalitarian; all the nations of the world are seen capable of living in peace under law in an association of equals devoted to harmony. This mixture of universalism, legalism, and equalitarianism diverts Americans from any suggestion that their attempt to spread the gospel might be imperialistic or self-serving; what is being sought is the common good, in the best interest of all. But the proselytizing contradicts the stated purpose, the method clashes with the intended outcome.

In the words of theologian Reinhold Niebuhr (and Heimert 1963:150), "Moral pretensions and political parochialism are the two weaknesses of the life of a messianic nation."

What are the consequences of the tendency to embrace such moralistic positions and rhetoric on US foreign policy choices and the debate over them?

Third, the American penchant for moral crusades also produces major contradictions between **principle versus pragmatism**. Despite its moralization, the actual conduct of US foreign policy often involves the pragmatic pursuit of national interests heavily informed by a national security ethos that existed before, and has continued to exist since, the Cold War. This means that policymakers engage in diplomacy, secrecy, bargaining, rewards, threats, force, and all of the other instruments associated with power politics in order to successfully promote their national interests as they define them. But such amoral and pragmatic behavior by the superpower, or great power, or hegemonic power of its day is not consistent with notions of American innocence, benevolence, and exceptionalism, to the point that much of US foreign policy has had to remain hidden and disguised from the public.

This contradiction has posed real problems for the leaders and makers of US foreign policy, producing a kind of "American dualism," the necessity to speak two different languages: the language of power and the language of peace and harmony (or democracy and freedom). "Of course," states Stanley Hoffmann (1968:178), "only a symbolic eagle can hold both the arrows and the olive branch easily at the same time." Americans' unwillingness to recognize, and deal with, these contradictions between morality and pragmatism in foreign policy has been a topic of concern for quite some time for such thinkers as George Kennan (1951), Hans Morgenthau (1952), and Reinhold Niebuhr (1944).

Fourth, American leaders often feel the need to oversell their policies in order to legitimate them with the public by simplifying them and infusing them with moral purpose in the process. It matters little whether political leaders themselves share these same cultural and nationalistic values—most do, some do not (at least in varying degrees). The fact is that the pragmatic majority is generally uninterested and uninformed about world affairs, and so political overstatement and oversell is deemed necessary to attract public attention and support, especially when foreign policy changes or the use of force is involved. This compels leaders to speak in terms of power and peace and to rely on the politics of symbolism to legitimize their policies.

To arouse public support, political leaders link issues to moral symbols and values with which most Americans identify. To gain congressional support for military assistance to Greece and Turkey in 1947, Secretary of State Dean Acheson testified about what was at stake through use of an analogy for what would become the domino theory, a "Soviet break-through [in the Near East] might open three continents to Soviet penetration. Like apples in a barrel infected by the corruption of one rotten one, the corruption of Greece would infect Iran and all to the East . . . Africa . . . Italy and France . . . . Not since Rome and Carthage had there been such a polarization of power on this earth." Senator Arthur Vandenberg, Republican chair of the Foreign Relations Committee, literally told senior Truman officials that the only way to overcome post–World War II isolationist tendencies and to get full congressional and public support was to "scare the hell out of the American people" about the threat of communism to freedom, democracy, and the American way of life. Such was the language of the Truman Doctrine (Yergin 1978:281).

This helps to explain the power of anti-communism, and the free market, in the making of foreign policy since World War II. Likewise, the war on terrorism is sold and legitimized for the American public as necessary to protect democracy, freedom, and the American way of life by exterminating terrorism, ultimately embodied by the most evil and omnipresent figure of first Osama bin Laden and then Saddam Hussein. Phrases such as the war to "end evil" and characterizations of adversaries as an "axis of evil" further illustrate this point. It also is an important foundation behind contemporary appeals to "make America great again."

Fifth, US political culture and national style often breed strong doses of American **nationalism** and intolerance abroad and at home. Nationalism is often a positive force, for it helps to promote a strong sense of community among members of society in support of a common effort—an essential quality in both war and peace. One of the major problems with a strong sense of nationalism, however, is that patriotism often turns into intolerance and **super-patriotism**. Such attitudes have the tendency to dehumanize adversaries and repress domestic criticism and dissent in the name of national security. Intolerance is particularly evident during periods of national emergency and war, when people feel threats to their values and to their country's security—such as after the 9/11 attacks.

A strong sense of nationalism also has made it difficult for Americans to accept criticism from abroad, including from the country's closest allies, thus reflecting deep-seated isolationist and unilateralist sentiments. As Hoffmann (1968:195) has argued, American foreign policy easily leads to "an activism that others see as imperialistic: for we expect them to join the consensus, we ignore the boundaries and differences between 'them' and 'us,' we prod them out of conviction that we act for their own good, and we do not take resistance gracefully." Americans have such a strong faith in American virtue and progress that it is difficult for them to understand, let alone accept, the value of alternative paths to economic and political development divorced from the American model. Or as was often asked after the 9/11 attacks, how could the United States (and Americans) be so loved and so hated? Moreover, this sense also leads Americans to justify behavior they would quickly condemn in others. Consider, for example, current debates over border security and the treatment of those—especially women and children—seeking asylum and refuge.

A final consequence of American political culture and nationalism is its tendency to contribute to major swings in **public moods** or sentiments with respect to US foreign policy. It is commonly argued that "twentieth-century exceptionalism has fueled both interventionism and isolationism" (Davis and Lynn-Jones 1987:24). As Louis Hartz (1955:286) has stated, "Americas seem to oscillate between fleeing from the rest of the world and embracing it with too ardent a passion. An absolute national morality is inspired either to withdraw from 'alien' things or to transform them: it cannot live in comfort constantly by their side." Richard Barnet (1972:259), in fact, has argued that "the internationalist versus isolationist debate is really an argument about little more than military strategy" abroad, in which both competing perspectives ultimately reflect an underlying sense of unilateralism among the mass public and in America's national style. Or as Stanley Hoffmann (1968:191) has stated, "Both quietism and activism are compensatory assertions of total independence."

Conservatives and liberals possess strong nationalist sentiments and continue to believe in America, but in different ways. Conservatives and the right believe that American innocence, benevolence, and exceptionalism have prevailed throughout American history; in contrast, liberals and the left are more prone to see the good, the bad, and the ugly in American history, while still believing in the possibility of building an America where innocence, benevolence, and exceptionalism reign supreme. As Robertson (1980:348) has put it, "As a New World, many Americans believe their country to be the last, best hope of the world, a place of youth, of new beginnings, of booming. Even those who believe that America is, in reality, no such place of hope or virtue believe it somehow ought to be."

Most members of the mass public, being more pragmatic and centrist, probably entertain both sets of feelings at different times—what they manifest depends on the salience of the issues and how they are played out politically at the time. A kind of "pessimistic-optimistic dualism," in other words, operates among members of the mass public, since they share a certain cynicism about American politics while still maintaining an optimistic image of American innocence, benevolence, and exceptionalism. This helps to explain how both liberal and conservative views—as embodied, for example, in Carter's human rights policies, Reagan's anti-communism, and George W. Bush's war on terrorism—were initially attractive to most members of the public. This may also help to explain why Obama received so much initial mass support behind his policies to revive the economy despite major governmental activism within the so-called free market system. Such appears to be the contradictory nature of America's political culture and national style in the complex politics of US foreign policy.

PUBLIC OPINION AND FOREIGN POLICYMAKING

The public's role in US foreign policymaking stems from three layers of beliefs. American political culture and national style set the broad context within which the politics of US foreign policy transpire. Then the ideological and foreign policy beliefs of Americans further narrow what is possible and probable within domestic politics and the policymaking process. Finally, public opinion—of elites, the attentive public, and the mass public—affects the foreign policy process.

However, before we finish our discussion of the role of public opinion, we need to add one final piece to the puzzle. As Douglas Foyle (1999) argues, in addition to the three layers we have examined, a key part of the equation for the role and influence of public opinion is how key policymakers themselves think it should fit into their efforts. As Foyle suggests, the influence of public opinion varies in part due to different beliefs about its value and significance held by America's leaders, especially the president. Depending on what they think about the need to consider public opinion in decision making and/or to seek the public's support once decisions are made, presidents fall into one of four categories:

- Delegates: favor public input and seek its support

- Executors: desire public input; do not seek its support

- Pragmatists: ignore public input; want public support

- Guardians: neither seek public input nor require public support

For Foyle, guardians include Reagan and Truman, while Clinton is a good example of a delegate. Carter is an example of an executor. Finally, Eisenhower and George H. W. Bush are examples of pragmatists.

With this last piece of the puzzle in place, we can connect the dots to identify three channels of connection and influence between public opinion, broadly defined, and foreign policymaking. As Knecht (2010) argues (see Figure 11.9), these are a "political leadership" channel, in which policymakers shape and guide public opinion; a "political representation" channel, in which policymakers and the public share and mutually shape each other's preferences, both guided by the broader layers of ideology/orientation and culture/national style; and a "political responsiveness" channel in which public opinion leads policymakers and their policy preferences.

With regard to public opinion, prolonged lack of interest, information, and thought about national and international affairs—especially in the mass public—will not change overnight. Beyond the elite and attentive publics, Americans are likely to retain very short attention spans, as well as superficial knowledge and simplistic understandings of national and international affairs despite the rise of globalization and the increasing impact of world politics and foreign policy on their lives. In the complicated world of the present, diversity of ideological and foreign policy beliefs is also likely to continue. While anti-communism was the foundation of the ideological and foreign policy consensus

FIGURE 11.9

The Public Opinion–Foreign Policy Connections

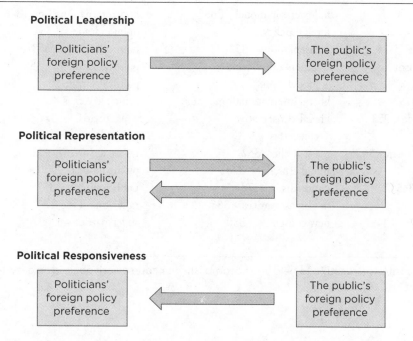

Political Leadership

Politicians' foreign policy preference → The public's foreign policy preference

Political Representation

Politicians' foreign policy preference → ← The public's foreign policy preference

Political Responsiveness

Politicians' foreign policy preference ← The public's foreign policy preference

Source: Adapted from Thomas Knecht, *Paying Attention to Foreign Affairs: How Public Opinion Affects Presidential Decision Making* (University Park: Pennsylvania State University Press, 2010).

during the Cold War, the end of the Cold War, 9/11, the Iraq War, changes wrought by the global economy, and the changing nature of American power and leadership in the world have given rise to a new great debate. Whatever the case, one thing that can be predicted with great certainty is that the competing foreign policy orientations and the response of public opinion will reflect the moral foundation of American political culture and national style, which together will directly and indirectly impact the making of US foreign policy in the future.

THINK ABOUT THIS

As we noted earlier in this chapter, Henry Kissinger once argued that public support is "the acid test of foreign policy." Think about this chapter's discussion of the nature and role of public opinion.

What factors shape the role and influence of public opinion in US foreign policymaking?

KEY TERMS

Almond-Lippmann
consensus   348
American benevolence   374
American exceptionalism   374
American innocence   374
American mission   375
American national style   353
attentive public   351
Cold War internationalism   362
conservative
internationalism   365
elite public   351
elitist view of the public   349

followership model   368
foreign policy
orientations   352
fragmentation/swing
model   368
liberal internationalism   365
liberal-conservative
consensus   363
mass public   352
moral crusader   376
nationalism   378
neo-conservatives   366
new consensus   350

non-internationalism   366
opinion leaders   351
political culture   353
political ideology   352
political socialization   350
principle versus
pragmatism   377
public approval   354
public attitudes   352
public moods   379
public opinion   352
rally around the flag   353
super-patriotism   378

Visit **edge.sagepub.com/scottrosati7e** to help you accomplish your coursework goals in an easy-to-use learning environment.

Interest Groups and Foreign Policy

12

PHOTO 12.1 Lobbyists seeking access to lawmakers.

AP Photo/Rick Bowmer

LEARNING OBJECTIVES

1. Understand the context of interest group activity in US political participation.

2. Identify the origins and development of interest groups and social movements.

3. Explain the strategies of influence by interest groups.

4. Describe the nature and evolution of interest groups and their influence in US foreign policymaking in the Cold War, post-Vietnam, and post–Cold War contexts.

In 2018, lobbying firms in the United States—professional firms hired by individuals, organizations, and companies to influence political decisions in government—spent more than $3.4 billion to advocate for their clients. That marked the eleventh straight year in which more than $3 billion was spent for lobbying, a value that never exceeded $1.5 billion prior to 1999. A variety of interests groups pay for lobbying and engage in other activities to influence to US government. These interests include business, labor, consumer, environmental, religious, ethnic, civic, and veterans groups; national security organizations; and foreign countries. One area of increasing activity is in foreign policy, as more and more interests cross borders and concern foreign and intermestic affairs.

In this chapter, we examine a second key component of the societal context—interest groups and foreign policy. We first consider the context of interest group activity and then discuss their influence strategies and their evolving role and influence over time. As we will see, group politics have significantly affected the politics and process of US foreign policy, engaging with both the executive and legislative branches.

CONTEMPORARY POLITICAL PARTICIPATION

Citizens have many avenues to engage in civic life. They may vote, respond to a public opinion poll, write to their elected representatives, write letters to newspaper or magazine editors, give money for a cause, join an organization or a group, work for a candidate or political party, lobby and petition, demonstrate, or become involved in mass movements. While people engage in these activities in elections—by voting and being involved in political parties—they may also actively engage in group politics through interest groups and social movements, which are the focus of this chapter.

Most Americans participate infrequently in the political process, and when they do so, it is mainly through voting. Many Americans, in fact, have completely opted out of any form of political participation. Indeed, although more and more Americans vote in each election cycle as the US population grows, turnout (i.e., of eligible voters actually casting ballots) has generally ranged between 50 and 55 percent of the voting-age population since 1972, and it has not exceeded 60 percent since the 1960s, which was the norm for most post–World War II elections until then. Much smaller percentages have voted in presidential primary elections, congressional elections, and state and local elections (the lowest rates in any developed democracy). Increasingly since the Vietnam War, many voters register as Independents as opposed to Democrats or Republicans, reflecting a **dealignment**, in which there is no longer a consistent majority party over time. However, although only a minority of the US population participates in interest groups and social movements, this form of participation has increased over time. The rise of interest group and mass movement participation is particularly noticeable if one compares the post–Vietnam War era to the Cold War era.

Who participates? Members of the elite public (and the attentive public) tend to be more likely than the mass public to vote, join interest groups, and become politically active. As we discussed in Chapter 11, compared to the mass public, members of the elite and attentive publics tend to be more interested and better informed about politics and also tend to have greater resources at their disposal—especially information and money—and a greater sense of political efficacy. Members of the mass public also participate, but they do so less frequently than people who come from higher socioeconomic classes and who have higher levels of education. Among the mass public, there has been an overall decline in political efficacy and trust in political officials and Washington politics—that is, a sense of powerlessness, mass apathy, and cynicism about the ability to effect change through the political process. Age is another important factor: Older people tend to vote more often; younger people, less often. At the same time, younger people tend to become more politically active in social movements and interest group politics than do older people.

People participate to further both their own interests and the interests of their country. Interests fluctuate from person to person and depend on how people see the world, which is predominantly a function of their beliefs—that is, of political culture, political ideology, and public opinion (the topics of Chapter 11). While most people who participate do so through voting and, to a lesser extent, through joining groups and giving money, others are more politically "activist"—they give their time and become personally involved (see Neuman 1986; Verba and Nye 1972; Zukin et al 2006).

INTEREST GROUPS AND SOCIAL
MOVEMENTS: ORIGINS AND DEVELOPMENT

Interest groups are organizations made up of people who share common interests and work together to advocate for those interests with the government. Interest groups tend to form in waves, usually in reaction to salient problems and key events often related to political or economic instability or turmoil. For example, large numbers of interest groups formed during the 1930s in response to the Great Depression, during the 1940s and early 1950s in response to World War II and the Cold War, and during the late 1960s and 1970s in response to events such as the Vietnam War. These time periods are often characterized by "negative" events—that is, events that hurt people or are perceived to be counterproductive for people's lives. Such events activate people, many of whom previously may have been apathetic and politically passive.

Periods of political instability and turmoil can also produce **social movements**—large coalitions of individuals and groups that unite loosely around certain issues, usually in opposition to the status quo. Social movements involve thousands, sometimes millions, of people. They usually involve a change in the way people think about an issue, and these changes in attitudes usually remain even after the social movement fades. Social movements involve dozens, sometimes hundreds, of interest groups—both those that have been around for a while and more recent groups that have arisen in reaction to the political climate of the times (Cigler and Loomis 2015; Wilson 1995).

Social movements and interest groups tend to go through life cycles. Social movements tend to have a relatively short life span. Initially highly visible and potentially influential, they wither away as the issue dies due to either success or failure. Interest groups tend to go through a longer life cycle. Groups in their formative stages tend to be more informally structured and nonbureaucratic. New interest groups, like the social movements of which they are often a part, also tend to be more purposive, as group leaders and members are motivated to accomplish certain goals. They also tend to be **challenging groups** in the sense that group leaders and followers are usually unhappy with things as they currently exist and are change oriented, challenging some aspect of the status quo, such as established groups.

With time, interest groups tend to become more formal and less purposive. The activities of older groups tend to be much more bureaucratic and institutionalized. Members of older, **established groups** also tend to join for material and solidarity (social) reasons—for example, in order to defend certain policies, preserve or acquire certain services, or socialize with others. Every political system, according to David Truman (1971:xii) "of course, tends to discriminate in favor of established groups of interests, and it may deny to new groups access to points of decision." Established groups tend to support the status quo and thus promote continuity in the policymaking process, especially if they are accepted or legitimate in society and have been somewhat successful in fulfilling their original purposive goals.

American group politics tends to go through different phases of political stability and instability. During more stable periods, established groups and the status quo tend to dominate. Challenging groups exist, but they are often few in number, small in size and support, and invisible to most Americans. However, times of greater political instability produce considerable social movement activity and interest group expansion. During these periods, major political challenges of the status quo occur in which efforts are made to change the ideological beliefs and institutions that dominate society and the government. While the forces supporting the status quo usually have an advantage in resisting challenging groups, it is during these times that political changes have the greatest potential and likelihood of occurring.

Challenging groups, in contrast, attempt to change domestic politics and the policy-making process. How successful are challenging groups at surviving, being accepted within society, and achieving their goals? Sociologist William Gamson (1975) performed a classic in-depth study of more than fifty major challenging groups throughout American history. As Figure 12.1 shows, he found that fewer than half of the challenging groups were able to survive and gain minimal acceptance within society. Furthermore, only half of the groups were successful in gaining at least some of their goals. Overall, roughly 40 percent of the challenging groups were successful in both gaining some legitimacy and achieving some of their goals, but more than 40 percent collapsed entirely. Some groups were "preempted"—in which some of their goals were embraced by the status quo groups, while the challenger was excluded—or "coopted," in which the challenger group was brought (or bought off) into the process, while their goals were not. As Gamson (1975:140) concludes,

> The central difference among political actors is captured by the idea of being inside or outside of the polity. Those who are inside are members whose interest is vested—that is, recognized as valid by other members. Those who are outside are challengers. They lack the basic prerogative of members—routine access to decisions that affect them.

FIGURE 12.1

Political Outcomes for Challenging Groups

| | | LEGITIMACY Minimal Acceptance | |
		Yes	No
GOALS Some Achieved	Yes	Full Response 38% (20)	Preemption 11% (6)
	No	Cooptation 9% (5)	Collapse 42% (22)

N = 53

Source: William A. Gamson, The Strategy of Social Protest (Homewood, Ill.: Dorsey Press, 1975), p. 37.

Many different factors account for these outcomes. However, challenging groups tend to have their greatest impact on those issues with great salience and visibility in domestic politics. Such issues become politicized and attract the attention of the elite and mass publics throughout society beyond the confines of government policymakers and established groups. However, for issues of low salience—the normal state of affairs for most issues—challenging groups are usually unable to overcome the lack of public attention and penetrate the web of relations that exists between government policymakers and established groups.

So, while status quo interest groups tend to have advantages over challenging interest groups, and low salience issues tend to advantage established interest groups, most recent studies of interest groups tend to emphasize a combination of several additional factors as critical for their influence and success (e.g., Austen-Smith 1993; Baumgartner et al 2009; Bernhagen, Dür, and Marshall 2014; McKay 2012). Money is central, with wealthier interest groups generally having advantages over those with fewer resources. Membership is also important, with larger groups having some advantages over smaller groups. Group cohesiveness and leadership are also factors, with advantages going to those with broadly shared focus and goals, enthusiasm, and effective leaders. Finally, as we have suggested, the political and policy climate is also important. As Kingdon (2002) suggests, the nature of the "problem stream" may empower some groups that seize on the problems or issues in the public eye, whether they be emergencies, crises, or other attention-getting matters.

Clearly, group politics is demanding and rough. It tends to pit people from new and challenging interest groups and social movements against people from more established and status quo–oriented groups. Success for new and challenging groups is an uphill battle because more established groups tend to enjoy considerable support from much of society and the government. However, challenging groups that succeed in gaining legitimacy and promoting their goals are able to affect the public and their beliefs, political participation, domestic politics, and the governmental policymaking process.

INFLUENCE STRATEGIES IN GROUP POLITICS

How do interest groups and social movements attempt to influence government policymaking? We can organize interest group strategies into direct and indirect approaches through which groups try to influence the political agenda, public beliefs and behavior, and electoral politics. They use access, information, money, and membership to advocate for their causes directly with policymakers, or more indirectly by trying to frame the public debate and influence public opinion. In some cases, well-established groups in more closed policy systems may be consulted by policymakers and participate in the policy process itself.

As political scientist Chung-in Moon (1988) makes clear, groups typically engage in four general strategies to influence the politics of foreign policy:

- The access-to-power approach
- The technocratic approach
- The coalition-building approach
- The grassroots mobilization approach

In perhaps the most well-known approach, groups **lobby** policymakers involved in the policy process. In the *access-to-power approach*, interest groups use high-powered power brokers, law firms, public relations firms, and consultants to gain direct access to top policymakers within the government. The *technocratic approach* is another form of direct lobbying, in which groups retain lawyers and technical consultants who use their expertise and contacts to influence mid-level decision makers in government, the media, and other relevant groups in society. The other two **lobbying strategies** used by groups and social movements attempt to affect the policymaking process more indirectly by targeting electoral politics and domestic politics in general. The *coalition-building approach* emphasizes the formation of group alliances based on mutual interests in order to politicize issues, get issues on the political agenda, and place pressure on the government's policymaking process. Finally, *the grassroots mobilization approach* attempts to rally mass support in order to politicize issues, affect electoral and group politics, and increase public pressure on the policymaking process. As Hedrick Smith (1988:ch. 9) points out, the old game of **inside politics** within the Washington community has been supplemented by a new game of **outside politics** since Vietnam.

Social movements and groups are politically active because of their potential impact on domestic politics and, more specifically, on the government's policymaking process. With respect to Congress, for example, a study by the Congressional Research Service (2001:38) concluded:

> Groups come to represent significant allies, or formidable opponents, when they are well organized; when they represent a sizable, well-educated, and middle- to upper-class constituency and when the positions they wish members of Congress to support are viewed as mainstream and respectable, entailing little or no political cost, and some political gains (e.g., support for Israel, Greece, Taiwan, Ireland, etc.); when the groups confront no significant internal counter-lobbies in the private sector or can count on the neutral stance of much of the public when an opinion is yet unformed.

As Smith (1988:71) explains, "Access is bread and butter . . . . Without it, your case doesn't get heard; you can't be a player in the power game. Obviously that's why corporations, unions, and lobbyists of all sorts pay enormous fees for prestigious Washington lawyers or pump millions into campaigning. They are buying access, if not more."

But outside politics has also been growing among groups, both domestically and transnationally. This has probably become most visible in the economic arena, where individuals and a variety of groups concerned with the effects of the globalization of market forces—such as on the environment, jobs and poverty, and growing national and global inequality—have been building coalitions and engaging in grassroots mobilization against multinational corporations, Western governments, and international organizations such as the International Monetary Fund (IMF), the World Bank, and the World Trade Organization (WTO). This has resulted in major political demonstrations against economic and political leaders, often when they meet to discuss the international economy. Examples include demonstrations at the World Trade Organization meetings in Seattle in 1999 (Aaronson 2002), and the "99%" or "Occupy Wall

Street" demonstrations against elitism, corporate greed, and the influence of the wealthy over government. So-called Tea Party demonstrations during the Obama administration are also examples of this phenomenon.

In other words, these social movements and interest groups try to influence the political agenda and policymaking by gaining access to policymakers and participating in policymaking, providing information, contributing campaign funds and other money, actively campaigning, engaging in litigation, demonstrating, attracting media coverage, networking with other groups, attempting to gain general public support, having individuals appointed to governmental positions, and undertaking international activity.

THE EVOLUTION OF GROUP POLITICS IN US FOREIGN POLICY

Interest groups and social movements have become increasingly active, consequential, and complex for the making of US foreign policy since World War II. Overall, group politics in foreign policy has gone through two major eras: (1) the Cold War years and (2) the post–Vietnam years to the present. Before World War II, the group process played a vital role in domestic politics and the policy process of US foreign policymaking, especially with respect to economic issues of trade and protectionism. For most interest groups and social movements, however, national security was relatively unimportant and "low" policy compared to economic and domestic issues. Those few groups that were devoted exclusively to foreign policy rarely had much influence over the policymaking process. This situation changed permanently with American intervention in World War II, the rise of the Cold War, and American hegemonic power abroad.

Interest Group Politics during the Cold War

During the 1940s and 1950s, new and established groups in American society became heavily involved in the foreign policymaking process. Most of these groups were overwhelmingly anti-communist and conservative in their foreign policy orientations, reinforced by the rise of extremely conservative social movements at the time, represented by the forces of McCarthyism. This contributed to the Cold War Consensus that benefited the presidential leadership, the expansion of the foreign policy bureaucracy, and a supportive Congress and public. Groups and movements that challenged containment policies from the political left did exist during the Cold War years. However, they were small in numbers and resources and constantly on the political defensive, remaining primarily outside the realm of mainstream domestic politics.

Foreign Policy and Cold War-Oriented Groups. The 1940s and 1950s resulted in the rise of numerous interest groups that became active in the politics of US foreign policy. These included (1) national security and public policy groups, (2) veterans and military support groups, (3) political and civic groups, (4) businesses and corporations, (5) labor unions, (6) religious groups, and (7) ethnic groups. There were certainly differences in perceptions among leaders and members of these groups concerning the intensity of the Soviet communist threat and the particulars of US national security policy; some were more anti-communist than others. However, these groups all tended to share a general Cold War internationalist orientation that formed the basis of a consensus in the making of US foreign policy.

National security and public policy groups became increasingly active and prominent in the making of US foreign policy during World War II and the Cold War. Among others, these groups included foundations, policy institutes, and think tanks such as the Carnegie Endowment for International Peace, the Committee on the Present Danger, the Council on Foreign Relations, the Ford and Rockefeller Foundations, the Foreign Policy Research Institute, and the Rand Corporation. Membership and involvement in most of these groups were limited to proponents of American Cold War policies, including select government officials (both current and former), business leaders, academics, journalists, and other opinion leaders within American society. The activities of these groups typically consisted of group seminars on important issues, involvement in policy research and proposals, and the publication and communication of members' work. Not only did these activities affect the beliefs of the attentive and mass publics, but many of these groups also became extremely important sources of ideas and personnel for the government during the Cold War years, especially the Council on Foreign Relations.

Headquartered in New York City, the **Council on Foreign Relations** not only provided a significant forum for generating ideas and policies for opinion leaders and government officials but also was a significant source of political recruitment. Many important government positions throughout the foreign policy bureaucracy were often filled by presidential appointment of council members, including those at the secretary level and the national security adviser. As Robert Schulzinger (1984) concluded in his history of the Council on Foreign Relations, entitled *The Wise Men of Foreign Affairs*, its members filled the role of a "professional clergy" for the foreign policy community in and out of government.

Veterans and military support organizations were staunchly anti-communist supporters of American Cold War policies and emphasized a large defense buildup and reliance on force. These organizations included the major veterans' organizations, such as the American Legion and the Veterans of Foreign Wars, and military support organizations, such as the Navy League and the American Ordnance Association.

Broad-based **political and civic organizations** also became participants in the anti-communist foreign policy consensus in American politics. Americans for Democratic Action, for example, was launched in the early 1950s by prominent American Democrats and liberals as a means to support the government's Cold War policies.

Business and labor groups were also part of the consensus supporting US foreign policy. Business had long played a prominent role in American politics and government, especially since the rise of industrialization and the development of modern corporations. Much of this was because business leaders were regularly recruited into government policymaking positions by political leaders and because of the increasing scale of activities of American business abroad, especially in Latin America. With World War II and the onset of the Cold War, business groups such as the Chamber of Commerce, the Committee for Economic Development, and the National Association of Manufacturers became strong supporters of the government's containment policy. Industry involvement in foreign policy was reinforced by the growing role of big business in defense production. As a result, a type of big business and government partnership developed in support of US national security and economic policy during the Cold War years.

For example, as American banks and companies became increasingly multinationalized following World War II, they located in countries where there was a strong US governmental presence abroad, such as in Latin America and Europe. One can debate whether the American "flag" led the American "dollar" abroad, or vice versa. Regardless, both business and government were driven to promote an open door or free market ethos in US foreign policy during the Cold War years. The government-business relationship was generally interactive and supportive: The increasing global presence of American government and the relocation of American multinational industry abroad led to greater mutual dependency between American business and government. US governmental actions to assist postwar reconstruction of Western Europe through the Marshall Plan also relied on American private investment in the region; in addition, America's military and economy became increasingly dependent on continued access to oil by American petroleum companies, especially in the Middle East. As Michael Stoff (1980:208) concluded, private corporations, not the government, "became the agents of national policy" (see also Ikenberry 1988; Yergin 1990). In turn, American multinational corporations expected the US government to promote American private investment abroad and prevent nationalization by foreign governments.

Organized labor was also a strong supporter of anti-communism at home and abroad. This fact may come as a surprise to many Americans given the popular impression of labor-management conflict and labor's pre–World War II history. However, by the 1930s, as part of Roosevelt's New Deal policies, the government officially recognized the right of workers to form unions, and the often-fierce opposition to unions by business and government abated. More important, organized labor's growing legitimacy and moderation in goals, the postwar return of economic prosperity, Republican and McCarthyist attacks against New Deal policies and unionization, and the national security demands of World War II and the Cold War produced unions that were much more comfortable and supportive of the status quo.

After World War II, the **American Federation of Labor–Congress of Industrial Organizations (AFL-CIO)**, the umbrella organization to which most American unions belonged during the 1950s, strongly supported the government's Cold War policies at home and abroad. The AFL-CIO Institute for Free Labor Development was active, for example, in supporting anti-communist unionization and movements in Latin America (and often worked in conjunction with the CIA). Hence, while many American unions historically were the source of liberalism and the political left, they too became part of the anti-communist consensus during the Cold War (Fraser and Gerstle 1989).

Religious and ethnic groups also played prominent anti-communist roles during the Cold War. Religious movements and groups have always played a powerful role throughout American history. As Garry Wills (1990:25) argues, "Religion has been at the center of our major political crises, which are always moral crises—the supporting and opposing of wars, of slavery, of corporate power, of civil rights, of sexual codes, of 'the West,' of American separatism and claims to empire." Given this background, it is perhaps not surprising that religion played a prominent role in the rise of the anti-communist consensus during the post–World War II years. For example, the Catholic Church historically was extremely critical of communism and its atheistic views, rallying American Catholics behind the government's Cold War policies. The late 1940s and early 1950s also witnessed the rise of Protestant fundamentalism against the secular trends of modern society, a movement that provided support for McCarthyism during the Cold War years.

The United States is also a country of great ethnic diversity, and ethnic groups have actively influenced the making of US foreign policy. For example, the Soviet Union's domination of Eastern Europe provoked a strong anti-communist response from ethnic groups with ties to the region. Polish Americans, reinforced by their Catholicism, were particularly vocal over the fate of Poland. Furthermore, they also represented a large bloc of potential voters in a number of key industrial states. This domestic political background helps to explain why Stalin's eventual consolidation of power in Poland was one of the important postwar developments during the late 1940s in hardening attitudes within the Truman administration and throughout society around the issue of anti-communism.

The famed **China lobby**, or Taiwan lobby, gained great prominence during the Cold War years. The China lobby consisted of Nationalist Chinese officials and Americans, including government officials, Protestant missionaries, China watchers and journalists, American business leaders, and a broad coalition of diverse anti-communist groups, such as the American China Policy Association, the Committee to Defend America by Aiding Anti-Communist China, and the Committee for One Million (against the admission of communist China into the United Nations). These groups shared a common concern over the so-called fall of China and identified with the nationalist Chinese government in Taiwan. Participants within the China lobby tended to emphasize the greater importance of Asia over Europe as a market, for national security reasons as symbolized by the Korean War, and for the future of Christianity. Members of the China lobby attacked the Truman administration for its Eurocentric and inadequate foreign policies, played a prominent role in the rise of McCarthyism, and helped forge an anti-communist consensus throughout society and the government during the Cold War years. Their efforts help to explain why American presidents and their advisers were always more concerned about the political threat posed by the right than by those on the left (Bachrack 1976; Koen 1974; US Congress, House Committee on Foreign Affairs 1982).

In sum, the prevalent interest groups during the Cold War together helped to promote and reinforce the development of an anti-communist consensus, a strong national security, and a free market ethos throughout American society, in electoral and domestic politics, and in the governmental policymaking process. The prominence of these groups and their Cold War orientation contributed to development of a consensus behind a strong anti-communist foreign policy, along with presidential leadership, the expansion of the national security and economic bureaucracies, and the development of a supportive and bipartisan Congress—all with strong public support throughout society and the domestic political environment.

The Military-Industrial-Scientific Infrastructure. Before World War II, few institutions within the government or throughout American society were oriented toward foreign affairs and national security. World War II changed this situation dramatically and permanently.

Almost overnight, the US government redirected itself to waging a global war in which the military expanded enormously, civilian agencies grew to assist the president in fighting the conflict, and the economy and society took on a war footing to provide the necessary personnel, equipment, and services to achieve allied victory. In this process, a military-industrial-scientific infrastructure began to develop. Unlike previous US wars, after World War II the US military demobilized for only a short time. With the rise of anti-communism and the Cold War, the United States sustained, and even expanded, this infrastructure, which has played a prominent role in defense politics and the making of US foreign policy ever since.

The **military-industrial complex** is a term popularized by President Dwight Eisenhower during his farewell address to the nation (see "A Closer Look: Eisenhower Warns of a Military-Industrial Complex"). He used it to describe the existence of various segments of society with complementary interests that were mutually dependent on one another and together played a vital role in the politics of US foreign policy. Instead of a small collection of individuals within the military and private industry who conspired to dominate American national security policy against the wishes of the American people, Eisenhower argued that a broad complex of private, academic, and governmental bureaucratic institutions was an inevitable outcome of a society permanently mobilized for war, necessitated by containment and deterrence policies. Hence, **military-industrial-scientific infrastructure** (or national security infrastructure) is a more accurate term than military-industrial complex (Yarmolinsky 1971).

A Closer Look

EISENHOWER WARNS OF A MILITARY-INDUSTRIAL COMPLEX

On January 17, 1961, President Dwight Eisenhower, former general and commander of all allied forces in the European theater during World War II, made his farewell address to the American people, imploring them to be knowledgeable citizens alert to the threats and opportunities that the United States faced both abroad and at home. It is in this speech that the term "military-industrial complex" was first used, as Eisenhower warned Americans of the dangers it posed for the workings of democracy. Because he was retiring from public office, Eisenhower's farewell address may have represented a public airing of his most personal thoughts and feelings.

In his address, Eisenhower warned of a permanent military-industrial complex: "A vital element in keeping the peace is our military establishment. Our arms must be mighty, ready for instant action, so that no potential aggressor may be tempted to risk his own destruction." Yet as he pointed out,

> Our military organization today bears little relation to that known by any of my predecessors in peacetime, or indeed by the fighting men of World War II or Korea. Until the latest of our world conflicts, the United States had no armaments industry. American makers of plowshares could, with time and as required, make swords as well.

But according to Eisenhower

> We can no longer risk emergency improvisation of national defense; we have been compelled to create a permanent

(Continued)

(Continued)

armaments industry of vast proportions. Added to this, three and a half million men and women are directly engaged in the defense establishment. This conjunction of an immense military establishment and a large arms industry is "new" in the American experience. The total influence—economic, political, even spiritual—is felt in every city, every State house, every office of the Federal government.

Although Eisenhower recognized "the imperative need for this development," he also believed that Americans "must not fail to comprehend its grave implications. Our toil, resources and livelihood are all involved; so is the very structure of our society."

Eisenhower, therefore, emphasized the need for vigilance: "In the councils of government, we must guard against the acquisition of unwarranted influence, whether sought or unsought, by the military-industrial complex. The potential for the disastrous rise of misplaced power exists and will persist." Eisenhower continued

We must never let the weight of this combination endanger our liberties or democratic processes. We should take nothing for granted. Only an alert and knowledgeable citizenry can compel the proper meshing of the huge industrial and military machinery of defense with our peaceful methods and goals, so that security and liberty may prosper together.

Eisenhower also warned of the threat of the connection to science and academic that this complex raised:

Akin to, and largely responsible for the sweeping changes in our industrial-military posture, has been the technological revolution during the recent decades. In this revolution, research has become central; it also becomes more formalized, complex, and costly. A steadily increasing share is conducted for, by, or at the direction of, the federal government.

This technological revolution has changed the nature of academia and the conduct of science. As Eisenhower explained, "Today, the solitary inventor, tinkering in his shop, has been overshadowed by task forces of scientists in laboratories and testing fields. In the same fashion, the free university, historically the fountainhead of free ideas and scientific discovery, has experienced a revolution in the conduct of research." One of the consequences is that "partly because of the huge costs involved, a government contract becomes virtually a substitute for intellectual curiosity." Given these changes, Eisenhower warned that

the prospect of domination of the nation's scholars by federal employment, project allocations, and the power of money is ever present—and is gravely to be regarded. Yet, in holding scientific research and discovery in respect, as we should, we must also be alert to the equal and opposite danger that public policy could itself become the captive of a scientific-technological elite.

What does President Eisenhower's warning tell us about the nature of US foreign policymaking?

Source: President Dwight D. Eisenhower, "Farewell Address" (January 17, 1961).

This infrastructure involves four major segments of society: (1) the military establishment within the executive branch, (2) industry and business, (3) Congress, and (4) academia and the scientific community. Each segment has complementary interests: Members of the military establishment want weaponry and equipment to engage in their national security missions, which during the Cold War meant contributing to the containment strategy.

Industry wants to expand and make money by building and selling the equipment to the military. Members of Congress want military bases and defense industries in their districts to provide jobs and local economic benefits and, thus, secure the votes of happy constituents. Scientists want the prestige and prominence that came with large grants and direct involvement in government and policymaking.

As we discussed in Chapter 5, the military establishment, especially the Department of Defense, grew enormously in size and scope as a result of World War II and the Cold War. Demands for personnel, weaponry, and equipment were equally enormous. The government relied on its own production process, supervised by the Atomic Energy Commission and operated by private industry, for building nuclear weapons. However, the military contracted out to private industry to meet its needs in virtually all other areas, from conventional weapons to uniforms to base construction.

American industry became directly involved in equipping the military as a result of the Cold War. This transformation began with US entry into World War II, when the production of civilian materials and services changed to military production to defeat Germany and Japan. Large US companies such as General Motors, Chrysler, McDonnell Douglas, and Boeing retooled their assembly lines to produce tanks and bombers rather than cars and commercial airplanes. With the rise of the Cold War, these same companies continued working for the government and the Defense Department. By the 1950s, many Fortune 500 companies were **defense contractors** for the US government. Some companies, such as General Dynamics, Lockheed and Martin-Marietta (now merged as Lockheed Martin), and Rockwell International (now broken up into multiple spin-off companies), became mostly dependent on defense production. For other companies, such as General Electric, defense work was only a part of their business. Smaller, local businesses also became involved in defense work through the subcontracting of weapons systems or provision of services at local military bases. Taken together, defense-related industries provided millions of jobs for Americans, gaining the support of organized labor and workers in general (see Barnet 1985; Hartung 2012; Ledbetter 2011). These relationships were reinforced by the development of a **revolving door system** through which members of the military were hired by the defense industry upon retirement, defense industry leaders were appointed to important positions within the Department of Defense, and so on (US Congress 1989a).

Congress also helped to reinforce these "**iron triangle**" networks of relationships that developed in defense politics. Members of Congress had to approve the defense programs and budget for the government. This role gave them considerable power, especially within the armed services and appropriations committees. In return for political support, the Pentagon and defense industry built their military bases and businesses in the states and districts of key members of Congress. Not surprisingly, the military came to operate hundreds of bases located in every state, and major weapons systems were typically subcontracted out to dozens of businesses throughout the country. Although many basing and contracting decisions may have been made for sound national security and financial reasons, they also were made in order to win the political support of members of Congress. In this way, members of Congress were able to claim responsibility for economic growth and jobs back home, attracting local constituent support for their reelection.

Although it has typically been deemphasized in discussions of the military-industrial complex, academia and the scientific community represent the final element in the military-industrial-scientific infrastructure. The ties between science and the government date back to the nineteenth century. However, the major drive to bring scientists together to work for the US government began with the Manhattan Project, the effort to develop the atomic bomb during World War II (Rhodes 1986). Since that time, scientists in physics, chemistry, and other natural sciences have been employed by government, academia, and research and policy institutes to provide the know-how for designing weapons and turning ideas into reality. Led by the more prominent universities, such as Yale University, Massachusetts Institute of Technology, Stanford University, and the University of California at Berkeley, the **militarization of research** occurred as social scientists and other academics provided many of the ideas that became the basis of US national security policy during the Cold War years, such as nuclear deterrence theory, the theory of limited war, intelligence analysis and operations, counterinsurgency warfare, and Third World development strategies for nation-building and modernization (Kaplan 1983; Latham 2000; Leslie 1994; Packenham 1973; Simpson 1994; Winks 1996). In fact, scholarship in international relations proliferated and graduate programs in international studies grew to become a key source of recruitment and expertise for US government foreign affairs personnel (Hoffmann 1977).

The net result of these activities was that each organized segment of society could claim that its activities contributed to strengthening American national security while they were enmeshed in the politics of national defense:

> The influence of politics on national defense is so pervasive, so deeply embedded at every level, that it becomes difficult even to identify. Virtually every American is involved, directly or indirectly. Selfish political and economic interests in military affairs are often carefully wrapped in the American flag, and defended with the most elegant, sophisticated, and technically complex rationales.... Politics influences literally thousands of decisions that constantly must be made to create the treaties, strategies, forces, bases, and weapons that collectively make up our national defense. (Kotz 1988:viii)

The development of a national security infrastructure and the politics of national defense contributed not only to the development of the anti-communist consensus and a permanent large military establishment in support of the requirements of the containment strategy during the Cold War era but also to waste, corruption, vested interests, and resistance to any challenges to the status quo. This also had a major impact in exacerbating the tensions between the demands of national security and the requirements of democracy. Aware of this possibility, Eisenhower's farewell address to the country warned Americans to be "knowledgeable and alert" concerning the consequences of a military-industrial complex for the functioning of American democracy (see "A Closer Look," earlier in this chapter).

The Foreign Policy Establishment. The Cold War years also saw the rise of a **foreign policy establishment**, an informal network of prominent, like-minded individuals who shared an anti-communist consensus and moved in and out of high-level policymaking positions within the executive branch, exerting great influence on the making of US foreign policy. They have been referred to as the "best and the brightest," "national security managers," and the "wise men." By constantly shifting between high-level positions in government and in the private world, they also provided critical bridges among the president, the national security bureaucracy, and key groups and institutions throughout American society.

The members of the foreign policy establishment shared five commonalities (Hodgson 1973). First, they shared a common history. Contrary to popular opinion, this common history was not principally membership in the upper class, although "it may help you to rise in the establishment if you have inherited wealth, or family connections with powerful men in it, or an Ivy League education" (Hodgson 1973:6–7). Rather, they consisted of hundreds of individuals of varying degrees of prominence who came to know each other (or of each other) through governmental service, work outside the government, and social interaction. The crucial common experience was World War II. They were initially recruited to staff the war effort in the War Department, the State Department, and the Office of Strategic Services (OSS). It wasn't long before many of these people began to interact with each other and work together, forming working networks of relationships that continued after the war.

Second, the foreign policy establishment shared common emphases on anti-isolationism and anti-communism in foreign policy. This approach to foreign policy was heavily conditioned by a realpolitik—or power politics—view of the world in which states competed for power, wealth, and status, where threats to international stability and order came from unsatisfied and revolutionary great powers, and the threat and use of force (more than diplomacy) were considered the most effective instruments of statecraft. They were particularly concerned with the threat of the Soviet Union and communist expansion in Europe but had little fear of domestic communism like the political right and McCarthyism.

Third, the foreign policy establishment shared a commitment to global moral and political leadership. They "wanted to succeed Britain as the military and economic guarantor and moral leader of an enlightened, liberal, democratic, and capitalist world order" who felt that the postwar years represented the "American century" (Hodgson 1973:11). This outlook probably reached its height working under President Kennedy, where

> they carried with them an exciting sense of American elitism, a sense that the best men had been summoned forth from the country to harness this dream to a new American nationalism, bringing a new, strong, dynamic spirit to our historic role in world affairs, not necessarily to bring the American dream to reality here at home, but to bring it to reality elsewhere in the world. (Halberstam 1969:41,100; see also Isaacson and Thomas 1986)

Fourth, the establishment shared a preference for the political center. As Hodgson (1973:12) put it, "The characteristic men of the establishment—Stimson, McCloy, Acheson, Rusk, Bundy—have always seen themselves as the men of judicious, pragmatic wisdom, avoiding ideology and steering the middle course between the Yahoos of the right and the impractical sentimentality of the left." This reflected a long tradition going back to Teddy Roosevelt, of "an aristocracy come to power, convinced of its own disinterested quality, believing itself above both petty partisan interest and material greed" and viewing their role as service (Halberstam 1969:49)—most considered themselves moderate Republicans or Democrats, and many never even registered to vote.

Finally, the establishment's preferred "technique" was to operate out of public view and within the executive branch, especially the White House. Members of the establishment virtually never ran for elective office, and they tended to be distrustful and fearful of mass opinion. They were usually appointed by the president to policymaking positions within the foreign policy bureaucracy, revolving continually from government to the private world and back through membership in prominent foreign policy groups, most notably the Council on Foreign Relations. They played roles in every post–World War II administration and contributed to a fundamental consistency and consensus through the Vietnam War.

INTEREST GROUP POLITICS AFTER VIETNAM

As the liberal-conservative ideological consensus that dominated the Cold War years collapsed during the 1960s and 1970s, it was replaced by greater ideological, electoral, and group competition in American politics. The breakdown of the foreign policy consensus affected the post–Vietnam role of group politics in the making of US foreign policy in three ways, with two of the patterns representing change and one representing continuity: (1) The foreign policy establishment collapsed; (2) there was a proliferation of groups, ideological diversity and partisanship, and political activism; yet (3) the military-industrial-scientific infrastructure continued to pervade society. Thus, some Cold War patterns continued but were accompanied by new patterns of change. These patterns generally persisted and intensified in the post–Cold War and post-9/11 years.

Collapse of the Foreign Policy Establishment

The last time individuals within the foreign policy establishment would operate with a consensus and act in unison was in March 1968. The war in Vietnam was going badly, and the country was being torn apart at home. As he had in the past, President Johnson convened a meeting of his major advisers and a group of senior policy advisers from outside the government, who were referred to as the "wise men." Johnson met with this collection of prominent individuals, many of whom had held high-level government positions in previous administrations under Presidents Truman, Eisenhower, and Kennedy, to discuss what to do about US policy in Vietnam. In effect, the participants represented a who's who of the foreign policy establishment, and they surprised President Johnson by telling him that they no longer supported further escalation of the war. According to Godfrey Hodgson (1973:24), the participants were discouraged by the lack of progress in the war and the relative decline of the United States economically, so they "made a characteristic decision not to put good money after bad."

The consensus in foreign policy views of the establishment had collapsed and splintered, contributing to the ideological and foreign policy diversity that would permeate among the elite and mass publics. By the early 1970s, the establishment was bitterly divided over Vietnam and the future of US foreign policy. Walt Rostow and Dean Rusk, Johnson's national security adviser and secretary of state, continued to believe that the war was justified and that no major avoidable mistakes had been made in the way it was waged.

Others, such as McGeorge Bundy, Kennedy's national security adviser, believed that the war was justified but that mistakes were made in its conduct. However, some members of the establishment, such as Clark Clifford, adviser to Truman and secretary of defense under Johnson, believed that the Vietnam War was a mistake. Some, such as Paul Warnke and George Ball, high-level Johnson officials in the Defense and State Departments, held not only that the Vietnam War was a mistake but that the pursuit of containment in a non-European context was misguided, as well. Finally, people such as Daniel Ellsberg, a prominent Defense Department official, believed that containment and US intervention throughout the world was not only inappropriate but also a fundamentally unjust policy. These prominent individuals within American society would continue to receive attention and exercise influence, but they would no longer do so as a unified force in support of America's Cold War policies. Instead, they would compete with each other for influence in the making of US foreign policy by choosing sides in the group politics since Vietnam.

As the foreign policy establishment collapsed, the Vietnam War also generated new movements from both the left and the right. From the left, an **antiwar movement** representing a broad coalition of Americans united against the escalation and continuation of the Vietnam War emerged during the mid-1960s. At its height, the antiwar movement was supported by a large segment of society and staged peaceful demonstrations involving millions of people throughout the country. Not only did more than half a million men refuse to be drafted, but more and more soldiers went AWOL (absent without leave) and service people joined the peace marches as well (Benedetti and Chatfield 1990; Gitlin 1987; Powers 1973).

By 1968, the Tet Offensive; the assassinations of Martin Luther King Jr. and Robert F. Kennedy, two powerful advocates for peace; and the results of the 1968 Democratic National Convention (in Chicago)—which produced the nomination of Hubert Humphrey, the endorsement of Lyndon Johnson's Vietnam policies, and dramatic opposition efforts in the streets of Chicago—combined to further alienate and radicalize members of the antiwar movement. The domestic conflicts and violence also further splintered an unbelieving public that was watching the war at home on television (the role of the media is the focus of the next chapter). As a result, much of the public—the so-called silent majority—would turn against the demonstrators and toward Richard Nixon, the Republican presidential nominee. The civil rights and antiwar movements also were responsible for generating new social movements and politically active groups in areas such as feminism, native American and Hispanic rights, gay rights, consumer rights (and Ralph Nader), and environmentalism. Many women, for example, were active in the civil rights movement, the antiwar movement, and the new left, an important element in the mobilization of the modern women's movement (Evans 1979). The pro-choice, nuclear freeze, antiapartheid, and human rights movements that arose in prominence after the 1970s are legacies of the civil rights and antiwar movements (Epstein 1991; Waller 1987). Overall, liberalism and the new left became active and influential forces in group and domestic politics in the 1960s.

The events and social movements of the 1960s also contributed to the resurgence of movements and groups reflecting conservatism and the **political right**. Conservatives and members of the political right were aghast over the loss of Vietnam to communism, the increasing power of the Soviet Union relative to the United States, the growth of government intervention in the economy and the welfare state represented by President Johnson's Great Society programs, the rise of individualism and sexual promiscuity, and the decline of law and order. Many conservatives believed that America was in a state of "moral decline" caused by the rise of liberalism and the left. Some—including disgruntled liberals and leftists such as Irving Kristol and Norman Podhoretz, eventually known as neoconservatives, or neocons—became concerned by the dovishness of the left and what they characterized as the left's failure to confront and challenge communism, and they abandoned the left and pressed for more aggressive and militant foreign policy. Hence, social movements representing broad coalitions of conservative-oriented groups within society arose in support of anti-communism, private enterprise, and social issues such as school prayer and abortion (Blumenthal 1986; Himmelstein 1991; Nash 1976).

Expansion of Group Politics

The rise of social movements of the left and right led not only to the collapse of the anti-communist consensus and the foreign policy establishment but also to the expansion of group politics. Fed by dealignment and the weakening of the two major political parties, the events and movements of the 1960s and 1970s resulted in the proliferation of groups in American politics; increased ideological diversity, competition, and partisanship among groups; and more individual political participation in social movements and group politics. As one former member of Congress characterized the years after 1965,

> The last four decades have . . . seen a proliferation of groups outside of government seeking to influence foreign policy: the business community, labor unions, ethnic constituencies, nonprofit organizations, foreign countries, former officials, international organizations, think tanks, universities—and the list goes on. All of these groups and individuals seek to advance their views on Capitol Hill and in the White House. (Hamilton 2006:273)

This trend, which began in the wake of Vietnam, accelerated after the end of the Cold War.

Let us consider some of the more salient features of this explosion of group activity. Since the 1970s, there has been, first of all, a dramatic expansion in the number of **issue- and cause-oriented groups**—including single-issue groups—seeking to influence US foreign policymakers. For example, liberal and left-leaning groups have actively supported a US foreign policy that promotes human rights and self-determination, arms control and disarmament, the eradication of Third World hunger and poverty, antiapartheid, and global environmentalism. At the same time, more conservative and right-wing groups first emphasized the problems associated with the expansion of Soviet power and communism, the need for a US defense buildup, and support for Third World allies and market economies abroad in the 1970s and 1980s, and then emphasized other security threats, the preservation of American power, sovereignty, and other causes in the 1990s.

After the 9/11 attacks, the left and right bitterly divided over the proper ways to counter the threat of terrorism, the liberty-security trade-offs of domestic measures to reduce the risk of terrorist attacks, and the role of diplomacy and force in US foreign policy. Political, economic, and social developments since 2005 produced intense partisan differences over how to address the economic collapse and recession within the US and the global political economy. Even more recently, anti-immigration groups have emerged and pressed hard within the Trump administration and Congress on border security, immigration, and related matters (e.g., Goodman 2018; Shear 2019). Hence, the Cold War Consensus was replaced by considerable national fragmentation, competition, and partisanship, especially among the elite and attentive publics. This prompted more activist Americans and interest groups to attempt to influence American politics and US foreign policy, both in national security and economic affairs.

Another area of expanded group activity is in the efforts of foreign policy organizations. For example, groups such as the Carnegie Endowment for International Peace, the Council on Foreign Relations, the Foreign Policy Research Institute, and the Rand Corporation continued to function after Vietnam and were complemented by new groups such as the Trilateral Commission. However, since the 1970s, these centrist groups were joined by more conservative groups such as the American Enterprise Institute, the Heritage Foundation, the Hoover Institution, the Center for Strategic and International Studies, a new Committee on the Present Danger (formed in the 1970s against the Soviet threat and reborn in 2004 against the threat of Islamic terrorism), and the Joseph Coors and John Scaife Foundations. At the same time, more liberal groups were formed and became prominent as well, including the Arms Control Association, Brookings Institution, the Center for Defense Information, the Institute for Policy Studies, the World Policy Institute, and Worldwatch Institute. These institutions were also joined by those advocating a semi-isolationist orientation, such as the more libertarian Cato Institute.

By the late 1960s and early 1970s, old **think tanks** began to grow and new ones were established, and these were increasingly prone to take independent policy initiatives (as opposed to rely on contract work). Overall, of the more than 100 or so policy research groups, or think tanks, in Washington, DC (some having fewer than a dozen employees, others employing up to 250), two-thirds were set up after 1970. According to Ricci (1993:208),

> Every year, these institutes conduct thousands of conferences, luncheons, forums, and seminars, while publishing hundreds of books and innumerable pamphlets, reports, newsletters, backgrounders, and occasional essays. In addition, their members write scores of op-ed articles that appear in dozens of newspapers, and their most articulate fellows perform as commentators on radio and television news programs, often coast-to-coast.

The foreign policy specialists of these groups increasingly came to wage campaigns in support of or against the policy directions of the administration in power. In fact, many of these think tanks became fertile grounds for administrations of one political stripe or the other to recruit personnel. For example, the Heritage Foundation supplied many people for the Reagan administration and the Trump administration, while the Clinton administration turned to the Brookings Institution. The American Enterprise Institute was a key source for the neoconservatives of George W. Bush's administration, while Barack Obama turned to Brookings, the Carnegie Endowment for International Peace, and the newer Atlantic Council and the Center for American Progress. The net result is that since Vietnam, foreign policy expertise and personnel are no longer monopolized by a few old establishment groups, a development that reflects greater ideological diversity, among intellectuals as well (see Table 12.1 for a list of the most prominent groups or think tanks involved in foreign policy).

A third area for the expansion of group activity involved **commercial interests**. As the anti-communist and free trade consensus shattered in the aftermath of the Vietnam War and the Bretton Woods international economic system no longer functioned as originally intended, labor and business (and governmental) interests increasingly splintered. For instance, the AFL-CIO turned increasingly against free trade (such

TABLE 12.1

Major Foreign Policy Think Tanks

Name Location	Year Began	Issue Orientation	Ideological Orientation
Carnegie Endowment for International Peace Washington, DC	1910	Foreign	Liberal
Foreign Policy Association New York	1918	Foreign	Centrist
Hoover Institution Palo Alto, CA	1919	Domestic and foreign	Conservative
Council on Foreign Relations New York	1921	Foreign	Centrist
Brookings Institution Washington, DC	1927	Domestic and foreign	Liberal
American Enterprise Institution Washington, DC	1943	Domestic and foreign	Conservative
Rand Corporation Santa Monica, CA	1948	Domestic and foreign	Centrist
Aspen Institute Washington, DC	1951	Foreign	Liberal
Foreign Policy Research Institute Philadelphia	1955	Foreign	Conservative
Hudson Institute New York	1961	Domestic and foreign	Conservative
Atlantic Council Washington, DC	1961	Foreign	Liberal
Center for Strategic and International Studies Washington, DC	1962	Foreign	Conservative

Name Location	Year Began	Issue Orientation	Ideological Orientation
Institute for Policy Studies Washington, DC	1963	Domestic and foreign	Liberal
Center for Defense Information Washington, DC	1972	Foreign	Liberal
Trilateral Commission New York	1973	Domestic and foreign	Centrist
Heritage Foundation Washington, DC	1974	Domestic and foreign	Conservative
World Watch Institute Washington, DC	1974	Foreign	Liberal
Cato Institute Washington, DC	1977	Domestic and foreign	Non-internationalist
Institute for International Economics Washington, DC	1981	Foreign	Liberal
Carter Center Atlanta	1982	Domestic and foreign	Liberal
World Policy Institute New York	1983	Foreign	Liberal
Center for American Progress Washington, DC	2003	Domestic and foreign	Liberal

as the NAFTA negotiations) in order to protect American jobs as foreign economic competition increased. Within the business community, domestic-oriented companies began to push for protectionist measures by the government as large American multi-national corporations, such as major US banks and other financial institutions, became the champions of free trade and globalization (Barnet and Muller 1976; Milner 1989).

On the question of policy toward China, especially during the debates over trade, sanctions, and normal trade relations in the 1990s, for example, businesses in the aviation and automobile sectors, including Boeing, Ford, General Motors, and others, were advocates of normal trade relations and opponents of sanctions; other businesses, such as the music and entertainment industry, opposed normal trade relations. Labor, which generally opposed normal trade, also worried about Chinese countersanctions that might cost American jobs (Rourke and Clark 1998). One well-known observer noted this vast array of competing commercial interests and bemoaned the fragmentation of foreign policy purposes it spawned, worrying that broad strategies and purposes that characterized foreign policy in the Cold War were lost to commercial particularism (Huntington 1997).

Not surprisingly, as commercial interests have multiplied, their presence in Washington, DC, also has grown substantially. Before World War II, there were no more than a dozen trade associations in town; by the 1960s, however, about 100 corporations and 1,000 trade associations maintained offices in Washington. By the 1990s, there were more than 1,300 corporations and 3,500 trade associations lobbying government and promoting their special interests. In fact, in the late 1980s, more than 80,000 people in Washington worked for trade associations alone (Judis 1989:7). These numbers have only increased in the twenty-first century, as more and more businesses and sectors of the US economy are engaged in international trade. Indeed, according to Open Secrets, the top-spending lobbyist every year from 2000 to 2018 was the US Chamber of Commerce, which spent $95 million in 2018. Thus, commercial interests continue to exert a heavy influence on governmental policies but in a much more complex and contradictory fashion than prevailed during the Cold War. Many of these corporations and the interest groups representing them contributed to decreasing governmental regulation and oversight.

A fourth area of increased group activity and fragmentation involves religious and ethnic lobbies. With respect to religious groups, one scholar put it this way:

> While religious lobbies were particularly prominent on foreign policy issues during the Vietnam War in the 1960s and 1970s and over El Salvador, Nicaragua and the nuclear freeze issues in the 1980s, these groups have not declined in activism. Indeed, the end of the Cold War has actually sparked renewed activity and involvement to infuse a moral and ethical component into American foreign policy. (McCormick 1998)

Like the issue- and cause-oriented groups we discussed earlier, religious groups run the gamut from conservative to liberal concerns and have actively promoted policies to contend with disease and suffering, promote human rights, fight religious persecution, and oppose family planning and access to abortions overseas (Hertzke 1988; Martin 1999). Over the past ten years, for example, religious groups were heavily active and instrumental in the passage of the International Religious Freedom Act of 1998, the Sudan Peace Act of 2002, the North Korea Human Act of 2004, and a variety of new initiatives in foreign aid designed to alleviate poverty, disease, and suffering in the developing world.

With respect to ethnic groups, since Vietnam "the number of politically active ethnic groups has grown tremendously, and their lobbying techniques have become much more sophisticated. The ethnic groups with the most influence are those that are well funded and have large numbers nationally, heavy concentrations in particular areas of the country, or positions of power in society" (Hamilton 2006:273). Even as the old China lobby declined as a force, especially with the establishment of diplomatic relations with the People's Republic of China in 1978, new ethnic groups grew in prominence. For example, Greek American groups promoted the American embargo of Turkey during the 1970s; African American groups played an important role in the antiapartheid forces leading to US sanctions against South Africa; and Cuban American groups remained hostile to Fidel Castro and continue to oppose any normalization in American-Cuban relations to the present day.

Some of the key factors that contribute to influence by ethnic groups include the group's size, commitment, resources, skills, whether it seeks to preserve the status quo or overturn it, and the range and power of interests who support or oppose the group's preferences (Rubenzer 2008). Not only does ethnicity play a role in group politics, but politicians sometimes are very sensitive to the political clout of ethnic groups for electoral politics, especially in key states (see "A Different Perspective: How Powerful Is the Israeli or Jewish Lobby?").

A Different Perspective

HOW POWERFUL IS THE ISRAELI OR JEWISH LOBBY?

The so-called Israeli or Jewish lobby, which includes a variety of individuals and groups, such as the American Israel Public Affairs Committee (AIPAC), is widely considered the most powerful of all the ethnic groups. It was not really powerful, well organized, or connected until after the 1967 Arab-Israeli War. A controversial article entitled "Unrestricted Access: What the Israel Lobby Wants, It Too Often Gets" and a subsequent book by John Mearsheimer and Stephen Walt (2006, 2007) credit the Israeli lobby with having gained the backing of members of Congress, as well as the president, to provide unwavering support and assistance to the state of Israel—to the tune of $3 billion of US foreign assistance per year for the state of Israel and its 6 million citizens—as well as being the major provider of military weaponry. This book set off a political firestorm, although the existence and clout of the Israeli lobby has been a recurring controversy over the years. Indeed, controversial comments in 2019 by Rep. Ilhan Omar, a freshman Democrat from Minnesota about the influence of AIPAC ignited a fierce round of discussion and criticism.

New York Senator Charles Schumer, a Democrat, described three levels of Israeli political strength in the United States: "The most pro-Israeli group in America is the Congress. Next are the American people. The White House is least of the three because they have to deal with all of the Arab states and the variety of foreign policy factors at work" (Diamond and Piec 2002). Presidents nevertheless have usually been strong supporters of Israel, especially publicly, given the number of Jews in such critical states as California, New York, and Florida. Given this context, presidents have had to manage a difficult balancing act between supporting Israel and trying to act as a third party and even-handed broker to help resolve the long-standing Arab-Israeli conflict in the Middle East.

President Carter was the most successful in beginning the peace process with the Camp David Accords in 1978. President George W. Bush was considerably more pro-Israeli and struggled as conflict intensified between Israel and the Palestinians (and Arabs), especially after the 9/11 attacks. Early in his first year, President Obama strongly signaled a more even-handed approach, insisting on a viable two-state solution and a cessation in Israeli settlement-building in the West Bank. While pressuring Israeli leaders for concessions, Obama also took a more open and conciliatory tone toward Palestinians and the Arab world and visited a number of Arab and Muslim countries in an effort to generate early progress toward a peaceful resolution. President Trump has been conspicuously pro-Israel and, in fact, pro-Netanyahu—expressing very public support for long-serving Israeli Prime Minister Benjamin Netanyahu and his policies. Trump even took the unusual step of publicly endorsing Netanyahu's efforts to form a coalition government following the Israeli leader's narrow election victory in 2019.

How does the Israeli or Jewish lobby influence US foreign policymaking and affect efforts to pursue a peaceful settlement to the Arab-Israeli conflict in Palestine and the Middle East?

Another prominent ethnic lobby represents Cuban Americans, whose influence over US policy toward Cuba is frequently discussed. This is partly due to the concentration of Cuban Americans in electorally critical states such as Florida and partly due to the cohesive message they deliver. As Haney and Vanderbush (1999) describe, the Cuban lobby has been a key player, helping to preserve restrictions, fighting moves toward normalization, and even extending sanctions in the 1990s on Cuba and other countries engaging in relations with Cuba. Moreover, as Vanderbush (2009) documents, the Cuban lobby illustrates an underappreciated aspect of group influence: the role of ethnic groups in marketing administration policies to help the administration shape public opinion and the policy debate. As Vanderbush (2009:291) puts it, "The greatest impact that these groups have is when they cooperate with government officials to sell the public on policies." The Cuban lobby performed this role in many ways, perhaps most recently in the successful passage of the LIBERTAD legislation, also known as the Helms-Burton Act, in the mid-1990s. Iraqi exiles performed a similar function in the run-up to the Iraq War in 2002–2003.

Immigrants from India represent another group becoming more active and potentially important in US foreign policy. As one analyst suggests, the growing population of immigrants and families of immigrants from India "are affluent and interested in India, [and] China's rising power and India's decision to move toward a market economy means their calls for a more 'India-Friendly' foreign policy are likely to meet a receptive audience in Washington" (Lindsay 2002:38). Indian Americans have become significantly more active in politics in recent years, and the Congressional Caucus on India and Indian Americans now has more than 120 members. For example, as Kirk (2008) argues, the aggressive efforts and mobilization of Indian Americans was a crucial factor behind the generation of congressional support for nuclear trade and cooperation agreements between India and the United States in 2006. This clearly has not helped US–Pakistani relations in general or against terrorism, especially given the ongoing war in Afghanistan.

The newest forms of interest groups gaining prominence in US foreign policy have been consulting firms and foreign lobbies. **Private consulting firms** representing different clients, corporations in particular, have proliferated since the 1970s. Henry Kissinger, for example, founded the consulting firm Kissinger Associates in 1982. For annual fees reported to start at $100,000, clients, including some of the largest multinational corporations in the world, meet with Kissinger and his associates in his New York office overlooking Park Avenue in order to get information about world politics and gain access to policymakers around the world (Feeney 2001). Two of Kissinger's associates, Brent Scowcroft and Lawrence Eagleburger, subsequently became President George H. W. Bush's national security adviser and deputy secretary of state. In another example, Kissinger Associates was a part of the US-Iraq Business Forum during the 1980s: a conglomeration of predominantly large American corporations—such as Amoco, Bell Helicopter, Caterpillar, General Motors, Mobil, Westinghouse, and Xerox—responsible for increasing business and trade with the Iraqi regime, thus contributing to Saddam Hussein's buildup of his military into a regional threat. With its officers and staff based in Washington, DC, the US-Iraq Business Forum pressured the Reagan and Bush administrations to continue to provide government credits and loan guarantees to Iraq and oppose congressional sanctions, despite Iraq's terrible human rights record. Nevertheless, when Iraq invaded Kuwait in 1990, Kissinger, speaking as a former national security adviser and secretary of state, was a leading proponent of expelling Iraq with the use of force (Conason 1990). Even more recently, key members of the Trump campaign and administration, including General Michael Flynn and Paul Manafort, came under fire—and investigation—for their efforts to lobby on behalf on foreign interests.

Closely related to the rise of consulting firms is the growth of **foreign lobbies** through which foreign governments (and private interests) attempt to influence American domestic politics and the policymaking process. Foreign lobbies rely heavily on American expertise, such as in consulting, law, and advertising firms, and operate in a fashion similar to domestic pressure groups. In fact, foreign lobbies have existed throughout American history and often work closely with their domestic counterparts, such as ethnic groups. The Jewish lobby, for example, has always had strong ties with the state of Israel. By 2007, more than 140 countries had secured representation in Washington, DC, by professional lobbying firms. Among the most prominent contemporary examples of the foreign lobby are Saudi Arabia and Japan. The Japan lobby, for example, is quite multifaceted, ranging from cultural organizations that try to promote favorable American attitudes toward Japan (such as the Japan Foundation) to professional economic organizations (such as the Japanese Economic Institute of America) and direct lobbying activities that represent Japanese business interests. Concerning the latter, according to journalist John Judis (1989:7), "The Japanese alone have hired about 125 former government officials. These include two of the last three special trade representatives, three of the last four Democratic National Committee chairmen, and the last two Republican chairs."

More recently, the countries of the former Soviet Union, Eastern Europe, Africa, and every other corner of the world have expanded their presence and lobbying activities as well. In 2017–2018 alone, foreign lobbyists and their hired agents spent $535 million to influence the US government. According to Open Secrets, "An examination of the records since 2017 shows more than 300 lobbying firms and other registrants representing more than 350 foreign clients, including governments, political parties, non-profits, businesses, and individuals" (see Figure 12.2).

One final recent development involves the **direct international activities of various groups**. Such direct international activities impact international politics and affect the conduct and making of US foreign policy. Although individuals and groups have long played direct roles in world events (e.g., Doyle 1986), such widespread efforts are a relatively recent phenomenon. Some examples are the missionary activities of American Christian religious organizations, including certain Protestant, Catholic, and Mormon denominations. Moreover, with gross sales often greater than the gross national product of many Third World countries, the business activities of American multinational corporations abroad are extensive and their lobbying efforts can be quite pervasive.

But other types of private groups are active abroad, as well. Many **private consulting firms** and individuals, for instance, sell their services to foreign governments to provide advice on domestic and foreign policies. Moreover, a number of think tanks are now self-styled "action tanks" engaged in a variety of hands-on work around the world rather than the traditional educational and policy analysis work for which they received their traditional

FIGURE 12.2

Top 10 Countries in Foreign Lobbying in the US, 2017–2018

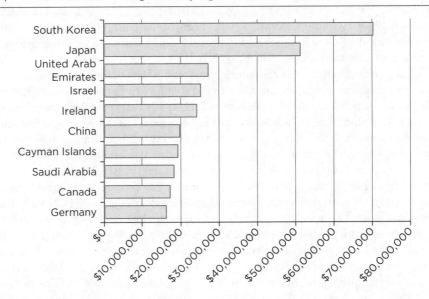

Source: Adapted from Center for Responsive Politics, https://www.opensecrets.org/news/2018/08/foreign-interests-fara-lobby-watch-exclusive/.

label (Scott 1999). Such activity became particularly noticeable in Eastern Europe with the end of the Cold War, a region in which many American firms and individuals (often with the support of the US government and the IMF) instructed Eastern Europeans on transitioning from communist systems to, it was hoped, democracies and market economies. This both eased their entry into an expanding European Union while also contributing to the rise of the large sovereign (governmental) deficits and debts that played a role in the economic crises in Europe and the United States after 2007. Even private individuals, such as former President Carter, through the Carter Center in Atlanta, have pursued their own foreign policy agendas abroad, revolving around democratic and economic development (which has increased Carter's public approval since he left the Oval Office and for which he was awarded the Nobel Peace Prize in 2002).

The international activities of **private voluntary organizations (PVOs)**, such as CARE, Catholic Relief Services, and Lutheran World Relief—many of them religiously affiliated—have proliferated since Vietnam as well. They originated primarily as relief organizations during and immediately after World War II and focused most of their attention on the war-torn countries of Europe. Over the past forty years, these and newer PVOs have diversified their activities and geographic focus to emphasize emergency and developmental assistance to Third World countries. In the 1980s, for example, more than 125 US PVOs received over $740 million from the United States Agency for International

Development (USAID) in support of their overseas work—a tenfold increase since the 1960s (Smith 1984:116). This trend of subcontracting out foreign assistance has increased to the present day. In the early twenty-first century, PVOs were dispensing considerably more aid than the United Nations system.

Another facet of this recent development, especially evident in the aftermath of the 2003 Iraq War, is the increasing use of **private military contractors (PMCs)**—a new type of interest group (and also a unique type of defense contractor as part of the military-industrial-scientific infrastructure). At least 30,000 private employees from more than sixty different PMCs were under contract to the US government to provide logistical support and security services in Iraq as of 2006. (Another 50,000 to 70,000 unarmed civilians—many from PVOs—are under government contract in Iraq to provide other services, from delivering mail to rebuilding essential infrastructure.) The use of PMCs has grown steadily since the early 1990s. During the 1991 Gulf War, the ratio of soldiers to private security contractors was fifty to one; today, it is closer to five to one, and even three to one, depending on the conflict.

In fact, according to Peter Singer (2005:122), the US military is increasingly "out-sourcing war" and "[p]rivate military companies are not only supporting a shrinking U.S. force in Iraq; they are also playing critical roles for both state and non-state actors in stabilization, drug interdiction, and humanitarian operations" (see also Singer 2003). The United States has increasingly relied on PMCs in the war in Afghanistan, especially given President Obama's decision to withdraw American combat troops after the surge and the fact that the civilian agencies such as the State Department and USAID have neither the resources nor the personnel to provide sufficient support for the Iraqi and Afghani transitions. Therefore, **corporate warriors** through "private companies are becoming significant players in conflicts around the world, supplying not merely the goods but also the services of war" (Singer 2005:119, 2007).

In sum, the post–Vietnam War and post–Cold War years have been accompanied by a proliferation of interest group and social movement activity in foreign policy. Older, Cold War–oriented groups have been joined by more liberal and more conservative groups. Ideologically motivated groups have been joined by hundreds of other groups representing specialized interests, including business, ethnic, and foreign interests. Such groups have flocked to Washington, DC, which explains the explosion of lobbyists (365 were officially registered in 1961; by 2018 the number had skyrocketed to more than 12,000), lawyers (the District of Columbia Bar Association listed roughly 12,000 members in 1961 and more than 100,000 in 2019), and journalists (1,500 were accredited to congressional press galleries in 1961; in 2015 there were more than 6,800). According to Thomas Mann (1990b:16), a major implication is that "conflict between the President and Congress must be seen as a consequence of a broader set of developments affecting America's place in the world and domestic political interests and processes." The Cold War Consensus years in group politics have been replaced by group competition for public support and control of the government. Domestic politics continue to be more divisive, complex, and fluid than during the Cold War. Therefore, as Mann concludes, "It is no wonder that the President today occupies a less than dominant position in American foreign policy."

Continuation of the Military-Industrial-Scientific Infrastructure

Although the foreign policy establishment collapsed while groups proliferated and became more diverse, a massive military-industrial-scientific infrastructure still pervades the government and American society. Defense spending has represented a smaller percentage of the federal government's budget and the domestic economy since Vietnam, and has been more open to criticism, but the national security infrastructure remains huge and remains embedded in American society. Indeed, at $750 billion proposed by the Trump administration in 2019, the defense budget is more than double that of 1976, even after adjusting for inflation. According to a *Los Angeles Times* analysis on the US defense establishment during the 1970s and 1980s,

> The jobs of one out of ten Americans depend directly or indirectly on defense spending. The Pentagon is the largest single purchaser of goods and services in the nation. Defense industries account for 10 percent of all US manufacturing. In certain states, including California, defense-related employment is the largest single source of personal income. Defense employs more than 25 percent of all the nation's scientists and engineers. (Tempest 1983b:1)

Throughout the 1980s, the federal government continued to devote the largest share of its budget to defense spending—roughly 30 percent. Defense products, such as arms, also accounted for more than one-third of American exports abroad.

Defense Department domestic spending (which includes procurement contracts, payroll, military pensions, and grants) declined somewhat with the end of the Cold War. However, in the wake of the 9/11 attacks, defense spending surged to more than $500 billion in base budget for fiscal year 2009 (excluding funds for nuclear weapons research, maintenance and production, veteran's affairs, and other supplemental funding necessary for the wars in Iraq and Afghanistan), with an additional $70 billion "emergency allowance" for the war on terrorism. According to the Pentagon, in 2018 the top three states receiving federal defense dollars were California ($49 billion), Virginia ($46 billion), and Texas ($38 billion). And this does not include domestic spending by other national security–oriented government agencies, such as the Department of Energy, NASA, the Department of Justice, and the Department of Homeland Security.

The **pork barrel politics** of defense spending has become more sophisticated. Known as "**Beltway bandits**," hundreds of private defense think tanks, lobbying offices, corporate government-relations offices, and law firms specializing in military contracts have sprung up around Washington, DC, in order to lobby for defense spending and support the military establishment. According to the Fairfax County Office of Economic Development, during the 1980s, more than 620 high-tech firms with 47,000 employees, more than 70 percent of whom work on defense-sponsored projects, were located in the four northern Virginia cities closest to Washington (Tempest 1983a:14). And the revolving door system remains alive and well. As Gordon Adams (1982) documented in *The Iron Triangle*, "Our review of DOD data showed that 1,942 individuals (uniformed and civilian) moved between DOD/NASA and the eight [largest defense] companies between 1970 and 1979.

Of these, 1,672 were hired by the companies, while 270 company employees went to work for DOD and NASA." In 2018, Open Secrets showed that seventy-six of Lockheed Martin's lobbyists in the 2017–2018 period previously held government jobs.

These types of developments have intensified the mutually supportive networks existing among members of the military establishment, Congress, private industry, and academia at national and local levels. The building and production of the B-1 bomber is a typical illustration of the dynamics of the military-industrial-scientific infrastructure (see "A Closer Look: The Politics of the B-1 Bomber").

A Closer Look

THE POLITICS OF THE B-1 BOMBER

As David Wood (1983:8–9) explains, "The story of the B-1 bomber provides a casebook example of how the military-industrial complex works, how the personal, professional, political and economic interests of thousands of individuals and institutions in government and the defense industries intertwine to influence what America does in the name of national security." Since the late 1950s, the Air Force had wanted a new bomber to replace the B-52. However, critics emphasized the B-1's cost, limited capabilities, and unclear mission.

For three years beginning in 1975, Air Force and Rockwell International officials planned, coordinated, and executed a major political campaign on behalf of the struggling **B-1 bomber program**, which was on the verge of cancellation. Under President Reagan, Congress finally agreed to the full-scale production of 100 B-1s at a cost of almost $500 million per plane. The Air Force and its supporters not only finally acquired the B-1 bomber but, to their delight, the B-2 "Stealth" bomber as well (at a cost of more than $1 billion per plane). Kotz (1988:22) concluded that over the years

the Air Force and its allies in science, industry, labor, and politics have relentlessly pursued their goals—and other groups have opposed them. On both sides, the motives of patriotism, financial gain, career ambition, political aggrandizement, and loyalty to an institution or idea were often so mixed that it is hard to tell what was narrow self-interest and what was concern for the national good.

Once approval is given for its production, the geography and politics of production virtually guarantee the future of a weapons system such as the B-1 bomber. Although Rockwell International was awarded the $40 billion–plus contract, as many as 5,200 subcontractors were involved in the forty-eight continental states. These subcontractors included most of the largest defense contractors, such as Boeing, TRW, Westinghouse, General Electric, Goodyear, Singer, Sperry, Bendix, Martin Marietta, Northrop, Litton, Westinghouse, IBM, and others. Unions such as the United Auto Workers and the International Association of Machinists and Aerospace Workers were also involved. "Contract spreading" involved as many as 400 of the 435 congressional districts. For many Americans, this meant jobs—good-paying jobs. Thus, thousands of individuals and groups at the local and national levels had a vested interest in providing support for B-1 production (see Figure 12.3).

(Continued)

(Continued)

FIGURE 12.3

The Geography of the B-1 Bomber

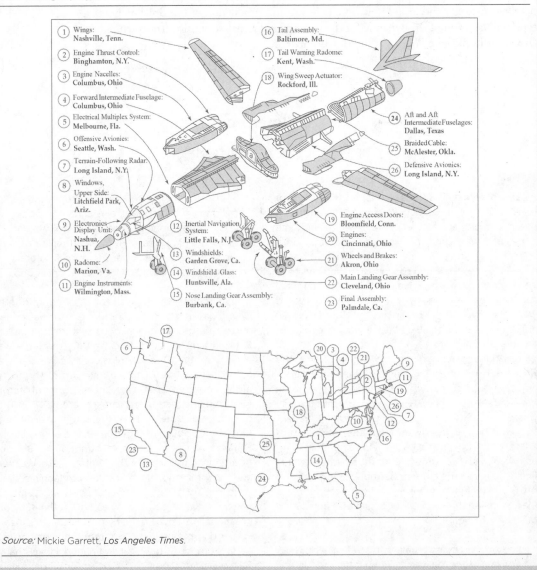

Source: Mickie Garrett, *Los Angeles Times*.

What are the economic and political consequences of these influential networks and weapons programs | for the national security policies and economic performance of the United States?

Nevertheless, according to the Government Accountability Office (GAO), the dynamics of the weapons procurement process remain problematic at the beginning of the twenty-first century. Procurement of a new weapons system is so laborious and lengthy—averaging at least eleven years from start to finish—that any sense of program continuity and personal accountability is nearly impossible to maintain. "This means that from drawing board to actual deployment, the average procurement project conceivably could outlast the involvement of four program managers, five program executive officers, eight service-acquisition executives, five chairmen of the Joint Chiefs, seven secretaries or undersecretaries of defense and three presidents" (US Congress, General Accounting Office 1982:23). The GAO comptroller general recommended that "trying to reduce the acquisition cycle to no longer than five years from technology development to production (as many private companies do) and slowing the revolving door in key management positions might help reduce the number of major projects that are over budget, behind schedule and without focus" (Paige 2000:47).

Furthermore, despite government efforts to crack down on fraud and corruption in the defense procurement process, fraud and corruption have been endemic in defense procurement and military spending (and nation-building) among all four elements of military-industrial-scientific infrastructure since the initial growth of the modern military establishment during the 1940s and 1950s (see, e.g., US Congress, US General Accounting Office 1982). For example, as of January 2012, the Defense and State Departments and USAID had reported 88,380 contracting actions, projects, and grants in Iraq, totaling $40.31 billion for reconstruction since the beginning of the 2003 war. Currently, there are about 15,000 employees of US-funded contractors and grantees in Iraq (a decline by 72 percent from the 53,447 registered as of September 2011), and more than $2 billion worth of contracts appear to be completely unaccounted for (Isenberg, 2012). Even more recently, in November 2018, the independent auditing firm Ernst and Young announced that it could not complete its contracted audit of the Department of Defense because "DoD's financial records were riddled with so many bookkeeping deficiencies, irregularities, and errors that a reliable audit was simply impossible" (Lindorff 2018). Moreover, this audit revealed the misleading—even fraudulent—budget tactics used by the Defense Department to secure and expand its funding.

Since the end of the Cold War, there has been a greater concentration of the defense industry, which has an impact not only on the politics of defense but on people and communities as well. For example, in 1997, Boeing Company (with $20 billion in revenues—about one-third of them military oriented) acquired McDonnell Douglas Corporation (with $15 billion in revenues—about two-thirds military oriented) in a $14 billion deal. Boeing Company replaced Lockheed Martin Corporation (which was formed in 1995 after a merger of Lockheed and Martin Marietta corporations) as the world's largest aerospace company, making it the only manufacturer of commercial jets in the United States. Although Boeing had 145,000 employees and McDonnell Douglas had 64,000 located in various plants throughout the country, corporate mergers are usually accompanied by considerable streamlining and cutbacks, to minimize overlap and duplication and to cut costs. Such concentration raises serious questions about the future of defense politics. The net result is a few megacompanies with "tremendous political clout" (Korb 1996).

In 2018, the leading defense contractors were Lockheed Martin ($30.5 billion), Boeing ($22 billion), General Dynamics ($13.5 billion), Raytheon ($11.8 billion), and Northrop Grumman ($11.5 billion). And how do companies like these preserve and exercise their clout? In addition to the dynamics of the iron triangle we discussed earlier, consider the practices of Lockheed Martin in the 2018 election cycle. According to Open Secrets, Lockheed Martin and its employees contributed $4.7 million to candidates, party committees, other political action committees, outside groups, or 527 groups (typically parties, candidates, committees, or associations organized to influence policy, appointments, or elections) in the cycle. Lockheed Martin also spent more than $13 million lobbying the government. As Table 12.2 shows, the manner in which Lockheed Martin distributed its contributions reveals another aspect of such efforts and their influence. As the table shows, Lockheed Martin supported candidates and organizations from both political parties.

INTEREST GROUP POLITICS IN THE FUTURE

As we have seen, interest group politics has experienced considerable change, as well as some important continuities, from the Cold War era to the present. Following World War II, the rise of foreign policy and Cold War–oriented groups, of a military-industrial-scientific infrastructure, and of a foreign policy establishment provided a significant foundation and domestic context for the politics of anti-communism and the policy of containment. This context made presidents particularly powerful in foreign policy while allowing the demands of national security to prevail.

The end of the Cold War Consensus led to the collapse of the foreign policy establishment and the proliferation of new and old groups in American politics with increased

TABLE 12.2

Top Recipients of Lockheed Martin Contributions in 2018

Recipient	Total	From Individuals	From Organizations
Kay Granger (R-TX)	$131,940	$121,940	$10,000
Defend America PAC	$111,750	$101,750	$10,000
Republican National Committee	$72,328	$42,328	$30,000
Democratic Congressional Campaign Committee	$67,978	$37,978	$30,000
DNC Services Corp.	$63,582	$37,978	$30,000
Lindsey Graham (R-SC)	$58,700	$56,700	$2,000
Ted Cruz (R-TX)	$54,301	$54,301	$0
Pete Visclosky (D-IN)	$49,800	$39,800	$10,000
National Republican Congressional Committee	$49,636	$19,636	$30,000
Patrick Leahy (D-VT)	$49,200	$49,200	$0

*Source.*Center for Responsive Politics, https://www.opensecrets.org/orgs/summary.php?id=d000000104.

ideological diversity and competition. This contributed to a decline in presidential leadership in foreign policy and the growth of divided government since Vietnam, even while the military-industrial-scientific infrastructure continued to operate and exert substantial influence. After the end of the Cold War and the 9/11 attacks, ideological divisions and partisanship intensified, making it even more difficult for any president, regardless of person or party, to lead, govern, or overcome political gridlock in Washington, DC. Interest groups are thus an increasingly competitive and influential element of the societal circle of our analytical framework and a significant force in the politics of US foreign policy.

THINK ABOUT THIS

Since World War II, the landscape of interest group activity in US foreign policy has grown increasingly complex and competitive. Think about the discussion of interest groups and their nature, role, and influence in this chapter.

How do group interests and activities shape the politics of US foreign policy?

KEY TERMS

American Federation of
   Labor–Congress of
   Industrial Organizations
   (AFL-CIO)   391
antiwar movement   399
B-1 bomber program   411
Beltway bandits   410
business and labor groups   390
challenging groups   385
China lobby   392
commercial interests   402
corporate warriors   409
Council on Foreign Relations   390
dealignment   384
defense contractors   395
direct international activities of
   various groups   407

established groups   385
foreign lobbies   407
foreign policy
   establishment   396
inside politics   388
interest groups   385
iron triangle   395
issue- and cause-oriented
   groups   400
lobby   388
lobbying strategies   388
militarization of research   396
military-industrial complex   393
military-industrial-scientific
   infrastructure   393
national security and public
   policy groups   390

outside politics   388
political and civic
   organizations   390
political right   399
pork barrel politics   410
private consulting firms   406
private military contractors
   (PMCs)   409
private voluntary organizations
   (PVOs)   408
religious and ethnic
   groups   391
revolving door system   395
social movements   385
think tanks   401
veterans and military support
   organizations   390

Visit **edge.sagepub.com/scottrosati7e** to help you accomplish your coursework goals in an easy-to-use learning environment.

The Media and Foreign Policy

$$13$$

Mandel Ngan/AFP/Getty Images

PHOTO 13.1 President Donald Trump at a 2018 press conference.

LEARNING OBJECTIVES

1. Understand the conventional wisdom and the more complex reality about the media and foreign policy.

2. Identify the sources and main features of the news and its coverage of foreign policy.

3. Explain the evolving nature of the media and its coverage of foreign policy since World War II.

4. Describe the main features of the role and influence of the media in the foreign policy process.

Our final piece of the foreign policymaking puzzle is the third major element of the societal context—the media. While the role of the media in foreign policy—and politics in general—has been hotly debated, their role and influence are even more significant and controversial in the current context. Certainly, much of the information, knowledge, and images that individuals gather about the world—whether the mass public, the elite public, or policymakers—comes from the mass media. This makes for a mediated reality in which the American mass media and the communications process play an important role. However, transformations in the media environment, including the increasingly important role of social media, have affected this role and process in important ways. Moreover, the media have always been part of a two-way process: They play a role and have influence with policymakers, the public, and the policy process, but they are also used by policymakers in the process. In this chapter, we examine the nature and role of the media in foreign policy. We first lay out the landscape of the American media and the historical patterns of news coverage. We then consider the role and influence of the media in foreign policy.

CONVENTIONAL WISDOM
AND COMPLEX REALITY

The mass media and the communications process have become significant elements in the politics of US foreign policy. Almost 100 years ago, Walter Lippmann (1922) argued that the US news media play a central role in transforming the "world outside" into "the pictures in our heads," which affects public opinion and US foreign policy. Among other things, this has an important agenda-setting affect. As Bernard Cohen (1963, 13) once put it, the media "may not be successful much of the time in telling people what to think, but it is stunningly successful in telling its readers what to think about" when it comes to foreign affairs.

As society and the global environment have grown in complexity and become increasingly important in the lives of Americans, people have developed a greater need for information about national and international affairs. Furthermore, a communications revolution occurred during the twentieth century that has enabled the mass media to rapidly communicate information anywhere on the planet. In the twenty-first century, the increasingly important arena of alternative and social media has further complicated the media landscape and its role and influence. Across these dynamics, as Shanto Iyengar and Donald R. Kinder (1987) demonstrate, the news media provide "news that matters" and this has important policymaking consequences.

Three competing views seem prevalent throughout American society. Conservatives tend to argue that the media play a powerful role in American politics and that there is a "liberal bias" in the American news media. Liberals tend to agree that the media play a powerful role, but they believe there is a "conservative bias" in the news media. Journalists, however, tend to argue that the power of the media has been overblown, that the news media are "neutral" and simply attempt to mirror reality, reporting events and the facts as they exist. Very simply, all three views tend to be overly stereotypical and self-serving: The media are not consistently liberal, conservative, or objective.

The complex reality is that there are contradictory implications of people's dependence on the news media and their reliance on the mainstream media. In many ways, the news media coverage today is better than ever before. The mainstream media are more informative regarding national and international affairs. The quality of journalism has improved and become more professional. More public affairs programs are on television than in the past. Quality newspapers, such as the *New York Times,* the *Washington Post,* and the *Wall Street Journal,* are readily available in urban areas throughout the country and digitally on everyone's cell phones, tablets, and computers. Indeed, the Internet has made news incredibly accessible to almost anybody. In sum, members of the public who rely on the mainstream media can gain considerable information about national and international affairs if they are interested, especially if they already possess a good base of information.

At the same time, the news media are highly selective and inconsistent with respect to which events are covered and how they are presented: sometimes being more liberal, other times more conservative, and sometimes more neutral. Many public affairs programs provide soft (as opposed to hard) news. Television news coverage is usually brief and simplistic, appealing to a mass public by emphasizing drama and the least common denominator. Investigative reporting by the mainstream media is common but often oversimplified.

Finally, much of the public typically has a short attention span and demonstrates little interest in becoming truly informed. As a result, the net result of reliance on the mainstream media is often a simplistic understanding of reality.

It is also true that this greater accessibility involves an explosion of information from alternative and social media sources outside the mainstream media. Certainly, this has made more information more readily available to more Americans. But it has also complicated the situation. As a recent Gallup-Knight Foundation poll reported, "By 58% to 38%, Americans say it is harder rather than easier to be informed today due to the plethora of information and news sources available" (Knight Foundation 2018). The explanation? Key aspects include concern over the spread of inaccurate information via the Internet and social media, which 73 percent of Americans consider to be a major problem. But it also includes concerns over the effectiveness of the mainstream media in separating fact from opinion, which 66 percent of Americans believe to be an issue (up from 42 percent in 1984).

UNDERSTANDING SOURCES AND COVERAGE OF THE NEWS

Let's begin by discussing where most Americans get whatever information they have about national and international affairs, followed by the nature of the coverage that is provided to most people by the media in the United States—including the revolution in **information and communications technology**, especially the Internet.

Sources of News

Most Americans get their information about national and international affairs from the **mainstream media**—the major newspapers, radio stations, and television stations available in their communities and from the Internet—but things are changing. First, Americans increasingly turn to the Internet and streaming video for this news. Second, Americans' reliance on social media for news has also been on the rise. According to a recent study by the Pew Research Center (2011), "In short, instead of replacing traditional news platforms, Americans are increasingly integrating new technologies into their news consumption habits."

In the area of news, it could be argued that **national media**—sometimes referred to as the elite press—developed and became the primary source of information on national and international affairs for most Americans. The national media consist of the following organizations: ABC, NBC, CBS, Fox, CNN (Cable News Network), the *New York Times*, the *Washington Post*, the *Los Angeles Times*, the *Wall Street Journal*, and the Associated Press (AP). One could also include *Newsweek, Time,* and *US News & World Report* for the attentive public. Other large urban media organizations, such as the *Boston Globe*, the *Chicago Tribune*, the *Miami Herald*, and the *Philadelphia Inquirer*, are junior partners of the national media, for they generally lack regular national reach beyond their regional markets. Each of these media organizations provides its news both in broadcast or print form as well as electronically through its website. In addition to serving as a direct source of information, the national media also operate **wire services**. For example, the AP and

Reuters, unknown to most Americans, are a significant part of the national media because they make available to other media organizations a large number of news stories from their reporters throughout the world (at a cost) through their wire services. Finally, newer **Internet-based sources** such as Politico.com and Vox.com are more frequent sources of news for many Americans, especially among the elite and attentive publics.

The mass public, being relatively uninterested and uninformed about national and international affairs, tends to be most receptive to **headline news** from mainstream sources, such as lead stories on the front page of the newspaper and, especially, on television. According to the Pew Research Center, at the end of 2018, almost half (49 percent) of Americans frequently relied on television news, especially local news, more than any other source, although that figure represents a decline from 57 percent just three years earlier. At the same time, the percentage of Americans frequently relying on print media for news has declined to just 16 percent and is now the least relied on source. About a third of the American public now frequently rely on news websites, and, at 20 percent, the proportion relying on social media is now greater than that relying on print media.

Even if they rely on the Internet, most Americans rely on the mainstream and national media for their news, if they pay attention at all. But there are also some interesting patterns and differences to note. Older Americans tend to rely on television and print media more, while younger Americans more often turn to websites and social media for their news (see Figure 13.1). The elite public follows the media's coverage of the news

FIGURE 13.1

Sources of News for Americans

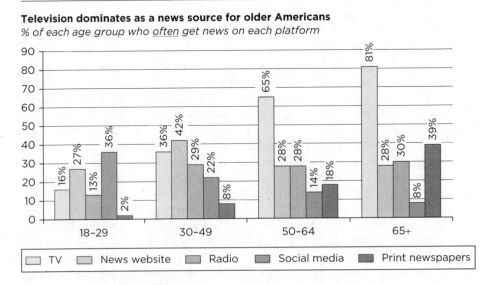

Television dominates as a news source for older Americans
% of each age group who <u>often</u> get news on each platform

Source: Elisa Shearer, "Social Media Outpaces Printer Newspapers in the U.S. as a News Source," Pew Research Center, December 10 (https://www.pewresearch.org/fact-tank/2018/12/10/social-media-outpaces-print-newspapers-in-the-u-s-as-a-news-source/).

more closely and is most likely to go beyond the headlines and supplement its information beyond television and the local newspaper (especially through use of the Internet), although most still rely on national media sources (see Bennett 2011; Graber 2009; Pew Research Center 2010; Stacks 2004).

Contemporary News Coverage

What do we know about mainstream and national media coverage of contemporary national and international affairs? For one thing, we know that the news media display considerable **selective attention** to the world around them. Most of the American media focus on national and local news, with little attention given to international news. Most studies examining media coverage have found that the percentage of news stories devoted to international affairs by major mainstream media organizations ranged from a low of 10 percent to a high of 40 percent (with the percentage declining over time), representing anywhere from five to fifteen international news stories daily. In 2013, for instance, a study by Aalberg et al. (2013) reported that television news reduced coverage of international affairs by more than 70 percent after the end of the Cold War. By 1995, only 14 percent of coverage was international, a level at which it remained until 2013, with some variation for times of pressing international events such as the terrorist attacks of September 11, 2001, and the Iraq War.

Media coverage of international affairs also varies to a considerable extent depending on the medium. The print media, especially newspapers, usually cover more news stories and devote more space to each story than the television media. National news on television has a higher percentage of stories devoted to international affairs, but they are few in number. National television news programs may broadcast an average of five to seven international stories (representing a total of seven to eleven minutes) out of fifteen to seventeen stories broadcast daily. At best, national news shown on a major television network, such as ABC, CBS, or NBC, provides only a brief digest of national and international events in less than twenty-one minutes—not much time to cover the world (the regular one-hour news show on CNN provides a longer version of similar coverage). The networks' Internet sites tend to reflect these patterns as well, although there may be more overall coverage (given the Internet's more flexible and dynamic, nonphysical, virtual nature).

International coverage by major newspapers represents a smaller percentage of their total news coverage, but newspapers tend to cover more international stories overall. For example, the *New York Times*—considered the best daily American source of international news—averages thirteen to twenty international news stories per day. Overall, only a limited number of events and issues become news, especially in the media's coverage of the world beyond American shores. Or as H. D. Wu (1998:507) concluded after reviewing and synthesizing fifty-five different media studies of American international news coverage, "One cannot help but realize that the everyday representation of the world via news media is far from a direct reflection of global realities. International news is selected, sifted, edited and mostly discarded through a myriad of processes by the news organizations and professionals."

The medium also is important because it affects not only the space available for news coverage but also how the news is presented. Television news stories, in particular, are unique because they are accompanied by video pictures (and sound) that provide viewers with a greater sense of immediacy—of "being there"—which further affects viewers' perceptions. The power of television (and increasingly the Internet with video feeds such as YouTube) is particularly noticeable during crisis reporting, when issues and stories that are part of the crisis are highlighted and most vulnerable to being sensationalized. According to Hedrick Smith (1988:395), "Television is driven to dramatize the news, to give it plot, theme, and continuity to make it comprehensive to a mass audience. Television needs action and drama. It needs to boil down complexities. It needs identifiable characters. Hence the focus on personality, preferably one personality." Television also has a greater "tendency to present (and understand) politics in terms of demons and friends, good guys and bad guys" (Smith 1988:395).

Overall, television news coverage simplifies reality the most because it tends to be more incomplete and provide less depth than the print media. At the same time, its visual images make it more compelling and powerful. Television is, nevertheless, the major medium by which most Americans gain their information and understanding of national and international affairs. Given the selectivity and the medium, which international topics tend to be covered by the American media?

Research has found that, in order to receive mainstream and national media coverage on television or in print as well as on the Internet, foreign news in general must be more consequential, especially for Americans; must involve people of higher status; and must entail more violence or disaster than national news. According to *Deciding What's News*, a classic 1979 study of CBS, NBC, *Newsweek*, and *Time* by Herbert Gans (1979), the following international topics tended to receive the most attention by the national media:

1. American activities abroad (especially official visits)

2. Foreign events directly affecting the United States (involving especially national security and economic affairs)

3. East-West governmental relations

4. Changes in heads of state (with a special interest in European royalty)

5. Dramatic political conflicts (such as wars, coups, revolutions, and terrorism)

6. Natural disasters

7. Excesses of foreign dictators

Not much changed after the collapse of the Soviet Union and communism in Eastern Europe, nor after September 11, 2001, or with the growing popularity of the Internet, with the exception that attention to East-West governmental relations has been replaced by the war on terrorism and the wars in Iraq and Afghanistan (see also Hess 1996; Pew Research Center 2005, 2010; Seplow 2002). According to the 2018 Tyndall Report on news coverage, for example, international events coverage by ABC, CBS, and NBC in 2018

FIGURE 13.2

(a) International and (b) Foreign Policy News Coverage by ABC, CBS, and NBC

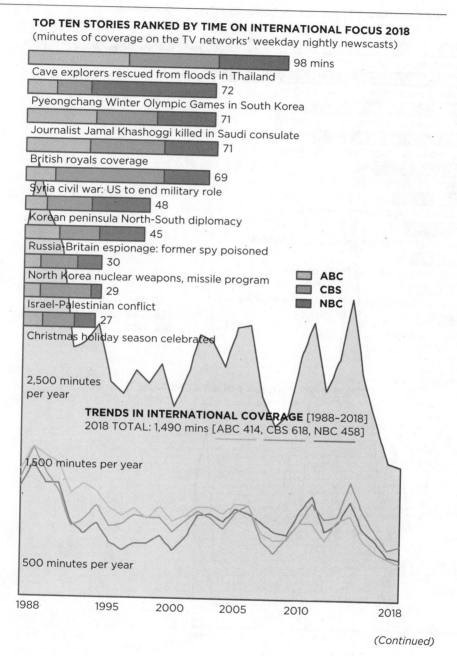

TOP TEN STORIES RANKED BY TIME ON INTERNATIONAL FOCUS 2018
(minutes of coverage on the TV networks' weekday nightly newscasts)

98 mins — Cave explorers rescued from floods in Thailand

72 — Pyeongchang Winter Olympic Games in South Korea

71 — Journalist Jamal Khashoggi killed in Saudi consulate

71 — British royals coverage

69 — Syria civil war: US to end military role

48 — Korean peninsula North-South diplomacy

45 — Russia-Britain espionage: former spy poisoned

30 — North Korea nuclear weapons, missile program

29 — Israel-Palestinian conflict

27 — Christmas holiday season celebrated

ABC
CBS
NBC

TRENDS IN INTERNATIONAL COVERAGE [1988–2018]
2018 TOTAL: 1,490 mins [ABC 414, CBS 618, NBC 458]

2,500 minutes per year

1,500 minutes per year

500 minutes per year

1988   1995   2000   2005   2010   2018

(Continued)

FIGURE 13.2
(Continued)

TOP TEN STORIES RANKED BY TIME ON US FOREIGN POLICY FOCUS 2018
(minutes of coverage on the TV networks' weekday nightly newscasts)

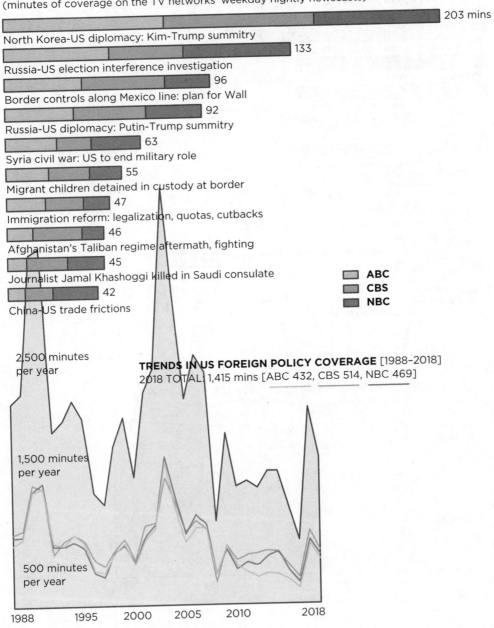

203 mins

North Korea-US diplomacy: Kim-Trump summitry

133

Russia-US election interference investigation

96

Border controls along Mexico line: plan for Wall

92

Russia-US diplomacy: Putin-Trump summitry

63

Syria civil war: US to end military role

55

Migrant children detained in custody at border

47

Immigration reform: legalization, quotas, cutbacks

46

Afghanistan's Taliban regime aftermath, fighting

45

Journalist Jamal Khashoggi killed in Saudi consulate

42

China-US trade frictions

ABC
CBS
NBC

2,500 minutes per year

TRENDS IN US FOREIGN POLICY COVERAGE [1988–2018]
2018 TOTAL: 1,415 mins [ABC 432, CBS 514, NBC 469]

1,500 minutes per year

500 minutes per year

1988   1995   2000   2005   2010   2018

Source: Tyndall Report (2019a, 2019b); tyndallreport.com.

averaged about 500 minutes total (about 3.5 percent of airtime) across the networks, the lowest of any year from 1988 to 2018. Major stories (and coverage) included the murder of journalist and permanent US resident Jamal Khashoggi by the Saudi Arabian regime and US involvement in the Syrian civil war (Tyndall Report 2019b). About the same amount of time was devoted to foreign policy matters. Topping the list were stories on US–North Korea relations and negotiations over nuclear weapons, Russian interference in US elections, and US border security issues with Mexico (Tyndall Report 2019a).

A typical conclusion is that the American mainstream and national press devote more attention to some countries than to others, with wealthy, powerful, and culturally similar countries getting more attention (e.g., Friedman 2013; Likes 2014; Semmel 1976). According to Hawkins (2011), when it comes to conflict, for example, many of the world's deadliest are also the most ignored, as the American media selectively pay attention to conflicts in countries with political significance, close proximity, (geographically and culturally), and political and national interests for Americans, to the exclusion of others.

News coverage of events abroad by the US media tends to be American- and Western-centric; focus on government officials, emphasize so-called negative events such as conflict, and highlight political and national security issues. The emphasis on political and national security news remains problematic in informing the public about the workings of the international political economy. Not only do issues in the developing world receive little attention, but when they do get covered, they often entail more sensational items (military coups, wars, natural disasters, accidents, and crime).

This selective and volatile coverage is intensified during times of crisis, whether domestic or international. Crisis coverage is often so great that most other national and international news of consequence disappears entirely. James Reston (1967:195) of the *New York Times* explained the reactive nature of media crisis coverage this way:

> We are fascinated by events but not by the things that cause the events. We will send 500 correspondents to Vietnam after the war breaks out, and fill the front pages with their reports, meanwhile ignoring the rest of the world, but we will not send five reporters there when the danger of war is developing.

Such was the case during the Bush administration for months following the September 11 attacks and the launching of the war on terrorism.

Crisis coverage by the American news media also tends to be limited to events that affect the United States or in which it is heavily involved; little or no media coverage would be given to a civil war or a disaster in another country where the United States has little involvement, even though this may clearly be a crisis situation for the people and the region involved (compare coverage of Hurricane Katrina in 2005 or Hurricane Sandy in 2012 with the 2005 earthquake in Pakistan, where more than 150,000 people died). Similarly, the Afghan War received considerable coverage during the winter of 2001–2002 when the United States intervened militarily, but once victory was declared, coverage virtually disappeared despite the resultant "mess in Afghanistan," until it received more attention after the United States withdrew from Iraq (Rashid 2004). Subsequent coverage tended to occur only in the case of American actions or casualties. Likewise, domestic and international economics received lots of attention in 2008–2010, but once the economic collapse was forestalled, the emphasis again became the domestic economy and the recovery. President Trump's embrace of tariffs and protectionism pushed news coverage episodically as well. But, in the interim, most stories returned to the business and finance sections or outlets.

NEWS AND FOREIGN POLICY SINCE WORLD WAR II

Let's take a historical look at the foreign policy coverage of the US mainstream and national media since World War II to shed light on its evolving nature and role. To begin, consider the words of Doris Graber (2009:29) in *Mass Media and American Politics*:

> The mass media are more than passive transmission agents for available information. Decisions made by media personnel determine what information becomes available to media audiences and what remains unavailable. By putting stories into perspective and interpreting them, media personnel assign meaning to the information and indicate the values by which it ought to be judged. News shaping is unavoidable because space is limited and because facts do not speak for themselves. Hence the media select and shape much of the raw material needed by political elites and the general public for thinking about the political world and planning political action.

News coverage during World War II neatly illustrates Graber's point. Once the US government declared war on Japan and entered World War II, the American mainstream and national media quickly acted to rally mass support behind the cause. The media became the principal means by which pictures of the enemy were portrayed to the American public and acted as an important source for unifying the country against the Axis powers. The media depicted the Allied countries as righteous defenders of democracy and freedom against the aggression and evil represented by Germany and Japan. Among other things, this contributed to a West Coast hysteria concerning Japanese sabotage, which led to the internment of Japanese Americans in concentration camps during the war (Roeder 1993; Sweeney 2001). American leaders also used the media to preach the value of Soviet-American friendship and continued cooperation following the war. The media popularized the Soviet Union as the great ally of the United States, frequently referring to Joseph Stalin as "Uncle Joe."

Since World War II, there have been three broad patterns in mainstream news media coverage as it has related to the making of US foreign policy: (1) During the Cold War, news media coverage generally reflected and reinforced the anti-communist consensus prevailing in society and the government, strengthening presidential leadership, especially in national security; (2) after the Vietnam War, news media coverage tended to be more critical and reflected more diverse views, presenting some challenges to policymaking and presidential leadership; and (3) after the Cold War ended, the rise of the Internet, more ideological news sources, and social media combined to present new challenges, both for the functions of the media and for their impact on politics.

Cold War Coverage

After World War II, the American news media began to reflect greater diversity of views, reflecting the great political debate raging over the future of US foreign policy. However, with the onset of the Cold War, mainstream and national media coverage again began to narrow and reflect the growing anti-communist political environment. The administrations of Harry Truman and Dwight Eisenhower communicated their fears of communism through the media to educate the mass public and rally support for the containment policy. Such media coverage both reflected and contributed to the rise of the political right—including the rise and then, once the political climate in Washington, DC, shifted, the fall of Senator Joseph McCarthy and McCarthyism—and anti-communism, further narrowing public debate (e.g., Bayley 1981).

There was no outright government censorship of the news media during the Cold War (except for Korean War coverage)—there didn't need to be, given the consensus of thought and McCarthyism. In fact, as Carl Bernstein (1977) of Watergate fame has reported, more than 400 American journalists occasionally worked closely with the CIA, and many carried out assignments for the intelligence community (not always knowingly). This included major executives and reporters in the field from every major news organization in the country, as well as a few minor ones. As pointed out by the Senate's Church Committee investigation in 1975, such cozy relationships between the mainstream media and the intelligence community raised serious concerns about the "potential, inherent in covert media operations, for manipulating or incidentally misleading the American public" and the "damage to the credibility and independence of a free press" (US Congress 1976:197).

Although the national media are credited with being critical of the Vietnam War, it is usually forgotten that in their Vietnam War coverage during the late 1950s and early 1960s the media dutifully communicated the government's position and promoted the Americanization of the Vietnam War. As David Halberstam (2000:446) observed,

> The great heads of the media were anxious to be good and loyal citizens, and the working reporters had almost without question accepted the word of the White House on foreign policy. . . . The press corps might be congenitally skeptical in assessing the intentions and ambitions of domestic politicians, but it brought no such toughness of mind to the politics of foreign policy.

Thus, the media contributed to and reinforced the Cold War Consensus and presidential leadership in foreign affairs and facilitated a national security ethos in which the demands of national security often prevailed over the demands of democracy.

Post-Vietnam War Coverage

As the Cold War Consensus broke down among US policymakers and elites in the mid- and late 1960s, the national news media's coverage of the Vietnam War became more critical of the government (e.g., Hallin 1986). As long as consensus prevailed within the government, national media coverage reflected this consensus and supported government policy. It was only when dissent increased within the government—both in Congress and in the Johnson administration—that media coverage became more critical of the war and the government's policies.

By the late 1960s and early 1970s, national media coverage increasingly reflected the collapse of the Cold War Consensus in the government and society. The Watergate crisis and its aftermath, in fact, represented a prime example of the **"watchdog" press**—a critical and cynical media independent of the administration and engaged in investigative reporting. Still, the American failure in the Vietnam War was one of the few times that the popular interpretation—that Vietnam did not represent a vital interest and that the war was a mistake—became inconsistent with the presidential view.

After Vietnam the president no longer monopolized media coverage. With the collapse of the Cold War Consensus, the national media in particular were more likely to represent a greater diversity of foreign policy thought (especially in the area of national security), rely on more sources of information throughout society and in the policymaking process, and present news in a more critical and cynical fashion. This contributed to the rise of Congress, the proliferation of group politics in the making of US foreign policy, and the expansion of news programs in the electronic media and on the Internet. In this more complicated post-Vietnam context, sometimes national news media coverage was more supportive of the president and sometimes it was more critical. Much depended on the nature of the issue, the political environment, and the times. Presidents Nixon, Ford, Carter, and Reagan all experienced positive and negative coverage during their terms in office, but overall the media were more skeptical and critical.

Coverage after the Cold War

As we discussed in previous chapters, the end of the Cold War contributed to increasing fragmentation over foreign policy means and ends, which had an impact on the media. Simply put, the more complicated foreign policy environment and the lack of consensus among US policymakers fostered highly contentious debates over policy, while rising polarization and partisanship fueled discord and disagreement. Such political and policy disagreements fuel media coverage, and the widening number of voices and access points provided the media with more opportunities for reporting, while also increasing the number of policymakers seeking out the media for their own ends. After the Cold War, the "golden triangle" of the White House, Pentagon, and State Department no longer dominated media access (e.g., Bennett 1994a).

Of course, the nature of media coverage still depended on the nature of the issue, the political environment, and the times. For example, for months after 9/11, the media and the country rallied behind President Bush's war on terrorism—giving him the highest presidential approval ratings in modern history. But within months of Bush's spring 2003 announcement that the Iraq War was over, questions and criticisms occasionally began to be raised about the administration's foreign policy toward the Middle East and terrorism and, in particular, relative to the decision to invade Iraq and overthrow Saddam Hussein. Following the 2004 presidential election and especially in 2005, the mainstream media became much more critical in response to the continued difficulties of the so-called postwar occupation, efforts at nation-building, and increasing casualties of American soldiers—reflecting and promoting the public's growing disapproval of the president's handling of the war. Initially, President Obama received positive coverage based in part on his pledge for "hope and change." However, the positive tone evaporated by the end of 2009 due to the slow pace of the economic recovery and short-term, "what are you doing for me today" aspects of media coverage. These news cycles may have a faster and more intense pace with constant changes in information and communications technology. Most recently, media coverage during the Trump administration tended to seize on the most controversial aspects of the administration and its foreign policy, including the issues related to Russian interference in the 2016 election and the administration's subsequent responses to the investigation of that interference, as well as President Trump's own inflammatory use of Twitter to advance his (often factually dubious and/or negative) perspectives and interpretations of events and people.

Three additional developments since the end of the Cold War warrant attention: (1) the growth of the Internet, (2) the rise of more ideological news sources, and (3) the rise of social media.

Growth of the Internet. The growth of the Internet has had important implications for media coverage. For one, it has greatly expanded access to and dissemination of information and perspectives. All of the components of the national media are accessible nationwide via their websites, although many maintain paywalls for some or all of their content. A good many media sources are entirely online as well, without print or broadcast versions.

However, the explosion of the Internet over the past three decades has also greatly diversified and decentralized these sources of information. This has opened the media world to amateur online journalists, bloggers, and many others. According to the Center for Communication and Civic Engagement (n.d.) at the University of Washington:

> While some traditional news outlets are reacting with fear and uncertainty, many are adopting open publishing features to their own online versions. The Guardian and other mainstream media outlets have added blogs to their sites. The BBC's web site posts reader's photos, and other sites solicit and use reader-contributed content. Mainstream news outlets are increasingly scanning blogs and other online sources for leads on news items, and some are hiring journalists from the blogging ranks. Journalists are blogging live from courtrooms, from Baghdad, and elsewhere, allowing them to post frequent updates in near real-time. As the public turns toward participatory forms of online journalism, and as mainstream news outlets adopt more of those interactive features in their online versions, the media environment is shifting, slowly and incrementally, away from the broadcast model where the few communicate to the many, toward a more inclusive model in which publics and audiences also have voices.

But there is a price to this, as the explosion of information creates new challenges for sorting out truth from fiction. Indeed, as we noted earlier in this chapter, Americans are finding it much harder to be informed *because* of the volume of information that is available, and almost three out of four Americans are very concerned about access to and the spread of inaccurate information via the Internet and social media.

The Internet revolution has had another notable impact, which is to generate increasing challenges for the news media to sustain themselves profitably amid the more decentralized and digital landscape. Indeed, according to the Pew Research Center, while cable news revenues (e.g., Fox, MSNBC, CNN) have been stable or growing, newspapers and magazines, as well as local television and radio, have suffered from declining revenues (Barthel 2018). This has forced a variety of adjustments, the most notable of which are reductions in newsroom staffing and, most important for our focus, a dramatic decline in foreign correspondents and foreign bureaus.

According to the Pew Research Center, employment of reporters, editors, photographers, and videographers in newspaper, radio, broadcast television, cable, and digital-native newsrooms declined by 23 percent between 2008 and 2017 (Grieco 2018). The decline was particularly steep for newspapers, which drove the overall result (see Figure 13.3).

FIGURE 13.3

Newsroom Employment, 2008–2017

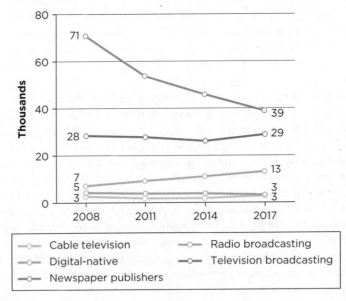

Newspaper newsroom employees declined by 45% between 2008 and 2017

Number of U.S. newsroom employees in each news industry, in thousands

Source: Grieco, Elizabeth. "U.S. newsroom employment has dropped by a quarter since 2008, with greatest decline at newspapers." Pew Research Center, Washington, D.C. (July 9, 2019) https://www.pewresearch.org/fact-tank/2019/07/09/u-s-newsroom-employment-has-dropped-by-a-quarter-since-2008/.

Even more troubling for our focus, the news media have steadily and systematically been dismantling their **foreign bureaus** and firing their **foreign correspondents**. The US media once maintained an extensive network of foreign correspondents and foreign bureaus to contribute to reporting on international affairs and foreign policy matters. One of the very few media organizations with extensive global geographic coverage is the Associated Press, the largest American wire service (which submits stories that have to be selected and purchased by news media outlets; see Hannerz 2004; Hess 1996). As Table 13.1 shows, although smaller than during the Cold War, major American news organizations had many foreign bureaus and correspondents as of the time of the terrorist attacks on 9/11. Since then, however, major news organizations have sharply reduced those numbers. According to Kaphle (2015), by 2011, for example, "at least 20 US newspapers and other media outlets eliminated all their foreign bureaus, according to *American Journalism Review.* Elsewhere, the number and size of those bureaus have shrunk dramatically." News organizations like the *Washington Post*, the *New York Times*, the *Los Angeles Times*, ABC, CBS, NBC, and others have scaled back significantly (World Tribune Staff 2018). And, where "foreign bureaus" are maintained, increasingly they are staffed by just one person (Martin 2012).

TABLE 13.1

Foreign Correspondents and Bureaus of Major Media Organizations (as of September 1, 2001)

Organization	Bureaus	Correspondents
Associated Press	10	150
New York Times	26	40
Los Angeles Times	21	26
Washington Post	20	26
Knight Ridder	4	14
USA Today	4	4
Time	7	19
Newsweek	11	16
CNN	30	55
CBS	4	9
NBC	5	8
ABC	6	7
Fox	6	6

Regional papers with five or more bureaus: *Chicago Tribune* (10), *Dallas News* (5), *Baltimore Sun* (5), and *Boston Globe* (5).

Source: Michael Parks, "Foreign News: What's Next?" *Columbia Journalism Review* 40 (January/February 2002), p. 53.

Even the *Wall Street Journal*, which maintained a sizable staff of foreign correspondents to serve its international reach and publication in different global regions, resorted to cutting its foreign staff in dramatic waves of layoffs in recent years. As one *Wall Street Journal* employee described it:

> The Moscow bureau has lost two reporters, reducing the size of the office—a particularly key outpost in the context of the ongoing revelations since the campaign about Russia and Trump—to just a small handful of staff. The Warsaw bureau lost one of its two reporters, and the Budapest bureau has been shut down, as has the bureau in Madrid. The one-man Riyadh bureau has also been closed. The paper's operation in India has lost two reporters, according to a source with knowledge of the reduction. All staff in Scandinavia have been laid off except for one. The Berlin bureau is said to have been reduced by one .... There's "nobody left between Stockholm and Greece, and between Berlin and Moscow there is nobody" except for the remaining reporter in Warsaw, said a former reporter in one of the European bureaus who was laid off in the latest round. (Gray 2017)

How might these steps affect the role and influence of the media in foreign policy?

The Rise of More Ideological News Sources. Connected in some ways to the growth of the Internet, the past three decades are notable for the rise of more **ideological news sources**, with Fox News being the clearest, but not only, example among the national media. Perhaps unsurprisingly, as the political landscape in the United States became more fragmented, polarized, and partisan, the media took on those characteristics as well. In contrast to the days in which the media prized accuracy and objectivity, since the end of the Cold War the national media landscape has become populated by organizations taking a much more pronounced ideological stance.

In part a reaction by the political right to what it long regarded as a liberal bias in the mainstream media (discussed later in this chapter), the establishment of Fox News as a major player in the national media landscape changed the equation markedly. Rupert Murdoch's network, part of his broader News Corporation business (which also owns the *Wall Street Journal*), has "grown steadily to become one of the most influential right-wing media voices in the US since it first aired on 7 October 1996" (Somerlad 2018). Its operations also reflect a related trend that contributes to this increasingly ideological landscape, which is the blending of the news reporting functions and the news commentary and opinion functions at many major networks. Fox News adopted its increasingly partisan approach (see Mayer 2019), for example, first embracing George W. Bush, then relentlessly criticizing and opposing Barack Obama, and finally aggressively advocating for and defending Donald Trump. Other major networks adapted, some following suit, although none to the degree of Fox (see Figure 13.4).

At the same time, a wide variety of other news outlets, some with even more defined and extreme ideological perspectives, popped up on the left and right, contributing further to the increasingly partisan landscape of the media (see Figure 13.5 and 13.6).

FIGURE 13.4

Political Ideology for Fox, MSNBC, and CNN since 2000

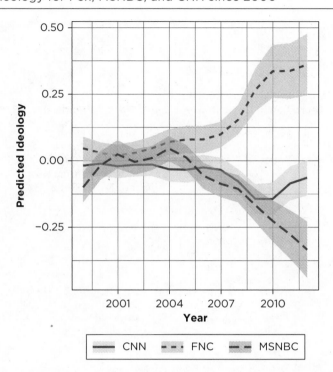

Source: Gregory J. Martin and Ali Yurukoglu, "Bias in Cable News: Persuasion and Polarization" (https://web.stanford.edu/~ayurukog/cable_news.pdf).

The Rise of Social Media. The rise of **social media** has greatly affected consumption and coverage of the news. Also fueled by the growth of the Internet, social media are ubiquitous in today's world, with Americans (and the world) making broad use of such outlets as Facebook, Twitter, Instagram, YouTube, Reddit, and many others. In terms of the news, as we noted earlier, a growing segment of the US population relies on social media frequently for news. Despite concerns about accuracy, by 2018 almost two-thirds of the American public got its news from social media, with almost half doing so often or sometimes, according the Pew Research Center (Shearer and Matsa 2018). Facebook, by far, led all social media sources in this regard.

At least three aspects of the growing importance of social media are significant for our consideration here. First, reliance on social media contributes to the creation and maintenance of "information bubbles" in which like-minded networks of individuals tend to access and share a narrow range of information sources, which often limits their exposure to a variety of opinions. Second, for policymakers, social media offers a highly appealing channel for communication to the public, unfiltered by the more traditional

FIGURE 13.5

The Ideological and Partisan Landscape of the Media, by Source and Audience

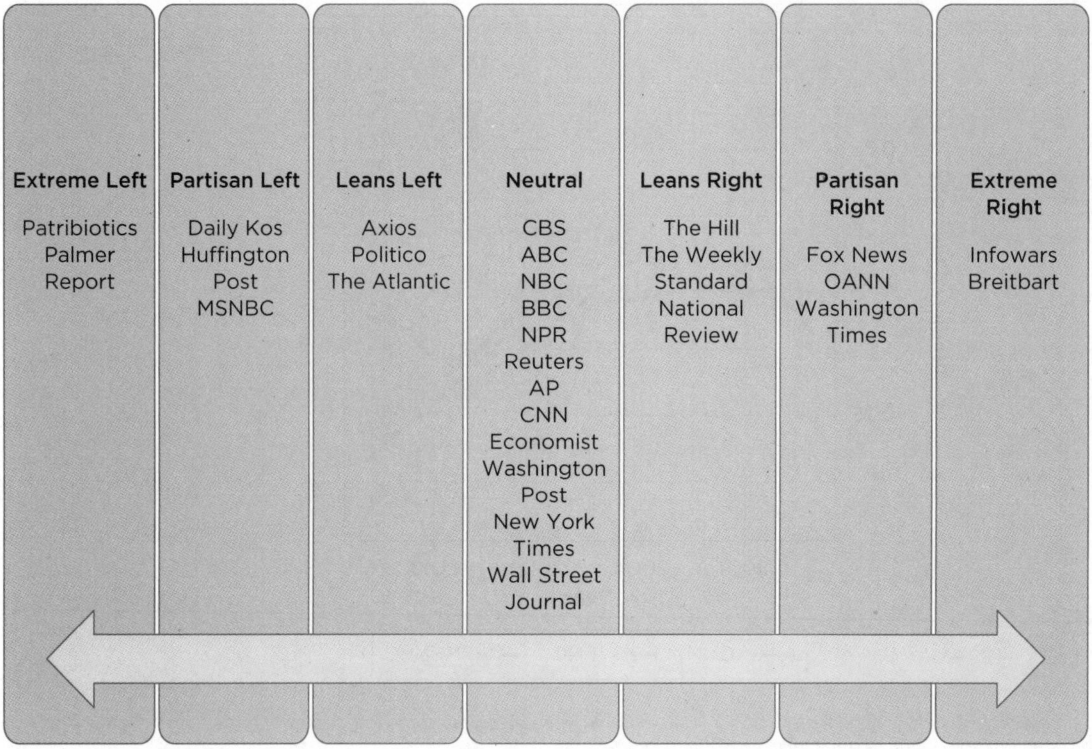

Extreme Left	Partisan Left	Leans Left	Neutral	Leans Right	Partisan Right	Extreme Right
Patribiotics Palmer Report	Daily Kos Huffington Post MSNBC	Axios Politico The Atlantic	CBS ABC NBC BBC NPR Reuters AP CNN Economist Washington Post New York Times Wall Street Journal	The Hill The Weekly Standard National Review	Fox News OANN Washington Times	Infowars Breitbart

Source: Adapted from the Shorenstein Center (https://mediabiasfactcheck.com/shorenstein-center/), Allsides (https://www.allsides.com/media-bias/media-bias-ratings), The Media Bias Chart (http://www.adfontesmedia.com/the-chart-version-3-0-what-exactly-are-we-reading/).

news media. For example, Donald Trump's Facebook strategy targeting specific slices of the voting public for Facebook ads was critical to his election victory in 2016, particularly in key battleground states such as Pennsylvania, Michigan, Wisconsin, and a few others. This effort was aided by Facebook's loose privacy standards and its controversial sharing of Facebook member information with Cambridge Analytica, which the Trump administration had hired—the data analytics and voter research firm was later disbanded after it came under investigation. Of course, President Trump's aggressive and controversial use of Twitter while in office provides another example. Third, significant problems with slanted, inaccurate, and "fake news" abound in this outlet, further contributing to discord and political conflict, not to mention challenges for public knowledge and awareness. See "A Closer Look: 'Fake News' and Social Media" for further discussion.

FIGURE 13.6

Ideological Placement of Source Audiences

Ideological Placement of Each Source's Audience

Average ideological placement on a 10-point scale of ideological consistency of those who got news from each source in the past week . . . .

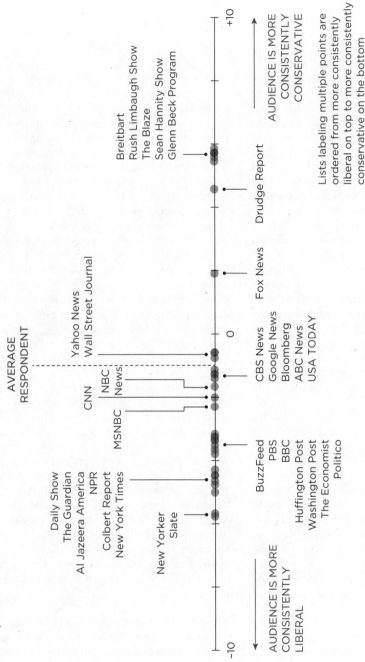

American Trends Panel (wave 1). Survey conducted March 19–April 29, 2014. Q22. Based on all web respondents. Ideological consistency based on a scale of 10 political values questions (see About the Survey for more details.) ThinkProgress, DailyKos, Mother Jones, and The Ed Schultz Show are not included in this graphic because audience sample sizes are too small to analyze.

Source: Amy Mitchell, Jocelyn Kiley, Jeffrey Gottfried, and Katerina Eva Matsa, "Political Polarization & Media Habits," Pew Research Center, October 21, 2014 (https://www.journalism.org/2014/10/21/political-polarization-media-habits/).

A Closer Look

"FAKE NEWS" AND SOCIAL MEDIA

One does not have to look far to find charges of "fake news" in the contemporary political arena. Indeed, President Trump has made the "fake" or "phony" charge increasingly more often and more expansively on his controversial Twitter feed since 2017 (Keith 2018). The president takes great pride in his claims about mainstream news as well, telling Fox News, "If you look at it from the day I started running to now, I'm so proud that I have been able to convince people how fake it is," and even claiming responsibility for the term (Schwartz 2017).

However, virtually all of what Trump labels as fake news is really just reporting or other matters he disagrees with or that he finds to be critical of himself, his family, or his administration. Well before he appropriated the term as a political weapon to mobilize his supporters, "fake news" had emerged as a different, and much more serious problem, aided and abetted by the increasing prominence of social media in American lives. In fact, "fake news" refers to "any piece of misinformation intended to sway and confuse the public. It often spreads via websites designed to help misinformation circulate as widely as possible" (Shalby 2019).

The fake news problem really surfaced during the 2016 election. It rests on the activities of individuals and groups that write false stories, create fake headlines, and/or produce doctored photos and videos and then share them via social media, hoping that they will "go viral" via Facebook, Twitter, YouTube, or other avenues. In a recent example from 2019, a right-wing sports blogger from the Bronx posted a doctored video of House Speaker Nancy Pelosi that altered actual footage to make her appear to be drunk and slurring her speech. The video went viral on Facebook and triggered a firestorm of controversy. It even prompted a congressional investigation on such "deep fake" phenomena.

Understood in this more accurate fashion, fake news and its pervasiveness stem from several sources. First, individuals and groups create made-up headlines and stories, doctored photos or videos, and memes based on moments that never really happened to share on social media to support views, policies, candidates, and policymakers they prefer, or to attack those they dislike. These can go viral as they are shared by individuals and their networks. Candidates and campaigns have even helped to spread them, wittingly or not. Second, "trolls," fake accounts, and automated bots on Facebook and Twitter amplify stories to spread them as widely as possible (e.g., Temming 2018). Third, and perhaps most troubling of all—as documented by numerous studies (e.g., Jamieson 2018; Shuster and Afraimova 2018; Watts 2018) and Special Counsel Robert Mueller's report on the investigation into Russian interference in the 2016 election—foreign countries and their intelligence services, especially Russia, have engaged in widespread efforts to create and disseminate fake news to interfere in the politics of the United States and other countries.

The effects? Fake news on social media has certainly clouded the political debate in the United States. Not all members of the public are equally susceptible—studies find that less educated, older, and more conservative individuals tend to read and share more fake news (Allcott and Gentzkow 2017; Guess, Nagler, and Tucker 2019; Shalby 2019)—but the phenomenon certainly complicates the likelihood of an informed and knowledgable public. Some studies (e.g., Allcott and Gentzkow 2017; Jamieson 2018) find that fake news played an important role in the outcome of the 2016 election. And, of course, it is the accessible and extensive networks of social media that make this fake news possible.

What are the implications of the fake news phenomenon, properly understood, for the role of the media in politics and foreign policy?

THE MEDIA AND FOREIGN POLICY POLITICS

We finish our examination of the media and foreign policy by building on the previous discussion to consider the media's role and influence in the politics of foreign policy. Our starting point, stemming from the previous sections, is that the news media must select, simplify, and, consequently, distort reality, a point on which conservative and liberal critics of the American media agree. Due to the increasing complexity of the world and the changing technology of communications, the news media can provide only a **mediated reality** yet one that has an important impact on the politics of US foreign policy. To better understand this basic point and its consequences for the politics of foreign policy, we consider the nature and diversity of the media, the factors shaping coverage, and the effects on the policy process.

Characteristics of the News Business

Let's start with some key aspects of the media that shape their role and influence. At first blush, our preceding discussion, especially of the effects of the Internet, suggests that diversity is a major story about the nature of the media. It is certainly true that Americans can now find "news" from an increasing variety of sources, including many alternative and "new media" outlets. However, there is another, perhaps far bigger story that is quite relevant to the media's role and influence, and that is the increasing **concentration of ownership** of the mainstream media. In fact, today, a handful of corporations—even a handful of people—own and control most of the American media.

Of the 1,500 daily newspapers that existed in the 1990s, 99 percent were local monopolies, and about a dozen corporations controlled most of the country's circulation. Independently owned newspapers, once dominant, have been replaced by large media chains, such as Gannett, which operates *USA Today* and more than 100 other daily newspapers and almost a thousand weekly publications; Knight Ridder, now owned by McClatchy, which runs the *Philadelphia Inquirer*, the *Miami Herald*, and thirty other daily newspapers; the New York Times Company, which operates the *New York Times*, the *Boston Globe*, and more than thirty other dailies (as well as numerous magazines and television and radio stations); and Tribune Media, which owns the *Chicago Tribune*, the *Los Angeles Times,* and the *Baltimore Sun* (as well as other regional newspapers and radio stations and some forty television stations).

When the first edition of this book was published in 1983, about 90 percent of the media were owned by about fifty corporations. At that time, the strategy of most of the fifty biggest firms was to gain market domination in one medium—to have the largest market share solely in newspapers, for example, or in magazines, or broadcasting, or books, or movies, but not in all of them. Since then, ownership has steadily concentrated into the hands of fewer and fewer corporations and individuals. Today, just five firms or conglomerates dominate about 90 percent of the American mass media. The five conglomerates are AT&T, which owns CNN; the Walt Disney Company, which owns ABC; Murdoch's News Corporation, based in Australia, which owns Fox; Comcast, which owns NBC; and National Amusements, which owns CBS

FIGURE 13.7

The "Big Five" Media Conglomerates

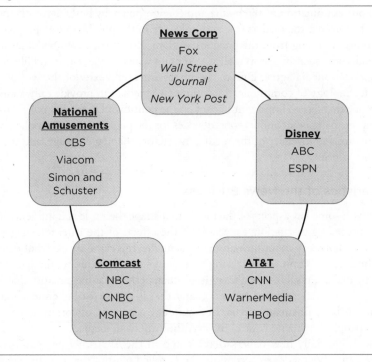

and Viacom (see Figure 13.7 on these "big five" and a few of their key subsidiaries). Indeed, according to *Forbes*, much of the American media is controlled by fifteen billionaires, including such people as Rupert Murdoch, Michael Bloomberg, and Jeff Bezos, the Amazon.com executive who purchased the *Washington Post* in 2013 (Vinton 2016).

So the mainstream media and the national media have become the basic source of national and international news through which most Americans acquire information about the world around them, and they are mostly owned by five global conglomerates. While the existence of so many news sources provides the appearance of considerable diversity, the national media and their overall concentration tend to present **homogeneous news coverage** rather than a diverse picture of the news and the world. Regardless of which of the national television news programs or newspapers one watches or reads, all of these sources usually select the same lead news item, cover the same stories, and provide similar information and interpretations. In recent years, Fox News represents a notable exception, often departing from the reports common to other news sources to emphasize stories that more closely fit its more partisan alignment.

We should note another aspect of the news business that also has important implications. One reason the news media have become concentrated and their coverage so homogenized is that the mass media have increasingly become a big business. Historically, the American press used to consist of small, independent operations that were usually quite partisan. Presses frequently were operated to make money and provide a living for those involved. In addition, many were financed by wealthy patrons who were more interested in providing news and political interpretation, even at a financial loss. With the rise of industrialization, urbanization, and mass society, however, the media have become a big business where the bottom line—financial worth and profit—predominates.

As economics has replaced politics as the basic source of motivation within the news business, some observers would argue that critical and investigative journalism—especially in the broadcast media—has declined. Overall, growing concern with generating revenue and maintaining profitability has led to the mass media's preoccupation with maximizing their appeal to very broad as well as very specialized audiences, reinforcing the tendency to provide a selective and homogenized picture of national and international politics, if any is provided at all. This factor drives the competitive nature of the media, especially in the sense that it reflects their business and profit motives. The phrase used by one scholar to describe this situation is that the mass media are **"rivals in conformity"** for audiences and advertisers, which has little to do with improving the quality of media coverage (Bigman 1949). The news media, as in any business, attempt to increase their market share because their revenues are obtained predominantly through advertising. Hence, a key concern of national media organizations is to present news in such a way that attracts, not alienates, audiences and advertisers—that, in other words, takes into consideration the beliefs of the mass and elite publics, or of particular sectors of them. This would include not alienating business in particular, since it is the major source of most media advertising.

Television is probably the most competitive and "infotainment oriented" because the national networks compete for the same viewing audience (and the same national advertisers). Although advertising rates are lower for news than for entertainment programs, it still costs advertisers an average of about $250,000 a minute for a commercial on one of the nightly network news shows (as opposed to more than $5 million for a thirty-second ad during the Super Bowl). Having a larger or smaller audience means a difference of millions of dollars in yearly revenues. This competitiveness, ironically, tends to promote what might be called a "risk-avoidance approach." Their fear of losing viewers and offending corporate sponsors makes the media act with great caution in their programming, usually preferring to emulate the news organizations (or the entertainment shows) currently enjoying the greatest amount of success. "Soft" public affairs programs such as *The Today Show* that emphasize entertainment and personalities, and news opinion or commentary shows such as *The Sean Hannity Show* and *The Rachel Maddow Show*, have proliferated.

Factors Shaping News Coverage

Within this context, a series of factors shape the nature of news coverage as it relates to politics and foreign policy. These include key aspects of our preceding discussion, such as the rise of more ideological media sources, the media's increasingly concentrated ownership and business/profit demands, and the decline of foreign reporting that stems from it. But it also includes a few other important factors.

National media organizations are large, complex bureaucratic enterprises involving thousands of people organized in terms of hierarchy, specialization, and routines. They are also heavily influenced by a media subculture based on certain norms and standards of professional journalism. This affects how the news media portray contemporary national and international affairs in terms of which issues, places, and events get covered (or do not get covered), how those topics are reported, which stories are finally run, and how they are presented to the public, including through the Internet. Presidents and political leaders can try to manage and manipulate the press, but this is difficult to do across the board, although different presidents may find more sympathetic partners in parts of the media.

Within these organizations, editors and executives at the top of the bureaucratic hierarchy also play an important role, for they supervise and oversee the news production and **editorial process**. They make crucial decisions concerning which journalists are hired, what gets covered and by whom, which stories are published, the length and location of the stories, and their final presentation and wording. The importance of this is evident, for example, in studies that have found a much higher proportion of stories on the Third World in the AP and United Press International wire services than appear in the American press (Gerbner and Marvanyi 1977; Stacks, 2004). The recent experience of the *Wall Street Journal*'s former editor in chief—Gerard Baker—is instructive on this. Baker's stormy tenure at the *Journal* included controversy over his gatekeeping role on reporting and content, including his insistence on more favorable and sensitive treatment of Donald Trump. Interestingly, when Baker was replaced, he moved on to a weekly show on Fox Business Network, another Rupert Murdoch–owned outlet. In more subtle fashion, journalists of major news organizations who work in the field recognize that editors have certain idiosyncrasies and beliefs that make them more receptive to certain kinds of information and news angles than others. In this sense, a type of "self-censorship" occurs within the news process, as it does in all professions, given the incentives and disincentives built into the media bureaucracy and the journalistic profession.

Among the mainstream media, coverage is heavily affected by the subculture of the journalism profession. First, journalists tend to be generalists, not specialists. What a generalist gains in terms of breadth of information is offset by limited depth of knowledge and understanding relative to any particular issue or area. More important, historically the contemporary mainstream media have taken a so-called nonpartisan approach in their news coverage—often referred to as **objective journalism**. Journalistic norms emphasize independence (acting free of "outside" political pressures), objectivity (presenting the facts without prejudice or distortion), and impartiality (avoiding partisanship and providing balance in representing without favor the views of contending parties). Although this may result in less personal bias, the emphasis becomes on what is "factual" in a news story from "establishment" sources (the opposite may be true for the political blogs on the Internet). As we noted, however, the past several decades have seen sharp deviations from this norm and practice among some parts of media. Yet, both conservative groups that perceive a liberal bias and liberal groups that perceive a conservative bias oversimplify the ideological nature of the news media. For the mainstream and national media, the personal beliefs of journalists are often moderated by their professional journalistic roles, for they must operate within the constraints of mainstream media that are concentrated, run as a business, competitive, and bureaucratic within a larger cultural and political environment. See "A Different Perspective: Are the Media Biased?" for some additional insights on the question of media bias.

A Different Perspective

ARE THE MEDIA BIASED?

The norms and practices of professional journalism emphasize objectivity. Even so, charges of media bias abound throughout government and society today. President Trump routinely attacks the mainstream media as partisan and hostile to Republicans, while Democrats regularly point to Fox News and decry its increasingly partisan practices. As noted in a recent study of the media by political scientist Adam Schiffer (2017):

> Accusations of media bias are everywhere . . . . It is likely the most commonly held opinion about the news media. It is often the most strongly held, or even the only, attitude toward the press that a politically aware student brings to class or that an uncle brings to the Thanksgiving table or your social-media feed. Talk-radio hosts, bloggers, and Fox News obsess over it, and several interest groups are devoted entirely to exposing it. (pp. 1–2)

How do we evaluate these concerns? Are the media biased? Empirical research casts doubt on these claims. In more than four decades of careful analysis by researchers in political science and mass communication, "the preponderance of evidence finds no overall, systematic bias in the mainstream press toward one side of the political spectrum" (p. 17). In particular, "the popular claim of an overall, systematic leftward tilt is unsupported" (p. 33).

At the same time, we should not ignore the increasing divide between the more ideologically driven news outlets. Liberal, conservative, and other ideological outlets are abundant, especially on radio and the Internet (and MSNBC and Fox News on cable). While the "average" of the coverage works out to a centrist balance, viewers relying on one or the other receive a very different depiction of issues and events compared to the more mainstream news media on which most of the mass public relies—reinforcing partisan politics among the most politically attentive and active. How, then, can we assess bias?

Schiffer provides direction in his recent book, *Evaluating Media Bias*. According to Schiffer (p. 55),

> Bias charges succumb to many pathologies. Among the most common are that the charge attacks journalists or owners rather than their product, the charger fails to specify a standard, the standard is ideologically loaded and thus is more of a partisan talking point than a valid media criticism, the charger expects balance between unbalanced phenomena, an alleged imbalance can be explained by factors other than media bias, the charger cherry-picks confirming evidence and ignores disconfirming content, or a charger with a vested interest in a particular conclusion makes a subjective assessment of news slant.

A better approach requires more careful analysis. Schiffer offers a helpful framework. As he summarizes, "A valid bias charge should (1) set a nonideological normative expectation (the 'ideal') for high-quality news content, (2) derive

(Continued)

(Continued)

a clear standard (the 'baseline') for what would constitute unbiased coverage in that context, and (3) provide a social-scientifically valid demonstration (the 'evidence') of the alleged deviation from the standard" (p. 54). Thus, assessing media bias requires the following:

- Definition of partisan bias: "when news content deviates from an ideal, to the benefit of one side of the American political divide" (p. 40).

- Clear establishment of a non-ideological baseline or "standard by which to measure the news content in question" that rests on . . . "a belief about how the news media should behave that derives from commonly accepted principles of good journalism" (pp. 41, 42). As Schiffer elaborates, "A valid accusation must state, or clearly imply, criteria for unbiased coverage in that context. Otherwise, a charge against one or more news stories, with no apparent standard for what would have constituted unbiased coverage, is merely empty rhetoric with no logical heft" (p. 44).

- Evidence: "The final component is the most straightforward: All bias charges must present concrete evidence of the alleged bias" (p. 45).

What are the implications of this perspective on the charges of media bias and the broader politics of US foreign policymaking?

Much of the news is a function of the **beat system**, in which reporters are given responsibility for covering a particular issue or institution. Although journalists like to talk about the age of investigative reporting following the Vietnam War and Watergate, there are actually very few investigative reporters per se who make a concerted effort to uncover as many relevant sources and pieces of information as possible in putting a story together. Instead, "beat reporters" are assigned by their media organizations to cover established political and national security institutions, such as government (including the White House, Pentagon, State Department, Congress, and Supreme Court), and rely on the authorities available as their basic source of information. Naturally, the most prestigious beat is the White House.

In addition to finances, journalists and the major media organizations are preoccupied with getting the story first and being the "number one" source of news. This concern with being the media leader tends to result in the phenomenon of **pack journalism**, in which journalists chase the same headline stories. This tendency to congregate while in search of the same story is reinforced by the strong *esprit de corps* that develops among journalists (see also Sabato 1991). Pack journalism is most noticeable, for instance, during crisis coverage or with the media's effort to cover election campaigns (as depicted by Timothy Crouse's 1972 classic *The Boys on the Bus*).

Not surprisingly, much of the political news is about what government officials from these institutions have said or done. Thus, the news media tend to practice **source journalism** (versus **investigative journalism**). "Very few newspaper stories are the result of reporters digging through files; poring over documents; or interviewing experts, dissenters, or ordinary people. The overwhelming majority of stories are based on official sources—on information provided by members of Congress, presidential aides, and other political insiders" (Karp 1989:61). As Carl Bernstein (1992:22), who was critical in breaking the Watergate story has pointed out:

> America's news organizations assigned only fourteen of those 2,000 men and women [reporters working in Washington, D.C.] to cover the Watergate story on a fulltime basis. And of those fourteen, only six were assigned to the story on what might be called an "investigative" basis, that is, to go beyond recording the obvious daily statements and court proceedings, and try to find out exactly what had happened.

And according to Bernstein, not much has changed in post-Watergate journalism.

For instance, Leon Sigal (1973) found that, in the *New York Times* and the *Washington Post*, stories from regularly covered beats outnumbered off-beat stories two to one, including front-page headlines. Because so many journalists cover the same institutions and issues while operating under the same time constraints, the beat system also sets the stage for pack journalism. As Stephen Hess (1981:118) argues, "Washington news gathering, in other words, is an interaction among elites. One elite reports on another elite."

As we discussed earlier, international coverage is heavily a function of foreign bureaus and foreign correspondents. Historically, they have tended to be stationed in countries that are allied with the US government and located in major cities. At their peak, at least half of roughly 700 foreign correspondents were routinely stationed in Europe, while fewer than 10 percent were stationed in each of the three regions of Africa, Latin America, and the Middle East. Moreover, as we described in the preceding section, since the end of the Cold War, most media organizations have cut back on the number of their foreign bureaus and foreign correspondents.

Media, Politics, and the Policy Process

It is time now to bring our discussion to a close and consider the role and influence of the media in the politics of US foreign policy. To begin, what we have considered to this point suggests four broad channels of influence that reflect related but different roles for the media (see Figure 13.8). The first two are relatively straightforward and reflect the idea that the media influence politics and processes. First, the media may shape policymaker views and priorities directly, both through agenda setting—calling attention to particular problems—and by the nature of their coverage of those problems. Second, the media may shape public opinion by calling the public's attention to particular problems and issues, and by influencing how the public understands and responds to those matters. To repeat the words of Cohen (1963:13), the press "is stunningly successful in telling its readers what to think about" in foreign affairs and, to a certain extent, what to think. This in turn can significantly shape and constrain what policymakers do.

Perhaps the most well-known theory related to how the media can set the agenda for both the public and policymakers is the so-called **CNN effect**, which argues that

FIGURE 13.8

Channels of Influence for the Media and Foreign Policymaking

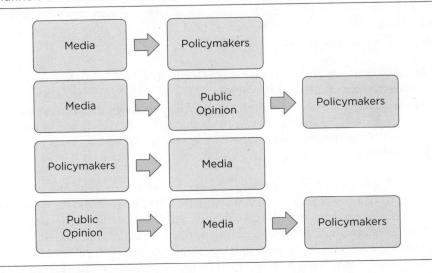

media attention to and coverage of some issues over others—and, in particular, the images associated with such coverage—can serve to reorder the foreign policy priorities of policy-makers, accelerate the decision-making process, and/or limit the policy options available to policymakers. This occurs as policymakers—and the public—are emotionally affected by images and stories contained in news coverage. Typically, this theory has been applied to cases involving humanitarian crises and whether the United States should intervene, but it has been extended to other policy areas as well. The CNN effect is therefore particularly relevant to the first two channels. However, empirical studies have mostly found little evidence supporting the argument that such an effect exists (e.g., Gilboa 2005; Livingston and Eachus 1995). Some do indicate that the *lack* of media coverage might increase the likelihood that a problem will be ignored by policymakers (e.g., Hawkins 2011), and others conclude that policymakers are particularly aware of the potential for public backlash if the costs of intervention (or other policies, for that matter) become too high (e.g., Livingston 1997; Mueller 1973, 2005; Robinson 2002).

The other two channels reflect a different role for the media, one in which it responds to, rather than affects, the public or policymakers. The third channel suggests that media attention and coverage respond to policymakers and/or reflect the efforts of policymakers to use it to frame issues, push their preferences, and shape public opinion. Indeed, a major explanation of the role and influence of the media is the "**indexing**" argument (e.g., Bennett 1990, 1994a, 1994b; Bennett et al., 2007). This explanation rests on the close connections among media coverage, the opinions and priorities of elites, and the source-driven nature of journalism to posit that media coverage tends to follow the attention and debates of elites, particularly in the White House and the Senate. As Daniel Hallin (1986) argues, the national media tend to reflect the views of leaders and government officials: When they agree, the news media reflect the consensus view; when they disagree, the media reflect their level of diversity. Thus, in the words of Mermin (1999:143), "The media act, for the most part, as a vehicle for government officials to criticize each other" and, as a result, make "no independent contribution (except at the margins) to foreign policy debate."

Other scholars, however, have suggested that the indexing argument is far too limiting and overly simplistic in its assessment of the role of the press in the foreign policymaking process. Entman's (2003, 2004) "**cascading activation**" model, for example, suggests that it is not enough merely to assess the level of disagreement among policymakers to predict how the news media might cover a particular problem or issue; we must also consider the sources on whom journalists tend to rely in news coverage and whether the content of what those sources are saying resonates with the broader public. Specifically, some officials—for example, White House and military officials, followed by members of Congress—tend to have more access and be more influential in shaping news content on foreign affairs than others—for example, ex-government officials, academics, policy experts, and journalists. Nonetheless, each of these sets of actors possesses at least some capability to shape news coverage and, in turn, influence how policymakers evaluate and respond to problems or issues. As several scholars have indicated, this largely depends on the extent to which this information appeals to and reinforces the political predispositions and national identity of the broader citizenry (e.g., Rowling, Jones, and Sheets 2011; Rowling, Sheets, and Jones 2015). Thus, instead of a top-down process in which elites dictate news coverage and, in turn, public opinion, cascading activation allows for bottom-up pressures—in terms of both what nonofficials say and what the public demands—in shaping the relationships among officials, the press, and the public within the foreign policymaking process.

The fourth and final channel represents the possibility that the media may respond to public attention or opinion—particularly in more salient and intense matters—to shift its coverage. In this explanation, because the public is the market for the media's products, it tends to follow public attention pretty closely, which conditions its role and relationship to the elites. According to Baum and Potter (2019; see also Baum and Potter 2008), for example, while the public was unengaged, uninterested, and inattentive, the media acted as a "lapdog," following elites. However, with public attention and engagement, the media became a "watchdog"—providing the public with information; conducting investigations; and exposing failure, scandal, and other problems with policy or policymaking.

Three additional observations and their implications bring this section to a close. First, as our previous discussion indicates, and Baum and Potter (2019) show, changes in the media since the end of the Cold War have increased the silos within which Americans live, reducing their exposure to a broad range of perspectives and information. Driven by the twin trends of the rise of ideological media and the growth of social media—with algorithms generating more of what we like rather than broad perspectives—this has made it harder to create and sustain an informed public, and easier for that public to be manipulated. As Baum and Potter (2019) suggest,

> Information distribution patterns on social media have evolved in ways that exacerbate rather than mitigate hyper-fragmentation (Stroud 2011) . . . . Moreover, the algorithms developed by social media platforms are designed

to keep eyeballs locked in place by buffering against exposure to alternative viewpoints .... As platforms learn what we most like to consume, they become increasingly adept at serving it up to the exclusion of contrary information that might induce us to look elsewhere. The end result is a public that is more fragmented and polarized than ever and so more difficult than ever for leaders to reach with their messages. The paradox is that too much information, when combined with fragmentation, can contribute to a less informed public.

With respect to foreign policymaking, there are many implications. Jeong and Quirk (2017), Schultz (2018), and Baum and Potter (2019) note several, including the reduction of bipartisanship; complications for learning, adaptation, and correction of policy failures; the media's contribution to dramatic policy swings and the accompanying difficulties these swings create for reputation, policy consistency, and relations with both allies and adversaries; and the increasing vulnerability to foreign interference and manipulation of American politics.

Second, this trend, and other elements of our previous discussion, highlight and enhance the role and impact of policymaker tactics when it comes to making use of the media. As we have seen, the news media are directly affected by the political dynamics of the policymaking process and domestic politics. In fact, government officials and societal groups attempt to influence and manipulate the media's coverage of domestic and international affairs because they understand that the images communicated by the media, especially television, have a powerful influence on domestic politics and the policymaking process. Indeed, media images affect the political agenda and general climate of public opinion about politics and policy problems. Policymakers have a number of ways of doing this.

For one, policymakers know the deadlines of important publications and broadcast media, such as the *New York Times*, the *Wall Street Journal*, *Time*, *Newsweek*, and network television news. They schedule events and news releases so that stories arrive in gatekeepers' offices precisely when needed. If their releases are attractively presented and meet newsworthiness criteria, journalists find it hard to resist using them. If news sources want to stifle publicity, they can announce the news just past the deadlines, preferably on weekends when few newscasts are scheduled.

Moreover, the **politics of symbolism and legitimacy** has been important throughout history. Power, for the president or any political actor, depends heavily on the illusion of power and the politics of symbolism. This was a key to Reagan's success and his "television presidency." As Hedrick Smith (1988:345) explained it, "Reagan is so natural onstage that, unlike most politicians, he creates the illusion of not being onstage." Furthermore, "Reagan has a political genius for selling his message—like the genius of Franklin Roosevelt. His secret is his mastery of political shorthand. He knows how to make ideas accessible and popular." The politics of symbolism is particularly prominent in situations of security threats and whenever the US government has relied on the use of force abroad.

A favorite technique of symbolic politics, especially given the decline in public trust of government officials, is **blame game politics**. When the policymaking process becomes gridlocked, when policies fail, or when they are poorly received by the public—which has been occurring pretty regularly from the Clinton administration through the Trump administration—all government and private parties involved rush to disclaim any responsibility and blame others: The president blames Congress, members of Congress blame the president, Republicans blame Democrats, and Democrats blame Republicans.

Finally, the institution most successful in gaining access to the news media and influencing their coverage is the government and, in particular, the presidency. Rightly or wrongly, with the president often considered the center of foreign policy activity, the national media, with their beat system and norms of objective journalism, have become heavily dependent on the government and especially the executive branch for much of their information concerning US foreign policy and international affairs. As Jon Western (2005:18) argues, "Most correspondents are reluctant to challenge executive sources openly," and they tend to accept administration assumptions, definitions, and so on as legitimate. As Bernard Cohen (1963:28) explained in his classic *The Press and Foreign Policy*, "The more 'neutral' the press is . . . the more easily it lends itself to the uses of others, and particularly to public officials whom reporters have come to regard as prime sources of news merely by virtue of their positions in government. This is unquestionably the case at the Presidential level." Or according to Daniel Hallin (1986:8), with the rise of so-called objective journalism, "journalists gave up the right to speak with a political voice of their own, and in turn they were granted a regular right of access to the inner councils of government, a right they had never enjoyed in the era of partisan journalism."

Thus, the president—the top governmental official—has a unique advantage in gaining access to the news media and having them communicate his or her views and preferences to the American public, most visibly during the early stages of a foreign policy crisis. Whatever and whenever the president speaks or acts, it is newsworthy by definition. Recently, President Obama exemplified this through his numerous public statements, press conferences, and interviews before the media. President Trump also exemplifies this, relying on his Twitter feed to force the media and others to respond, while avoiding formal press conferences in favor of informal "stop and talk" moments on the White House driveway or lawn, which the media dutifully report. Trump's unprecedented relationship and interactions with Fox News also serves as a good example, while further illustrating the rise and importance of ideological media sources (see "A Closer Look: The Fox News Presidency").

A Closer Look

THE FOX NEWS PRESIDENCY

The relationship between President Donald Trump and Fox News is really unprecedented. As Jane Mayer (2019) reports, in January 2019, President Trump gave his forty-second interview to Fox. At that point, he had given a total of only ten interviews to the other major networks and none of those interviews was with CNN. That same month, Fox talk-show host Sean Hannity appeared with Trump at a campaign event, and not as a reporter or commentator, crossing a line long observed by members of the media. The Trump

(Continued)

(Continued)

administration has been full of former Fox employees and contributors, including Bill Shine, who served as the administration's director of communication and deputy chief of staff from July 2018 to March 2019. Shine had been director of programming at Fox News prior to that. Both Fox and the White House paid Shine. Furthermore, many former Trump administration advisers are now employed by Fox as regular contributors.

Beyond these connections, Trump himself relies on Fox for an inordinate proportion of his daily activity. As we discussed in Chapter 3, a large portion of the president's time is what the White House calls "executive time." This unstructured time dominates the president's daily schedule, which itself is dominated by watching television, mostly Fox. According to Mayer, longtime Washington political insider Charlie Black told her that "Trump gets up and watches 'Fox & Friends' and thinks these are his friends. He thinks anything on Fox is friendly. But the problem is he gets unvetted ideas."

Matthew Gertz (2018) describes an especially unsettling aspect of this relationship: President Trump appears to be "live-tweeting" Fox News programs, with the show Fox & Friends particularly central to his attention. While Trump's penchant for tweeting about what he watches has been well-established by reporting, according to Gertz the practice is even more extensive than recognized. As Gertz (2018) puts it:

After comparing the president's tweets with Fox's coverage every day since October, I can tell you that the Fox-Trump feedback loop is happening far more often than you think. . . . Here's what's also shocking: A man with unparalleled access to the world's most powerful information-gathering machine,

with an intelligence budget estimated at $73 billion last year, prefers to rely on conservative cable news hosts to understand current events.

Trump may not be trying to divert the media, but the media definitely gets distracted. Trump's morning tweets upend the news cycle, with cable news producers and assignment editors redistributing time and resources to cover his latest comments. Statements from the president are inherently newsworthy. But the result is certainly a positive one for Fox: The network's partisan programming gets validation from the president and forces the rest of the press to cover Fox's obsessions whether they are newsworthy or not.

In December, Mediaite put the co-hosts of Fox & Friends at the top of its "Most Influential in Media" list, pointing out "the topics they cover essentially set the national agenda for the rest of the day." Mediaite is not wrong. Soon after White House counselor Kellyanne Conway congratulated the co-hosts for the designation during an interview on the show, Trump weighed in, urging the "many Fake News Hate Shows" to "study your formula for success!" He had been watching.

What are the implications of President Trump's devotion to Fox News (and vice versa) for the media's role and influence in the politics and processes of US foreign policy?

Source: "I've Studied the Trump-Fox Feedback Loop for Months. It's Crazier Than You Think," by Matthew Gertz. Politico, January 5, 2018 (https://www.politico.com/magazine/story/2018/01/05/trump-media-feedback-loop-216248).

As this brief summary suggests, presidents have a number of tools at their disposal to influence media coverage of national and, in particular, international affairs (Cohen 2008). First, realizing that presidential acts are "newsworthy," presidential appearances in public are often "staged" to maximize positive news coverage and communicate the desired information and message. According to David Gergen, a member of the White House staff to Presidents Nixon, Reagan, and Clinton, "We had a rule in the Nixon operation that before any public event was put on his schedule, you had to know what the headline out of that event was going to be, what the picture was going to be, and what the lead paragraph would be. You had to think of it in those terms, and if you couldn't justify it, it didn't go on the [president's] schedule" (quoted in Smith 1988:401).

A second important advantage is that the government is perceived as a "highly credible source" of information. Under the beat system, government officials are able to control the release of information through press releases, briefings, and public statements. During foreign policy crises, the news media are almost exclusively dependent (or allow themselves to become almost exclusively dependent) on the executive branch for their information.

A third way that the executive branch controls information is to take advantage of the "classification of information." This can be done by "denying" or through **leaks** of information. As Hedrick Smith (1988:80) points out, "On Wall Street, passing insider information to others is an indictable offense. In Washington, it is the regular stuff of the power game." Although leaking is widespread throughout the Washington community, it tends to be more frequent within the executive branch, especially the closer one gets to the president (these are, in fact, the primary sources that journalist Bob Woodward, of Woodward and Bernstein Watergate fame, relies on for his insider books).

As did most administrations before it, the Obama administration, especially the White House, routinely leaked information. For example, many people believe that the *Rolling Stone* article written by Michael Hastings (2010) on "The Runaway General" Stanley McCrystal was based on a White House leak countering unauthorized leaks by the Pentagon in favor of an Afghan surge. The article led to a more involved president and deliberative process in fall 2009 about McCrystal's request for a surge in troops and ultimately led to his being fired as commander of American forces in Afghanistan and replaced by General Petraeus (who was demoted from combat commander of CENTCOM, as discussed in Chapter 6). In the Trump administration, leaking has been pronounced, with both dissenters and advocates adopting the tactic.

Current administrations have also illustrated the related tactic of the use of **propaganda and censorship**. Members of the executive branch occasionally orchestrate public relations campaigns with propaganda (consciously distorting information and lying), employ disinformation (knowingly manufacturing false information), and resort to censorship (based on secret classified information)—to manipulate the media and rally public support for their foreign policy efforts. The Persian Gulf and Iraq Wars serve as excellent examples of presidential censorship and propaganda. According to one assessment, "One casualty of the Gulf War appears to be the independent, itinerant war correspondent. The press pool system used in the Gulf encouraged the most docile sort of pack journalism" in which "members of the national media competed in tandem for whatever censored information and video images that the White House and the Pentagon allowed them to communicate" (Schmeisser 1991:21). As Michael Deaver, President Reagan's deputy chief of staff and communications chief, assessed it,

The Department of Defense has done an excellent job of managing the news in an almost classic way. There's plenty of access to some things and at least one visual a day. If you were going to hire a public relations firm to do the media relations for an international event, it couldn't be done any better than this is being done. (quoted in Jones 1991:A9)

The administration of President George W. Bush and Vice President Dick Cheney has been accused of being among the most secretive in controlling information in modern presidential history. Bush administration officials have been accused of using knowingly false information about weapons of mass destruction (WMDs) and al-Qaeda's links with Saddam Hussein in rallying public (and international) support for its invasion of Iraq. Michael Massing (2005:43) highlights how the mainstream media, focusing on the *New York Times*, missed (or buried) the story about Iraq's WMDs before the attack—the heart of the president's case for war: "In the period before the war, US journalists were far too reliant on sources sympathetic to the administration. Those with dissenting views—and there were more than a few—were shut out. Reflecting this, the coverage was highly deferential to the White House." The Trump administration has also been aggressive in these kinds of efforts through a variety of means, including excluding and bullying journalists critical of its actions and controlling the dissemination of information in reports and on government websites to serve its own ends and shape the public debate.

Finally, government officials often promote favorable news media coverage by building on their many contacts and personal relationships within the media. Henry Kissinger was a master, for example, at wooing the media in order to promote his foreign policy purposes. He was a constant source of information, often classified, anonymously provided to the media in general or to selected journalists, which they would then attribute to a "senior government official." As Stanley Hoffmann (1968:308) pointed out long ago:

The closeness to official Washington of the nation's leading columnists and reporters, writing for the main newspapers and television networks, is especially responsible for numbing the mass media's capacity to question and challenge. . . . Enjoying the confidence of the great usually kills the urge to investigate. Officials disarm these men by giving them the illusion of being admitted to the mysteries of decision-making, and by making them sympathize with their ordeals.

CONCLUSIONS ON THE MEDIA AND FOREIGN POLICY

Overall, our discussion in this chapter suggests several general conclusions. First, most Americans are dependent on the news media, especially the national media, for information and understanding of national and international affairs. Second, the national media provide a considerable amount of information regarding national and international affairs. Third, coverage tends to be selective, disjointed, and American-centric as stories come and go with little history or context provided. Fourth, the mainstream and national media represent a business and a bureaucratic profession. Fifth, media coverage is influenced by politics and political actors (such as the president) and it also influences domestic politics and the policymaking process. It has thus been affected by the growing polarization and partisanship of the foreign policy landscape and has also contributed to it. Finally, these patterns are magnified by the revolution in information and communications technology.

The nature of the news business and the political environment in American society have made the news media more dependent on the government, especially the president and the executive branch. At the same time, the president and the government have become more dependent on the media. The president and the executive branch have considerable advantages in promoting positive news media coverage, especially early in an administration, over issues of foreign policy and during crises, when presidential legitimacy and support are at their highest. But, even with all its advantages, the presidency in the post–Vietnam War and post–Cold War eras has been unable to dominate and influence media coverage to the same extent it did during the Cold War, even in the area of foreign policy.

Most broadly, because Americans are dependent on the media as their fundamental source of information concerning national and international affairs, the news media have a major impact on public knowledge and democratic citizenship in the politics of US foreign policy. At best, most Americans acquire a simplistic awareness of and familiarity with the world around them. This is because the mass public, as discussed in Chapter 11, tends to be uninterested, inattentive, uninformed, and, therefore, most receptive to media headlines. This simplistic awareness is also due to the public's tendency to be "over-newsed" and "under-informed" by the media, especially now in the age of the Internet. This problem is much more severe with respect to international news, because most Americans lack the context to make sense of the information and images being communicated to them about "foreign" places abroad. The net result is a mass public that bears little resemblance to the "alert and knowledgeable citizenry" called for by President Eisenhower in his farewell address. Instead, the nature of media coverage contributes to a relatively poorly informed public, increasingly immersed in bubbles reflecting their own views and predispositions, and vulnerable to wild fluctuations and significant manipulation.

THINK ABOUT THIS

The author George Orwell once said, "The people will believe what the media tells them they believe." Think about the discussion of the media and foreign policy in this chapter, especially the two-way process of influence involving the media, policymakers, and the public.

How does the nature, role, and behavior of the media shape the politics of US foreign policy?

KEY TERMS

beat system   442

blame game politics   446

cascading activation   445

CNN effect   443

concentration of ownership   437

editorial process   440

foreign bureaus   431

foreign correspondents   431

headline news   420

homogeneous news
    coverage   438

ideological news sources   432

Visit **edge.sagepub.com/scottrosati7e** to help you accomplish your coursework goals in an easy-to-use learning environment.

PART IV

Conclusion

In our last chapter, we offer some broad conclusions about the major patterns and processes discussed throughout the book and implications for the future politics of US foreign policy.

Patterns, Processes, and Foreign Policymaking

LEARNING OBJECTIVES

1. Reflect on key questions about the politics of US foreign policy.

2. Describe the patterns and politics of US foreign policy since World War II.

3. Identify the shifting patterns of policy leadership in US foreign policy.

SAUL LOEB/AFP/Getty Images

PHOTO 14.1 The White House Situation Room.

We have now come to the end of our examination of the players, processes, and politics that drive US decisions and involvement in the global political system. At the outset, we emphasized the complexity and political nature of US foreign policymaking, and we asked you to keep a single, overarching question in mind: *What are the factors that shape and determine the foreign policy choices of the United States?* We hope that, by now, you understand the variety of actors who play a role and that the struggle over competing values, purposes, meanings, and interests is never far from the surface of foreign policy.

In the preceding chapters, we examined the historical and global context of US foreign policy (Part I); the government and the policymaking process, focusing on the president, the foreign policy and foreign economic bureaucracies, and policymaking processes and explanations (Part II); and the role of society and domestic politics, concentrating on public opinion, interest groups, and the media (Part III). We hope by now that you agree with us on the utility of our Shifting Leadership and Politics analytical framework, which provides the basic structure or frame of reference for organizing and thinking about the politics and processes of US foreign policy (see Figure 14.1). Overall, it should be clear at this point that the commonly held view that presidents make foreign policy in the United States is a gross oversimplification at best, and an outright inaccuracy at worst.

Unlike the Presidential Preeminence framework (see Figure 1.1), which is the conventional approach, the Shifting Leadership and Politics framework recognizes the complex and messy politics of the US foreign policy process and the varying roles and leadership of the president; presidential advisers; the agencies of the foreign policy bureaucracy; Congress and its members; societal forces and actors such as public opinion, interest groups, and the media; and international factors. As we have seen throughout the pages of this text, the president and the White House may lead in US foreign policy, but they do not necessarily *always* do so. Moreover, even when the executive branch does lead, that does not necessarily mean it is the president at the helm. Thus, although presidential leadership is a key aspect of US foreign policymaking, our analytical framework encourages consideration of the conditions under which it is more or less likely. In particular, other actors have leadership roles to play in the foreign policy process—from the foreign policy bureaucracy to Congress—and they bring unique resources to the process as well.

In this conception, policymaking involves a political process of conflict, compromise, and incrementalism due to the multiplicity of actors attempting to reconcile competing goals. Thus, as Hilsman (1964:13) recognized long ago, a nation is moved as a result of "the interaction of the President, the Congress, the press, and special interests" and "the rivalries of the great Executive departments, State, Defense, and the Central Intelligence Agency, as they clash in the actual making of policy." According to Hilsman (1964:561–62), the implications of such a political and messy policymaking process are that

> over some of this at certain times, the president may merely preside—if it is a matter of slight interest to him and has little impact on his position. But if he is an advocate or if the outcome affects his position and power, then the

FIGURE 14.1

The Shifting Leadership and Politics Framework

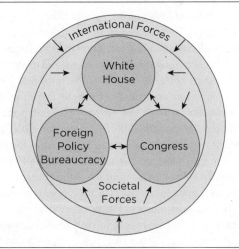

president, too, must engage in the politics of policymaking. In the field of foreign affairs, the president's power is immense. . . . But he, too, must build a consensus for his policy if it is to succeed. . . . [H]e must bring along enough of the different factions in Congress to forestall revolt, and he must contend for the support of wider constituencies, the press, interest groups, and "attentive publics." Even within the Executive Branch itself, his policy will not succeed merely at his command, and he must build co-operation and support, obtain approval from some, acquiescence from others, and enthusiasm from enough to carry it to completion.

In this concluding chapter, we revisit some of the key takeaways from our earlier discussions of the patterns and processes of US foreign policy. We do so with the two central themes of our text in mind: (1) the patterns and changes in the politics of US foreign policy and (2) the conditions for and challenges to presidential leadership of foreign policy. We end by considering the implications for future politics of US foreign policy.

UNDERSTANDING US FOREIGN POLICY SINCE WORLD WAR II

To begin, let's raise a few questions that you should consider in light of the material we have covered in the preceding chapters. First, review and reflect on the overall picture, and think about three core questions:

- What makes foreign policy political?

- What are the central challenges of foreign policymaking in the United States?

- What are the key tasks that must be accomplished for good foreign policymaking?

As you think about these three questions, be sure to reflect on the international and societal contexts and forces that help to shape US foreign policymaking. Also, carefully consider the complicated governmental context and what it means for the politics and processes of policymaking. And, keep your focus on the policymaking process. If you were advising the next president, what would you emphasize about these things? How would you guide the next president to understand and approach the politics and processes of foreign policymaking in order to be effective?

Now, let's be more specific. Again, review and reflect on the preceding chapters, and think about five more questions:

- What factors impact presidential leadership on foreign policy?

- How does the foreign policy bureaucracy influence and create challenges for policymaking?

- When is Congress most likely to engage in and influence foreign policymaking?

- How does "society" shape and influence foreign policy?

- How has the global context affected the politics, processes, and policies of the United States?

As you think about these questions, try to pull from and synthesize across the preceding chapters to identify some patterns and themes that integrate the material we have considered.

POLITICS AND PATTERNS

In Chapter 10, we referred to the aphorism about policymaking that "the only decision that is final is the one you agree with." As a point of departure for our effort to summarize our exploration of the politics of US foreign policy, this saying seems quite useful. In many ways, the story of US foreign policymaking since World War II reflects it.

Broadly speaking, as we have seen throughout the text, for the politics of US foreign policy the most important pattern of the past seventy years or so involves the shift from White House–dominated policymaking during the Cold War to a more complicated landscape involving more players. The president was, and remains, central to the process but, over time, the elements of the paradox of presidential power that we discussed in Chapter 3 became more and more challenging. This is, surely, the subtext of Lyndon Johnson's comment as he left office ("It ain't exactly as advertised"), which we introduced early in Chapter 1, and it also helps us to understand the meaning behind Bill Clinton's "Gosh, I miss the Cold War" comment in 1993.

As we have elaborated across the preceding chapters, beginning with Chapter 2's discussion of the global and historical context, the Cold War context really fostered White House–dominated foreign policy politics and processes. The Cold War context—especially of American leadership, the clarity of the threat context, the crisis atmosphere, and the broad Cold War Consensus, which we considered in most of the preceding chapters—contributed to a focus, priorities, and broad agreement that helped to place the president in the driver's seat. Part of the explanation for this rests in the "shortcuts" provided by the Cold War to US foreign policymakers. Contending with a complex world was made easier by the Cold War Consensus, which narrowed and simplified both problem interpretation and policy prescription. This consensus included basic agreement on the nature of the world conflict (a zero-sum game between the United States and the Soviet Union), the role of the United States in the world (leadership), and US policy orientation (containment of the Soviet Union and communism and promotion of an open, multilateral economy). In effect, during the period in which this consensus was strongest, debate in the United States tended to be more about narrow policy tactics and less about broader strategy or purposes.

This consensus generated substantial societal support for an internationalist foreign policy orientation. The American public tended to support (or, at least, acquiesce to) US leadership in the world in part because it was predicated on a clear threat, substantial security concerns, and a sharply defined sense of moral purpose. Second, this consensus generated a tendency toward executive branch (especially White House) leadership in the making of US foreign policy. While this presidential leadership was predicated on numerous factors, one central aspect was simple policy agreement. During the Cold War, power became increasingly concentrated within the executive branch—especially in the White House and the national security bureaucracy—and in its linkages to key private groups, especially more prominent corporations, foreign policy groups such as the Council on Foreign Relations, and academic institutions. Furthermore, the politics that permeated society and government operated within a Cold War Consensus that drove Congress to be more supportive of presidential foreign policy leadership, in part because of simple policy agreement. This same consensus also resulted in considerable bipartisanship among the most politically active supported by a more inattentive and compliant mass public.

Our examination explored the nuances of Cold War foreign policy politics in a number of ways. The common theme across the chapters is that the particular configuration of the international and societal contexts and the governmental players and institutions served to balance the paradox of presidential power in favor of the White House. Perhaps the first big challenge to this favorable balance emerged as the foreign policy bureaucracy expanded after World War II, creating a much more larger and challenging array of agencies, institutions, and players, requiring White House management and coordination, and making the White House work to achieve leadership even in the executive branch itself. In effect, securing agreement in the executive branch was an early challenge in the politics and processes of US foreign policy.

Of course, that is not to say that foreign policymaking was without controversy, that politics was irrelevant, or that the president and executive branch had free rein during this time. But the range of disagreement and competition—the politics—was definitely muted in some really important ways, as the preceding chapters have indicated. However, the politics shifted in the 1960s and early 1970s. The disastrous experience of the Vietnam War, along with international and societal changes, cracked the clarity and consensus of the Cold War context. Without the glue of the Cold War Consensus to bind up the politics and processes of US foreign policy, competing perspectives and interests drove an increasingly fractious politics. The policymaking elite no longer shared consensus over the outlines and purposes of American engagement in the world, and societal forces reflected much more disagreement than was previously the case. As a consequence, as we have seen in the preceding chapters, Congress, the public, interest groups, and the media all engaged in different, and more competitive, fashion to define American interests, goals, and foreign policies in an increasingly complicated post-Vietnam world. These changes did not mean that presidents were irrelevant or sidelined—to be sure, they continued to be central—but the end of the broad agreement opened the politics of US foreign policy to a more competitive process in which the White House could no longer count on support and deference or dominate policymaking.

From this broad view, the end of the Cold War in 1989 completed the shift. The end of the Cold War international structure and its central competition between the United States and the Soviet Union contributed to even more complex foreign policy politics and processes. As our discussion throughout the text has detailed, the end of the Cold

War altered the international "playing field" for American foreign policy and contributed to a changing policymaking environment. The very different threat context and power dynamics of the post–Cold War world, along with the twin forces of globalization and interdependence, posed myriad new challenges for American foreign policymakers attempting to determine US interests in a given situation. As the "post-Vietnam Cold War era" yielded to the "post–Cold War world," the politics and processes of US foreign policymaking were affected, sometimes dramatically. As we have seen, a variety of factors stemming from the effect of the post–Cold War changes ensured this: reduced interest in world affairs on the part of many Americans; reduced consensus over American goals and interests; reduced emphasis on national security, with a corresponding reduction in the role of the government's national security apparatus; a rise in the importance of economics and issues of prosperity and economic security; and multiplying interests, voices, and agendas.

Above all, the end of the Cold War removed the last vestiges of the shortcuts that made US foreign policy during the Cold War a simpler task. Role, interests, and priorities had to be reconsidered and revised in light of the changing world. At the same time, however, the more complex and international context worked against consensus on the proper role, important interests, and necessary actions of the United States in the world. If, as former director of central intelligence James Woolsey suggested, the Cold War's dragon was slain, the snake-filled jungle that remained was perhaps even more difficult to navigate. To push the analogy further, it is more difficult to see the snakes, tell whether they are poisonous, and know how to react to them. In the post–Cold War period, indeed, in a growing trend since the shattering of the Cold War Consensus in the late 1960s and early 1970s, policymakers and the public are increasingly divided over foreign policy goals and instruments and now do not agree on even more basic issues such as the appropriate role of the United States in the world. In this context, the politics of US foreign policy took a turn toward the kinds of struggles more common in domestic politics.

Among other things, the post–Cold War characteristics sketched out here have had the following effects on US foreign policymaking:

- The ambiguity in the threat-interest-cost equation has intensified the tendency in the American public toward ambivalence (or reluctance) concerning international involvement.

- Expanding globalization, interdependence, and transnationalism have raised the stakes for domestic interests, making foreign policymaking more like domestic policymaking—subject to conflict, bargaining, and persuasion among competing groups within and outside the government—in part due to the increasingly important link between domestic interests and international events, which has given rise to the expansion of "intermestic" issues.

- The lack of consensus has made policy leadership by any element of the US government more difficult and has encouraged elements of many parts of the government to press for their own policy preferences.

- Agenda change has expanded the elements of the bureaucracy with "foreign policy" concerns (especially the foreign economic bureaucracy) and increased the scope of the "intermestic" arena (thereby prompting more activity by Congress and societal forces—i.e., interest groups), making both White House management (of the bureaucracy) and leadership (of policy) more difficult.

To return to the aphorism about the importance of agreement, White House dominance depends as much on substantive agreement on the purposes and instruments of US foreign policy as it does on institutional powers and levers of influence. The lack of consensus, therefore, contributes to the diffusion of leadership ability.

And now? The past two decades have been a "post–Cold War plus" phenomenon. To be sure, there have been moments of clarity and focus such as those generated by the consensus-fostering terrorist attacks on September 11, 2001. Yet, neither the 9/11 attacks nor subsequent crises such as the global economic crisis that began in 2007 fundamentally altered the pattern. Instead, changes in global power dynamics; the broadening and deepening of globalization and its consequences; and the complicated challenges of transnational problems such as terrorism, the global environment, immigration, and others further complicated the politics of US foreign policy. To these complicating factors we must add the divisive effects of political polarization and partisanship that characterize so much of American politics, foreign and domestic. And the result? The fragmented and pluralist political environment that has prevailed since Vietnam—with its important effects for the paradox of presidential power—is likely to continue as we proceed in the twenty-first century. Indeed, all of America's most recent presidents—George H. W. Bush, Bill Clinton, George W. Bush, Barack Obama, and Donald Trump—have experienced this. In many ways, the aphorism "the only decision that is final is the one you agree with" is truer now than ever for the broad policymaking landscape and all the players.

LEADERSHIP IN US FOREIGN POLICYMAKING

Let's bring our final chapter to a close by returning to our Shifting Leadership and Politics framework to draw out some broad observations about the patterns of policy leadership we have observed in the preceding chapters. As we know, our framework calls our attention to three circles of policymakers whose nature and interactions shape the policy process and ensuing policies. These actors are embedded in and affected by societal forces (and actors such as public opinion, interest groups, and the media) and the international context. As we have seen in the preceding section and chapters, these international and societal circles shape, constrain, and offer opportunities for policymakers and policymaking. What patterns of policy leadership do our framework and discussion lead us to observe?

The Context of Foreign Policy Leadership

First, remember the nature of the three circles of governmental players. The role of the president and top aides and advisers (the White House) stems from the president's position as the chief executive. This circle commands the executive branch and thus has access to its expertise, information, and capabilities for implementing policy. Moreover, this group has the ability to set the agenda and seize the initiative, mobilize opinion, set the bureaucracy in motion, exert pressure on Congress, and force it to react.

The foreign policy bureaucracy is also a significant player in the governmental circle. As we have seen, this circle consists of the State Department, the Defense Department, the intelligence community, and a number of economic and trade agencies created to provide advice and implement policy decisions. The bureaucracy's expertise and control of information put it in a position to shape the formulation of policy by performing much of the generation and consideration of policy alternatives. Moreover, the various agencies of the foreign policy bureaucracy shape policy with their primary role in its implementation. In both of these roles, disagreements among different officials and agencies affect both the nature of the policy and the process by which it is formulated and implemented. The policy behavior of the foreign policy bureaucracy is affected by its central characteristics—hierarchy, specialization, and routinization—but also by its missions and subcultures, fragmentation, disagreements, "turf wars," and other organizational characteristics.

Congress includes the leadership, committees, and individual members of both houses. While members and the institution are limited by many structural characteristics (including size, decentralization, procedures, segmentation of and limited access to information, and electoral constraints), the institution and its individual members have access to potentially potent avenues of influence. These include tools such as their ability to legislate; their constitutional and statutory authority to hold oversight hearings, require reports, and request briefings by executive branch officials; their advise-and-consent authority over treaties and appointments; and their "power of the purse." In addition, instruments such as threatening to legislate, expressing a "mood," issuing requests and warnings directly to executive branch personnel, or passing nonbinding resolutions also provide a means for congressional influence, as do the abilities to frame opinion and enact procedural legislation.

Our Shifting Leadership and Politics framework—and the discussion of the preceding chapters that it has guided—calls our attention to the varying roles and influence of these players. Our framework suggests that the patterns of interaction and leadership are dynamic, with the White House, foreign policy bureaucracy, and Congress playing important, and often shifting, roles and exercising varying degrees of leadership at different times. Presidential leadership, while possible, is a variable, not a given. As we suggested in Chapter 1, our framework cues our attention to a number of different leadership patterns:

- *White House leadership* based on the premises of the Presidential Preeminence framework, in which foreign policy is seen as a product of presidential policymaking and leadership, which assumes that discussion and debate lead to presidential decisions that are then implemented. Since the White House is dominant, the president and a small group of advisers and their personal characteristics, group dynamics, and policy preferences will be of great importance. In addition, the capacity to structure an "interagency process" centered on the White House also strengthens presidential leadership, while providing opportunities to manage or channel some of the rivalries and processes inherent in bureaucratic politics.

- *Bureaucratic leadership* based on the premise that some foreign policy is made and conducted primarily in the mid- to lower levels of the executive branch because of both the range and complexity of policy and because high-level officials in either branch are limited in their time and interest. The most significant patterns of behavior from this constellation stem from the nature of bureaucracy, which may cause compromise, bargaining, incrementalism, competition, and/or stalemate. The features of bureaucratic policymaking include risk avoidance (i.e., cautious and noninventive policy), routinization, and institutional conflict.

- *Congressional leadership* based on the premise that the avenues of influence afforded by the Constitution, the law, and practice give Congress and its members their own opportunities to shape foreign policy. Members of Congress may formulate and select the option through the legislative process, which is presented to the president, implemented by the White House and the foreign policy bureaucracy, and supervised and evaluated by members of Congress through the institution's oversight powers.

- *Interbranch politics* based on the premise that all three governmental circles share responsibility and interact in the policy process, which may take one of at least four strains (see Jentleson 1990): *cooperation*, in which the circles work together to make policy; *constructive compromise*, in which members of the circles devise solutions that garner enough support for policy to proceed, although these sometimes satisfy no group completely and contain inherent contradictions; *institutional competition*, involving legislative-executive or interagency contention (actors may pursue parallel policymaking, seeking to act independently of one another to make policy); or *confrontation and stalemate*, in which each circle, endowed with some "negative power," blocks the preferences of the others.

The Patterns of Foreign Policy Leadership

So, what does our examination of the politics of US foreign policymaking suggest about the shifting patterns of foreign policy leadership?

White House Leadership. The president is central to US foreign policy, but the White House is not always the center of policymaking. As we have seen, the executive power gives the president a series of "chief" roles in the foreign policymaking arena that make the White House central: constitutional roles as chief executive, commander in chief, and chief diplomat; and less formal but still vital roles of chief communicator, chief legislator, and, perhaps, chief lobbyist. Together these roles put the president in a position to initiate and/or shape efforts to forge foreign policy.

Our discussion describes a cluster of roles for the White House that place the president in a key leadership position. First, the White House plays a vital role in foreign policy agenda-setting—the process of identifying problems, setting priorities, and the like. Ordering policy reviews, requiring the development of options on one issue and not another, and assigning responsibilities to certain executive branch structures and agencies rather than others, among other abilities, enables the president to influence heavily the foreign policy agenda. This, of course, does not ensure the White House's ability to enact the option of its choice. However, a key aspect of White House influence and leadership concerns its ability to structure initial efforts to formulate an option or options.

Second, a principal element of White House leadership stems from the ability to initiate action, a function of the chief executive, chief diplomat, and commander-in-chief hats worn by the president. Although this is closely related to the agenda-setting power possessed by the White House, it goes beyond the ability to determine the problems to be considered and into the capability to actually take action, forcing others (e.g., members of the bureaucracy, Congress, and society) to respond. Obviously, however, as our discussions in Chapters 3 and 9 suggest, policy instruments really matter in this area: Some are more obviously executive dominated (allowing for White House initiation of action), such as diplomacy, executive agreements, some aspects of military action, and the like; others are clearly more susceptible to influence by Congress (trade agreements, foreign aid requests, and perhaps the war power as well).

The White House also has enormous "negative" power—the power to say no. This means the president may have a remarkable ability to determine what will *not* be foreign policy. In this sense, the other elements in the government circle have a difficult, if not impossible, time making foreign policy on many issues without the White House.

Nevertheless, the president does not *make* foreign policy. Other elements in the governmental circle also have negative powers that enable them to obstruct or block presidential preferences. Moreover, presidential actions are clearly shaped and constrained by the preferences and actions of these other elements. Hence, the White House must often persuade, bargain or compromise with, or even accede to the preferences of other players. Moreover, the actions or preferences of other elements of the foreign policy arena may be instrumental in White House choices regarding the agenda, and they may also structure initial formulating and actions. As we described earlier in the text, such a situation is one of "anticipated reactions."

What factors affect White House leadership? Aside from the already-noted factors related to the nature of the international and societal contexts, our discussion highlights several things. First, presidential style and management can enhance or detract from White House leadership. Think about how such factors influenced presidential leadership and policymaking in our discussions in Chapters 3, 7, 8, and 10. Second, the nature of presidential advisers, their relationships with the president, and their relationships with each other also greatly impact successful leadership. Third, politics—especially the role of partisanship and divided government—shapes leadership opportunities as well, especially since Vietnam. Fourth, what we called the presidential life cycle has a significant effect as well. Finally, a cluster of factors related to policy context are also significant, including the policy situation (e.g., crisis or noncrisis); the policy type and issue area; and the policy instrument (e.g., aid, troop deployment, diplomacy). Which ones are most conducive to White House leadership?

Bureaucratic Leadership. As our discussion, especially in Chapters 4–8, suggests, the foreign policy bureaucracy is big, complex, and complicated. It will not coordinate by default and it must be managed, but it often is not. Its core characteristics shape its behavior and affect its impact on policymaking. Because the bureaucracy plays a role in both executive branch formulation and implementation of foreign policy, it always matters. As we have seen in our discussion, bureaucratic influence in US foreign policymaking has definitely become more complex, and this has helped to diminish the opportunity for White House leadership (and, probably, congressional leadership as well). Bureaucratic agencies continue to exert great influence over policymaking in a number of ways: (1) Substantial bureaucratic control over implementation allows the shaping of policy on the back end; (2) reliance on bureaucratic actors for information, advice, and options planning allows great influence over policy on the front end; and (3) their characteristics and the bureaucratic politics they spawn can stymie effective leadership by both the White House and Congress. All told, our discussion suggests that bureaucratic leadership is most common when high-level attention by the White House and Congress is least. In such situations, policymaking tends to exhibit those classic characteristics of bureaucratic politics—including incrementalism; fragmented, agency-specific efforts; and others. Can you suggest examples of bureaucratic leadership in foreign policymaking that you recall from the text?

Congressional Leadership. The preceding chapters also suggest that members of Congress can be quite important in foreign policy. In general, members of Congress (1) have been less deferential to the White House in foreign policy after the Cold War than during it; (2) have had more opportunities to affect foreign policy since the end of the Cold War; and (3) have many tools with which to shape policy. Moreover, public opinion and interest group activity can provide substantial political incentives for congressional involvement. These factors, and the actions and avenues discussed here, point to a more vigilant, engaged, and influential Congress.

Post–Cold War foreign policy seems to suggest a number of characteristics about the involvement of Congress in foreign policymaking. First, the overall environment works to increase, rather than restrain, congressional involvement and influence. For example, the rise of economic and intermestic issues entails domestic winners and losers, prompting more congressional involvement. The emphasis on aid and trade also hard-wires members of Congress into the policy process. Moreover, given concerns about public support for military operations, members of Congress have tended to be less deferential on most such issues since the Cold War. Furthermore, fiscal constraints mean that any foreign policy issue that involves the expenditure of funds is potentially a budgetary issue as well as a foreign policy concern, subject to congressional disposal.

As we have seen, Congress does not necessarily have to act for members to influence foreign policy. Of course, the institution may go through its formal, legislative process and produce issue-specific legislation that shapes US foreign policy. In addition, members rely often on the oversight responsibility to gain information, make policy statements, and generate momentum for further policy actions.

However, members of Congress also exert influence through nonlegislative or other, less direct means. First, members attempt to "frame opinion" to shape the policy debate and generate pressure for or constraints on the administration. In addition, members resort to the *threat* of legislative action as leverage to bring administration proposals or actions into line with their preferences. These actions—which occur through measures such as simple public or floor statements, letters to the White House, nonbinding resolutions, and even the introduction of legislation—often persuade an administration to adjust a policy. Such "anticipated reactions" take two forms. In *congressional signaling*, members offer signals about a desired course of action through informal statements, speeches and media appearances, letters, hearings, and the like. In effect, some members warn of the possibility of further legislative action or actually begin such action by proposing legislation. In *congressional conditioning*, the backdrop of previous congressional actions and/or preferences prompts the administration to try to preempt congressional activity by incorporating some features of member preferences into policy, placing the stamp of congressional influence on the policy.

Furthermore, interested individuals from Congress can exert powerful influence on a foreign policy even if the full institution never really takes it up. The ability of various leaders, committee and subcommittee chairs, and individual congressional "foreign policy entrepreneurs" to utilize their positions and powers can be extremely significant. Such individuals can block action; hold up legislation; and, in the case of the Senate, obstruct treaties, personnel appointments, and so on. In combination with legislation, framing, and anticipated reactions, such actions by these members can force policy adjustments (i.e., accommodation by the administration), stalemate, or wider institutional action.

But congressional leadership? Members of Congress have more negative power than positive power, even though they are hard-wired into the process by which foreign policy is made. This is, in part, because of the White House's substantial negative power, and because no matter what Congress directs, foreign policy tools are in the hands of the executive branch (e.g., although Congress can mandate diplomacy, its members have limited power to control negotiations). Hence, *congressional leadership* is likely to be rare for the life of a policy, even if it occurs in a particular stage or cycle of the policy process. Yet, virtually all foreign policies must come to Congress for authorizing legislation, funding, or evaluation (in the oversight process). So, members have opportunities, and in the post–Cold War world they seem also to have greater incentives.

Indeed, even though members attempt to frame, signal, or condition initial administration choices, they often tend to react to executive branch initiatives, agendas, and actions rather than initiate their own foreign policies. Members of Congress tend initially to defer to the executive branch, preferring to try to channel, push, or shape administration approaches at first. However, greater congressional assertiveness—and thus congressional leadership—tends to follow (1) failed presidents, including those whose efforts and preferences do not secure support and are unpopular, and those who "overshoot and collapse" or face scandals; (2) failed policies, including a failure by the administration to act on an issue, or the failure of the particular actions an administration takes; (3) a failure by the administration to respond to congressional signals regarding its actions on an issue; (4) new developments or "crises" that call into question the administration's approach to an issue; and (5) divided government, in which the opposition party controls sufficient majorities in Congress to take action.

Our discussion suggests that congressional leadership generally occurs only when consensus exists within the institution. In that case, Congress may act as a unified institution and legislate policy. As Carter and Scott (2009) have argued, this is particularly likely, given consensus, when agreement on the need for a policy exists but the president or executive branch has not acted (i.e., a policy vacuum), or when an administration adopts a policy that a substantial part of Congress rejects (i.e., a policy disagreement). In general, although it rarely occurs throughout an entire policy, congressional leadership occurs occasionally during certain periods or stages of a policy. Can you describe situations or examples of congressional leadership from the preceding chapters?

Interbranch Politics. Our discussion strongly suggests that, since Vietnam, the conditions and incentives for interbranch politics have increased substantially, making it much more likely to be a regular feature of the politics of US foreign policy. As we suggested in Chapter 10, on the legislative-executive dimension, the nature of interbranch politics introduces the possibility of supportive, compliant, competitive, and strategic behavior by Congress, and the cooperation, constructive compromise, institutional competition, and confrontation and stalemate strains that we noted in this chapter. Our previous discussions suggest that the nature and extent of interbranch politics is highly conditional on a number of factors, including public opinion; converging or diverging policy preferences; partisanship; the nature of the policy process, with initial policy stages or cycles more subject to White House leadership, and subsequent and/or extended stages and cycles more likely to involve Congress; the policy context (e.g., crisis/noncrisis, policy type, and issue area); the success or failure of initial policy actions; the policy instrument; and others. Which of these factors are most conducive to interbranch politics?

CONCLUSION: THE FUTURE OF US FOREIGN POLICYMAKING

When it comes to the politics of US foreign policy, what seems to exist then, is a "post–Cold War Dissensus" (e.g., Carter and Scott 2009). This appears to be the case for a host of reasons, including the lack of consensus over US goals and interests, the heightened importance of economic policy, the increased involvement of societal actors and nongovernmental actors, and the complicated nature of the international context. In this dissensus, politics is king.

Tradition, as well as the president's roles as chief executive, manager of the sprawling foreign policy bureaucracy, and a number of other formal and informal roles, guarantees presidential involvement, if not dominance. Members of Congress have a formidable set of tools and, if anything, have greater motives for foreign policy activity. The erosion of consensus over foreign policy goals and appropriate instruments signals the likelihood of congressional activism on substantive grounds, while expanding interdependence and growing intermestic policy issues reduce the gap between foreign and domestic policy, thus increasing the political incentives for activism. Furthermore, the post–Cold War period indicates greater bureaucratic fragmentation as well. The changing agenda in which economic concerns challenge traditional security issues for saliency suggests two results: (1) an expanding definition of the foreign policy bureaucracy, which will increasingly include economic and other, more traditionally domestic, agencies and (2) an increasingly broad spectrum of interests and perspectives, combined with new bureaucratic missions to be defended. These changes in the foreign policy bureaucracy point to greater difficulty for presidential control, more access for members of Congress, and more numerous points of contact for groups and individuals from the societal circle in our analytical framework.

Foreign policy leadership in this dissensus is highly challenging. The two-presidencies scenario—weak in domestic policy, strong in foreign policy—has been replaced by a paradox of presidential power, which requires the exercise of strong presidential leadership to govern, even in the making of US foreign policy. The crisis of governance facing most post–Vietnam War presidents, however, is so severe that a president has great difficulty fulfilling the high expectations created among the public and, consequently, is prone to experience failure. The president and the executive branch retain significant advantages in the politics of US foreign policy, but presidents have experienced less support and have faced considerably stronger constraints in foreign policy leadership since Vietnam. Significantly, a president can no longer exercise prerogative government with virtual impunity, as occurred during the Cold War years. To do so is to risk "overshoot and collapse" or "political backlash." Presidents Nixon, Reagan, George W. Bush, and Obama all experienced this to one degree or another. Will the controversial approach of Donald Trump; his preference for prerogative government; and his administration's disdain for the norms, rules, and constraints of democratic policymaking result in the same?

The complex politics of US foreign policy slows down the process and makes it more difficult to produce policy. It also seems to ensure politicization and the need for bargaining, persuasion, and compromise. Moreover, it makes stalemate possible and allows for conflict and contradictory actions. In the fragmented, pluralist US environment, consensus is necessary for coherent, sustained, White House–led foreign policy. Consensus, however, rests on clarity of threat, purpose, and interest, making it a rare commodity since the Vietnam War.

THINK ABOUT THIS

Early in the text, we quoted President Lyndon Johnson on presidential power and leadership as it relates to foreign policymaking: "It ain't exactly as advertised." Think about the discussions of the players, processes, and politics of US foreign policy in the preceding chapters. Now, consider the following two statements:

- The president is central to, but not necessarily the center of, US foreign policymaking.

- Presidential leadership depends as much on policy agreement as it does on the powers and behavior of the president.

Reflect on and react to these assertions.

What factors shape and determine the politics, processes, and policy choices of US foreign policy?

Visit **edge.sagepub.com/scottrosati7e** to help you accomplish your coursework goals in an easy-to-use learning environment.

468   PART IV   CONCLUSION

References

Aalberg, Toril, Stylianos Papathanassopoulos, Stuart Soroka, James Curran, Kaori Hayashi, Shanto Iyengar, . . . & Rodney Tiffen. (2013). International TV News, Foreign Affairs Interest and Public Knowledge. *Journalism Studies* 14: 387–406.

Aaronson, Susan Ariel. (2002). *Taking Trade to the Streets: The Lost History of Public Efforts to Shape Globalization.* Ann Arbor: University of Michigan Press.

Aberbach, Joel D. (1990). *Keeping a Watchful Eye: The Politics of Congressional Oversight.* Washington, DC: Brookings Institution Press.

Ackerman, Spender. (2006). Our Myopic Spooks: Under Analysis. *New Republic.*

Adams, Gordon. (1982). *The Politics of Defense Contracting: The Iron Triangle.* New Brunswick, NJ: Transaction Publishers.

Adkin, Mark. (1989). *Urgent Fury: The Battle for Grenada.* Lexington, MA: Lexington Books.

Adler, Kenneth P. (1984). Polling the Attentive Public. *Annals of the American Academy of Political and Social Science* 472: 143–54.

Albright, Joseph, and Marcia Kunstel. (1990). CIA Tip Led to '62 Arrest of Mandela: Ex-Official Tells of U.S. "Coup" to Aid S. Africa. *Atlanta Constitution,* June 10, p. A14.

Allcott, Hunt, and Matthew Gentzkow. (2017). Social Media and Fake News in the 2016 Election. *Journal of Economic Perspectives* 31: 211–36.

Allen, Mike. (2004). Rice Is Named Secretary of State. *Washington Post,* November 17, p. A1.

Allison, Graham T. (1971). *Essence of Decision: Explaining the Cuban Missile Crisis.* Boston, MA: Little, Brown.

Allison, Graham. (2017). *Destined for War: Can America and China Escape Thucydides's Trap?* New York: Houghton Mifflin Harcourt.

Allison, Graham T., and Morton H. Halperin. (1972). Bureaucratic Politics: A Paradigm and Some Policy Implications. *World Politics* 24: 40–79.

Allison, Graham T., and Philip Zelikow. (1999). *Essence of Decision: Explaining the Cuban Missile Crisis.* New York: Longman.

Almond, Gabriel. (1960). *The American People and Foreign Policy.* New York: Praeger.

Alter, Jonathan. (2010). *The Promise: President Obama, Year 1.* New York: Simon and Schuster.

Andrews, Edmund L. (2009). Forget Aloof, Bernanke Goes Barnstorming. *New York Times,* July 26, p. A1.

Auerswald, David P., and Forrest Maltzman. (2003). Policymaking Through Advice and Consent: Treaty Consideration by the United States Senate. *Journal of Politics* 65: 1097–110.

Auerswald, David P., and Peter F. Cowhey. (1997). Ballotbox Diplomacy: The War Powers Resolution and the Use of Force. *International Studies Quarterly* 41: 505–28.

Austen-Smith, D. (1993). Information and Influence: Lobbying for Agendas and Votes. *American Journal of Political Science* 37: 799–833.

Ayres, B. Drummond, Jr. (1983a). A New Breed of Diplomat. *New York Times Magazine,* September 11, pp. 66–67, 70–73, 105.

Ayres, B. Drummond, Jr. (1983b). Grenada Invasion. *New York Times,* November 14, pp. A1, A6.

Bacchus, William I. (1983). *Staffing for Foreign Affairs: Personnel Systems for the 1980's and 1990's.* Princeton, NJ: Princeton University Press.

Bacevich, Andrew J. (1994). Charles Beard, Properly Understood. *National Interest* 35: 73–83.

Bachrack, Stanley D. (1976). *The Committee of One Million: "China Lobby" Politics, 1953–1971.* New York: Columbia University Press.

Badie, Dina. (2010). Groupthink, Iraq, and the War on Terror: Explaining US Policy Shift toward Iraq. *Foreign Policy Analysis* 6 (October): 277–96.

Baer, Robert. (2002). *See No Evil: The True Story of a Ground Soldier in the CIA's War on Terror.* New York: Arrow Books.

Baer, Robert. (2009). Independent Intel: High Stakes in a CIA Turf War. *Time*, June 12 (http://content.time.com/time/politics/article/0,8599,1904284,00.html).

Bailey, Thomas. (1961). America's Emergence as a World Power: The Myth and the Verity. *Pacific Historical Review* 30: 1–16.

Baker, Peter. (2005). President Acknowledges Approving Secretive Eavesdropping. *Washington Post*, December 18, p. A1.

Baker, Russell. (2008). Condi and the Boys. *The New York Review of Books*, April 3.

Balz, Dan and Bob Woodward. (2002). Ten Days in September. *Washington Post*, January 27–February 3, p. A1.

Bamford, James. (1982). *The Puzzle Palace: Inside America's Most Secret Intelligence Organization*. New York: Penguin.

Bamford, James. (2001). *Body of Secrets: Anatomy of the UltraSecret National Security Agency*. New York: Doubleday.

Bamford, James. (2002). Eyes to the Sky, Ears to the War, and Still Wanting. *New York Times*, September 8, p. 5.

Barber, J. D. (1972) *The Presidential Character: Predicting Performance in the White House*. Englewood Cliffs: Prentice-Hall.

Bardes, Barbara A., and Robert W. Oldendick. (2002). *Public Opinion: Measuring the American Mind*. Belmont, CA: Wadsworth.

Baritz, Loren. (1985). *Backfire: A History of How American Culture Led Us into Vietnam and Made Us Fight the Way We Did*. New York: William Morrow.

Barnes, Julian E., and Adam Goldman. (2019). Gina Haspel Relies on Spy Skills to Connect With Trump. He Doesn't Always Listen. *New York Times*, April 16 (https://www.nytimes.com/2019/04/16/us/politics/gina-haspel-trump.html).

Barnes, Julian E., Adam Goldman, and David E. Sanger. (2019). C.I.A. Informant Extracted From Russia Had Sent Secrets to U.S. for Decades. *New York Times*, September 9 (https://www.nytimes.com/2019/09/09/us/politics/cia-informant-russia.html).

Barnet, Richard J. (1972). *Roots of War: Men and Institutions Behind U.S. Foreign Policy*. New York: Penguin.

Barnet, Richard J. (1985). *The Permanent War Economy: American Capitalism in Decline*. New York: Touchstone.

Barnet, Richard J., and Ronald E. Muller. (1976). *Global Reach: The Power of Multinational Corporations*. New York: Simon and Schuster.

Barrett, David M. (1988). The Mythology Surrounding Lyndon Johnson, His Advisers, and the 1965 Decision to Escalate the Vietnam War. *Political Science Quarterly* 103: 637–64.

Barrett, David M. (1989). *Uncertain Warriors: Lyndon Johnson and His Vietnam Advisors*. Lawrence: University of Kansas Press.

Barrett, David M. (2005). *The CIA and Congress: The Untold Story from Truman to Kennedy*. Lawrence: University of Kansas.

Barthel, Michael. (2018). 5 Facts about the State of the News Media in 2017. Pew Research Center, August 21 (https://www.pewresearch.org/fact-tank/2018/08/21/5-facts-about-the-state-of-the-news-media-in-2017/).

Baum, Mathew, and Philip Potter. (2008). The Relationships between Mass Media, Public Opinion, and Foreign Policy: Toward a Theoretical Synthesis. *Annual Review of Political Science* 11:39–65.

Baum, Mathew, and Philip Potter. (2019). Media, Public Opinion, and Foreign Policy in the Age of Trump. *Journal of Politics* 81: 747–56.

Baumgartner, F. R., J. M. Berry, M. Hojnacki, D. C. Kimball, and B. L. Leech. (2009). *Lobbying and Policy Change: Who Wins, Who Loses, and Why*. Chicago, IL: University of Chicago Press.

Bax, Frans R. (1977). The Legislative-Executive Relationship in Foreign Policy: New Partnership or New Competition? *Orbis* 20: 881–904.

Bayley, Edwin R. (1981). *Joe McCarthy and the Press*. Madison: The University of Wisconsin Press.

Bayoumy, Yara. (2019). Trump's Disdain for Diplomacy. *The Atlantic*, January 13 (https://www.theatlantic.com/politics/archive/2019/01/why-was-rex-tillerson-fired/580009/).

Belasco, Amy. (2011). *The Cost of Iraq, Afghanistan, and Other Global War on Terror Operations Since 9/11*. Congressional Research Service RL33110, March 29.

Bender, Michael, and Vivian Salama. (2019). John Bolton Ousted by Trump as National Security Adviser. *Wall Street Journal*, September 10 (https://www.wsj.com/articles/trump-says-john-bolton-is-leaving-white-house-11568131727).

Benedetti, Charles De, and Charles Chatfield. (1990). *An American Ordeal: The Antiwar Movement of the Vietnam Era.* Syracuse, NY: Syracuse University Press.

Benen, Steve. (2019). Congress Quietly Makes History with Rebuke of Key Trump Foreign Policy. MSNBC, April 5. (http://www.msnbc.com/rachel-maddow-show/congress-quietly-makes-history-rebuke-key-trump-foreign-policy).

Bennett, Stephen Earl. (1996). Know Nothings' Revisited Again. *Political Behavior* 18: 1–22.

Bennett, W. Lance. (1990). Toward a Theory of Press-State Relations in the United States. *Journal of Communication* 40:103–27.

Bennett, W. Lance. (1994a). The Media and the Foreign Policy Process. In *The New Politics of American Foreign Policy*, edited by David Deese, pp. 165–88. New York: St. Martin's Press.

Bennett, W. Lance. (1994b). The News about Foreign Policy. In *Taken by Storm: The Media, Public Opinion, and US Foreign Policy in the Gulf War*, edited by W. L. Bennett and D. L. Paletz, pp. 12–42. Chicago: University of Chicago Press.

Bennett, W. Lance. (2011). *News: The Politics of Illusion.* New York: Longman.

Bennett, W. Lance, Regina G. Lawrence, and Steven Livingston. (2007). *When the Press Fails: Political Power and the News Media from Iraq to Katrina.* Chicago: University of Chicago Press.

Berman, Larry. (1989). *Lyndon Johnson's War: The Road to Stalemate in Vietnam.* New York: W.W. Norton.

Bern, Daryl J. (1970). *Beliefs, Attitudes, and Human Affairs.* Belmont, CA: Brooks/Cole.

Bernanke, Ben. (2009). I'm as Disgusted as You Are. *CBS News.*

Bernhagen, P., A. Dür, and D. Marshall. (2014). Measuring Interest Group Success Spatially. *Interest Groups & Advocacy* 3, 202–18.

Bernstein, Carl. (1977). The CIA and the Media. *Rolling Stone*, October 20, pp. 55–67.

Bernstein, Carl. (1992). The Idiot Culture. *New Republic*, June 8, pp. 22–26.

Bernstein, Paul, and William Freudenberg. (1977). Ending the Vietnam War: Components of Change in Senate Voting on Vietnam War Bills. *American Journal of Sociology* 82: 991–1006.

Beschloss, Michael, and Strobe Talbott. (1994). *At the Highest Levels: The Inside Story of the End of the Cold War.* Boston, MA: Little, Brown.

Betts, Richard K. (1977). *Soldiers, Statesmen, and Cold War Crises.* Cambridge, MA: Harvard University Press.

Betts, Richard K. (1978). Analysis, War, and Decision: Why Intelligence Failures Are Inevitable. *World Politics* 31: 61–90.

Betts, Richard K. (2002). The Soft Underbelly of American Primacy: Tactical Advantages of Terror. *Political Science Quarterly* 117: 19–36.

Beutler, Brian. (2016). Obama Is Warning America about Trump's Presidency. Are You Listening? *New Republic*, November 15 (https://newrepublic.com/article/138757/obama-warning-america-trumps-presidency-listening).

Biddle, Stephen. (2003). Afghanistan and the Future of War. *Foreign Affairs* 82: 31–46.

Bigman, Stanley K. (1949). Rivals in Conformity: A Study of Two Competing Dailies. *Journalism Quarterly* 25: 127–31.

Bill, James A. (1988). *The Eagle and the Lion: The Tragedy of American-Iranian Relations.* New Haven, CT: Yale University Press.

Blechman, Barry M., and Stephen S. Kaplan. (1978). *Force Without War: U.S. Armed Forces as a Political Instrument.* Washington, DC: Brookings Institution Press.

Bleifuss, Joel. (1990). The First Stone. *In These Times.*

Blumenthal, Sidney. (1986). *The Rise of the Counter-Establishment: From Conservative Ideology to Political Power.* New York: Basic Books.

Bohan, Caren, Andy Sullivan, and Thomas Ferraro. (2011). Special Report: How Washington Took the U.S. to the Brink. *Reuters*, August 4.

Boot, Max. (2003). The New American Way of War. *Foreign Affairs* 82: 41–58.

Boot, Max. (2005). The Struggle to Transform the Military. *Foreign Affairs* 84: 103–18.

Braumoeller, Bear F. (2010). The Myth of American Isolationism. *Foreign Policy Analysis* 6 (October): 349–71.

Bremmer, Ian. (2016). *Superpower: Three Choices for America's Role in the World*. New York: Penguin/RandomHouse.

Broder, David. (2005). Finally, Congress Stands Up. *Washington Post*, December 4, p. B7.

Brodie, Bernard. (1973). *War and Politics*. New York: Macmillan.

Brody, Richard A. (1991). *Assessing the President: The Media, Elite Opinion, and Public Support*. Stanford, CA: Stanford University Press.

Brooks, Stephen G., and William C. Wohlforth (2002). American Primacy in Perspective. *Foreign Affairs*, July/August.

Burke, John P. (2005). The Contemporary Presidency: Condoleezza Rice as NSC Advisor: A Case Study of the Honest Broker Role. *Presidential Studies Quarterly* 35: 554–75.

Burke, John P. (2009a). The Obama National Security System and Process: At the Six Month Mark. *White House Transition Project Report*. Online Edition.

Burke, John P. (2009b). *Honest Broker? The National Security Advisor and Presidential Decision Making*. College Station, TX: A&M University Press.

Burns, Edward M. 1957. *The American Idea of Mission: Concepts of National Purpose and Destiny*. New Brunswick, NJ: Rutgers University Press.

Burns, James MacGregor. (1989). *The Crosswinds of Freedom*. New York: Vintage.

Calmes, Jackie. (2009). Obama's Economic Circle Keeps Tensions High. *New York Times*, June 8, p. A1.

Campbell, Colton C. (2001). *Discharging Congress: Government by Commission*. Westport, CT: Praeger.

Campbell, John Franklin. (1971). *The Foreign Affairs Fudge Factory*. New York: Basic Books.

Cannon, Lou. (1991). *President Reagan: The Role of a Lifetime*. New York: Simon and Schuster.

Carden, James. (2018). A New Poll Shows the Public Is Overwhelmingly Opposed to Endless US Military Interventions. *Nation*, January 9 (https://www.thenation.com/article/new-poll-shows-public-overwhelmingly-opposed-to-endless-us-military-interventions/).

Carter, Ralph G., and James M. Scott. (2009). *Choosing to Lead: Understanding Congressional Foreign Policy Entrepreneurs*. Durham, NC: Duke University Press.

Carter, Ralph G., and James M. Scott. (2010). Understanding Congressional Foreign Policy Innovators: Mapping Entrepreneurs and Their Strategies. *Social Science Journal* 47: 418–38.

Center for Communication & Civic Engagement. (n.d.) The Internet's Impact on News Media (https://depts.washington.edu/ccce/digitalMedia/newsimpact.html).

Center for the Study of Political Change. 2006. European Elites Survey: Survey of Members of the European Parliament and Top European Commission Officials; Key Findings 2006. University of Siena (www.circap.unisi.it/ees/ees_overview).

Chapman, Matthew. (2019). Trump's Ambassadors, the Least Qualified in 40 Years, Gave Him Record Amounts of Money. *Salon*, February 25 (https://www.salon.com/2019/02/25/trumps-ambassadors-are-the-least-qualified-in-40-years-but-they-gave-record-amounts-of-money-him_partner/).

Chaudoin, Stephen, Helen V. Milner, and Dustin H. Tingley. (2010). The Center Still Holds: Liberal Internationalism Survives. *International Security* 35: 75–94.

Chicago Council on Global Affairs. (2008). Anxious Americans Seek a New Direction in United States Foreign Policy (www.thechicagocouncil.org/UserFiles/File/POS_Topline%20Reports/POS%202008/2008%20Public%20Opinion%202008_US%20Survey%20Results.pdf).

Chicago Council on Global Affairs. (2018). 2019 Chicago Council Survey of American Public Opinion (https://digital.thechicagocouncil.org/lcc/rejecting-retreat?utm_source=tw&utm_campaign=rpt&utm_medium=social&utm_term=rejecting-retreat&utm_content=text).

Cigler, Allan J., and Burdett A. Loomis. (2015). *Interest Group Politics* (9th ed.). Washington, DC: Congressional Quarterly Press.

Clarke, Duncan. (1987). Why State Can't Lead. *Foreign Policy*, pp. 128–42.

Clarke, Richard. (2004). *Against All Enemies: Inside America's War on Terror*. New York: Free Press.

Clinton, Bill, and Al Gore, Jr. (1992). *Putting People First: How We Can All Change America*. New York: Random House.

Clodfelter, Mark. (1989). *The Limits of Air Power: The American Bombing of North Vietnam*. New York: Free Press.

Coates, James, and Michael Kilian. (1985). *Heavy Losses: The Dangerous Decline of American Defense*. New York: Penguin Press.

Coats, Daniel R. (2019). Statement for the Record, Worldwide Threat Assessment of the US Intelligence Community. Senate Select Committee on Intelligence, January 29, p. 14 (https://www.dni.gov/files/ODNI/documents/2019-ATA-SFR---SSCI.pdf).

Cochran, Thomas B., William M. Arkin, Robert S. Norris, and Milton M. Hoenig. (1987). *Nuclear Weapons Databook*. Cambridge, MA: Ballinger Press.

Cohen, Bernard C. (1963). *The Press and Foreign Policy*. Princeton, NJ: Princeton University Press.

Cohen, Bernard C. (1973). *The Public's Impact on Foreign Policy*. Boston, MA: Little, Brown.

Cohen, David B., Chris J. Dolan, and Jerel A. Rosati. (2002). A Place at the Table: The Emerging Roles of the White House Chief of Staff. *Congress and the Presidency*.

Cohen, Eliot A. (1984). Constraints on America's Conduct of Small Wars. *International Security* 9: 151–81.

Cohen, Eliot A. (1991). After the Battle. *New Republic*, April 1, pp. 19–26.

Cohen, Jeffrey E. (2008). *The Presidency in the Era of 24-Hour News*. Princeton, NJ: Princeton University Press.

Cohen, Stephen D. (2000). *The Making of United States International Economic Policy: Principles, Problems, and Proposals for Reform* (5th ed.). New York: Praeger.

Cohen, William I. (1987). *Empire Without Tears: America's Foreign Relations, 1921–1933*. New York: Knopf.

Coll, Steve. (2004). *Ghost Wars: The Secret History of the CIA, Afghanistan, and Bin Laden, from the Soviet Invasion to September 10, 2001*. New York: Penguin.

Collins, Kaitlan, Kevin Liptak, and Zachary Cohen. (2019). Bolton-Pompeo Relationship Hits New Low as Foreign Policy Tests Mount. CNN, September 6 (https://www.cnn.com/2019/09/06/politics/bolton-pompeo-not-speaking-tension/index.html).

Commission on the Roles and Capabilities of the United States Intelligence Community. (1996). *Preparing for the 21st Century: An Appraisal of U.S. Intelligence* (http://www.gpo.gov/fdsys/pkg/GPO-INTELLIGENCE/content-detail.html).

Conason, Joe. (1990). The Iraq Lobby. *New Republic*, October 1, pp. 14–17.

Congressional Research Service. (2001). *Foreign Policy Interest Groups*. Washington, DC: Congressional Research Service.

Conley, Richard S. (2004). *Transforming the American Polity: George W. Bush and the War on Terrorism*. Upper Saddle River, NJ: Prentice Hall.

Cook, Nancy, and Andrew Restuccia. (2017). Trump's Trade Warrior Prowls the West Wing. *Politico*, July 17 (https://www.politico.com/story/2017/07/17/peter-navarro-trump-trade-240611).

Cooper, Matthew, and Melinda Liu. (1997). Bright Light. *Newsweek*, February 10, pp. 22–29.

Cordesman, Anthony H. (2012). Afghanistan: The Death of a Strategy. *CSIS: Center for Strategic & International Studies*, February 27.

Corrigan, Jack, and Government Executive [Anonymous]. (2018). The Hollowing Out of the State Department Continues. *The Atlantic*, February (https://www.theatlantic.com/international/archive/2018/02/tillerson-trump-state-foreign-service/553034/).

Corwin, Edward S. (1957). *The President: Office and Powers, 1787–1957*. New York: New York University Press.

Council on Foreign Relations. (1996). *Making Intelligence Smarter: The Future of U.S. Intelligence*.

CQ Press. (1999). *CQ Almanac*. Washington, DC: CQ Press.

Crabb, Cecil V. (1982). *The Doctrine of American Foreign Policy: Their Meaning, Role, and Future*. Baton Rouge: Louisiana State University Press.

Crabb, Cecil V., Jr., and Pat M. Holt. (1992). *Invitation to Struggle: Congress, the President, and Foreign Policy*. Washington, DC: Congressional Quarterly Press.

Cronin, Thomas E. (1979). Presidential Power Revised and Reappraised. *Western Political Quarterly* 32: 381–95.

Cronin, Thomas E., and Michael A. Genovese. (2009). *The Paradoxes of the American Presidency*. New York: Oxford University Press.

Crosby, Harry. (1991). Too at Home Abroad: Swilling Beer, Licking Boots, and Ignoring the Natives with One of Jim Baker's Finest. *Washington Monthly*, September, pp. 16–20.

Crouse, Timothy. (1972). *The Boys on the Bus*. New York: Ballantine Books.

Crowley, Michael. (2004). Playing Defense: Bush's Disastrous Homeland Security Department. *New Republic*, March 15, pp. 17–21.

Cutler, Robert. (1956). The Development of the National Security Council. *Foreign Affairs*, April.

Daalder, Ivo H., and I. M. Destler. (2001). Prepared Statement before the Committee on Governmental Affairs, US Senate, October 12.

Daalder, Ivo H., and I. M. Destler. (2009). *In the Shadow of the Oval Office: Profiles of the National Security Advisers and the Presidents They Served—From JFK to George W. Bush.* New York: Simon and Schuster.

Daalder, Ivo H., and James M. Lindsay. (2003). *America Unbound: The Bush Revolution in Foreign Policy.* Washington, DC: Brookings Institution Press.

Danner, Mark. (1997). Marooned in the Cold War: America, the Alliance, and the Quest for a Vanished World. *World Policy Journal* 14: 1–23.

Davidson, Janine A. (2010). *Lifting the Fog of Peace: How Americans Learned to Fight Modern War*. Ann Arbor: University of Michigan Press.

Davis, T. R., and S. M. Lynn-Jones. (1987). City upon a Hill. *Foreign Policy* 66: 20–38.

Davis, Vincent. (1967). *The Admiral's Lobby*. Chapel Hill: University of North Carolina Press.

de Tocqueville, Alexis. (1945). *Democracy in America*. New York: Vintage.

Deering, Christopher J. (2002). Alarms and Patrols: Legislative Oversight in Foreign and Defense Policy. In *Congress and the Politics of Foreign Policy*, edited by Colton C. Campbell, Nicol C. Rae, and John F. Stack Jr., pp. 112–38. Upper Saddle River, NJ: Prentice Hall.

Deibel, Terry L. (1991). Bush's Foreign Policy: Mastery and Inaction. *Foreign Policy* 84: 3–23.

DeLaet, C. James, Charles M. Rowling, and James M. Scott. (2007). Partisanship, Ideology, and Weapons of Mass Destruction in the Post-Cold War Congress: The Chemical Weapons and Comprehensive Test Ban Cases. *Illinois Political Science Review* 11: 2–35.

DeLaet, C. James, and James M. Scott. (2006). Treaty-Making and Partisan Politics: Arms Control and the U.S. Senate, 1960–2001. *Foreign Policy Analysis* 2: 177–200.

Delli Carpini, Michael X., and Scott Keeter. (1991). Stability and Change in the U.S. Public's Knowledge of Politics. *Public Opinion Quarterly* 55: 583–612.

Delli Carpini, Michael X., and Scott Keeter. (1997). *What Americans Know About Politics and Why It Matters*. New Haven, CT: Yale University Press.

DeLuce, Dan. (2017). Senators to Trump: Show Resolve with Beijing in South China Sea. *Foreign Policy*, May 10 (http://foreignpolicy.com/2017/05/10/senators-to-trump-show-resolve-with-beijing-in-south-china-sea/).

Denison, Benjamin. (2019). Confusion in the Pivot: The Muddled Shift from Peripheral War to Great Power Competition. War on the Rocks (https://warontherocks.com/2019/02/confusion-in-the-pivot-the-muddled-shift-from-peripheral-war-to-great-power-competition/).

Destler, I. M. (1972). *Presidents, Bureaucrats, and Foreign Policy*. Princeton, NJ: Princeton University Press.

Destler, I. M. (1994). A Government Divided: The Security Complex and the Economic Complex. In *The New Politics of American Foreign Policy*, edited by David A. Deese, pp. 132–47. New York: St. Martin's Press.

Destler, I. M. (1996). *The National Economic Council: A Work in Progress*. Washington, DC: Brookings Institution Press.

Destler, I. M. (2005). *American Trade Politics*. Washington, DC: Brookings Institution Press.

Destler, I. M. (2009). Jonestown: Will Obama's National Security Council Be Dramatically Different? *Foreign Affairs*, April 30.

Destler, I. M., Leslie H. Gelb, and Anthony Lake. (1984). *Our Own Worst Enemy: The Unmaking of American Foreign Policy*. New York: Simon and Schuster.

Deudney, Daniel, and G. John Ikenberry. (1992). The International Sources of Soviet Change. *International Security* 16: 74–118.

Devroy, Ann, and R. Jeffrey Smith. (1993). Clinton Reexamines a Foreign Policy Under Siege. *Washington Post*, October 17 (https://www.washingtonpost.com/archive/politics/1993/10/17/clinton-reexamines-a-foreign-policy-under-siege/794fbbd6-349c-44d4-94b2-65868bd53587/).

DeYoung, Karen. (2009). Obama's NSC Will Get New Power. *Washington Post*, February 8, p. A1.

DeYoung, Karen. (2019). Collapse of Afghanistan Peace Talks Spotlights Internal Trump Administration Divisions. *Washington Post*, September 9 (https://beta.washington post.com/national-security/collapse-of-afghanistan-peace-talks-spotlights-internal-trump-administration-divisions/2019/09/08/c7d57412-d24b-11e9-86ac-0f250 cc91758_story.html).

DeYoung, Karen, Greg Jaffe, John Hudson, and Josh Dawsey. (2019). John Bolton Puts His Singular Stamp on Trump's National Security Council. *Washington Post*, March 4 (https://www.washingtonpost.com/world/national-security/john-bolton...854a-7a14d7fec96a_story.html).

Diamond, John, and Brianna B. Piec. (2002). Thousands March in Support of Israel: Pro-Israel Lobby Remains Strong Force in D.C. *Knight Rider/Tribune News Service*, April 15.

Diehl, Jackson. (2005). The Rice Touch. *Washington Post*, May 9, p. A23.

Dizard, Wilson P. (2001). *Digital Diplomacy: U.S. Foreign Policy in the Information Age*. Westport, CT: Greenwood Press.

Dolan, Chris J. (2001). *Striking a Balance: Presidential Power and the National Economic Council*. Columbia: University of South Carolina.

Dolan, Chris J. (2008). The Shape of Elite Opinion on U.S. Foreign Policy, 1992 to 2004. *Politics and Policy* 36: 545.

Dolan, Chris J., and Jerel A. Rosati. (2006). U.S. Foreign Economic Policy and the Significance of the National Economic Council. *International Studies Perspectives* 7: 102–23.

Donner, Frank M. (1981). *The Age of Surveillance*. New York: Vintage.

Dorman, Shawn, ed. (2011). *Inside a U.S. Embassy: How the Foreign Service Works for America* (3rd ed.). (Washington, DC: American Foreign Service Association).

Doyle, Michael W. (1986). *Empires*. Ithaca, NY: Cornell University Press.

Doyle, Michael W. (1997). *Ways of War and Peace: Realism, Liberalism, and Socialism*. New York: W.W. Norton.

Draper, Theodore. (1997). Is the CIA Still Necessary? *New York Review of Books*, August 14, p. 5.

Drew, Elizabeth. (2009). The Thirty Days of Barack Obama. *New York Review of Books*, March 26 (http://www.nybooks.com/articles/22450).

Drezner, Daniel. (2003). Barely Managing. *New Republic Online*, NP.

Duffy, Michael. (2003). Could It Happen Again? *Time*, August 4.

Duffy, Michael, and Elaine Shannon. (2005). Condi on the Rise. *Time*, March 20, pp. 36–38.

Eckes, Alfred E., Jr. (1995). *Opening America's Market: U.S. Foreign Trade Policy Since 1776*. Chapel Hill: University of North Carolina.

Edwards III, George C., and Stephen J. Wayne. (2005). *Presidential Leadership: Politics and Policy Making*. New York: Wadsworth Publishing.

Edwards III, James C. (2009). *The Strategic President: Persuasion and Opportunity in Presidential Leadership*. Princeton, NJ: Princeton University Press.

Ehrman, John. (1995). *The Rise of Neoconservatism: Intellectuals and Foreign Affairs 1945–1994*. New Haven, CT: Yale University Press.

Eichenwald, Kurt. (2012). The Deafness before the Storm. *New York Times*. September 10, 2012 (http://www.nytimes.com/2012/09/11/opinion/the-bush-white-house-was-deaf-to-9-11-warnings.html?_r=1).

Elliott, Michael. (2002). They Had a Plan. *Time*, August 12, pp. 28–43.

Elliott, Michael, and Massimo Calabresi. (2004). Is Condi the Problem? *Time*, April 5, pp. 32–37.

Emery, Fred. (1994). *Watergate: The Corruption of American Politics and the Fall of Richard Nixon*. New York: Times Books.

Enten, Harry. (2018). How Trump Ranks in Popularity vs. Past Presidents. FiveThirtyEight.com, January 19 (https://fivethirtyeight.com/features/the-year-in-trumps-approval-rating/).

Entman, R. M. (2003). Cascading Activation: Contesting the White House's Frame after 9/11. *Political Communication* 20: 415–23.

Entman, R. M. (2004). *Projections of Power: Framing News, Public Opinion, and US Foreign Policy*. Chicago: University of Chicago Press.

Epstein, Barbara. (1991). *Political Protest and Cultural Revolution: Nonviolent Direct Action in the 1970s and 1980s.* Berkeley and Los Angeles: University of California Press.

Erskine, H. G. (1962). The Polls: The Informed Public. *Public Opinion Quarterly* 26: 669–77.

Erskine, H. G. (1963). The Polls: Textbook Knowledge. *Public Opinion Quarterly* 27: 133–41.

Etheredge, Lloyd S. (1985). *Can Governments Learn? American Foreign Policy and Central American Revolutions.* New York: Pergamon Press.

Evangelista, Matthew. (1989). Issue Area and Foreign Policy Revisited. *International Organization* 43: 147–71.

Evans, Sara. (1979). *Personal Politics: The Roots of Women's Liberation in the Civil Rights Movement & the New Left.* New York: Vintage.

Fallows, James. (2004). Blind into Baghdad. *Atlantic Monthly,* January/February, pp. 52–74.

Farber, Farber, ed. (2008). *Security vs. Liberty: Conflicts Between Civil Liberties and National Security in American History.* New York: Sage Foundation.

Farnham, Barbara. (2004). Impact of the Political Context on Foreign Policy Decision-Making. *Political Psychology* 25: 441–63.

Farrow, Ronan. (2018). Inside Rex Tillerson's Ouster. *The New Yorker,* April 19 (https://www.newyorker.com/books/page-turner/inside-rex-tillersons-ouster/).

Feeney, Mark. (2001). All the World's His Stage Revered or Reviled, Henry Kissinger Remains Diplomatic in Spotlight's Glare. *Boston Globe,* June 21.

Fenno, Richard F., Jr. (1978). *Home Style: House Members in Their Districts.* Boston, MA: Little, Brown.

Ferguson, Niall. (2004). *Colossus: The Rise and Fall of the American Empire.* New York: Penguin.

Fessenden, Helen. (2005). The Limits of Intelligence Reform. *Foreign Affairs* 84: 106–20.

Fineman, Howard. (2003). Bush and God. *Newsweek,* March 10, pp. 22–30.

Fisher, Louis. (2004a). *The Politics of Executive Privilege.* Durham, NC: Carolina Academic Press.

Fisher, Louis. (2004b). *Presidential War Power.* Manhattan: University Press of Kansas.

Fisher, Louis. (2007). Invoking Inherent Presidential Powers: A Primer. *Presidential Studies Quarterly* 37: 1–22.

Fiske, Susan T., and Shelley E. Taylor. (1999). *Social Cognition.* New York: McGraw-Hill.

Fleisher, Richard, Jon R. Bond, Glen S. Krutz, and Stephen Hanna. (2000). The Demise of the Two Presidencies. *American Politics Quarterly* 28: 3–25.

Fordham, Benjamin. (1998). The Politics of Threat Perception and the Use of Force: A Political Economy Model of U.S. Uses of Force, 1949–1994. *International Studies Quarterly* 42: 567–90.

Foyle, Douglas C. (1999). *Counting the Public In: Presidents, Public Opinion, and Foreign Policy.* New York: Columbia University Press.

Franck, Thomas, and Edward Weisband. (1979). *Foreign Policy by Congress.* New York: Oxford University Press.

Fraser, Steve, and Gary Gerstle, eds. (1989). *The Rise and Fall of the New Deal Order, 1930–1980.* Princeton, NJ: Princeton University Press.

Freeland, Chrystia. (2009). Lunch with Larry Summers. *Financial Times,* July 10.

Friedman, Thomas L., and Elaine Sciolino. (1993). Clinton and Foreign Issues: Spasms of Attention. *New York Times,* March 22, p. A3.

Friedman, Uri. (2013). How Three Decades of News Coverage Has Shaped Our View of the World. *The Atlantic,* November 19 (https://www.theatlantic.com/international/archive/2013/11/how-three-decades-of-news-coverage-has-shaped-our-view-of-the-world/281613/).

Fukuyama, Francis. (1989). The End of History? *National Interest* 16: 3–18.

Fulbright, J. William. (1966). *The Arrogance of Power.* New York: Vintage.

Gamson, William A. (1975). *The Strategy of Social Protest.* Homewood, IL: Dorsey Press.

Gans, Herbert J. (1979). *Deciding What's News: A Study of CBS Evening News, NBC Nightly News, Newsweek, and Time.* New York: Pantheon.

Gardiner, Harris. (2017). Diplomats Sound the Alarm as They Are Pushed Out in Droves. *New York Times,* November 25, p. A1 (https://www.nytimes.com/2017/11/24/us/politics/state-department-tillerson.html).

Gardner, Richard N. (1980). *Sterling-Dollar Diplomacy in Current Perspective: The Origins and Prospects of Our International Economic Order*. New York: Columbia University Press.

Garrison, Jean, Jerel Rosati, and James Scott. (2012, April) *President Obama and the "Team of Rivals" Model in Foreign Policy Decision Making: Presidential Style, DecisionMaking Structure, and Policymaking Consequences*. Paper presented at the 2012 International Studies Association Annual Conference, San Diego, California, April 1–4.

Garrison, Jean, Jerel Rosati, and James M. Scott. (2014). The Two Obamas? Presidential Styles, Structures and Policymaking Consequences. *White House Studies* 13, 21–46.

Geithner, Timothy F. (2009). *Remarks Before the Economic Club of Washington*, April 25.

Gelb, Leslie H. (1972). The Essential Domino: American Politics and Vietnam. *Foreign Affairs* 50: 459–75.

Gellman, Barton. (2008). *Angler: The Cheney Vice Presidency*. New York: Penguin.

Gellman, Barton, and Dafnia Linzer. (2005). Pursuing the Limits of Wartime Powers. *Washington Post*, December 18, p. A1.

Gelpi, Christopher, Peter D. Feaver, and Jason Reifler. (2005/2006). Success Matters: Casualty Sensitivity and the War in Iraq. *International Security* 30: 7–46.

Geltzer, Joshua. (2019). So This Is What Congress' Getting Involved in Foreign Affairs Looks Like. *Just Security*, February 14 (https://www.justsecurity.org/62591/congress-involved-foreign-affairs/).

George, Alexander L. (1980a). Domestic Constraints on Regime Change in U.S. Foreign Policy: The Need for Policy Legitimacy. In *Changes in the International System*, edited by Ole R. Holsti, Randolph Siverson, and Alexander L. George, pp. 233–262. Boulder, CO: Westview Press.

George, Alexander L. (1980b). *Presidential Decision Making in Foreign Policy: The Effective Use of Information and Advice*. Boulder, CO: Westview Press.

George, Alexander L., and Eric K. Stern. (2001). Harnessing Conflict in Foreign Policy Making: From Devil's Advocate to Multiple Advocacy. *Presidential Studies Quarterly* 31: 484–508.

George, Alexander L., and Juliette L. George. (1956). *Woodrow Wilson and Colonel House: A Personality Study*. New York: Dover.

George, Alexander L., and Richard Smoke. (1974). *Deterrence in American Foreign Policy: Theory and Practice*. New York: Columbia University Press.

Gerbner, George, and George Marvanyi. (1977). The Many Worlds of the World's Press. *Journal of Communication* 27: 52–66.

Gertz, Matthew. (2018). I've Studied the Trump-Fox Feedback Loop for Months. It's Crazier Than You Think. *Politico*, January 5 (https://www.politico.com/magazine/story/2018/01/05/trump-media-feedback-loop-216248).

Gibbs, Nancy. (1997). The Many Lives of Madeleine. *Time*, February 17, pp. 52–61.

Gilboa, E. (2005). Global Television News and Foreign Policy: Debating the CNN Effect. *International Studies Perspectives* 3: 325–41.

Gilpin, Robert. (1981). *War and Change in World Politics*. Cambridge, UK: Cambridge University Press.

Gitlin, Todd. (1987). *The Sixties: Years of Hope, Days of Rage*. New York: Bantam.

Glad, Betty. (1980). *Jimmy Carter*. New York: W.W. Norton.

Glasser, Susan. (2019). Trump Finally Fired John Bolton, but Does It Really Matter? *The New Yorker*, September 11 (https://www.newyorker.com/news/letter-from-trumps-washington/trump-finally-fired-john-bolton-but-does-it-really-matter).

Glasser, Susan B., and Michael Grunwald. (2005). DHS Undermined from the Start. *Washington Post*, December 22, p. A1.

Goddard, C. Roe. (1993). *U.S. Foreign Economic Policy and the Latin American Debt Issue*. New York: Garland Publishers.

Godson, Roy. (2000). *Dirty Tricks or Trump Cards: U.S. Covert Action and Counterintelligence*. New Brunswick, NJ: Transaction Publishers.

Goldgeier, James. (2000). *Not Whether but When: The U.S. Decision to Enlarge*. Washington, DC: Brookings Institution Press.

Goldman, Adam. (2018). New Charges in Huge CIA Breach Known as Vault 7. *New York Times*, June 18 (https://www.nytimes.com/2018/06/18/us/politics/charges-cia-breach-vault-7.html).

Goldsmith, Jack L. (2007). *The Terror Presidency: Law and Judgment Inside the Bush Administration*. New York: W.W. Norton.

Golshan, Tara. (2019). Trump Vetoes Congress's Directive to End US Involvement in Bloody Saudi-Led War in Yemen. *Vox*, April 17 (https://www.vox.com/2019/4/17/18411863/trump-veto-yemen-resolution-saudi-bernie-sanders).

Goodman, Carly. (2018). The Shadowy Network Shaping Trump's Anti-immigration Policies. *Washington Post*, September 27 (https://www.washingtonpost.com/outlook/2018/09/27/shadowy-network-shaping-trumps-anti-immigration-policies/).

Goodman, Melvin A. (1997). Ending the CIA's Cold War Legacy. *Foreign Policy* 106: 128–43.

Goodwin, Doris Kearns. (1991). *Lyndon Johnson and the American Dream*. New York: St. Martin's Press.

Goodwin, Doris Kearns. (2006). *Team of Rivals*. New York: Simon and Schuster.

Gordon, Michael R. (2004). The Strategy to Secure Iraq Did Not Foresee a 2nd War. *New York Times*, October 19, p. A1.

Gorman, Siobhan. (2005). Cutbacks Likely Ahead for NSA. *Baltimore Sun*, October 27, p. 1A.

Gould, Joe. (2019). Senate's Pentagon Budget Bill Would Obstruct Trump from Leaving NATO. *Defense News*, May 23 (https://www.defensenews.com/congress/2019/05/23/senates-pentagon-budget-bill-would-obstruct-trump-from-leaving-nato/).

Graber, Doris A. (2009). *Mass Media and American Politics*. Washington, DC: CQ Press.

Gray, Rosie. (2017). The Wall Street Journal's Global Retrenchment. *The Atlantic*, February 16 (https://www.theatlantic.com/politics/archive/2017/02/wall-street-journal-retrenches-around-the-world/516915/).

Green, Joshua. (2010). Inside Man. *The Atlantic*, April.

Greenstein, Fred I. (1992). Can Personality and Politics Be Studied Systematically? *Political Psychology* 13, 105–28.

Greenstein, Fred I. (1994). The Two Leadership Styles of William Jefferson Clinton. *Political Psychology* 15: 351–62.

Greenstein, Fred I. (2009). *The Presidential Difference: Leadership Style from FDR to Barack Obama*. New York: Free Press.

Greider, William. (1987). *Secrets of the Temple: How the Federal Reserve Runs the Country*. New York: Simon and Schuster.

Grieco, Elizabeth. (2018). U.S. Newsroom Employment Has Dropped by a Quarter since 2008, with Greatest Decline at Newspapers. Pew Research Center, July 30 (https://www.pewresearch.org/fact-tank/2018/07/30/newsroom-employment-dropped-nearly-a-quarter-in-less-than-10-years-with-greatest-decline-at-newspapers/).

Grose, Peter. (1995). *Gentleman Spy: The Life of Allen Dulles*. Boston, MA: Houghton Mifflin.

Guess, Andrew, Jonathan Nagler, and Joshua Tucker. (2019). Less Than You Think: Prevalence and Predictors of Fake News Dissemination on Facebook. *Science Advances* 5 (https://advances.sciencemag.org/content/5/1/eaau4586).

Halberstam, David. (1969). *The Best and the Brightest*. New York: Random House.

Halberstam, David. (1973). *The Best and the Brightest*. New York: Pocket Books.

Halberstam, David. (2000). *The Powers That Be*. Champaign: University of Illinois.

Halberstam, David. (2001). *War in a Time of Peace: Bush, Clinton, and the Generals*. New York: Scribner.

Halberstam, David. (2007). *The Coldest Winter: America and the Korean War*. New York: Hyperion.

Hallin, Daniel C. (1986). *The Uncensored War: The Media and Vietnam*. Los Angeles: University of California Press.

Halperin, Morton H. (1974). *Bureaucratic Politics and Foreign Policy*. Washington, DC: Brookings Institution Press.

Halperin, Morton H., and Arnold Kanter. (1973). *Readings in American Foreign Policy: A Bureaucratic Perspective*. Boston, MA: Little, Brown.

Halperin, Morton H., and David Halperin. (1984). The Key West Key. *Foreign Policy* 52: 114–30.

Hamilton, Lee H. (2006). The Making of U.S. Foreign Policy: The Roles of the President and Congress over Four Decades. In *Rivals for Power: Presidential-Congressional Relations*, edited by Jordan Tama, p. 273. New York: Rowman and Littlefield.

Hamilton, Lee H., and Jordan Tama. (2003). *Creative Tension: The Foreign Policy Roles of the President and Congress.* Washington, DC: Woodrow Wilson Center Press.

Hammer, Joshua. (2004). Uncivil Military. *New Republic,* March 1, pp. 16–18.

Haney, Patrick J., and Walt Vanderbush. (1999). The Role of Ethnic Interest Groups in U.S. Foreign Policy: The Case of the Cuban American National Foundation. *International Studies Quarterly* 43: 341–61.

Hannerz, Ulf. (2004). *Foreign News: Exploring the World of Foreign Correspondents.* Chicago, IL: University of Chicago Press.

Hansen, Allen C. (1984). *U.S. Information Agency: Public Diplomacy in the Computer Age.* New York: Praeger.

Harman, Jane. (2009). What the CIA Hid from Congress. *Los Angeles Times,* July 25 (http://articles.latimes.com/2009/jul/25/opinion/oe-harman25).

Harris, John F. (2005). *The Survivor: Bill Clinton in the White House.* New York: Random House.

Harris, Shane, and Ellen Nakashima. (2019). U.S. Got Key Asset Out of Russia Following Election Hacking. *Washington Post,* September 10 (https://beta.washingtonpost.com/national-security/us-got-key-asset-out-of-russia-following-election-hacking/2019/09/09/c8820f70-d344-11e9-9343-40db57cf6abd_story.html).

Hartung, William. (2012). *Prophets of War: Lockheed Martin and the Making of the Military-Industrial Complex.* New York: Bold Type Books.

Hartz, Louis. (1955). *The Liberal Tradition in America.* New York: Harcourt Brace and World.

Hastings, Michael. (2010). The Runaway General. *Rolling Stone,* June 25.

Hastings, Michael. (2011). King David's War. *Rolling Stone,* February 11.

Hawkins, V. (2011). Media Selectivity and the Other Side of the CNN Effect: The Consequences of Not Paying Attention to Conflict. *Media, War & Conflict* 4: 55–69.

Heclo, Hugh. (1977). *A Government of Strangers: Executive Politics in Washington.* Washington, DC: Brookings Institution Press.

Heclo, Hugh. (1988). The In-and-Outer System. *Political Science Quarterly* 102: 37–56.

Heilemann, John, and Mark Halperin. (2010). *Game Change: Obama and the Clintons, McCain and Palin, and the Race of a Lifetime.* New York: Harper.

Henkin, Louis. (1987). Foreign Affairs and the Constitution. *Foreign Affairs* 66: 284–310.

Henkin, Louis. (1996). *Foreign Affairs and the Constitution.* Mineola, NY: Foundation Press.

Hermann, Charles F. (1969). International Crises as a Situational Variable. In *International Politics and Foreign Policy,* edited by James N. Rosenau, pp. 409–21. New York: Free Press.

Hermann, Charles F. (1972). *International Crises: Insights from Behavioral Research.* New York: Free Press.

Hermann, Charles F., ed. (2011). *When Things Go Wrong: Foreign Policy Decision Making under Adverse Feedback.* New York: Routledge.

Hermann, Margaret G. (1986). Ingredients of Leadership. In *Political Psychology: Contemporary Problems and Issues,* edited by M. G. Hermann, pp. 167–92. San Francisco: Jossey-Bass.

Hermann, Margaret G., and Thomas Preston. (1994). Presidents, Advisers, and Foreign Policy: The Effect of Leadership Style on Executive Arrangements. *Political Psychology* 15, 75–96.

Hersh, Burton. (1992). *The Old Boys: The American Elite and the Origins of the CIA.* New York: Scribner.

Hersh, Seymour H. (1983). *The Price of Power: Kissinger in the Nixon White House.* New York: Summit Books.

Hersh, Seymour H. (2004). The Gray Zone: How a Secret Program Came to Abu Ghraib. *New Yorker,* May 24, p. 38.

Hersman, Rebecca K. C. (2000). *Friends and Foes: How Congress and the President Really Make Foreign Policy.* Washington, DC: Brookings Institution Press.

Hertzke, Allen D. (1988). *Representing God in Washington: The Role of Religious Lobbies in the American Polity.* Knoxville: University of Tennessee Press.

Hess, Stephen. (1981). *The Washington Reporters.* Washington, DC: Brookings Institution Press.

Hess, Stephen. (1996). *International News and Foreign Correspondents.* Washington, DC: Brookings Institution Press.

Hicks, Kathleen H., Louis Lauter, Colin McElhinny, et al. (2018). *Beyond the Water's Edge: Measuring the Internationalism of Congress*. Washington, DC: Center for Strategic & International Studies.

Hilsman, Roger. (1964). *To Move a Nation: The Politics of Foreign Policy in the Administration of John F. Kennedy*. New York: Delta.

Hilsman, Roger. (1993). *The Politics of Policymaking in Defense and Foreign Affairs*. New York: Prentice Hall.

Himmelstein, Jerome L. (1991). *To the Right: The Transformation of American Conservatism*. Berkeley and Los Angeles: University of California Press.

Hinckley, Barbara. (1994). *Less than Meets the Eye: Congress, the President, and Foreign Policy*. Chicago, IL: University of Chicago Press.

Hirsh, Michael. (2002). Bush and the World. *Foreign Affairs* 81: 18–43.

Hoagland, Jim. (2009). White House Fault Lines. *Washington Post*, July 12 (http://www.washingtonpost.com/wp-dyn/content/article/2009/07/10/AR2009071002936.html).

Hodgson, Godfrey. (1973). The Establishment. *Foreign Policy*, pp. 3–40.

Hodgson, Godfrey. (1976). *America in Our Time*. Princeton, NJ: Princeton University Press.

Hoffmann, Stanley. (1968). *Gulliver's Troubles, or the Setting of American Foreign Policy*. New York: McGraw-Hill.

Hoffmann, Stanley. (1977). An American Social Science: International Relations. *Daedalus* 106: 41–60.

Hofstadter, Richard. (1965). *The Paranoid Style in American Politics, and Other Essays*. New York: Knopf.

Holsti, Ole R. (1967). Cognitive Dynamics and Images of the Enemy: Dulles and Russia. In *Image and Reality in World Politics*, edited by John C. Farrell and Asa P. Smith, pp. 16–39. New York: Columbia University Press.

Holsti, Ole R. (1979). The Three-Headed Eagle: The United States and System Change. *International Studies Quarterly* 23: 345.

Holsti, Ole R. (1990). Crisis Management. In *Psychological Dimensions of War*, edited by Betty Glad, pp. 116–42. Newberry Park, CA: Sage.

Holsti, Ole R. (1992). Public Opinion and Foreign Policy: Challenges to the Almond-Lippmann Consensus. *International Studies Quarterly* 36: 439–66.

Holsti, Ole R. (1994). *Public Opinion and American Foreign Policy*. Ann Arbor: University of Michigan Press.

Holsti, Ole R. (2004). *Public Opinion and American Foreign Policy* (revised ed.). Ann Arbor: University of Michigan Press.

Holsti, Ole R., and James N. Rosenau. (1984). *American Leadership in World Affairs: Vietnam and the Breakdown of Consensus*. New York: Allen and Unwin.

Hook Steven, and James M. Scott, eds. (2012). *U.S. Foreign Policy Today: American Renewal?* Washington, DC: CQ Press.

Hopkins, Raymond F. (1978). Global Management Networks: The Internationalization of Domestic Bureaucracies. *International Social Science Journal* 30: 31–45.

Howell, William, Saul Jackman, and Ron Rogowski. (2013). *The Wartime President: Executive Influence and the Nationalizing Politics of Threat*. Chicago: University of Chicago Press.

Howell, William G., and Jon C. Pevehouse. (2007). *While Dangers Gather: Congressional Checks on Presidential War Powers*. Princeton, NJ: Princeton University Press.

Hulse, Carl. (2005). Senate G.O.P. Push for Plan on Ending War. *New York Times*, November 15, p. A1.

Huntington, Samuel P. (1957). *The Soldier and the State: The Theory and Politics of Civil-Military Relations*. Cambridge, MA: Harvard University Press.

Huntington, Samuel P. (1997). The Erosion of American National Interests. *Foreign Affairs* 76: 28–49.

Ifill, Gwen. (1993). The Economic Czar Behind the Economic Czars. *New York Times*, March 22, p. A1.

Ignatius, David. (2018). How Mike Pompeo Is Succeeding Where Rex Tillerson Failed. *Washington Post*, August 9 (https://www.washingtonpost.com/opinions/how-mike-pompeo-is-succe...3e-9c19-11e8-b60b-1c897f17e185_story.html).

Ikenberry, G. John. (1988). *Reasons of State: Oil Politics and the Capacities of American Government*. Ithaca, NY: Cornell University Press.

Ikenberry, G. John. (1989). Rethinking the Origins of American Hegemony. *Political Science Quarterly* 104, 375–400.

Ikenberry, G. John. (1992). A World Economy Restored: Expert Consensus and the Anglo-American Post-War Settlement. *International Organization* 46: 289–321.

Ikenberry, G. John (2011). *Liberal Leviathan: The Origins, Crisis, and Transformation of the American World Order.* Princeton, NJ: Princeton University Press.

Ikenberry, G. John. (2017). The Plot Against American Foreign Policy: Can the Liberal Order Survive? *Foreign Affairs*, April (https://www.foreignaffairs.com/articles/united-states/2017-04-17/plot-against-american-foreign-policy).

Immelman, A. (2017). The Leadership Style of U.S. President Donald J. Trump (Working Paper No. 1.2). Collegeville and St. Joseph, MN: St. John's University and the College of St. Benedict, Unit for the Study of Personality in Politics (http://digitalcommons.csbsju.edu/psychology_pubs/107/).

Immerman, Richard H. (1982). *The CIA in Guatemala: The Foreign Policy of Intervention.* Austin: University of Texas Press.

In Bob We Trust. (1994). *Economist*, December 10, p. 28.

Isaacson, Walter. (1999). Madeleine's War. *Time*, May 17, pp. 26–36.

Isaacson, Walter, and Evan Thomas. (1986). *The Wise Men: Six Friends and the World They Made.* New York: Touchstone.

Isenberg, David. (2012). SIGIR Reports: Hey, Anybody Know What Happened to the $2 Billion? *Huffington Post*, February 6.

Isenstadt, Alex. (2009). *Committee Will Investigate CIA* (http://www.politico.com/news/stories/0709/25094.html).

Isikoff, Michael. (2006). The Other Big Brother. *Newsweek*, January 30, pp. 32–34.

Iyengar, Shanto, and Donald R. Kinder. (1987). *News That Matters: Television and American Opinion.* Chicago, IL: University of Chicago Press.

Jackson, Michael Gordon. (2012). *A Dramatically Different NSC: President Obama's Use of the National Security Council.* Paper presented at the 2012 meeting of the Western Political Science Association, March 22–24.

Jamieson, Kathleen Hall. (2018). *Cyberwar: How Russian Hackers and Trolls Helped Elect a President; What We Don't, Can't, and Do Know.* New York: Oxford University Press.

Janis, Irving L. (1982). *Groupthink.* New York: Houghton Mifflin.

Jeffreys-Jones, Rhodri. (1989). *The CIA and American Democracy.* New Haven, CT: Yale University Press.

Jehl, Douglas. (1993). C.I.A. Nominee Wary of Budget Cuts. *New York Times*, February 3 (https://www.nytimes.com/1993/02/03/us/cia-nominee-wary-of-budget-cuts.html).

Jentleson, Bruce W. (1987). American Commitments in the Third World: Theory vs. Practice. *International Organization* 41: 667–704.

Jentleson, Bruce W. (1990). American Diplomacy: Around the World and Along Pennsylvania Avenue. In *A Question of Balance: The President, the Congress and Foreign Policy,* edited by Thomas E. Mann, pp. 146–200. Washington, DC: Brookings Institution Press.

Jentleson, Bruce W. (1992). The Pretty Prudent Public: PostVietnam American Opinion on the Use of Military Force. *International Studies Quarterly* 36: 49–74.

Jeong, Gyung-Ho, and Paul J. Quirk. (2017). Division at the Water's Edge: The Polarization of Foreign Policy. *American Politics Research* 47: 58–87.

Jervis, Robert. (1976). *Perception and Misperception in International Politics.* Princeton, NJ: Princeton University Press.

Jochim, Ashley E., and Bryan D. Jones. (2012). Issue Politics in a Polarized Congress. *Political Research Quarterly* 66: 352–69.

Johnson, Loch K. (1985). *The Making of International Agreements: Congress Confronts the Executive.* New York: New York University Press.

Johnson, Loch K. (1989). Covert Action and Accountability: Decision-Making for America's Foreign Policy. *International Studies Quarterly* 33: 81–109.

Johnson, Loch K. (2000). *Bombs, Bugs, Drugs, and Thugs: Intelligence and America's Quest for Security.* New York: New York University Press.

Johnson, Loch K. (2004). The Contemporary Presidency: Presidents, Lawmakers, and Spies: Intelligence Accountability in the United States. *Presidential Studies Quarterly* 34: 828–37.

Johnson, Loch K. (2005). Accountability and America's Secret Foreign Policy: Keeping a Legislative Eye on the

Central Intelligence Agency. *Foreign Policy Analysis* 1: 99–120.

Johnson, Loch K., and James Wirtz. (2004). *Strategic Intelligence: Windows into a Secret World*. Los Angeles, CA: Roxbury Publishing.

Johnson, Richard Tanner. (1974). *Managing the White House: An Intimate Study of the Presidency*. New York: Harper and Row.

Johnson, Robert David. 2006. *Congress and the Cold War*. New York: Cambridge University Press.

Johnson, Simon. (2009). An Emerging Split That Matters: Treasury vs. The National Economic Council. *New York Times*, July 2 (http://economix.blogs.nytimes.com/2009/07/02/an-emerging-split-that-matters-treasury-vsthe-nec/).

Jones, Alex S. (1991). War in the Gulf: The Press; Process of News Reporting on Display. *Washington Post*, February 15, p. A9.

Jones, Christopher M. (1998). The Foreign Policy Bureaucracy in a New Era. In *After the End, Making US Foreign Policy in the Post-Cold War World* (pp. 57–88), edited by James M. Scott. Durham, NC: Duke University Press.

Jones, David C. (1982). What's Wrong with Our Defense Establishment. *New York Times Magazine*, November 7, pp. 38–42, 70–83.

Jordan, Hamilton. (1982). *Crisis: The Last Year of the Carter Presidency*. New York: G.P. Putnam's Sons.

Jost, Tyler, and Robert Schub. (2019). Trump Tweeted There's 'No Infighting' on U.S. Policy on Iran. But Does He Have All the Information? *Washington Post*, May 18 (https://washingtonpost.com/politics/2019/05/18/trump-tweeted-theres-no-infighting-us-policy-iran-does-he-have-all-information/).

Judis, John B. (1989). K Street's Rise to Power of Special Interests to U.S. *In These Times*, November 1, p. 7.

Judis, John B. (1993). Old Master. *New Republic*, December 13, pp. 21–28.

Juster, Kenneth I., and Simon Lazarus. (1997). *Making Economic Policy: An Assessment of the National Economic Council*. Washington, DC: Brookings Institution Press.

Kagan, Robert. (1996). *A Twilight Struggle: American Power and Nicaragua, 1977–1990*. New York: The Free Press.

Kahl, Colin, and Hal Brands. (2017). Trump's Grand Strategic Trainwreck. *Foreign Policy*, January 31 (https://foreignpolicy.com/2017/01/31/trumps-grand-strategic-train-wreck/).

Kahn, Chris. (2019). Half of American Adults Expect War with Iran "Within Next Few Years." *Reuters*, May 19 (https://www.reuters.com/article/us-usa-iran-poll/half-of-american-adults-expect-war-with-iran-within-next-few-years-reuters-ipsos-poll-idUSKCN1SR27K).

Kalb, Madeleine G. (1981). *The Congo Cables: The Cold War in Africa from Eisenhower to Kennedy*. New York: Macmillan.

Kane, Paul, and Ben Pershing. (2009). Secret Program Fuels CIA-Congress Dispute. *Washington Post*, July 10 (www.washingtonpost.com/wp-dyn/content/arti-cle/2009/07/09/AR2009070903017.html).

Kaphle, Anup. (2015). The Foreign Desk in Transition. *Columbia Journalism Review*, March/April (https://www.cjr.org/analysis/the_foreign_desk_in_transition.php).

Kaplan, Fred. (1983). *The Wizards of Armageddon*. New York: Touchstone.

Kaplan, Lawrence F. (2004). State's Rights. *New Republic*, December 7, pp. 16–17.

Kaplan, Robert D. (1994). *The Arabists: The Romance of an American Elite*. New York: Free Press.

Kaplan, Robert D. (2005). *Imperial Grunts: The American Military on the Ground*. New York: Random House.

Karp, Walter. (1989). Who Decides What Is News? (Hint: It's Not Journalists). *Utne Reader*, pp. 60–68.

Kassop, Nancy. (2003). The War Power and Its Limits. *Presidential Studies Quarterly* 33: 509–29.

Kearns, Doris. (1976). *Lyndon Johnson and the American Dream*. New York: New American Library.

Keating, Peter. (2009). The Good Soldier: Hillary Clinton as Secretary of State. *New York Magazine*, June 14 (http://nymag.com/daily/intel/2009/06/hillary_clinton_as_secretary_o.html).

Keith, Tamara. (2018). President Trump's Description of What's "Fake" Is Expanding. *NPR*, September 2 (https://www.npr.org/2018/09/02/643761979/president-trumps-description-of-whats-fake-is-expanding).

Kennan, George F. (1951). *American Diplomacy, 1900–1950*. New York: Mentor.

Kennedy, Paul. (1987). *The Rise and Fall of the Great Powers: Economic Change and Military Conflict from 1500 to 2000.* New York: Random House.

Kennedy, Paul. (2002). "The Eagle Has Landed." *Financial Times*, February 2.

Keohane, Robert, and Joseph Nye, Jr. (2011). *Power and Interdependence* (4th ed.) New York: Longman.

Keohane, Robert O., and Joseph S. Nye, Jr. (2011). *Power and Interdependence: World Politics in Transition* (4th ed.). Boston, MA: Little, Brown.

Kessler, Glenn. (2003). U.S. Decision on Iraq Has Puzzling Past. *Washington Post*, January 12, p. A1.

Kessler, Glenn, and Thomas E. Ricks. (2004). Rice's NSC Tenure Complicates New Post: Failure to Manage Agency Infighting Cited. *Washington Post*, November 16, p. A7.

Kessler, Ronald. (1994). *The FBI: Inside the World's Most Powerful Law Enforcement Agency.* New York: Pocket Books.

Khong, Yuen Foong. (1992). *Analogies at War: Korea, Munich, Dien Bien Phu, and the Vietnam Decisions of 1965.* Princeton, NJ: Princeton University Press.

Kilcullen, David. (2009). *The Accidental Guerrilla: Fighting Small Wars in the Midst of a Big One.* London: Hurst & Company.

Kindleberger, Charles P. (1977). U.S. Foreign Economic Policy, 1776–1976. *Foreign Affairs* 55: 395–417.

Kingdon, John W. (1984). *Agendas, Alternatives, and Public Policies.* Boston, MA: Little, Brown.

Kingdon, John. (2002). *Agendas, Alternatives, and Public Policies* (2nd ed.). New York: Pearson.

Kirk, Jason. (2008). Indian-Americans and the U.S.– India Nuclear Agreement: Consolidation of an Ethnic Lobby? *Foreign Policy Analysis* 4: 275–300.

Kirschten, Dick. (1993). Rescuing Aid. *National Journal* 25: 2369–72.

Kitfield, James. (1995). *Prodigal Soldiers: How the Generation of Officers Born of Vietnam Revolutionized the American Style of War.* New York: Simon and Schuster.

Kitfield, James. (2001). A Diplomat Handy with a Bayonet. *National Journal* 33: 250.

Knecht, Thomas. (2010). *Paying Attention to Foreign Affairs: How Public Opinion Affects Presidential Decision Making.* University Park: Pennsylvania State University Press.

Knight Foundation. (2018). American Views: Trust, Media and Democracy, January 15 (https://knightfoundation.org/reports/american-views-trust-media-and-democracy).

Knutsen, Trobjorn L. (1997). *A History of International Relations Theory.* Manchester, UK: Manchester University Press.

Koen, Ross Y. (1974). *The China Lobby in American Politics.* New York: Harper and Row.

Kopp, Harry, and Charles Gillespie. (2008). *Career Diplomacy: Life and Work in the Foreign Service.* Washington, DC: Georgetown University Press.

Korb, Lawrence J. (1996). A Military Monopoly. *New York Times*, December 21, p. 25.

Kornblut, Anne E., Scott Wilson, and Karen DeYoung. (2009). Obama Pressed for Faster Surge: Afghan Review a Marathon. *Washington Post*, December 6.

Kotz, Nick. (1988). *Wild Blue Yonder and the B-1 Bomber.* Princeton, NJ: Princeton University Press.

Krasner, Stephen D. (1972). Are Bureaucracies Important? (Or Allison Wonderland). *Foreign Policy* 7: 159–79.

Krasner, Stephen D. (1982). American Policy and Global Economic Stability. In *America in a Changing World Political Economy,* edited by William P. Avery and David P. Rapkin, pp. 29–48. New York: Longman.

Krauthammer, Charles. (1990). The Unipolar Moment. *Foreign Affairs*, September (https://www.foreignaffairs.com/articles/1991-02-01/unipolar-moment).

Krepinevich, Andrew F. (1986). *The Army and Vietnam.* Baltimore, MD: Johns Hopkins University Press.

Kriner, Douglas. (2010). *After the Rubicon: Congress, Presidents, and the Politics of Waging War.* Chicago: University of Chicago Press.

Kuttner, Robert. (1991). *The End of Laissez-Faire: National Purpose and the Global Economy After the Cold War.* New York: Knopf.

Kwitny, Jonathan. (1984). *Endless Enemies: The Making of an Unfriendly World.* New York: Penguin.

Lacey, Marc, and Raymond Bonner. (2001). A Mad Scramble by Donors for Plum Ambassadorships. *New York Times*, March 19, p. 19.

LaFeber, Walter. (1994). *The American Age: United States Foreign Policy at Home and Abroad: 1750 to the Present* (2nd ed.) New York: W. W. Norton.

LaFranchi, Howard. (2001). In PR War, US Gets Ready to Turn up Volume. *Christian Science Monitor*, November 1, pp. 7–13.

Landler, Mark. (2017). Trump, the Insurgent, Breaks with 70 Years of American Foreign Policy. *New York Times*, December 28 (https://www.nytimes.com/2017/12/28/us/politics/trump-world-diplomacy.html).

Lantis, Jeffrey S. (2019). *Foreign Policy Advocacy and Entrepreneurship*. Stanford, CA: Stanford University Press.

Lasswell, Harold D. (1938). *Politics: Who Gets What, When and How*. New York: McGraw-Hill.

Latham, Michael E. (2000). *Modernization as Ideology: American Social Science and "Nation-Building" in the Kennedy Era*. Chapel Hill: University of North Carolina Press.

Lawrence, Jill. (2008). Obama: Keeping Cool, Focusing on "Common Purpose." *USA Today*, October 8, p. A1.

Layne, Christopher. (1997). From Preponderance to Offshore Balancing: America's Future Grand Strategy. *International Security* 22: 86–124.

Lebow, Richard Ned. (1981). *Between Peace and War: The Nature of International Crisis*. Baltimore, MD: John Hopkins University Press.

Ledbetter, James. (2011). *Unwarranted Influence: Dwight D. Eisenhower and the Military-Industrial Complex*. New Haven, CT: Yale University Press.

Lee, Carol E., and Gordon Lubold. (2010). Donilon to Replace Jones. *Politico*, October 8.

Lee, Carol E., Kristen Welker, Stephanie Ruhle, and Dafna Linzer. (2017). Tillerson's Fury at Trump Required an Intervention from VP Pence. NBC News, October 4 (https://www.nbcnews.com/politics/white-house/tillerson-s-fury-trump-required-intervention-pence-n806451).

Leibovich, Mark. (2012). For a Blunt Biden, an Uneasy Supporting Role. *New York Times*, May 7.

Lemann, Nicholas. (2002). The Next World Order: The Bush Administration May Have a Brand-New Doctrine of Power. *New Yorker*, April 1, p. 42.

Leslie, Stuart W. (1994). *The Cold War and American Science: The Military-Industrial Complex at MIT and Stanford*. New York: Columbia University Press.

Leuchtenburg, William E. (2009). *In the Shadow of FDR: From Harry Truman to Barack Obama*. Ithaca, NY: Cornell University Press.

Levy, Jack S. (1994). Learning and Foreign Policy: Sweeping a Conceptual Minefield. *International Organization* 48: 279–312.

Light, Paul C. (1984). *Vice Presidential Power: Advice and Influence in the White House*. Baltimore: John Hopkins University Press.

Likes, Terry. (2014). Does Anyone Care? The State of International News Coverage Among U.S. Media. *Electronic News* 8(1): 64–67.

Lindblom, Charles E. (1959). The Science of "Muddling" Through. *Public Administration Review* 19: 79–88.

Lindorff, Dave. (2018). Massive Accounting Fraud Exposed. *The Nation*, November 27 (https://www.thenation.com/article/pentagon-audit-budget-fraud/).

Lindsay, James M. (1994). *Congress and the Politics of U.S. Foreign Policy*. Baltimore, MD: Johns Hopkins University Press.

Lindsay, James M. (2000). The New Apathy: How an Uninterested Public Is Shaping Foreign Policy. *Foreign Affairs* 79: 2–8.

Lindsay, James M. (2002). Getting Uncle Sam's Ear: Will Ethnic Lobbies Cramp America's Foreign Policy Style? *Brookings Review* 20: 37–40.

Lindsay, James M. (2003). Deference and Defiance: The Shifting Rhythms of Executive-Legislative Relations in Foreign Policy. *Presidential Studies Quarterly* 33: 530–46.

Lippmann, Walter. (1922). *Public Opinion*. New York: The Free Press.

Liptak, Kevin, Dan Merica, Jeff Zeleny, and Elise Labott. (2017). Tense and Difficult Meeting Preceded Tillerson's "Moron" Comment. CNN, October 12 (https://www.cnn.com/2017/10/11/politics/tillerson-moron-comment/index.html).

Lissner, Rebecca Friedman, and Mira Rapp-Hooper. (2018). The Day after Trump: American Strategy for a New International Order. *Washington Quarterly* 41: 7–25.

Livingston, Steven. (1997). *Clarifying the CNN Effect: An Examination of Media Effects According to Type of Military Intervention.* Cambridge, MA: Joan Shorenstein Center on the Press Politics and Public Policy, John F. Kennedy School of Government, Harvard University.

Livingston, Steven, and Todd Eachus. (1995). Humanitarian Crises and US Foreign Policy: Somalia and the CNN Effect Reconsidered. *Political Communication* 12: 413–29.

Lizza, Ryan. (2002). White House Watch: Big Deal. *New Republic*, June 24, pp. 10–12.

Lizza, Ryan. (2010). Inside the Crisis: Larry Summers and the White House Economic Team. *The New Yorker*, October 19.

Lizza, Ryan. (2011). The Consequentialist: How the Arab Spring Remade Obama's Foreign Policy. *The New Yorker*, May 2.

Locker, James R., III. (2002). *Victory on the Potomac: The Goldwater-Nichols Act Unifies the Pentagon.* Bryan, TX: A&M University Press.

Lowenthal, Mark M. (2011). *Intelligence: From Secrets to Policy.* Washington, DC: Congressional Quarterly Press.

Luttwak, Edward N. (1985). *The Pentagon and the Art of War.* New York: Simon and Schuster.

Madrick, Jeff. (2009). How We Were Ruined & What We Can Do. *New York Review of Books*, February 12.

Maechling, Charles, Jr. (1976). Foreign Policy Makers: The Weakest Link? *Virginia Quarterly Review* 52: 1–23.

Malmgren, Harald B. (1972). Managing Foreign Economic Policy. *Foreign Policy* 6: 42–63.

Mann, James. (2004). *The Rise of the Vulcans: The History of Bush's War Cabinet.* New York: Vikings Press.

Mann, Thomas E. (1990a). Making Foreign Policy: President and Congress. In *A Question of Balance: The President, the Congress, and Foreign Policy*, edited by Thomas E. Mann, pp. 1–34. Washington, DC: Brookings Institution Press.

Mann, Thomas E. (1990b). *A Question of Balance: The President, the Congress, and Foreign Policy.* Washington, DC: Brookings Institution Press.

Manning, Bayless. (1977). The Congress, the Executive, and Intermestic Affairs: Three Proposals. *Foreign Affairs* 55: 306–22.

Marsh, Kevin, and Jeffrey S. Lantis. (2018). Are All Foreign Policy Innovators Created Equal? The New Generation of Congressional Foreign Policy Entrepreneurship. *Foreign Policy Analysis* 14: 212–34.

Marshall, Bryan W., and Brandon C. Prins. (2002). The Pendulum of Congressional Power: Agenda Change, Partisanship and the Demise of the Post-World War II Foreign Policy Consensus. *Congress and the Presidency* 29: 195–212.

Martin, Justin D. (2012). Loneliness at the Foreign "Bureau." *Columbia Journalism Review*, April 23 (https://archives.cjr.org/behind_the_news/loneliness_at_the_foreign_bureau.php).

Martin, Lisa L. (2000). *Democratic Commitments: Legislatures and International Cooperation.* Princeton, NJ: Princeton University Press.

Martin, William. (1999). The Christian Right and American Foreign Policy. *Foreign Policy* 114, 66–80.

Martini, Nicholas F. (2015). Foreign Policy Ideology and Conflict Preferences: A Look at Afghanistan and Libya. *Foreign Policy Analysis* 11: 417–434.

Mascaro, Lisa. (2019). Senate Reasserts Foreign Policy Role, Reshapes Trump Agenda. Associated Press, February 2 (https://www.theoaklandpress.com/news/nation-world-news/senate-reas...es-trump-agenda/article_638ca336-271a-11e9-8edd-cff1f3088ad8.html).

Massing, Michael. (2005). The Press: The Enemy Within. *New York Review of Books* 52: 20.

Mastanduno, Michael. (1985). Strategies of Economic Containment: U.S. Trade Relations with the Soviet Union. *World Politics* 37: 503–31.

Mayer, Jane. (2019). The Making of the Fox News White House. *The New Yorker*, March 11 (https://www.newyorker.com/magazine/2019/03/11/the-making-of-the-fox-news-white-house).

Mayhew, David R. (1974). *Congress: The Electoral Connection.* New York: Yale University Press.

Mazzetti, Mark. (2009). Five Years after Overhaul, U.S. Spy Chiefs Still Fight over Turf. *New York Times*, June 9, p. A10.

McAdams, Dan. (2016). The Mind of Donald Trump. *The Atlantic*, June (https://www.theatlantic.com/magazine/archive/2016/06/the-mind-of-donald-trump/480771/).

McCammond, Alexi, and Jonathan Swan. (2019). Insider Leaks Trump's "Executive Time"-Filled Private Schedules. *Axios*, Feburary 3 (https://www.axios.com/donald-trump-private-schedules-leak-executive-time-34e67fbb-3af6-48df-aefb-52e02c334255.html).

McCormick, James M. (1998). Interest Groups and the Media in Post-Cold War U.S. Foreign Policy. In *After the End: Making U.S. Foreign Policy in the Post-Cold War World*, edited by James M. Scott, pp. 170–98. Durham, NC: Duke University Press.

McCormick, James M., Eugene R. Wittkopf, and David Danna. (1997). Politics and Bipartisanship at the Water's Edge: A Note on Bush and Clinton. *Polity* 30: 133–50.

McGeary, Johanna. (2001). Odd Man Out. *Time*, September 10, pp. 24–32.

McGuinness, Damien. (2017). How a Cyber Attack Transformed Estonia. BBC News, April 27 (http://www.bbc.com/news/39655415).

McKay, A. (2012). Buying Policy? The Effects of Lobbyists' Resources on Their Policy Success. *Political Research Quarterly* 65, 908–23.

McManus, Doyle. (2018). Almost Half the Top Jobs in Trump's State Department Are Still Empty. *The Atlantic*, November 4 (https://www.theatlantic.com/politics/archive/2018/11/state-department-empty-ambassador-to-australi/574831/).

Mearsheimer, John, and Stephen Walt. (2006). The Israel Lobby. *London Review of Books* 28: 3–12.

Mearsheimer, John, and Stephen Walt. (2007). *The Israel Lobby and U.S. Foreign Policy*. New York: Farrar, Strauss, and Giroux.

Melanson, Richard A. (1990). *Reconstructing Consensus: American Foreign Policy Since the Vietnam War*. New York: St. Martin's Press.

Melanson, Richard A. (2005). *American Foreign Policy since the Vietnam War*. Armonk, NY: M.E. Sharpe.

Melanson, Richard A. (2015). *American Foreign Policy Since the Vietnam War: The Search for Consensus from Richard Nixon to George W. Bush*. New York: Routledge.

Mermin, Jonathan. (1999). *Debating War and Peace: Media Coverage of U.S. Intervention in the Post-Vietnam Era*. Princeton, NJ: Princeton Universty Press.

Milbank, Dana. (2001, November 20). In War, It's Power to the President. *Washington Post*, p. A1.

Milbank, Dana, and Bradley Graham. (2001). No Time for "Strategy." *Washington Post, Weekly Edition*, October 15–21, p. 13.

Milner, Helen V. (1989). *Resisting Protectionism: Global Industries and the Politics of International Trade*. Princeton, NJ: Princeton University Press.

Milner, Helen V., and Dustin Tingley. 2015. *Sailing the Water's Edge: The Domestic Politics of American Foreign Policy*. Princeton, NJ: Princeton University Press.

Moens, Alexander. (1990). *Foreign Policy under Carter: Testing Multiple Advocacy Decision Making*. Boulder, CO: Westview Press.

Moon, Chung-in. (1988). Complex Interdependence and Transnational Lobbying: South Korea in the United States. *International Studies Quarterly* 32: 67–89.

Morgan, Wesley, and Nahal Toosi. (2019). Trump Again Overrules Top Brass. *Politico*, April 8 (https://www.politico.com/story/2019/04/08/trump-iran-revolutionary-guard-pentagon-1261448).

Morgenthau, Hans J. (1952). *In Defense of the National Interest: A Critical Examination of American Foreign Policy*. New York: Knopf.

Morley, Jefferson. (2012). David Petraeus and the Signature of US Terror. *Salon*, April 19.

Morris, Roger. (1977). *Uncertain Greatness: Henry Kissinger and American Foreign Policy*. New York: Harper and Row.

Morse, Edward L. (1973). *Foreign Policy and Interdependence in Gaullist France*. Princeton, NJ: Princeton University Press.

Mueller, John E. (1973). *War, Presidents, and Public Opinion*. New York: John Wiley.

Mueller, John E. (2005). The Iraq Syndrome. *Foreign Affairs* 84: 44–54.

Mueller, Robert S., and US Department of Justice Special Counsel's Office. (2019). Executive Summary of Volume 1. In *Report on the Investigation into Russian Interference in the 2016 Presidential Election* (https://www.justice.gov/storage/report_volume1.pdf).

Mulcahy, Kevin V. (1991). The Bush Administration and National Security Policy-Making: A Preliminary Assessment. *Governance* 4: 207–20.

Naftali, Timothy. (2005). *Blind Spot: The Secret History of American Counterterrorism*. New York: Basic Books.

Nai, Allesandro, Ferran Martinez i Coma, and Jurgen Maier. (2019). Donald Trump, Populism, and the Age of Extremes: Comparing the Personality Traits and Campaigning Styles of Trump and Other Leaders Worldwide. *Presidential Studies Quarterly* 22. doi:10.1111/psq.12511

Nakashima, Ellen, and Bradley Graham. (2001). Direct Authority Called Key in Homeland Agency. *Washington Post*, September 27, p. A7.

Nash, George H. (1976). *The Conservative Intellectual Movement in America*. New York: Basic Books.

Nathan, James A. (1975). The Missile Crisis: His Finest Hour Now. *World Politics* 27: 256–81.

National Commission on Terrorist Attacks upon the United States. (2003). *The 9/11 Commission Report: Final Report of the National Commission on Terrorist Attacks upon the United States*. Washington, DC: US Government Printing Office.

National Security Council Project. (1999a). *The Bush Administration National Security Council*. Washington, DC: Brookings Institution Press.

National Security Council Project. (1999b). *The Role of the National Security Advisor*. Washington, DC: Brookings Institution Press.

National Security Council Project. (2000). *The Clinton Administration National Security Council*. Washington, DC: Brookings Institution Press.

Neumann, W. Russell. (1986). *The Paradox of Mass Politics: Knowledge and Opinion in the American Electorate*. Cambridge, MA: Harvard University Press.

Neustadt, Richard A. (1960). *Presidential Power: The Politics of Leadership*. New York: John Wiley.

Neustadt, Richard E. (1991). *Presidential Power and Modern Presidents*. New York: Simon and Schuster.

Newhouse, John. (1973). *Cold Dawn: The Story of Salt*. New York: Holt, Rinehart, and Winston.

Niebuhr, Reinhold. (1944). *The Children of Light and the Children of Darkness*. New York: Charles Scribner's Sons.

Niebuhr, Reinhold, and Alan Heimert. (1963). *A Nation So Conceived*. New York: Charles Scribner's Sons.

Nisbet, Robert A. (1988). *The Present Age: Progress and Anarchy in Modern America*. New York: Harper and Row.

Nollen, Stanley D., and Dennis P. Quinn. (1994). Free Trade, Fair Trade, Strategic Trade, and Protectionism in the U.S. Congress, 1987–1988. *International Organization* 48: 491–525.

Nye, Joseph S., Jr. (1992). What New World Order? *Foreign Affairs*, Spring (https://www.foreignaffairs.com/articles/1992-03-01/what-new-world-order).

Obama, Barack. (2009). *Press Conference*. Hilton Hotel. Port of Spain, Trinidad and Tobago, April 19.

O'Brien, David M. (2003). Presidential and Congressional Relations in Foreign Affairs: The Treaty-Making Power and the Rise of Executive Agreements. In *Congress and the Politics of Foreign Policy*, edited by Colton C. Campbell, Nicol C. Rae, and John F. Stack, Jr., pp. 70–89. Englewood Cliffs, NJ: Prentice Hall.

Office of the Director of National Intelligence. (2019a). Who We Are (https://www.dni.gov/index.php/who-we-are/organizations).

Office of the Director of National Intelligence. (2019b). US Intelligence Community Budget (https://www.dni.gov/index.php/what-we-do/ic-budget).

O'Hanlon, Michael E. (2016). Making the Grade? Assessing John Kerry's Record as Secretary of State. *Brookings, Order from Chaos*, January 20 (https://www.brookings.edu/blog/order-from-chaos/2016/01/20/making-the-grade-assessing-john-kerrys-record-as-secretary-of-state/).

Oldfield, Duane M., and Aaron Wildavsky. (1991). Reconsidering the Two Presidencies. In *The Two Presidencies: A Quarter Century Assessment*, edited by Steve A. Shull, pp. 181–90. Chicago, IL: Nelson Hall.

Oleszek, Walter. (2003). *Congressional Procedures and the Policy Process*. Washington, DC: Congressional Quarterly Press.

Olmsted, M. S., B. Baer, J. Joyce, and G. Prince. (1984). *Women at State: An Inquiry into the Status of Women in the United States Department of State*. Washington, DC: Women's Research and Education Institute of the Congressional Caucus for Women's Issues.

Oneal, John R. (1988). The Rationality of Decision Making during International Crises. *Polity* 20: 598–622.

Ornstein, Norman, and Thomas Donilon. (2000). The Confirmation Clog. *Foreign Affairs* 79: 87–99.

Pace, Julie. (2014). Susan Rice Remains Powerful Force as National Security Advisor. *Christian Science Monitor*, June 1 (http://www.csmonitor.com/layout/set/print/USA/Latest-News-Wires/2014/0601/Susan-Rice-remains-powerful-force-as-national-security-advisor).

Packenham, Robert A. (1973). *Liberal America and the Third World: Political Development Ideas in Foreign Aid and Social Science*. Princeton, NJ: Princeton University Press.

Packer, George. (2005). *The Assassin's Gate: America in Iraq*. New York: Farrar, Straus, and Giroux.

Page, Benjamin I., and Robert Y. Shapiro. (1992). *The Rational Public: Fifty Years of Trends in Americans' Policy Preferences*. Chicago, IL: University of Chicago Press.

Paige, Sean. (2000). Projects Lose Way in Pentagon's Revolving Door. *Insight on the News*, May 29, p. 47.

Parker, Ashley, and Philip Rucker. (2019). "You Are a Prop in the Back": Advisers Struggle to Obey Trump's Kafkaesque Rules. *Washington Post*, September 11 (https://beta.washingtonpost.com/politics/youre-a-prop-in-the-back-advisers-struggle-to-obey-trumps-kafkaesque-rules/2019/09/11/35bbf622-d4a9-11e9-9610-fb56c5522e1c_story.html).

Parker, Charles F., and Eric K. Stern. (2005). Bolt from the Blue or Avoidable Failure? Revisiting September 11 and the Origins of Strategic Surprise. *Foreign Policy Analysis* 1: 301–31.

Pastor, Robert A. (1981). *Congress and the Politics of U. S. Foreign Economic Policy*. Oakland: University of California Press.

Pastor, Robert A. (1992). *Whirlpool: U.S. Foreign Policy toward Latin America and the Caribbean*. Princeton, NJ: Princeton University Press.

Patterson, Bradley H., and James P. Pfiffner. (2001). The White House Office of Presidential Personnel. *Presidential Studies Quarterly* 31: 415–38.

Peake, Jeffrey S. (2017). The Domestic Politics of US Treaty Ratification: Bilateral Treaties from 1949 to 2012. *Foreign Policy Analysis* 13: 832–53.

Pear, Robert. (1989). Confusion Is Operative Word in U.S. Policy Toward Japan. *New York Times*, March 20, p. 1.

Penney, Joe, Eric Schmitt, Rukmini Callimachi, and Christoph Koettl. (2018). CIA Drone Mission, Curtailed by Obama, Is expanded in Africa Under Trump. *New York Times*, September 9 (https://www.nytimes.com/2018/09/09/world/africa/cia-drones-africa-military.html).

Perlmutter-Gumbiner, Elyse, Ken Dilanian, and Courtney Kube. (2019). On Trump's Calendar, Just 17 Intelligence Briefings in 85 Days. NBC News, February 6 (https://www.nbcnews.com/politics/national-security/trump-s-calendar-just-17-intelligence-briefings-85-days-n967386).

Perry, Mark. (1989). *Four Stars*. Boston, MA: Houghton Mifflin.

Perry, Mark. (2018). McMaster's Problem Isn't Trump. It's Mattis and Kelly. *Foreign Policy*, March 7 (https://foreignpolicy.com/2018/03/07/mcmasters-problem-isnt-trump-its-mattis-and-kelly/).

Pew Research Center. (2005). *The State of the News Media 2004: An Annual Report on News Journalism*.

Pew Research Center. (2010). Americans Spending More Time Following the News. Ideological News Sources: Who Watches and Why, September 12 (https://www.people-press.org/2010/09/12/americans-spending-more-time-following-the-news/).

Pew Research Center. (2011). What the Public Knows—In Words and Pictures, November 7 (http://www.people-press.org/files/legacy-pdf/11-7-11%20Knowledge%20Release.pdf).

Pew Research Center. (2013). Majority Says U.S. Should "Mind Its Own Business Internationally," December 3 (https://www.people-press.org/2013/12/03/public-sees-u-s-power-declining-as-support-for-global-engagement-slips/12-3-2013-2/).

Pew Research Center. (2016). Key Findings on How Americans View the U.S. Role in the World, May 5 (https://www.pewresearch.org/fact-tank/2016/05/05/key-findings-on-how-americans-view-the-u-s-role-in-the-world/ft_16-05-04_apwtakeaways_global-2/).

Pew Research Center. (2017). Continued Partisan Divides in Views of the Impact of Free Trade Agreements, April 24 (https://www.pewresearch.org/fact-tank/2017/04/25/support-for-free-trade-agreements-rebounds-modestly-but-wide-partisan-differences-remain/ft_17-04-24_free trade_usviews_2/).

Pillar, Paul R. (2010). Unintelligent Design. *The National Interest*, September/October.

Pincus, Walter. (2001). Intelligence Shakeup Would Boost CIA. *Washington Post*, November 8, p. A1.

Pious, Richard M. (1979). *The American Presidency*. New York: Basic Books.

Pious, Richard M. (2002). Why Do Presidents Fail? *Presidential Studies Quarterly* 32: 724–42.

Piper, Richard. (1994). Situational Constitutionalism and Presidential Power: The Rise and Fall of the Liberal Presidential Government. *Presidential Studies Quarterly* 24: 577–94.

Pollack, Kenneth M. (2004). Spies, Lies, and Weapons: What Went Wrong. *Atlantic Monthly*, January/February, pp. 78–92.

Popkin, Samuel L. (1991). *The Reasoning Voter: Communication and Persuasion in Presidential Campaigns*. Chicago, IL: University of Chicago Press.

Posen, Barry. (2018). The Rise of Illiberal Hegemony: Trump's Surprising Grand Strategy. *Foreign Affairs*, March/April (https://www.foreignaffairs.com/articles/2018-02-13/rise-illiberal-hegemony).

Posen, Barry R., and Andrew L. Ross. (1996). Competing Visions for U.S. Grand Strategy. *International Security* 21: 5–53.

Powell, Colin. (2012). *It Worked for Me: In Life and Leadership*. New York: Harper.

Powers, Thomas. (1973). *The War at Home: Vietnam and the American People, 1964–1968*. New York: Grossman.

Powers, Thomas. (1979). *The Man Who Kept the Secrets*. New York: Pocket Books.

Powers, Thomas. (2003). The Vanishing Case for War. *New York Review of Books*, December 4, p. 12.

Prados, John. (1986). *President's Secret Wars: CIA and Pentagon Operations Since World War II*. New York: William Morrow.

Preston, Thomas. (1997). "Following the Leader": The Impact of U.S. Presidential Style Upon Advisory Group Dynamics, Structure, and Decision. In *Beyond Groupthink: Political Group Dynamics and Foreign Policymaking*, edited by P. 't Hart, E. Stern, and B. Sundelius, pp. 191–248. Ann Arbor: University of Michigan Press.

Preston, Thomas. (2001). *The President and His Inner Circle: Leadership Style and Advisory Process in Foreign Policy Making*. New York: Columbia University Press.

Preston, Thomas. (2017). Leadership and Foreign Policy Analysis. *Oxford Research Encyclopedias: International Studies*. New York: Oxford University Press. doi:10.1093/acrefore/9780190846626.013.255

Preston, Thomas, and Paul 't Hart. (1999). Understanding and Evaluating Bureaucratic Politics: The Nexus between Political Leaders and Advisory Systems. *Political Psychology* 20: 48–98.

Priest, Dana. (2003). *The Mission: Waging War and Keeping Peace with America's Military*. New York: W.W. Norton.

Program on International Policy Attitudes. (2006). World Public Says Iraq War Has Increased Global Terrorist Threat. World Public Opinion, Global Public Opinion on International Affairs (www.worldpublicopinion.org/pipa/articles/international_security_bt/172.php).

Ranelagh, John. (1986). *The Agency: The Rise and Decline of the CIA*. New York: Simon and Schuster.

Ransom, Harry Howe. (1983). Strategic Intelligence and Intermestic Politics. In *Perspectives on American Foreign Policy: Selected Readings*, edited by Charles W. Kegley, Jr. and Eugene R. Wittkopf, pp. 299–319. New York: St. Martin's Press.

Rashid, Ahmed. (2004). The Mess in Afghanistan. *New York Review of Books*, February 12, pp. 24–27.

Ratnesar, Romesh. (2005). The Condi Doctrine. *Time*, August 15, pp. 36–42.

Recer, Paul. (2002). Geography Knowledge Lacking. *State*, November 21, p. A4.

Renshon, Stanley A. (2000). After the Fall: The Clinton Presidency in Perspective. *Political Science Quarterly* 115: 41–65.

Renshon, Stanley A. (2004). *In His Father's Shadow: The Transformations of George W. Bush*. New York: Palgrave/Macmillan.

Resnick, Brian. (2019). 9 Essential Lessons from Psychology to Understand the Trump Era. *Vox*, January 10 9https://www.vox.com/science-and-health/2018/4/11/16897062/political-psychology-trump-explain-studies-research-science-motivated-reasoning-bias-fake-news).

Reston, James. (1967). *The Artillery of the Press*. New York: Harper.

Restuccia, Andrew, Nahal Toosi, and Tara Palmeri. (2017). John Kelly Folds Navarro's Trade Shop into National Economic Council. *Politico*, September 29 (https://www.politico.eu/article/kelly-folds-navarros-trade-shop-into-national-economic-council/).

Rhodes, Richard. (1986). *The Making of the Atomic Bomb*. New York: Simon and Schuster.

Ricci, David M. (1993). *The Transformation of American Politics: The New Washington and the Rise of Think Tanks*. New Haven, CT: Yale University Press.

Rice, Condoleezza. (2000). Promoting the National Interest. *Foreign Affairs* 79: 45–62.

Rice, Susan. (2017). Reflecting on the National Security Council's Greatest Asset: Its People (https://obamawhitehouse.archives.gov/blog/2017/01/17/reflecting-nscs-greatest-asset-its-people-0).

Richelson, Jeffrey. (2002). *Wizards of Langley: Inside the CIA's Directorate of Science and Technology*. Boulder, CO: Westview Press.

Ricks, Thomas E. (2009). *The Gamble: General David Petraeus and the American Military Adventure in Iraq, 2006–2008*. New York: Penguin.

Riebling, Mark. (2002). *Wedge: From Pearl Harbor to 9/11—How the Secret War between the FBI and CIA Has Endangered National Security*. New York: Simon and Schuster.

Rieff, David. (2003). Blueprint for a Mess. *New York Times Magazine*, November 2, pp. 28–33.

Ripley, Randall B. (1988). *Congress: Process and Policy*. New York: W.W. Norton.

Ripley, Randall B., and Grace A. Franklin. (1990). *Congress, the Bureaucracy, and Public Policy* (5th ed.). Boston, MA: Houghton Mifflin Harcourt.

Ripley, Randall B., and James M. Lindsay. (1993). Foreign and Defense Policy in Congress: An Overview and Preview. In *Congress Resurgent: Foreign and Defense Policy on Capitol Hill*, edited by Randall Ripley and James Lindsay. Ann Arbor: University of Michigan Press.

Risen, James. (2000). The Clinton Administration's See-No-Evil CIA. *New York Times*, September 10, p. 5.

Risen, James. (2001). In Hindsight, CIA Sees Flaws That Hindered Efforts on Terror. *New York Times*, October 7, p. A1.

Risen, James. (2006). *State of War: The Secret History of the CIA and the Bush Administration*. New York: Free Press.

Robertson, James Oliver. (1980). *American Myth, American Reality*. New York: Hill and Wang.

Robinson, Piers. (2002). *The CNN Effect: The Myth of News, Foreign Policy, and Intervention*. Oxford, UK: Routledge.

Rochefort, David A., and Roger W. Cobb. (1993). Problem Definition, Agenda Access, and Policy Choice. *Policy Studies Journal* 21: 56–71.

Rockman, Bert A. (1981). America's Department of State: Irregular and Regular Syndromes of Policy Making. *American Political Science Review* 75: 911–27.

Roeder, George H., Jr. (1993). *The Censored War: American Visual Experience during World War II*. New Haven, CT: Yale University Press.

Rogin, Josh. (2017). Vice President Pence Is Quietly Becoming a Foreign Policy Power Player. *Washington Post*, March 5 (https://www.washingtonpost.com/opinions/global-opinions/vice-president-pence-is-quietly-becoming-a-foreign-policy-power-player/2017/03/05/e347c394-0048-11e7-8f41-ea6ed597e4ca_story.html).

Rohde, David. (1994). Partisan Leadership and Congressional Assertiveness in Foreign and Defense Policy. In *The New Politics of American Foreign Policy*, edited by David A. Deese. New York: St. Martin's Press.

Roman, Peter J., and David W. Tarr. (1998). The Joint Chiefs of Staff: From Service Parochialism to Jointness. *Political Science Quarterly* 113: 91–122.

Romano, Luis. (2010). Hillary Clinton Widens Her Circle at the State Department. *Washington Post*, March 11.

Rosati, Jerel A. (1981). Developing a Systematic DecisionMaking Framework: Bureaucratic Politics in Perspective. *World Politics* 33: 234–52.

Rosati, Jerel A. (1987). *The Carter Administration's Quest for Global Community: Beliefs and Their Impact on Behavior*. New York: Harper and Row.

Rosati, Jerel A. (1997). United States Leadership into the Next Millennium: A Question of Politics. *International Affairs* 52: 297–315.

Rosati, Jerel A. (2000). The Power of Human Cognition in the Study of World Politics. *International Studies Review* 2: 45–75.

Rosati, Jerel A. (2010a). Ignoring the Essence of Decision. *International Studies Review* 3 (Spring): 178–81.

Rosati, Jerel. (2010b). Political Psychology, Cognition and Foreign Policy Analysis. In *Compendium of International Studies*, edited by Bob Denmark, Vol. IX, pp. 5732–5755. ISA and Blackwell.

Rosati, Jerel A., and John Creed. (1997). Extending the Three-Headed and Four-Headed Eagles: The Foreign Policy Operations of American Elites during the 80s and 90s. *Political Psychology* 18: 583–623.

Rosenau, James N. (1961). *Public Opinion and Foreign Policy*. New York: Random House.

Rosenau, James N. (1976). The Study of Foreign Policy. In *World Politics*, edited by James N. Rosenau, Gavin Boyd, and Kenneth W. Thompson, pp. 15–35. New York: Free Press.

Rosenberg, Emily S. (1982). *Spreading the American Dream: American Economic and Cultural Expansion, 1890–1945*. New York: Hill and Wang.

Rossiter, Clinton. (1960). *The American Presidency*. New York: Harcourt, Brace, Jovanovich.

Rothkopf, David J. (2005). *Running the World: The Inside Story of the National Security Council and the Architects of American Power*. New York: Public Affairs.

Rothkopf, David J. (2009). It's 3 A.M. Do You Know Where Hillary Clinton Is? *Washington Post*, August 23 (www. washingtonpost.com/wp-dyn/content/article/2009/08/21/AR2009082101772.html).

Rothkopf, David. (2019). Why the Trump-Bolton Marriage Was Doomed From the Start. *The Daily Beast*, September 11 (https://www.thedailybeast.com/why-the-trump-bolton-marriage-was-doomed-from-the-start).

Roubini, Nouriel, and Stephen Mihm. (2010). *Crisis Economics: A Crash Course in the Future of Finance*. New York: Penguin Press.

Rourke, John, and Richard Clark. (1998). Making U.S. Foreign Policy toward China in the Clinton Administration. In *After the End: Making U.S. Foreign Policy in the Post-Cold War World*, edited by James M. Scott, pp. 201–24. Durham, NC: Duke University Press.

Rourke, John T., Ralph G. Carter, and Mark A. Boyer. (1996). *Making American Foreign Policy* (2nd ed.). Madison, WI: Brown and Benchmark.

Rowling, C. M., Penelope Sheets, and Timothy M. Jones. (2015). American Atrocity Revisited: National Identity, Cascading Frames, and the My Lai Massacre. *Political Communication* 32:310–30.

Rowling, C. M., Timothy M. Jones, and Penelope Sheets. (2011). Some Dared Call It Torture: Cultural Resonance, Abu Ghraib, and a Selectively Echoing Press. *Journal of Communication* 61:1043–61.

Rozen, Laura. (2005). He's Done. *American Prospect*, November 20, pp. 27–32.

Rozen, Laura. (2009). Obama's NSC Takes Power. *Cable*, March 3 (http://thecable.foreignpolicy.com/posts/2009/03/03/jones_s_nsc_moves_to_assert_greater_control_over_interagency_process).

Rubenzer, Trevor. (2008). Ethnic Minority Interest Group Attributes and U.S. Foreign Policy Influence: A Qualitative Comparative Analysis. *Foreign Policy Analysis* 4: 169–85.

Rubin, Barry. (1985). *Secrets of State: The State Department and the Struggle over U.S. Foreign Policy*. New York: Oxford University Press.

Rudalevige, Andrew. (2005). The Executive Branch and the Legislative Process. In *The Executive Branch*, edited by Joel D. Aberbach and Mark A. Peterson, pp. 419–51. New York: The Annenberg Foundation Trust at Sunnylands/Oxford University Press.

Rudalevige, Andrew. (2009). *Rivals or a Team? Competitive Advisory Institutions and the Obama Administration*. Paper presented at the American Political Science Association Annual Meeting, September 3–6.

Ruttan, Vernon W. (1996). *United States Development Assistance Policy: The Domestic Politics of Foreign Economic Aid*. Baltimore, MD: Johns Hopkins University Press.

Sabato, Larry. (1991). *Feeding Frenzy: How Attack Journalism Has Transformed American Politics*. New York: Free Press.

Salazar Torreon, Barbara, and Sofia Plagakis. (2018). *Instances of Use of United States Armed Forces Abroad, 1798–2018*. Congressional Research Service R2738, December 28.

Sanger, David E. (2001). Bush Plans to Stress Effects of Economics on Security. *New York Times*, January 18, p. A10.

Savage, Charles, and Mark Landler. (2011). White House Defense Continuing US Role in Libya Operation. *New York Times*, June 15.

Schake, Kori N. (2012). *State of Disrepair: Fixing the Culture and Practices of the State Department*. Stanford, CA: Hoover Institution Press.

Schiffer, Adam. (2017). *Evaluating Media Bias*. New York: Rowman and Littlefield.

Schilling, Warner R., Paul T. Hammond, and Glenn H. Snyder. (1962). *Strategy, Politics, and Defense Budgets*. New York: Columbia University Press.

Schlesinger, Arthur, Jr. (1989). *The Imperial Presidency*. New York: Houghton Mifflin.

Schlesinger, Arthur, Jr. (2005). *War and the American Presidency*. New York: W.W. Norton.

Schlesinger, Stephen, and Stephen Kinzer. (1982). *Bitter Fruit: The Untold Story of the American Coup in Guatemala*. New York: Doubleday.

Schmeisser, Peter. (1991). Shooting Pool: How the Press Lost the Gulf War. *New Republic*, March 18, p. 22.

Schmidle, Nicholas. (2011). Getting Bin Laden. *The New Yorker*, August 8.

Schmitt, Eric, Mark Landler, and Julian Barnes. (2018). Fraying Ties with Trump Put Jim Mattis's Fate in Doubt. *New York Times*, September 15 (https://www.nytimes.com/2018/09/15/us/politics/jim-mattis-trump-de...elationship.html).

Schneider, William. (1983). Conservatism, Not Interventionism: Trends in Foreign Policy Opinion. In *Eagle Defiant: United States Foreign Policy in the 1980s*, edited by Kenneth A. Oye, Robert J. Leiber, and Donald Rothchild, pp. 33–64. Boston, MA: Little, Brown.

Schneider, William. (1987). "Rambo" and Reality: Having It Both Ways. In *Eagle Resurgent? The Reagan Era in American Foreign Policy*, edited by Kenneth A. Oye, Robert J. Leiber, and Donald Rothchild, pp. 41–74 Boston, MA: Little, Brown.

Schraeder, Peter J. (1994). *United States Foreign Policy toward Africa: Incrementalism, Crisis and Change*. Cambridge, UK: Cambridge University Press.

Schroen, Gary. (2005). *First In: An Insider's Account of How the CIA Spearheaded the War on Terror in Afghanistan*. New York: Presidio Press.

Schultz, Kenneth. (2018). Perils of Polarization for US Foreign Policy. *Washington Quarterly* 40(4): 7–28.

Schulzinger, Robert D. (1984). *The Wise Men of Foreign Affairs: The History of the Council on Foreign Relations*. New York: Columbia University Press.

Schwartz, Drew. (2017). Trump's "Proud" of Starting "This Whole Fake News Thing." *Vice*, October 26 (https://www.vice.com/en_ca/article/7x4b5y/trumps-proud-of-starting-this-whole-fake-news-thingo).

Schwartz, Mattathias. (2019). Mike Pompeo's Mission: Clean Up Trump's Messes. *New York Time Magazine*, February 26 (https://www.nytimes.com/2019/02/26/magazine/mike-pompeo-translates-trump.html).

Sciolino, Elaine. (1989). Friends as Ambassadors: How Many Is Too Many? *New York Times*, November 7, pp. 1, 6.

Scott, Andrew M. (1969). The Department of State: Formal Organization and Informal Culture. *International Studies Quarterly* 12: 1–18.

Scott, James M. (1996). *Deciding to Intervene: The Reagan Doctrine and American Foreign Policy*. Durham, NC: Duke University Press.

Scott, James M. (1997). In the Loop: Congressional Influence in American Foreign Policy. *Journal of Political and Military Sociology* 25: 47–76.

Scott, James M, ed. (1998). *After the End: Making U.S. Foreign Policy in the Post-Cold War World*. Durham, NC: Duke University Press.

Scott, James M. (1999). Transnationalizing Democracy Promotion: The Role of Western Political Foundations and Think-Tanks. *Democratization* 6: 146–70.

Scott, James M. (2018). The Challenge of the South China Sea: Congressional Engagement and the U.S. Policy Response. *All Azimuth* 7: 1–26.

Scott, James M., and Ralph G. Carter. (2002). Acting on the Hill: Congressional Assertiveness in U.S. Foreign Policy. *Congress and the Presidency* 22: 151–70.

Scott, James M., and Ralph G. Carter. (2014). The Not-So-Silent Partner: Patterns of Legislative-Executive Interaction on the War on Terror. *International Studies Perspectives* 15: 186–208.

Scott, James M., and Elizabeth A. Rexford. (1997). Finding a Place for Women in the World of Diplomacy: Evidence of

Progress toward Gender Equity and Speculation on Policy Outcomes. *Review of Public Personnel Administration* 17: 31–56.

Scowcroft, Brent, and Samuel R. Berger. (2005). In the Wake of War: Getting Serious About Nation-Building. *National Interest* 81: 49–53.

Semmel, Andrew K. (1976). Foreign News in Four U.S. Elite Dailies: Some Comparisons. *Journalism Quarterly* 53: 732–36.

Seplow, Stephen. (2002). Closer to Home. *American Journalism Review* 14: 6.

Sestanovich, Stephen. (2017). The Brilliant Incoherence of Donald Trump's Foreign Policy. *The Atlantic*, May (https://www.theatlantic.com/magazine/archive/2017/05/the-brilliant-incoherence-of-trumps-foreign-policy/521430/).

Shafer, Michael D. (1988). *Deadly Paradigms: The Failure of U.S. Counterinsurgency*. Princeton, NJ: Princeton University Press.

Shalby, Colleen. (2019). Facts about Fake News's Influence on U.S. Elections and the Fight against Misinformation. *Los Angeles Times*, March 19 (https://www.latimes.com/science/sciencenow/la-sci-sn-fake-news-election-2019031919-story.html).

Shane, Scott. (2004). Official Reveals Budget for U.S. Intelligence. *New York Times*, November 8, p. A18.

Shane, Scott, Nicole Perlroth, and David Sanger. (2017). Security Breach and Spilled Secrets Have Shaken the NSA to Its Core. *New York Times*, November 12 (https://www.nytimes.com/2017/11/12/us/nsa-shadow-brokers.html).

Shear, Mark. (2019). Anti-Immigration Groups See Trump's Calls for More Legal Immigrants as a Betrayal. *New York Times*, March 8 (https://www.nytimes.com/2019/03/08/us/politics/trump-anti-immigration-groups-betrayal.html).

Shearer, Elisa, and Katerina Eva Matsa. (2018). News Use across Social Media Platforms 2018. Pew Research Center, September 10 (https://www.journalism.org/2018/09/10/news-use-across-social-media-platforms-2018/).

Sheridan, Mary Beth, and William Branigin. (2010). Senate Ratifies New US-Russia Nuclear Weapons Treaty. *Washington Post*, December 22.

Sherman, Ryne. (2015). The Personality of Donald Trump. *Psychology Today*, September 17 (https://www.psychologytoday.com/us/blog/the-situation-lab/201509/the-personality-donald-trump).

Shull, Steven A. (1991). *The Two Presidencies: A Quarter Century Assessment*. Chicago, IL: Nelson Hall.

Shuster, Simon, and Sandra Afraimova. (2018). A Former Russian Troll Explains How to Spread Fake News. *Time*, March 14 (http://time.com/5168202/russia-troll-internet-research-agency/).

Sick, Gary. (1985). *All Fall Down: America's Tragic Encounter with Iran*. New York: Penguin.

Sigal, Leon V. (1973). *Reporters and Officials: The Organization and Politics of Newsmaking*. Lexington, MA: D.C. Heath.

Simpson, Christopher. (1994). *Science of Coercion: Communication Research and Psychological Warfare, 1945–1960*. New York: Oxford University Press.

Sinclair, Barbara. (1993). Congressional Party Leaders in the Foreign and Defense Policy Arena. In *Congress Resurgent: Foreign and Defense Policy on Capitol Hill*, edited by Randall B. Ripley and James M. Lindsay. Ann Arbor: University of Michigan Press.

Sinclair, Barbara. (2000). *Unorthodox Lawmaking: New Legislative Procedures in the U.S. Congress* (2nd ed.). Washington, DC: Congressional Quarterly Press.

Singer, P. W. (2003). *Corporate Warriors: The Rise of the Privatized Military Industry*. Ithaca, NY: Cornell University Press.

Singer, P. W. (2005). Outsourcing War. *Foreign Affairs* 84: 119–33.

Singer, P. W. (2007). *Corporate Warriors: The Rise of the Privatized Military Industry*. Ithaca, NY: Cornell University Press.

Skowronek, Stephen. (2011). *Presidential Leadership in Political Time: Reprise and Reappraisal*. Lawrence: University of Kansas Press.

Smeltz, Dina, Ivo Daalder, Karl Friedhoff, Craig Kafura, and Lily Wojtowicz. (2018). *America Engaged: American Public Opinion and US Foreign Policy*. Chicago Council on Global Affairs (https://digital.thechicagocouncil.org/america-engaged).

Smist, Frank J., Jr. (1994). *Congress Oversees the Intelligence Community*. Knoxville: University of Tennessee Press.

Smith, Bruce H. (1984). U.S. and Canadian PVOs as Transnational Development Institutions. In *Private*

Voluntary Organizations as Agents of Development, edited by Robert F. Gorman, pp. 115–64. London: Westview Press.

Smith, Hedrick. (1988). *The Power Game: How Washington Works*. New York: Random House.

Smith, Joseph B. (1976). *Portrait of a Cold Warrior*. New York: Ballantine Books.

Smith, Steven. (1994). Congressional Party Leaders. In *The President, the Congress, and the Making of Foreign Policy*, edited by Paul E. Peterson, pp. 129–57. Norman: University of Oklahoma Press.

Snyder, Jack L. (1978). Rationality at the Brink: The Role of Cognitive Processes in Failures of Deterrence. *World Politics* 30: 344–65.

Snyder, Richard C. (1958). A Decision-Making Approach to the Study of Political Phenomena. In *Approaches to the Study of Politics*, edited by R. Young, pp. 3–37. Evanston, IL: Northwestern University Press.

Somerlad, Joe. (2018). Fox News: How the Right-Wing Network Became One of America's Most Influential Political Voices. *The Independent*, May 30 (https://www.independent.co.uk/news/world/americas/us-politics/fox-news-network-america-trump-right-wing-republicans-rupert-murdoch-tv-station-a8375236.html).

Sorensen, Theodore C. (1963). *Decision-Making in the White House: The Olive Branch or the Arrows*. New York: Columbia University Press.

Spero, Joan Edelman, and Jeffrey A. Hart. (2009). *The Politics of International Economic Relations*. Belmont, CA: Wadsworth.

Stack, John F., and Colton C. Campbell. (2003). Congress: How Silent a Partner? In *Congress and the Politics of Foreign Policy*, edited by Colton C. Campbell, Nicol C. Rae, and John F. Stack, pp. 22–43. New York: Longman.

Stacks, John F. (2004). Hard Times for Hard News: A Clinical Look at U.S. Foreign Coverage. *World Policy Journal* XX: 12–21.

Steinbruner, John D. (1974). *The Cybernetic Theory of Decision*. Princeton, NJ: Princeton University Press.

Steiner, Miriam. (1983). The Search for Order in a Disorderly World: Worldviews and Prescriptive Decision Paradigms. *International Organization* 37: 373–413.

Stephanson, Anders. (1995). *Manifest Destiny: American Expansion and the Empire of Right*. New York: Hill and Wang.

Stockwell, John. (1978). *In Search of Enemies: A CIA Story*. New York: W.W. Norton.

Stoff, Michael B. (1980). *Oil, War, and American Security: The Search for a National Policy on Foreign Oil, 1941–1947*. New Haven, CT: Yale University Press.

Stokes, Bruce. (1993). Elevating Economics. *National Journal* (March 13): 615–19.

Stone, Geoffrey. (2007). *War and Liberty: An American Dilemma: 1790 to the Present*. New York: W.W. Norton.

Stroud, Natalie Jomini. (2011). *Niche News the Politics of News Choice*. New York: Oxford University Press.

Summers, Harry G., Jr. (1982). *On Strategy*. Novato, CA: Presidio Press.

Suskind, Ron. (2011). *Confidence Men: Wall Street, Washington, and the Education of a President*. New York: HarperCollins.

Sweeney, Michael S. (2001). *Secrets to Victory: The Office of Censorship and the American Press and Radio in World War II*. New Haven, CT: Yale University Press.

Swift, Art. (2017). Putin's Image Rises in U.S., Mostly Among Republicans (https://news.gallup.com/poll/204191/putin-image-rises-mostly-among-republicans.aspx).

Szoldra, Paul. (2015). A Day in the Life of the President of the United States. *Business Insider*, February 16 (https://www.businessinsider.com/day-in-the-life-of-president-obama-2015-2).

't Hart, Paul, Eric K. Stern, and Bengt Sundelius. (1997). *Beyond Groupthink: Political Group Dynamics and Foreign Policy-Making*. Ann Arbor: University of Michigan Press.

Tama, Jordan. (2018a). The Multiple Forms of Bipartisanship: Political Alignments in US Foreign Policy Items: Insights from the Social Sciences. Social Science Research Council (https://items.ssrc.org/the-multiple-forms-of-bipartisanship-political-alignments-in-us-foreign-policy/).

Tama, Jordan. (2018b). Congress, Trump, and Internationalism in U.S. Foreign Policy. Duck of Minerva (https://duckofminerva.com/2018/10/congress-trump-and-internationalism-in-u-s-foreign-policy.html).

Tammen, Ronald L., Mark Abdollohian, Carole Alsharabati, Brian Efird, Jacek Kugler, Douglas Lemke, Allan C. Stam III, and A. F. K Organski. (2000). *Power Transitions: Strategies for the 21st Century*. London: Chatham House.

Tankel, Steven. (2018). Donald Trump's Shadow War. *Politico*, May 9 (https://www.politico.com/magazine/story/2018/05/09/donald-trumps-shadow-war-218327).

Tapper, Jake, and Jim Acosta. (2019). "Like Pulling Teeth" to Get White House to Focus on Russian Election Interference, Official Says. CNN, April 24 (https://www.cnn.com/2019/04/24/politics/kirstjen-nielsen-trump-election-security/index.html).

Tarnoff, Curt, and Marian Lawson. (2018). *Foreign Aid: An Introduction to U.S. Programs and Policy*. Congressional Research Service R40213, April 25 (https://fas.org/sgp/crs/row/R40213.pdf).

Tatum, Sophie, and Laura Jarrett. (2019). Booker Asks Administration to Retract Controversial Immigration Report. CNN, January 9 (https://www.cnn.com/2019/01/09/politics/cory-booker-doj-dhs/index.html).

Taubman, Philip. (1983). Casey and His CIA on the Rebound. *New York Times Magazine*, January 16, p. 20.

Taylor, Stuart, Jr. (1983). In Wake of Invasion, Much Official Misinformation by U.S. Comes to Light. *New York Times*, November 6, p. A20.

Temming, Maria. (2018). How Twitter Bots Get People to Spread Fake New. *Science News*, November 20 (https://www.sciencenews.org/article/twitter-bots-fake-news-2016-election).

Tempest, Rone. (1983a). Beltway Bandits Ring Washington. *Los Angeles Times*, July 10, p. 14.

Tempest, Rone. (1983b). U.S. Defense Establishment Wields a Pervasive Power. *Los Angeles Times*, July 10, p. 1.

Tetlock, Philip. (2006). *Expert Political Judgment: How Good Is It? How Can We Know?* Princeton, NJ: Princeton University Press.

Thomas, Evan. (2002a). Chemistry in the War Cabinet. *Newsweek*, January 28, pp. 26–31.

Thomas, Evan. (2002b). He Has Saddam in His Sights. *Newsweek*, March 4, pp. 18–24.

Thomas, Evan. (2005). Bush in the Bubble. *Newsweek*, December 19, pp. 33, 34, 37.

Toosi, Nahal. (2019). Inside the Chaotic Early Days of Trump's Foreign Policy. *Politico Magazine*, March 1 (https://www.politico.com/magazine/story/2019/03/01/trump-national-security-council-225442).

Tower Commission. (1987). *The Tower Commission Report*. New York: Bantam.

Trainor, Bernard E. (1989). Flaws in Panama Attack. *New York Times*, December 31, pp. A1, A6.

Treverton, Gregory. (1990). *Covert Action*. New York: Basic Books.

Trubowitz, Peter, and Nicole Mellow. (2011). Foreign Policy, Bipartisanship and the Paradox of Post-September 11 America. *International Politics* 48: 164–87.

Truman, David B. (1971). *The Governmental Process: Political Interests and Public Opinion*. Berkeley: University of California Press.

Turner, Stansfield. (2005). *Burn before Reading: Presidents, CIA Directors, and Secret Intelligence*. New York: Hyperion.

Tyndall Report. (2019a). Top Ten Stories Ranked by Time on Foreign Policy Focus 2018 (http://tyndallreport.com/yearinreview2018/foreignpolicy/).

Tyndall Report. (2019b). Top Ten Stories Ranked by Time on International Focus 2018 (http://tyndallreport.com/yearinreview2018/international/).

Ungar, Sanford J. (2005). Pitch Imperfect: The Trouble at the Voice of America. *Foreign Affairs*.

US-CERT. (2017). Alert (TA17-318A): HIDDEN COBRA – North Korean Remote Administration Tool: FALLCHILL. US Computer Emergency Readiness Team, November 14, 2017 (https://www.us-cert.gov/ncas/alerts/TA17-318A).

US Congress. (1976). Final Report of the Select Committee to Study Governmental Operations with Respect to Intelligence Activities. *Congressional Report* 1: 197–98.

US Congress. (1989a). *DOD Revolving Door*. Washington, DC: US Government Printing Office.

US Congress. (1989b). *State Department: Minorities and Women Are Underrepresented in the Foreign Service*. Washington, DC: US Government Printing Office.

US Congress. (1991). *Department of Defense: Professional Military Education at the Four Intermediate Service Schools*. Washington, DC: US Government Printing Office.

US Congress. (1994). *Cleaning up the Department of Energy's Nuclear Weapons Complex.* Washington, DC: US Government Printing Office.

US Congress. (2002). *Joint Inquiry in Intelligence Community Activities before and after the Terrorist Attacks of September 11, 2001.* Washington, DC: US Government Printing Office.

US Congress. (n.d.). Congressional Directory (https://www .govinfo.gov/app/collection/cdir/115/2018-10-29/L1).

US Congress, General Accounting Office. (1982). *Improper Lobbying Activities by the Department of Defense on the Proposed Procurement of the C-5B Aircraft.* Washington, DC: US Government Printing Office.

US Congress, General Accounting Office. (1993). *State Department: Survey of Administrative Issues Affecting Embassies.* Washington, DC: US Government Printing Office.

US Congress, House Committee on Foreign Affairs. (1982). *Foreign Policy Interest Groups as Information Sources.* Washington, DC: US Government Printing Office.

US Congress, Senate Committee on Foreign Relations. (1981). *The Ambassador in U.S. Foreign Policy: Changing Patterns in Roles, Selection, and Designations.* Washington, DC: US Government Printing Office.

US Department of the Army. (2006). *Counterinsurgency Field Manual 3-24*, December.

US Department of Defense. (2009). *The National Defense Strategy FY2008.* Washington, DC: US Government Printing Office.

US Department of State. (1992). *State 2000: A New Model for Managing Foreign Affairs.* Washington, DC: US Government Printing Office.

US House of Representatives, Permanent Select Committee on Intelligence. (1996). *Intelligence Community in the 21st Century.* Washington, DC: US Government Printing Office.

US National Intelligence Council. (2005). *Estimative Products on Vietnam, 1948–1975.* Washington, DC: US Government Printing Office.

US Senate, Committee on Foreign Relations. (1997). *Legislative Activities Report of the Committee on Foreign Relations.* Washington: US Government Printing Office.

US Senate, Committee on Foreign Relations. (1989). *United States Foreign Policy Objectives and Overseas Military Installations.* Washington, DC: US Government Printing Office.

US Senate, Select Committee on Intelligence. (2004). *Report on the U.S. Intelligence Community's Prewar Assessments on Iraq.* Washington, DC: US Government Printing Office.

USAID. (2004). *U.S. Foreign Aid: Meeting the Challenges of the Twenty-First Century.* Washington, DC: USAID.

Van Alstyne, Richard W. (1960). *The American Empire: Its Historical Pattern and Evolution.* General Series Pamphlet No. 43. London: Historical Association.

Van Alstyne, Richard W. (1974). *The Rising American Empire.* New York: W.W. Norton.

Van Creveld, Martin. (1989). *Technology and War: From 2000 B.C. to the Present.* New York: Macmillan.

Vanderbush, Walt. (2009). Exiles and the Marketing of U.S. Policy toward Cuba and Iraq. *Foreign Policy Analysis* 5: 287–306.

Verba, S., and N. Nye. (1972). *Participation in America.* New York: Harper and Row.

Vinton, Kate. (2016). These 15 Billionaires Own America's News Media Companies. Forbes, June 1 (https://www .forbes.com/sites/katevinton/2016/06/01/these-15-billionaires-own-americas-news-media-companies/#653d 2e73660a).

Volkan, Vamik D. (1988). *The Need to Have Enemies and Allies: From Clinical Practice to International Relationships.* Northvale, NJ: Jason Aronson.

Walcott, Charles E., and Karen M. Holt. (2003). The Bush Staff and Cabinet System. *Perspectives on Political Science* 32: 150–55.

Walcott, Charles E., Shirley Anne Warshaw, and Stephen J. Wayne. (2001). The Chief of Staff. *Presidential Studies Quarterly* 31: 464–89.

Walcott, John. (2019). "Willful Ignorance." Inside President Trump's Troubled Intelligence Briefings. *Time*, February 5 (https://time.com/5518947/donald-trump-intelligence-briefings-national-security/).

Waller, Douglas C. (1987). *Congress and the Nuclear Freeze: An Inside Look at the Politics of a Mass Movement.* Amherst: University of Massachusetts Press.

Waller, Douglas C. (1991). The CIA Called It—But Nobody Listened. *Newsweek*, September 2, p. 44.

Walsh, Kenneth T. (2008). The Leadership Style of the Next President. *U.S. News and World Report*, October 17, p. 35.

Walt, Stephen. (2005). *Taming American Power: The Global Responses to U.S. Primacy*. New York: W.W. Norton.

Waltz, Kenneth N. (1959). *Man, the State, and War*. New York: Columbia University Press.

Watson, Jack H., Jr. (1993). The Clinton White House. *Presidential Studies Quarterly* 23: 431–36.

Watts, Clint. (2018). *Messing with the Enemy*. New York: Harper.

Wawro, Gregory. (2001). *Legislative Entrepreneurship in the U.S. House of Representatives*. Ann Arbor: University of Michigan Press.

Weeks, William Earl. (1996). *Building the Continental Empire: American Expansion from the Revolution to the Civil War*. Chicago, IL: Ivan R. Dee.

Weil, Martin. (1978). *A Pretty Good Club*. New York: W.W. Norton.

Weinraub, B. (1985). New Rose among White House Press Thorns. *New York Times*, October 16, p. A24.

Westerfield, H. Bradford. (1995). *Inside the CIA's Private World*. New Haven, CT: Yale University Press.

Western, Jon. (2005). *Selling Intervention and War: The Presidency, the Media, and the American Public*. Baltimore, MD: The Johns Hopkins University Press.

White, Ralph K. (1968). *Nobody Wanted War: Misperception in Vietnam and Other Wars*. Garden City, NY: Doubleday.

Whyte, William. (1956). *The Organization Man*. New York: Simon and Schuster.

Wiarda, Howard. (2000). Beyond the Pale: The Bureaucratic Politics of United States Policy in Mexico. *World Affairs* 162: 174–90.

Wildavsky, Aaron. (1966). The Two Presidencies Thesis. *Transaction* 4: 7–14.

Wildavsky, Ben. (1996). Under the Gun. *National Journal* 26: 1417.

Williams, William A. (1988). *The Tragedy of American Diplomacy*. New York: W.W. Norton.

Wills, Garry. (1988). *Reagan's America*. New York: Penguin.

Wills, Garry. (1990). *Under God: Religion and American Politics*. New York: Simon and Schuster.

Wilson, James Q. (1989). *Bureaucracy: What Government Agencies Do and Why They Do It*. New York: Basic Books.

Wilson, James Q. (1995). *Political Organizations*. Princeton, NJ: Princeton University Press.

Wines, Michael. (1990). The Iraqi Invasion; U.S. Says Bush Surprised by Iraqi Strike. *New York Times*, August 5, p. 8.

Winks, Robin. (1996). *Cloak and Gown Scholars in the Secret War, 1939–1961*. New Haven, CT: Yale University Press.

Wise, David, and Thomas Ross. (1990). *The Invisible Government*. New York: Vintage.

Wittkopf, Eugene. (1990). *Faces of Internationalism: Public Opinion and American Foreign Policy*. Durham, NC: Duke University Press.

Wittkopf, Eugene R., and James M. McCormick. (1998). Congress, the President, and the End of the Cold War. *Journal of Conflict Resolution* 42: 440–67.

Wolffe, Richard. (2010). *Revival: The Struggle for Survival Inside the Obama White House*. New York: Crown Publishers.

Wood, David. (1983). B-1 Symbolizes Power of Military-Industrial Complex. *Los Angeles Times*, July 10, pp. 8–9.

Woodward, Bob. (1987). *Veil: The Secret Wars of the CIA, 1981–1987*. New York: Simon and Schuster.

Woodward, Bob. (1991). *The Commanders*. New York: Simon and Schuster.

Woodward, Bob. (2002). *Bush at War*. New York: Simon and Schuster.

Woodward, Bob. (2004). *Plan of Attack*. New York: Simon and Schuster.

Woodward, Bob. (2007). *State of Denial*. New York: Simon and Schuster.

Woodward, Bob. (2010). *Obama's Wars*. New York: Simon and Schuster.

Woodward, Bob. (2018). *Fear: Trump in the White House*. New York: Simon and Schuster.

Woodward, Bob, and Carl Bernstein (1974). *All the President's Men*. New York: Warner.

WorldPublicOpinion.org. (2010). American Public Opinion on Foreign Aid (http://worldpublicopinion.net/wp-content/uploads/2017/08/ForeignAid_Nov10_quaire.pdf).

World Tribune Staff. (2018). U.S. Foreign Correspondents Once Shaped America's World View; Now Russian, Chinese Replacements Do. *World Tribune*, September 12 (https://www.worldtribune.com/u-s-foreign-correspondents-once-shaped-americas-world-view-now-russian-chinese-replacements-do/).

Wright, Robin, and Thomas Ricks. (2004). Wider FBI Probe of Pentagon Leaks Includes Chalabi. *Washington Post*, September 3, p. A1.

Wu, H. D. (1998). Investigating the Determinants of International News Flow: A Meta-Analysis. *International Communication Gazette* 60: 493–512.

Wylie, J. C. (1966). *Military Strategy: A General Theory of Power Control*. New Brunswick, NJ: Rutgers University Press.

Yarmolinsky, Adam. (1971). *The Military Establishment: Its Impact on American Society*. New York: Harper and Row.

Yergin, Daniel. (1978). *Shattered Peace: The Origins of the Cold War and the National Security State*. Boston, MA: Houghton Mifflin.

Yergin, Daniel. (1990). *The Prize: The Epic Quest for Money, Oil, and Power*. New York: Simon and Schuster.

Yoffe, Emily. (2008). The Supervisor, the Champion, and the Promoter: What Psychological Personality Tests Reveal about Clinton, Obama, and McCain. *Slate* (http://www.slate.com/articles/news_and_politics/politics/2008/02/the_supervisor_the_champion_and_the_ promoter.html).

Yoo, John C. (1996). The Continuation of Politics by Other Means: The Original Understanding of War Powers. *California Law Review* 84: 170–305.

Yoo, John C. (2005). *The Powers of War and Peace: The Constitution and Foreign Affairs after 9/11*. Chicago, IL: University of Chicago Press.

Zegart, Amy B. (1999). *Flawed by Design: The Evolution of the CIA, JCS, and NSC*. Stanford, CA: Stanford University Press.

Zegart, Amy B. (2005). September 11 and the Adaptation Failure of the U.S. Intelligence Agencies. *International Security* 29: 78–111.

Zegart, Amy B., and Michael Morell. (2019). Spies, Lies, and Algorithms: Why U.S. Intelligence Agencies Must Adapt or Fail. *Foreign Affairs*, April 19 (https://www.foreignaffairs.com/print/1124170).

Zeleny, Jeff. (2017). West Wing Real Estate: Who Has Proximity to Trump. CNN, February 3 (https://www.cnn.com/2017/02/03/politics/west-wing-office-map-oval-office-real-estate/index.html).

Zenko, Micah, and Rebecca Friedman Lissner. (2017). Trump Is Going to Regret Not Having a Grand Strategy. *Foreign Policy*, January (https://foreignpolicy.com/2017/01/13/trump-is-going-to-regret-not-having-a-grand-strategy/).

Zetter, Kim. (2014). *Countdown to Zero Day: Stuxnet and the Launch of the World's First Digital Weapon*. New York: Crown.

Zimmerman, Tim. (1997). Twilight of the Diplomats. *U.S. News & World Report*, January 27, pp. 48–50.

Zukin, Cliff, Scott Keeter, Molly Adolina, Krista Jenkins, and Michael X. Delli Carpini. (2006). *Political Participation, Civic Life, and the Changing American Citizen*. New York: Oxford University Press.

Index

military specialization, 131
unification period, 129
Arrogance of Power, The (Fulbright), 32
Aspin, Les, 228
Aspin-Brown Commission, 305
Assassin's Gate, The (Packer), 329
Assistant secretary, 101–102
Associated Press, 419–420, 431, 440
Asymmetrical warfare, 163
Atlantic Council, 401
AT&T, 437–438
Attentive public, 351
Attrition warfare, 144
Authorization process, 300–302
Avenues of influence, 276–277
Axelrod, David, 233

Backfire (Baritz), 373–374
Baker, Gerard, 440
Baker, Howard, 224, 225
Baker, James, 121*t*, 135, 177, 224, 227
Ball, George, 311, 399
Bannon, Steve, 235–236
Baritz, L., 373–374
Bay of Pigs (1961), 176, 221
Beat system, 442, 443
Begin, Menachem, 51
Beirut, 148, 294
Bellinger, John, 231
Beltway bandits, 410–412
Bendix Corporation, 411
Benghazi, (2012), 305
Bentsen, Lloyd, 258
Berger, Sandy, 228
Berlin Wall (1989), 129
Bernanke, Ben, 262–263, 264–265
Best and the Brightest, The (Halberstam), 323
Betts, R., 135
Beyond Groupthink ('t Hart, Stern, Sundelius), 325
Bezos, Jeff, 438
Biden, Joe, 66, 156, 318
Biegun, Stephen, 98
Bin Laden, Osama, 38, 41, 175, 182, 194, 207
Bipartisanship, 287–288
Bipolar world, 27
Blacklist, 29
Blair, Dennis, 181, 182
Blair, Rob, 237
Blame game politics, 446–447

Bloomberg, Michael, 438
Boeing, 395, 411
Bolten, Joshua, 65
Bolton, John, 105, 158, 236–237, 337
B-1 bomber program, 411–412
Boston Globe, 419
Bowen, Stuart, 231
Bremer, Paul, 152
Brennan, John, 178
Bretton Woods II, 28
Bretton Woods system, 25, 32, 243–244, 300
Brezhnev Doctrine, 34
Broadcasting Board of Governors, 109
Brookings Institution, 401
Brzezinski, Zbigniew, 223
Budget and Impoundment Control Act (1974), 282
Budget and personnel systems, 134
Bully pulpit, 53
Bundy, McGeorge, 221, 311, 399
Bureau, 101
Bureaucracy:
    characteristics, 92–93
    complexity of, 94–95
    coordination issues, 92–93
    defined, 92
    foreign policy bureaucracy, 93, 94*t*
    hierarchy of, 92
    historical development, 95–97
    internationalization of domestic bureaucracies, 95
    mission of, 93
    National Security Act (1947), 96
    routinization of, 92
    size of, 93, 94*t*
    specialization of, 92
    standard operating procedures, 93
    study guide, 125–126
Bureaucracy (Wilson), 110
Bureaucratic politics, 334–337
Bureaucratic Politics and Foreign Policy (Halperin), 336
Bureaucratic process, 104–105
Bureau for Economic and Business Affairs, 250
Bureau of African Affairs, 101*f*, 102
Bureau of Industry and Security, 251
Bureau of Intelligence and Research (INR), 173, 177
Bureau of International Labor Affairs, 251
Bush, George H. W.:
    commander in chief, 52
    congressional foreign policy, 274, 296, 305

Department of State, 106, 112, 119
foreign economic policy, 245
foreign policymaking process, 320
intelligence community, 193–194, 205
National Security Council (NCS) system, 217, 218*t*, 219, 220, 225, 226–227
new world order, 36–37
partisanship approval, 359*f*
Persian Gulf War (1991), 52, 84, 320, 354*f*
public opinion, 354*f*, 358*f*
secretary of state, 121*t*
U.S. Department of Defense, 135
Bush, George W.:
Afghanistan (2001), 52, 85–86
bureaucracy, 95, 96
Bush Doctrine, 38–39
chief of staff, 65
commander in chief, 52
congressional foreign policy, 275, 289, 290–291, 294–295, 300
daily schedule, 54–56
Department of Defense, 150–152
Department of State, 106, 109, 110, 113, 118, 119–120
European approval ratings, 43*f*
foreign economic policy, 245–246
foreign policymaking process, 315–316, 320–323, 329, 332–333, 342
intelligence community, 185, 191–192, 206
interest groups, 405
Iraq (2003), 52, 85–86, 316
liberty-security objectives, 29–30
media coverage, 428–429, 432, 450
National Economic Council (NEC), 256*t*, 261–262
National Security Council (NCS) system, 214, 218*t*, 228–232
partisanship approval, 359*f*
political polarization, 7
prerogative power, 71
presidential leadership, 85–86
public opinion, 355*f*, 358*f*
secretary of state, 121*t*, 122
unitary executive theory, 85–86
war on terrorism, 38–39, 85–86, 205, 294–295, 315–316, 320–321, 329, 332–333
weapons of mass destruction (WMDs), 86, 191–192
Business and labor groups, 390–391
Byrnes, James, 121*t*

Cabinet government, 214
Cable traffic, 98–99
Campbell v. Clinton (1999), 274
Camp David Accords (1978), 51
Card, Andrew, 65, 229
Cardin, Benjamin, 276, 304
CARE, 408
Careerism, 143
Careerist-appointee issues, 107
Carlucci, Frank, 224
Carnegie Endowment for International Peace, 390.401
Carter, Ashton, 141
Carter, Jimmy:
chief diplomat role, 51
congressional foreign policy, 298–299, 301
intelligence community, 204
interest groups, 405, 408
leadership style, 63
National Security Council (NCS) system, 218*t*, 223
partisanship approval, 359*f*
presidential leadership, 82–83
secretary of state, 121*t*
Cascade network activation model, 445
Case Act (1972), 298
Casey, William, 191, 204, 315
Castillo Armas, Carlos, 200
Castro, Fidel, 176, 202
Catholic Relief Services, 408
CBS, 419, 421, 422, 423–424*f*, 425
Censorship, 427, 449–450
Center for American Progress, 401
Center for Defense Information, 401
Center for Strategic and International Studies, 401
Central American Free Trade Agreement, 300
Central Intelligence Agency (CIA):
Bay of Pigs (1961), 176
counterintelligence, 183
covert operations, 173, 186, 197–208
intelligence collection, 173, 175, 178–179, 183, 186, 197–208
CEO style, 231
Chair of the JCS (CJCS), 132–137
Challenger space shuttle, 318–319
Challenging groups, 385–387
Chamber of Commerce, 390–391
Checks and balances, 273
Chemical Weapons Convention (1997), 297–298, 299

Executive-dominated instruments, 340
Executive Office of the Presidency (EOP), 63–64
Executive privilege, 275
Export-Import Bank, 252

Fake news, 434, 436
Fast-track authority, 300
Federal Bureau of Investigation (FBI), 177, 183, 186
Federal Open Market Committee, 251–252
Federal Reserve Banks, 251
Federal Reserve Board, 251–252
Feith, Douglas, 151, 322–323
Finished intelligence, 172
First World, 14
Flake, Jeff, 275–276
Flynn, Michael, 235, 236, 237–238, 407
Followership model, 368
Food for Peace Program, 250
Ford, Gerald:
    intelligence community, 203–204
    leadership style, 63
    National Security Council (NCS) system, 218*t*, 223
    presidential leadership, 79, 82
Ford Foundation, 390
Foreign Affairs Reform and Restructuring Act (1998),
        107, 109, 297–298
Foreign Agricultural Service, 250
Foreign aid, 107, 108
Foreign assistance, 108
Foreign bureaus, 431–432
Foreign Commercial Service, 250–251
Foreign correspondents, 431–432
Foreign Credit Insurance Association, 252
Foreign economic bureaucracy:
    Bretton Woods system, 243–244
    bureaucratic management, 253–255
    Cold War, 254–255
    Council of Economic Advisers, 252–253
    Department of Agriculture, 250, 253–254
    Department of Commerce, 250–251
    Department of Energy, 251, 253–254
    Department of Labor, 251
    Department of State, 250, 253=–254
    Department of the Treasury, 248–250, 254, 255
    economic security perspective, 246–247
    Export-Import Bank, 252
    Federal Reserve Board, 251–252
    Great Depression, 244

    historical context, 244–248
    International Trade Commission, 252
    liberal international economic order (LIEO), 243–244
    Office of Management and Budget (OMB), 254
    Office of the US Trade Representative (USTR),
        254–255
    Organization of Petroleum Exporting Countries
        (OPEC), 245
    Overseas Private Investment Corporation, 252
    presidential leadership, 253–255
    relevant governmental agencies, 248–253
    secretary of the treasury, 248–250
    study guide, 270
    trade growth (1900-2020), 245*f*
    See also National Economic Council (NEC)
Foreign lobbies, 407, 408*f*
Foreign policy:
    analytical frameworks for, 7–9, 456–457
    bureaucratic leadership, 463, 464–465
    complexity of, 5–7
    congressional leadership, 463, 465–467
    defined, 3
    future trends, 467–468
    historical patterns, 458–461
    impact of, 4–5
    interbranch politics, 463, 467
    key questions, 457–458
    leadership context, 461–463
    leadership patterns, 463–467
    national interest, 6
    policymaking process, 3–4
    politics, 6
    presidential leadership, 462, 463–464
    Presidential Preeminence framework, 7, 8*f*
    Shifting Leadership and Politics framework, 7–9,
        456–457
    study guide, 468
Foreign policy bureaucracy, 93, 94*t*
Foreign policy establishment, 396–400
Foreign policy orientations, 352–353, 362–373
Foreign policy process:
    agenda-setting stage, 310–311
    bureaucratic politics, 334–337
    cognition and perception, 326–329
    cognitive consistency, 327
    Cold War, 328, 329
    congressional behavior models, 338
    counterinsurgency strategy, 318

Outside politics, 388
Overseas Private Investment Corporation, 252

Packer, G., 329
Pack journalism, 442
Pakistan:
  Afghanistan-Pakistan War, 153, 155 (map), 156
  foreign policymaking process, 317–318
  presidential leadership, 52, 87
Palmer Raids (1919), 29
Panama (1989), 52, 149
Panama Canal treaties (1978), 298–299
Panama Canal Zone, 23
Panetta, Leon, 65, 182, 195, 207, 228, 234
Paradox of presidential power, 50–61
Paris Accord (2015), 87, 299
Partisanship, 286–288
Passive-negative leadership, 62
Passive-positive leadership, 62
Paulsen, Henry, 261, 262
Peace Corps, 107, 108
Pelosi, Nancy, 300, 436
Pence, Mike, 66
Pentagon Papers, 275
Perdue, Sonny, 266–267
Perry, Matthew C., 21
Perry, William, 228
Persian Gulf (1987), 52
Persian Gulf War (1991), 52, 84, 149–150, 320, 354*f*
Personality, 329–334
Personal staffs, 284
Petraeus, David, 152, 153, 155, 156, 318
Philadelphia Inquirer, 419
Philippines, 21, 23
Phoenix program, 202
Podhoertz, Norman, 400
Poindexter, John, 224, 315
Polarization, 286–288
Policy corrections, 340
Policy formulation, 310–311
Policy implementation, 310–311
Policy vacuums, 340
Political and civic organizations, 390
Political appointments, 105–107
Political culture, 353, 373–379
Political ideology, 352–353, 362–373
Political questions, 274
Political resultant, 318

Political right, 399–400
Political socialization, 350
Politicization of intelligence, 190–192
Politico.com, 420
Politics, 6
Politics of Policymaking in Defense and Foreign Affairs, The (Hilsman), 323
Politics of symbolism and legitimacy, 446–447
Politics of threat, 289–290
Pompeo, Mike, 121*t,* 124, 158, 177, 237, 238
Pork barrel politics, 410–412
Porter, Ross, 267, 268
Post-9/11 (2002-present):
  global and historical context, 37–41
  intelligence community, 183, 185–186, 205, 206–208
  presidential leadership, 76, 85–88
Post-Cold War (1989-2001):
  congressional foreign policy, 278*f,* 285–292
  global and historical context, 34–37, 459–461
  intelligence community, 204, 205
  media coverage, 426, 428–436
  presidential leadership, 76, 83–85
Post-Vietnam War (1968-1988):
  congressional foreign policy, 278*f,* 281–285
  interest groups, 398–414
  media coverage, 426, 427–428
  public opinion, 364–366
Powell, Colin, 120, 121*t,* 122, 133, 135–136, 227, 228–232, 316
Power, 72–73
Power Game, The (Smith), 6, 310
Power of the purse, 301–302
Power to persuade, 69–70
Prerogative government, 70–71, 87–88
Presidential character, 62
Presidential choices, 70
Presidential finding, 203–204
Presidential leadership:
  active-negative style, 62
  active-positive style, 62
  advice and consent, 67
  analyst/innovator, 63
  bully pulpit power, 53
  bureaucratic constraints, 58–59
  chief diplomat, 51
  chief executive officer, 52, 62
  chief legislator, 52
  chief of staff, 64–65

defined, 352
direct-immediate impact, 353–357
elite public, 349–350, 351, 352
elitist view of public, 349
followership model, 368
foreign policy impact, 348–350, 353–357, 358f, 376–381
foreign policy orientations, 352–353, 362–373
fragmentation/swing model, 368–369
inattentive public, 359, 360–361
indirect-long term impact, 357, 358f, 359f
isolationism policy, 369–372
liberal-conservative consensus, 363–364
liberal internationalism, 365
limits-driven orientation, 368
mass public, 352
moral crusader style, 376–378
nationalism, 375–376, 378–379
neo-conservatives, 366
new consensus, 349–350, 351–352
non-internationalism, 366
opinion leaders, 351
order-driven orientation, 367–368
patterns of, 358–361
political culture, 353, 373–379
political ideology, 352–353, 362–373
political leadership channel, 380, 381f
political representation channel, 380, 381f
political responsiveness channel, 380, 381f
political socialization, 350
post-Vietnam War, 364–366
presidential leadership impact, 60
principle *versus* pragmatism, 377
public approval, 354–357, 358f
public attitudes, 352
public moods, 379
rally around the flag, 353
range of opinion, 352–353
reorientation of, 366–373
study guide, 381–382
super-patriotism, 378–379
traditional wisdom, 348–349, 353–354
types of public, 350–352
uniformed public, 359–361
values-driven orientation, 368
Vietnam War, 364–365
volatile public, 361
Public prestige, 70
Puerto Rico, 23

Punch-their-ticket expectation, 143
Putin, Vladimir, 51, 197–198

Race discrimination, 112
Radio Free Asia, 109
Radio Free Europe, 109
Radio Liberty, 109
Radio Marti, 109
Radio news, 420f
Radio Sawa, 109
Rally around the flag, 353
Rand Corporation, 390, 401
Ratcliffe, John, 181
Rational actor model, 311–313
Raymond, John W., 137
Raytheon, 414
Reagan, Ronald:
    Beirut (1982-1984), 294
    chief diplomat role, 51
    commander in chief, 52
    congressional foreign policy, 274, 294, 296, 301–302, 304–305
    Contras-Sandanistas (Nicaragua), 52, 204
    Department of State, 98
    foreign policymaking process, 314–315, 320
    Grenada (1983), 52, 320
    intelligence community, 190–191, 193, 204
    interest groups, 401, 411
    Iran-Contra affair, 71, 83, 314–315
    leadership style, 62
    Lebanon (1982), 52
    Libya (1986), 52
    National Security Council (NCS) system, 214, 218t, 220, 223–225
    Persian Gulf (1987), 52
    prerogative power, 71
    presidential leadership, 83
    public opinion, 358f
    secretary of state, 121t
    U.S. Department of Defense, 135
Reed, Jack, 276, 304
Regan, Donald, 224, 225
Relative economic decline, 32
Religious interest groups, 391–392, 404, 405
Reporting requirements, 305
Reuters, 419–420
Revolving door system, 395
Rice, Condoleezza, 113, 118, 121t, 122, 151, 185, 228–232, 261, 316

Rice, Susan, 234–235
Ridge, Tom, 185
Rivals in conformity, 439
Robertson, Pat, 106
Rockefeller Commission, 305
Rockefeller Foundation, 390
Rockwell International, 395, 411
Rogers, William, 121t, 222
Rogowski, R., 289
Roll call votes, 284
Rolling Stone, 449
Romney, Mitt, 41
Roos, John, 106
Roosevelt, Franklin:
  bureaucracy, 95
  foreign economic policy, 254
  Good Neighbor policy, 23
  leadership style, 63
  National Security Council (NCS) system, 216
  staff and advisers, 63
  two presidencies thesis, 77
  World War II, 25–26
Roosevelt, Theodore, 22–23, 95
Ross, Wilbur, 266–267
Rostow, Walt, 221, 332, 398
Routinization of bureaucracy, 92
Rove, Karl, 229
Rubin, Robert, 257–258
Rubio, Marco, 276, 304
Rumsfeld, Donald, 120, 144, 150, 223, 228–229, 230, 231, 316, 321, 322
Rusk, Dean, 121t, 221, 311, 332, 398
Russia:
  Alaskan purchase (1867), 19
  cyberwarfare, 164–165
  election interference (2016), 190, 192, 195–196, 198
  New START treaty, 87, 291, 299, 325

Sadat, Anwar, 51
Saltonstall, Leverett, 304
Schatz, Brian, 304
Schemas, 327
Schiffer, A., 441–442
Schlesinger, A., Jr., 289
Schneider, Rene, 202
Schulzinger, R., 390
Scowcroft, Brent, 135, 212, 219, 223, 225, 226, 227, 304–305, 337, 406
Secchia, Peter, 106

Secretary of state, 99, 120–124
Secretary of the treasury, 248–250
Sedition Act (1918), 29
Seko, Mobutu Sese, 202
Selective attention, 421
Separate institutions sharing power, 273
Services, 131
Sex discrimination, 112–113
Shaheen, Jeanne, 275
Shanahan, Patrick, 159
Shifting Leadership and Politics framework, 7–9, 456–457
Shine, Bill, 448
Shultz, George, 121t, 135, 177, 224, 225, 315
Signal-to-noise problem, 192
Singer Corporation, 411
Singularity power, 53
Skinner, Samuel, 227
Smith, Chris, 276
Smith, H., 6, 310
Snow, Jack, 261–262
Social globalism, 14
Social media, 420f, 433–434, 436
Social movements, 385
Soft-power policy, 40, 87
Soldiers, Statesmen, and Cold War Crises (Betts), 135
Somalia (1993), 85
Sorensen, Theodore, 311
Source journalism, 442–443
South China Sea and East China Sea Sanctions Act (2017), 304
Soviet Union:
  Cold War Consensus (1947-1968), 26–31
  Cuban Missile Crisis, 31
  dissolution, 34–35, 193
  World War II, 25–26
Space Command, 137, 138t
Spain, 19
Spanish-American War (1898), 21
Specialization of bureaucracy, 92
Specter, Arlen, 303
Sperling, Gene, 262–263, 265, 266
Sperry Corporation, 411
Sphere of influence, 23
Standard operating procedures, 93, 319
State 2000 (Department of State), 125
State Department-centered system, 214
Steinberg, James, 122
Stern, E., 325